W9-DEZ-718

...POLITICAL RUMOUR / CULTURAL LANDSCAPE / PRESENT IMPERFECT / RUINS IN REVERSE / ZONES OF CONTINGENCY / UNDER CONSTRUCTION / SPIRITUAL NOISES / PROJECT AND ACCUSATION / LANDSCAPE MANUAL / ENCOUNTER WITH AMBIGUITY / CITY FOLDED OVER ONTO ITSELF / TWO WAY MIRROR / DOUBLE EXPOSURE / BIPOLAR CITY / POWER OF IDENTITY / POTEMKIN VILLAGE / STAGED MATRIX / TRICKLAND / SILENT FACTORY...

○ ○ ○ WITH ALL DUE INTENT

urated by Marta Kuzma and Massimiliano Gioni

WORKS

KOLDO MITXELENA

MUSEO SAN TELMO

KUBO KUTXA KURSAAL

SOTO

it is no accident

Joxe Juan Gonzalez de Txabarri
Deputy General of Gipuzkoa

It is no accident that Donostia-San Sebastian was chosen to host Manifesta 5, or that it should take place in the Basque Country, a country with a strong political and cultural identity and a clear commitment to opening up and engaging with other cultures and identities.

It is no accident that there has never before been such a galaxy of Basque artists interacting in the international network of contemporary art with artists who are living, training, working and exhibiting in so many different cities around the world.

It is no accident that Basque institutions should support contemporary art. I speak only for the institution at which I have the honour to preside, the Statutory Delegation of Gipuzkoa, whose support has taken concrete form in the history of Arteleku, a space devoted to reflection on, experimentation in, and diffusion of emerging art, or in the established programme of the Koldo Mitxelena Gallery, or in the creation of the centre for contemporary culture in Tabacalera.

It is no accident that the North and the South, the East and the West of Europe should be present in Manifesta. Neither is it an accident that Manifesta should posit the bipolarity between Donostia-San Sebastian and Pasaia as a symbol of others bipolarities in the world today.

None of this is accidental; it is a consequence of the will to engage through art with a complex, changing reality in order to commit ourselves to transform it, make it more habitable and, in short, more worthy of living in.

All of this belongs in the framework of an international context in which video is very forcefully present as one of the preferred supports for so many contemporary artists, and in which art can often seem 'blurred', close to the everyday and to the languages we find around us in the street and in which the protagonism is assumed by a wide spectrum of viewpoints that place the emphasis on apparently humdrum, down-to-earth motives as much as on the major tensions that run through contemporary society.

I would like to conclude with some words of Eduardo Chillida's that sum up a thoroughly contemporary attitude towards life and art:

I understand almost nothing, but I share the blue, the yellow and the wind.
Of death, reason says to me:
definitive.
Of reason, reason says to me:
limited.

art in the city

Odon Elorza
Mayor of Donostia-San Sebastián

Gabriel Celaya, our celebrated Donostiarra poet, described Donostia-San Sebastian as an open city. The concept itself is open to a great many interpretations. In the case of Manifesta 5, it seems to me that it corresponds to the spirit of openness with which our city welcomes this biennial of contemporary art, in which young artists from many different countries will fill our urban landscape with their creations. In this we are taking our place alongside other European cities with a prestigious cultural tradition, such as Rotterdam, Luxembourg, Ljubljana and Frankfurt.

The city is also opening itself up to the surrounding conurbation by extending this celebration of culture to Pasaia, in this way twining different landscapes and different problems that share a common project of progress. In doing so, the Curators of the exhibition have sought to go beyond the exclusively artistic domain to engage with the urbanistic, cultural and social development of the area as a whole.

We are thus being offered something new and avant-garde that will no doubt give rise to a collective reflection on the latest forms of artistic expression, combining sculpture with audio-visual formats, and reflecting a variety of settings of significance in the cultural life of the city. The sheer number of different nationalities represented here, combined with the participation of local artists, ensures a creative diversity that will provide a wide-ranging vision of contemporary art.

Manifesta 5 also serves to demonstrate the importance of collaboration between institutions, the Spanish Ministry of Culture among them, in the development of major cultural projects. For us, this is a point of departure that will encourage and give a great impetus to the future International Centre of Contemporary Culture in Tabacalera, a strategic project of impressive scope that marks a quantitative and qualitative leap in the cultural life of the Basque Country.

It only remains now to look forward to the participation of the local people with a spirit of openness in this very special event. Because art and culture are nothing without the necessary communion between the creators and the public. I am sure that the efforts of the General Co-ordinator and the Curators of this Biennial, to whom I wish to express my thanks, will be amply rewarded by the popular success of the biennial.

manifesta 5

Miren Azkarate Villar
Minister for Culture
of the Basque Government

Manifesta 5, the European Contemporary Art Biennial in Donostia-San Sebastian, will serve as a valid and reliable tool for showing the current state of plastic and visual expression in Europe. It is a meeting place where artists and cultural agents from around Europe will be able to interact. This ambitious project will allow us to glimpse one of the project's main strengths: its support of new artistic expression and its relation to international art and new tendencies.

Manifesta 5 demonstrates the openness of Basque society and culture. It is a symbol of a people that is working on building its future whilst recognizing culture as an essential part of the welfare and modernization of 21st century societies.

At the same time it is a form of recognition of the Basque Country's vitality and dynamism in the contemporary art world. The Basque Government and Basque institutions in general – provincial governments and local councils- are fully aware of the importance of culture in society's development. That is why a tremendous amount of investment is being poured in to plastic and visual arts in the Basque Country such as never has been witnessed before.

In Donostia-San Sebastian Manifesta 5 will become a reference point for the whole of the Basque metropolis. In fact, with a population density which is double the European Union average and triple Europe's Atlantic regions, over 90% of the Basque population lives within less than a one and a half-hour radius of the setting for Manifesta.

The geographical location of Donostia-San Sebastian, Gipuzkoa and the Basque Country also makes it the nexus of a major European regional area. A location which directly relates to the long term strategic objective of the International Manifesta Foundation: that of striking a balance between the north and south of Europe in all its areas of activity.

Manifesta 5, the European Contemporary Art Biennial in Donostia-San Sebastian, is organized jointly by the International Manifesta Foundation, the Basque Government, the Provincial Government of Gipuzkoa and the Donostia-San Sebastian Local Council – Basque institutions that have come together in the Donostia San Sebastian International Centre for Contemporary Culture (CICC). The CICC and Manifesta 5 form a part of the idea of the Basque Government, Provincial Government of Gipuzkoa and Donostia-San Sebastian Council to make San Sebastian an international reference point for contemporary culture and in this way increase what the Basque Country already offers in this field.

International Foundation Manifesta
Hedwig Fijen
Director

On behalf of the Board of the International Foundation Manifesta:
Daniel Birnbaum, Francesco Bonami, Iara Boubnova, Lourdes Fernández, Martin Fritz, Henry Meyric Hughes (President)**, Maaretta Jaukkuri, Gilane Tawadros, Vicente Todolí and Igor Zabel.**

Since its founding in the early 1990s, Manifesta has been creating relationships with specific cities and regions in Europe in order to foster exchange between local configurations and external networks. Our goal has been to build bridges between artists, professionals, mediators, and audiences. Manifesta's concept originated in the growing synergy between, on the one hand, geographical and cultural contexts and, on the other, social and political environments.

Although some have accused the Biennial of showcasing only the 'hottest' young contemporary artists, Manifesta sees itself, in its nomadic enterprise, more as a multilateral mediator, which because of its independent, non-governmental status is able to provide a basic organisational framework every two years in a different setting. During the period leading up to the exhibitions, Manifesta's entire programme focuses specifically on the exchange of knowledge, providing a structure in areas of Europe where there appears to be mutual interest in collaboration and in exploring new connections. The temporary invasion of the public space of a city or region can only be justifiable if this process helps to establish dynamic platforms that offers a new scope for creativity.

Our goal of creating new relationships between various socio-political entities and Europe's art communities and audiences requires a special format. Manifesta's format is distinguished by its nomadic nature, as well as by its curatorial team, constituted anew each time, who represent a range of cultural and generational backgrounds. This kind of continual self-reinvention, re-examining its methodologies and adapting its critical apparatus so as to remain always attentive to new contexts, is one of Manifesta's guiding principles.

Since its debut in Rotterdam in 1996, Manifesta's concentration on research and new presentational modes has been closely tied to the topic of East–West relationships, culminating with the holding of Manifesta 3 in Ljubljana in 2000. Two years later, however, Manifesta returned to the centre of the cultural infrastructure, setting its fourth edition in Frankfurt-am-Main.

Why should Manifesta now move to Donostia-San Sebastian in the Basque Country? Why choose this beautiful seaside setting, which is, at the same time, characterised by a history of ethnic polarity and a long tradition of bilingualism? In what way can Donostia-San Sebastian provide Manifesta 5 with new sources of inspiration and an infrastructural network different from the institutional contexts of Rotterdam, Luxembourg, Ljubljana or Frankfurt?

When Donostia-San Sebastian was selected two years ago as the Host City for Manifesta 5, it was due in large part to its multi-layered intersections and historical trans-regional context. The structural pluralism of the region, its multiculturalism, identity issues, languages and political turmoil presented Manifesta with many previously unexplored challenges. What is more, these political and contextual issues have clear and direct relevance for an analysis of the current feelings of instability in Europe. Our hope was that Manifesta's latest venture might represent an experimental integration with the area's co-existent urban extremes. When Manifesta 5 took up residence in the Basque Country, with its passionately cherished cultural autonomy, it came with a mission. Can this Manifesta represent a visualisation of the current moment in European history, with the Basque situation representing, *pars pro toto*, the global moment?

Manifesta, indeed, is using art and art systems as a means of action in the urban space, developing models of integration and reflecting cross-cultural relations through art, as a response to local challenges. Manifesta´s efforts strive to be not only local and concrete but also to situate this local approach in a more general horizon, as a model of negotiating cultural and social tensions. Donostia-San Sebastian can show us a different Europe, one that has been fragmented into regional entities but now has a chance to rephrase its history in a more vertical dimension.

For Manifesta in general, the world-wide growth of large-scale art projects and cultural festivals with an orientation toward marketing has persuaded us to step back gradually from this sort of event, lowering the expectations of all kinds of stakeholders and concentrating our activities. Consequently, Manifesta has opted for closely integrating artistic practice in a more compact and more articulated community in order to de-territorialise itself from commercial constraints and so reclaim its humanity. Over the next few years, this means a policy of inviting distinctly transitional areas to host Manifesta, and slowly withdrawing from the Western art circuit in order to create closer connections and collaborations with new communities. In this way, Manifesta signals to the art circuit its intention to diversify and modify current structures – instead of simply invading countries still untouched by the international art world scene.

By the same token, Manifesta seeks to maintain and cultivate its philosophy of person-to-person relations. This entails a fluid working methodology whereby the main task of producers, mediators and curators is shaped under the pressure of close collaboration with artists so as to create an abundance of rich experiences in which audiences are seen as active participants and not casually ignored as if they were mere passers-by.

The success of this philosophy has been confirmed by the experiences of former board members, foundation staff, co-ordinators, curators and artists who maintain their relationships even after their formal role within Manifesta has come to an end. This has led to the creation of an extensive network, which continues to shape the development and basic concept of Manifesta towards a concentration on a knowledge-based exchange process.

From the start, Manifesta adopted a deliberately nomadic structure, relocating itself in a different European Host City every two years (Rotterdam, 1996; Luxembourg, 1998; Ljubljana, 2000; Frankfurt, 2002,; and now Donostia-San Sebastian). It also established a firm spirit of collaboration, determining that Manifesta's curators should work together as a team and in situations that are both internally and externally complex. The curators are asked to integrate artistic practices and relate these to the existing socio-political context. They must commit themselves wholeheartedly to the principles of active collaboration and co-operation, without falling into the trap of facile consensus. Establishing Manifesta on a more permanent basis has meant that people now have much higher expectations of the organisation. How will Manifesta respond to these expectations?

Manifesta and its curatorial teams have in the past pursued active involvement in the contemporary art world by creating opportunities for young artists, curators and writers who are not yet fully established. We have also taken a keen interest in the art theory emanating from areas of Europe that have customarily failed to attract the attention they deserve. Manifesta believes that art should be of its time and that new working practices and new forms of artistic response will develop from an engagement with the wider issues of the day. But at the same time, we must seek to ensure that Manifesta continues to inhabit a clearly defined in-between space, not only geographically, but also institutionally, politically, artistically and commercially.

Thus we find ourselves now, as we launch Manifesta 5, in a very open and fluid situation, in which it seems only right to re-examine some basic assumptions. Is Manifesta willing to change its working methodology in order to create greater exchange between various fields and projects both within and outside the organisation? How can such changes be implemented? And should we try to relate Manifesta to an even wider range of socio-cultural public platforms? Clearly, new strategies are needed to stimulate critical reflection and debate about the positioning of current art practices and the role of curators within the structural model provided by Manifesta. In general, Manifesta's curatorial teams should continue to endeavour to make a radical distinction between Manifesta and other biennials and large-scale art events, and Manifesta itself should offer new perspectives and models that can mediate flexibly between various levels of artistic communication and presentation. (In this regard, we especially appreciate the innovative approach of the curatorial team of Manifesta 5, who initiated the Office of Alternative Urban Planning, a collaborative effort with the Rotterdam-based Berlage Institute, a post-graduate laboratory for architectural and urban research). Finally, Manifesta should continue to work hard, at all times, to develop close working relations with its local partners.

The International Manifesta Foundation's Network Programme may offer a new way forward on a number of fronts. The launch of *Manifesta Journal (MJ)*, which focuses on contemporary curatorial practices, conditions and contexts, provides an important self-critical interface for assessing our network activities.

Over the next three years, through a series of programmes facilitated by the Foundation and produced in conjunction with outside partners, we hope to redefine the context for Manifesta's framework, to create additional platforms for co-operation with others on many levels, and to develop solid relationships with a broader audience. The Manifesta at Home archive in Amsterdam promises to serve as an important instrument of mediation, enabling us both to enlist the participation of others and to play a part in determining the nature of that participation.

One of the challenges the International Foundation Manifesta now faces is to find a way to convert our expanding information resources into a site-based platform for Manifesta's Biennial programme, one that can serve both as a repository of knowledge and as a direct stimulus to the efforts of curators and other art professionals. In this way, the fully networked archive will not only help to make information more widely available but will also engage the active participation of curators/mediators and audiences alike.

Every two years, with each Biennial, new teams of art professionals gets acquainted with each another through Manifesta.

We are greatly indebted to the two curators of Manifesta 5, Marta Kuzma and Massimiliano Gioni, who took up the challenge of working together for the first time and temporarily put aside other commitments in order to reside for an extensive period in Donostia-San Sebastian. At the same time, we wish to express our deepest appreciation to the artists who have participated in both the preparations for Manifesta 5 and the exhibition itself; almost all of them have spent a substantial period of time in the Basque Country and each has made a unique contribution to the success of the event. The curators and the artists committed themselves to analysing the multi-layered complexity of the Basque Country and getting beyond clichés and stereotypes. They have sought to show that Basque identity consists of much more than picturesque towns and tourist attractions, and is more than a beautiful natural setting with spectacular views.

We would also like to thank the most important stakeholders in the event, who deserve our deepest respect for the support and trust with which they responded when the International Foundation Manifesta approached them with the invitation to collaborate:

The Honourable Odón Elorza, *Mayor of the City of Donostia-San Sebastian, The Honourable* Joxe Joan Gonzalez Gonzalez de Txabarri, *current Deputy General of Gipuzkoa, and The Honourable* Miren Azkarate, *Cultural Adviser to the Basque Government.*

We also thank especially our colleague and board member, Mr. Vicente Todolí , now director of the Tate Modern in London, and Mr. Bartomeu Marí , currently senior curator at the Museu d'Art Contemporani de Barcelona (MACBA), for their initial interest in bringing the Basque Country and its people into the Manifesta network. We would also like to thank Mr. Román Sudupe, former Deputy General of Gipuzkoa, who helped start up Manifesta 5 in Donostia-San Sebastian.

The curators Marta Kuzma and Massimiliano Gioni could not have done their job without the inspiring co-ordination efforts of the local team, led by Manifesta 5's General Co-ordinator Lourdes Fernández — whose ingenuity helped us out of many difficult situations — and Manager José Miguel Ayerza. The whole team worked intensively with the community of Donostia-San Sebastian in order to make a significant contribution to the city; at the same time, they invited local art professionals to create numerous interventions. Manifesta's role as agent and mediator between different communities took on special significance in regard to the bilingual cultural traditions and social history of the region.

The organisation and execution of Manifesta 5 was entrusted to the Centro Internacional de Cultura Contemporánea (CICC), and we would like to thank the centre's President Joxe Joan Gonzalez de Txabarri for his unfailing good will and ready co-operation.

The Manifesta 5 team who took on the task of developing this project also deserves our deepest gratitude; the enterprise would not have been possible without the magnificent work of Carmen Ruiz, José Ignacio Abanda, Saioa Riba, Tevi de la Torre, Elixabete Azpiroz, Eider Córdoba, and Begoña Galparsoro, as well as the team of talented interns who provided Manifesta 5 with invaluable support.

Last but not least, I would like to thank the staff at the Manifesta Foundation, the backbone structure and initiator of the Manifesta projects. Our colleagues, Marieke van Hal and Julia Schleyerbach, have been responsible for the day-to-day execution of the Foundation's tasks in regard to the start-up of the Biennials and the monitoring of the Network Programme. At the same time, Manifesta at Home — as the headquarters in Amsterdam is called — ensures the long-term continuity of Manifesta's activities, as well as the implementation of process and project management in the Host Cities.

The Basque Government, the Provincial Council of Gipuzkoa and the Donostia-San Sebastian City Council all receive our sincere thanks for their generous support and willingness to open up the Basque Country to European cultural infrastructures.

We also would like to express our gratitude to the Ministry of Culture of Spain for its generous support.

We are deeply grateful, too, for the valuable backing we received from the Culture 2000 Framework Program of the European Commission, the Kutxa Obra Social Foundation, the Allianz Cultural Foundation and *El Diario Vasco*. We would also like to thank Mr. Lu van Orshoven, director of the multimedia company Vidisquare, for sponsoring their third edition of Manifesta, and the Mondriaan Foundation and the Prins Bernhard Cultural Fund, both in the Netherlands, for their support of Manifesta's Network Programme in Amsterdam.

Manifesta is honoured by the continued support of the individuals, foundations and private organisations who have helped us in the past. They have demonstrated such tremendous commitment to us, in some cases for almost a decade now, and we look forward to strengthening our relationships with them in the future.

this wild dark-ness

Massimiliano Gioni

Everything tends to make us believe that there exists a certain point of the mind at which life and death, the real and the imagined, past and future, the communicable and the incommunicable, cease to be perceived as contradictions.
–André Breton, *Deuxième manifeste de Surréalisme*, 1929.

CAN'T GET OUT OF MY HEAD

Maybe we have been asking for too much: we want art to tell us everything about racial conflicts, peripheral geographies, global economics and social, possibly interactive, practices. Or alternatively, we expect art to reveal the mechanisms of fashion, the up and downs of pop culture, the hallucinations of consumerism, the spirals of electro-nets and the ebbs and flows of corporate hyper-modernity.

In the midst of all this frenzy, we might have forgotten what goes on behind closed doors, what happens in those obscure spaces we call minds.

The head – we all know – is round, so that thoughts can run in circles. The brain is a labyrinth, sometimes more tortuous than the world outside. The paths connecting our minds to reality are complex, often interrupted, always convoluted. As a matter of fact, art might not be about understanding or reflecting our world, but about creating new, possible universes.

The most grotesque and fantastic conceits haunted him in his bed at night. A universe of ineffable gaudiness spun itself out in his brain while the clock ticked on the wash-stand and the moon soaked with wet light his tangled clothes upon the floor. Each night he added to the pattern of his fancies until drowsiness closed down upon some vivid scene with an oblivious embrace. For a while these reveries provided an outlet for his imagination; they were a satisfactory hint of the unreality of reality, a promise that the rock of the world was founded securely on a fairy's wing.
–Francis Scott Fitzgerald, *The Great Gatsby*, 1925.

The works of many artists in this edition of Manifesta suggest the possibility of discovering the world by closing our eyes, and diverting our attention towards the inside or towards our immediate surroundings. It's not a retreat, nor a form of escapism, but rather an immersion in a constellation of microcosms founded on individual, at times even maniacal, rules.

As debates, discussions and struggles about borders, territories and occupations abound, some artists feel the urge to proclaim their own autonomous state – a state of mind. They write intricate laws and proclaim private systems of belief, they draft intimate mindscapes, they trace the boundaries of psychological geographies, while inventing personal idioms and secret codes. Their languages gain strength from a radical obscurity: suddenly they seem not to care about some kind of international Esperanto.

They each practice a vernacular form of speech, adopting and forging cryptic signs. It's not so important to be immediately translatable, or perfectly transparent. Opacity, instead, becomes valuable: ambiguous metaphors proliferate; idiosyncratic symbolisms generate misunderstandings and short-circuits of logic. Some even turn to mystical thinking. Evoking is more important than identifying: suggestions are preferred over absolute definitions.

> *When Europe first began to take shape as an idea and as a political reality, between Merovingian times and the High Middle Ages, what people spoke was unproblematic. It was called "romance" or "theodisc" – peoplish. Only somewhat later, lingua vulgaris became the common denominator distinguishing popular speech from the Latin of administration and doctrine. Since Roman times, a person's first language was the patrius sermo, the language of the male head of the household. Each such sermo or speech was perceived as a separate language. Neither in ancient Greece nor in the Middle Ages did people make the modern distinction between mutually understandable dialects and different languages. The same holds true today, for example, at the grass roots in India. What we know today as monolingual communities were and, in fact, are exceptions. From the Balkans to Indochina's western frontiers, it is still rare to find a village in which one cannot get along in more than two or three tongues. While it is assumed that each person has his patrius sermo, it is equally taken for granted that most persons speak several "vulgar" tongues, each in a vernacular, untaught way. Thus the vernacular, in opposition to specialized, learned language – Latin for the Church, Frankish for the Court – was as obvious in its variety as the taste of local wines and food, as the shapes of house and hoe.*
> –Ivan Illich, *Vernacular Values*, 1980.

THIS LAND IS MY LAND

John Bock has taken the practice of multi-linguistics to the furthest extent. His lectures and performances are assemblages of derailed trains of thoughts, suspended somewhere between James Joyce on speed and a hyperbolic medieval storyteller. In the video *Gast*, a hare happily runs around a small playground: it is finally freed from Joseph Beuys' pedantic teachings and historical reflections. Beuys had invented a mythological land that extended from Germany all the way to Asia. Bock's Eurasia is nothing more than a living room, but one so fragmented, detailed and transfigured that it expands much further than a whole continent. Bock's micro-universes, just like the parallel realities described by many artists in this exhibition, don't develop horizontally, or subscribe to the rules of geography; they grow deeper and deeper.

In Külli K. Kaats' world, speaking has been replaced by cooing, chirping and twittering. Half shaman and half ornithologist, Kaats is learning the lost language of birds. Her hermetic jargon is meticulously planned and carefully studied, as are the music scores and notations for her performances and videos. And yet something absolutely visceral hovers above this world, like a primal scream in the middle of the night.

It's probably the same sound roared by the creatures in Yevgeniy Yufit's films. Yufit goes as far as imagining a whole cosmology and writing a personal theory of evolution. His film *Killed by Lightning* is a foundation myth narrated as a detective story, unraveling according to slow, almost geological rhythms. But it's also an ambitious exercise in imagination, a hallucinatory tour de force, suggesting that the whole world can be re-invented.

> *We can call the gods upon stage, we can trace magic circles around the untouchable characters of an imagined myth. We must introduce on stage the irrational and monstrous logic of dreams, the logic that can show you a face within the gesture of one hand, and suggest the passage of a hurricane with one single, excited ear-whisper. It is this technique that in the everyday language we call metaphor.*
> –Antonin Artaud, *Un Medea sin fuego*, 1936.

A ROOM OF ONE'S OWN

Some prefer to start from more domestic scenarios, mapping the route of a sentimental journey or preparing the conditions for long, distant, armchair travels.

Mark Manders' sculptures and installations – resembling waiting rooms and desolate alcoves – are direct projections of his imagination, and the artist stresses this relationship by describing all of his objects, drawings and constructions as self-portraits. Manders has built a private, often mysterious, iconography of forms, that are repeated, endlessly transformed and re-combined, their places permutated and their associations slightly modified, as recurring elements in a grammar. Solidifications of a lexicon in perennial metamorphosis, Manders' rooms and buildings always remain at a chilling distance, as though they were not filtered through an optical perception, but rather observed from a cerebral perspective.

Micol Assaël opens the doors of modest, industrial quarters to the fury of elements: ice, wind, water, fire, and smoke swipe through empty offices and sealed chambers. It's yet another materialization of a mental landscape, where the vastness of Siberian plains can be compressed into the intimate, at times oppressive, perimeter of a cell.

Carlos Bunga's maquettes and installations delimit rough and precarious living spaces, cross-fading between the geometrical precision of modernist architecture and the improvised cacophony of shanty towns. After erecting his cardboard houses, with one single gesture Bunga makes his own world crumble and collapse, leaving behind just the shadows of his edifices, like the remains of a dream strangely allowed to enter into daylight.

Daniel Roth's fastidiously executed maps, dioramas and scenarios also share the hypnotic power of debris, but they do not come out of the past; they are relics of a future that has never arrived. An untiring explorer of impossible topographies and secret passages, Roth lays out an atlas of imaginary nations, clandestine societies and unknown civilizations where paranoia takes over geography, and transforms it into conspiracy theory.

> *Yes, it must be admitted – Pool had lost faith in actuality. He regarded his surroundings as a function of his own mental condition rather than as a separate and independent background. He was like a balloon that had slipped through a child's gasp – the world where he had spent his first three decades, the world he had shared with millions, had floated away when he wasn't looking.*
> –Thomas Palmer, *Dream Science*, 1990.

LIFE: A USER'S MANUAL

A skeptical attitude towards reality informs many of the artists working today. Doubts flourish, theorems are arbitrarily applied and absurd speculations are carried out with clinical precision.

Kirsten Pieroth postulates a weird science, based on suspicions and lies. Her research into the life of inventor Thomas Edison does not aim to reveal the verifiable facts of his biography or illustrate his many discoveries. Instead, Pieroth is writing a historical, fictional novel. Documents are counterfeited, photographs and objects are collected and transformed into sculptures. As on the scene of a crime, evidence is produced, catalogued, and archived, but only to prove the disappearance of reality.

The real doesn't offer much resistance against Paola Pivi's gestures either. Pushing the readymade to a cyclopean dimension, Pivi flips airplanes upside down, transports exotic animals into incongruous contexts or reproduces entire islands in actual size. Pivi's systematic embrace of paradox gives birth to artificial paradises where zebras live on snowy mountains, kids roll down soft, grassy hills, and user-friendly robots gently shiver when approached by humans.

While Pivi and Pieroth seem to rely on a rarefied, abstract order that can be grasped only by suspending our disbelief, other artists base their experiments on the principle of trial and error. It's a much more physical interpretation of science, but the results are just as illogical and anti-practical: giant, cranky bachelor machines, running on empty, or fragile interventions that can subvert any routine.

Conrad Shawcross' nervous systems and exoskeletons are complex anatomical studies and elaborate mechanisms to measure the infinite. Interpreting the role of a bricoleur or that of a mad scientist, Shawcross prepares the tools to survive in a world where micro and macro dimensions seem to collide.

Michael Sailstorfer is more interested in recycling. His do-it-yourself constructions result from a cut and paste furore, shot in with a boyish enthusiasm: aircrafts broken to pieces and re-assembled as small huts on a tree; trailers and caravans transformed into country hideaways; police vans reduced to drum sets; street lamps used as projectiles... Anything is possible, as long as one can invent his own rules and try out new combinations.

> *When I make a show it's like when you arrive at home and you open your fridge at night and there's two potatoes and one sausage and two eggs, and with all that you make something to eat. I try to make something with what is in my fridge.*
> –Christian Boltanski, *Studio Visit*, 2002.

ONE FOR ALL, AND ALL FOR ONE

Inventing your own rules doesn't mean withdrawing completely from reality or living in a world of absolute solipsistic illusion. Many artists still believe that art can serve as a testing ground for experimentation with possible alternatives to the real. But these transformations, before being applied on a grand scale, have to be tried out within smaller groups. In an attempt to negotiate the space between collective needs and one's own desires, artists imagine micro-societies where individuals behave like organisms of a larger body, entertaining parasitic relationships or more symbiotic functions.

Leopold Kessler acts as a social engineer under cover; his discreet, at times invisible interventions open small fractures in the tight fabric of everyday life. Trash cans are raised to become baskets for some new urban sport, while street lights get clandestinely connected to a remote control so that they can be switched on and off according to the artist's will. With his small deeds of kindness and his imperceptible gestures of exploitation, Kessler prepares the conditions for a silent revolution of roles and a gentle subversion of public authorities.

A spontaneous intolerance against official powers also emerges from Iñaki Garmendia's work. His installations and videos are built with a rough immediacy: colors are often saturated, excessive; objects are thrown together with a punk, fuck it all attitude; eccentric, almost incomprehensible gestures are carried out by restless characters. A certain adolescent discontent seems to be the key to understanding these strange rituals of aggregation and aggression, which mimic mechanisms of inclusion and exclusion in youth movements: it's this primal, almost tribal sense of belonging to a group, that makes Garmendia's work even more hypnotic.

The secret codes and private languages invented and spoken by different subcultures seem to be the epicenter of Kim Hiorthøy's drawings and murals. Departing from the world of music and crossing the territory of street life, Hiorthøy produces large paintings and wall works that recall the overcharged style of tazebao and teenage posters. At the same time, the artist is engaged in the creation of small, enchanted drawings that act as a visual diary of quotidian moments of loss – the seismograph of an infantile and almost fragile soul that struggles to find a place in the world.

Patrick Tuttofuoco works at the intersection between the most basic, even repressed, desires and the most superfluous, inducted needs. His installations are often conceived as material realizations of the dreams formulated by small communities and groups of friends. Whether customizing vehicles according to specific and yet absurd requirements or building giant toys for eternal, overgrown children, Tuttofuoco's constructions appear as elaborate prostheses for transforming reality into a giant playground.

A ludic atmosphere also pervades Jeremy Deller's research, but his approach is also permeated by a more systematic, almost anthropological, curiosity. Through his installations, videos, and performances, Deller investigates how cultures, societies, and associations are built and around which symbols they gravitate. Always ambitious and at times verging on encyclopedic precision, Deller's practice examines and reproduces social phenomena as diverse as fanaticism, nationalism, political engagement and folkloric rites. Moved by a democratic idealism, Jeremy Deller often leaves the central stage to ordinary people and working class heroes, who are invited to take control of festive, choral events. Deller's parades thus become anarchic and yet self-regulated universes, where – if only for a moment – a delicate balance between individual and shared needs emerges.

There is no such thing as the social production of reality on the one hand, and a desiring production that is mere fantasy on the other... The truth of the matter is that social production is purely and simply desiring-production itself under determinate conditions. We maintain that the social field is immediately invested by desire, that it is the historically determined product of desire, and that libido has no need of any mediation or sublimation, any psychic operation, any transformation, in order to invade and invest the productive forces and the relations of production. There is only desire and the social, and nothing else.

–Gilles Deleuze and Felix Guattari, *L'anti-Oedipe*, 1972.

REALITY CHECK

To many other artists the real appears as a much more polemical and threatening space, cut to pieces by ethnic tumults and cultural clashes. Rather than experimenting with alternative microcosms, some feel the need to document their own surroundings and describe that nebulous territory where international politics and individual psychologies overlap. This particular form of reportage, this para-journalistic approach, never claims to have access to a final, superior truth. It proceeds by posing questions, instead of formulating straight answers; and it often prefers the format of the personal confession to the presentation of some kind of omniscient, detached author. That's why many documentaries produced by artists and filmmakers today deploy fragmented narratives and convoluted stories, while often bringing together different temporalities and sudden flashbacks. Often filmed with very basic means and shaky hand held cameras, these documentaries filter the world through the eyes of individuals, as though the trauma of conflicts had damaged our ability to experience reality objectively or at least collectively.

Whether depicting the life of professional international peace corps or exploring the physical effects of weapons on our bodies, the films of Olivier Zabat are incessant digressions into the life of multiple characters, who only seem to share painful experiences and terrible losses. Looking beyond war zones, Zabat's documentaries describe a world of psychological tension that stretches from the mountains of Kosovo to the peripheries of Paris and the mine fields of Cambodia, suggesting that our predisposition to violence is not simply related to geographic reasons or ideological struggles; it is instead an inescapable condition of humanity.

Similar conclusions arises in the film *Route 181* by Eyal Sivan and Michel Khleifi who traveled across Israel and Palestine interviewing hundreds of people on both sides of the conflict. Again, rather than operating as a political treatise on the responsibilities of terrorists' warfare and military occupation, the film provides a collection of partial and often irreconcilable points of views. *Route 181* is a documentary that does not unveil a solution, but rather captures the complexity of a situation in the very moment it changes, depending on who is trying to describe it.

The slippery nature of truth is also the subject of Hito Steyerl's *November*, in which vintage images of kung fu fighting girls and juvenile delinquency à la Russ Meyer are intersected with short sentences and reflections on the inadequacy of cinema to portray reality. More than a documentary, Steyerl's movie is a visual elegy for a lost friend who has disappeared after joining a clandestine, revolutionary group in the Middle East. But it's not so much the detailed, biographical aspects that attract the attention of the artist; Steyerl's film functions like a script for constructing a private mythology, in which the vagueness of memory adds to the mystery of a character suspended between reality and fiction.

> *The more the global flows of capital, technology and information become abstract, the more relevant becomes the communal and concrete experience of local territories, histories, languages, religions and the sense of ethnic belonging.*
> –Manuel Castells, *El poder de la identidad*, 2003.

PLAYING AMONG THE RUINS

Geography has become a fixation, imposing itself as the exclusive paradigm used to describe our world and contemporary art alike. And yet, as we were too busy debating borders and global transitions and national quotas, we haven't realized that many artists were already looking elsewhere, embarking on a trip along the spirals of time. History has slowly crept in with ruins and debris casting shadows in the work of many young artists; the stratified and complex wealth of local traditions and personal memories become a reservoir of images and inspirations. There is nothing regressive or conservative in this attitude, especially because the past no longer appears as heroic or monumental, but rather consumed and decayed. Nobody seems to care about a triumphal conquest of one's own origins. Instead, a feeling of loss and longing emanate from the works of many European artists of today, like a romantic spleen updated.

In Amelie von Wulffen's drawings, collages and photographs, old interiors, ancient landscapes and deserted houses come to the surface as if washed in by sudden recollections, only to sink immediately into the background under the pressure of some art noveau motif scribbled in a corner just next to a portrait of John Travolta or a snapshot stolen from a TV program. Like some kind of exquisite corpse, the drawings of Amelie von Wulffen bring together distant images that have been buried in the storage room of German history and in the secret corridors of the artist's memory.

Silke Schatz' models and large-scale drawings also attempt to find a physical manifestation for the volatile substance of reminiscences. Her architectural plans, at first sight so coldly detached, appear upon a closer look as evocative as Piranesi's inventions: imaginary landscapes and immense chambers from which one contemplates the past and faces the ephemeral brevity of the present.

The chaotic assemblages of Angela de la Cruz are also ruins of a sort.

Digesting and reprocessing the tradition of modernist abstraction, de la Cruz paints large monochromatic canvases, which then get destroyed, compressed and transformed into unstable sculptures. Referring to her structures as "clutters" to stress their precarious and promiscuous nature, the artist envisions a world in continuous transformation, where objects and art works are endlessly recycled in a perennial struggle between shining novelty and instant archaism.

Cathy Wilkes' installations are instead sparse, often delicate and dispersed. They are born out of a mental tension rather than a physical confrontation with materials. And yet, Wilkes' sculptures seem to preserve the memory of something anthropomorphic, as though these geometrical shapes and every day objects were to be interpreted as human figures that are bent, fractured and broken. Seen in this perspective, Wilkes' installations appear as dark mementos of our fragility.

Now he has departed from this strange world a little ahead of me. That means nothing. People like us, who believe in physics, know that the distinction between past, present, and future is only a stubbornly persistent illusion.
–Albert Einstein, *Out of My Later Years*, 1950.

HIROSHIMA MON AMOUR

There is something sublime in recognizing our weaknesses. And, in the works of many artists of today, landscapes have returned to appear threatening and menacingly vast. It's as though, in spite of digital connections and information technologies, artists still perceive the world as a mysterious space.

Anu Pennanen's composite video installation *Monument to the Invisible* departs from this feeling of a clear, imminent danger. The cold immensity of corporate architecture serves as a backdrop to the wanderings of a blind woman, who carefully and just as slowly moves through a scenery of gigantic proportions.

Geert Goiris' photographs are desolate views of Nordic panoramas, frozen with glacial precision, that are immersed in a warm, painterly patina. His lonely barracks somehow transplanted into cold and lunar landscapes depict a hostile reality almost devoid of any human presence.

Laura Horrelli films the construction of a cruise ship, revealing the hidden side of the holiday and entertainment industry. Similar to Goiris' photos, Horrelli's films speak of the never-ending struggle between humanity and nature, but this romantic opposition is now tinted with more prosaic details. Today we have to fight against a much more dangerous enemy than the vehemence of the elements; we have to fight against our own mediocrity.

Hüseyin Alptekin's hotel signs can be read as a parody of our global concerns. Transforming exotic destinations into familiar signage that, in turn, gets displayed out of context in unexpected situations, Alptekin's work dwells in the ragged no man's land of international tourism. The dismal atmosphere evoked by his cheap hotel names – a litany that brings together disparate and random geographies such as Sarajevo, Tibet or Copa Cabana – brings to mind cheap thrills and all inclusive holiday vacations that roll by like subtitles to the end of the world news.

> *The alien looks up and says "E.T. phone home."*
> *Elliott screams with joy.*
> *"Home, home, home, home" says E.T.*
> -Steven Spielberg, *E.T., the Extra-Terrestrial*, 1982.

(DON'T) LOOK BACK

Others have traveled alone, crossing the ocean, in search of the miraculous. Bas Jan Ader's poetic interpretation of conceptualism, and the myth surrounding his disappearance at sea, makes him almost an epic figure. Both rigorous and sentimental, his work appears enveloped in an aura of tragedy, as a blurred melancholy infuses all of his gestures. In Bas Jan Ader's films, as in his trip across the Atlantic Ocean, what is left behind and left unspoken seems even more relevant than what is clearly stated. His is an art of evocations and secret epiphanies.

A suggestive, obscure symbolism also emerges from Victor Alimpiev and Sergey Vishnevsky's film *Deer*: set in a Russian forest but also edited to sequences shot in claustrophobic interiors, *Deer* portrays two distant lovers caught in some kind of torment and passionate sickness.

In Andrea Faciu's video *Le Luneux*, we witness another heartbreaking story of love and sweet violence, as narrated by a traditional song. As less and less artists from younger generations seem interested in shock tactics and frontal attacks, capturing impalpable emotions and states of being becomes crucial. Dark and ghostly manifestations permeate these films, like phantoms called upon a séance.

The same creatures probably haunt Jan De Cock's massive installations, but his ghosts do not belong to the past: De Cock's wooden constructions and intersections into old buildings are literally ruins in reverse; their obsolescence being carefully planned. Updating the life of museums and other institutionalized spaces, De Cock's installations also look strangely outmoded, as though they were bound to disappear – site specificity becomes a matter of time. Like metastases growing inside a body, De Cock's constructions both control and consume the space they occupy, reminding their inhabitants that the end is always near.

> *I came home from the office one day and Holly said, "Gordon Matta-Clark wants to cut a house in half, have you got one?" After it had been cut, I felt nervous being in the house. I thought it would collapse at any minute. I really didn't enjoy being in it.*
> –Horace Solomon, *Gordon Matta-Clark*, 1985.

HOME, WHERE THE HURT IS

Contemporary art has defined itself as a practice of displacement, whether through the endless variations of the readymade or the more recent fascination with geography. Obviously many young artists are proceeding on this path but they are also attempting to discover the route that connects displacement with nostalgia. Rather than being preoccupied with global diasporas and international migrations, art has taken a more confessional approach, focusing on personal stories. Even when addressing cultural phenomena and social transformations, artists depart from an individual point of view in which history reveals itself slowly, emerging from the pages of a family album.

Darius Žiura's *Gustoniai* is precisely a simple, straightforward group portrait of the inhabitants of a small village in Lithuania. One by one, for one minute each, all the citizens of this miniscule community stand in front of his camera. It is easy to imagine the artist taking this film with him, anywhere he goes, to preserve intact the memory of his native land.

David Zink Yi's films and video installations are peregrinations across the biography of the artist and his intricate family tree, with its branches pointing out in different directions, from China to Peru, from Germany to Cuba. But Zink Yi never seems to play the role of the perfectly polished, international individual. His research instead is an immersion in local knowledge, in an attempt to preserve a certain foreignness and specificity to each culture, language and tradition. Music is the vehicle used by Zink Yi in his explorations, and the soundtrack of his films carries the subtleties and tastes of distant places. In his film *La Cumbia* the artist goes as far as performing a traditional dance with just two fingers on his naked body – it's both an emblem of solitude and homesickness, but also the proof of how deep, down under our skin, our roots are cast.

Something similar happens in Maria Lusitano's film *Nostalgia*, which combines music and vintage images from a Portuguese family living in Mozambique during the crucial years just before the independence of the colony. While perfectly aware of how oppressive and violent any colonial regime is, Lusitano's film leads us to identify with the colonizers in a dangerous and yet empathic twist of our expectations. The dialectics of perpetrator and victim get completely subverted and we are left asking ourselves how deep are the ties that link us to the place we call home.

> *There is a secret agreement between past generations and the present one. Our coming was expected on earth. Like every generation that preceded us, we have been endowed with a weak Messianic power, a power to which the past has a claim. That claim cannot be settled cheaply.*
> –Walter Benjamin, *Angelus Novus*, first published in1961.

THE BIRTH OF A NATION

The complex system of symbols, allegories and beliefs that shape national consciousness are addressed by many artists in this edition of Manifesta. Again it's not so much a geopolitical fascination that leads this kind of research: it is instead a more psychological or anthropological approach, which aims at understanding how this sense of belonging is built and on which references and foundations it is maintained. It's not about the physical manifestations of nations, but rather about their mental images, the internally assimilated values that shape our credos.

These mechanisms of identification and projection are laid bare in Gillian Wearing's *Tedi*, in which children perform the role of guides to national monuments and fictional local traditions in a pantomime of chauvinistic rhetoric.

Vangelis Vlahos also treats architectures and buildings as totemic figures around which national ideals revolve. His sculptures and hard-edged technical drawings dissect embassies and bureaucratic offices, neutralizing their symbolic power, by reducing them to arid paper models.

Asier Mendizabal employs and subverts stereotypes of national representations in his series of views of typical Basque villages and portraits of local policemen, accompanied by the music played by a traditional brass band. Often working on the dangerous liaisons that tie desire to group gatherings and politics, Mendizabal creates sculptures and installations that have a raw power to them, like barricades built in the middle of the night.

Marc Quer also examines public spaces as territories of conflicts between different identities and ethnic groups. By installing in the Arab neighborhoods of Marseilles a series of posters depicting 19th century colonial scenes, in which the Arab population appears passively serving the needs and stereotypes of the French occupants, Quer initiated a spontaneous and inflammatory reaction. In a few days the posters were covered by graffiti, comments and insults that re-appropriated and re-directed the meaning of the images, clarifying that there is no such thing as the history of a nation, but just a history in favor of someone and against someone else.

Most likely there is no better definition of history than the following: history is the science of changes and, in many cases, it is a science of differences.
–Marc Bloch, *Qu'est-ce que on peut demander à l'histoire?*, 1937.

LOST IN THE ARCHIVE

Time has become a privileged site of investigation for many artists. Moving along the vertical axis of history, they unearth public tales and forgotten myths in a sort of anti-systematic archeology of knowledge. Again, it is a strategy that aims to question national beliefs and official narratives, but also a way to give a personal shape to the past. Time thus emerges as a torn cloth that can be continuously woven and taken to threads – a multi-layered stratification of time zones.

Iliya Chichkan and Kyrill Protsenko accumulate images gathered from the Ukranian National Archive, collecting propaganda films and documentaries. The group DAE, working on the border between artistic and curatorial tactics, scrutinize the past of the Basque history of art by presenting a rare film in which the sculptor Jorge Oteiza collaborates with musicians, directors and industrialists in an attempt to reform the premises of art production. Zbyněk Baladrán digs out old Czech movies, short animations and brief sequences of historical moments captured on film, and edits them to odd bits and pieces of music, found sounds, and mumbling noises. All together, and each in their individual way, these artists experiment with archival images and cinematic, perched moments, creating a tapestry of visions and sounds, a magic lantern that projects chimeras and sudden revelations of our social unconscious.

A communal history emerges from Boris Mikhailov's sepia tinted photographs. Displayed in vitrines like testimonies of some ancient empire, they act as time capsules, preserving the gloomy atmosphere of social cataclysms and cultural transitions.

Cengiz Çekil has built a collection of newspapers in which texts and titles have been erased only to leave room to images of dramatic events. It's a frail catalogue of historical breaks and traumas, in which words are left out, as victims of some collateral damage.

Serhiy Bratkov's scattered installations of photographs create unexpected narratives by generating connections and detours. The editing and the clashing of images produce an emotional distortion that replicates the gaze of Bratkov's characters and sitters, who often appear tortured and scared, never at ease.

A sense of anxiety penetrates Mark Leckey's films and his by now almost legendary *Fiorucci Made Me Hardcore*, a cut and paste collective hallucination built by assembling footage of raves and disco scenes from British television. A visual essay on psychosis and mass cults – like *Rock My Religion* reloaded – *Fiorucci Made Me Hardcore* preserves and, at the same time, erases memory, as in a potlatch ritual of dissipation.

> *This is your last chance. After this, there is no going back. You take the blue pill and the story ends. You wake in your bed and you believe whatever you want to believe. You take the red pill and you stay in Wonderland and I show you how deep the rabbit hole goes.*
> –Larry and Andy Wachowski, *The Matrix*, 1999.

MY DARK PLACES

What we forget is often as significant as what we obstinately remember. In the lapses of memory, in its ruptures and holes, we store images and fears, which can suddenly jump to the surface. As many artists seem to declare a renovated interest in the secret space of our mind, they are also discovering the obscure place where images disappear, the black holes of our brain.

Amnesia, analyzed both as an individual pathology and as a metaphor of culture's infinite processes of repression, is at the center of many works in this edition of Manifesta.

In the video *Johan*, Sven Augustijen portrays a man affected by an acute form of aphasia. He struggles to connect his thoughts to the appropriate wordings, he seems unable to retain or express any information, his linguistic skills completely erased. As we witness his painful exercises in a clinic, a glimpse in the man's eyes betrays that he might actually be conscious of his own disease, as if his amnesia had only interrupted the path that leads from his brain to his mouth, while leaving intact the perception of his own desperate condition.

The distance between thoughts and their clear expressions is the space in which Johannes Kahrs' figures seem to dwell. His hazy paintings depict blurred shapes and fragments of bodies resisting both the pressure and the violence of becoming complete, recognizable images.

In Markus Schinwald's films, eerie, ectoplasmatic creatures move, often trapped in reiterated movements and repetitive actions. Dust particles seem to fall on the surroundings as landscapes fade in and out of each other, driven by inexplicable sympathies and abrupt fractures.

Michael Borremans' paintings are made of broken gestures and moments of suspension: characters are transformed into automatons, smashed dolls become victims of medical experiments, helpless patients are handled by teams of doctors or strange engineers – their eyes always obtuse, alienated. Immersed in a lacteous light, Borremans' canvases seem enveloped in a vacuum, like fragments of recollections obscured by the fog of forgotten thoughts.

History is a nightmare from which I'm trying to awake.
–James Joyce, *Finnegan's Wake*, 1939.

GUIDED BY VOICES

Out there, slogans and catch phrases get sharper and sharper: the dictatorship of communication and branding has imposed super-effective refrains and jingles. To this over-simplistic, often one sided, perception of reality, many artists have reacted by staging and occupying schizophrenic environments, increasing the degree of complexity and the obscurity of their languages – they are speaking in tongues. As reflected through these works, the corridors of our minds seem to be resonating with impenetrable rattles, broken words, spiritual noises – it's the hiccup of reason – the stutter of confusion.

Duncan Campbell's monologues accompany his visions of Belfast's youth with sobbing sounds, thick accents and labyrinthine plots. It's a personal syntax of expressions and images that emerges from a muddy stream of consciousness.

Garrett Phelan's drawings and installations scatter maniacal scribbles over the walls of abandoned buildings. Like intricate Rorschach tests of our paranoia, Phelan's drawings seem executed by a disturbed subject who declares to have found some secret code to the universe. His equations and speculations betray the belief in a perfect correspondence between one's own obsessions and the external world.

This faith can be tinted with mystical connotations: it's the illusion – at times liberating, other times simply desperate – of controlling the world by discovering the secret affinities that regulate it. Misha Stroj's complex vocabulary – sprung at the intersection between philosophy, linguistics, mathematics and religion, with Pasolini in the role of the high priest – summarizes reality in a set of 181 problems and questions. His work thus becomes an exercise in endless combinations and analyses, which paradoxically don't lead to a close, practical system, but rather to an explosion of doubts, reminding us that there are no solutions, only problems.

Estragon: What were you saying when?
Vladimir: At the very beginning
Estragon: The very beginning of WHAT?
Vladimir: This evening... I was saying... I was saying...
Estragon: I'm not a historian
Vladimir: Wait... Do you not remember?
Estragon: I'm tired
–Samuel Beckett, *En attendant Godot*, 1952.

the staged ma-trix

Marta Kuzma

A man in his underwear can tramp around the city only if he is in police custody, and only if he's going to one place – the police station!... One should know that when you see such a man, you should begin to blow your whistle without a moment's delay.
–The Incident at Gribodyedov
From Bulgakov's *Master and Margarita*

This is not the time for political works of art, rather politics has migrated to the autonomous work of art, and it has penetrated most deeply into works that present themselves as politically dead.
–*Critique of Committed Art*
Theodor Adorno

The city as a project and accusation, willingly surrendering to arbitrariness, was viewed by the architectural historian Manfredo Tafuri as the construction of a utopia of dissolute form. Referring specifically to Piranesi's drawings of Campo Marzio, Tafuri found the "optimal clash of organisms, immersed in a sea of fragments, dissolving even the most remote memory of the city as a place of form."[2] This interpretation of place as a contradiction between the demand for order and the will to formlessness, bracketing the rational and irrational, offers an architectonic point of departure in envisioning a possible trajectory for Manifesta as a concept. With open-endedness and fragment as part of its matrix, Manifesta's very flexibility benefits from its genre as a project but one equivalent to a city if we are to consider the city as part of a broader territory.

Manifesta's critical validity as emergent and developing is invested in the project's form as an abstract temporal structure, totalizing history from the standpoint of the ever-vanishing and ever-present, embracing a conflicting plurality of projects, relational points and possible futures. Through an endeavor to claim the city and its possible other (Pasaia), Manifesta extends beyond abstract theoretical applications to invent a series of scenarios, constellations and conspiracies that enable the very dimensions of the city to become personified. In doing so, it resists General Potemkin's example of merely building a makeshift village of canvas and pasteboard to transform the landscape for the sake of the imperial court of viewers. By effectively extending the parameters of the city, Manifesta transforms the place into an evental site that anticipates a future.

Manifesta arrives in San Sebastian in the Basque autonomous region vociferously; perhaps one of the most critical sites since its inception. Located in the very seat of a movement focused on cultural autonomy centered on the proliferation of a unique language, Manifesta develops in an emphatically singular place where supermodernity, accelerated space and characterization of the artwork as the site of non-place may only proceed cautiously. As an international art event, or what Manuel Castells calls the space of flows[3], it is

LANDSCAPE

MANUAL

J. WALL

25¢

FROM AND FOR A WORK IN PROGRESS

Toward a defeatured landscape on all levels, without any sense of loss, negation, subversion, etc.---reams of tiny photographs.

The beginning of a continuing interpenetration with as yet untaken photographs, with as yet unreceived signals from the as yet existenceless future. This date, September 27, 1969, 7:15 p.m., will mark the"outset" of this endless experiment.

The work in progress: sequences, interspersed with situations and spaces of a specific, dense nature---a sequence which is subtly altered, manipulated in a particular way, one procedure from a vault of endless possibilities. I myself sit here---or possibly ride in a car---and am somewhat more than just a "recording machine".

The outlines of the region of concrete reactions---reactions "lived" in complex (i.e.--timeless) time & remembered in "neural" time--complex but different. Instead of being an expository work, the work should be a particular procedure itself, carried out as the writing (etc.) is carried out, becoming, in effect indistinguishable from the procedure itself---not subordinate to any other particular physical etc. process, but instead, as concrete as any other particular procedure. Typewriting as "physical" activity: interadtion with materials, etc., as interaction with stone, steel, ## clay, etc. Interaction with materials as primarily "structural"; i.e.--participation in any process is a condition of relating which demands a complete structural "metaphysics", and we can see more & more clearly that this demand & its response should be made as consciously as possible. When words are used, this necessity obviously becomes most apparent---(close attention to interface of vagueness/clarity---apparent "opposition" of mistakes to "correct procedure")

"no documents"

Look carefully onto the page; pattern might see the surface as a (preliminary) , a particular articulation of many simultaneous functions, propositions, etc.---this "surface" articulation a particular and necessary structure, and, as such, intimately related to extended regions of abstraction, each simpler than the previous---all connected in organic "crystalline" fashion, like the interchange on the broad high-speed freeway under the wheels of a car (1968 Dodge Monaco convertible), then the gleaming approaches, the long straight secondary highways with rutted gravel shoulders, and further and further away, the complex and simultaneous network of suburban drives, crescents and avenues---the white lines carrying speakers out of hearing range. The road-landscape exists, then, as a region of primary involvement, carried to the page with real, primary words and actual chemical photographs.

VAST DEFEATURED REGION

The "regions" which make up the content of the ongoing system are of little importance in & for themselves. Because what we know, or what we actually work with when we work at all, is an awareness of structures---when we make abstractions from these structures to qualitatively different kinds of structures---we understand that what we are doing involves a manipulation of elements or of maybe "objects" which are not important to us except in the manner in which we manipulate them.

I am riding in a car; the sun breaks and slants in through the windows. The car is full of noise---the engine, the wind tearing in through rolled-down windows and wide-open vents under the dashboard. On my lap lies a camera in a leather case. My hands are at my sides and I am looking to my right out the window. Books and papers cover the back seat. The landscape issues out through the rear windows of the car and slips away much too quickly to be contained; nevertheless, from time to time I snap a photograph through one of the car's windows.

From Jeff Wall's *Landscape Manual*, 1969-1970

contrasted against an environment of intermittent insurgency where power may appear nowhere tangible and even ghostly in appearance. As an implicit site of tension, the region is detached from a global or synthetic notion of the present or of history. This places Manifesta in the position of a critical cultural manifestation that has the fortunate challenge of working with contingency, though this is not fetishized for the sake of its own glamour. Nevertheless, it is the contingency which inevitably leads actions and strategies to be interpreted and coded by this real politic first and foremost. Subsequently, the project leads to inevitable questions of intelligibility and resolution as being abstract and unstable, inscribed as they are within a dialectical site that is marked by a consciousness of temporality, one that represents a structural present and a gesture towards a future.

To abstract from the social experience of the city of Manifesta's inception implies a departure from the logic of its difference that influences the syntax and semantics of the cultural. By referring to the architectonics of place, there is an attempt to reveal the essence of something that articulates the simultaneously economic, political, historical, and aesthetic. It prompts one to seek out what lies beneath the surface of the appearance of its rationalist coherence - beyond the linearity, the ritual, and the regimented. What is it in the nature of its particular, its vernacular even, that leads it to find a constellation for its broader meaning? How is it possible to use the elements of place, as Steven Izenour proposed, to create and quote a sense of the importance of the ordinary aspects of the everyday into a kind of monumentality?[4] In this way, how is it possible to formulate a project that interweaves itself into the fabric of the city in an intertwined way so that it evolves into something further?

LOCATING A FORM FOR THE POLITICAL

A picture of war is not war.
-From Hito Steyerl's film *November*

Within a zone of contingency marked as the Basque region, the malleability of time and space evokes the omnipresence of change and unpredictability as endemic to its structure. Within this structure, the nature of change serves as its own constellation. Marx's infamous statement that history appears first as tragedy and later as farce may find its inverse in a reconsideration of modern Spanish history in relation to developments in recent months. ETA's involvement in the death of Carrero Blanco essentially ended Francoism and changed the course of modern Spanish history. Nevertheless, ETA remained a plaguing

Building of the Set for Fritz Lang's *Metropolis*.

separatist group for nearly three decades thereafter and served as the central target within Aznar's authoritarian stylization of a "new strategic culture" against terrorism. Wielding influence over the media and public opinion, this campaign equated the more complex issues relating to the territorial structure of Spain with black-and-white incentives to violence. This clothing of politics in the murkiness of moralistic ambiguity on the premise of promoting greater national security involved strategies that, as stated by the former Vice President of the Catalan Government, Josep-Lluí s Carod-Rovira, "illustrated the ability and success with which the Popular Party's government criminalized differences, cultural and linguistic diversity, to influence institutional representatives who should otherwise be seen as guaranteeing impartiality." Despite the zeal with which the government coerced a self-censorship that pervaded the political, social and cultural sphere, it was the unexpected turn in the March 2004 electoral vote in the immediate aftermath of the tragic Atocha bombings that ironically led to a shift in public opinion within a period of forty-eight hours and effectively and unexpectedly ousted the incumbent government. This second unforeseen turn in modern Spanish history was one that extended beyond the country itself, further reshaping and greatly influencing European politics. In this particular case, however, it was not the activity of ETA that brought about the change but the purported rumour of ETA's possible activity that prompted nearly two million voters to engage unexpectedly in the national elections. What ensued was a reshuffling of political activity that resulted in an immediate about-face and a reversing of the policies of the previous government.

The "Basque problem" is plagued by what is connoted internationally and nationally by the clandestine nature of ETA. The realpolitik of the territory, however, transcends this clandestine aspect and is, in actuality, framed moreover by aspirations to self-determination and autonomy as claimed in the controversial "Ibarretxe Plan" for Basque sovereignty. This proposal in the form of a claim, even if it is dismissed as political rumour and as regional rancour by its opponents, is nevertheless publicly articulated and challenged in the canons of the regional parliament. The plan as it stands is, quite simply, incompatible with today's Europe. Faintly echoed in the European and world media, the plan challenges the traditional notion of the nation state in Europe. The possible fracture insinuated by its potential is what prompted the newly elected Zapatero to make his first telephone call as Prime Minister to Juan José Ibarretxe, the regional premier of the Basque Territory, to restore the relations that had been severed by Aznar in 2001. Among these resulting irregularities and discrepancies in this traditional flow of city, region, province, and state,

☛ *La justicia, aunque anda cojeando, rara vez deja de alcanzar al criminal en su carrera (Horacio)*

EL MUND

VIERNES 21 de febrero de 2003
Año XIV. Número: 4.826

PAIS VASCO / GIPUZKOA

MOVILES / Una avería deja sin teléfono a 8,6 millones de clientes de Vo

Cuatro agentes de la Guardia Civil precintan, ayer, las instalaciones de «Egunkaria» en Bilbao. / IÑAKI ANDRES / CARLOS GARCIA

Un juez cierra el único diario en euskara al relacionarlo con la trama financiera de ETA

▸ Un nota conjunta del magistrado Del Olmo y el Ministerio del Interior señala que «se pretende demostrar la intervención» de la banda en 'Egunkaria' ▸ El líder radical Xabier Alegría, entre los 10 detenidos

BILBAO.– El juez de la Audiencia Nacional Juan del Olmo clausuró ayer el diario abertzale *Euskaldunon Egunkaria*, único periódico editado en euskara. El juez y el Ministerio del Interior, en una nota pactada por ambos, aseguran que la investigación pretende demostrar «la intervención de ETA en la financiación del rotativo».

El magistrado ordenó la operación a la Guardia Civil, que practicó una veintena de registros y detuvo a 10 personas. Entre los arrestados se encuentran el dirigente radical Xabier Alegria y el director del diario, Martxelo Otamendi.

Trescientos agentes de la Guardia Civil intervinieron en este operativo que incluyó también 21 registros y que permitió la incautación de abundante documentación. Con ella y con la información policial que ha dado pie a esta actuación judicial, el juez Del Olmo intenta confirmar la «presunta instrumentali zación de las sociedades mercanti les» ligadas al periódico clausurad dentro de «la estrategia terrorista» El cierre de *Egunkaria* provoc ayer el rechazo de importantes sec tores políticos y educativos relacio nados con el euskara que ya ha anunciado movilizaciones com una marcha que recorrerá mañan sábado San Sebastián.

Páginas 8 a 1
Editorial en pág.

«A la gente le da igual que ETA atente contra un periodista de Madrid», aseguró el año pasado el director de 'Egunkaria' en una entrevista para una tesis doctoral

Página 10

it is possible to consider the juxtaposition of the rational and irrational and its relevance in relation to art. Certainly, it is not the intent of this project to legitimize these political initiatives. The incentive of Manifesta remains to abstract from the social experience of the Basque region, one conscious of autonomy and self-determination, to locate a parallel discourse that leads to a consideration of the autonomous work of art, one that is characterized by dissonance and tension in its construction. In doing so, its challenge is not to privilege the regime of the spectacle, nor some kind of organicist fantasy about the overcoming of the state and the end of politics as shared by the nihilistic attitudes of the Situationists. But neither is it in its interest to deny the existing realities to reduce them merely to a private matter. It is an attempt to broaden the canvas of what we regard as contemporary history to locate an aesthetic frame to project art's possibility as a social agency that assumes a form of resistance through a construction that reaffirms its power of reflection through its very performativity, and not through its attempt at clarity and immediacy.

IRRECONCILABLE DIFFERENCES AS A CRITICAL SITE FOR ART

> *When I was taking photographs in the late 70's, I clearly made a mistake in valuing our (Soviet) lives from the point of view of our mediocre technology. My understanding of the visual image was informed by the square, the cube, the cell, as a constructivist element that arrived out of the transformation and the disruption of a straight line. This reaffirmed my interest to locate the set of coordinates that designated a point somewhere in this time. This served as my point of departure in constructing art.*
> -Boris Mikhailov

> *I want to make something that is just as beautiful as a plant, or a computer. In my case, it is a fictitious person in the form of a large building.*
> –Mark Manders

How are sites of resistance to be understood spatially, temporally, theoretically, and practically? It is necessary to review how the question of function has been interpreted historically to arrive at an answer. Ever since Adolf Loos referred to architecture as a "cry into emptiness," art has drawn from the debates around critical architecture to renounce its artificiality and its propensity toward artifact. Architectural ideology has contributed to the formulation of a performative aesthetics that endows art with the potential, as an independent agency, to recollect that which no longer exists and anticipate what has yet to exist in a vision of an alternative world. Within the spatial premise of modernity centered on the construct of the city, and through architectural theory's focus on the plan, art has sought a political logic of resistance.

Although the cooperation between architecture and art has evolved into a dominant art form, it is important to point out what distinguishes each discipline as thought and practice to begin to understand why their entanglement has evolved into what is already commonplace in contemporary art practice. As architecture moves toward the condition of conceptual art, it ceases to be architecture. Artworks, on the other hand, require cunning. If the individual impulses of artworks were left to their own immediacy, to themselves, they would blow away without a trace.[5] Art, in order to be art, writes architectural theorist Andrew Benjamin, must negate the present, otherwise it would be in its service. Architecture, while having to function, cannot negate men as they are, and yet its possibility, its approaching towards art, is given by its projected autonomy and thus by its negation of men as they actually are.[6]

The central consideration in the historical entanglement of art and architecture returns to the basic question of functionalism. This is not to consider function in its static and practical state but function as gauged against its historical dynamic – that which was functional yesterday is not so today (i.e. that which was valid yesterday is superfluous today). Utopian considerations of functionalism arriving out of an effacement of ornament as commenced by Loos steadily became contested by the mid 20th century. What was inscribed into the plan for social utopia in the 1920s eventually divided European culture between the Expressionist and Neue Sachlichkeit movements. While the latter called for the destruction of the object and its substitution by a process to be lived as such, Expressionism called for the exasperation of the object. Neue Sachlichkeit's agenda centered on pure white constructions unfettered by the imaginative forms of the past, entered into architecture's agenda at the Congrès Internationaux d'Architecture Moderne (CIAM). The Functionalist city evolved as a model based on Ludwig Hilberseimer's cell as a standardized form reflecting the categorization and reorganization of production in the face of the new techniques of production employed by modernist architecture. What evolved into a symbol of rationalism and functionalism constituted, as the architectural historian Manfredo Tafuri noted, the primary element of the continuous production line that concluded the city. The cell as a paradigmatic unit arrived as a dominant form that remained implanted in mass produced post-war architecture and was usurped into a stylization of the modern that continues to the present day. The historical dynamic contained within the concept of ornament that reaffirmed Loos' claim that articles lose their meaning as soon as they are displaced or disengaged in such a way that their use is no longer required, led to an understanding of the usefulness of functionalist architecture as useless. Its oppressive nature was made apparent within the emergence of a social irrationality previously latent in historical development.[7] The architectural cell, initially imposed as part of a program of liberal thought, arrived as a symbol of a repressive capitalist order associated with mechanisms of pacification and control. A younger generation of architects arriving in the 1950s protested against Le Corbusier's dominant position in CIAM and called for a revision of the functionalist codes outlined in CIAM's original charter with respect to the propagation of the grid, the cell and prefabricated structures. Shadrach Woods and Alison and Peter Smithson in the form of Team 10 proposed an alternative organic, open structure for planning and living that centered less on the creation of a plan than on a way of planning. In their proposal plan for Val d'Asua in Bilbao at the 1962 Team 10 meetings, Woods noted that - "our intention is to create a stem tied to the pedestrian system... where the paseo would happen – you know the old Spanish thing – Las Ramblas of Barcelona, Plaza Real in Salamanca – a place where people could be and at the same time see all these things happening without being disturbed by them."[8]

Postwar critical thought returned to the cultural field in the 1960s with the roots of its revival in the Frankfurt School accompanied by an atmosphere of what amounted to a crisis in urbanism throughout Europe. What emerged was a divergence of views over the notion of the subject in relation to the built environment. It was a time when the original utopian values promoted by the Russian Revolution had been overtaken by the USSR's increasingly technocratic bureaucracy and overbearing state machinery. France under de Gaulle was not very far removed from the restrictive policies of Franco's regime. The Algerian War promoted further intellectual dissent in France which made for clandestine movements such as 'Manifeste des 121' against the government. How did the zeitgeist of the 60s contribute to the understanding that architecture had surpassed its premise as ideology? How did art, then, attempt to proceed apart from the cycle of production and consumption of late capitalism to stand apart from the increasingly compromised position of architecture? How did art evolve as the only remaining mediator from which architecture might borrow to empower its imagination and fathom its other possibilities? Basque sculptor Jorge Oteiza, who left the art world after his presentation of *Operation H* in the Bienal de São Paulo in 1957, sought out alternative possibilities for cultural production as available through the modes of production available in the factory and documented on film with the aim of extending the construction metaphor in relation to sculptural production. In a letter written to a colleague in 1965, he expressed his views about a "new functionalist approach to the art gallery" marking a departure from what he viewed as a former prevalence of concrete rationalism and the geometric reasoning of place prevalent in previous decades toward the emergence of the reasoning of the irrational, spontaneous, subjective, informal conditions of expression.[9] Art began to extend rather than recite the language of architecture by referring to its logic while remaining separate to its aspirations to practical function and adherence to monocular perspective.

This gradual architecturalisation of art was not solely rooted in a historical activism in relation to the rational and built environment. The inter-articulation of architecture and art can also be attributed to the disillusionment on the part of architects who, even in the 1960s, had lost their credibility as ideologists. As Tafuri notes, the architect steadily became "aware of the enormous technological possibilities available for rationalizing cities and territories, coupled with the daily spectacle of their waste to create an atmosphere of anxiety. The reorganization of the global market and productive development left little extraneous to architectural design. As there was no remaining possibility for a class political economy," but only for a critique of political economy, so too there was no class aesthetic, art or architecture but only a class critique of the aesthetic, of art, of architecture, and of the city itself. The resulting unification of art, architecture, and city arose out of the crisis in the ideological function of architecture and art's own objective commercialization. The only possible alternative for architecture lay not in the finality of a structure but in seeking out architecture's other possibility.[10] Alterity served as architecture's only critical alternative, and the imagining of its alternatives was subsequently co-opted by art.

The early 1960's saw an international revision of the social significance of architecture that oscillated between handicraft and imagination and its subordination to rationality. The city became the central site where questions of the architectonic collided with the social in areas that related to the existence or non-existence of the social subject. Theodor Adorno referenced these oscillating arguments between rationality and expression relevant within the debates of architecture in a little-noted, but seminal essay entitled *Functionalism Today* presented to the German Werkbund in 1965. Adorno's text was drafted nearly four years after Berlin had been divided along Ackerstrasse, a street that during the postwar period served as a shared and functioning border between two economic systems – the market system and the Socialist system. During the Bauhaus period, Ackerstrasse also symbolized the boulevard of progress where the industrial designs of Peter Behrens were rendered in the form of the AEG and Siemens factories. Ackerstrasse was pivotal in releasing Adorno's arguments from the traditional categories of function and ornament framed in the first half of the 20th century to revise these concepts in confrontation with the current socio-historical situation and the emerging global economy. By inter-articulating the contrasting approaches of the "outmoded modernist" Le Corbusier and the expressive complexity of Hans Scharoun, Adorno structured a logic that invested critical architecture as the foundation for understanding the autonomous work of art by unraveling the irreconcilability of function. By focusing on Le Corbursier's exaltation of the architect's power of imagination as a perpetual organizer and reorganizer and on Sharoun's response to complex geometry and openendedness, Adorno emphasized the irreconcilability of function and expression as the optimal condition. In doing so, he structured a logic to explain why architecture inhabits culture before culture inhabits architecture, and how architecture tends to construct the visual before it is placed in the visual. This logic would provide a foundation for exploring why the more critical works of art produced within the last century have been those entangled with architecture, either in approximating architectural structures, by simulating their functions, or by contesting architecture outright.

THE CRY INTO EMPTINESS

> *Suffering from aphasia, François gropes at a certain moment his head with his hands: 'I would like to know what is going on up here upstairs...*
> *my spirit can't grasp all this anymore!*
> –An excerpt from *François*
> Sven Augustijnen

> *The "Wall Built from One Brick" is an idea related to the invention of the brick as a sort of trick... the original brick from which the construction departs is finally disguised with the remainder of the bricks and the entirety of the construction.*
> –From the proposal *Wall Built from One Brick*
> Kirsten Pieroth

> *Ondartxo evolves as a museum under construction whereby the paper architecture of its plans becomes a witness to the possible future development of that space. It becomes an outline of the core... as a search for the essence and life of things.*
> –From the proposal for *Denkmal 2* at Ondartxo, Pasaia
> Jan de Cock

Architecture as a discipline lodged in the future fathoms the possibilities of what has yet to be. In its projection toward the future, architecture relies on a kind of staging process that resists the literal to try to convey that even though a building is built, it is at the same time incomplete, despite its completedness. It is "privileged yet, in the end, it is attributed the status of an artwork precisely because it contains the gap to which the allusion has been made."[11] This contradiction in terms is made evident by architecture's binding relationship to space, which is gauged against this notion of staged time versus built time in the generation of form. Within the matrix of staged time, it is possible to unlock time from a purely singular concept to gain its complexity in the interplay of form and function through alterity. In alterity, or the understanding of otherness, the logic of architectural thought allows the aesthetic to surpass the materiality of art by means of an imagination that Adorno refers to as "innervated." This innervated imagination is what constitutes an artistic imagination that "awakens the accumulated elements by becoming aware of the innate problematic of material – just as in music, which emphasizes the primacy of an individual tone, it has to discover a more complex relationship of its components."[12] Imagination allows for the development of the immateriality of excess that assumes an enigmatic form reaffirming the irreconcilability of differences and dissonance within the construction of a work of art. Adorno illustrates this point further in *Functionalism Today*:

> *Architecture inquires: how can a certain purpose become space, through which forms, which materials? All factors relate reciprocally to one another. Architectonic imagination, involves the ability to articulate space purposefully. It permits purposes to become space. It constructs according to purposes. Conversely, space and the sense of space can become more than impoverished purpose only when imagination impregnates them with purposefulness. Imagination breaks out of the immanent connections of purpose, to which it owes its very existence.* [13]

Architecture, moreover, and the thinking of architecture and its articulation of spaces, is inscribed by a gap – that between the structural present and a gesturing toward a future – marking a site of tension and potential. Whereas function is linked to utility, alterity or the striving for an otherness is bound to human potential. It involves an unconstrained gesture toward freedom present in the most functionally driven object and it repeats the position of the art object in the logic of its negation. It is in this gap, this striving for that which has yet to be defined, implicit within both art and architecture, that a future may be projected to overcome the present by yielding a completion to come.[14] In this projection, function extends beyond a question of what is practical and useful to encompass "that which may be." This "what has yet to be" refers to alterity as the pivotal mechanism that distinguishes art from a real project to allow it to retain its critical status as an art work lodged between the probable and the possible.

The autonomous work of art is inscribed by a tendency that may find its metaphor in the performative. As an artwork is constituted according to its internal logic, it is determined by the integral organization of all its elements so that nothing remains of the ornamental. It strives toward becoming a more opaque and unintelligible object so that its effective de-arting is essential to its constitution. Assuming the form of the enigma, it adopts the metaphor of the puzzle or the riddle whose solution takes the form of the comprehension of the puzzle without a solution. In this way, art works within the paradox of its own incomprehensibility to lead to an understanding of art as more of a tendency and a gesture than a result. This allows for the production of emotional effects, if even in the form of the invisible, to produce "the more" or what Adorno refers to as the "crackling noise" of art.[15] It is possible to refer to the work of Bas Jan Ader to explain this structure. In the series of films entitled *Falling*, distinguished as *Falling (geometric)* and *Falling (organic)*, Ader explores human subjectivity by positing his body as a construction set against the forces of gravity. Although the motion is initiated by the artist and the foundation of his constructions based on mathematical relations, he eventually relinquishes control in order to be driven into unforeseen trajectories and paths. Ader employs his body as a pivotal vortex within a rational construction – his leaning against a chair, his standing on the roof of a house – to assume the performative in contrast to what could otherwise be read as a formalist motion study. He proceeds from the geometry of motion to engage with the construction of the expressive in the film *I'm Too Sad To Tell You*, in which he documents his being driven to tears. This "being driven to" is what stands as essential throughout the artist's oeuvre and not in the residual tears of its formation. Ader's propensity to explore the more expressive elements that arrive out of rational logic is what prompts one to suspect the resolution of his final project, *In Search of the Miraculous*, as a mistaken detour. Intended as a voyage into the Atlantic, it is difficult not to interpret the excursion as a homage to Le Corbusier, who also walked into the sea for an endless voyage.

Architecture remains the privileged site in demonstrating the performative construction as one that arrives as expression qua construction. By its very nature, it holds the configuration of the space between the real and the imaginary to characterize a gap between what our understanding can grasp and what can only be declared logically possible.[16] Architecture is the site that can be assigned the status of an artwork because it holds the gap that interconnects purpose and imagination in a dialectical interplay. Yet, art resists reducing imagination to the anticipatory adaptation to material ends, and the interarticulation of expression and construction drawn from architectural examples provides the foundation for elaborating on the autonomy of art – "in recognizing that functionalism today, prototypically in architecture, would have to push expression so far as to win expression."[17] Construction, according to Adorno, gains expression through its coldness but cannot, as a form of human content, wait to be filled with expression.[18] Expression and construction dialectically combine in such a way that they are realized only through one another. It is in this dialectic of reconciliation and non-reconciliation generated by the artwork that the critical status of the work is retained.[19]

FATHOMING ANOTHER PLACE

> *Retraction from a black below grey horizon, flat except for the shape of the horses, grazing silenty. The window, shuttered by two red doors, is open but reflective.*
> (Day)
> –A Stage Direction from *Diarios (To You)*
> Markus Schinwald

The particularities of place lead to the possibility of conceptualizing various futures without departing from the real factors and forces moulding the future forms of this place. San Sebastian is a leisure-oriented space, a potlatch of surplus objects, symbols and energies, with an accent on sports, reinvigoration and the carnivalesque, rather than on rest, relaxation and asceticism. The illusion of naturalness exhibited by the city makes space for another illusion: that of a centralized, organized, symbolized and programmed space facilitating the production of a representational space. In its spontaneously induced eroticism, it holds material for the development of ample discursive sites for interrogation and investigation. As a predominantly figurative city by virtue of a neoclassical reconstruction designed by Pedro Manuel de Ugartemendia after a devastating fire in 1813, San Sebastian reeks of narrative to the point that would inevitably lead Adolf Loos to scream: "ornament and crime".[20] Extended to its very edges by the abstract volumes of Rafael Moneo's Kursaal, the city as discursive and shifting meets the sea, which is, in contrast, a kind of solid defined in history, identities and functions. Moneo's orthogonal tectonic spaces silhouetting the headlands of Mont Urgull and Ulia employ a compositional device of rotation that draws from the Bahia de La Concha to other critical sites for intervention. As a Derridean marker of the limit and the delimited, the interior and the anterior, it announces the sublime as the ontological condition of this particular place. Situated within the *as if*, San Sebastian envisions itself as "other" through a critical exploration of contemporary culture and aesthetics in the form of a project.

The consideration of the limit is not in the sense of a marker but as a means of discriminating between a certain order and a certain disorder – that which falls within the limit is subject to the law and that beyond it is devoid of law and form. In this sense, nature points to a hybrid domain that refers back to the cult of ruin that holds within it a force of resistance that expresses a history and yet is compelling. As an example, the surroundings of San Sebastian falsely invite an innate faith in natural beauty that in reality has been subject to the incursions of technology in the production of a man-made landscape along the coast. What Humboldt referred to as the craggy Basque landscape, is in large part an illusion and an imitation that constitutes it as artifactal - a "cultural landscape" from which it is possible to abstract to find the relational in the aesthetics of nature to the philosophy of art. At its very core, nature is a reality that points to something other – to the difference between what we interpret as the reality of nature and a certain fiction that the idea of nature imposes. It is not merely a division of what is visible and invisible but an alluding to 'a something more' that leads to suspension and the unthinkable, to an undeterminable detour that is marked by a perpetual movement of withdrawal and to reinscription.[21] Nature points to an otherness that presents to thought the concept of alterity. The aesthetic attitude toward nature – that of contemplation, that of correspondence and the experience of nature as a prototype, implies different modes of experiencing temporality. As the experience of contemplation relates to the present as a passing moment, the experience of correspondence relates to the past, and the experience of an imagination to the future. These attitudes imply aesthetic experiences of landscape wherein the experience of nature in correspondence plays a predominant role in architecture bound by a time and space relationship that extends beyond the language of existing buildings and structures and questions of practicality and function.[22]

The 19th-century Romantic understanding of the sublime as portrayed in the seascapes of Caspar David Friedrich has been gauged against the historic dynamic of landscape to depart from a Kantian understanding of aesthetics in relation to natural beauty. The experience of the sublime relocates within the present-day space of the abject – within container-ridden port areas and industrial lots common within the outlying industrial belts of San Sebastian in Lezo or the nearby industrial ghost-town of Eibar, an architectural wonder of small scale modernist factories on the verge of demolition. As communicated within the genre of Andreas Gursky's landscapes, natural beauty, mediated by technology, industrial waste and the proliferation of increasing global economy, has been transformed into a caricature of itself.[23] The present-day experience of the sublime, then, locates human subjectivity in an otherness outside of what is experienced as the myth of natural beauty, to remind us that not everything is to be reduced to exchange value, and that not everything must submit to the control of an instrumental reason subject to a location within the grid of definitions and categories. The prior systems of classification and belief are subject to a historical dynamic that calls for the need for revision and reinterpretation. And art therefore requires the sublime in order to extend out of its frame of mere appearances to become, as Adorno claims, an active independent agency and not merely a reservoir of historical frustrations of failed dreams and projects of human emancipation.

Why is art "art" anyway, if anyone would even care to ask? Adorno answers enigmatically that art most resembles the phrase "Here I am" or "This is what I Am," or even "I am a Rhinoceros - for there is no place/without eyes to see you." Cryptic as this may sound, the analogy promotes an understanding of art that defers from identification and tends towards a reliance on the interdependence of entities that locks in a binding object-subject relationship.[24] Art is by its nature animated, continually speaking back to us. It acts like a subject by engaging the subject and, ironically, it is the gaze of the artwork that engages the subject and constitutes expression. What essentially makes art "art" is the residue of the subject in the artwork that remains thereafter and within. This is the way that subjectivity defines itself in the object and understands itself through the object. Although the artwork requires the intentional mediation of the artist, the subject remains the medium of truth, and the spirit of the work is something that artists may have very little relation to. And although a work of art may activate the intellect, and call to our rational side, it must also respond to a natural sense and intuition to engage.

VIOLENCE OF THE IMAGINATION AND NEGATION

> *On one of its sides, poetry makes sense, but on another it unmakes it. It distances speech, and if it restores it to us, it is from afar. It binds dangerously the possibility of speaking to an impossibility that becomes, as it were, its very condition. It allows us to write 'I am unhappy,' but this initial expression of unhappiness, by depriving us of already-formed, familiar, and reliable thoughts, exposes us to an experience full of risks, and more than that, to a silent drone, a stammering, whose perfection does not prevent us from acknowledging it as a lack.*
> –From *Le Paradoxe d'Aytré*
> Maurice Blanchot

Vandalism. The territory is intermittently vandalized by graffiti and by virtue of the immediate recourse taken by the authorities to remove the traces, the inscriptions read as invasive acts. This roving interventionism continually threatens the space to stand accused without an alibi through the mechanism of a spontaneous event, a project, a deed. The city's identity consequently evolves as a possible fiction, if one is to consider Mikhail Bakhtin's formulation that identity could be fiction[25], and at the same time universally present in assumptions made about one's status as an individual, in human social experience, language and even in scientific speculation. Other clues persist in proximity to San Sebastian. A recently built museum dedicated to the exhibition of cement as a cultural and historical artifact is offered as a tourist site and yet a museum of cement strokes Valéry's notion of the museum as mausoleum[26] with critical work being found everywhere else but there. The Museo del Cemento Rezola is located within a composite environment that includes a sports ground, kiosk, bar and neighboring factory.[27] With declamatory banners hung prominently throughout, a cultural space evolves similar to El Lissitsky's *PROUN*, as a type of abstraction of a propaganda hoarding, cryptic and unintelligible while at the same time communicating urgency. The signs without instructional function appear as head-on collisions announcing a fracture that prompts investigation. Posted banners in apparent protest read as painted writing functioning like Corday's letter in the hand of David's *Marat* - a discursive form that is not necessarily decipherable. [28] At this point, it is possible to cite Mayakovsky's poetry or Malevich's battle cry – U el el el teka! It points to a breakdown in the order of meaning and claims all as null and void.

Artworks rely on these very toxins to allow for an existence beyond a mere thingness, "killing what they objectify by tearing away from the immediacy of its life." They do so through the language of the mute or through what Beckett describes as the desecration of silence and the enigmatic. Nevertheless, their protest lies in the logic of negation which allows them the possibility of simply being resigned as things among things.[29] Negation, as written extensively by Jeff Wall in relation to Dan Graham's *Kammerspiel*, is central to functionalist art as the mechanism that counters the alienation resulting from a technologized society. In a determinate negation of contemporary social reality by recollecting what society represses, it is possible for art to anticipate how society might evolve. Although the functionalist work of art may approximate the appearance of usefulness, it does not respond to any external or practical function.[30] Wall notes that through the incorporation of architectural tropes and planning rhetoric, the functionalist work of art is an alteration in the actualization of a critical negation of the built environment, realized with the intent to cut through the contradictions in an effort to overcome them, not by covering them up, but by pursuing them.[31] Functionalist art therefore criticizes rationality without withdrawing from it, and in doing so, it retains its status as an aesthetic work.

Without the intent to be fulfilled as architecture, art continues in architecture's vein to strive to articulate the seemingly functional in order to pose questions as to how the nature of domestic, institutional, or public space can play a role in the formation of the human subject. Although architecture has historically provided art with a critical language, architecture has resisted following art's example. Architect Peter Eisenman interpreted this as contemporary architecture's very weakness - in its resistance to proceed from those questions initially asked by Piranesi in relation to the Panopticon to challenge the traditional subject-object relationships. Eisenman noted that it was the investigations by artists such as Dan Graham, Gordon Matta-Clark, and Robert Smithson, who throughout the 60's and 70's displaced the viewing subject from his/her position in an anthropocentric stability, "comfortably upright on a flat, tabular ground." These artists challenged the naturalism of the 17th, 18th, and 19th centuries to provide a non-objective sense of site made more complex by aerial photography and air transport in the 60s that brought into view the surface features of a world of shifting perspectives.[32] Smithson's *Towards the Development of an Air Terminal* (1967)[33], for example, in assuming the form of a plan, places Smithson in the role of an artist-consultant who studies the possibilities in the development of an air terminal without aspiring to ever being identified as an architect or engineer. Furthermore, discussions around the air terminal are not intended to operate on any presupposed notion of art, engineering or architecture but to serve the very purpose of open-endedness. This is rendered as an exploration, and not for the purpose of fulfilling any practical investigation or function to be applied as a feasibility study. As Schlegel proceeded within the early German Romantic tradition to adopt the form of notebooks and philosophical fragments, uncompleted drafts and sketches, these items were invested with cultural value. Similarly, in Smithson's project the air terminal was not defined in terms of a plan for a finalized structure but considered in its relation to aircraft. By approaching the air terminal against the enormous scale of runways, Smithson isolated aircraft into "buildings" for short spaces of time. As temporary buildings, the aircraft would eventually disappear, and as containers, they would be subject to a constant relocation throughout a vectored space that would result in a continual reconfiguration of the air terminal site. In this context, landscape and land-surveying define a program in which land and buildings disappear as they develop. As a future project, the air terminal, both as an idea and as a thing defined as a set of coordinates among the straight lines of landing fields and runways, stood against the prevalence on the part of artists to create critical empty signifiers produced in the form of cells and containers without any further critical investigation. These kind of encounters with the plan, as invested by Smithson, continually challenge contemporary art's preoccupation with the result and its fear of the inability to achieve a realization that connotes innate failure. Nevertheless, something is retained by art's wish not to be presented as something real as a way of resisting the social, as a space that truly holds within it a delusion.

LIKE A PORCUPINE

Despite the failure of the student revolts of 1968, art still had the possibility to contribute to a liberation in the recognition, that even if a revolution takes place, art will not come to an end. And a revolution will not be achieved, if one thinks about the end of art.
–On Marcuse's *Counterrevolution and Art*, 1972
Alexander Garcia Duttmann

I believe architecture and urbanism are activities that should grow in harsh reality. The problem is when you do not have enough independence to transcend that reality, and get trapped into it.
–A planning meeting for TOOAUP, San Sebastian
Alejandro Zaera-Polo

If I were to remain onto you a hundred years or more, I would bestow the agedness of my vitality to break you into the very fragments from the ambition you held for what only a joke and a whim. The wonder lies in the illusion and not in the application.
–On winning a game of Monopoly to a bad loser
Oksana Pasaiko.

How is it possible for a project such as Manifesta to learn from the structure of an artwork in order to behave socially and politically without having to immerse itself into reality? To find the possibility of articulating from a distance, but nevertheless poignantly, in approaching the subject but not only one defined as the viewing subject? How is it then possible to build this into the process of Manifesta as an internal critique of both its own development and the place that has essentially consigned its form as a way to promote culture as a reflection of the city? If Manifesta, by its very nature, is a category of representation that links art with the specifics of the urban, how then can a project such as this one help to extend the language of architecture and urbanism in order to explore how culture may serve to catalyze change rather than be something purely ornamental? In these circumstances, when everything seems to be written on the sleeve of the place of Manifesta's inception, the key still lies in looking for what is not there and finding it elsewhere, although not too far from home.

Driving several kilometers inland, past San Sebastian's first beach and the monumental Kursaal, one encounters a port that is altogether antithetical to the picturesque San Sebastian in almost every way – politically, socially, economically and demographically. Decaying ships and vacant warehouses indicate a port and a surrounding town that seem to have been short-circuited from their former construction, maritime, trade and fishing activities. To contrast the two areas simply, San Sebastian, characterized by a tertiary economy, symbolizes leisure at its very essence, and Pasaia, a secondary economy, points to labour in decline. Although it had been Manifesta's initial intent to inhabit Pasaia to reflect the spectral doubling that characterizes San Sebastian, what evolved was far more critical than merely establishing a metaphorical dimension for an exhibition. The more rational collaboration sought out with the Berlage Institute in the form of the Office of Alternative Urban Planning and the expressive sculpting into Ondartxo as an open-ended and evolving museum – these projects broke Manifesta out of the immediacy of its scheduled time bracket and interwove it into the fabric of city and regional planning. The resulting inter-articulation of San Sebastian and Pasaia anticipated the possibilities of a future construction of behavior that overrode the debates about possible results. As noted by Sebastian Khourian, the contingency endemic to the region was observed as a vital force rather than a weakness in order to create the possibility for entrance to a place that formerly prevented entry.

It is art's privilege to defer political activism and to retain its power in promoting an awareness on the part of the subject of the social limits imposed by the city planning or by governments. As Adorno claims, perhaps autonomous art does not necessarily change political attitudes, but its effectiveness under advanced capitalist conditions lies in its ability to mount crucial resistance, which may inevitably lead to such changes. Adorno writes that "the artist can no longer proceed naively on a prescribed path" but must pursue "aesthetic thought energetically, at risk of lapsing into dilletantish hypotheses and groping justifications for the sake of defending an intellectual construct."[34] Insofar as a social function can be predicated for artworks, their social essence requires a double reflection on their being for themselves and on their relations to society. By crystallizing in itself something unique onto itself, rather than complying with existing social norms and qualifying as socially useful, the artwork criticizes society by merely existing.[35] Artworks arrive as the most profound instances of social alienation, their objectivity – the distance between the subject and freedom – constituting the artwork as a testament and a reminder of unfreedom.[36]

Just as Kracauer compares the lobby of the hotel to the traditional church in *Hotelhalle* [37] in contrasting the modern society of the transient and disconnected with the community of believers Manifesta posits a third point in this spatial comparison. The project is installed between San Sebastian and Pasaia as a labyrinth leading between temporal rupture and intention in a process of research whose very possibility is due to its uncertainty. A former monastery dating from the 16th century, Museo San Telmo, explores a national psyche in which folklore, history, politics, mysticism, eroticism, nationalism and perversion are intermingled. In the apse of its cathedral, Manifesta can comfortably accommodate the artist who stands central in the chapel, enigmatically indicted - for reductivist tendencies or, alternatively, for preaching the identity of difference in a public place. Within a dialectical site of project and accusation, Manifesta has had the opportunity to lead a concerted investigation among ornament and crime, identity and fiction, intent and alibi, rings and obstacles,[38] sea and constellation,[39] and fireworks and apparitions.

Donostia / San Sebastian

Pasaia. Photos by Sebastián Khourian

Notes

1. The title, *Staged Matrix*, is borrowed from a performance staged by Markus Schinwald with Oleg Soulimenko for Tanzquartier, Vienna, Austria, 2003.
2. Manfredo Tafuri, *Architecture and Utopia: Design and Capital Development* (MIT Press, Cambridge, Mass., 1976), Chapter 1: 'Reason's Adventures.'
3. Peter Osborne, 'Non-places and the Spaces of Art,' in *The Journal of Architecture*, Volume 6, Summer 2001.
4. From the lecture by Steven Izenour, as part of the *Mutable Monument* series, WPA/Corcoran, February 23, 2001.
5. Theodor Adorno, *Aesthetic Theory*, tr. R. Hullot-Kentor, ed. Gretel, Adorno and Rolf Tiedermann (The Athlone Press, London, 1987), p.187.
6. Andrew Benjamin, 'Allowing Function Complexity: Notes on Adorno's "Functionalism Today," *AA Files* 41, 1999, p.44.
7. Theodor Adorno, 'Functionalism Today,' ed. Neil Leach, *Rethinking Architecture: A Reader in Cultural Theory* (Routledge, London, 1997), p.7.
8. Interview between Woods, Smithson, and Bakema, ed. by Alison Smithson, *Team 10 Meetings* (Rizzoli, New York, 1991), p. 90.
9. See D.A.E. the project on *Operación H*, Manifesta 5.
10. Manfredo Tafuri, *Architecture and Utopia: Design and Capitalist Development*, pp.178-182.
11.Andrew Benjamin, 'Allowing Function Complexity', p.43.
12. Theodor Adorno, 'Functionalism Today', p.14.
13. Ibid. p.14.
14. Andrew Benjamin, 'Allowing Function Complexity', p.41.
15. Thedor Adorno, *Aesthetic Theory*, p.79.
16. Andrew Benjamin, 'Allowing Function Complexity', p.41.
17.Theodor Adorno, 'Functionalism Today', p.9.
18. Theodor Adorno, *Aesthetic Theory*, p.44.
19. Peter Osborne, "Adorno and the Metaphysics of Modernism: The Problem of a 'Postmodern' Art," ed. by Andrew Benjamin, *The Problem of Modernity: Adorno and Benjamin* (Routledge, London, 1989), pp.31-32.
20. Adolf Loos, 'Ornament and Crime' in Yehuda Safran and Wilfried Wang (eds), *The Architecture of Adolf Loos* (London, 1987). Loos' concern with ornament is inseparable from a conception of modernity. Ornament is not a sign of the times, rather it shows that the sign is already timed. The time is historical.
21. Theodor Adorno, *Aesthetic Theory*, pp.64-65.
22. Heinz Paetzold, 'Adorno's Notion of Natural Beauty,' ed. T. Huhn and L. Zuidervaart, *The Semblance of Subjectivity: Essays in Adorno's Aesthetic Theory*, p.228.
23. Theodor Adorno, *Aesthetic Theory*, p.67.
24. Theodor Adorno, *Aesthetic Theory*, p.112.
25. Michael Holquist, *Dialogism: Bakhtin and his World* (Routledge, London, 1990). Bakhtin's architectonics provides a conceptual armature enabling an exploration of relations in terms of spatial and temporal parameters specifically in relation to situation as a site that is defined by its "relation to elements other than itself in space, and situation as time implicated in elements other than itself."
26. Theodor Adorno, 'Valéry Proust Museum' in *Prisms* (MIT Press, Cambridge, Mass., 1981) p.175.
27. The reference is to the Rezola Cement Museum, Avda. Anorga, 36, San Sebastian, which

'takes a look at the culture of this traditional company and covers the history of cement and its importance to our civilization. It also compiles a history of manufacturing through various different thematic areas as well as housing temporary exhibitions of a historical nature,' according to the tourist brochure. Idazti, *Donostia-San Sebastian Tourist Brochure*, Centre of Attraction and Tourism of Donostia-San Sebastian, 2002.

28. The reference is to Ch. 1 'Painting in the Year 2' in T. J. Clark, *Farewell to an Idea* (Yale, New Haven, 1999). Clark marks the beginning of modernism from 25 Vendémiaire Year 2 (16 October 1793), the first public showing of Jacques-Louis David's painting, *Death of Marat*.

29. Theodor Adorno, *Aesthetic Theory*, p. 133. With regard to negation, Adorno writes: "Artworks kill what they objectify by tearing it away from the immediacy of its own life. Their own life preys on death. This defines the qualitative threshold to modern art. Modern works relinquish themselves mimetically to reification, their principle of death. The effort to escape this element is art's illusory element which, since Baudelaire, art has wanted to discard without resigning itself to the status of a thing among things."

30. Jeff Wall, 'Introduction', in Dan Graham, *Two-Way Mirror Power: Selected Writings by Dan Graham on His Art*, ed. Alexander Alberro (MIT Press, Cambridge, Mass., 1999), p.17.

31. Jeff Wall, *Dan Graham's Kammerspiel* (Art Metropole, Toronto, 1991), p.11.

32. Peter Eisenman, 'Visions' Unfolding. Architecture in the Age of Electronic Media', *Domus* 22, January, 1992, p.22.

33. Jack Flam (ed.), *Robert Smithson: The Collected Writings*, pp. 51-60.

34. Theodor Adorno, 'Functionalism Today', p.18.

35. Theodor Adorno, *Aesthetic Theory*, p.226.

36. The reference is to Herbert Marcuse's paradoxical notion of culture whereby cultural freedom appears as unfreedom, and cultural progress, the result of constraint.

37. Siegfried Kracauer, 'Hotelhalle', in *Der Detektiv-Roman. Ein philosophischer Traktat*, in *Schriften I: Soziologie als Wissenschaft, Der Detektiv-Roman, Die Angestellten* (Suhrkamp, Frankfurt, 1971).

38. The reference is to the 'vol-poom', an obstacle first employed at the Equestrian Competition for Military Riding in San Sebastian in September 1909. This novel approach in showjumping promoted a natural balance between the rider and the horse and led to further investigations in motion studies.

39. Theodor Adorno, *Aeshetic Theory* (Athlone Press, London, 1997). Adorno writes about constellations and the phenomenon of fireworks as prototypical for artworks: "fireworks are apparitions appearing empirically yet liberated from the burden of the empirical, which is the obligation of their duration."

art as displaced urbanism: notes on a new con-structivism of the exhibition form

Peter Osborne

What does it mean for the art in an exhibition when that exhibition is conceived as an 'instrument of investigation' into its site and a means of cultural and economic 'reinvigoration' of the surrounding area? What does it mean, that is, for our understanding of it as art, rather than the mere occasion for the pursuit of a set of independently defined social goals? What does it mean not only that this *might* be so (that an exhibition might be so conceived), but that it is so, and is so, moreover, as a matter of course? What does it tell us about contemporary art that such a contextualization is a normal part of art's cultural functioning and, furthermore, that it is a central part of art's *critical* functioning as art? What does it tell us about what art is; that is, about what art has become? What does it tell us about what art is becoming? What kind of thing is this kind of art?

One set of answers to these questions revolves around the concept of construction. With the renewed convergence of artistic and architectural practices since the 1960s, and the ongoing subjection of architecture to urbanism, 'construction' has re-emerged as the main term through which art approaches urbanism, via architecture. At the same time, philosophically, where once it was notions of design, foundation and, later, 'ground' (*Grund*) that metaphorically bound philosophical thought to architecture, now, in the wake of various critiques of philosophical 'foundationalism' (be they historicist, pragmatism, contextualist, or deconstructive in form), it is construction that most often plays that role. And construction, it is argued, is a process that is fraught with contingency, with the indeterminacies of dialogue, and the '*mystery* of applicability'.[1] This critique of the original architectural metaphor of philosophy broadly corresponds to changes in architecture itself.

If Western philosophy has, in one of its central impulses, been but 'another name' for the will to architecture, historically this took the form of a will to the first principle, an intellectual absolutization or ideation of the *techné* (skill) of the *architectón* (the original or principle craftsman): design. But the *techné* of the *architectón* is no longer to be identified with design. Today, with the subjection of architecture to urbanism (planning), and of urbanism to the tripartite logic of capitalist economics (production, circulation, consumption), '[n]othing is less relevant to the reality of architecture than the idea that it is the realization of a design *qua* idea.'[2] Indeed, it never was, outside of an absolutist ideology of architecture, which derived its credibility from its inscription within a particular system of power. In the early 20th century, for Le Corbusier, the architect became 'an organizer, not a designer of objects'; after the crisis of the modern movement (the crisis of the ideological function of architecture as utopian planning), the architect has become a technician and organizer of building production.[3] Thus it is construction in its most general sense that 'architecture' has become.

It is out of a growing interplay between the theoretical discourses of philosophy, architecture, art and urbanism that the idea of a 'new constructivism' emerges. In the 1950s it was asked, 'What is existentialism?'; in the 1960s and early 70s, 'What is structuralism?'; in the late 1970s and 80s, 'What is poststructuralism?' and 'What is deconstruction?'. Now, increasingly, it is asked, 'What is constructivism today?'[4] To answer this question, it is necessary first to return briefly to an earlier phase of constructivism: the Russian Constructivism of the 1920s. For it is there that we find the dialectic of constructivism outlined in its elemental form. And just as Russian Constructivism was split at the outset between a radically political, Soviet social variant and an interpretation that returned it to its art-historical condition (formalism) – with which it remained identified in the West until well into the 1970s –[5] so the idea of a new constructivism comes in differing theoretical and ideological variants today. In particular, on the one hand there is a *philosophical* constructivism and libertarian architectonics that follows the thought of Gilles Deleuze, which would place philosophy, art, architecture and urbanism on a single 'plane of immanence', breaking with socio-historical analysis to affirm simultaneously a new philosophy, a new architecture and a new conception of the work of art, at the level of thought alone.[6] On the other hand there is that dense network of historical and conceptual ties that links a certain post-conceptual *art criticism, practice and exhibition* to the Constructivism of the 1920s, while at the same time registering a definitive distance from it. The former re-enacts the ideology of the avant-garde at its most abstract, as the permanent invention of beginnings, in the 'positive', non-dialectical form of 'an experimental art of singularizing space'.[7] The latter works through the historical contradictions of Constructivism under the changed conditions of the present. What follows sketches the conceptual shape of this latter working-through as the tentative emergence of a 'post-autonomous' art. This is an art that, if it is to be more than ironic, increasingly depends upon the constructivism of its exhibition context.

CONSTRUCTION AND CONSTRUCTIVISM

The principle of construction refers to the building up of an object through a combination of independently pre-existent parts. Long familiar in architecture, mathematics and philosophy,[8] it was first applied to artistic production in the early years of the second decade of the 20th century, in the Cubist pictorial compositions, collages, *papiers collés* and reliefs of Braque and Picasso. However, it only became explicit as a general principle of artistic production – independent of a critical dialogue with traditional forms – on the basis of Tatlin's self-consciously abstract counter-reliefs of 1914–15, which inspired the explicitly designated spatial 'constructions' of Klyun and Bruni of 1916–17, and laid the formal basis for the constructivism to come. As a formal principle, construction is independent of any particular materials. It is central to a non-visual art such as music, for example. Nonetheless, a certain *kind* of materials is required, since construction presupposes the independent 'givenness' of the elements of the constructive process as self-sufficient objects or units. This type of materials is intrinsic to the technologies and division of labour of machinofacture. This connection is central to the social meaning of construction, which derives from both the formal principle and the historical condition of the constructed materials.

It is for this reason, for example, that it is important to distinguish the 1915–19 'constructions' of the Russian artist Naum Gabo (whose formalist works were long synonymous with constructivism in the West) from even the early work of Tatlin. As one commentator has put it:

> *Whereas Tatlin's starting point was an interest in the qualities of the materials and their juxtaposition and interaction in space, Gabo's was a precise analysis of the structure of form and its internal spatial implications. He began with the idea or image which he then executed in a formal material. There was no exploitation of the* objet trouvé *or any chance combinations of materials.*[9]

It is this relative indifference to materials that is the basis of the social and political indifference of Gabo's formalist version of constructivism, set out in *The Realistic Manifesto* (1920). It contrasts sharply with the social utilitarianism and polemically anti-art stance of the First Working Group of Constructivists, founded the same year, with which the term is more properly, and richly, associated. For construction is a rational-instrumental process with historically specific social, material and technological conditions. The 'factual rationalization of artistic labour' that it meant for the First Working Group also meant (reflecting on these conditions) integrating artistic labour into the total social labour out of which its principle arose (machine labour), as part of a collective practice of 'social construction'.[10] This is the central, guiding concept of Constructivism: social construction. In this respect, the project of the First Working Group was nothing less than 'to realize the communist expression of material structures.'[11] And the materials of those structures were, principally, those of the industrial technologies of the day. Hence the emblematic significance of an early, pre-Constructivist work of Tatlin's such as *Selection of Materials: Iron, Stucco, Glass, Asphalt* (1914), which, while 'non-utilitarian', nonetheless still has more affinities with the laboratory work of Constructivism proper (formal experimentation within the horizon of social use) than with Gabo's self-sufficient interest in pure spatio-temporal forms.

In its broadest historical meaning, construction is a manifestation of that wider process of societal rationalization theorized by Max Weber as means-end or instrumental rationality (*Zweckrationalität*), which was generalized by the Frankfurt School into the dominant principle of modern societies. In fact, Weber himself applied this theoretical framework to the analysis of musical developments as early as 1911 in his *The Rational and Social Foundations of Music* (although it was not published until 1921). In this respect, construction embodies a historical structure of social experience that is a condition of significance in modern art in general. However, there are complexities involved in its artistic use that make it a profoundly dialectical affair. These have to do, first, with the contradictory political dynamics and implications of formalism, and second, with the relationship of construction to expression, which lies at the heart of the question of materials, in both formalist ('non-utilitarian') and social utilitarian applications of the principle.

Formal construction was a historical and conceptual condition of social-utilitarian or revolutionary Constructivism. For formalism destroyed the conventional symbolic attributes of traditional artistic media, as a condition for its rearticulation of their material elements on the basis of a complete freedom of relations (aestheticism). This opened up the contrary possibility of a utilitarian deployment of forms (rationalization). Indifference to the traditional uses and significations of materials was thus the condition of *both* formalist-aestheticism *and* anti-aesthetic instrumentalization, the two opposing currents within constructivism itself.[12] This was a politically contradictory process in two ways. First, formalist construction became a metonym for the freedom of experimentation associated with social revolution; but it was 'anti-revolutionary' in its social confinement of such experimentation to the domain of 'art', cut off from the everyday life and needs of the people. Second, the principle of rationalization is itself inherently politically contradictory. In the revolutionary moment of an anti-traditionalist collectivism, it could appear unambiguously progressive – as it did to the First Working Group – as agreement about social ends overshadowed disputes over means. But in the more clearly transitional period of the New Economic Policy and after, its instrumentality could equally denote alienation: alienation from the social process of determining means. 'Revolutionary' constructivism could then appear as a form of unfreedom in comparison with the aesthetically unlimited (albeit socially confined) scope of formalism. This is the Cold War reading of Soviet Constructivism. And in fact the experimental character of Constructivism was inevitably compromised by the practicalities of social production, as the distinction between Constructivism and Productivism (constructive artistic labour and production-art) dissolved as the 1920s progressed. The consolidation of new social forms became a constraint upon forms of construction, and experimentation retreated back to the non-utilitarian domain. This is the familiar dialectic of the historical and the neo-avant-gardes: 'art into life' versus the autonomy of the artwork.[13]

The first contradiction above (between the revolutionary and anti-revolutionary aspects of formalism) was temporarily mediated by the idea of 'laboratory works' – formal exercises undertaken not for their own sake but as research for future instrumental uses. But the second contradiction, internal to the social process of rationalization under conditions of scarcity, was intractable. It led, inevitably, to the restoration of an independent artistic domain. The politics of that domain were, however, henceforth put on a new footing. For it became a political requirement of the good faith of the artwork that it in some way confront the bad faith of its own autonomy (its withdrawal from the social domain), reflectively, within its own structure. Indeed, subsequently, elsewhere, under the conditions of the capitalist cultural industry, this would become a condition of autonomy itself. Hence the centrality of the dialectic of art and anti-art, internal to the modernist work, to its status as art – the critically constitutive role of anti-art within contemporary art. Art had to become 'critical' once it had failed to become universally actual, if it was to continue to be associated with both the freedom and the social possibilities for critically significant expression that it had acquired in the formalist/aestheticist critique of tradition. From that point on, critical artistic meaning became inextricably but problematically tied to the question of the relationship of the individual artwork to the rationality (and irrationality) of social forms. This problematic relationship is manifest internally, within the work, in the dialectic of construction and expression. It appears externally, at the level of cultural form, in the contradictory character of the social space of art.

CONSTRUCTION AND EXPRESSION

For all its interest in materials, motivated by their technological potential and everyday uses (including pleasure in technological forms), the utopian presuppositions of revolutionary Constructivism inhibited it from seeing in materials the site of a possible contradiction between construction and expression. For Constructivism, revolutionary-utilitarian construction was *immediately* Communist expression. There was an identity of economic function and political meaning. As economic function and political meaning diverge, however, and economic function becomes the site of social conflict, construction enters into opposition to expression. This opposition appears within the (non-utilitarian) artwork in the fact that the very principle of construction seems to negate the materials' immanent capacity for expression. As Adorno put it:

> *What distinguishes construction from composition in the encompassing sense of pictorial composition, is the ruthless subordination not only of everything that originated from outside the artwork, but also of all partial elements immanent to the work. To this extent construction is the extension of subjective domination ... [It] tears the elements of reality out of their primary context and transforms them to the point where they are once again capable of forming a unity, one that is no less imposed on them internally than was the heteronomous unity to which they were subjected externally. ... if the synthesis of construction is to succeed, it must in spite of all aversion be read out of the elements themselves, and they never wholly accede in themselves to what is imposed on them ... This is the utopia of construction; its fallibility, on the other hand, is that it necessarily has a penchant to destroy what it integrates and [thereby - PO] to arrest the process in which it has its life.*[14]

This contradiction is not contingent but structural. It arises out of the contradictory character – the irrational rationality – of instrumental reason itself. For the concept of rationalization to which Constructivism was, at least initially, bound (prior to Tatlin's late 'organic' constructivism) was that of the domination of nature. It had no consciousness of the dialectic of Enlightenment rationality. This dialectic determines the primary meaning of expression as expression not of communism, but of suffering.

The subjugation of the elements of the work to the constructive principle expresses the suffering of an inner nature subjected to the domination of the concept, for which the rational side of the subject is itself the agent. Construction is not simply logical in form, but as such, a *mimesis* (imitation) of rationality. Constructivism is a negative expressionism. It is thus *through*, rather than as a 'corrective' to, construction that expression occurs – 'construction gains expression through coldness'[15] – but only negatively and individualistically. On the other hand, to the extent to which construction in art is successful (that is, imposes its principle of organization through, as well as against, its elements, in a reflective process of what Adorno calls 'determinate irreconcilability'), it represents 'the effort to bear up under the suffering of alienation by exceeding it on the horizon of an undiminished and thus no longer violent rationality'. This is its continuing, if fragile, utopian function: its 'anticipation of a reconciled condition'.[16]

Ultimately, though, the principle of construction, essential to the ability of modern art to express social form, seems fated to drive that art into an impasse not unlike that of Constructivism itself. Constructivism took for granted the rationality of construction. Adorno takes for granted the irrationality of this rationality. He thus attributes the compromising of the experimental dimension of constructivism (which was the effect of a socio-political restriction on utilitarian form) to the principle of construction itself: 'constructivism no longer grants any role to inspiration (*Einfall*), which is unplanned arbitrariness ... [This is] the fatality inherent to rationalization'.[17] It is the restoration of the recognition of 'unplanned arbitrariness' that is the goal of the new philosophical constructivism of Deleuze. Yet on Adorno's own account, construction cannot eradicate the mimetic basis of the artwork (construction in art *imitates* the form of logicality). This regulates the application of the principle of construction in an undetermined or at least an unconscious or 'free' way. This is precisely the advantage of non-utilitarian art's 'functionlessness' over utilitarian forms of artistic labour. Unplanned arbitrariness is in this respect ineradicable from the work of art. The threat is thus a threat to art itself. The problem becomes how to find new artistic materials and new forms of construction capable of expressing the latest forms of social (ir)rationality autonomously yet in a way that is nonetheless at the same time critical of the social limitations imposed by the current institutionalization of autonomy itself. This is the critical problematic of that contemporary art – post-conceptual art – which is grounded on a continued working through, transformation and development of the contradictions of constructivism – contradictions which are exemplary of those of the historical avant-garde in general.[18]

INSTITUTIONAL CRITIQUE

One way of reading the critical trajectory of the European and North American art of the 1960s and 1970s is as a displaced repetition of a series of relationships between art forms and movements of the 1920s and 1930s. However, this has generally been understood in terms of the repetition of 'artistic paradigms' – grid formation, monochrome, readymade, collage, assemblage, photomontage – rather than in terms of the contradictory conceptual structure of the artwork itself.[19] There has thus been a tendency in this work to identify a break with the dialectic of historical and neo- avant-gardes at precisely the point at which it reimposed itself most intensely, moving to a new stage of development: in the practice of an art of institutional critique.[20]

From the standpoint of the contradictory structure of the artwork, the movement from Minimalism, via Conceptual art, to Institutional Critique appears as a displaced repetition of the movement from formal construction, via Constructivism, to the functionalism of Productivism. Institutional critique appears as a political functionalism turned inward, against the social relations of autonomy that are responsible for art's lack of 'productivity' and social impotence. But it is also thereby a functionalism that is turned against the institutional conditions of its own functioning as critique – 'critique' being the one function compatible with art's functionlessness: the function of functionlessness itself. Institutional critique can only be an art of direct practicality by restricting itself to a terrain on which critique is the only form of practicality, the only social use-value: autonomous art. However, it thereby implicitly affirms the critical value of the art institution, the political conditions and social impotence of which it simultaneously exposes. Ironically, this helps the institution to survive its own critique. The very existence of this critique within the institution – the institution's acceptance of institutional critique – negates the practical function of that critique; although not its intellectual value. Institutional critique thus strengthens and develops the art institution.

At one level, this appears as failure: the liquidation of its aspiration to be immediately social or directly practical, a deepening of the sense of art's social impotence, even within its own highly restricted domain. At another level, however, as a critical artistic practice, it appears as a *constructed mimesis* of the ability of cultural institutions within developed capitalist societies to sustain and recuperate their own critique. Its so-called 'failure' is an operative dimension of this critical functioning. There is thus an additional irony here (an 'irony of irony', in Schlegel's sense): the irony of the ironic failure of institutional critique as a political practice is that it thereby succeeds critically as art. It succeeds in giving artistic expression to the irrational rationality of the art institution: the basis of its critical rationality in irrational (oppressive) socio-economic forms. Using institutional forms, histories and relations as artistic materials, and developing new forms of construction – establishing new relationships between the elements of its materials – it expresses an existing form of social (ir)rationality, autonomously, yet in a way that is nonetheless at the same time critical of the current institutionalization of autonomy itself. Furthermore, by expanding the range of artistic materials to include the social relations and practices of institutions, it renders the hitherto repressed social side of the ontology of the artwork explicit. However, by restricting its focus to established forms of art-institutionality (principally, the museum and the gallery), institutional critique retains the defensive structure of self-reference characteristic of formalist modernisms. It thus combines aspects of Formalism and Productivism, but it lacks the key element of Constructivism: social construction. It is in this respect that the 'architectural turn' in post-conceptual art practice and curating represents a new departure: it aspires to the broader social canvas of something like a new constructivism.

A NEW CONSTRUCTIVISM?

As the Canadian artist and critic Jeff Wall has argued (with regard to the work of Dan Graham, but the point is a general one): 'architecture emerges as the determining or decisive art form, because it most wholly reflects institutional structure, and influences behaviour through its definition of positionality.'[21] There are two things to note about this idea.

The first is the breadth of architecture's institutionality, such that it has come to be understood as 'the discourse of siting the effects of power generated by publicity, information and bureaucracy in the city.' The city becomes 'the single grand subject' of post-conceptual art.[22] The second is the difficult idea of influencing behaviour through 'definitions of positionality'. The notion of 'definitions of positionality' is the aspect of Wall's account which is perhaps most specific to Dan Graham's work; it is in 'influencing behaviour' that the constructivist aspect lies. A more explicitly constructivist position would construe such influence more directly, in terms of the construction not only of situations but of social relations and practices as well. The beginnings of a movement towards such constructions has occurred on the basis of recent transformations in the social space of art.

These are changes in both the social relations of artistic production and the social character of exhibition space. They have their origins in conceptual art: specifically, those kinds of conceptual art that attacked established modes of artistic autonomy, eroding the boundaries that had previously set modernist art apart from other cultural practices, especially communications and the media.[23] This was a possibility opened up by the use of language as an artistic material, and it involved taking cultural forms of all kinds as the objects of a new constructive intent. Such art is Constructivist – and hence 'post-autonomous' – to the extent that it is an immanently artistic functionalism: that is, to the extent that there is a simultaneous emergence of definitions of social function and new artistic forms. However, as Wall has argued, it remains 'a liminal type of autonomous art' to the extent that its functional goals are the outcome of artistic decision.[24] Yet this is perhaps to construe the matter too narrowly, since this kind of art is rarely the outcome of decisions made by the artist alone. The contemporary art of international exhibition space is largely the outcome of negotiations between artists and curators, museum or exhibition authorities, and often corporations, councils and governments (at local, regional and national levels), too. It is these practices of organization, co-ordination and negotiation – whether they be about 'production' or 'installation', the difference between which is increasingly tenuous – that make such art genuinely 'architectural'. They place it in a direct relation to urbanism. At its broadest, it depends upon a new kind of public exhibition: a constructivism of the exhibition form.

The institutional spaces of contemporary art are intimately related to the new global, informational, metropolitan 'non-place' of the city, both through the network character of the international art world and via the deep-rooted immanence of metropolitan experience to modern art itself.[25] If the white cube was once 'the single major convention through which art passed',[26] it is now subordinated to the international biennial, as a temporary network of a huge range of works, articulated in thematic clusters across a string of sites. These sets of sites might be relatively geographically stable (like the Venice Biennial) or, like Manifesta, nomadic. Either way, in this expanded and distributional spatial context, 'the exhibition has become the basic unit from which it is possible to conceive of relationships between art and ideology ushered in by technologies, to the detriment of the individual work.' And the constructive technologies are no longer just technologies of machinofacture, but primarily of communications. This is no longer the exhibition as 'store' (the original Constructivist metaphor), but the exhibition as 'set', within a general remodelling of the cinematic in line with the technologies of video.[27] The curator functions as director and the works of art function as elements of the constructive process of exhibition-building. Such works are intrinsically double-coded: they have their own ('liminally autonomous') significations and modes of experience, and they have the more fully 'post-autonomous' meanings that accrue to them as a result of their place within the overall (and often quite chaotic) logic of construction of the exhibition. This is a logic that is itself contradictory: divided between the presentation of the collective exhibition-value of the works and their putative use-values as models within a speculative programme of social construction. Such programmes are uneasy amalgams of art, economics and politics. (But then, what is 'culture' but such an amalgam?) And the use-values of individual works – and the programme itself – may, or may not, survive to be 'consumed' after the exhibition. But it is the horizon of expectation that they might that the practice depends upon for its constructive force. Walter Benjamin's accounts of architecture as 'the prototype of a work of art the reception of which is consummated by a collectivity in distraction', and of film as its 20th century model,[28] come together and are fused in the constructivism of this contemporary exhibition form.

Notes

1. Kojin Karatani, *Architecture as Metaphor: Language, Number, Money*, MIT Press, Cambridge MA and London, 1995, pp. 126–8. Karatani is thinking in particular of the late Wittgenstein and deconstruction. For Karatani, 'deconstruction could be realized only by exhaustive construction' and 'if formalized, is tantamount to Gödel's proof.' (pp. xxxiii–iv)
2. Ibid., pp. xxxii, 5, xxxix.
3. Manfredo Tafuri, *Architecture and Utopia: Design and Capitalist Development*, MIT Press, Cambridge MA and London, 1976, pp. 125, 182.
4. Cf. Gilles Deleuze, 'How Do We Recognize Structuralism?' (1972), in his *Desert Islands and Other Texts 1953–1974*, trans. Michael Taormina, ed. David Lapoujade, Semiotext(e), Los Angeles and New York, 2004, p. 170.
5. See Christina Lodder, ''Postscript to Russian Constructivism: The Western Dimension', in her *Russian Constructivism*, Yale University Press, New Haven, 1983, pp. 225–38, and Benjamin H. D. Buchloh, 'Cold War Constructivism', in Serge Guilbaut (ed.), *Reconstructing Modernism: Art in New York, Paris and Montreal, 1945–1964*, MIT Press, Cambridge MA and London, 1990, pp. 85–112.
6. See, for example, John Rajchman, *Constructions*, MIT Press, Cambridge MA and London, 1998, and *The Deleuze Connections*, MIT Press, Cambridge MA and London, 2000.
7. Rajchman, *Constructions*, p. 9.
8. In mathematics a construction is a proof of existence of a mathematical entity via its reduction to other demonstrably existing mathematical entities. In philosophy, Schelling used the term for his method of meeting the formal need of a post-Kantian philosophical system to reconcile philosophical principle with recognition of the wealth of contingent particularities, by deriving the latter from the former. It re-emerged later in a radical empiricist form in Carnap's *The Logical Construction of the World*, 1928. Each of these uses demonstrates that abstraction of the intellectual logic of construction from the practice of building that is also the theoretical basis of Constructivism.
9. Lodder, *Russian Constructivism*, p. 38.
10. 'Statement by the First Working Group of Constructivists' in the catalogue of the *First Discussional Exhibition of Associations of Active Revolutionary Art* (1924), in John E. Bowlt (ed.), *Russian Art of the Avant-Garde: Theory and Criticism, 1902–1934*, Thames and Hudson, London, 1988, pp. 241–3. Gabo and Pevsner's *The Realistic Manifesto* is translated in ibid., pp. 208–14. The reiteration in the former of the 1920 slogan 'we declare implacable war on art' contrasts starkly with the latter's appeal to 'people to whom Art is ... the source of real exhaltation, our word and deed.' The First Working Group was made up of Aleksei Gan (their theorist), Aleksandr Rodchencko, Varvara Stepanova, Karl Ioganson, Vladimir Stenberg, Georgii Stenberg and Konstantin Medunestskii.
11. 'Programme of the First Working Group of Constructivists, Institute of Artistic Culture', March 1921, quoted in Lodder, *Russian Constructivism*, p. 3.
12. Cf. Tafuri, *Architecture and Utopia*, pp. 153–6. The precursor of Tafuri's analysis is Walter Benjamin's understanding of Surrealism as the 'secret cargo' of aestheticism. See Walter Benjamin, 'Surrealism: The Last Snapshot of the European Intelligensia' (1929), in his *One-Way Street and Other Writings*, trans. Edmund Jephcott and Kingsley Short, New Left Books, London, 1979, p. 231.
13. See Peter Bürger, *Theory of the Avant-Garde* (1974), University of Minnesota Press, Minneapolis, 1984. Bürger himself notoriously sees this relationship less as a dialectical one than as a historical fall. He thus tends merely to judge, rather than comprehend, the condition of art in capitalist societies after World War II.

14. Theodor W. Adorno, *Aesthetic Theory*, trans. Robert Hullot-Kentor, Athlone Press, London, 1997, pp. 57–8.
15. Ibid., p. 44.
16. Ibid., pp. 168, 257, 225.
17. Ibid., 304. Adorno is writing here about constructivism in music, but his point is a general one.
18. For the concept of post-conceptual art, see Peter Osborne, 'Art Beyond Aesthetics: Philosophical Criticism, Art History and Contemporary Art', *Art History*, Vol. 27, no. 3 (Spring 2004).
19. The model of paradigm repetition has its source in Buchloh's critique of Bürger. See Benjamin Buchloh, 'Theorizing the Avant-Garde', *Art in America*, November 1984 and *Neo-Avantgarde and Culture Industry: Essays on European and American Art from 1955 to 1975*, MIT Press, Cambridge MA and London, 2000. See also, Hal Foster, 'Who's Afraid of the Neo-Avant-Garde?', in his *The Return of the Real*, MIT Press, Cambridge MA and London, 1996, pp. 1–34, where it acquires a psychoanalytical inflection.
20. See Buchloh, *Neo-Avantgarde and Culture Industry*, p. xxiv.
21. Jeff Wall, *Dan Graham's Kammerspiel*, Art Metropole, Toronto, 1991, p. 33.
22. Ibid., pp. 11, 28.
23. See Peter Osborne (ed.), *Conceptual Art*, Phaidon, London and New York, pp. 18–19, 35–45.
24. Jeff Wall, 'Introduction' to Dan Graham, *Two-Way Mirror Power: Selected Writings by Dan Graham on his Art*, ed. Alexander Alberro, Cambridge MA and London, 1999, p. xvii.
25. See Peter Osborne, 'Non-Places and the Spaces of Art', *Journal of Architecture*, Vol. 6 (Summer 2001), pp. 183–94.
26. Brian O'Doherty, *Inside the White Cube: The Ideology of Gallery Space* (1976), University of California Press, Berkeley, 1999, p. 44.
27. Nicolas Bourriaud, *Relational Aesthetics*, les presses du réel, 2002, pp. 72–3.
28. Walter Benjamin, 'The Work of Art in the Age of Mechanical Reproduction', in *Illuminations*, Fontana/Collins, 1973, pp. 219–53, pp. 241–2.

for a new functional approach to an art gallery

Jorge Oteiza

FORMS AND COMMITMENTS: A PREFACE TO A LETTER

In the mid-sixties the first Basque artists' collective was created, GAUR (Basque for "Today"). Reflecting the *zeitgeist* of the times, their aim was to consolidate a "Basque School". The collective was formed by eight artists from San Sebastian and its surroundings. Their first exhibition took place at Galerí a Barandiarán. Conceived as a private production centre, this gallery included an experimental group of artists and experts, who prioritised an activity inspired by the principle of the integration of the different arts, paying special attention to education and popular traditional art expressions. For this reason, the gallery was renamed "Galerí a Barandiarán, Productora de Arte Compuesto" ("Composed Art Producer").

In this letter addressed to the painter and filmmaker José Antonio Sistiaga, the sculptor Jorge Oteiza offers some conceptual bases for the creation of a new exhibition space in anticipation of times to come. The depiction of this future scenario followed Oteiza's decision to abandon sculpture in order to dedicate himself to direct intervention in reality; a decision taken in 1959 that caused a heated public debate. Following this decision, the end of the formalisation in arts as part of the modern project had to inaugurate a new stage through education, new and old folkloric expressions, creation of new cultural institutions and the socialization of aesthetic models.

Galerí a Barandiarán was the "hot-spot" for this local avant-garde, born from the desire to galvanise shared dreams. The gallery was an attempt to develop an organisational structure in which artists had an ideal exhibition space that would also serve as a public meeting space for audiences of experimental music concerts, poetry readings and children's workshops.

This "periodisation" of the 60's in the local context can be now viewed as a possibility to analyse contemporary art production conditions, jumping from a local situation to a global one. The future landscape outlined by Oteiza related to many of the subjects still at issue in the present time.

Galerí a Barandiarán became an exemplary model that created a renewed sense of art organisations and productive structures, by reconfiguring the use of space, the self-involvement of artists in organizational systems, the role of galleries and the definition of new curatorial positions, amongst other issues.

Peio Aguirre and Leire Vergara

The following is a letter written by Jorge Oteiza in September 1965 to his colleage José Antonio Sistiaga, who had been in negotiations with Dionisio Barandiaran for the creation of a new contemporary art gallery in San Sebastian.

The current situation.
The prevailing trend in contemporary art questions the very existence of the art gallery. Sculptors and painters have been in contact with their public within exhibition spaces in much the same way as musicians have related to their audience in concert halls and as poets have interacted with their readership through journals and books. The arts have been classified according to their specific language of expression as artists have lived and created through their own highly specialized means of communication with audiences that have been generally different. At present, the barriers dividing the arts are lifting. Artists have collectively begun to produce a new type of cultural object reflecting an integrated approach between the artistic disciplines and for a broader public. The exhibition space as a venue for visual art is dying. There will be numerous attempts at its transformation and it is to our advantage to anticipate these transformations.

In what way can we be ahead of this transformation?
In other countries, the stratification in the economic and artistic relationships between the gallery, the artist and society has hindered the possibility for a more flexible and rapid transformation of their organization. In our country, the very absence of an organized artistic and cultural life, our forced withdrawal from what is essentially real life, has provided the artist with the opportunity to be located within theoretical activity in a state of being constantly alert, prepared at all times to respond to the first possibility to organize his life, from a point of knowledge and clarity, virtual structure and advanced projects. This attitude, arriving out of a comparative research in the interdisciplinary nature of the arts, is essential today for the reconsideration of a new art and a new way of organizing, producing and creating. This has been developing around us for some years now, while abroad there was an absence of this sense of urgency as artists were preoccupied with an overwhelming material attention to their work.

The immediate antecedents of the present trends.
Around 1957, two experimental styles coincided. One style was drawing to an end – this was the trend rooted in concrete rationalism that explored the objective conditions of space and the geometric reasoning of the site in the universe of communication. The other style, in the form of a more experimental movement, was already under way exploring the rational, spontaneous, subjective, informal conditions of personal actions guiding expression. At the present moment, sixty years on in the historical process

of contemporary art, these two trajectories of artistic investigation, that nevertheless constantly alternate with one another in a developing, progressive experimentation, are preparing to move into everyday life and out of the artist's private laboratory. There two experimental fields, supplemented by the memory of the achievements of former movements, are joining together to launch a new tendency grounded in the conjugation of all the arts (of the spatialist rationalism: Op Art and the concrete poetic prolongation of irrationalism: Pop Art).

The experimental programme of today's artist.
This new panorama for today's artist is truly complex, difficult and yet, fascinating. It will develop and manifest itself in the first experiences resulting in the revision in the organization of the art gallery in form and direction. To speak about the nature of these experiences is to announce the nature of the organization and structure of these new galleries.
We should try to anticipate a possible first idea to define amongst ourselves such a gallery focused on the immediate worldwide future. To do so, let us summarize the objective and fundamental areas that define the current direction of creative activity. These are the general objectives: a) the experimental field of interarticulation of different arts; b) the elaboration of a new popular art, whereby the traditional techniques of popular expression are readjusted in the domains anticipated by contemporary art; c) the conjugation of the two previous objectives which are understood as forthcoming following a particular period of preparation with its experiences already advanced. The appropriate approach on the part of the artist in the development of these issues will chart out the practical evolution of art and will give international relevance to the contribution made by countries, groups of artists and art galleries. I mention galleries because their role will be fundamental: no longer passive, as they have been until now but fundamental in the creation and the very production of the work of art. Let us now try to anticipate some of their characteristics.

A new art gallery (notes to be organized and completed).

The company or the owner of the property of a new gallery provides the very industrial element the artist has been waiting for – the industrialization through which art will evolve creatively, pedagogically, politically and culturally to the people. The owner of a gallery used to be a dealer. Nowadays, he has to be an industrialist and entrepreneur.

The gallery is no longer a place in which to exhibit the work of art. Today the gallery is where the work is created and produced. The gallery has to be organized according to its responsibility in the process of creation. The gallery is like a publishing house or a production company. The gallery is the real creator of the exhibition.

Exhibitions are not made by the exhibitors alone but are created fundamentally with the collaboration of an experimental team made up of specialists in the different artistic disciplines. The immediate objective of the gallery is not the selection of the private work of an artist, but of the gallery's experimental team.

The painting or sculpture that is being shown in an exhibition room at present is the point of departure, the first draft script for the production of the exhibition. We may think of this as the first stage in a current exhibition: the traditional exhibition-goer, the same public as always, visits this group of paintings and sculpture. The second stage – the analysis and comparative account of other artistic expressions. The work in the show is used as a score to test out its equivalence, its translation, variants, developments, etc., in terms of other languages. In this form, it is as if a group of visitors, the audience, attends an experimental show, creatively and pedagogically. The audience in the new laboratory of the artist serves as an experimental group whose experience is similar to, but richer than watching the making of a film on the production set, witnessing an integrated creative performance of painting and sculpture together with music, ballet, poetry, theatre, etc. The third stage – fixing and editing these experiments in a narrative audio-visual format, as a document that can be industrially reproduced simply onto a reel of film which has the following two lines of exhibition: a) the creative performance can be reproduced in the local area by repeating the installation of painting and sculpture together with tests of their translation and conjugation, together with the participation of other participants, other versions, and of extended experience, and b) the results, which may be one or several, are fixed in an easily transportable installation (including static work such as photographs, slides, audio tapes) or are fixed more definitely on film for further distribution, exchange, education, lease, sale, etc.

Dear Sistiaga, I believe that this is my first report and from my point of view, one that could serve to broaden your reflections and discussions. I have little time for further notes, although I will continue at the first possible

opportunity. Please study the designation of a permanent and founding experimental team and enlist the first contacts with the composer, singer, and choir who may make take the first experiments. Note your thoughts with precision and have a writer or scriptwriter accompany you...a theatre professional to be able to stage the scenes and to articulate the dialogues in the form of small texts and presentation of facts addressed to the audience. This man, this poet, this journalist, if possible, this director over the theatre set (the young Bertolt Brecht, our young Piscator) is truly fundamental. I do not know who he may be although he will not be fully mature, you have to find him. He has to have a real vocation and to be passionate about this experiment and to commit himself completely to this venture. He should be the very first man on the team to be secured and hired for the developing gallery. You must start a diary, telegraphically, but you must also take charge of the theory and the reality of this experimental mission from this point forward. Otherwise, all will be as it had been up until now, only to begin again from point zero. This diary represents the possibility to account for these experiences, of this course, which will have international repercussions. It will need to be published.
Warmest regards.
Irun.9-9-65

Projection of this gallery.
We will have to take into account that the cultural task of this gallery should project its influence over the renaissance of all expressions of our popular tradition. And, at the same time, it should act as an active Department of Cultural Extension in the service of official and private education (its minister of courses, classes, in primary and secondary schools and at all levels of education) that is not yet available in this country. This gallery as an institution of cultural extension has an unforeseeable potential. It is a good thing that it starts as a private venture: contacts and supports, requests for official and private sponsorships will not be long in coming. Nor will it be necessary to wait for the multiple relationships, artistic or economic, with other countries. But we must start out with intelligence and with the necessary means. It has occurred to me that this project should be linked to a private enterprise – a Cultural Economic Fund – that is defining itself in similar terms.

Concentrate specifically on the gallery, on the first effective team and the figures, and I will see to the rest. We will be seeing one another.

art in relation to architecture/architecture in relation to art

Dan Graham

While American Pop art of the early 1960's referred to the surrounding media world for a framework, Minimal art of the mid- through late 1960s would seem to refer to the gallery's interior cube as the ultimate contextual frame of reference for the work. This reference was only compositional; in place of an internal compositional reading, the art's formal structure would appear in relation to the gallery's interior architectural structure. That the work was equated to the architectural container tended to literalize it. Both the architectural container and the work it contained were meant to be seen as nonillusionistic, neutral and objectively factual—that is, simply as material. The gallery functioned literally as part of the art. One artist's work of this period (although not always his later work) examined how specific, functional architectural elements of the gallery interior prescribed meaning and determined specific readings for the art defined within its architectural frame: Dan Flavin's fluorescent light installations.

The lighting—even light fixtures—within the architectural setting of the gallery are normally disregarded, or considered merely functional or minor interior decoration. As gallery space is meant to appear neutral, the lighting, which creates this neutrality as much as the white walls, and at the same time is used to highlight and center attention on the art work on the wall or floor, is kept inconspicuous. While the background in general makes the artworks visible, the lighting literally makes the works visible. The lighting system, within which the specific light fixtures of a gallery arrangement function, is both part of the gallery apparatus and part of the larger, existing (non-art) system of electric lighting in general use: "I believe that the changing standard lighting system should support my idea within it."[1] Flavin's installations make use of this double functioning (inside and outside the gallery/art context) as well as the double connotation of lighting as minor decoration and the anonymously functional creator of the gallery's neutrality: "I believe that art is shedding its vaunted mystery for a common sense of keenly realized decoration. Symbolizing is dwindling—becoming slight. We are pressing downward toward no art—a mutual sense of psychologically indifferent decoration—a neutral pleasure of seeing known to everyone."[2]

Flavin's arrangements of light fixtures in a gallery depend contextually for significance upon the function of the gallery, and the socially determined architectural use of electric lighting. Electric light is related to a specific time in history. Flavin has observed that when the existing system of electric lighting ceases to exist, his art will no longer function. Made of standardized, replaceable units that, in Flavin's words, "can be bought in any hardware store," his arrangements of fluorescent tubes within the interior (or adjacent exterior) architectural frame of the exhibition space function only in situ and upon completion of the exhibition cease to function artistically. Unlike the self-defined or conceptual artwork, for example Duchamp's "found objects,"[3] they take on meaning by being placed in relation to other works of art or specific architectural features in an exhibition space; being part of the architecture/lighting of the gallery, they tend to underscore both the function of the space and other art's dependence upon the standard illumination of the gallery setting. Placed within a group of other paintings and sculpture, Flavin's lights radically disturb the other art's functioning, for it is then unable to rely on the neutral white ground of the gallery walls. The fluorescent illumination plays on the surfaces of paintings, highlighting or creating shadows that disturb their illusionary planes, undercutting (and so revealing) the latent illusionism employed in their construction. Similarly, the space in which the spectator stands is highlighted and dramatized. The effect is both constructivist and expressionist. In one installation, the use of all green lights plunged the interior space into lurid green, while turning the view from outside, defined pictorially by the windows of the gallery, into its after-image, a lavender-purple. The effect can be read ironically, as reversed illusionism, or, literally, as (physical) light and the obverse of the illusionary illumination radiating from the conventional painting.

Systematically, Flavin has investigated this gallery architecture by placing his arrangements of fluorescent tubes:

a) on the wall in either vertical, horizontal and diagonal bands;
b) in the comers of the room;
c) on the floor;
d) relative to exterior light-sources (near windows, open doors);
e) as partially visible/partially invisible, behind columns, architectural supports, or in niches;
f) in the hallway before the spectator enters the gallery, thus altering the spectator's perception when he enters to view the work;
g) in outside space, which serves as an entranceway or antechamber to the gallery/museum itself.

Just as art is internalized within society, the architecture which displays it is defined by the needs of society at large, and by art as an institutional internal need. Art as an institution produces ideological meanings and positions that regulate and contain the subjective experiences of the people placed inside its boundaries. Daniel Buren's work and writing focus on the specific architectural/cultural function of the gallery in producing art's institutional meaning. In general, all institutional space provides a background having the function of inversely defining what it places in the foreground. Since the Enlightenment, public interiors have been largely unornamented, geometrical, utilitarian and idealized. Thus they provide a seamless, clinical, recessive, white ground to set off Man's enlarged activities. The art gallery is an aristocratic relative of this conventional white cube. Its major task is to place the art object, and the spectator's focused consciousness of it, at eye-level center in the interior, and, in so doing, to conceal from the spectator any awareness of its own presence and function. So:

> Nothing which is not the work (of art) manages to distract the eye... A work is thus dramatized or emphasized (against its will or by request) by the so-called neutral architecture, or indeed the work turns up its nose at any external influence and attempts, despite everything, to attract the eye regardless of the context... In most normal artistic settings, which we have seen in the majority of cases are white cubes, the problems set by the architecture attempt to conceal themselves, in order to support (artificially) the triumph of a bourgeois art, which thus given value can assert itself "freely," within the soft shelter which receives it.[4]

The Modern Movement in architecture is the history of two conflicting conceptions of the role of the architect. On one hand, the architect is seen as an engineer, on the other, as an artist. Functionalism, from the Russian Constructivists through Le Corbusier, culminating in the Bauhaus School of Gropius, can be seen as a method of resolving this conflict as well as the contradictions between two bourgeois value systems: humanism and technological operationalism. The solution, as envisaged by the Bauhaus, lay in subjecting the architectural work and men's needs to a "scientific" analysis in order to produce a functional system.

Man's needs were seen as social needs and were to be incorporated into a unified (total) formal (esthetic) program. An abstract language composed "scientifically," like the basic elements of physics, would be used to produce a materialist architecture built from a language of elemental, ideal forms. Based on a total, reductive analysis of esthetic form, social needs and technical requirements, this approach enabled science and technology to be wedded to esthetics in the interests of social progress. Art/architecture was to be constructed of democratic, recomposible, open modular units (in opposition to totalitarian blocks). Art/architecture, as pure technology, came to be identified with the earlier notion of "art for art's sake," as the Bauhaus architects saw the function of their architecture as the creation of a language of "its" own. This language was liberalist–antirhetorical, antisymbolic and (supposedly) free from ideological contamination, a utopian language of pure function and pure materiality.

Because in the functionalist building symbolic form—ornament—is (apparently) eliminated from the building (form and content being merged), there is no distinction between the form and its material structure; that is, the form represents nothing more or less than the material; second, a form or structure is seen to represent only its contained function, the building's structural and functional efficiency being equated with its real utility for those who use it. Esthetically, this idea is expressed in the formula: *efficient form is beautiful and beautiful form is efficient*. This has a "moral" dimension; "efficient" connotes a pragmatically "scientific" approach seemingly uncontaminated by "ideology," which has (capitalistic) use value ("efficiency" is how well a building contributes to the operations of the company housed within it).

One can examine the later buildings of Mies van der Rohe, especially his corporate office buildings. These use transparent glass "curtain walls" to eliminate the distinction—and contradiction—between outside and inside. Glass and steel are used as "pure" materials, for the sake of their materiality. Until recently, these Bauhaus-derived buildings were sheathed in transparent glass. They read from inside out, making evident their functional construction. The function of the building is expressed in terms of the structural, evident materiality of the glass and steel that are exposed directly to view, as are the human activities within the building. The *social* function of building is subsumed into its formal disclosure of its technical, material and formal (self) construction. The neutrality of the surface, its "objectivity," focuses the viewer's gaze only on the surface material/structural qualities, deflecting it from the building's meaning/use in the social system's hierarchy. The glass gives the viewer the illusion that what is seen is seen exactly as it is. Through it one sees the technical workings of the company and the technical engineering of the building's structure. Yet the glass's literal transparency not only falsely objectifies reality; it is a paradoxical camouflage: for while the actual function of the corporation may be to concentrate its self-contained power and to control by secreting information, its architectural facade gives the impression of absolute openness. The transparency is visual only: glass separates the visual from the verbal, insulating outsiders from the locus of decision-making and from the invisible, but real, links between company operations and society.[5]

In attempting to eliminate the disparity between the facade (which conventionally mediates its relation to the outside environment) and its private, institutional function, this type of architecture appears to eliminate the distinction between outer form and inner function. The self-contained, transparent glass building denies that it has an outside and that it participates as an element in the language of the surrounding buildings in the environment. Rather than coming to terms, within its formal statement, with the social language of the surrounding commercially built environment of which it forms a part, the classic modernist building is aloof and noncommunicative. It does not acknowledge that it, too, is usually a commercial proposition. The building's functionalism conceals its less apparent ideological function, justifying one use of technology or technocratic bureaucracy by large corporations or government to impart their particular version of order upon society. Where other buildings have conventional signs of their function oriented toward public scrutiny, the glass building's facade is invisible and unrhetorical. The esthetic purity of the glass building, standing apart from the common environment, is transformed by its owner into social alibi for the institution it houses. The building claims esthetic autonomy over the environment (through its formal self-containment), yet it evinces transparent "openness" to the environment (it *incorporates* the natural environment). This rhetorical ploy efficiently legitimizes/naturalizes the corporate institution's claim to autonomy ("The World of General Motors"); the building builds the corporate myth. A building with glass on four sides seems open to visual inspection; in fact, the "interior" is lost to the architectural generality, to the apparent materiality of the outward form, or to "Nature" (light, sun, sky or the landscape glimpsed through the building on the other side.) Thus, the building stands apart from any language but its own.

Esthetic formalism and Functionalism in architecture are philosophically similar. By the same token, Functionalist architecture and Minimal art have in common an underlying belief in the Kantian notion of artistic form as a perceptual/mental "thing-in-itself," which presumes that art objects are the only category of objects "not for use," objects in which the spectator takes pleasure without interest. Minimal art and post-Bauhaus architecture also compare in their abstract materialism and their formally reductive methodology. They share a belief in "objective" form and in an internal self-articulation of the formal structure in apparent isolation from symbolic (and representational) codes of meaning. Both Minimal art and Functionalist architecture deny connotative, social meanings and the context of other, surrounding art or architecture.

By the end of the war, three Bauhaus architects, Gropius, Mies van der Rohe and Breuer, had emigrated to the United States and established themselves as influential teachers in large university architecture departments. There, as advocates of the Modern Movement, they trained a new generation of American architects. The architects as well as the architecture produced by them and their former Bauhaus teachers were given the name "International Style" by the architectural historians Henry-Russell Hitchcock and Philip Johnson. Mies' classicist glass office towers and apartment buildings became the new standard of American technology, especially as this style was easily exported to other areas of the world by American big business. Mies' classicism was based on an apparent trueness to materials (materials being seen for what they were, instead of disguised by the use of ornamentation) wedded to an idealized, "universal," and highly abstract, notion of space. These modernist structures soon became popular packages for international (multinational) corporate branch offices in the capitals of the "Free World." Used as an overseas branch office, the International Style building functions ideologically as a neutral and objectified rationale for U.S. export capitalism, although it would like to be taken as merely an abstract (not symbolic) form. Karl Beveridge and Ian Burn have indicated this symbolic rationale, which America had for its activities and which the form of its corporate architecture (and art) reflected during the postwar period:

> ...a technology which is democratic because it is good, neutral, and progressive, a technology which is equally available to everyone—the means for a better life, and free from ideological bias. The American artists of the sixties and seventies have reproduced this pattern, becoming the cultural engineers of "International art."[6]

Not that some American artists and architects have been unaware of the dilemma of their work's possible expropriation, once it is in the public sector, in the interests of the elite "Establishment" and also by commercialized mass culture. Politically conscious American artists have evolved two basic esthetic strategies to deal with this twofold social expropriation. The first is to avoid having the art product packaged automatically by the media by the simple procedure of having the art package itself. The American Pop artists of the early to middle 1960s equivocated between imitating the cultural clichés prepackaged by the media (in one sense, accepting the popular or vernacular code/reading) and various formal distancing devices making the "common" and ordinary appear strange (as these devices are formal and artistic method, this also allowed their works to be read as "art for art's sake"). A second strategy was to use popular techniques and subject matter *and at the same time (in the same work)* allow the work to read alternatively from a formal, "high" art perspective. A work by Lichtenstein, for example, can be both "art for art's sake" and something assimilable to popular cultural meanings. Both readings are simultaneously correct. Owing to its seeming ephermerality in terms of the popular code, such work cannot immediately be assimilated into the institutions of "higher" culture; conversely, the work cannot be immediately assimilated into the value-system of commercial, popular culture (although it speaks the same language) because of its anchorage in "high" art. The aspect of two equivalent, total/complete readings allows a work to question the position for the spectator which either one of these two readings poses and it also permits a questioning of both "popular" and "high" art's formal assumptions, As Lichtenstein told Gene Swenson:

> I think that my work is different from comic strips—but I wouldn't call it transformation; I don't think that whatever is meant by it is important to art. What I do is form, whereas the comic strip is not formed in the sense I'm using the word; the comics have shapes but there has been no effort to make them intensely unified. The purpose is different, one intends to depict and I intend to unify... The heroes depicted in comic books are fascist types, but I don't take them seriously in these paintings—maybe there is a point in not taking them seriously, a political point. I use them for purely formal reasons, and that's not what those heroes were invented for. Pop art has very immediate and of-the-moment meanings which will vanish—that kind of thing is ephemeral—and Pop takes advantage of this "meaning" which is not supposed to last, to distract you from its formal content. I think the formal statement in my work will become clearer in time.[7]

Lichtenstein's choice of indirect, and ultimately artistically self-referring, esthetic "political" strategies is a typical one for "progressive" artists of the '60s, who believed that, at best, the radicality of their art activities could "trickle down" to society at large, despite the fact that the art might utilize mass media—popular clichés—for its "content." But Lichtenstein's work, whether reproduced ("second-hand") in the mass media or viewed in art galleries, did allow for such a dual reading. Lichtenstein is ambivalent about whether he wants to consider his work political. In American culture to define a work as ostensibly "political" automatically categorizes it as academic or "high" art; mass culture will have little interest in it, because it assumes what for the mass public is a patronizing attitude. As a category, "the political" is negatively coded: it means, "no fun." Andy Warhol's films, his Brillo boxes presented as sculptures, "Mary Hartman, Mary Hartman,"[8] and the rock group, "The Ramones" are various examples of self-conscious works placed in the public media and capable of dual readings as both "high" and "low" cultural forms, but, ironically, being neither one or the other.

It is easy to condemn this approach from a rationalist Marxist perspective, because the work appears to equivocate in its attitudes toward commercial, vulgarized mass culture, even adopting some of its conventions and sentiments. Instead of negating (and proposing an alternative to) degraded American popular culture, it seems either passively to reflect or actively to celebrate it. European "leftist" architectural critics unconsciously equate mass culture with Fascist irrationalism, seeing rationalist socialism as both a "negation" of "degraded" mass culture and as the *only* "constructive" solution to the problems it confronts. They see present-day American society in terms of Europe of the 1930's. Similarly, in their critique of the use to which American International Style architecture is put, they use an idealist and historical model as an implicit standard. "Revolutionary" art for them is identified, for historical reasons, with the Russian Constructivist period. In fact, the work of Russian art and architecture after the Revolution was contextualized to real conditions and needs at that time; architects wished to purge personally symbolic (aristocratic-"art-for-art's-sake") elements from the architectural language to functionalize and socialize the means of artistic/architectural production. El Lissitzky summarized this approach:

> (1) The negation of art as mere emotional, individualistic, and romantic affair
> (2) 'Objective' work, undertaken with the silent hope that the end product will be regarded as a work of art.
> (3) Consciously goal-directed work in architecture, which will have a concise artistic effect on the basis of well-prepared objective-scientific criteria.
> Such an architecture will actively raise the general standard of living.[9]

The difficulty with applying Constructivist standards to present-day architectural/social problems is that they impose a blinder on reality as it exists at present. The neo-Constructivist theoretician wishes to remake this reality in accord with "revolutionary" (in fact highly elitist) solutions "from above" and only in terms of his own specialist and theoretical language.

Like International Style Functionalist architecture, Minimal and Conceptual art of the 1960's seemed to claim autonomy from the surrounding social environment. It represented only itself, as a factual, structurally self-referring language. It deliberately sought to suppress both interior (illusionistic) and exterior (representational) relationships to achieve a zero degree of signification. Beveridge and Burn point out that when this type of art is used by big business, the government or the cultural Establishment, either domestically or as a cultural export, it functions perhaps contrarily to the artist's intentions -to affirm America's apolitical, technocratic ideology. For: "to reproduce a form of art which denies political or social content... in fact provides a cultural rationalization for just such a denial."

In rejecting the reductivism and utopianism of modernist architectural doctrine, Robert Venturi and his collaborators propose an architecture that accepts the actual conditions, social realities and given economics of a particular situation. This means, for commercial buildings in a capitalist society, taking the syntax of the commercial vernacular seriously, including the building's relation to the surrounding built environment, the program of the client on whose behalf it was built, and the public's reading and cultural appropriation of the building. A Venturi and Rauch building relies on both popular taste and specialist codes. By displaying its rhetoric and (social) function openly, and by using contradictory conventional codes in the same building, Venturi opts for a realist (conventional) and multivalent architecture, one whose structure is conventional (semiotic) rather than abstract or materialistic, and whose aim is basically communicative. Venturi and Rauch's unbuilt 1967 project for the National Football Hall of Fame is an example of combining architectural allusion with communicative devices taken from the commercial vernacular.

Unlike modern "masters" who advocate unconventional solutions, Venturi advocates using known conventions, even humdrum ones. In dispensing with the myth of the "heroic and original" building, which in its search for new forms and expressive use of materials has simply fueled the surplus economy of late capitalism and helped to provide large corporations with the alibi of "high culture," Venturi and his associates' approach implies a critique of post-Bauhaus ideology. The Bauhaus had associated efficiency and the notion of technical/formal innovation: "revolutionary" design would be efficient design. Today "efficient" design is more symbolic than real; it symbolizes not cost efficiency, but the corporation that has built the structure's hegemonic power (possibly due to its efficient use of social technology). Although the building's structure may read as "revolutionary" (in an esthetic sense), its function (in a social sense) is more often than not reactionary, Venturi prefers to take the ideological or symbolic assumptions of a cultural vernacular at their face value in determining his program. "Democracy" and pragmatic "pluralism" as given ideological values and cultural conventions of the local vernacular can be assumed to be part of the architectural object and, as they are taken into consideration, are free to emerge in terms of the building's rhetoric with alternative meanings/ readings.

Venturi and Rauch's advocacy of conventional forms and techniques has an economic dimension. In public building it is usually more (cost) efficient, in both capitalist and Bauhaus formal terms, to build conventionally. If "good design" costs twice as much, then "good design" is not realistic and needs redefinition. And, as Denise Scott Brown notes, in practice Bauhaus-style total design, usually advocated by governmental planning boards, is often "used" to betray rather than support the social concerns from which...it sprang."[10]

The question that the work of the American and British Pop artists and Venturi raise is the relation and socio-political effect of art and architecture to its *immediate* environment. Actually, this issue is implicit, merely on a daily, pragmatic basis, in all architectural work. What Venturi appropriates from the Pop artists is the understanding that not only can the internal structure of the architectural work be seen in terms of a relation of signs, but that the entire built (cultural) environment with which the building is inflected is constructed from signs. Pop art acknowledges a common code of schematic signs, conventionalized meanings and symbols which link vernacular, environmental signs to artistic/architectural signs. Abstract art's opposition to representational realism denies that an abstract work speaks the same language as its surrounding environment. The ideology of abstract art equates realism with representational art and, in turn, with an illusionism that can be manipulated to convey univalent, ideologically reactionary information to the masses, who might only understand the older convention (an often cited example is the Socialist Realism of Stalinist Russia). Modernist art has been committed to a purge of illusionist/connotative meaning in order to forge a purely formal, abstract and functional language. For the modernist, realism is identified not only with representational art, but with a morally pejorative pragmatism. If both the cultural and the "real" environment are seen in terms of a culturally connected semiotic coding, and if in practice an abstract work also functions, symbolically, in relation to other cultural signs, then a "new realism" whose basis is the function of the sign in the environment is necessary.

Signs in architecture can be either denotative, *architectural* signs, referring to building itself; or connotative, representing what is to be found within the building (literally or metaphorically), or to alternative—perhaps contradictory—meanings elsewhere. Both types of architectural sign connect with the codified sign system of which they are a part and to all

other signs in the cultural environment.
Unlike the buildings of Mies and his followers, whose idealistic purism veils a corporation's less than pristine business practices, Venturi and Rauch buildings incorporate the "commercial" in their code, which allows them, ironically, to comment upon the predominant capitalist commercial environment of the American built landscape. This is also an acknowledgment that meanings in architecture are not inherent to or exclusively framed within the work of architecture itself, but already exist as part of the environment in which the building is placed. A good example is the Guild House where, instead of idealizing or sugar-coating the realities of the lives of the elderly, or of the rather banal environment surrounding the building, or its institutional nature, the building simply tries to make evident what those assumptions are. This is done by building a clearly standard, cheap building and by expressing an ideology (shown in the building's aspirations to elegance) that suggests alternative symbolic meanings. Thus Venturi and Rauch build conventionally, but use this "conventionality" unconventionally to express human conditions in a realistic, discursive manner.

In this anti-utopian, anti introspective merging of realism and irony, the approach parallels that of Pop art. For Roy Lichtenstein Pop art assumes

> an involvement with what I think to be the most brazen and threatening characteristics of our culture, things which are also powerful in their impingement on us. I think art since Cézanne has become extremely romantic and unrealistic, feeding on art; it is utopian. It has had less to do with the world, it looks inward–neo–Zen and all that. This is not so much a criticism as an obvious observation. Outside is the world; it's there. Pop art looks out into the world, it appears to accept its environment, which is not good or bad but different—another state of mind.[11]

Venturi specifically acknowledges the influence of Pop art as well as "popular" culture.[12] Venturi prefers to make a building's symbolic function apparent by emphasizing it; this is done in a code which is understood not only in the architectural world, but also in the vernacular. An example is the proposal for a Town Hall, part of a larger city plan, for Canton, Ohio, from 1965,

> whose front is more important than its back... The change in size and scale in the front of the town hall is analogous... to the false fronts of western towns, and for the same reasons to acknowledge the urban spatial demands of the street... The front screen wall... is faced with very thin white marble slabs to reemphasize the contrast between the front and the back... The enormous flag is perpendicular to the street so that it reads up the street like a commercial sign.[13]

The flag displayed on a public building emotively signifies, in a code understandable to all Americans, at least two related readings: the pride of American citizens in their country and, especially when the flag is displayed on a commercial building, the confusion of capitalism with the American system (of government).

It is interesting to compare Venturi's use of a symbolic, heraldic flag on a public building to recent works of Daniel Buren using flaglike hangings in his conventional vertical-strip pattern. *In the Wind: A Displacement*, done in 1978 as part of the exhibition "Europe in the Seventies: Aspects of Recent Art" at the Hirshhorn Museum, Washington, D. C., featured eight flags hung from flagpoles in the museum's central courtyard (an area that reads as interior when viewed from the inner windows of the museum but which is exterior from the point of view of people outside the museum, as it is an extension of the entrance courtyard). The flags hang perpendicular to the building with their flagpoles tilted slightly upward, in other words, the vertical stripes read the same relative to spectator and to the ground as do conventionally displayed American flags. The flags were arranged in a circular sequence; so if the first flag is blue and white, the second is black and white, the third is orange and white, the fourth is black and white, the fifth is green and white, the sixth is black and white, the seventh is yellow and white, and the eighth is black and white. While Venturi and Rauch's project ironically acknowledges the symbolic potency of the U.S. flag, Buren's work neutralizes any connotational reading for the work, allowing it to refer back to its architectural positioning and to help render the architecture's/art's assumptions and functions more apparent. Buren's work is designed to negate its own potential appropriation as either "high" art or symbolic content. For instance, the use of alternate black-and-white-striped flags between each of the colored flags is a way to cancel the presence of rival symbolic content which the work (a sum of flags) might take in relation to the symbolic function of (other) flags.

Unlike the Functionalist building and unlike the neutrality of Buren's material means, Venturi's architecture acknowledges the same communicative codes that vernacular architecture exploits (usually to sell products). In *Learning From Las Vegas* Venturi, Brown and Izenour criticize the new Boston City Hall (and modernist megastructures in general) for not overtly acknowledging its symbolic assumptions of, or aspirations to, monumentality. They observe that it would have been cheaper (more efficient) for the architects to have built a conventional building to satisfy the Hall's functional requirements topped by a large sign: "The Boston City

Hall and its urban complex are the archetype of enlightened urban renewal. The profusion of symbolic forms... and the revival of the medieval piazza and its *palazzo pubblico* are in the end a bore. It is too, architectural. A conventional loft would accommodate a bureaucracy better, perhaps with a blinking sign on top saying I AM A MONUMENT."[14]

As Venturi and Rauch's buildings admit more than one linguistic code, they can sometimes express conflicting present-day values rather than being tied to a "higher" language of unified form. Venturi, Brown and Izenour criticize upper-middle-class American architects for their rejection of the forms and symbolic importance of architecture of their own vernacular:

> They understand the symbolism of Levittown and do not like it, nor are they prepared to suspend judgment on it in order to learn and, by learning, to make subsequent judgment more sensitive to the content of the symbols...Architects who find middle-class social aspirations distasteful and like uncluttered architectural form see only too well the symbolism in the suburban residential landscape...They recognize the symbolization; but they do not accept it. To them the symbolic decoration of the split-level suburban sheds represents the debased, materialistic values of a consumer economy where people are brainwashed by mass marketing and have no choice but to move to the ticky-tacky, with its vulgar violations of the nature of materials and its visual pollution of architectural sensibilities... They build for Man rather than for people—this means, to suit themselves, that is, to suit their own particular upper-middle-class values, which they assign to everyone... Another obvious point is that "visual pollution" (usually someone else's house or business) is not the same order of phenomenon as air or water pollution. You can like billboards without approving strip mining.[15]

Similarly, "beautification" substitutes for serious ecological planning and is aggressively promoted by Lady Bird Johnson, big land developers and Exxon; it clearly serves the ideological interests of those who have the most to lose if the idea of American dependence upon a consumer economy and overuse of energy is seriously challenged.

Venturi and Rauch will mix the "low" commercial code with the "high" architectural code, so that the commercial look of one of their buildings tends to subvert its reading as "high"-value architecture. And in a reverse fashion, the specific historical-architectural references in their buildings tend to question, to put into historical perspective, the usually immediate, unexamined assumptions communicated through commercial, popular codes. This commercial code has evolved to merge the interests of middle-class desires. The code of "high" architecture is a coalition of upper-middle-class "cultured" values, upper–echelon Establishment "taste," with values of the architectural profession as institution. The International Style unifies upper-middle-class and upper-class values in the interest of corporate business and government; at the same time, it looks down upon the "blight" and "visual pollution" it discerns in the complex diversity of smaller, less organized and lower-class codes, all representing alternative value-systems.

Venturi uses irony as a way to acknowledge contradictory political realities, rather than to suppress or to resolve them in a (false) transcendence, employing it to make certain assumptions of a building's given program overt. This use of irony as a "distancing" device suggests Brecht's notion of the self-aware style of acting (as found in classical Chinese theatre): "The Chinese performer limits himself to simply quoting the character played... The performer's self-observation, an artful and artistic art of self-alienation, stops the spectator from losing himself in the character completely... Yet the spectator's empathy is not entirely rejected... The artist's object is to appear strange and surprising to the audience... Everyday things are thereby raised above the level of the obvious and automatic."[16]

In the commercial environment "pure" architectural forms are often modified or violated by applied verbal signs. This is common, as Walter Benjamin and Roland Barthes have both noted, for communications media in general:

> Today, at the level of mass communications it appears that the linguistic message is present and independent in every image: as title, caption, accompanying press article, film dialogue, comic strip balloon.[17]

> Picture magazines begin to put up signposts for him [the viewer], right ones or wrong ones, no matter. For the first time, captions have become obligatory. And it is clear that they have an altogether different character than the title of a painting. The directives which the captions give to those looking at pictures in illustrated magazines become even more explicit and more imperative in the film where the meaning of each simple picture appears to be prescribed by the sequence of all preceding ones.[18]

Venturi and Rauch facades often function as linguistic modifiers of the building to which they are attached. For example, beneath the quartz-light fixture that illuminates the large painted number "4" at the top of Fire Station 4 in Columbia, Indiana (1965), itself a verbal and heraldic sign, two black bricks are set into the white brickwork that constitutes the facade to underline the light fixture; the line functions as literary irony and in the decorative/architectural modes simultaneously.

Walking along Main Street or driving in an automobile one sees a row of signs in sequence. Each sign stands out from the signs preceding and following it, having a prescribed, separate meaning in relation to the other signs that surround (and define) it in terms of its position. For a sign to convey meaning, it must conform to the general code shared by the surrounding signs and distinguish itself from—establish its position relative to—other signs. Each sign depends ultimately for its meaning upon its position in relation to the others. Signs change (and react to change in other signs) relative to their function, to general changes within the code of signs, and to shifts in the sequence of signs of which they are a part. Functions of buildings change (a real-estate office might become a medical clinic and then a used-car showroom or an art gallery), which is reflected in their representation in the sign-system.

By the early 1970's this notion of art as continual innovation came to be seriously questioned. Ecological concerns had generated a new cultural ethos that did not accept an idea of progress with its imperative to experiment with nature in order to create an ever-new future. Conservation of natural resources went along with conservation of the past. These changes in social perspective were reflected culturally in the 1970s fashion for "historical" re-creations of past decades, in the "new nostalgia," as well as in the neo-Colonial look of the facades/decor of vernacular architectural forms.

The historically eclectic, domestic (national, indigenous, vernacular and "homespun" as opposed to International Style) and "rustic" aspects of this style owed something to the "high" architecture of the late 1960s post-modernists (Venturi, Charles Moore and others), but used these influences for its own ideological purposes. It is possible that revivalism, in its nostalgic aspect, doesn't intend to clarify, but is meant to veil an accurate reading of the recent past: the connection between "the way we were" and the position we are in now, in place of integrity, postwar history to the present is broken into a confusion of delimited, self-contained decades, as first the '30s, then the '50s, and now the '60s are revived. The public's access to these "magic" eras is further confused with personal nostalgia: history as "memory": memory associated by media with the time when we "grew up." Like the cultural form of the western, the culturally mediated memory of coming of age in one of these recently past decades mythically stands for America's Past. In media representations the present appears confused with the particular "past" time being revived. In films and in television series such as "Happy Days," "Laverne and Shirley " and "The Waltons," one sees the projection of present-day, largely middle-class "problems," represented by lower-middle-class characters (possibly "our" family forebears, one generation removed) situated back in the half-accurately depicted, half-nostalgically recalled decades of the '50s, the '30s, the '40s or the '60s.

The problem of the authenticity of historical reconstructions is now seen to be crucial, not only in the "new nostalgia" of popular culture, but in the recent, clearly parallel, interest of architecture in the nature of historical syntax: What makes a building real or fake? And what constitutes an architectural tradition?

> Consider... [these] buildings, the restored Raleigh Tavern in Colonial Williamsburg, and the 1970's gas station called "Williamsburg." If the claim for authenticity is that they must actually have been built in the 18th century, or as an exact replica of the same, then, alas, the gas station and the conjecturally reconstructed parts of Williamsburg must be called fake. And even the use of indoor plumbing and electricity in Gunston Hall would have to be viewed as a compromise. Clearly, such an unrealistic definition of authenticity presumes that architectural tradition cannot change over time without losing validity or collapsing altogether...
> An architectural tradition is composed both of references to an ideal type and of accommodations to particular circumstances. Viewed in this way, the Colonial tradition is more than just a set of 18th-century buildings or latter-day replicas. In other words, the Colonial tradition is a collection of architectural elements to be used in contemporary buildings to evoke to the modern eye (and in the modern heart) both the shapes and the size and, finally, the feel of 18th-century America.[19]

The historical, in the form of an architectural allusion, signifies an ideal; but its specific meaning only has relevance in its relation to surrounding, present-day meanings, expressed by surrounding signs in the environment. And this is never neutral, but an active, present representation of one ideological view's explanation of the past in relation to present reality. The past is symbolic, never "factual." In architecture a sign of the past signifies a myth larger than the mere architectural function. "History" is a highly deceptive concept, as there are only histories, each serving some specific present-day ideological need.

Venturi and Rauch's 1968 restoration for the Saint Francis de Sales Church in Philadelphia heuristically overlaps present and past. It was constructed because the newly introduced (actually revived ancient) liturgical practice of the Catholic Church required a free-standing altar to replace the traditional one against the wall. Instead of destroying the old sanctuary, Venturi and Rauch left it as it was and installed an electric cathode light tube (since removed) suspended on a wire, ten feet high, parallel to the ground and just above the eye-level of seated parishioners. The electric line defined an ellipsoidal semicircle inflected inward, and following the perspective of the parishioners' line of sight, as well as the line of the old altar. It ran from just behind the new altar, following the curve of the apse behind it, to define a boundary that separated the old, rear altar from the new altar whose activities its light functionally illuminated.

Here the light tube functioned only as a sign (replacing nothing), a two-dimensional, graphic indicator, drawing a (mental) line through the old altar (thus leaving it in relative darkness) without physically destroying it. It literally illuminated/delineated the new area and so juxtaposed the old and the new, placing them in an historical, or archeological, relation to each other. Venturi proposed the word "hybrids" for such works that combine two contradictory or mutually exclusive categories of meaning/description: "I like elements which are hybrid rather than 'pure'... ambiguous rather than 'articulated'... I include the non sequitur and proclaim the duality... I prefer 'both-and' to 'either-or,' black and white, and sometimes gray, to black and white."[20] Again: "Our scheme for the F.D.R. Memorial was architecture and landscape; our foundation for the Philadelphia Fairmount Park Commission was architecture and sculpture; our design for Copley Plaza, architecture and urban design ... [while that for] the National Football Hall of Fame is a building and a billboard."[21]

The task of the work of art or architecture is not the resolution of social or ideological conflict in a beautiful artwork, and not the construction of a new ideological counter-content; instead the artwork directs attention to the seams in various ideological representations (revealing the conflicting variety of ideological readings).[22] To do this the work uses a hybrid form, one which partakes of both the popular code of mass media and the "high" code of art/architecture, of both the popular code of entertainment and a theoretically based political analysis of form, and of both the code of information and of the esthetically formal.

The article "Art in Relation to Architecture / Architecture in Relation to Art" was originally published in *Artforum*, February 1979, pp. 22-29. It was reprinted in *Rock my Religion*, ed. Brian Wallis, MIT, 1993.

Notes

1. Dan Flavin, "Some Remarks . . . ; . . . Excerpts from a Spleenish Journal," *Artforum*, December 1966.
2. Flavin, "Some Other Comments," *Artforum*, December 1967.
3. People tend to compare Flavin's fluorescents to Duchamp's readymades. It is important to make a distinction. Duchamp took an object produced as a commodity from the non-art sector and introduced it into the art gallery in apparent contradiction of both the usual function of the gallery (which is to designate certain objects "art" and to exclude others) and of other "non-contaminated" arts objects within the gallery. This would seem to question, on the level of abstract or logical truth, the aristocratic function of art and of the art gallery as institution. In fact, Duchamp's critique is only on the conceptual/philosophical level, and was immediately integrated back into the art institution's definitions of what constitutes (the function of) art without directing the spectator's attention to the specific details/practice of the functioning of the gallery or of art in relation to society at a specific historical moment. Duchamp's work resolves the contradiction between gallery art and art in relation to society into a totalizing abstraction; further, it is ahistorical: the condition of "art" is seen as neither social nor as subject to change. By contrast, Flavin's fluorescents only "work" through specific situation installation, either through necessity or esthetic calculation.
4. Daniel Buren, "Notes on Work in Connection with the Places Where It Is Situated, Taken Between 1967 and 1975," *Studio International*, September-October 1975.
5. In recent years the transparent glass style has been inverted with the glass façade being replaced by use of reflective (or semireflective, one-way) mirror-glass. Unlike the earlier transparent glass structures, which openly revealed their structural framework, the glass building now presents the viewer on the outside with a purely abstract form (from the inside it allows the corporate worker a concealed vantage point)—a cube, hexagon, trapezoid, or pyramid.
6. Karl Beveridge and Ian Bum, "Don Judd," *The Fox*, No. 2, 1975, pp. 129-42, esp. p. 138.
7. Roy Lichtenstein, as interviewed by G.R. Swenson, *Art News*, November 1965.
8. The American television series "Mary Hartman, Mary Hartman" functioned in a way not dissimilar to Lichtenstein's art. On one level it could be read as "soap opera." It was impossible for the viewer to know if it was one or the other. Its adherence to principles of identification with characters in a narrative format, its emotional directness, and other conventions of "soap opera," allowed it to be a believable "soap." In "Mary Hartman, Mary Hartman" the validity of the satire itself was continually undercut by the emotional' "reality" of the characters' problems, which, in fact, resembled those of most Americans. Because the show was conceived in this fashion as a form of both "high" and "vernacular" art, the writers and actors on the show never deluded themselves into thinking that the program was a "higher" form of art, nor did they take themselves totally seriously as "stars" or media-manipulators.
9. El Lissitzky, "Ideological Superstructure," (Moscow, 1929), in *Russia: An Architecture for World Revolution*, tr. Eric Diuhosch, Cambridge, Mass., 1970, pp. 70-71.
10. Denise Scott Brown, "An Alternative Proposal That Builds on the Character and Population of South Philadelphia," *Architectural Forum*, October 1971.
11. Lichtenstein, interview (note 7).
12. Robert Venturi, Denise Scott Brown and Steve Izenour, *Learning From Las Vegas*, Cambridge, Mass., 1972.
13. Robert Venturi, *Complexity and Contradiction in Architecture* (Museum of Modern Art Papers on Architecture, I), New York, 1966.
14. Venturi, Brown and Izenour, *Learning* (note 12).

15. *Ibid.*
16. Bertolt Brecht, "Alienation Effects in Chinese Acting", in *Brecht on Theatre*, trans. and ed. John Willett, New York, 1964, pp. 91–99.
17. Roland Barthes, The Rhetoric of the Image," in his *Image–Music–Text*, trans. and ed. Stephen Heath. London, 1977, pp. 32–51.
18. Walter Benjamin, "The Work of Art in the Age of Mechanical Reproduction," in his *Illuminations*, ed. Hannah Arendt, trans. Harry Zohn, New York, 1969, pp. 217–42.
19. Richard Oliver and Nancy Ferguson, "The Environment is a Diary," *Architectural Record*, February 1978.
20. Venturi, *Complexity* (note 13), p. 23.
21. Robert Venturi, quoted in Robert Maxwell, "The Venturi Effect," in *Venturi and Rauch: The Public Buildings*, New York, 1978.
22. This runs parallel in French semiotic theory to Julia Kristeva's critique of the unitary text based on "the construction of a single identity (with its own consistent identity)." She advocates instead a plurivocal text "where (various) discourses confront each other... in opposition" and which is "an apparatus for exposing and exhausting ideologies in their confrontation."
Julia Kristeva, "The Ruin of a Poetics," *20th-Century Studies*, 7/8, 1972.

judging terrorism

Andrew Benjamin

1. *Terrorist attacks are watched in disbelief.*
Terrorist attacks are watched as completely believable.
Terrorist attacks are condemned without equivocation.
Terrorist attacks engender equivocation concerning the relationship between means and ends.
Describing an event as a terrorist attack may be accurate.
Describing an event as a terrorist attack is a political stance used to deny the presence of a founding injustice.

Interrupting this list necessitates recognizing that there are moments of truth in every instance. As a term, therefore, 'terrorism' is inserted in a network of activities and is deployed and redeployed in the formulation of conflicting ethical and political positions. Rather than attempt to clarify this state of affairs by defining, absolutely, the way terrorism is to be understood and so determine in advance who the terrorist may be, a different approach will be taken. The inherent ambivalence will be allowed to endure. An initial justification for the position resides in the fact that what cannot be precluded is the possibility that within any conflict both sides could use the means of terrorism. (This would not simply be the claim by one side that the other deployed the means of terrorism; it could actually be the case.) The bombing of a sovereign power by another will be viewed by those bombed as an act of terrorism. The bulldozing of houses and villages as a form of reprisal will be viewed by those made homeless as an act of terrorism. The destruction caused by a suicide bomber in a dense urban setting will for its inhabitants, and by extension for everyone affected by the act, count as terrorism. It is precisely this predicament that makes it impossible to approach terrorism in abstract terms as though a general definition could account for its particular use. Whatever the term is finally taken to mean, terrorism is not the province of one group. It is not the case that in any one conflict one side is the terrorist and the other is not. This is the setting within which the term 'terrorism' will be approached.

2. One of the most obvious effects of a terrorist attack is the conception of object with which it works. (Object, in this context, is the one attacked; the subject is the one launching the attack.) When a bomb is placed in order to kill Protestants, or Muslims, or Israelis, etc, the act of destruction is necessarily indiscriminate. It is not just that it does not discriminate between those against whom the attack is aimed directly and others who may become directly involved although the attack was not aimed at them; it turns all those against whom the attack was directed into versions of the same, where sameness is defined by race, religion, ethnicity, nationality, etc. While this may seem to be a claim about the particularization of a universal humanity, it is not. Something else is involved. What is indicated is that terrorism is necessarily connected to the philosophical problem of identity.

The terrorist attack is always against an identity and in the name of another identity. Part of any response to terrorism has to recognize that it is inextricably bound up with this problem. Indeed, in order both to understand the issues involved and then to define the criteria in terms of which it is possible to develop arguments in relation to terrorism – and it is vital to add that what is important are arguments and not simple posturing – the connection to identity is of central importance. The argument is not that the question of identity is resolved and therefore closed in advance. The claim is that in order to understand what is occurring it is necessary to begin with the way in which identity works as the organizing term. Once it is possible to ask in whose name an attack is carried out, then the name cannot be easily, if at all, detached from the question of how the identity of the named is understood. It is therefore important here to give a degree of specificity to the conception of identity involved. Precisely because it concerns a conception of identity that is bound up with a conception of sameness, it can be designated the *sameness of identity*. Such a formulation is important because the terrorist attack has to have a homogeneous conception of its object. Questions pertaining to the judgment of terror have to begin with this failure to discriminate. The politics of terrorism are thus bound up with the politics of essentialism. This is still the case even when it can be argued that there is a justification for the terrorist attack. The justification is that it is a calculated response against a movement that essentialises.

An act of terrorism, understood as a response, is the counter to an essentialising movement that comes from the outside. The mistake, however, is to think that this movement towards sameness of identity is a denial of individuality and is thus to be understood as the staging of an enforced anonymity. Precisely the opposite is the case. The terrorist attack, and here an analogy can be drawn with history of the concentration camp and with the 'ethnic cleansing' that characterized the recent conflict in Bosnia, always has a specifically determined object, because it determines its object as the object. The terrorist attack is bound up with and is only possible because of that determination. While it is clear that individuals are involved, what is under attack is not individuality having become anonymous, it is the group interpolated within the sameness of identity.

As such what this establishes is an important link between this conception of sameness on the one hand, and violence and terror on the other.

While a distinction needs to be drawn between acts of terrorism and the situation in which, in Arendt's words, 'violence rules absolutely', these have an important affinity. She describes the latter situation in the following terms.

> *Where violence rules absolutely, as for example in the concentration camps of totalitarian regimes, not only the laws –* les lois se taisent, *as the French Revolution phrased it – but everything and everybody else must fall silent. It is because of this silence that violence is a marginal phenomenon in the political realm; for man, to the extent that he is a political being, is endowed with the power of speech.*[1] (18-19)

For Arendt, that violence, which has become identified with the operation of a political regime in necessitating silence, allows for its own interruption, sinceit stands opposed to the defining character of human being. While the social nature of being human and the articulation of that being through speech and argument cannot defend themselves against the actualization of violence's possibility, violence cannot use the means of speech and argument. Silence, while imposed, brings with it the ground of its own overcoming. The point of affinity between the act of violence and 'regime' is human being. This is not a claim about human beings or about humanity as an abstraction but about the being of being human understood as an ontological category. And yet, as Arendt points out, the tradition is marked by acts of founding or constituting violence. What must be questioned is the extent to which such acts of constituting violence play a role in developing an understanding of terror. As will emerge, the value of Arendt's formulation is that in positioning violence and silence in opposition to speech, this will allow speech – although reworked in terms of the endlessness of negotiation – to be that which provides a basis on which both to judge and to counter claims either about terror or about terror's possible justification. Leaving aside questions of their mythic status – though such questions will in the end be necessary – constituting acts of violence can either stand outside the realm of the human and thus appear as divine or as unmediated violence, or, in being incorporated into the realm of the human, mark violence as mediated from the start.

The first understanding of constituting violence stands in need of the demythologizing move that would occur as a consequence of maintaining the position that violence is always mediated from the start. Once all these elements are taken together what can be seen to emerge is the setting in which the terrorist act can be approached. The elements that mark it out include two central interarticulations. The first is between terror and the sameness of identity. The second is between the social and the ontological. What is important is how the components of this entire set-up interact. Again, there is an implicit philosophical argument here. What is being suggested is that not only does it have to be the case that terrorism can only be understood by thinking through the concept of identity articulated within it, but also the additional claim that it necessitates – again in order for it to be understood – the setting of the ontology of human being.

What, however, of the constituting act of violence? The insistence of this question lies in its inescapable link to a conception of the political that defines sovereignty in terms of war or opposition. Machiavelli, Hobbes and Schmitt, among others, will all figure in such a set-up.[2] One of the constituting acts of violence to which Arendt refers is Cain's murder of Abel. Arendt's own interpretation will not be central here, despite its acuity, since it does not take up the problem of mediation. Nonetheless, there is an element of the story that is of fundamental importance to these present undertakings. What is interesting about the story of the murder is the way it can be construed as a uniquely human concern.

3. The entire section of *Genesis* IV, 1-15. in which this occurrence takes place is concerned with fraternity, forgiveness and estrangement. Each of these terms involves alterity. An examination of 'fraternity' within the Hebrew bible reveals that what is at stake is the other person. Cain's transgression elicits the plea for forgiveness, and for the murder he is condemned to the life of the stranger. There is almost a folding of the story back in on itself. While there is no doubt that a murder has occurred, verse 10 stages a formulation that makes the question of alterity a human question. In verse 9 God asks Cain where his brother is. On a literal level the text is unproblematic. God must have known that Cain's actual brother (Abel) has been murdered, and yet another reading would have God asking Cain about the presence of the other (the 'brother' as the sign of an ineliminable and thus primordial alterity; the other to the same). Cain's reply has a certain infamy 'I know not, am I my brother's keeper?' This is the question addressed by Cain to God. God's response is the exclamation that Cain has murdered both his brother and future generations. The move from the present to the future (present in the text in the use of the plural 'bloods'[3]) indicates that Cain's question has greater extension than the mere moment of its being asked. What, however, of the question asked by

Cain? It should be remembered that this is a question to which God could have replied. Moreover, it is a question concerning human relations. After all, what is under examination is the question of the obligations alterity brings with it. The question is asked in verse 9 and the verses continue with the recognition of the deed and the punishment, without there being at any time a return to the question. The temptation is to say that the question is left in suspension without being addressed. However, that would make the failure to respond no more than a mere oversight. The important conclusion to be drawn is that God's silence means that the relation to the other is a fundamentally human concern. While elsewhere there will be an important discussion concerning how the stranger is to be understood (*Leviticus* XIX, 33), it remains the case that fundamental to all these discussions is that self/other relations both define the human predicament – indeed they are the human predicament – and have to be regulated as part of human life. If there is an act of constituting violence then it occurs within the set-up in which ethics was ethos from the start.[4] It is not external and as such an act of violence would constitute that which took place as a consequence. Violence is always already internal to the construction of social being. What is also there from the start, therefore, is the possibility of violence. However, it is neither divine nor pure violence. On the contrary, it is the violence that is an inherent possibility within self/other relations. As such it is uniquely human. It is the idea of an inherent possibility that is of fundamental importance. An inherent possibility exists as a potential. Since there has to be a type of distinction between potential and its realization, this will have to mean that the actualization of this inherent possibility necessitates mediation. (The move from potential being to actual being involves mediation, otherwise all that would be actualized would be the potential; moreover it would be actualized in toto.) The problem posed by the relationship between potential and actual existence is of great significance in this context because the move from a primordial self/other relation to the sameness of identity involves this potentiality.

As has already been made clear, an 'inherent possibility' is linked to potentiality. Human being needs to be defined in terms of the relationship between potential and actual being. The task is one of determining how potential is to be understood. In the first instance it should be noted that it necessitates that violence always be mediated. Violence, while inherent, is never actualized as such. And yet, at first glance it could be argued that the potential, rather than account for the inescapable presence of mediation, is the human's capacity for its own annihilation. It would be as though what founds human being brings with it the capacity for its own destruction.[5] However, such an argument would misunderstand the relationship between potential and actual being. It is not as though violence is an option that has to be mastered continually or that expresses itself absolutely. This would only be possible if violence could be presented as unmediated. The necessity of mediation means that, in the move from a potential to its realization, the distinction should not be thought of as absolute but as a continuum. In other words, while violence is always mediated, violence *is* – is what it is – in its always being mediated. There is no violence outside mediation, existing in a state of divine purity. While violence is a potential, the fact that its actualization is always specific means that the site of violence is the site of human being. In the same ways as action is always mediated, human being is always mediated by its involving the plurality of human actions.[6]

In a general sense what marks self/other relations is the possible refusal of alterity; hence the force of Cain's question. Refusal is a form of mediation. That refusal extends as much to the other as it does to oneself. Indeed, it is this twofold extension that indicates how the refusal needs to be understood. Refusal is not as simple as the denial of alterity. It also brings with it the denial of sameness. There is no pure alterity. What therefore emerges as a generalized position is that any form of original purity is impossible. This is not because there is a founding trace that marks the origin but because any form of actualization is a mediation. In this context, there is only the co-presence of sameness and alterity. The other is both the same and other. What makes ethics ethos is that the predicament of human being is that the other is both the same and other. What exists as an inherent possibility is the refusal of this founding complexity. Cain's question needs to be rewritten. It is not as though the already present nature of self/other relations has to be recognized, it is also the case that the relations mark out the self's relation to itself. Care becomes an original condition. It is not a duty to the other that has a ground outside that which determines human being, but that this emerges because of the ineliminable self/other relations that define human being.[7] What 'potential' means in this context is that which allows for its own interruption as the moment in which an act takes place. Precisely because the self/other relation constitutes human being, that act may involve refusal; refusal may take the form of violence.

Cain's question is therefore the mark of a refusal. That fratricide is a possibility entails nothing more or less than the denial of the other's presence as that which is given in the continual oscillation between the same and other. The continuity of an oscillation allowing for individuation – allowing, that is, for subjectivity – means that the source of violence is as much the refusal of sameness as it is of alterity. To insist that a face on the level of its appearance is completely other is to deny those elements that remain the same.[8] To insist that it is the same is to deny its alterity. (Outside of pragmatic determinations, neither element can be privileged.) Human being involves the continuity of a negotiation with that which is, *ab initio*, the same and different. Violence is not refusal *tout court* since violence is always mediated. Rather, violence is a form that refusal can take. While a great deal more needs to be adduced in order to develop how the primordiality of self/other relations is to be understood, a link between that relation and what was identified above as the sameness of identity needs to be introduced at this point.[9]

Prior to proceeding with establishing this link a note needs to be added on individuality. The reason for this addition is straightforward. It may seem that the individual is counterposed to all essentialising moves. The individual would be prior to any attribution of identity; moreover, the individual would have the status of being unique. What is unique has to be prior, and have priority over all other attributions of identity. The difficulty with the term 'individual' is that it is an abstraction. The individual has to be identified as that individual and in being thus identified the individual can be named. However, precisely because the individual cannot control or have mastery over everything that is done with that name, or in the name of that name – and here there is an important opening up of the individual to the philosophical and political problem of proper names – what this indicates is the extent to which, even at the limit, the proper name is subject to the same process of individuation that yields subjectivity. Individuality is an abstraction that once given specificity brings questions of identity and alterity into play. It is not as though there is any particularity marked out by the assertion of individuality.

4. What was identified above as the sameness of identity can be understood as that move which attributes identity. The position from which the attribution is made is always external to the group being identified; moreover, the group may be constituted as such by the ascription of an identity. Once discrimination is 'legitimated' by its inscription in legislation, once it occupies the realm of popular culture by its incorporation into a chant or slogan, those named within it are given an identity.[10] While that identity may be contested, or as is more likely have its meaning refused, what occurs to the group thus determined takes place as a result of the ascription of that identity. For the National Socialist there were exact regulations determining who was a Jew and who was not. The ascription of being a Jew was sufficient to deny German citizenship. (German citizenship had been 'legally' removed from Jews by the Nuremberg laws.) While not as rigorous, nor necessarily as horrifying, it remains the case that tests for the right to obtain or maintain citizenship continue to exist. The difficulty with arguments to do with autonomy as an end in itself occurs at this precise point, insofar as the condition for autonomy may be the very moments of particularity that are effaced in its acquisition.

The terrorist attack positions those against whom it is launched as the same. In a brute physical sense this is the nature of the bomb blast. It is not anonymous flesh that is damaged or blown apart. It is always determined and thus mediated flesh. (Flesh is only ever embodied.) And, as has already been suggested, this may be in response to a similar, although not necessarily as violent, ascription of the sameness of identity. What is occurring in such a situation would therefore be a clash between forced conceptions of identity. Both forms of actions – the terrorist attack and that which may have prompted it – are themselves acts with ends. In neither case would it be possible to given an abstract or generalized account of these ends. Each instance would be specific. And yet, even in allowing for that specificity is there a ground of judgment outside mere political utility – the utility of ends and means? The starkest question to which terrorism gives rise is the possibility of judgment that takes the setting – the complex of interarticulations identified above – into real consideration. The point needs to be made clear. There is no attempt to develop a justification. Rather, the real question is the ground of judgment; i.e. developing a ground from which any condemnation of an act of terrorism would take place. (Again it should be remembered that terrorism is as much the province of states – even democratically elected states – as it is of those branded as 'terrorists' by such states.)

The ground of judgment has to be one that recognizes the particularity of terrorist violence. What, then, is the relationship between the act of terror and the primordiality of self/other relations? What is the connection between Cain's question and acts of terror? The answer cannot be that terror undermines self/other relations. Or that terror strikes against humanity. Both claims involve a generalization or an abstraction that cannot be substantiated. Both the primordiality of self/other relations and any claim about humanity (where the latter claim is understood as referring to the being of being human) cannot be posed in complete differentiation from the continuity of their actualization What the primordiality of the self/other relation entails – and this will be the case no matter what particularity is given to that relation – is a site of activity. It is not just that action involves the other or that it involves alterity of necessity. It is more emphatically that actions involve sites of negotiation. Actions begin to make up social being. The judgment of actions concerns the way they allow the continuity of social being to hold together. Part of that holding together is the possibility of activity within the domain of social being. If, for example, all women, all Muslims, all Palestinians are restricted in virtue of an essentialising form of identity attributed to them, then this is not wrong because it infringes on their autonomy or their individual liberty. It is an act that can be judged as it signals a failure to negotiate the primordiality of self/other relation. Acts of restriction or exclusion that are based on the identity of sameness are premised on a refusal to accept the predicament of human being. Expressed in this way, this means that attempts to rectify the situation – or even to engage with such situations – cannot take place as though all that were necessary were arguments to do with equality. Equality, understood as a version of sameness, is fundamental, and yet it cannot be assumed as an end in itself. Those arguments and practices, be they philosophical, cultural or political, will – if they seek to maintain the primordiality of self/other relations – be different from those based on securing (or negatively opposing) equality.

It is in terms of the possibility of judgment – a possibility bound up as much with evaluation as it is with the formulation of policy – that the difference between what allows for the ineliminable presence of self/other relations and the position that seeks to overcome them in the name of sameness can be rewritten in terms of a difference between dissymmetry and symmetry. Maintaining dissymmetry involves working with more than the already present status of difference. There are two components to this position. The first is that maintaining involves activity. Since the differences in question cannot be resolved but provide a continual state of negotiation, what is important are the activities, which, while allowing for pragmatic closures, nonetheless hold the sites of negotiation as continually open. The second pertains to how there could be a justification for such a set-up. In other words, what will provide the basis for this maintenance? The answer to this question has to do with the being of being human. Dissymmetry has to be understood as the original condition.[11] Given this original condition the response it can be said to envisage is one that is characterized by an affirmed reconciliation to irreconcilability. What would stand opposed to maintaining this set up would be the attempt to efface it in the name of symmetry. Again what is being adumbrated here is the context in which the terrorist act occurs.

The terrorist act refuses, in the first place, the maintenance of dissymmetry as that which entails an endless negotiation with ineliminable difference; a negotiation always interrupted by the pragmatic necessity for decisions. In the second place what is also refused is any conception of symmetry other than one driven by the identity of sameness. The terrorist act has as its end a synthetic political realm. Instituted in the name of a synthetic unity for a synthetic unity. This will account for why there is an important connection between the conception of identity at work within 'ethnic cleansing' and the terrorist act. While the terrorist attack involves these two different forms of refusal it only acquires particularity once it is brought into conjunction with what has already been described as the identity of sameness. The throwing of a bomb turns all against whom it is thrown into the same; i.e. they comprise the same object of attack and what is attacked is one and the same. It is an attack that refuses any type of negotiation; that refusal, in using the form of violence, is the mort emphatic form that refusal can take. While the terrorist attack may seek justification in the claim that it is the only possible response to actions – perhaps even State-sanctioned actions which themselves may warrant the description 'terrorist' – that themselves fail to discriminate and in so doing construct an identity of sameness, the justification will fail precisely because the refusal to negotiate differences is not a response to the refusal to negotiate differences. What will interrupt an initial refusal is the continual insistence on how a state in which a reconciliation to irreconcilability will predominate can be brought about.

The terrorist act can be identified as the act of violence that enforces an identity of sameness and in which the nature of the act can give rise to no other response than that of violence. (The response may be another attack, although more probably it will be an act 'legitimated' by a state and justified by either national or international law.) Both the terrorist act and such a response – a response open to the charge of terrorism - are characterized as forms of violence that are structured to refuse the possibility of negotiation. And here it is necessary to see a real confluence between pragmatic negotiations and the endless negotiation demanded by the primordiality of self/other relations.

MANIFESTA 5

ARTISTS' CONTRIBUTIONS

5

Finally, it should be noted that the point made above concerning different analyses giving rise to different cultural and political practices is central here. Once it can be argued that the response to the denial of difference is the affirmation of differences – and what that means as a strategic possibility will differ, of necessity, from one context to another – then the political and cultural activity flowing from it will be markedly different from those linked to the bomb or the bulldozer. The affirmation and the denial of difference has to be understood in terms of self/other relations which in being maintained enjoin the continuity envisaged by the formulation reconciliation to irreconcilability.

5. What is essential, and what has been attempted in the argument presented above, is that the terms 'terrorism' and 'terrorist' should not be identified with actions of a specific group, as though this attribution provided either a proper account of what terrorism is, or an adequate description of the nature of the group. Identifications of this kind do not stem from any real political analysis of the causes of such actions, and nor would they account for why the terminology of terrorism would be used to describe them. The only way of circumventing the charge and countercharge of terrorism is by giving an account of terrorism that situates it within the context of social being. What has to be precluded is the move that would seek to justify a specific act – and again this claim will have to be true for both parties to any real conflict – by arguing that it is the inevitable outcome of a particular political or cultural situation. The reason that such an approach has to fail is twofold. The first is that it works without any attempt to give an account of terrorism independently of its uses as a tactic by particular groups or states. Secondly, and relatedly, the impossibility of resolving the problem of relativity stems from the fact that the situation in which terrorism is possible and where some would seek to justify it is reproduced. Holding relativity to one side involves working with the recognition that terrorism is on the one hand bound up with the philosophical problem of identity, and equally has to be accounted for in terms of the nature of the relationship between violence and the primordiality of self/other relations. Once those relations are understood in terms of a founding and ineliminable dissymmetry – a dissymmetry that, while allowing for violence as a potential, is also sundered by such violence – then what this engenders is the ground in terms of which actions and policy can be judged. The challenge presented by terrorism is how to develop a conception of judgment that escapes the hold of both moralism and the politics of gestures. This can occur once it becomes possible to draw on speech. Speech needs to be understood as marking that which ties social being to the primordiality of self/other relations. Speech is the condition in which the endlessness of negotiation becomes possible. Maintaining speech, holding to its site, is to allow for that openness in which a reconciliation to irreconcilability can continue.

Notes

1 Hannah Arendt. *On Revolution*. Penguin Books. Harmondsworth. page 18-19.
2 One of the most emphatic presentations of this position is found in Schmitt's argument that 'the specific political distinction to which political actions and motives can be reduced is that between friend and enemy'. Carl Schmitt. *The Concept of the Political*. (trans George Schwab). University of Chicago Press. Chicago. 1996. Page 26.
3 It is not his 'brother's blood' that has been split, the text is more complex, but his 'brother's bloods'. Most commentators understood the plural to denote his 'possible descendents' (Rashi) Even on a 'literal' reading therefore the text opens beyond the moment.
4 Even though Arendt does not draw a distinction between the fratricide involving Cain and Able from the one involving Romulus and Remus, it is important, even for her own argument, to distinguish between them. The former affirms the impossibility of a position defined outside the realm of the social, while the latter locates the myth or origin outside sociality as its condition of existence. The latter therefore is mythic in structure.
5 It is clear that Ode to Man (330-375) in Sophocles's *Antigone*, is central in order to understand this potential. For Sophocles human being's capacity for acting in a way that places it beyond that which defines its being is part of what makes a given individual the strangest (δεινοτερον) of the strange (τα δεινα). Acting in a way that is contrary to an understanding of the political nature of justice – and here the political can involve respect for divine justice – means that the one who acts is, in virtue of those actions, απολισ. Being without a "polis" need not be taken literally. The state of affairs it suggests is a refusal on the part of the agent to act in accord with the propriety sanctioned, if not demanded by the being of being human. Despite its problematic status the most philosophically significant commentary on this passage of the play is Heidegger's. See Martin Heidegger. *An Introduction to Metaphysics*. (translated by Ralph Manheim) Yale University Press. New Have. Pages 146-65.
6 Taking this position a stage further necessitates developing an ontology of original plurality. While it cannot be argued for here I have attempted such an undertaking in *The Plural Event*. Routledge. London. 1993.
7 Allowing care such a role opens up two different t areas of investigation. The first would be to at the role played by 'care' (*Sorge*) in Heidegger's *Sein und Zeit*. The point of of investigation would be the the conception of identity and relatedness that emeeged in that context. The other would be to look at the construction of'care' (souci) developed by Foucault in *Le Souci de soi*.
8 That faces and bodies must always be the interaction of genders, races, ethnicities, abilities, disabilities will involve a complexity far greater than the simple logic of oppositions male/female, white/ black, able bodied /disabled, etc can provide. Here is the point at which a thinking of difference can take on a more directly political role. Again however the philosophical question

concerns how difference is thought given that difference cannot be simply posited. Pursuing this complexity can take many forms: see, amongst many others, Jean-Luc Nancy *L''il y a' du rapport sexuel*; Cronenburg *Crash*; Partrick White *The Twyborn Affair*; Franz Kafka *Metamorphoses*; Arthur Miller *Focus*.

9 It would be at this point that an engagement with Levinas would need to take place. When for example Levinas argues for an 'original irreducibility' as a way of describing the relation between self and other, the problematic element is how this apartness is to be understood. Dissymmetry, which is key to the relation is being presented the context of this paper in terms of an 'apartness' that is also an 'a apartness'. In 'Transcendence et hauteur' (in *Liberté et commandment*. Fata Morganna. Cognac. 1994). in regards to a concern with the 'rights of man' Levinas argues that;

Le droit de l'homme qu'il s'agit ainsi de faire reconnaître est le droit d'un Moi. L'homme est conçu comme un moi ou comme un citoyen - jamais dans l'originalité irréductible de son altérité à laquelle citoyen n'accède pas dans la réciprocité et la symétrie. (The right of man that is of concern has to be recognised as the right of an ego/self/I. Man is conceived as an ego/self or as a citizen. Never in terms of the original irreducibility of his alterity to which the citizen never accedes except in terms of reciprocity and symmetry.) (page 42)

While the argument for a founding dissymmetry is accepted that dissymmetry has to be set in the context of anoriginal relatedness.

10 There is, of course, an extra dimension that needs to be introduced here. Part of what is involved in the ascription of identity – the sameness of identity – signals the general presence of the crisis of identity. One of the disturbing elements is that the racist gains identity in hating. Racism is not the same as terrorism nonetheless the link between them is the crisis of identity. For an important psychoanalytic investigation of racism that is concerned with crisis of identity is Daniel Sibony. *Le 'racisme' ou la haine identitaire*. Editions du Seuil. Paris. 1997.

12 This is not to argue that this original condition is the state of nature. Nor is it to suggest that it is pre-social. The force of Arendt's Aristotelianism is that it locates human being within the realm of the polis and thus as always already engaged with the complex relationship between polis and nomos.

5

ARTISTS' CONTRIBUTIONS

BAS JAN ADER

A telephone conversation with Mary Sue Ader

Phone: Prrr... prrrrrr......
MSA: Hello?
LB: Hello, is this Mary Sue?
MSA: Yes it is. (...)
LB: I'd like to start with a few factual things.
When exactly did Bas leave for this piece, *In Search of the Miraculous*?
MSA: He left July 9th, 1975.
LB: Where did he leave from?
MSA: He left from Stage Harbor, Chatham, Cape Cod, Massachusetts. It's a yacht anchorage.
LB: Did he know it well, had he been there before?
MSA: No, uhhuh.
LB: Do you know how he happened to select this particular place to leave from?
MSA: Well, he selected Cape Cod in general because it was the furthest point East and South and he needed to be at that point to drop down to catch the... er...
LB: The Gulf stream.
MSA: Yeah, the Gulf stream.
LB: How exactly had he plotted the course, had he charted it?
MSA: Yeah.
WS: Where did he want to go?
MSA: He wanted to go to Land's End, England, to Falmouth.
WS: And how long did he expect the trip to take?
MSA: He expected it to take from 60 to 90 days. He actually expected to be there within 67 days.
WS: And how much food did he have, for how long?
MSA: He had food for, we think, approximately 180 days, and then he had fishing equipment, and he had water for 180 days. (...)
LB: When he didn't arrive, what happened?
MSA: I wasn't discouraged by the time I left, I expected him any week. When he didn't arrive within his set time period we decided that he had grossly miscalculated the time it would take him on such a small boat, and a lot of experienced sailors said that he could make it but it would probably take him up to 150 days. So we waited until 150 days were up and then we thought, well he still could make it, and we kept postponing...

LB: Did you...
MSA: I went over again at Christmas time and with his brother went to all the embassies of the governments bordering the Atlantic and informed them of the situation, and asked them to get the word out and try and see if there was any information about him at all.
WS: Was a search made along any kind of route?
MSA: Yes, there was a search made a couple of times out of England. The coastguard was informed the day he left in Cape Cod and they sent out radio messages that week and regularly during the time period he was gone, and then the British Coastguard was contacted, and they got a couple of reports of small boats, one sighting of a small boat and one sighting of a flare, and searched. They didn't turn anything up at the time.
WS: He had no radio or...
MSA: He had a short-wave receiver and an emergency locator transmitter that would transmit a beacon that would reach around the horizon and up to an airplane in the sky, and that apparently never went off. It was water-activated, if the antenna was pulled out, which is quite possible.
LB: Were there any heavy storms?
MSA: Quite a number of them, although I think on the whole the weather was rather mild – at the beginning and at the end.
WS: What do you think happened?
MSA: I think the boat was too small and not designed for that kind of a trip and it just couldn't take it.
WS: So you think that he's lost?
MSA: I'm convinced that he's lost. There's been a lot of speculation about him sailing off and taking on a different identity and stuff like that...
WS: Do you discount that?
MSA: Totally discount it. (...)
WS: Is there a history of anyone else accomplishing that goal?
MSA: There's a man who'd made approximately the same sail on the same route on the boat *Tinkerbelle*, and that was 14 feet 8 inches, and he held the record for the smallest boat crossing the Atlantic in 78 days.
WS: So Bas was looking to break the record?
MSA: Well, that was kind of a side aspect.
LB: How did he talk about this piece in the context of his work, did he think this was going to be some culmination of it?
MSA: He thought that it was a very special piece and very important in the development of his work. He thought it was a step ahead, I'm sure: progress,

not culmination. Otherwise I don't think he would have done it in this context. He felt very strongly about it, he was very sensitive about it, he had very romantic feelings about the whole effort and all of the...
LB: There's a line in the song on the back of the Bulletin: 'Like an eagle caged, I pine on this dull unchanging shore.'
MSA: That was very expressive of his feelings, the freedom of the ocean, the challenge of the seas. He had terrifically romantic feelings about all of that. (...)
MSA: He did the Fall pieces, the *Broken Fall (Organic)* and the *Broken Fall (Geometrical)*, he stood on a street that led up to the West Cappella lighthouse, which was a frequent subject of Mondrian's, and he stood next to a horse, a hobbyhorse that carpenters use, and he fell sideways over that horse, and it fell down with him. He called that *Geometrical* because he determined the time it would take to do it. In *Broken Fall (Organic)* he was hanging from the limb of a tree over a small canal that had a little bush next to it; he hung onto the branch as long as he could and then fell, the bush breaking his fall.
WS: So risk played a significant part in his work?
MSA: In a sense, yes, but it wasn't about that. It wasn't about risking his life.
WS: Then what was it about, essentially?
MSA: It wasn't about that in the sense that he was playing with the risk. It was more incidental. Of course, it was part of the piece, it was obvious that he was taking a risk, but I think it was about... er... His work was about falling in its many meanings, especially at that time, that was the central theme. (...)
LB: What did he feel as an artist in relation to the art world? He kept himself pretty much...
WS: ...Reclusive.
MSA: Yeah. He felt very much part of a group of people who are mostly quite singular people.
WS: Like?
MSA: Bill Leavitt was a very good friend of his, and Ger Van Elk. And I think he also felt very close to Mondrian and Yves Klein. Bas had studied Mondrian and his writings, he kept up an ongoing dialogue with him. He often referred to Mondrian's ideas about neo-classicism, and the colors red, yellow, blue, black and white. He felt very much like being identified as an individual instead of part of a movement. (...)
LB: He had a very strong interest in philosophy, didn't he?

MSA: He did work towards a doctorate in philosophy after he got his master's degree.
LB: In Descartes.
MSA: Yes, and Hegel. (...)
LB: What did he tell you specifically when he set sail from Chatham?
MSA: He wanted me to take some photographs and film... I have some 8mm film which I haven't seen yet... of him setting sail – the photograph on the Bulletin was from that – and of him getting ready.
LB: Did he do any physical training?
MSA: No, but he was in really good shape, he was slim and muscular and generally very active.
LB: Did he take anything to do with him on the boat?
MSA: He took, I believe, a tape recorder and cameras and movie cameras and a couple of books...
LB: What books?
MSA: I was trying to think. They were a couple of books on navigation, and a couple of books on Hegel. He didn't want to take a lot of books because he was sure he wouldn't have time to read them, or the space. He figured almost all of his waking time would be taken up by sailing and boat repairs, practical things.
WS: He expected to sail all the way, he didn't have a motor.
MSA: No. He had a self-steering wind vane. I think he could have floated if the mast had broken, he had had super strong sails made for the boat, and special rigging too, extra heavy rigging. I think he was also planning to write a journal, and to teach himself the songs that were to be sung in Groningen. (...)
MSA: They had rumors going for months that he was alive and well.
WS: There was no sense of him wanting that kind of thing or thinking...
MSA: Oh no.
WS: ...this was the ultimate piece and... er... committing suicide.
MSA: No, I'm absolutely convinced that was nowhere in his consciousness. We talked about it, and he assured me repeatedly these were not his intentions.

Excerpts from a telephone conversation between Mary Sue Ader, Willoughby Sharp and Liza Bear, published in *Avalanche*, 1976.

VICTOR ALIMPIEV AND SERGEY VISHNEVSKY

'Once upon a lovely grey day
The deer has run through a city.'

What is the 'lyrical'?

For example:
To give flowers - is awkward as a rule.
To fall on your face in a pie - is ridiculous as a rule.
To fall on your face in sweetness represents a flower glade.
To fall on your face, to get dirty in a substitute way – is a perfect comedy.
Early garbage comedy, which is not worthy of «Great Silent» yet.

To fall on your face and to fall asleep so.
And not to see your own reflection - crystal clear, yet fragmentary, in a substitute of substitutes, in a brilliant flower wrapper, in another's face, in the same face.
Hung by eternal, perfect Narcissus' dream. Already reflected Narcissus.
To present flowers – is awkward: they are already presented, stretched - each time. To give flowers – is a perfect utopia.

Two muddy, slightly dirty texts: let them live and reflect in each other with crystal clearness. Comedy. Utopia.

To put on a comedy as a utopia.
To conceive utopia as a comedy, maintaining Utopian awkwardness and necessary straightness at the same time.
Necessary straightness of a verb: perfect lyrical transmission.

So,
'Once upon a lovely grey day
The deer has run through a city.'
Forest deer - is in the distance.
He has escaped, has left - but has not disappeared.
Don't worry.
He has not disappeared.

What is the 'lyrical'?

Experience of 'something in the distance', something stretched.
Spatial experience.

HOTEL HOLIDAY

my way or High way,
third way
any way, Hemingway,
no way, Norway,
Bombay, subway...

---

one day

* * *

Via Bertiera, 13 - 40126 Bologna - Tel. 051/235326 (3 l. r.a.) - Telefax 051/235326

MICOL ASSAËL

3.11 OF COURSE WE HAVE TO ALLOW THAT THERE ARE ALL KINDS OF PROBLEMS ABOUT THE UNCONSCIOUS, SELF-DECEPTION, AND ALL THE REST OF THE UNKNOWN AND UNACKNOWLEDGED REASONS FOR ACTION. BUT IN THE IDEAL CASE WHERE I CONSCIOUSLY ACT ON A REASON AND AM CONSCIOUSLY AWARE OF ACTING ON A REASON, THE SPECIFICATION OF THE REASON AS THE EXPLANATION OF MY ACTION IS PERFECTLY ADEQUATE.

3. THERE ARE THUS TWO AVENUES TO THE GAP, AN EXPERIENTIAL AND A LINGUISTIC ONE. WE EXPERIENCE OURSELVES ACTING FREELY IN THE GAP, AND THIS EXPERIENCE IS REFLECTED IN THE LOGICAL STRUCTURE OF EXPLANATIONS THAT WE GIVE FOR OUR ACTIONS. WE EXPERIENCE OURSELVES ACTING AS RATIONAL AGENTS, AND OUR LINGUISTIC PRACTICE OF GIVING EXPLANATIONS REFLECTS THE GAP (BECAUSE THE EXPLANATIONS DO NOT CITE CAUSALLY SUFFICIENT CONDITIONS);

3.1 THE BRAIN IS SUCH THAT THE CONSCIOUS SELF IS ABLE TO MAKE AND CARRY OUT DECISIONS IN THE GAP, WHERE NEITHER DECISION NOR ACTION IS DETERMINED IN ADVANCE, BY CAUSALLY SUFFICIENT CONDITIONS, YET BOTH ARE RATIONALLY EXPLAINED BY THE REASONS THE AGENT IS ACTING ON

2.11 THERE ARE NOT TWO SETS OF CAUSES, THE CONSCIOUSNESS AND THE NEURONS; THERE IS JUST ONE SET, DESCRIBED AT DIFFERENT LEVELS. CONSCIOUSNESS, IS JUST THE STATE THAT THE SYSTEM OF NEURONS IS IN, IN THE SAME WAY THAT SOLIDITY IS JUST A STATE THAT THE SYSTEM OF MOLECULES IS IN.

2.1 CONSCIOUSNESS IS A FEATURE OF THE BRAIN IN A WAY THAT SOLIDITY IS A FEATURE OF THE WHEEL.

1.1 ASSUME WE HAD AN ACCOUNT OF HOW THE BRAIN PRODUCES MENTAL CAUSATION, AND AN ACCOUNT OF HOW IT PRODUCES THE EXPERIENCES OF RATIONAL AGENCY, HOW DO YOU GET RATIONAL INDETERMINISM INTO YOUR ACCOUNT OF BRAIN FUNCTION?

1. FREE WILL, IF IT EXISTS AT ALL, IS A PHENOMENON IN TIME.

1.12 THE STATE OF THE NEURONS DETERMINES THE STATE OF CONSCIOUSNESS. BUT ANY GIVEN STATE OF NEURONS/ CONSCIOUSNESS IS NOT CAUSALLY SUFFICIENT FOR THE NEXT STATE. *

2.12 BUT EVEN ASSUMING WE HAD A QUANTUM MECHANICAL EXPLANATION OF CONSCIOUSNESS, HOW DO WE GET FROM INDETERMINISM TO RATIONALITY? IF QUANTUM INDETERMINACY AMOUNTS TO RANDOMNESS THEN QUANTUM INDETERMINACY BY ITSELF SEEMS USELESS IN EXPLAINING THE PROBLEM OF FREE WILL BECAUSE FREE ACTIONS ARE NOT RANDOM.

2. FIRST WE KNOW THAT OUR EXPERIENCES OF FREE ACTION CONTAIN BOTH INDETERMINISM AND RATIONALITY AND THAT CONSCIOUSNESS IS ESSENTIAL TO THE FORMS THAT THESE TAKE. SECOND WE KNOW THAT QUANTUM INDETERMINISM IS THE ONLY FORM OF INDETERMINISM THAT IS INDISPUTABLY ESTABLISHED AS A FACT OF NATURE.**

1.11 AS LONG AS THE GAP IS EPIPHENOMENAL, THEN NO INDETERMINISM IN THE CAUSAL APPARATUS IS ESSENTIAL TO EXPLAIN HOW CONSCIOUSNESS IS CAUSED BY AND REALIZED IN BRAIN PROCESSES.

3.12 WE THOUGHT FREE WILL WAS A MYSTERY, BUT CONSCIOUSNESS AND QUANTUM MECHANICS WERE TWO SEPARATE AND DISTINCT MYSTERIES. NOW WE HAVE THE RESULT THAT IN ORDER TO SOLVE THE FIRST WE HAVE TO SOLVE THE SECOND AND INVOKE ONE OF THE MOST MYSTERIOUS ASPECTS OF THE THIRD TO SOLVE THE FIRST TWO.

.DS RH FILENAME: ROYALLON.DOC
.DS LH LAST DATE CORRECTED: 8 APRIL 01
BY JOHN R. SEARLE

SVEN AUGUSTIJNEN

Look at him.
About Johan and François, and eventually also about Eva, Michael, you and me.

A man is speaking to the camera. His name is Johan. We gather that he is in some sort of institution, but it is not clear what type that may be, a prison or a hospital. If the latter, is he suffering from some fatal illness or is he in a mental clinic? As he answers the questions of the filmmaker and a doctor in the room, it slowly becomes clear that he is suffering from aphasia, defined in the Collins English Dictionary as a 'disorder of the central nervous system, characterised by partial or total loss of the ability to communicate, especially in speech or writing.' At one point, Johan keeps responding to a prompt from the therapist by saying 'I want to know, I want to know.' She cannot get him to say 'what' he wants to know.

> *Is this not the position of the viewer in watching this 'documentary' by Sven Augustijnen? We want to know what is going on; we want to know more about this 'subject'; we want to know that the filmmaker will not abuse his position of power. And we can only know by trusting the filmmaker, by trusting the camera, by trusting that we (and Johan) will not be manipulated. But that, of course, is a contradiction in terms. Better to accept the manipulation and go from there.*
> –Michael Tarantino[1]

Reconstructing that hot summer of 2003, I realize now, while Michael, with his 'self-deprecating, downbeat wit, his hangdog, lugubrious look,'[2] was writing probably one of his last texts, I was editing 'François.'
Suffering from aphasia as well, François at a certain moment gropes his head with his hands: 'I would like to know what is going on here upstairs... My spirit can't grasp all this anymore!'
And then he looks into the camera and asks: 'Are you telling him my entire memory? You're not writing it down, I hope?'
Who is the 'him' I am telling his entire memory to? Or is it the camera that is telling...? Or regarding Michael's text, more abstract, that despite the manipulation, or better still by means of the manipulation... that all I can say is by means of somebody else's words?
Eva, the speech therapist, intervenes: 'Not writing, he's filming.'

-'He can film me.
That's okay. That looks smart.'
-'Look at him,' she remarks of his twinkling eyes, ready and proud for another prank.
I look at him and can't help smiling.
-'I can still drivel.
But that's the problem.
I can still drivel.
I can joke around.
But anything more serious...' He could keep on jumping nervously from one topic to the other, finally ending up with:'Seriously, I would like to know...'
What a smile can do! But how do they affect us?
How comfortable are we in the face of a once in a lifetime stroke or tumor?
'In the beginning was the word!... Why?' the child asks his father in the introductory scene of Tarkovsky's last film Sacrifice.
We have the answer on the tip of our tongues...

Brussels, April 2004

1. Michael Tarantino, 'The index of truth', (in *Wiel's* exhibition catalogue, Brussels, 2003).
2. Adrian Searle, 'Michael Tarantino, Creative curator of contemporary art' (Obituary, *The Guardian*, Friday December 5, 2003).

ZBYNĚK BALADRÁN

Projection / 1.2

Classified ads that I have placed here and there in various periodicals and on the Internet form a time-space co-ordinate of sorts at the point where I take possession of old motion pictures (8mm, 16mm, VHS, etc.). It's kind of like when an archaeologist more or less accidentally uncovers a layer of earth and finds traces of the past. The first thing he must do is draw the exact co-ordinates of the discovery. Then he must identify the layer in which the artefact is found and determine its approximate date. Another step consists of classifying the find in a context of time and space and interpreting the reasons for its creation and extinction. This is followed by a series of classifications, analyses of various indications and the ensuing composing and creation of images. Each of the images is part of our past and memory, even if it isn't a historical fact. The resulting image simultaneously presents a large amount of data; this is way to read the discovery.

Now – 2 min. 06 sec.
Footage from May 17th 1945, parade of Czechoslovak Army,
'Z. Nejedly talks to university students', 1947.
Czechoslovak newsreel film.
16mm black & white film, duration 20 min. 00 sec.
Footage provided by Radek Trojovsky.

The enthusiasm of people during a parade of the Czechoslovak Army that fought on the Eastern Front (soldiers fighting in the ranks of the British Army are excluded). Footage from a speech by the highest cultural personnel from later years. The path to implementing social realism.

End – 0 min. 42 sec.
Footage from 1930s to 1950s.
16mm black & white film, duration 49 min. 00 sec.
Sound - 16mm Meoclub 16 automatic projector.
Footage provided by Radek Trojovsky .
End, credits.

KG – 12 min. 11 sec.
Footage from 1948-1955 Czechoslovak newsreel films and unidentified footage

from the same years.
Black & white 16mm film, duration 45 min.
Music - Rudolf Cortez, 1950s, Supraphon .
Footage provided by Radek Trojovsky.

Footage from the Czechoslovak weekly newsreel films of the 1950s. These newsreels are full of Communist propaganda – reports of untrue successes in constructing Socialism and staged political trials. The trial of Milada Horáková (democratic politician, executed in 1950) and Rudolf Slánský (former secretary general of the Communist Party, executed in 1952). The funeral of Klement Gottwald, the first Communist president, who died shortly after Stalin's death in 1953.

Swimmer – 4 min. 14 sec.
Footage from 1965, Adriatic (sea).
Color 8mm film, duration 90 min. 00 sec.
Filmed by Vaclav Frk, duration 45 min. 00 sec.
Music - 'Starci na chmelu', 1965.
Footage provided by Milos Baladran.

A rare colour film, unique for the attractiveness of its underwater footage. The filmmaker told me that he used an ordinary Soviet-produced movie camera wrapped in a plastic bag.

Head – 1 min. 00 sec.
Footage from 1930's to 1950s.
8mm black & white film, duration 90 min. 00 sec.
Music - Vasta Burian 'Pred maturitou'.
Footage provided by Radek Trojovsky?

Kristian – 5 min. 15 sec.
Footage from 1939 and probably from 1946. Popular Czech film 'Kristian' from the beginning of the war with A. Mandlova and O. Novy and cartoon 'Perak and SS' by J. Brdecka and J.Trnka, dating from the end of the war.
VHS, black & white 16mm film, duration 97 min. 00 sec.
Music? R. A. Dvorsky orchestra and O. Novy .
Footage provided by Radek Trojovsky.

Kristian is a film by Czech director Mac Fri from 1939 (the year the Nazis began their occupation of the country). It is a romantic story of a man who

spends his evenings wooing women with his stories of adventures in the Orient, even though he is merely a clerk in a travel agency by day.
The second film is animated and dates from the period just after the war (1946), telling the story of a fictional hero, who is originally a chimney sweeper and takes on the Nazis as the elusive superhero 'Pérák'.

Document – 0 min. 42 sec.
Footage probably from 1940s.
duration 10 min. 00 sec.
16mm black & white film.
Collection of Radek Trojovsky.
Sound - present sounds.

Part of a documentary about the life of beasts of prey.

Asanation - 0 min. 42 sec.
Footage from the end of the 1960s.
Pardubice.
8mm black & white film, duration 90 min. 00 sec.
Music - Karel Vlach orchestra, 1940s.
Footage provided by Radek Trojovsky.

A view of the destruction at the end of the 1960s.
This shot consists of the demolition of part of the city of Pardubice.

Prior – 2 min. 09 sec.
Two excerpts from the TV series 'Zena za pultem' (The Woman Behind the Counter).
Story of the greengrocerer Jirinka, part II
VHS, duration 78 min. 00 sec.
Music - J. F. Fiser, Fisyo Dr. S. Konicek
KF Prague, 1977. Found material.

Through the screen a prominent actress of the 1970s and 1980s gazes at us in the leading role of a slanted series on the everyday worries of a person in Socialism, on the threshold of future Communism.

Tunnels – 4 min. 33 sec.
Footage from 1965, Adriatic coast

Ride on a motorcycle, mid 1960's.
Black & white 8mm film, dutration 45 min. 00 sec.
Filmed by Václav Frk.
Music – Antonin Dvorak, Serenade in E for strings, op. 22
II. Tempo di valse, Václav Talich,
CROPS, 1951, Supraphon.
Footage provided by Milos Baladran.

Amateur footage taken in the mid 1960's documenting one of the first holiday routes by car to the Mediterranean Sea. Middle-class Socialist families could usually only take trips to the seacoast in Yugoslavia, East Germany and Bulgaria. This was virtually the only opportunity for travel abroad within the Socialist bloc.

Carousel - 5 min. 16 sec.
Family footage from 1940s and 1950s.
8mm black & white film, duration 90 min. 00 sec.
Music – 'Tise pada snih', Karel Vlach orchestra.

A short sequence from a family film from the 1940s or 1950s.

Hic sunt leones - 0 min. 52 sec.
8mm black & white film, duration 16 min. 00 sec.
Music ? R. A. Dvorsky, 1930s

Agents - 2 min. 26 sec.
Footage from the late 1970s.
StB agents watching J. Hajek and F. Kriegel.
VHS, duration - torso.
Music – 'Bye Bye Blues' by Fred Hamm, Dave Bennett, Bert Lown & Chauncey Gray, performed by Peter Molik. Found material.

This is probably footage from the 'Original Videojournal,' a dissident periodical from the second half of the 1980s. It shows StB secret police agents following two Prague pensioners who signed Charter 77 on their daily walk. All of the people in the film are StB agents (Communist Czechoslovak secret police).

JOHN BOCK

Maggot-Monologue II. (Excerpt)

(...)
A tiny maggot worms its way through the oesophagus
Leaves track of mucus-mire
Maggot devours solid
Remains of food
Maggot eats its way
Direction brainy mass
But brainy mass no longer there
There cave-like snug-warm hairgrease-mouse lives
Nibbles itself fully satiated with BrainMind
Out of the flooded and clogged ear, the deaf,
there roll mouse-droppings rolled.
The other ear nourishes an earth-bird.
Intestine filled with old BREWFOOD
Crisscrossed by tapeworm.
Nourishment-ritual à la bonne cuisine.
Masses-rich richness writhes heavy and snake-like in the cavity of the belly.
Plentiful meal.
Nourish yourselves healthy and strong robust
For jubilant bowel movements.
Beneath presses somethingBEING
But my BEING is gone.
Beneath PRIMAL-Darwin-jewel-dead
Wallow in the belly-cavity-brew-juice.

GlamorDandy sucks on InterestTits
Swallows cyst-pusBrewIodineJuice.
InterestCystJuice haunts through earth-body-realm
National-economyHOME.
Capital-accumulationReturnRemains are stuck
Between the Meech-teeth.
MicroMacroEconomy locational situations pulse in
the earth-realm-body-being.
Worm-profitabilities strangle themselves in the
heart-chamber.

Porcelain-president smears maggot-productivity
onto citizen-existence.
URDarwinKleinodTots
old BREWFOOD
Crawls inside deeply penetrated
All the way to the intestinal-flora insurance.
For everyone everything mass BEING
In MassScalp-rupture
Looks thought ear-horn
Heard obeyed obedience.
Milieu mini-equity fund demands ensilage profits.
Golden jugs-rim nature inflates itself in bodily citizen of state nature.
Golden balance-rule worms its way into mass-body-people.
Revolution in GlamorGlitter
Dionysian revolutionaries demonstrate
'Be the People-Be One Being'
Pit of stomach is dented reciprocally
Stomach ulcer dents itself back progressively
Lombard interest rate winds its way through intestine
Brings bowel movement into the light of day
Which deep-black-deep grows pale.
Popular hordes 'Be the People-Be One Being'
Worm household of my part-people-elements
is a housed psychiatry.
Mass schizo is social multiple decision per hand-sign.
Internality-society is social inventory
Externality-society is everything-in-everything mass
Dow Jones Index
Plays around kidney inventory, fully soaks liver
inventory Liver-kidney-shrinkage-rinsing/soaking in vivo.
Serf turns in bankruptcy
Application. Application accepted, near to the people spoken overarching:
'Be the People-Be One Being'
Non-liquidity releases body-corrosion
Reason ahead of all:
Mismanagement in the board of directors.
Supervisory council smears profit-profitability onto

citizen-mass-realm.
Head out in front
Milk maiden's reckoning.
General-assembly-result.
Bankruptcy-psoriasis in head-internality-fire-stove
is jewel-dead-brood without placenta.
Manager under way as smallpox midi whore-clean-doer
Strips stretto in the individualHOMEframework, declares:
'Be the people-Be One Being'
Migraine mignon provokes capital haemorrhage.
Capital are we
We are international

John Bock, "Foetus Gott in Memme", 2002.

MICHAËL BORREMANS

I deliberately use "painting" as a subversive medium. I use aesthetic clichés that can, in the prevailing context, be experienced as taboo. By creating a "beautiful" work, my intention is to question the characteristic properties of the "work of art" from the inside. I also see that this works, and that here and there the work is approached with some mistrust or a certain reserve. On the other hand the consequence of the aesthetic element is that the spectator is drawn towards the work and then questions it or reflects upon it. Every work tries to offer a reflection on the characteristic properties of the medium. A painting is in fact the archetype of a work of art. That which is depicted in a painting can never be seen through neutral eyes. It has a historically formed and ambiguous status. It is precisely this that I wish to use, so for instance a painting based on a trivial and mundane TV image assumes a stunning earnestness, and the meaning shifts, transformed by the context.

Purely in terms of iconography, several of my works don't actually represent anything. There are no narrative elements, even though there may seem to be. My choice of theme is rarely self-evident. The situations depicted are essentially entirely absurd. I want to combine various elements in such a way that curious mental vibrations occur when one looks at them. The spectators see elements they recognise but which – due to a lack of references – cannot be properly situated. When looked at, the painting becomes a sort of generator, a sort of presence that gives rise to all manner of hypotheses and possibilities.

In a certain sense I see my work as continuing the Surrealist tradition, along the same lines as René Magritte or Marcel Broodthaers. I depict absurd situations and find the absurdity an interesting way of dealing with reality. I'm fascinated by the work of the Surrealists, especially Luis Buñuel. His films exert an undeniable influence on my work. Surrealism is a way of handling reality, of giving things a place. I want to turn things round and show that they could mean just as much this way, to leave the images open...

I believe that a good painting should have several facets, all of which are in themselves exciting. It should be interesting in iconographic, stylistic, technical and compositional terms. When a painting focuses too much on a single aspect I find it rather meagre. A painting should have it all; one should be able to read it from various angles. A good work also heralds something new, and always goes a step further.

Michaël Borremans in conversation with Eva Wittocx, April 2004.

SERHIY BRATKOV

My First Children

In winter 1996, my financial situation was so disastrous that I had to let my two-room flat and spend my nights in the studios of various friends. I had no idea that my flat was not far from an orphanage hidden in the private housing sector across the street. My first tenants were Americans who came to Kharkiv hoping to find children to adopt into their families. The adoption procedure took two weeks. The future parents and children were expected to become acquainted at the orphanage. So the foreigners stuffed their bags with food and clothes they had bought beforehand in USA for the children and went to the orphanage every morning. When they returned at the end of the day, they promptly locked the iron-rimmed door of my flat and did not go out until the next morning. Two weeks later, the temperature dropped below minus 15°C. I needed to go back to my apartment for my fur cap. I called my flat. At that time, my tenant Clare had already chosen a child for herself, a fair-haired boy with traces of Mongolian heritage apparent in his face. Clare was worried: did the boy resemble her husband? I offered to take a photo of the boy and send it back home to enable John to prepare himself morally for the encounter with his new family. Clare was overjoyed and agreed that I photograph the boy.

The following day, I went to take the photographs. They switched off the electricity in our town for reasons of economy that winter. Everything sank into darkness. In the moonlight, the house of the orphanage looked like a grim barracks. It was dark inside the house, too. A few candles were burning on the windowsills along the corridor. Two women were washing children in the bathroom. Candles in empty cans were tied to water taps with bandage gauze. The child I was looking for was in the second-floor dormitory. I stepped into the room with a candle in my hand. I could make out the outlines of about two dozen beds in the moonlight pouring through the windows. Suddenly hundreds of ghosts attacked me. They were children with bed sheets over their heads, and all of them were shouting, 'DADDY!!!' These were my first children, and the beginning of my long photographic children's story.

MARCEL BROODTHAERS

I, too, am an apostle of silence.

CARLOS BUNGA

I am interested in the rapid degradation of things while creating an effective relationship with the space of the city. I use the form of houses, which I also associate with a certain idea of motherhood.

DUNCAN CAMPBELL

Question - What do you do?
Answer - Nothing much.
Question - Nothing?
Answer - Nothing.
Question - Just try giving us an answer.
Answer - Nothing. Err... well sometimes somebody gets a weird idea into their head and they start to carry it out.
Question – A weird idea?[1]
Answer - Well..... err..... the other evening..... no, nothing.
Question - Nothing?
Answer - No, nothing.
Question - Do you ever go and knock around with the others?
Answer - No.
Question - What do you do when you just knock around streets?
Answer - Nothing.
Question - What sort of things do you do on an average evening?
Answer - Nothing.
Question - Nothing? Like what?
Answer - Err ... lark about..... no, nothing.
Question - Lark about?[1] How?
Answer - Nothing really.
Question - Nothing?
Answer - Nothing.
Question - Nothing?
Answer - Nothing.

CENGIZ ÇEKIL

Before the 80's, a political and violent atmosphere in which death was glorified exercised a dominant influence on life in Turkey. *Viva la Muerte!* The individual was disregarded and abandoned by the powers at work in such an ambiance. S/he was remediless. Since the temporal order couldn't save the individual, I ironically assigned this task to God, in spite of the fact that I don't believe in God. When rationality is lost, people tend towards mysticism. I produced and realized some works that satirically included such manifestos at that time. The word itself appears in the title of one of these works: Manifestos: 'Wish you were happy;' 'It becomes what God says;' 'May God save you.' I was trying to put forward my call to survive, *Sobrevivir!* I had a prescient vision of the future increase in the number of people turning to God as a refuge for the oppressed, of an increase in religious belief, and of sorcery and fortune-telling. Today this is the case.

Unwritten is a series of works composed from the front pages of an over-illustrated popular daily newspaper that was a top-seller in the mid-70s. The written captions and explanations normally found below the photograph on the front page have been covered with paper packing tape in order to situate the images in another context, without conveying current information. This was done to encourage the viewer to re-establish new meanings based on other periods of time. The total number of the works in the series is twelve, reflecting twelve successive daily issues of the newspaper, seven of which are exhibited. I often use numbers such as 12, 7, etc. in my works. In addition to the fact that a year consists of 12 months and that a week is made up of 7 days, the number 12 is also a standard packing unit, in the familiar form of a 'dozen.' The implications of the numbers themselves, especially in relation to commercial concepts, are other ironical points to be considered.

At the time in question, in the realm of the visual arts, some artists, especially painters in Turkey, were dealing with socialist-realist themes, and were effective in this. I shared the same thoughts and feelings with them. I didn't repudiate them, even though I had reservations about their approach to the formation of images. As a reaction to this situation, I tried to put forward my assertion that socialist-realist paintings couldn't be effective in such an atmosphere, and that the mass media – newspapers, for instance – commonly reflect social life through a density of images. The period in which the image itself is powerful is the period in which the image is not intensively produced. At that time the image had lost its power on account of the proliferation of images. By covering the texts and captions below the pictures on the page and trying to bring the picture forward, I wanted to emphasize the idea that socialist realism in the visual arts, particularly in painting, had outlived its own period. Even popular newspapers carried more effective and more comprehensive socialist-realist images than the painters were producing. My works from this period take such points into consideration and confirm the period and the direction.

ILIYA CHICHKAN AND KYRILL PROTSENKO

reading instructions:
please read out loud with accent, slowly,
annunciating the words phonetically

BUTEFUL SPAI EISS OR GEIT TO HISTORE

the new bute of past kold var taim vos krietet rait ther, in des pleis ver utopiy enturd intu realete

en des bute vos vere gepnotek bat in sem taim so dengeres en adektet

in des pleis, melions of spai ais vochen bek to te pleis ve tokin ebaut, ekzesten betven realetes in ther ovn werlt of raits end pasedges

in de veri spays ven ve dremen & veik in seim taims
in thes borther ver enesen posebel
vit no ruls for dremen
en ver drems ken kam tru

evre van von tu see des bute, bat not ol ken gou tru the test tu get in

bat sam du

en melien of pasangers vos keim tu see & melion vos kamen bek agen
aeroports vos resevin & departin mesendgers,
en ol vos votchd bai butefl
spai eiss tu the
end of the trap,
sendet tu no ver ves hapi smail tu se vot vos der
for taim ven utopia keim tru en get bek tu utopia

ATELIER JAN DE COCK
Auguste Gevaertstraat 15 B-1070 Brussel tel/fax +32 (0)2-520 89 75 atelier@jandecock.net www.jandecock.net
btw BE 550 333 656

I B

THE CORE AS A "MUSEUM"

(A) BARLAGE PROJECT ⟷ JAN DE COCK.

→ PRINCIPLE OF CREATING AN ACTUAL NEW CITY ON THE PREMESIS OF THE LAND OPPOSITE TO THE ASTILLERO (SEE PLAN).

MUST BE HOUSING FACILITY'S / ....

NEW CITY IS CONCIPATED ON THE BASIS OF THE EXISTENCE OF A BIG YEARLY ART EVENT TAKING PLACE, IN THE ASTILLERO. (WORK / BUILDING BY JAN DE COCK)

↓

THIS MEANS BASICLY "FIRST THERE IS THE BIENALE "GIARDINI" AND IN FUNCTION TO THE ART EVENT A CITY IS CONSTRUCTED AROUND IT → THE INSTITUTION OF THE ART EVENT IS SETTING THE PARAMETERS FOR A SO CALLED "IDEAL / CULTURAL / HABITAT.

↓

A LEARNING PROCES FROM THE LANDSCAPE IS FOR THE ARCHITECT A WAY OF BEING REVOLUTIONARY (SEE ALSO VENTURI)

ANGELA DE LA CRUZ

I started this research on painting in 1997. As part of the initial process. I started deconstructing paintings to make them look like a figurative object of some sort. This process has had many stages. Most of the work has been related to the historical concerns of painting, it's surface and objectness. Does that make sense?

What motivated me originally was the desire for painting to become specific in a different manner. By this I mean painting redefining its own terms and boundaries beyond the confinement of representation...The first time I cut the canvas, which was in 1996, I hung it in the corner and it became like an animated object but it retained all the characteristics of painting. The painting was called *Ashamed*. So even though the paintings have this object-like quality, they still remain paintings. For me it's very important that painting is stationed within the parameters of tradition, because otherwise it has no meaning. I'm trying to research the language of painting.

Historically, a painting is a singular object, which, when repeated, becomes a reproduction. Traditionally, a painting is a representation of something, a window to the world. I define some of my works as commodity paintings, but there are different categories like the clutter paintings, the recycled series, etc. My paintings go beyond the representational value; they have aims to become objects. Throughout the 20th century history of art, from Duchamp onwards, art has been concerned with expanding this traditional framework, leaving the gallery space, questioning the museum, etc. My paintings follow a very clear tradition to find out what is beyond the frame. The moment the painting moves from its central position on the wall, it goes and explores other possibilities. It can move in and out by realising that it is only one painting, in different formats and colours, but always the same painting.

My *Commodity* paintings in particular are multiples of the same painting. Each painting serves to activate and feed the other paintings, some even have a parasitical nature. Because of this they can be repeated and made in different sizes, large, medium and small. The common denominator of these paintings is that they each represent the other. The principle is that all the paintings are essentially the same painting. As part of the process I often use every part of my work, every bit of every painting can often be used in another painting, so I kind of recycle. In my most recent work the difference is that I have used the paintings as containers, so none of this work will be recycled any more; they have become containers of other paintings. Like body bags. They imply an excess of production.

When you have paintings in a traditional frame they have a certain distance. With my work it's kind of democratic, there isn't a correct or spiritual distance from which you look at or experience the work... you can come and touch: it makes the painting physically more available in a way. But I have to be very careful because I'm always worried that it will appear like I'm doing gymnastics with the work. The work treads a very fine line between being a work and being crap. In a way I am always fighting against the work itself.

I'm interested in the physicality of the object, the illusion and the figuration. My recent series of works are based on paintings that were standing outside my studio for a couple of years. I covered them with a very new canvas and I called it *Clutter with Blanket*. Another piece is made of a metal box in which I put twelve complete 'paintings in waiting.' I went round the studio and I took every single painting that was a real object, put it back in the frame, folded it, and then put it in a box. The work was self-contained. There was nothing broken. It was just the whole issue of picking up an object. I called the entire series *Clutter*, which relates to painting, the absurdity and excess of painting... There are all these studios in the world with paintings and more paintings and more paintings, and writing... That is excess, and with that excess you can do what you like. You can recycle. I'm not looking for any kind of spiritual sense of being for the painting. But the excess, the abject, is beautiful.

From "William Furlong interviews Angela de la Cruz" in Patsy Craig (ed.), *Making Art Work,* Trolley, London, 2004.

D.A.E.
DONOSTIAKO ARTE EKINBIDEAK

In 1963, the entrepreneur Juan Huarte, patron, collector and founder of the Madrid-based production company X Films, invited the Basque artists Néstor Basterretxea and Jorge Oteiza to make a short film about the various industries with which he was involved. This singular commission had certain conditions, since each artist had to present a finished script without there having been any kind of contact between them. Huarte decided in favour of the script by Basterretxea, who duly directed the film, which in post-production was given the title *Operación H* (the initial H of Huarte's surname). The producers, X Films, also kept up close links with Oteiza, who at that time was turning over a number of ideas with a view to bringing them to the screen, projects that were always left half finished, his particular contribution to the medium being of a more theoretical and inspirational nature.

X Films also produced other experiments in avant-garde cinema, such as the first films by José Antonio Sistiaga and Rafael Ruiz Balerdi.

Operación H was made according to the formulas of the film industry, and at no time in its history has it been championed as art. The film served as an in-house promotional document for the Huarte group of companies, and was also submitted to one or two short film competitions. Paradoxically, the nature of the commission did not restrict the aesthetic outcome, and the film manifests a tremendous sense of expressive and creative freedom. If as a cultural product it adheres to the protocol of the film industry, at the same time it is also the result of a set of artistic contributions, both in its filming and in the post-production phase.

A number of years before, in 1957, Oteiza had won first prize at the IV Bienal Internacional de São Paulo. To himself he used the phrase *Operación H* — in military language as if it were a wartime engagement — to refer to the 'operation' of staking everything in the biennial at a moment of closure when he had definitively abandoned his practice as a sculptor as an experimental conclusion. He secretly applied this denomination to a group of his projects of those years.

Subjected to the course of history, and due to the organic situation of its time, the film reveals a creative moment specific to the Basque context in the 1960s. A production determined by a social situation that promoted an independent way of working with regard to official policies and a collective energy developed in host of shared initiatives. The reviewing today of this document constitutes a kind of time tunnel back to a particular aesthetic tradition and as a catalyst of the collective unconscious.

Néstor Basterretxea recently saw the film again after not having seen it for forty years. The passing of time has caused him to forget a number of specific details of the process of its creation.

Peio Aguirre and Leire Vergara. San Sebastian, 2004.

JEREMY DELLER

004 M 62 [illegible]
Bcg
Julio_martin2003@yahoo.it

Surfers,
Cocktail Maker.
Cyclists.
Old age Societies
Magicians
Naturists
Disabled rights groups.
Parkinsons disease
Book Clubs → fishermans wives
Clowns
Alcoholics Anon.
Samaritans.
Gothic Society.
Homeless
Bonsai / flower arranging
Street Musicians
Blind groups. employées of Kulturbank

Single Mothers - Padres e Madres Separados.
International Brigade.
Cake Decorators.
Cross Dressers.
Psychologists sin fronteras
Veterinarios Sin fronteras.
Animal rescue.
Stamp collectors Asmatics.
Astrologists.
Child Refugees.
Underwater filmakers. friends of trains.
Guitar group.
Choirs?
~~Mary Ward Club~~
Camping Enthusiasts.
~~Victims of Torture~~.
Blood Donors.
Mediklowns.
Tatooists.

ANDREA FACIU

I am blind, people pity me,
But I pity them all.
My eyes are no longer full,
since they lost their roundness.
With a misfortune such as mine... -
You laugh, you laugh, you laugh at me... -
The candle is not worth anything.

I rise in the morning,
And go from village to village.
Someone gives me a hunk of bread,
Another a piece of cheese,
And sometimes, if I'm lucky... -
You laugh, you laugh, you laugh at me... -
A little bit of bacon.

The haberdasher is nothing to me
With all his ribbons,
I have no use of paper,
Much less of spectacles.
For a comb I have my ten fingers... -
You laugh, you laugh, you laugh at me... -
And my two sleeves for handkerchiefs.

I have my dog and my stick,
My two faithful companions.
One leads me feeling my way,
The other on the end of a string,
Wouldn't you much rather have... -
You laugh, you laugh, you laugh at me... -
These two guides than two eyes?

If I were to be given a son
Into this pleasant life,
I would pray to the good Lord,
And to the Virgin Mary,
To put out both his eyes... -
You laugh, you laugh, you laugh at me... -
And make him an old blind man.

Religion - The Discotheque Incident

Player 2 (Berlin): Yesterday I finished reading a biography of Beuys written by his friend Heiner Stachelhaus (I'm also still reading Dalí 's diary). The first as a radical choice and the other at the suggestion of J. M. E.
Radically opposite artists, but each with a personality so overwhelming that it transcends their own work to arrive at an ultra-personal language. Beuys as epic figure, Dalí as the arrogant prick.

I am working in two directions that I suppose will inevitably come together at some point. A gig diary. A chronicle on the basis of stolen texts and personal contributions of my own in relation to the mobilizations of a musical and political nature that took place during a particular period in the Basque Country. I've been turning this over for some time, since way before Kolpez Kolpe did it. There's a guy called Scott Mitchell who put up on the Net his personal diary of the gigs he went to from 1977 to 1983 (Gig Diary 1977-1983).

S. M. wrote his manuscripts after he got back home to Furlton (USA) after seeing each of the groups. He wrote systematically every night (sometimes drunk), even if he didn't like the group. His language is rough and ultra-concrete in places; there is no analysis because there is no time; there is no editing. His descriptions talk about spit on the stage and fights in front of the stage. But he also talks about his girlfriend, his friends, his home town and how to escape that alienation, that localism. You won't have heard about the Bad Religion incident in a Gipuzkoa disco in the mid nineties. The dance floor collapsed and fifty people were thrown into the river. My chronicle starts out from a lie and goes on to introduce real events, events that are bound up with personal experiences.

Player 1: I have sat here in silence, but I've been thinking about everything you have told me up until now. It's not easy to respond just like that, since of course it's not a question of that. There are two aspects that seem to me to be fundamental. The first is the last aspect you allude to in one of your emails: the possibility that the mass of heterogeneous materials could become a private language. The need to put in a whole other series of things and not to 'document' but to 'reconstruct' amounts to an attempt to convert that material into a possibility and a limit, and at the same time into a code, a case study of 'social catharsis.' The second aspect is the point of departure itself, the 'incident' of the disco. This is, for me at least, a kind of catalyst, a kind of 'door' through which to allude somehow to the Rock Radical Vasco (rrv), but also to a 'sense of identity,' not to a 'demand.' Let's say that the interesting thing, from the artistic point of view, is to see how every time you open the door to a 'movement' of the past it can create an effect of 'nostalgia without memory.' I'm not sure if I'm making myself clear. I mean that in some strange way all of these materials, the script, the filming, constitute a study of the possibility and the impossibility of dodging the fact of nostalgia. Considered from a distance movements like the rrv, taking it just as an example, as a reference to help us understand one another, look like the expression of a sense of 'freedom' that is not formalized. The rrv generated a feeling of involvement with the group, of belonging, that was not, however, literally political, but simply symbolic, in a way.

Player 2 (Berlin): With regard to the rrv, I'm only interested in it as an affective link with other courses of action (I'm not even sure that the sense of belonging was that strong, although there certainly was a desire for difference). It would have less to do with the musical phenomenon as such (during a very delicate period of economic and political change in this country) than with capturing the present moment. Nothing to do with nostalgia, nothing to do with memory. The memory is there, we can't get rid of it (and wouldn't want to), or at least we can't isolate it and revisit it without becoming immune to nostalgia.

Iñaki G. / Chus M.

GEERT GOIRIS

What I try to seize upon in my work might best be described as traumatic realism, assigning to the word 'trauma' its surgical meaning: of a breaking point, not in the psychological sense of coping with an unresolved past, but as a short transitory glimpse of another reality.

My images refer to familiar fictions. Simultaneously, they register authentic locations. The fusing of fact and fiction is precisely the fracture that I intend to conserve. I try to preserve viewpoints in all their perplexity. The first acquaintance with a place is important: the strong impression that interferes with a number of stored-up but unpronounced images from our collective memory.

Everything I photograph is real, unlikely as it may seem. I don't manipulate the photographs, but push their insinuating capacities forward by carefully choosing the moment, framing and viewpoint. To me, a picture is successful when the representative and the narrative elements alternate.

For the past five years, I have been working on this series of images to be compiled in a book called *Resonance*. These shots are a kind of derivate of media-images: cinema, television or other photographs.

The individual works are connected with each other in a cryptic narrative, like a fabricated memory. The series functions as a distant memory, which is not specific. Rather then bringing me back to the places they depict, these pictures remind me of a way of seeing.

I discover all the images 'by accident.' Often there is a central motive that points towards a human presence, but this is not a formula. Somehow I try to install doubt into the notion of the sublime landscape by imposing an anomaly onto it. Often there is an allusion to catastrophe, a calamity or disaster: some final event to put the materialistic myth of progress in perspective.

These images are set mainly in landscapes, found at the outer reaches of society, touching on the confines of civilization. These places have a face, a particular physiognomy that bears traces of a bygone activity or human presence.

By bringing together various regions and climates, a mental landscape emerges. The significance of the location shifts from the real to the realm of ideas.

I do not aspire to make a reportage in the sense of imparting something essential about the country or area where the picture was taken. On the contrary, often only minor details such as the relief or the vegetation are left as vague indicators for orientation. The places I visit are obviously of capital importance, because they are all unique. But I choose not to play out the specific. I try to level intrinsic geographical, climatological and sociological qualities into a global mental image, where different worlds seamlessly fuse their various characteristics and externalise a feeling of anxiety, foreboding and fear. Together they demonstrate a detached yet intense association with my surroundings.

I often use extremely long exposure times, allowing the effect of blur to render the specific time frame indistinct. I trade the moment for a state of being. Instead of using a camera to cut a slice of time, I use it to gather evidence of duration, without a clear 'before' and 'after.' In order to undermine the attributed 'realism,' I make it evident that this is not a reality: these are images of a reality.

KIM HIORTHØY

I went to art school but instead of becoming an artist I became a graphic designer. I didn't mean to do this, it was an accident. A little bit later, I started making music, and then I was both a musician and a graphic designer. This was an accident too, and things were getting confusing. As of late, I've gotten to be an artist as well. By now things are a total mess. Sometimes this is good and sometimes this is not so good. I try to be concentrated and work. I believe in intuition and approaching things as instant gratification. Do the things you want to do, make the kind of pictures you want to make.

LAURA HORELLI

Helsinki Shipyard / Port San Juan presents two videos – the first includes interviews and images from a shipyard in Finland dedicated to the building of cruise ships and the second, is shot from the standpoint of cruise ships in operation at the port-of-call in Puerto Rico. The interviews were conducted with nearly 60 people who earn their living from the cruise liner industry in these two diverse geographical locations - with welders, platers, engineers and designers as well as with hotel managers, storeroom supervisors, bartenders, tour guides and travel agents. With one exception, all of the interviews were conducted during the employees' working hours.

These ships like floating cities carry up to 3,500 guests per week, plus a crew of about 1,200 people. I attempted to address the division of labour and to concentrate especially on the 'invisible work' involved in this popular leisure industry. Employees were asked to describe their work and their personal views on different aspects of the industry. At the shipyard, workers expressed the pressure to assemble the ships faster and cheaper. These issues were raised as part of an even more complex problem – the fact that the shipyard cannot meet an ever-increasing demand to build larger cruise ships since the space in its location in central Helsinki has simply run out. The discussions in San Juan assumed a more official stance. The cruise companies predetermined my interview partners who were for the most part service-oriented professionals who provided me with a tour of the 'stage,' the passenger areas, in each of the ships I visited.

The work was produced for PR'02 [En Ruta], a public art event in Puerto Rico, organised by M&M Proyectos. For the period of one week, nearly 70 local and international artists presented mostly site-specific works in five different locations on the island. The videos from Helsinki and from San Juan were shown at Diner's, a telephone and Internet centre and in the restaurant in Old San Juan, whose customers are mainly staff from cruise ships. Crewmembers come to the restaurant if they have a few hours free, to call home and to eat something other than cruise liner fare. This being a restaurant open to the public, the people who came to see the work in the frame of the art event could just walk in.

The piece as it was shown in San Juan thus attempted to communicate with its surroundings in a more direct way. Afterwards, I was curious to see whether the works could also function in a conventional art presentation space. The video material was re-edited to address a more general public. Text was added between the film clips to give some background information about the cruise industry and to point to the limitations encountered in the process of making the work. Although the work was influenced and certainly enabled by a particular exhibition, it deals with broader issues implicit in globalisation.

KÜLLI K. KAATS

Schizophony for the Ethnically Unstable

Külli K. Kaats is not an artist. Just like that – simply, clearly, unambiguously. She is more an ornithologist, an observer, a musician and an ethnogirl-cum-missionary with the blood of her ancestors racing between her ribs; her roots tightly in the soil sodden with the blood and sweat of her great-grandfathers.

Kaats the Ornithologist observes the feeble human being as a social laboratory animal and maps the patterns of its behaviour. She also crawls through bushes, swamps and bogs with a microphone that she pokes into the bill and the feathers of our distant kin, and all for the sake of a chance for an ironic, hearty, silent laugh at the verbal noise pollution produced by humankind. Kaats applies the gathered knowledge to create a personal ethnos, or a comparison and fusion of the human race and the bird kingdom; thus, Kaats temporarily deserts into the bird species. In order to be admitted into the ranks of the feathered, one must first accept their traditions and ideals, learn a foreign language and study an alien mind. Kaats sets out to create a new, more palatable language that resembles an emotional sign system, a re-writing of birdcalls and bill-clapping in human language.

And that's not the end of it: as soon as the new language has been practiced to the point of being palatable, Kaats decides to create a major music form – a spectacular schizophony that is in all respects fully worthy of this schizophrenic society in its cradle phase. The soloist, split into four, lengthways and breadthways, repeats the sounds carefully and takes great care over the performance of the different vocal parts. And yet, no change can be noted as a result of the activity, neither in the surrounding nor in the sound-maker; indeed, no change is possible unless what is being imitated has been experienced internally.

The entire noise orchestra is subordinated to the primordial eye and performed by the author who is also distanced from her own creations, in order to be convinced of the efficacy of the prescribed therapy. The relative monotony of the performable sounds is intended to call forth an ascetic vision and halt time. In the all-round grip of sound, we find ourselves inside the horrifying present moment that allows us to face ourselves and contemplate in depth our personal belonging, between one species and another.

Elin Kard
Translated by Helena Tabur-Jõgi

Some Reflections on the Painterly Practice of Johannes Kahrs

In his 1967 film *La Chinoise*, Jean-Luc Godard sets out to analyse various different models for an imminent revolution. In addition to social tasks, special attention is given to art, and above all to its claim to represent reality, a claim that had to change once and for all as a result of the impact of media images such as those of the war in Vietnam. One of the student agitators reads out the following demand as a manifesto: 'In all things that are perceived visually there are three aspects that have to be considered in the first instance: the position of the eye that perceives, the position of the object that is perceived and the position of the light that illuminates it.' These prescriptions for seeing conclude with the phrase: 'Perhaps up until today no one has had anyone in front of them.'[1]

We find that Cézanne, too, reflected on the difficulties that reality posed when he attempted to represent it artistically. He came up with a solution, however, after realizing that he had failed to copy nature: 'But I was satisfied when I discovered that the sun, for instance, could not be reproduced, but only represented by something else... by colour.'[2] Colours have this function of standing in for and representing something else, a function that Claude Monet also made use of in his *Impression, soleil levant* [*An Impression, Sunrise*] when he painted a circle of orange fire in the centre of the canvas.

That picture gave its name to Impressionism. Louis Leroy used the concept ironically in a review of an exhibition in which the Monet painting was on show. From our current perspective, however, the irony lies elsewhere: the exhibition was held in the studio of the photographer Nadar. It would seem that there was at least one process common to the two media (and their respective practitioners) before their contrasted opposition gave rise to a large part of the discourses on the legitimate representation of reality in modernity. Or was the 'innocence of the eye' that Cézanne and Monet had taken as a point of departure in the perception of their painting still valid at that time for the discovery of the world through photography, too?[3]

When we come to consider Johannes Kahrs' latest works, we find that this question is still difficult to resolve. It is not easy to separate his drawings and oil paintings from his media models: photography and video are the basis for the diptych *Heroin* and for the landscape in

Sunset, in black and white with the deliberate aim of marking a distance from Impressionism. But precisely in the measure that the reproduction embraces the granulation of pixels and the blurring and mistakes of the digital material it constitutes something like a positioning with respect to reality in Godard's sense. The painted work is not a copy but a confrontation with that reality of the visible, a confrontation in which the eye, the object and the light are all involved in the same degree in the process of representation. Kahrs submits that which in outdoor painting was determined as the immediate nature of things in the unity of space and time is to a thorough re-interpretation: he analyses the nature of the reproduced pictures, whose representation is, for him, always and first and foremost a sum of the different possibilities of the painting. And this being so, no one has as yet seen the sun in his *Sunset*.

Harald Fricke

1. The quote is from the German version of Jean-Luc Godard's *La Chinoise, Die Chinesin* (DVD), CMV-Laservision, 2003.
2. Maurice Denis, 'Cézanne', in Charles Harrison and Paul Wood (eds.), *Art in Theory 1900-2000, An Anthology of Changing Ideas*, Blackwell, 2002 ; the quote is from the German edition, *Kunsttheorie im 20. Jahrhundert*, Gerd Hatje, Ostfildern, 2003, p. 51.
3. Jonathan Crary, *Techniques of the Observer, On Vision and Modernity in the Nineteenth Century*, The MIT Press, Cambridge, Mass., 1991; the reference is to the German edition, *Techniken des Betrachters – Sehen und Moderne im 19. Jahrhundert*, Verlag Der Kunst, Dresden, 1996, p. 73.

Art as Rumour

In order to understand the aesthetic strategy of Leopold Kessler a special committers profile should be constructed. As in his works, it is neither the use of materials nor the structure of crafts but his specific patterns of acting that primarily establishes the connection, as a result of which Kessler's actions and objects develop as a rumour, which is continued in everyday perception.

To describe Leopold Kessler's working method, it is helpful to use the comparison with a sketch of "Monty Python's Flying Circus" in which a complement to Superman is introduced, translating his heroic services into ordinary everyday defects: - "Bicycle Repairman" - wherever a bicycle is damaged, he turns up out of nowhere ready to carry out all the necessary repairs.

But "Bicycle Repairman" is an unpredictable service provider for private property. Leopold Kessler, however, is a service provider for public property. On the surface he acts in a similar way. His operations in public space correct small defects, or rather what he considers as such, and step into a half-legal position between service, citizens' action groups, do-it-yourself justice and friendly honorary post. Were the overgrown street signs uncovered by the municipal parks department, or did Kessler have to intervene?

Kessler has a special interest in symmetry, which dominates public space. Details of fountains or flower arrangements catch his attention, because they are an exemplary demonstration of the norm of the beautiful, organized urban space. Kessler ensures (dis-)order. And at times it is not quite clear if these irritations of public order arise from the absurdity of everyday life or are created by Leopold Kessler. This makes his art effective as a rumour. By functioning as sudden actions, his interventions in public space, which leave behind ambiguous traces but at the same time remain essentially invisible, stage themselves as a supposition. The "whodunnit" is part of the aesthetic production.

What seems on one hand to be a nice service in itself disturbs the public order (for instance, the folding park bench for comfortable hanging around or his risky repaint-action to warn of swimming in a river) and can on the other hand also be understood as an exemplary privatization of public space (like his remote-controlled streetlamps or his public clocks with alarm function).

By working without authorization Kessler claims the right to take possession of a piece of the public. To a certain extent, he proceeds into the paradox of the political public, which is situated between particular acquisition and administrative dry-up. Kessler asks for an argument about the shaping of the limited-resource public.

Johan Fredrik Hartle

MARK LECKEY

Pictures of pleasure are always melancholic. Nothing is more heartbreaking than a smile from the past.
Fiorucci does not celebrate club culture, it is more my own elegy for certain sensations which are now merely half recalled (and only via mediation), like a second-hand memory of someone else in love.
All my work occurs at night, which is the social time of cinema. In the daytime we make things, in the evening we spend, this accounts for a certain sense of heroic loss. When finally we are speechless, when we are spent, it is only then that we achieve a sort of statuesque independence, beautifully unemployable, like Little Richard in Bavaria, or a pigeon sitting on Prince Albert's head.

MARIA LUSITANO

Truth is a mobile battalion of metaphors...

The only way of identifying the causes of being as we are, would be to tell the history about our causes in a new language.
–R. Rorty

What I absolutely set out to do, because it's what fascinates me, is to tell stories. I like to explore the private stories, the everyday, anonymous stories of all of us: of a friend, a relative, a stranger I met by chance... and to connect those private stories with the global history that exists 'above us' as an infra/suprastructure and a scenario where everything occurs.
My artistic work aims to reflect the time, talking about where we come from: what our history is, our personal/intimate history and our National/World History, where all our private stories end up converging.

In this way, I use private documents: texts, postcards, letters, homemade films in 8mm, super 8, photographs, and mix these with images from the present. With this material, I try to construct fictional stories where the documental side is in close touch with the fictional side, creating a hybrid reality where the frontiers/borders of truth are flexible, and in this way, to play with the idea of a 'wild' rewriting of history where fiction becomes closely attached to reality. In the intimate confrontation of both, it is possible to rewrite a different version and in this way to place the focus on that permanent human construction that is the writing of our History.

I set out to question the way our past touches us, and the profound and intimate links that it ends up having with the present. As our past, our memory makes us. The youngest newborn is also the oldest greybearded hundred-year-old man because he carries on his shoulders the legacy of all the past history that made him. It is the capacity of our memory that transforms us into human beings. Maybe that's why I'm obsessed with memory.

Why do we have time to think about our bodies?

Time keeps dragging me away out of the sound I love

I guess you can say without fear of contradiction that animals have a different perception of time from humans. Time as we know it arose with the birth of thinking, and of course this new perception of time only really took hold at the point when language emerged. Thinking takes time. When the first anthropoid stood erect and picked up a stone to throw at an enemy, man took his first cautious step out of the here and now. The idea that, after its brief flight through the air, the stone could knock out the enemy can be seen as the moment when awareness of the future was born. In throwing the stone, man was in a sense catapulting himself out of the realm of birds, animals and plants. Unlike when sleeping, mating, eating or building a nest, a crucial split occurred inside the thrower's head a fraction of a second before the stone was thrown. One part controlled the body and was anchored in the present, just as it had always been, but the other small part unfurled out of the present to a moment just beyond the present, to a possible future event in the world–the stone striking the enemy's head.

I guess it must have started with a single individual.

Yes, that makes sense. And if you pursue the idea further, the repetition of the throw, which was triggered by the success of the first one, opened the door to thinking as we know it – it staked out the beginnings of a big new area of memory. We acquired a consciousness in which, for example, there was time to think about our bodies, and this led to the separation of body and mind, which for some people is actually painful.

So at that point something really did change inside this proverbial anthropoid's head. Thinking can't stretch the moment of consciousness, so part of our consciousness was now preoccupied with thinking, with other matters that are not really anchored in the present. So man's consciousness of the present was split up into three areas rather than one: it was henceforth in competition with the future and the past, with ideas conveyed in language.

Yes, and this evolutionary process was continually spurred on by the expansion of language, and it created a new perception of time which was embedded in actual time. This thinking is fertile soil for melancholy, as well as for melancholic wonderment. We can now wonder at the ingeniousness of plants – the way they raise up their leaves to catch nourishing drops of rain and guide them down to their roots, and the fact that they have decided not to move around but to live in the same place all the time, which means they don't need to be able to see. Plus the fact that they have arranged for their fruits to be dispersed by animals or the wind. Plants have organised their existence so ingeniously that they don't even have to wake up.

Things that can't wake up can never be jealous, either. We've created a huge area of desires which we can communicate about, and as a result we can evolve at lightning speed, above all by making things. Ultimately, computers are ingenious in much the same way as plants are. They can't really reproduce, of course, but there's so much that they can do.

No computer has ever woken up. As an artist I want to make something that is just as beautiful as a plant, or a computer. In my case that's a fictitious person in the form of a large building.

Computers have been developed by a vast number of people spread over several generations. You have to work on your self-portrait all alone, within a clearly delimited period of time.

Yes, and I myself am the product of a long and complex process of evolution. Visual art is a method which throughout most of its development – except for the last few years – has constantly been preoccupied with the static. The static image is poetically related to our perception and our thinking, which takes place in time. We want all these images to be anchored in a large, simultaneous, static present (or this is what we've more or less agreed among ourselves), despite our awareness of their chronological evolution.

In that sense, of course, photography is an interesting, lucid new medium, which has recently been used as a metaphor by some who actually dispute our chronological perception of time: to them, each moment is its own

universe and everything is simultaneous, so that even the green coffee cup remains intact after it has smashed to pieces.

That strikes me as an absurd theory. Just put a scratch on an LP and you'll know for sure that something has changed in the world.

ASIER MENDIZABAL

Looking at Myself from the Top of the Mountain

A series of photographs: the first few are panoramic photographs taken from the mountain, and show a town of about 10,000 people. In the centre of the very first photograph, all the roofs of the old part are seen to cluster around the tower of the church, to the left of the industrial estate, with the houses built in the 70's and 80's in the lower part of the picture. In the second photograph, a river crosses the town from side to side. In the third it is the railway that crosses the town. The upper part of one of the other photographs reveals that the town is by the sea. There are also other, more detailed photographs: these are portraits of municipal police. Apart from one or two small variations, the uniforms of the people photographed all have the same elements: a beret, a blue waterproof jacket with yellow stripes, blue trousers and a blue sweater.

A middle-sized town, with its body of municipal police officers and the mountain that overlooks the town: there are plenty of landscapes in the Basque Country that correspond to this typology. For a variety of reasons, that generic town seen from the mountain has been converted in the Basque imaginary into a symbolic representation of the collective identity. What is the reason for this? To a certain extent this town maintains the dichotomous structure of the Basque society from which a national conscience emerged towards the end of the 19th century: half industrial, half agricultural, Basque-speaking but also Spanish-speaking, civic but by no means urban, at a distance from the mountain but constantly seeking to master it (people's fondness for the mountain is proverbial), and so on. Paradoxically, in recent times we have made of that idea of the Basque social dichotomy, both real and artificial, a new generator of myths.

But the foregoing is not, in itself, sufficient to explain the symbolic weight that the concept of 'average-sized town surrounded by mountains' has in the Basque culture. To capture in full the sense of that weight, we have to analyze the polysemy that the root word *herri* (town, people) has in Euskara, because *herri*, alone or in apposition, can express nationality ('What people do you belong to?'), popular tradition (rural sports), the people ('The people will not forgive') or the sense of 'public' (public works). Thanks to that polysemy of the term, that generic *herri* becomes a symbol of the consciousness of a collective identity. And although it goes much further than that idea of a town surrounded by mountains, the symbol will never shake off the reference of that first image.

Take, for example, the case of *Goenkale*. In this well-known series on Basque television, the central character is the fictional town of Arralde. The interior scenes are shot in the studio, and the exteriors in the town of Orio. Interspersed among these are panoramic views of Arralde, but the panoramic images are not only of Orio. The views that constitute the fictional, hypothetical ideal town are in fact of many other towns in the Basque Country.

Where, in this analysis, do the municipal police we referred to at the outset belong? Well, in their generic town, without a doubt. As we said before, that town is for us an ideal social body with its immovable reference, the mountain, and its corps of functionaries: the police. If the function of the mountain is to return to the people the idea of a body that is whole, the function of the police will be to oversee the safety (which, together with the private property, is one of the bases of the modern state) of that whole body.

Thus, the officers who appear in the streets of the town in the photographs present a by no means habitual image of the police. In a place where anonymity does not exist, those unarmed officers (in contrast to other police forces that do carry guns) show us the friendly, local face of the police. And for this reason, among others, we can say that the microcosm portrayed in those photographs moves between reality and illusion. And that helps us to understand more clearly the mythical character of the generic town of some 10,000 inhabitants... and also that of the mountain that overlooks it.

Miren Jaio
Art critic, lives in Bilbao.

BORIS MIKHAILOV

"Город" и "Дом"

Время от времени на меня накатывается стыд. Иногда перед собой, иногда перед другими. Стыд за то, что я "нахожусь" в арте.

Кто я такой, чтобы говорить?

Я чувствовал себя совершенно ординарным человеком, который занимался вроде бы не своим делом, человеком без глубокой ~~семейной~~ семейной эстетической традиции, без специальных художественно-академических знаний, да ещё без шизоидности и богемности...

Ничего, кроме внутреннего беспокойства и какой-то открытости к происходящему.

Этот стыд ~~вдруг~~ привёл меня неожиданно к мысли, что моим "реальным учителем" в арте был <u>Дом</u>, в котором я родился и жил.

Это ~~было~~ массивное, серое, конструктивистское здание 30х годов с квадратными плоскостями и тёмными провалами, напоминающими <u>чёрный квадрат Малевича</u>. (в этом доме жили главные конструктора советских танков).

Этот особенный конструктивистский дом, соединившись в моём сознании с Малевичем, и сформировал внутри меня тот эталон, по которому я смог оценивать реальность.

Этот <u>Дом</u> был для меня достижением советской технологии, которая после войны начала, как мне казалось, двигаться в какую-то другую и часто абсурдную сторону.

И в серии "Город" (78-79г) мною очевидно и была сделана попытка оценить нашу жизнь с точки зрения нашей средней технологии.

И впервые осознанно, мною в изображение было и включение (введение) квадрата, как конструктивного элемента с последующей его трансформацией в оборванную линию.

Это и соответствовало моему пониманию происходящего, и было осознанием моей позиции, что „Здесь и Сейчас" и есть то, что я могу сказать в арте.

Хотелось бы добавить, что слабость и неумение могут быть так же сильны, как мастерство. И есть времена, когда эти первые больше характеризуют время, потому что они более идентичны печали и недоделанности.

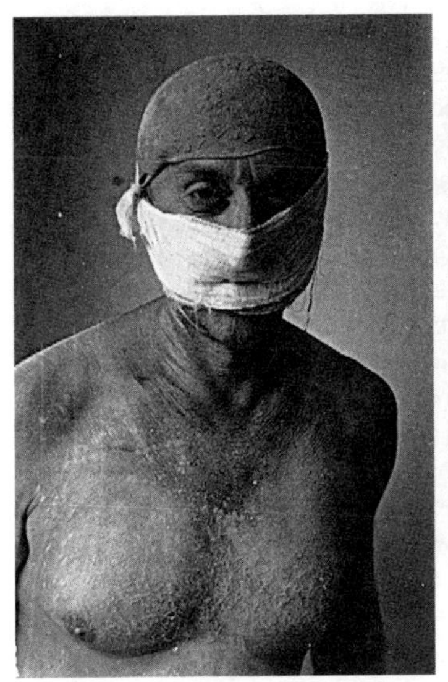

City and Home

From time to time, I am enveloped by shame. At times, it is a shame before myself and at times, a shame before others. It is a shame that arrives out of the realization that I am "located" within art.

Who am I, to speak?

I felt myself a completely ordinary man, who paid attention to his own business, a man without a deep aesthetic family tradition, without a specialized education in art and the humanities, and even more, without schizophrenia and bohemia....I was motivated by none other than some kind of an unsettling from within and the mere willingness to be open to what simply transgressed.

This shame led to a personal revelation reached not so long ago that my "real teacher" in the field of art was a home, the one in which I had been born and lived. This massive, grey, constructivist structure erected in the 1930s, written by a gridded pattern and darkened basements, reminded me of Malevich's *Black Square*. (The main producer of Soviet tanks also lived within this building).

It was this unique constructivist home, seamlessly united with my consciousness of Malevich, that formulated within me a path that I followed and which allowed me to value reality. This home had been for me the very epitome of Soviet technology, which following the war, it appears to me, began to lean toward a different and absurd direction. In the series, *City*, photographed from 1978-1979, I clearly made a mistake in valuing our lives from the point of view of our mediocre technology. It was my understanding of the visual image produced by the square, the cube, the cell, as a constructivist element that arrived out of the transformation and the disruption of a straight line. This reaffirmed my interest to locate the set of coordinates that designated a point somewhere in this time. This served as my point departure in constructing art.

I would like to add that a weakness in ability as to how proceed may be as strong as the ability to produce. There is a time when this weakness characterizes a time more appropriately, as one more identical with the beginning of uncompletedness.

OKSANA PASAIKO

Short Sad Text
(based on the borders of 14 countries)

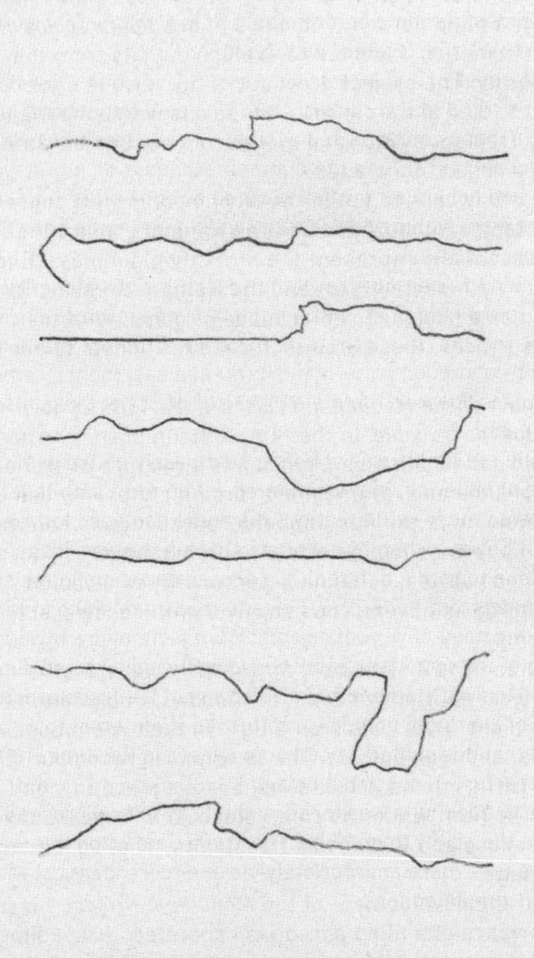

ANU PENNANEN

The Monument Project

The *Monument Project* is an investigation into urban Helsinki from the perspective of a blind person. The city's public space is heavily coded with visual information. I wanted to explore the city from the point of view of invisibility. The project grew out of my various interviews with the visually disabled and from my discussions with Johanna Röholm. Johanna is a freelance actor and mother of two. She became blind six years ago as a result of diabetes.

The urban study carried out in the *Monument Project* concentrates on the Ruoholahti neighborhood and the Kamppi construction site. These sites essentially represent the new city planning — Ruoholahti being the high-tech part of town and the Kamppi construction site projected as a shopping center made of glass. With their lit transparent surfaces, these architectural sites appeal to our visual senses.

A central part of the *Monument Project* is the 16mm short film *A Monument for the Invisible*. In the film, Röholm plays a fictional character also called Johanna. Johanna is a mixture of stories told by the real Johanna and my imagined version of her — a being between us. At the beginning of the film Johanna represents an anonymous blind person ho is engaged in her daily surroundings.
As the narration evolves, Johanna´s personality is revealed.
She appears to be an adventurous survivor with considerable skills such as fencing.

Installed alongside *A Monument for the Invisible* is another part of the *Monument Project* entitled *Windows*. In *Windows*, Ruoholahti residents are filmed at night. They switch on a light in their room appear at their windows, and look outside. The lit windows resemble film sets. The resident turns into an actor taking her/his place to signify the act of looking in the film. When the cinematographer cuts the take, the frames overexpose and flicker like flashlights creating a momentary loss of the image.

Throughout the development of the *Monument Project*, I learned that the experience of a blind person is concretely three-dimensional and bound to the present time. A blind person walking in the city must be constantly aware of her surroundings engaging all her senses.

With the hints provided by walking stick, Johanna maps her possible route. She is guided to alternative possibilities of relating to our environment. As such, Johanna builds a different monument in the public space, one that serves her own private needs and not for the generalised public eye.

GARRETT PHELAN

Scum of the Earth

He is speechless, in a dark room. In front of him a black and white image, human, pounds his head against a bed head, desperately attempting to communicate. He feels the figure's desperation, perhaps the desperation of speaking, communicating... He senses illness, or does he simply see it? Gradually, his response becomes the focus of his attention. Is he imposing alarm on the figure? Can he really read suffering here or has a neutral image stirred alarm in him? The piece is called Scum of the Earth. *He watches for about five minutes before the explicitly irregular nature of the edit alerts him to something. The figure is communicating, but in the language of Morse code. All he knows of Morse code is that it communicates through sound patterns of various lengths and punctuation. He begins to realise that the piece speaks a different language to that of the traditionally verbal. This strikes him as a very appropriate metaphor for an artwork that seems to be designed towards generating a sense of communicative breakdown, and perhaps even psychological breakdown.*

So how then to write about it, if the piece itself implies difficulty in communicating at a verbal level? The danger is that a narrative treatment of *Scum of the Earth* might be interpreted as an explication. It is necessary, then, to complement the manner in which *Scum of the Earth* communicates in an alternative discourse. A written treatment must draw attention to the work's self-conscious approach to verbal communication as communicative difficulty. And it should do this without suggesting that words can explain the function, or even the effect(s) of this work.

The careful reader will now recognise an essential schizophrenia here. While these comments acknowledge the linguistic turn away from transparent signifiers, at the same time they suggest that *Scum of the Earth* makes a clear point about the validity of alternative forms of discursive communication. Perhaps an appeal for calm can be made by referring the reader to certain pertinent contexts, which reinforce the view that *Scum of the Earth* indicates the presence of a non-verbal 'message.' Certainly, the Morse code communicates something, if only that the figure is attempting to communicate. Further, the framed image has been quarried from Dalton Trumbo's *Johnny got his Gun*, a little-known but humorous and memorable film about a war veteran deprived of all of his senses in battle.

Further, the Irish Museum of Modern Art, where *Scum of the Earth* was first exhibited, is housed in the Royal Hospital Kilmainham, which was originally built for retired and disabled British soldiers during the eighteenth century. The museum also looks out over the Wellington monument in Dublin's Phoenix Park and it is known that the Duke of Wellington suffered from post traumatic stress disorder, or what were then known as "dark moods."

But if this contextual excavation might seem essentialist, it is not an attempt to circumscribe either the directions that *Scum of the Earth* might take, or the expectations of the audiences that might encounter it. New Historicist approaches to temporal hermeneutics are useful here. How does one speak of the past with the tools of the present? Indeed, how do the discourses of the present define or alter the nature of the past?
The view that history is a series of past and present fictions reflecting the ideological position of its authors is pertinent when considering Phelan's work. In relation to *Scum of the Earth*, the artist made the choice to use an image that seems to communicate stress and trauma. The use of Morse code might localise this trauma in a twentieth century military context, but the fact that it simultaneously excludes a gallery audience from access to a message is also important. It seems to be a way of 'saying' that, in order to gain an understanding of the reality of war or war-induced trauma, it is perhaps necessary to know war as a communicable experience. Therefore, by suggesting that it cannot really communicate the experience of war but only represent it, *Scum of the Earth* is suitably self-effacing. Here, then, the Morse code works as a metaphor for an inability to speak about war, which is shared by combatants and non-combatants alike, although the reasons for their inarticulacy are radically different.
Moreover, and regardless of whether it evolved out of soldiers and eighteenth century hospitals, the wilful inarticulacy of *Scum of the Earth* suggests that it can also be interpreted as being unable to speak about history itself. In relation to the embedded text, there is also a very nice irony that further complements the piece's approach to history. If one chooses to translate the Morse code into English, one will have a text that will then be subject to the vagaries of interpretation, particularly if that virtual text is in any way figurative. Someone who would go to the trouble of translating the code in order to arrive at a final text would surely become aware that Scum of the Earth is in process. The meaning of the text is not the final element in the piece, as though *Scum of the Earth* were a riddle or jigsaw puzzle solved

by rendering it in the finality of verbal language. The embedded text is an important part of the process of the piece, because it illustrates that the verbal element of the work is subordinate to its audio-visual resonance, which grows exponentially as a result of submerging this verbal element. Also, given that Phelan's piece is looped, there is a multi-faceted movement away from narrative closure. How then could the meaning of the embedded text be fixed historically? Whatever narrative the embedded text of *Scum of the Earth* might elicit today could be rendered alien by the cultural permutations of tomorrow. In this light, Phelan's work is a valuable cultural artefact precisely because it signifies in speechlessness.

Rodney Sharkey

Works cited:

–Francis Barker, 1642: *Literature and Power in the Seventeenth Century* (University of Essex Press, 1981).
–Roland Barthes, "The Death of the Author," trans. Stephen Heath, from *Image-Music-Text* (Collins, 1980).
–Jean-François Lyotard, *The Differend: Phrases in Dispute*, trans. Georges Van Den.

KIRSTEN PIEROTH

It was some time during summer 2003 that I came across an original letter by the American inventor Thomas Alva Edison. The item was offered through a German autograph dealer, who in turn had bought the letter at an auction in New York. We agreed on a price and a few days later I received Edison's letter by post. It was of seemingly banal content, not mentioning an invention or anything of a related matter. However, after reading the letter several times, I contacted two Edison experts and subsequently a patents lawyer.
The following transcript includes the literal rendering of the correspondence with David Sloane, Edison's great-grandson and a lecturer on Edison's life and work; Paul Israel, the director of the Thomas Edison Papers at Rutgers University; and Klemens Schubert, a Berlin-based patents lawyer with a diploma in chemistry.

September 10, 1924

Dear Mr. Sproul:
I regret that a previous engagement prevents me from accepting your kind invitation to dinner at your home, on Thursday evening, September seventeenth.
Yours sincerely,
Thomas A. Edison

July 13, 2003

Dear David Sloane/Dear Paul Israel,
I am writing to you regarding a typewritten letter signed by Thomas Edison.
In the letter Edison cancels an invitation to dinner due to a previous engagement.
Do you think that Edison invented the excuse? I would be glad if you could give me your opinion. I have enclosed a copy of the original letter.
Yours sincerely,
Kirsten Pieroth

Undated

Dear Kirsten:
I don't know if Thomas Edison invented the excuse.
Yours truly,
David E. E. Sloane

September 2, 2003

Dear Kirsten,
I'm happy to write you regarding your Edison letter.
There is plenty of evidence regarding Thomas Edison's dislike of formal events due to his poor hearing. His daughter described how he did not like to entertain at dinner parties thrown by his wife at their home and that he would often feign illness. As she recalled, "he had this awful indigestion, usually before a party, not afterwards..." His official biography includes a chapter on the "Social Side of Edison," which notes that he did not like to be interrupted while working on a project and would even send visitors away without seeing them. I've personally seen letters of invitation that Edison either answered by indicating that he was too busy or by asking his secretary to make an excuse as to why he could not attend. So it is entirely possible that the letter you have is one that contains an "invented" excuse.
Sincerely,
Paul Israel

September 29, 2003
Re: Possibility to patent the letter from Thomas A. Edison from 10.9.1924

Dear Ms. Pieroth,
You wanted to know whether you could get a patent on the excuse formulated by Thomas A. Edison in his letter from September 10, 1924.
In general, patents are given for inventions that are new — based on an inventive activity, and that can be applied industrially. In my opinion the excuse of Mr. Edison lacks already the fact of being an invention in itself. Inventions need to have a technical character, which is lacking in such a verbal statement. This ensues, from our point of view, that a patent for an invention can't be taken into consideration. Additionally, this statement would have to be verified as being new, in the sense of intellectual property right. In regards to this we have considerable doubts, since the excuse to my opinion and knowledge, is often used and probably has been used already. Summarizing this, I have to ascertain that Mr. Edison, with his letter from September 10, 1924, neither made a new invention nor arrived at an outstanding creative achievement, for which a protection under an intellectual property right would come into question.
Kind regards,
Dr. Klemens Schubert

This is ridiculous, no goals!

As a shy and unassuming young man of 20, Doug Engelbart had read Vannevar Bush's article ("As We May Think") while serving in the US Navy in the autumn of 1945. He hadn't had a burning desire to enlist. "My eyes weren't good enough so I couldn't enlist in anything dramatic," he remembers, but he was drafted in 1944 anyway, and trained as a radar technician. Radar work had started to appeal to him back in high school. "I'd hear these rumours among the kids," he says, "about this thing called radar, and that the Navy had this program where they would train you by having you study, and you'd go behind closed fences and they'd take the books out of vaults and teach you and then search you when you left and put the books back in the vaults. It all sounded so dramatic!" Seduced by the mystery, he set his sights on radar. (...)

"This is ridiculous, no goals," he remembers thinking when he came home from work on that December day (1950). And so for the next few months he set about trying to find some. "For some reason I just picked that as an explicit, conscious thing to do," he recalls, "I had to figure out a good set of professional goals." Not motivated by money, Engelbart decided his new goal would involve helping humankind. But the question was how. "I remember reading about the people who would go in and lick malaria in an area. And then the population would grow so fast and the people didn't take care of the ecology and so pretty soon they were starving again, because not only couldn't they feed themselves, but the soil was eroding so fast that the productivity of the land was going to go down. So it's a case that the side-effects didn't produce what you thought the direct benefits would. I began to realize it's a very complex world." Thinking about this complexity, he saw that the probability of achieving any given goal was pretty low. And then it dawned on him that finding a way to increase this probability could be his goal.

Along with the growth in information Vannevar Bush had identified, Engelbart saw that the problems facing mankind were getting more and more complex and the time there was to solve them was getting shorter and shorter. "It suddenly flashed," recalls Engelbart, "that if you could do something to improve human capability to deal with that, then you'd really contribute something basic." At the same time he saw computers as an integral part of a tool that would help people cope with their rapidly changing environment. "Just to complete the vision," he recalls, "I also really got a clear picture that one's colleagues could be sitting in other rooms with similar work stations, tied to the same computer complex, and could be sharing and working and collaborating very closely." And also the assumption that there'd be a lot of new skills, new ways of thinking that would evolve, Engelbart decided that he would build this tool.

This was in early 1951, before computer workstations even existed, before Sputnik, and nearly two decades before the first computer networks. Computers themselves at the time were gargantuan calculating engines like the NPL's Pilot Ace, known only to a chosen few. To have had such a vision then is truly remarkable. It would be like imagining the road transport of the 1990s just after the invention of the wheel. But Engelbart's work as a radar technician fuelled his imagination, since he knew that cathode ray tubes (CRTs) could display anything you asked them to. He didn't know too much about computers, though. "I'll tell you what a computer was in those days," he says, "it was an underpaid woman sitting there with a hand calculator, and they'd have rooms full of them, that's how they got their computing done. So you'd say 'What's your job?' 'I'm a computer'." He did know enough about computers — the machines, not the women — to know that they could control CRTs, but he didn't know much more. So he left his job and...

Excerpts from: James Gillies and Robert Cailliau, *How the Web was Born*, Oxford University Press, New York, 2000.

MARC QUER

Algeria, France: Images

The photographs of colonial Algeria taken by Félix Moulin in 1856 were shown in Marseilles in 1998. This effectively 'historical' exhibition was organized by the photographer Estelle Fredet in the premises of an association situated in the Belsunce quarter: La Compagnie.
The idea was to show images that have always been present in the collective memory, to highlight the tensions that they still transmit, and to expose them to the gaze of different observers in order to give rise —in the light of current events and personal histories— to reflection and testimony. They were gathered in various ways and on various supports (audio tape, video, etc.).
In this same spirit, and by specific commission, I was prompted to transform some of these images by adding speech bubbles, as in a cartoon strip (the blank speech bubble is a direct invitation to write in it). The results, in the form of screen-printed posters, were pasted up in the Belsunce quarter, a traditional destination for immigrants arriving in Marseilles.
Two hundred posters were pasted up in this way in the streets, a hundred were recollected, and twenty-eight were shown as part of the historical exhibition.

DANIEL ROTH

It does not seem to me, Austerlitz added, that we understand the laws governing the return of the past, but I feel more and more as if time did not exist at all, only various spaces interlocking according to the rules of a higher form of stereometry, between which the living and the dead can move back and forth as they like, and the longer I think about it, the more it seems to me that we who are still alive are unreal in the eyes of the dead, that only occasionally, in certain lights and atmospheric conditions, do we appear in their field of vision.

Excerpt from W.G. Sebald, *Austerlitz*, Penguin Books, London, 2002 (first published in German by Carl Hanser Verlag, 2001, translated from the German by Anthea Bell, 2002).

EMAIL CONVERSATION 18 May, 2004

MARK GISBOURNE: Your work always seems to have a sense of that which was destroyed or derelict being first deconstructed and then reconstructed to serve new ends. What is the impulse behind this?

MICHAEL SAILSTORFER: I want my work to be close to life, if you like parallel to my life, that's why I decided to start to work with familiar things that surround me. To use them as material, I had to destroy the immediacy of their old function in order to make something new. The process of destruction is helpful to get to know the material you are working with. In an interview from last year I compared it to the grounding of the canvas.

MG: This second use value, which we might call its aesthetic value, is transposed but always with oblique references to its former existence. What I mean is say your work *D-IBRB* (2002) was a light aircraft that crashed (probably into a tree) and which you turned into a tree house. What do you mean by this?

MS: Yes, with those pieces it is always important that you can see where the material comes from. All the scratches and visible marks of their destruction are important as well. I want the whole process from A to B to be clearly visible in the final piece, to create a kind of timeline of a 'story'. I see this piece working from the tension between the catastrophe and the games children play. The other thing I am interested in is how the sculpture works formally in the tree; the dynamic of the air crash and the direction from which the light aircraft came.

MG: Many of your earlier works were self-consuming, as in *3 Ster mit Ausblick* (2002), or the obverse where a caravan (a potentially mobile home) is turned into the static object such as a house, as in say *Heimatlied*?

MS: I like the idea of creating something new by taking something away. The "Waldputz" project (2000) works in the same way. Creating an artificial space by cleaning the forest. That is something I want to keep on working with.

MG: In a certain sense there is a quality of variable permanence in your work. Nothing disappears but that it has become something else. Does this reflect your personal view of life?

MS: Yes, I think that is life, that's how most of the things work in the world, be it the human organism, cars, or the making of art.

MG: Personally I like to see you works as if they sort of ironic objects, and what I mean by this they convey one set of signifiers (original utility) turned to their opposite, a new uselessness posing a different set of cultural signifiers. If you like they have become art signifiers or aesthetic utility?

MS: Yes, I like very much this idea. That's how I think critical artistic practice should work. You take something from cultural life, change it or add something to it through your artistic practice in order to put it back into circulation.

MG: How much of the making is a sense of fun? What I mean is do you have any pre-conceived ideas before you begin, or do they simply evolve in the process of making?

MS: Most of the time it starts with an image coming in my mind. I find that the best ideas come, when I don't think about making art at all. That is to say, it's more like a sketch, without details. Then I check if the image is strong enough to be worth starting a project. This process can sometimes take months. The process of the making is very important. A lot of things can change in the studio. That is during the building all the decisions are made how the piece will finally look. But, yes, I always try to have as much fun as possible.

MG: In some of your works there is desire for interactivity, if you like some people could and can participate, as in *Und sie bewegt sich doch!* or your portable lampposts that can be fired as rockets and which you called *Sternschnuppe – Shooting Star*. Do you like to engage with spectator participation?

MS: I have thought a lot about interactivity and the participation of the viewer. For example when I show *Shooting-Star*. I would never shoot the lamppost in front of the viewer nor let the spectator do this performance himself. The same with the Mercedes of "Und sie bewegt sich doch!" The spectator is not allowed to drive the car. I am more interested in raising the expectation of the viewers desire to 'play with my toys', and which is finally unfulfilled. I haven't built a piece for purely interactive reasons, so far.

MG: Tell me about your new work, and where you see your work going from here on?

MS: I took this huge fan from the former fish factory, that is where one part of Manifesta 5 takes place, and moved it to the Museum space. I have almost rebuilt the negative room where it was installed before with plasterboard. It looks like an unfinished wall. The curve is new and I changed the scale a bit. However, the whole structure is on small wheels, as a negative pedestal and to underline the shift from one space to the other. There is a microphone on the top of the pipe to amplify the sound of the wind that the fan makes. The title is *Breadboard Construction Marilyn*. I thought a long time about this title, because I like this big, odd, unglamorous, industrial, phallic structure, as being a reference to Marilyn Monroe whispering Happy Birthday to the President. And it adds an extra layer to the piece, which I think is all to the good. But I have no idea what I will do next. You know, the idea of transformation and displacement is very important to me. And, I see that there are lots of possibilities as to how to deal with it.

Tuesday, 18 May 2004

SILKE SCHATZ

today - kalea foru
A Recollection. I was 18 in July/August 1985

A trip to Fuenterrabia, or rather Hondarrabia. During our summer vacation we – about five teenagers – travelled from Hannover, Germany, to Spain, or rather to the Basque Country. We had been in Hondarribia quite a few times because of Martina's single-handed trip to Barcelona and because of the holiday flat her new boyfriend's mother had there.

Hondarrabia is on the Atlantic coast just across the French border, an old sea port that has turned into a seaside resort, surrounded by mountains. We hardly had any notion what *Gora Euskadi* might mean. Having made friends with Basques who played in bands like Kortatu and took us along to their fiestas, we had got acquainted a bit.

We slept on a mountainside in the vicinity of Hondarrabia: Guadalupe, named after the small Catholic church on its top. It is filled with offerings from a 16th century sea captain. In memory of him two model ships sail around the crucifix beneath the roof. There is a gigantic subterranean castle from 1900 at the foot of the mountain. Although it was forbidden to enter, we found a way by a path that herds of sheep had trodden down before us. We slept not far from the castle under the starry sky, and were able to see many shooting stars in July or August 1985.

Early one afternoon, we drove down to Hondarrabia. We had changed the tire on our old Mercedes Benz. One of our fathers had advised us to drive slowly at first and then tighten the bolts again after driving for a while. On our trial run along the east coast road, the promenade of suburban Hondarrabia nowadays called *kalea foru*, we passed a small square. There stood a carousel and a candy-wagon. In the center of town, a fiesta was taking place for the day of the town's patron saint, I seem to remember, and the carousel was full. We kept on rolling. Suddenly ahead of us, parked cars were being pulled into the road. Barricades. We backed up a side street and immediately had a view of the open sea and the carousel and were surrounded by walls with villas and houses behind them.

The rear door of our car opened and a Basque friend jumped in and said: "If anything happens, I'm German." Then he fell silent. Ahead of us on the *kalea foru* was a pickup truck with an open back. On it, the Guardia Civil with their rubber-bullet guns in firing position had formed a circle.

The mothers and fathers at the carousel had formed a circle of protection for their children. The Guardia Civil shot at the mothers and fathers and at us. The bullets whizzed through the air and I was afraid we might be hit.

Then they were gone. I saw a man with a bloodstained shirt and the crowd at the carousel dispersed over the square.

Later I remembered that the doors of the houses and villas had been opened and that the people from the street had vanished behind them in order to seek shelter from the Guardia Civil.

Translated by Lothar Pollähne

MARKUS SCHINWALD

Retraction from a black below grey horizon, flat except for the shape of the horses, grazing silently. The window, shuttered by two red doors, is open but reflective.
(Day)

A folded Wing
–this suits you
a fluid wrist
–this suits you
a gentle hand

Interrupting. A meaningful pause, then with pregnancy:

Oval
Kiss
Undone

Shock

Give in
Exhale,
Collapse

Spring first, the fragile last
Starlit then, the morning vast.

Behind the dome. Fade up from black- it has rained. Birds shift and move against the building´s edge, flapping, crossing, descending to the ground:

You want to be an angry man,
Have tried to turn against the plan,
Now brutal, lost and vilified.
To you, the restless, half-unconscious queen
To you, the rejection of what was.
To you, the zest, the shine, the in-between.
To you, half done.

She steps into the streetlight, he turns hesitantly:

If only I could see you in a year.

Thoughts on *The Nervous Systems* and *Inversal*

I have been asked to write about my own work. I am slightly uneasy about this. While the ideas behind my work are paramount to me, I do not think they are necessarily important and perhaps may even be unhelpful to an audience. For while I acknowledge that the works are totally reliant on ideas for their conception, the work is not reliant on the explanation of these ideas for its reception. I think the conceptual strength of a work often lies in its ambiguity and can therefore be diminished by being explained and defined by the artist. Anyway, here are some of my thoughts behind *The Nervous Systems* and *Inversal*.

These recent pieces are concerned with the way we envisage and conceive of time. *The Nervous Systems* juxtaposes the slow orbit of coded bodies (the spools) with the gradual production of a linear structure (the rope.) This juxtaposition refers to the two main ways in which we envisage time. The first is as a line or timeline, the second is as a cycle or circle. The machine is based not so much on traditional rope machines as on old orreries and planetariums, except in place of the planets there are the spools. The machine, left on for the duration of the show, produces a continuous timeline and, as a result, any given point on the rope can be traced back to a particular moment in time during the show. One second is 2.2 millimetres. Two months is 482 metres.

Inversal conveys similar concerns as *The Nervous Systems*, but without the use of metaphor. From a distance, the piece seems stationary, but, on approach, it is clear that the spring-like toroid structure, while not moving in any direction, is moving through itself in perpetuity. The actual structure was born from investigations into both String Theory and Harmonics. It is composed of 24 loops, which are then joined back on themselves. In a way it is an exploded diagram of our 24-hour day: wheels within wheels, always repeating.

The way this piece moves, for me anyway, seems to be emotive of the passage of time suffered by all things. As we know, all objects exist inside the four dimensions of space and time. While the first three dimensions are easy, time has to be the most elusive, enigmatic and baffling thing that we have ever attempted to comprehend. My interest in time has brought me to science, and I have come to regard scientists as poets. Einstein's conception of time, for example, must have taken an immense imagination and a true poetry of perception. I will finish with one fact I gleaned from him, and quite possibly misunderstood, that I find truly inspiring:

We are all travelling through time, yet the slower we travel through space the faster we move through time and when, eventually, we are completely still, then, and only then, will we travel at the speed of light through time...

EYAL SIVAN AND MICHEL KHLEIFI

ROUTE 181, FRAGMENTS D'UN VOYAGE EN PALESTINE-ISRAËL

Since the start of the second Intifada, in October 2000, there has been no end to the bloodshed in Palestine-Israel. Walls and barbed wire are put up here and there, following in the steps of the solid walls in the minds of the citizens of both societies.

What can film do in the face of such a desperate situation, with no solution and no prospects for the future?

Faced with the tragic torments shaking our societies, we set out to perform a filmic act of faith.

We are both film-makers and friends. As chance would have it, we were also born in the same territory. Today, we both live in exile where, for fifteen years, we have pursued our respective film careers. One of us is Palestinian, the other Israeli. Our friendship remains untouched by the national identities that were imposed on us and in the name of which a bloody conflict has been fought for over fifty years.

Beyond the tribal membership with which we do not identify and on the basis of our common experience, we made the joint decision to return to a country, in order to re-find it, re-discover it and to reveal the geographical and mental reality in which the men and women of Palestine-Israel live today.

The demarcation line of the partition plan for Palestine, drawn and voted upon by the UN in 1947, was the point of departure for this cinematographic operation. It represented a documentary challenge and a human venture.

Our aim was to break with the usual procedure filming people, places and events that coincide with the film-maker's ideological mindset, a procedure that only serves to clarify already known and accepted political discourses regarding what is referred to as the 'the Israel-Palestine conflict.'

In the course of this non-existent route that we decided to take, independently of pre-established ideas, we filmed in such a way as to see things, men, women, and places as a sum total not yet revealed. Carried along by chance meetings, together we listened to words, nature, passions, and disillusions. We tried to induce – first in ourselves, then in the subjects we filmed – a loving relationship with the everyday, one full of danger and encounter with death. Men and women were provided the opportunity to speak – those who have forgotten the official discourse, but who are nonetheless the basis of the two societies, those on whose behalf the war is waged.

We still believe in the virtue of a shared life and peaceful coexistence, in a citizenship that accords equality of rights and responsibilities. Is this a utopia? No. We are both quite convinced that the only truly 'realistic' solution for the future lies in the prospect of a state in which citizens, be they Jews or Arabs, live together. The tragic situation of Near-Eastern 'reality' is an ideological and pathological construct made by men. These same men are capable of de-constructing it.

All we ask of this project is a shared experience. Without illusion or mystification, we are prepared to receive reality just as it is, in order to act on and with it.

November

> *An age that has lost its gestures is, for this reason, obsessed by them. For human beings who have lost every sense of naturalness, each single gesture becomes a destiny. And the more gestures lose their ease under the action of invisible powers, the more life becomes indecipherable.*
> –Agamben 2000: 53

When I was 17, my best friend was Andrea Wolf. Andrea died in 1998 when she was shot as a Kurdish terrorist in Eastern Anatolia.

When Andrea lived in Germany, there was a warrant out for her arrest as she was accused of having participated in terrorist activities, specifically in the case of the destruction of the deportation prison in Weiterstadt. She was also suspected of having been an associate of the Red Army Faction.

At this point, in 1996, Andrea chose to go to Kurdistan in order to join the women's army of the so-called PKK where she assumed the name 'Ronahi.' For some time, she remained there to train and live with the women's army mostly in camps in Northern Iraq. Then in October 1998, her unit was tracked by the Turkish army close to the border. A heavy firefight took place. Only a few of the unit's members remained alive. They were under heavy fire from Army helicopters. Most of the survivors took refuge in what is referred to as an earth hole. Surviving eyewitnesses who remained in the hole recall that she was shot either by army members or Kurdish village guards after having been dragged out as a prisoner. Her case is only one of the many illegal executions that structure this war.

"Gesture is the name of this intersection between life and art, act and power, general and particular, text and execution. It is a moment of life subtracted from the context of individual biography as well as the moment of art subtracted from the neutrality of aesthetics: it is pure praxis." (Agamben 2000:79)

This project tackles the question of what is called terrorism and used to be called internationalism, the spaces and subjectivites it can create, and their relationship to figures of popular culture, namely cinema. The film revolves around the gestures and postures in which a phenomenon called terrorism is created. Its point of departure is a feminist martial arts film that Andrea Wolf and I made together when we were 17 years old. Now this fictional martial arts flick has become a very specific type of document, namely a document of the fantasies that structured our posture and our desire. *November* is not a documentary about Andrea Wolf. It is not a film about the situation in Kurdistan. It deals with gestures of liberation after the end of history, as reflected through popular culture and traveling images. This project is a film about the era of November, when revolution seems to be over and only its gestures are still circulating.

Agamben, G. (2000) *Means Without End: 'Notes on Politics' (Theory Out of Bounds, V. 20)*, trans. Binetti, V. & Casarino, C., University of Minnesota Press.

first and foremost: the risk of 'integrity.' I presented my collected works in advance: "moma. the museum of the mechanical age. 119 problems," a plain collection of marginal experiences; a summary of decisive events which caused fundamental changes. there will be no more! note the double move: the singularity of the experiences includes but cannot escape their shared goal: the "collected works" (oeuvre) will definitively be the sum of a life spent.

(this kind of limitation of possible experiences should not deny its consequences. more than ever I insist on the openness of the conditions of life. still I feel as though I were in the middle of a fantastic, endless digression. This trajectory implies the perpetual menace of again reaching the point of exhaustion, which would demand the mentioned closure as completion. (119)

there will be no more! the most privileged position is to act posthumously. I reinterpret the possible totality of a life from a standpoint that will finally become my own. that's a necessary and simple conclusion which follows my initial premise: that my work was always inspired by the fascination with the actual material extension of ourselves; that is not just in space but in time: the simple truth, for example that every word spoken affects language, imagined as a whole; including all of tomorrow's discussions, all of tomorrow's diatribes. note the almost unendurable answerability and outrageous interference; returning into the museum of the 119 to reveal the most paradoxical figure: that the limitations of the museum of the 119 at the same time allow an intensification and expansion of experiences: to make them anew. for less pretentious experiments I think we do not have to insist on using the art form. (and the circus)

so the confessions are: control and limitation are at the heart of the work. this allows me to determine the basic idea which should not be forgotten throughout its execution. the idea is exhaustively interpreted in the phase of conception that concludes with the plot (compare it to developing a film-script). this phase is the exhaustive experiment of risking the idea in the necessary invasions and systematic destabilisations which come about in this moment.

returning from the colonization of the self, the numerous testimonies of impossibility of expression, of communication, the indescribability of the moment, (sung in tune) "parole! parole!" etc. Crossing the real threshold of this space is accepting the chance of mediation (also the contradiction), the continuous transformation of space and material into meaning as negotiated in the completed works.

crucial is the lapse from the plot to the final execution of the work. following the exhaustion of the conception, the work on-site follows a clear vision, that is, it is not an experiment and should not expose methodological considerations as they were extensively and emphatically explored before execution. the installation at manifesta demonstrates two ways (from 1 to 3 and from 4 to 6) of making this crucial move from a conceptual consideration to a clear vision, in which art retains an alchemistic, even magic touch, transforming control and limitation.

(the idea to be carried out at manifesta was: any given language is the style of the truth. STYLE is the agent, not just of any establishment. style allows productive limitations but also threatens to convert the limitation into restriction. the common speechlessness and alienation caused by given languages (spaces) is a challenge to art and at the same time demands its conquest. from here I start. still, the problem remains with the pretentiousness of theoretical conceptions. moma might be an excuse for the persisting distinction between conception and a practical execution. but why not be patient, allowing oneself this impoverishment, risking banality? art moves in the other direction favouring the joyful meandering living dead to the slavery of a planned economy. for more details try the second catalogue-contribution).

PATRICK TUTTOFUOCO

WHAT DO YOU DO ?

VANGELIS VLAHOS

Posted by Azcamadrid on 6:59 pm on July 12, 2002
–Athens is a very big city, it need a zone with skyscrapers and more investments.

Posted by gm2263 on 7:31 pm on July 12, 2002
–In the 1970's the Area of Ampelokipi where Kiffisias Avenue starts, was chosen to host the first highrise developments during the time of the military dictatorship (1967-1974). (...)
All towers built between 1971 and 1978. Nothing significant was added since then. New constructions moved to the north along Kiffisias Av., but unfortunately, the heights of the buildings diminished. I don't know if the architects believe that the democracy that succeeded the junta period has to do with low constructions since it was the dictators that allowed the constructions of tall buildings in the first place. (...)

Posted by De Snor on 8:02 pm on July 12, 2002
–I am always impressed by the density of Athens, but I would not give up hope for skyscrapers in that great city, the Olympics can put a enormous investment into a city AFTERWARDS→ look what happened to Montreal and Munchen in the 70's!

Posted by gm2263 on 8:15 pm on July 12, 2002
–I agree, first of all the investments in infrastructure in Athens and the works under development now are of an unprecedented magnitude and Athens needed them. You cannot build skyscrapers without proper infrastructure, that's for sure. (...)

Posted by yoyoalan on 5:20 pm on July 14, 2002
–I think the Acropolis will stay the tallest.

Posted by gm2263 on 5:58 pm on July 14, 2002
–The Acropolis rock is 150mt tall, a decent height for highrises in Athens. However, I doubt that they will ever build any highrises near it, ever. All Athens highrises are at a distance of least 10 km away.

Posted by KREZ on 7:20 am on July 15, 2002
–Don't worry gm2263, there is a HUGE hole in the supply of office towers in

Athens - that won't go unnoticed too long, trust me. Major investment is on the way...

Posted by gm2263 on 8:21 am on July 15, 2002
–Thenks Krez, True, the construction of highrises has to do with economy and lack of office space among other things, but at the same time, it's a matter of mentality of architects and acceptance from the public and the authorities. Just think that Italy, a country that belongs to the G-7 group with an economy much stronger than Greece, still has no tower taller than 150mt (i would die though to see a development like the Centro Direzionale in Naples – Napoli to be built in the northern suburbs of Athens). Italy's developments are few in numbers and certainly NOT reflecting the economic achievements of this great country.
I really wonder how the Italians manage to accommodate their businesses in this respect, not why the Greeks (a relatively wealthy country compared to the rest of the world) don't build highrises.
Anyway, I believe that to build highrises is a matter of culture besides engineering and architectural expertise. What makes me optimistic about Athens is that the cost of land is high at the moment and building vertical may be a solution. (...)

Posted by KREZ on 9:05 am on July 16, 2002
–Yeah, you make a good point. Cultural (maybe better put: political) acceptance is extremely important in the construction of tall buildings. (...)

Extract from *Athens Skyline Aerials*.
Read the whole topic at:
http://www.hoogbouw.nl/euroforums/cgi-bin/forums.cgi?forum=1&topic=904

GILLIAN WEARING

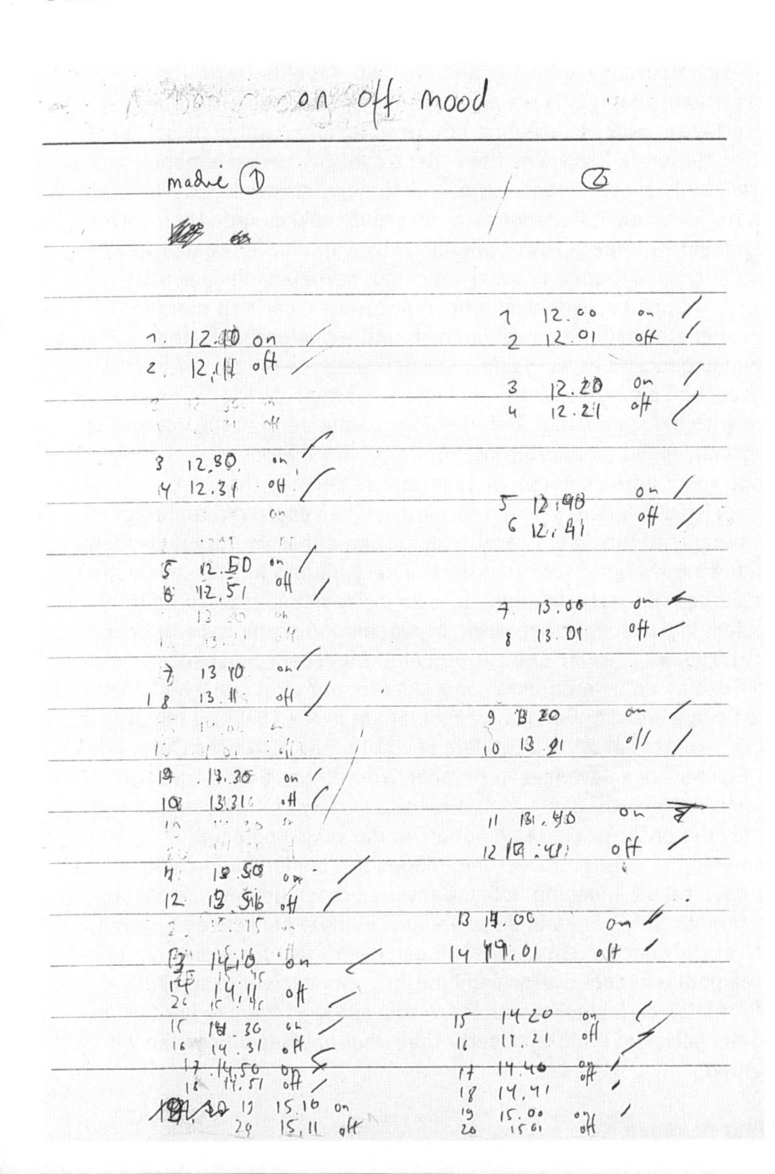
on off mood
machine 1
2

AMELIE VON WULFFEN

In fusing photography, drawing, and painting, Amelie von Wulffen creates dream-like hybrid scenarios rife with elisions, insertions, gaps, and overlays in order to create a new architecture vaulted by spikes in memory. Her work literalizes the artist's capacity to make mental space material, both in her collages, which confuse interior and exterior spaces, and in her drawing installations, which create spaces unto themselves.

Beginning with the verity of photographs, von Wulffen reappropriates images and gives them a broader meaning, perhaps a deeper truth. Almost in a Constructivist aesthetic, it becomes clear that montage is more complete than the polished finish of the photographic image. Instead of remaining locked in an instant, she activates the photos for her own purposes, linking images from art history, German history and personal history with her fluid hand. And in doing so, she iterates the notion that photography is not an appropriate metaphor for memory.

While von Wulffen's personal experiences pervade the work, such as the upper-middle class German furniture of her post-WWII upbringing and remnants of the John Travolta idolization of her youth, the pastiche technique serves better to recreate a history than to tell the anecdotes of her personal history. In addition to John Travolta, a cast of male characters resurfaces in her work, broadening in scope to be at once political, romantic, ironic and sentimental. Aleksandr Solzhenitsyn, the exiled Russian anti-Communist, and a personal moral idol whom von Wulffen connects with German conservatism in the 1970s, is honored in multiple, almost naively naturalistic portraits. She also uses Dürer, who fused Renaissance advances in perspective with the Gothic traditions of the North, in her collages, which employ a variety of multiple perspectives, with only the limits of the imagination as the vanishing point.

Like memory itself, the overlaid images are blended and confused, and sometimes result in gaping holes. Canyons breach domestic interiors, and cinematic self-portraits dissolve into the hazy sunsets and brambly forests of German Romanticism. The patchwork technique and double-exposed photos create overgrown interiors, like ancient ruins. With a certain matter-of-factness, coupled with a sense of longing bordering on melancholy, von Wulffen asserts that what has been forgotten will be reinvented.

Kathleen Eagan

Monologue of Small Girl from *Killed by Lightning*

Radio Announcer: And now our radio listeners will listen to the winner of the Palaeoanthropology competition...

The Girl: The latest discoveries in cryptozoology and palaeoanthropology have revealed serious mistakes made on the part of classical Evolutionary theorists. And, naturally, humanity again faces a mystery.

Radio Announcer: Do you think humanity will ever solve this mystery?

The Girl: When I become a scientist, I will make a very important discovery but people won't be happy about it and will even fear it. Fear.

Radio Announcer: But what kind of discovery?

The Girl: I will learn that the skull shape of all existing creatures, without exception — fishes and amphibians, amphibians and reptiles, birds and mammals — is changing from an elongated shape to a more spherical one. Perhaps stones... I will come to the conclusion that Evolution never took place. A stone and a human are units of one chain. Thus, humanity is not the pinnacle of evolution; it represents only one phase and its development is endless. The development of nature is a cycle without beginning or end.

And later, I will come to the conclusion that reproduction is not a mechanism of evolution because it is not enclosed in the human person, or in a bird, or in a tree, or in a stone, or in any other organism. Reproduction is probably only pathology, a mistake unprogrammed by nature. A man can suddenly be transformed into a different, absolutely new creature in the space of one human life. He can become the forefather of a stone, and a stone or a bird can be transformed into the forefather of a man. It is unnecessary for millions of years to pass for this process to occur. It can happen at any second. Within anybody.

Then I will probably leave the scientific world. And that's all.

OLIVIER ZABAT

'The only lasting form of beauty is that which is founded on a relation with natural beings. If we were to imagine beings in a state of rapid vicissitude, in which a painting merely represents a fleeting instant, all imagination would be superfluous. Beauty has the same foundation in the arts that truth has in philosophy.'

Denis Diderot

Excerpt from Olivier Zabat's film *1/3 des yeux*, 'Hôpital Percy' section.

DAVID ZINK YI

In some regions of the Andes, every mountain and stone is believed to be inhabited by a deity. Some deities are stronger, others weaker; then again they may be benevolent or malicious. I was told that to avoid feeling eerie there, one should take some earth and let it dissolve in one's mouth in order to become familiar with the local deity...

Letter written in February 2000, from Peru.

DARIUS ŽIURA

The Sketch of a Street Painter

Darius Žiura: I started to paint people's portraits near the Pompidou Centre in Paris. The following summer I worked in Palanga in Lithuania. It was the time before the 'Sekund's' bank collapsed, so it seemed that the affluent situation was going to last forever. It was the most opulent period for Palanga with people spending relentlessly. However the situation began to change soon. The profit in Palanga had dropped quickly and I went to Paris to join the 'big marathon' of street painting. It's like big sports with all the extreme things... although it's not considered an official sport.

Raimundas Malašauskas: I guess it's closer to illegal cock fights, no?

DŽ: There are certain parallels with the circus, since it's a show for a public. The whole thing has reached a certain sublimity at some point. Yet the government in Paris had changed and the new one outlawed any unofficial, unauthorized business. As you know, street painting is part of a complex phenomenon of all kinds of street exchanges and shady deals. Very soon the whole of our community was scattered by the police in a very methodical way.

RM: And you moved to another place?

DŽ: Then we resorted to our survival secrets. I know them, but would prefer not to reveal. Do you know what the Russian word 'panel' means?

RM: In what context?

DŽ: This is a very precise expression for a place where prostitutes wait to be picked up by their clients. The exact phrase is 'rabotat na panele' (to work on a panel) and this refers to a work with a client in unprotected and unauthorized street territory. This category is used both in the context of prostitution and in street painting. It also applies to taxi drivers.

RM: Well, I've read that a few years ago a social survey was held in some region in Russia asking kids about their dream professions and most chose DJ, mafia guy and prostitute. Prostitution is a channel to a better life.

Personally, I don't see anything wrong in it except the fact that workers are not protected enough.

DŽ: Prostitution has many aspects similar to street painting... first, it's work done in the street, and it involves a direct contact with a client.

RM: By the way, who is your average colleague 'on the panel'? I guess there must be a lot of Chinese painters.

DŽ: Chinese painting is bad and cheap.

RM: Dumping the business?

DŽ: Compromising the level.

RM: But if the client accepts that quality?

DŽ: In our practice, the client is totally a self-reflection-free element.

RM: Can you explain 'self-reflection-free element'? Does that mean free of self reflection?

DŽ: Exactly. The client is not allowed to make a free choice, he or she is denied such a possibility. In the situation of collective mass work, the client is usually a victim of psychological violence. Psychological violence is enough for certain 'geniuses' to make the biggest profit of all. 'Panel' is a jungle of relationships and nuances that are totally impossible for any cop to penetrate. To extract money from someone with a motive of making a portrait is a crime.

RM: I've read somewhere that the main reason for people go off for long periods on boats fishing in icy waters is actually not big money, but an addiction to extreme experiences. Yours sounds a bit similar.

DŽ: That's a very important moment. Many of my colleagues from street painting say, 'Well, I am sixty, I have my wife, a house, and could stay home,' but it's impossible because they are already hooked and addicted.

RM: Do you have any idea about the other life of your colleagues: how do they live when they get back home? Do they sustain any other artistic practice?

DŽ: A certain Dostoyevskian type prevails. Most often they do the same, paint some paintings, sell something. I haven't met anyone like myself. I don't touch a brush for the rest of the year.

RM: What do you think about when you do a portrait?

DŽ: It's a very intense experience. To me, it's basically a communication with a person, a type of communication that is very appropriate to me. I had thought about the phenomenon of a portrait many times in various ways. The portraits of 'Gustoniai' are also a very interesting thing, only I was shooting people on video for one minute instead of painting them. One could claim that a face is the most intimate part of the body. When painting on the street, it's great not to worry that you'll have to speak to the anonymous face. You are not committed to any social action. The painting session takes 30 to 40 minutes, and afterwards, the person goes away, and you have nothing in common with that person.

RM: Is there any feedback from the client?

DŽ: No. The session is over and then the next session starts. You forget everything and start again with a blank sheet of paper. It's a wonderful feeling. And after a day, you don't remember anything.

Vilnius, April 2004.

KOLDO MITXELENA

VICTOR ALIMPIEV AND SERGEY VISHNEVSKY

Deer, 2002. Video.

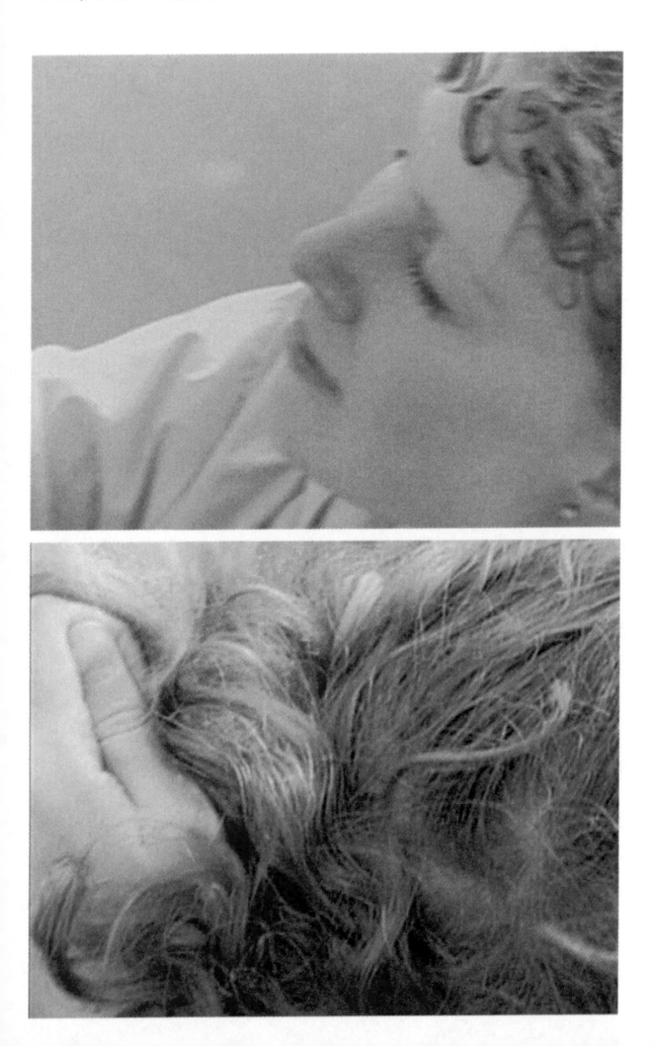

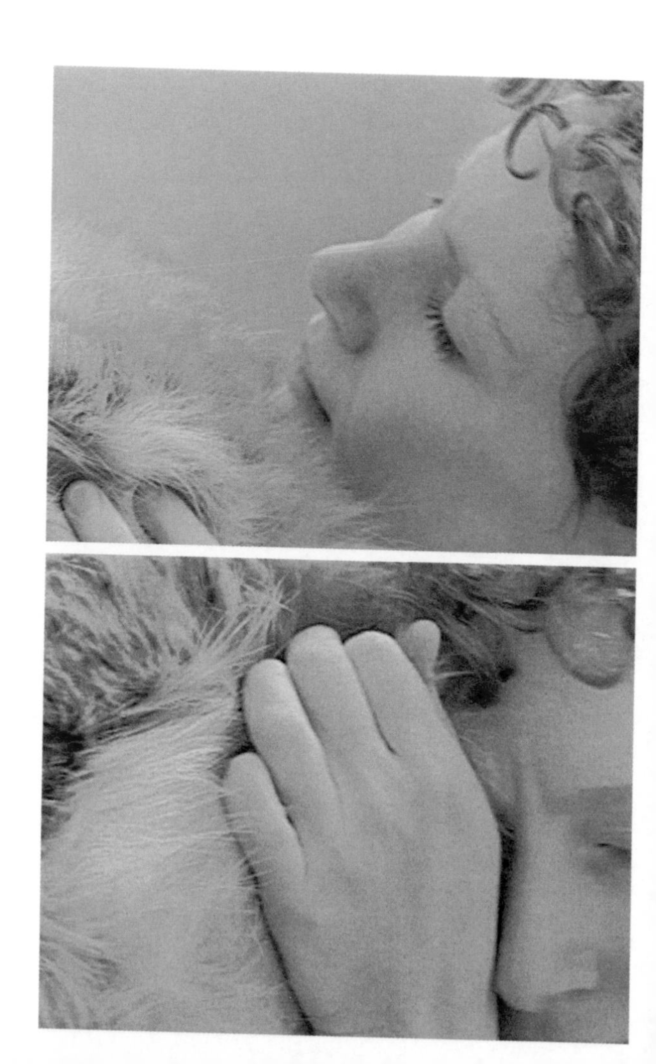

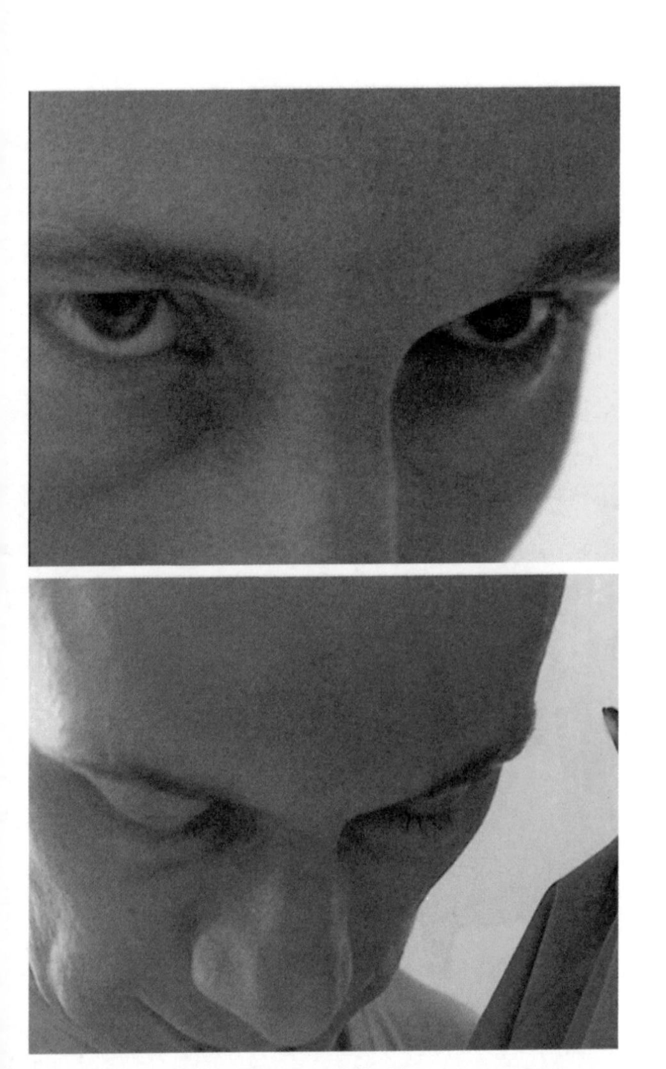

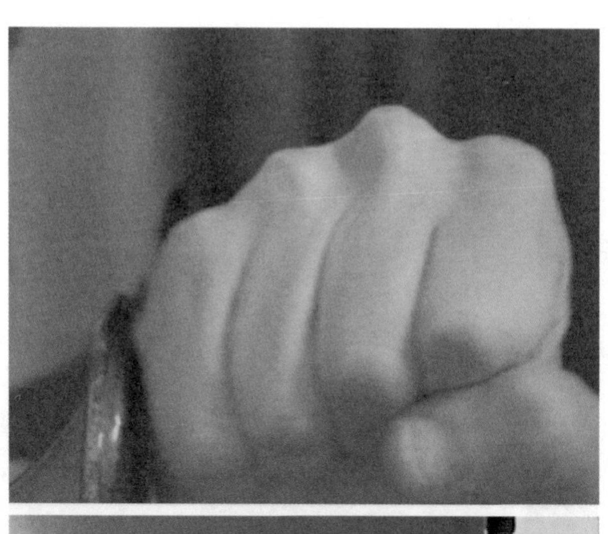

SVEN AUGUSTIJNEN

Johan, 2001. Video.

I can't...
- I don't understand.

François, 2003. Video.

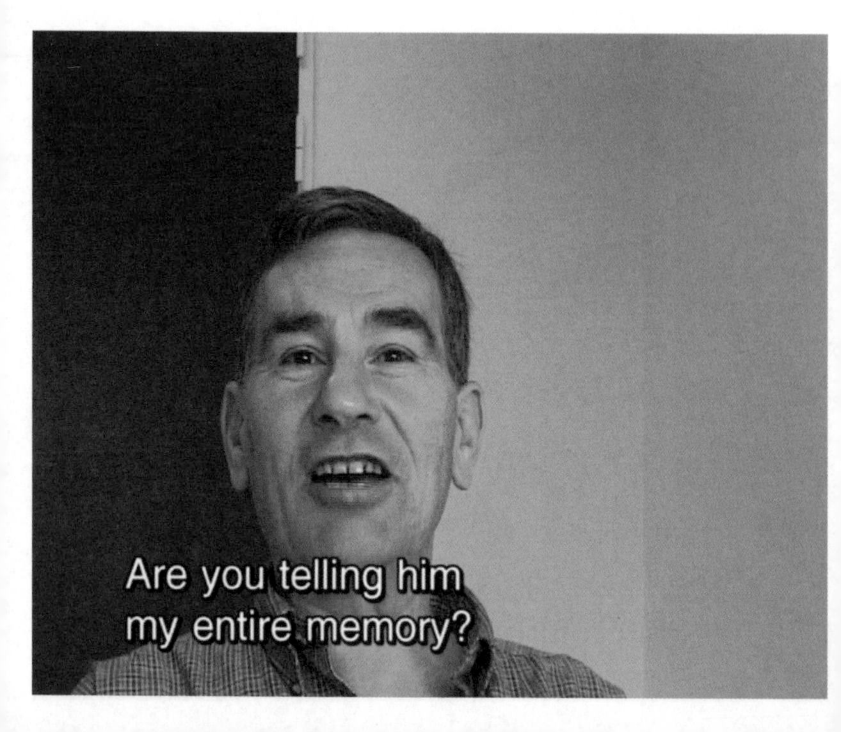

MICHAËL BORREMANS

Once At the Time, 2003. Oil on canvas, 85x100 cm.

The Preservation, 2001. Oil on canvas, 60x70 cm.

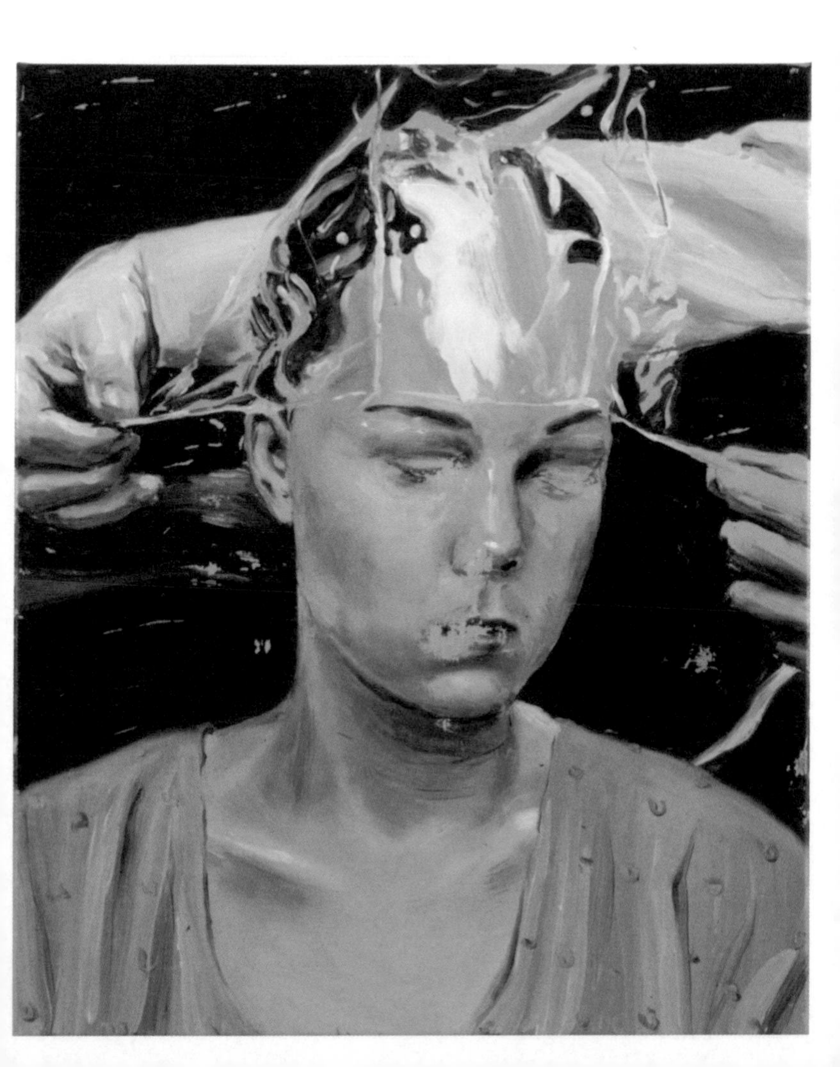

The Rendering, 2002. Oil on canvas, 74x124 cm.

Replacement I, 2004. Oil on canvas, 83x65 cm.

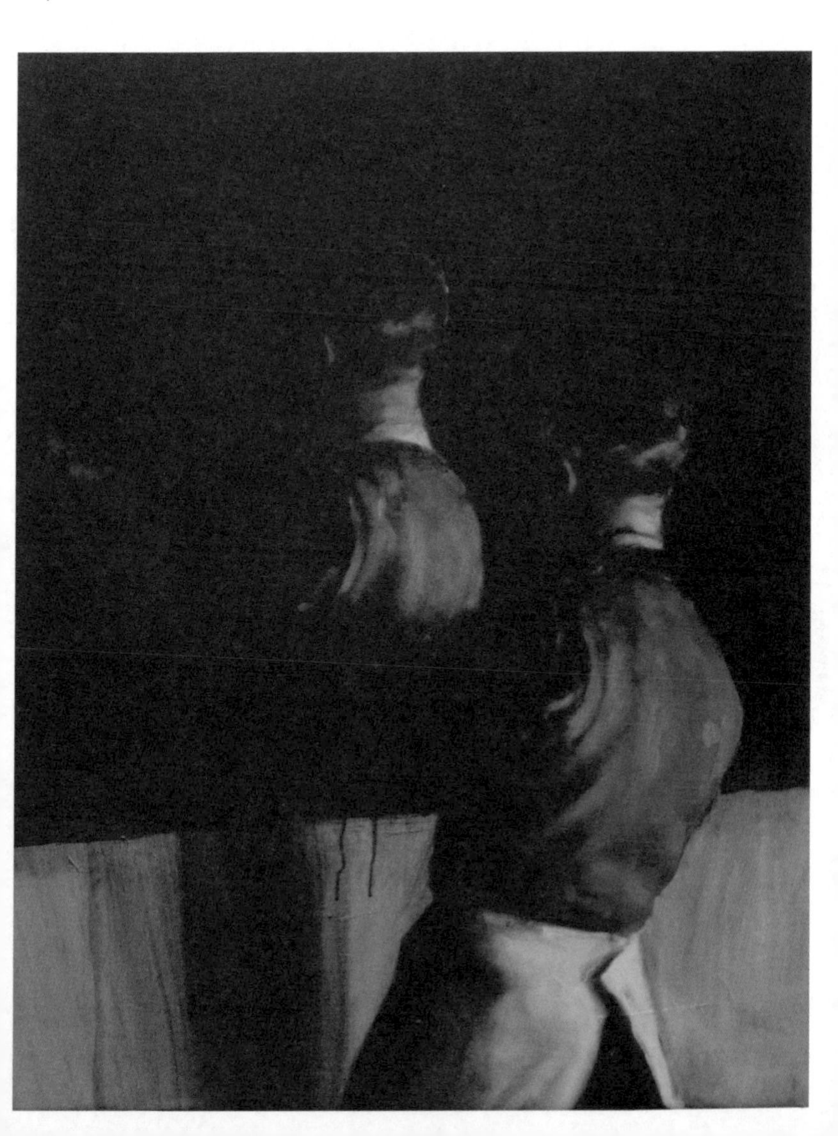

SERHIY BRATKOV

Birds, 1997.

Spetcraspredelitel, 2000.

ANDREA FACIU

Everything Nothing, 2004. Video.

Le Luneux, 2003. Video.

stel and charcoal on paper, 193x303 cm.

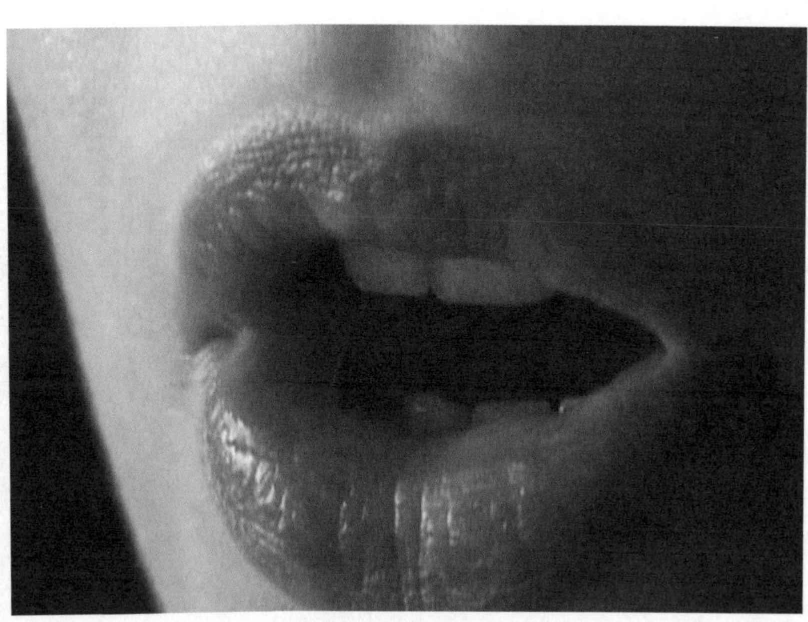

JOHANNES KAHRS

Spooky Love, 2002. Oil on canvas, 143x243 cm.

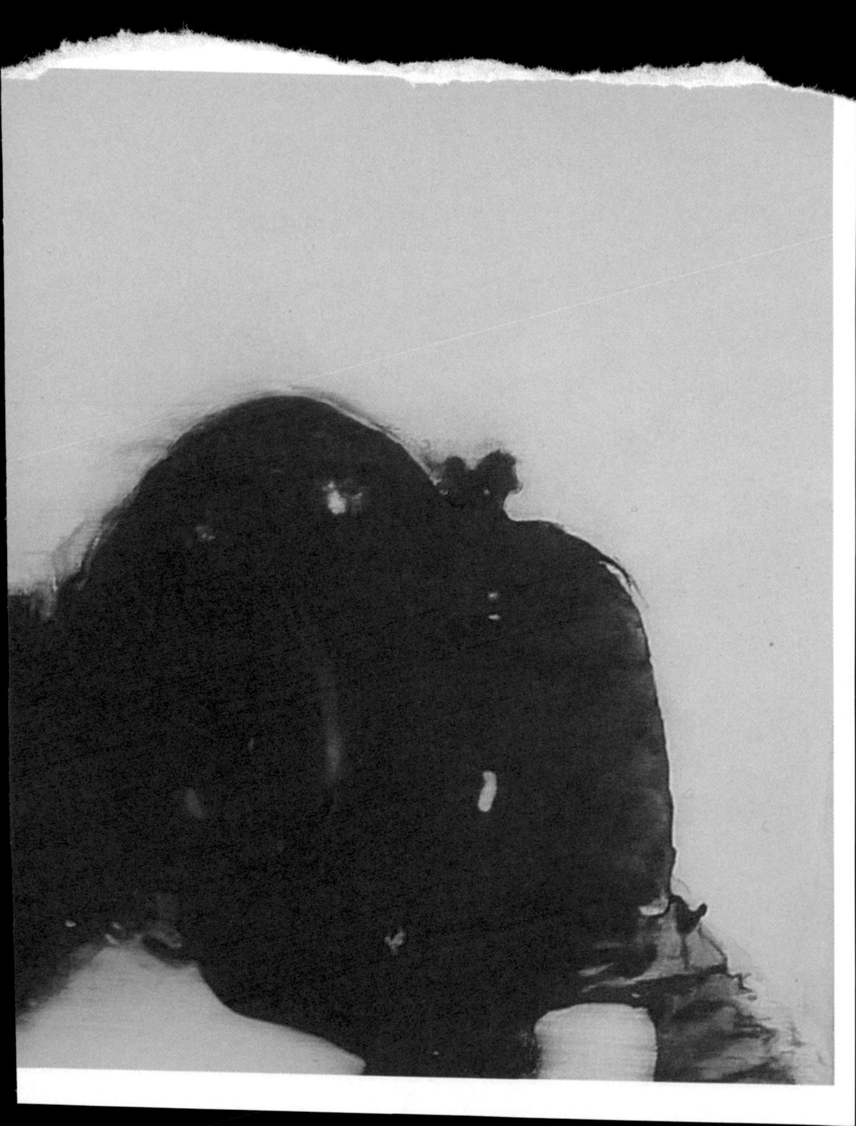

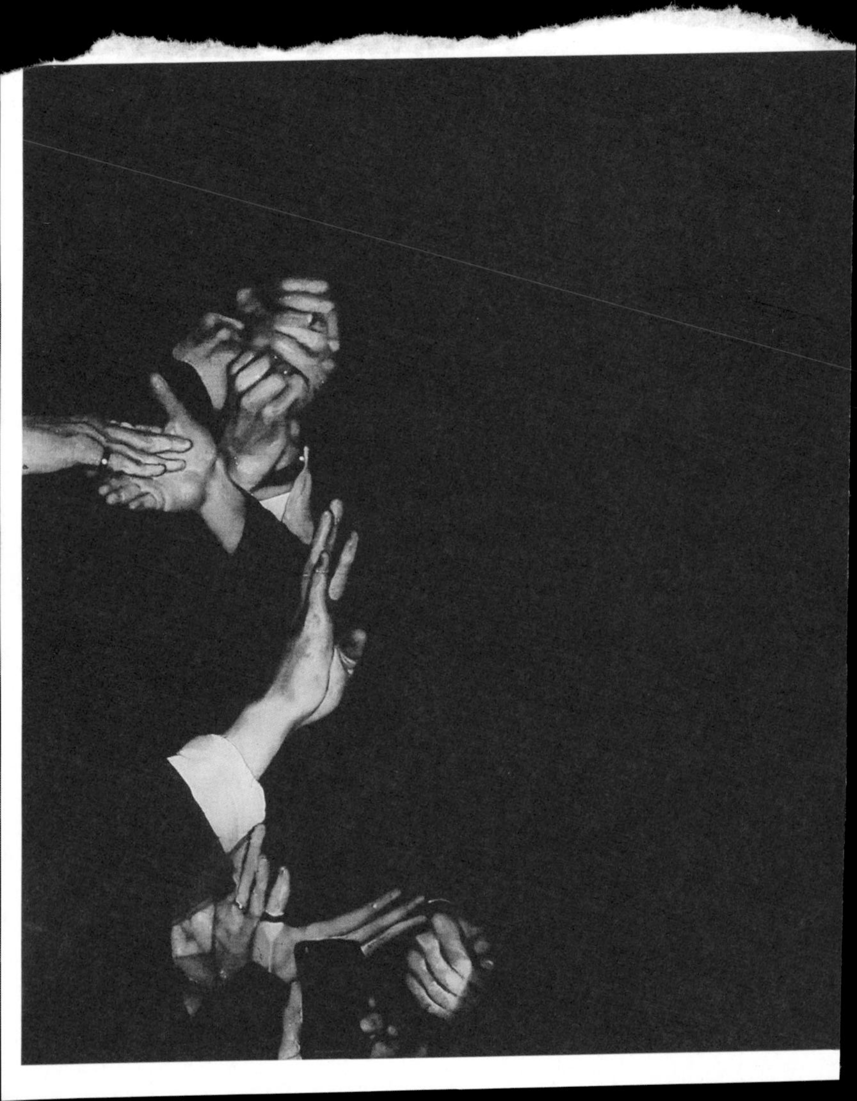

DANIEL ROTH

Cabrini Green Forest

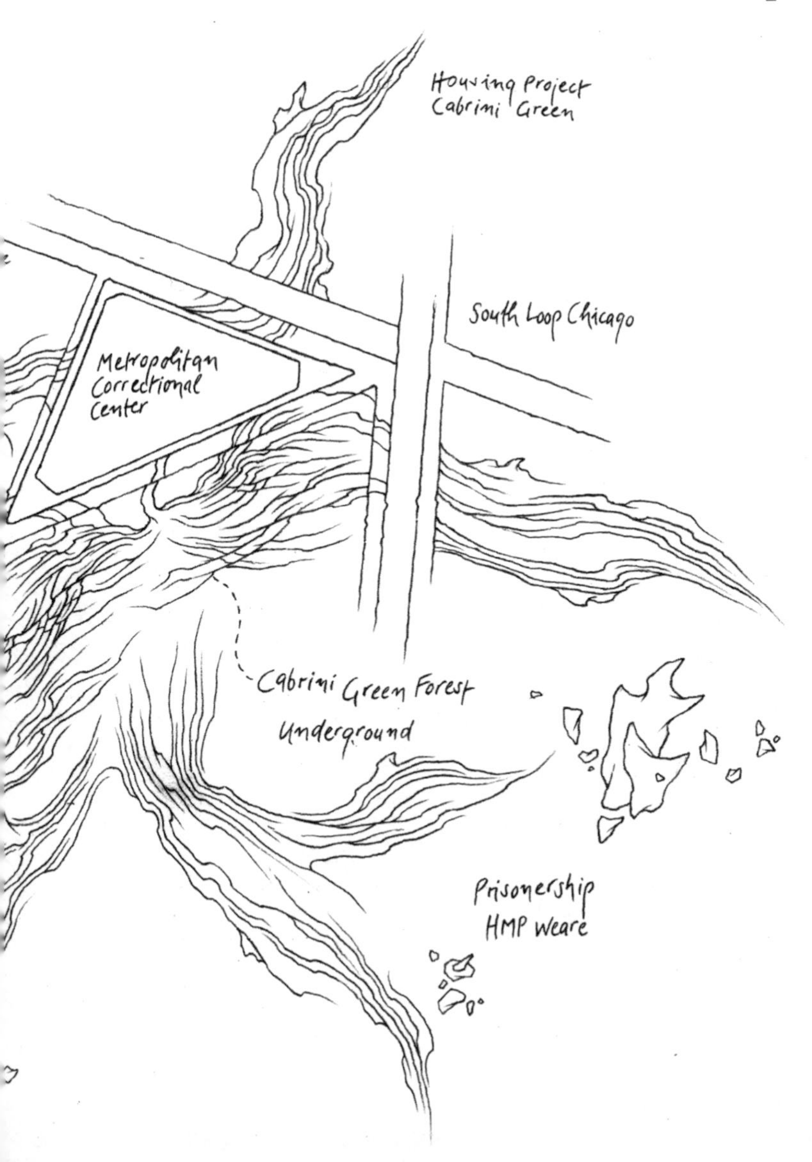
Housing Project
Cabrini Green
South Loop Chicago
Metropolitan
Correctional
Center
Cabrini Green Forest
Underground
Prisonership
HMP Weare

"The Metropolitan Correctional Center Chicago is a tower block at South Loop Chicago by architect Harry Weese that was built in 1975. Underground spaces originate from its basement, wherein a forest is slowly spreading out. This subterranean forest is being connected to a housing project in the city of Chicago called Cabrini Green, a prison ship in the United Kingdom named HMP Weare, and further extraterritorial prison ships that are sailing the oceans of the world."

Prisonership HMP Weare

Correctional Center Chicago

Housing Project Cabrini Green

MISHA STROJ

revenge style.

David Quigley reading the coming sculptures of Misha Stroj

1) Clinch

Floating sculptural moments, models for organizing memory (mnemotechno) and a fascination with giving form to the forces which constitute meaning and emotion. Movement of thought towards some specific point frozen in the special turn of the line, construction of space or the particular intonation and modulation of our words as we sing both in and out of tune. A shape or style which might hold thought steady for a while – maybe even reveal something about things to come. The tectonic is a force in itself with which we break away from the grasp of the tired boxer. The place where you are now, the physical construction of joyous investigation and doubt (also joyful) oscillates back and forth in the unbound progression of thought, paradoxically confirming that beginning is strangely the last and not the first step. This series is beyond the ordained procession: 1 to 6 and 6 to 1 starting at 4 and then confessing that we can't stop thinking about 3. Translating the hermetic thought processes of another into these words, confined but set free through the dogmatic structure, which anyway only works when laughing. Entering into the Museum of the Mechanical Age, forming a fragmentary totality, a complex negotiation and transformation of material which begins here in my body – breathing, confined, waiting and dreaming.

4) The rest

Production implies production of a world. Art as production of reality is the practice of exploring the realm of the unknown as it is simultaneously experienced by different individuals. Art produces discontinuities, which implies that it is immanently functional: The call to expand art to the outer limits of knowledge, to the realm of metaphysical investigation, but also to the limits of human practice, does not, however, imply moving art away from reality, but rather integrating it in the process of construction of the world itself. Negotiating the trickiness of actual desire: lapses, tropes, impossibilities and a general intuition of the fact that everything could be completely different. Here we must decide and act, but not because we have no other choice. The stuff is there before us and it is only a matter of moments. Here worlds and cosmologies are constructed as miracles.

2) Lapse. Reification.

If consciousness and identity are formed in the interplay of forces which flow within society as a whole, one must dive into the 'ebb and flow' of these forces to trace the general movements of massive currents as they enter into the formation of the individual. The real forces of ethics, exchange value and identity represent not only the limits and direction of movement within society as it concretely and historically unfolds; they also represent an integral dynamic within thought itself. In these forces constituting the present, the practice of the artist functions as an immanent exceptional situation, as a moment of material creation of value and meaning beyond the instrumentalizing, and limiting clichés of false-consciousness and ideology – but not merely in dialectical opposition to these. The questions and doubts are here as active reminders of the necessity to fight against these currents, but the

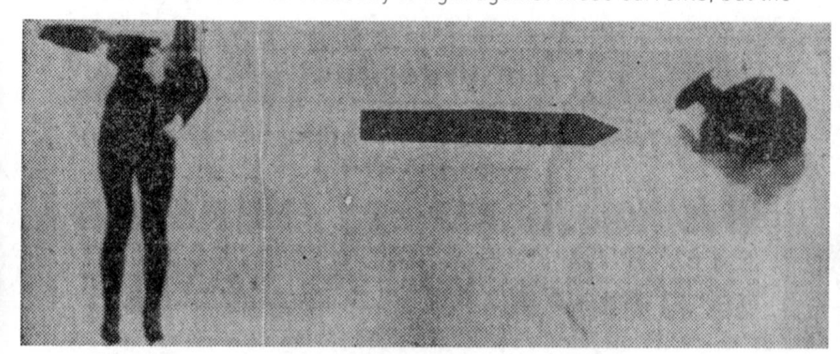

easily transmitted disease of resentment makes us tired and unable to formulate an alternative. This is the second step, but also the fifth. Record and form! Once whispered words are stored here on shelves as monuments to the inexplicable need to integrate ourselves into the prose of the world. Hark angels and recognize the mumbling, grumbling murmur-murmur of these written revelations. This moment is a non-dogmatic starting point for utopia.

5) The hedge (like a prayer)

Losing the way at first in this temporary space. Intimate revelations in changing topography. A continual process of seeing what has never before been seen. Chronologically linked to the progression from 1 to 6 and back again. The hedge is the other side of the lapse, crossing the water, the constellation of forces, and the tension of the eternal before – the trajectory towards the final zing. The hedge hesitates waiting to be moved. Sense, sensation and revolution. Falling out of order – joy and disaster.

3) Doors, messiahs and Greeks

Benjamin projects the power of any investigation into the material forces of the present as constellation, "blown to smithereens in the messianic now." This constellation is to be turned upon itself in the "little door" through which the Messiah arrives. But we must be careful to understand the singularity of this moment as it defines a particular expression. As Benjamin remarks in his notes: "Concerning the messianic standstill of events one could evoke Focillon's definition of style: A brief moment of complete possession of forms, coming about like a sudden joy, like the acme of the Greeks: so delicate that the pointer of the scale scarcely trembles. That which I expect to see is not the pointer dip down, even less the moment of absolute rest. I look at it instead in the miracle of this hesitant immobility, the slight trembling, imperceptible, which indicates that it is alive."

6) Empty pockets and broken bicycle

After a traditional story: In a village named Maria-Wörth on the day of great festivities honouring the Madonna, ships came from all sides of the lake bringing pilgrims from far and wide who were there to take part in the procession. A poor stable boy in Pritschitz had to stay at home and watch after the livestock because he had neither shoes nor clothes. There he stood in the fields looking across the lake to Maria-Wörth. In his mind's eye he could see the procession winding through the village and he could hear the prayers sounding in his ears, "Platschiken-Platschaken." The boy was deeply moved and felt himself drawn to the Holy Mother. He walked calmly to the lake, folded his hands with inner reverence, and, mimicking the sound of the prayer as it had reached his ears, he stepped out to cross the lake walking to the other side. Meanwhile in Maria-Wörth, the pilgrims and priest saw the child as he came over the lake. They hurried to the shore to witness the miracle from closer. There they heard to their amazement as the child spoke with reverence "Platschiken – Platschaken." Astounded, the priest said, "My child, what are you saying there? That's no prayer. That's no way to say a prayer." And he taught him the words of the prayer. "Now, my child, go back and say what you have learned from me." Obediently, the boy again walked across the water repeating the newly learned prayer. He soon disappeared into the waves.

CATHY WILKES

Little Joe (Dallesandro), 2004. Oil on canvas, 25x20 cm.

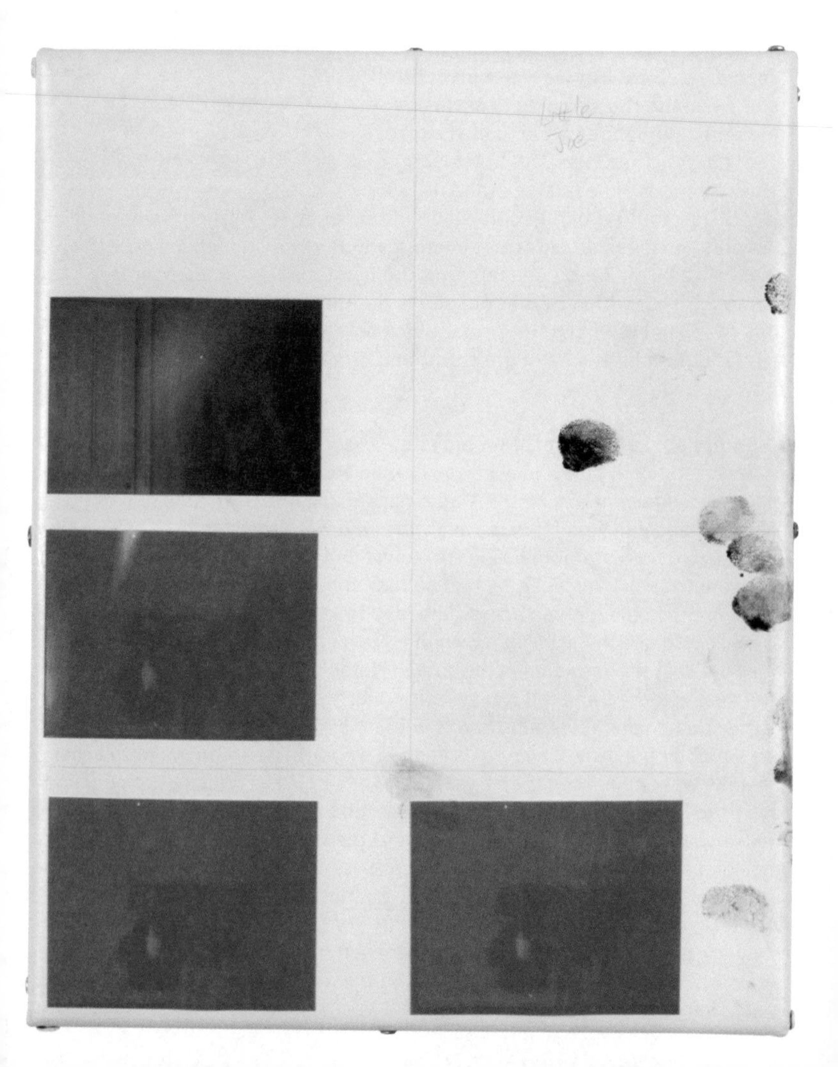

Start Speaking Cause I Screen Calls, 2004. Oil on canvas, 35x25 cm.

67 Francis Bacon Begin, 2003. Painting on catalogue plate, 27x20.5 cm.

Cara Studies Votes for Women, 2003. Painting on catalogue plate, 27x20 cm.

MUSEO SAN TELMO

BAS JAN ADER

Fall I, 1970. 16mm black and white film.

Fall II, 1970. 16mm black and white film.

Broken Fall (Organic), 1971. Gelatin-silver print, 45.7x62.2 cm.

I´m Too Sad To Tell You, 1971. 16mm black and white film.

JOHN BOCK

Gast, 2004. Video.

Wühl um die Klumpen, 2002. Documenta 11, Kassel.

(overleaf) **Installation view**, 2002. Documenta 11, Kassel.

CENGIZ ÇEKIL

Unwritten, 1976. From a series of 12 collages, 42.5x57.5 cm each.

18 Mart 1976
Cengiz

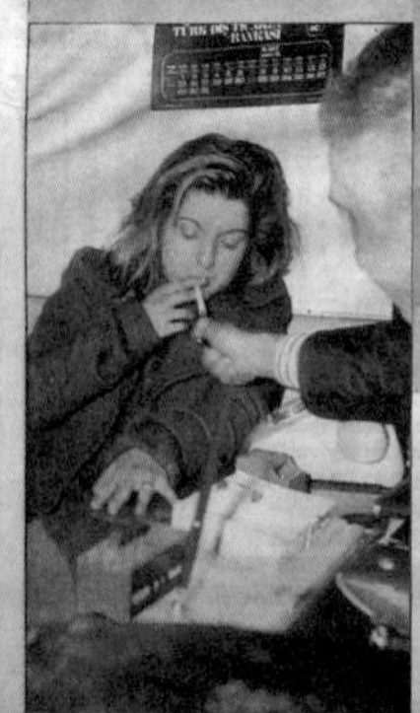

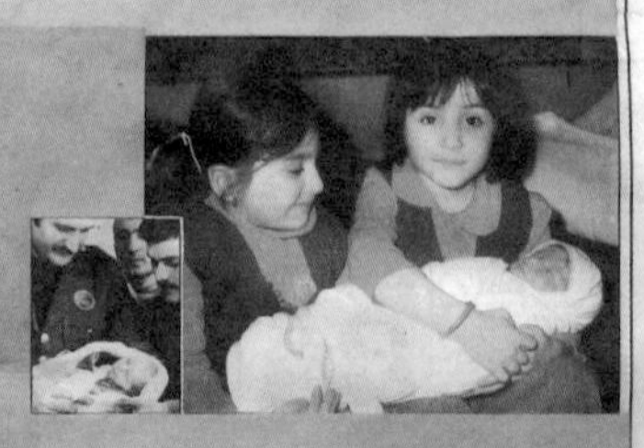

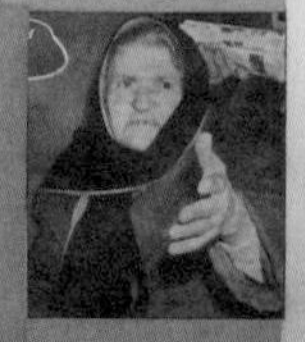

14 mart 1976

KÜLLI K. KAATS

(overleaf) **Avifauna**, 2002.DVD.

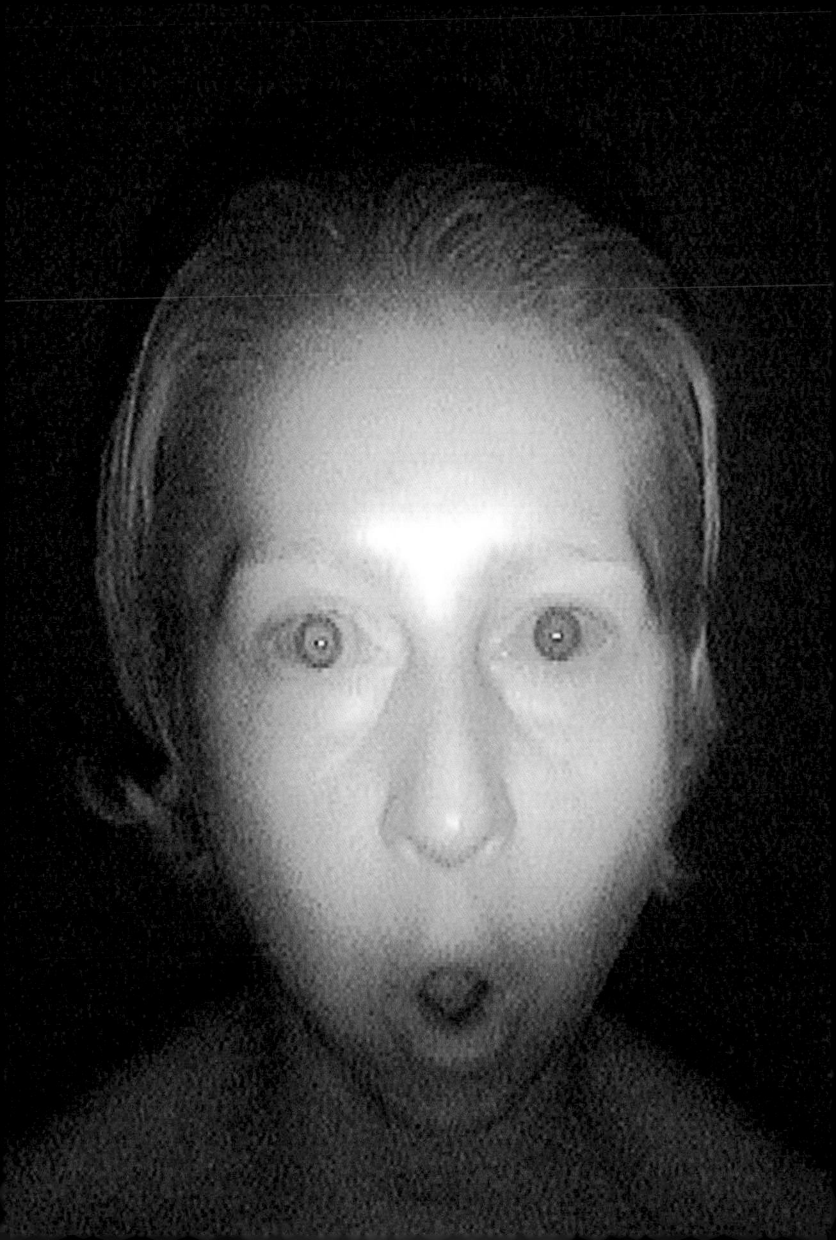

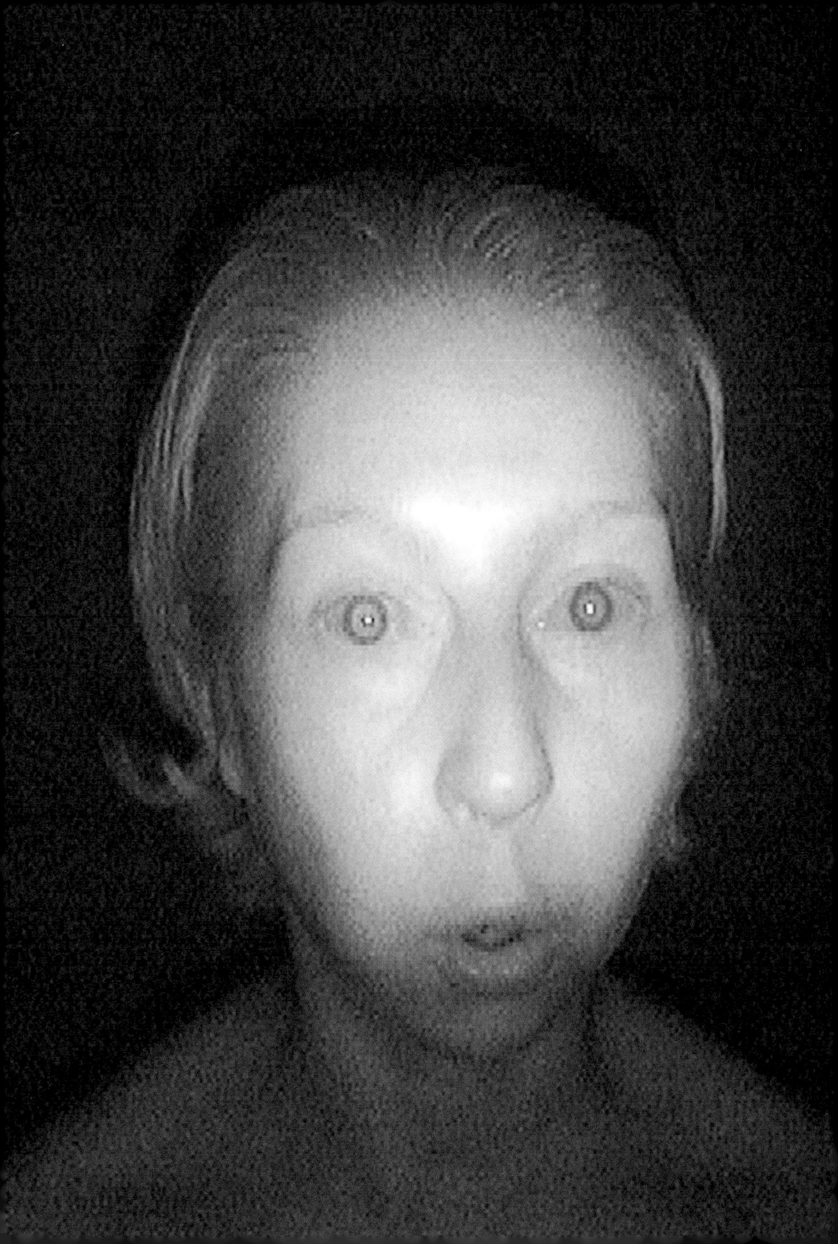

MARIA LUSITANO

Nostalgia, 2002. Video

PORTUGUESA
REPÚBLICA
$50
REPÚBLICA PORTUGUESA
1$00
ANGOLA
ANGOLA
LUANDA-C
Lisboa
Portugal
GABELA — ESCOLAS

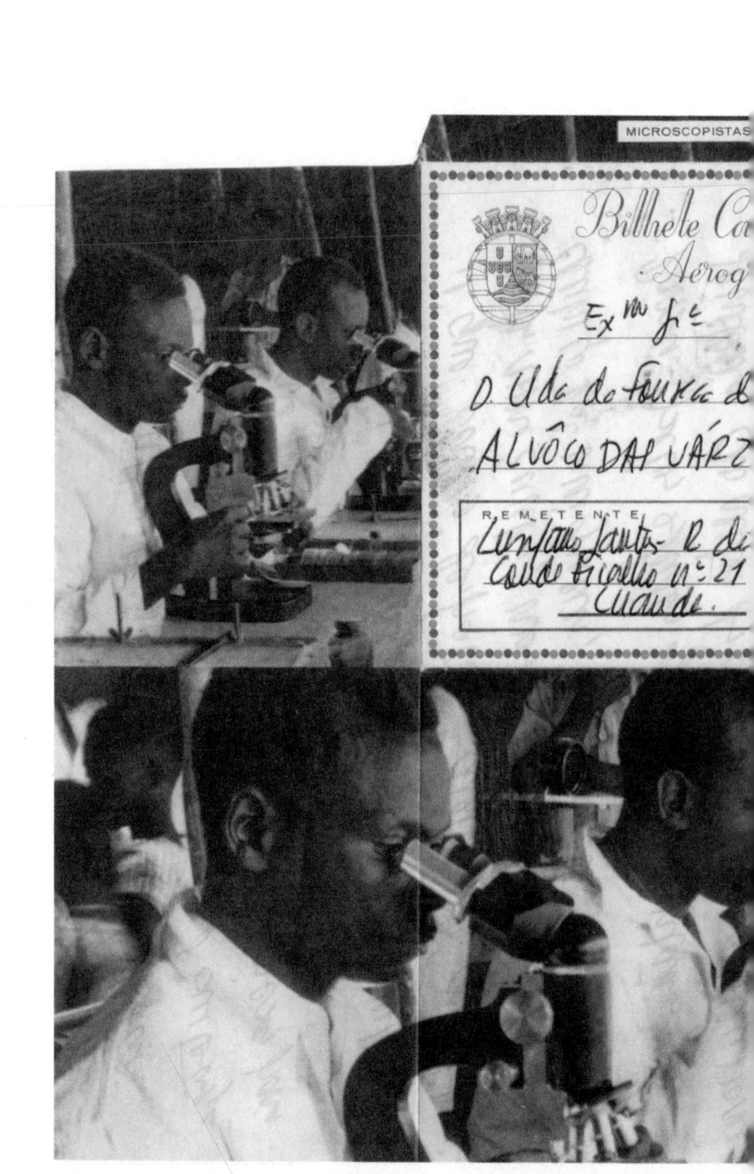
MICROSCOPISTAS
Bilhete Co
Aerog
REMETENTE

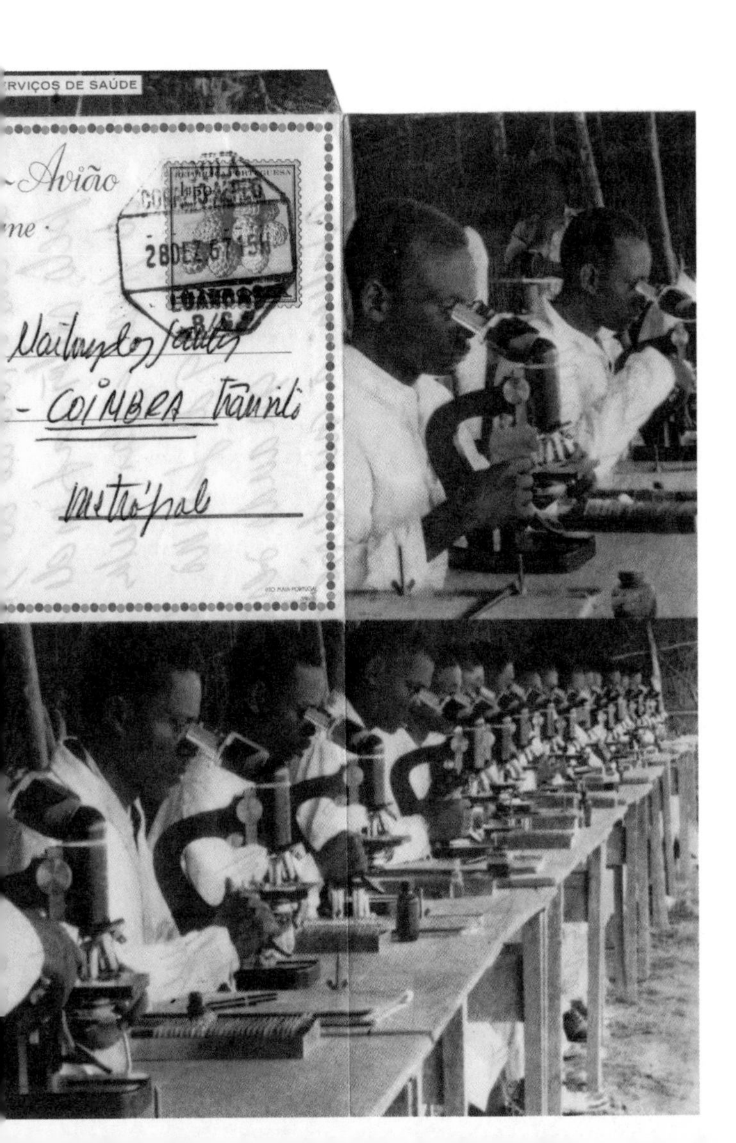
SERVIÇOS DE SAÚDE
Avião
REPÚBLICA PORTUGUESA
28DEZ.67
COIMBRA

MARK MANDERS

Page with Short Sentences, 2003.

/ Falling Earring / Staged Android / Silent Factory / Spain / Yellow Bathtub / Mark Manders / 1998 / Toilet with Reconstructed Nocturnal Garden Scene / Television Room with Vanishing Points / Expanded View / Notional Cupboard / Current Thoughts / Hallway with Sentences / 5 /
Room with Reduced Chair and Camouflaged Factory / Staged Reading Room / Writing Room / Fiction Machine / Isolated Landscape / Short Sad Thoughts / Reduced Rooms with Changing Arrest / Isolated Bathroom /
Self-portrait as a Building / China / Reduced Night Scene with One Beautiful Stone / Windy Saturday Drawing / Drawing with Vanishing Point / Drawing with Singing Sailors / Several Drawings on Top of Each Other / Silent Factory
Closet with Fives / Broom with Fives / Newspaper with Fives / Parallel Occurrence / A Place Where My Thoughts Are Frozen Together / Inhabited for a Survey / 82% Reduction of an Action that Probably Never Took Place Before /
Crumbled Tape / Landscape with the Sound of a Flag / Still-life with Broken Moments / Reduced Nightscene with Broken Moments / Dictated Drawings / Gathering of Mistakes /
Self-portrait in a Surrounding Area / Written Horror Vacui / Landscape with Countries / Landscape with Rain / 6 Self-portraits placed upon 5 Tables / Spit and Stare / Laptop on the Pavement / Kaleidoscope Night /
Reduced November Room / Kitchen / 1999 / Reduced Summer Garden Night Scene / Table with Paper Walls / One of the Various Contrivances by Which a Self-portrait is Fertilized by its Owner / Coloured Room with Black and White Scene /

Isolated Bathroom, 2003.

Page with Short Sentences, 2003.

/ Yellow Bathtub / Falling Earring / Staged Android / China /
Isolated Bathroom / Mark Manders / 5 / Silent Factory / 1999
/ 1998 / Toilet with Reconstructed Nocturnal Garden Scene /
Television Room with Vanishing Points / Expanded View / Hallway
with Sentences /
Room with Reduced Chair and Camouflaged Factory / Staged
Reading Room / Writing Room / Fiction Machine / Notional
Cupboard / Isolated Landscape / Reduced Rooms with Changing
Arrest / Drawing with Singing Sailors / Self-portrait as a Building /
Spain / Reduced Night Scene with One Beautiful Stone / Drawing
with Vanishing Point / Windy Saturday Drawing / Closet with Fives
/ Broom with Fives /
A Place Where My Thoughts Are Frozen Together / Inhabited for
a Survey / Parallel Occurrence / 82% Reduction of an Action that
Probably Never Took Place Before /
Crumbled Tape / Landscape with the Sound of a Flag / Current
Thoughts / Still-life with Broken Moments / Reduced Nightscene
with Broken Moments / Dictated Drawings / Short Sad Thoughts
/ Gathering of Mistakes / Self-portrait in a Surrounding Area /
Written Horror Vacui / Silent Factory
Reduced November Room / Kitchen / Reduced Summer Garden
Night Scene / Table with Paper Walls / One of the Various
Contrivances by Which a Self-portrait is Fertilized by its Owner /
Several Drawings on Top of Each Other / Coloured Room with
Black and White Scene /
Landscape with Countries / Landscape with Rain / 6 Self-portraits
placed upon 5 Tables / Spit and Stare / Laptop on the Pavement /
Newspaper with Fives / Kaleidoscope Night /

Toilet with Reconstructed Nocturnal Garden Scene, 2003.

MARC QUER

Algérie-France. Des papiers pour tous, 1998. Poster, mixed media.

Algérie-France. Vous nous devez 130 ans les français, 1998.
Poster, mixed media.

Algérie-France. Pas génial comme emplacement derrière les poubelles, 1998. Poster, mixed media.

Algérie-France, 1998. Poster, mixed media.

HITO STEYERL

November, 2004. DVD.

A picture of war is not war.

November

This is not a film about Kurdistan.

GILLIAN WEARING

Tedi, 2003. Production stills.

Work Towards World Peace, from *Signs That Say What You Want Them To Say. And Not Signs That Say What Someone Else Wants You To Say*. 1992/93. R-type color print.

The Political Situation In England Is Stable, from *Signs That Say What You Want Them To Say. And Not Signs That Say What Someone Else Wants You To Say*. 1992/93. R-type color print.

AMELIE VON WULFFEN

o.T. (Solschenizyn und handbemaltes Glasfläschchen), 2003.
Pencil and watercolor on paper, 50x73 cm.

o.T. (Doppelporträt Solschenizyn, Travolta), 2002-2003.
Pencil and watercolor on paper, 51x63 cm.

(overleaf) **Ohne Titel**, 2003. Photo, acrylic, ink on paper, 108x150 cm.

YEVGENIY YUFIT

Killed by Lightning, 2002. 35mm film.

DARIUS ŽIURA

Gustoniai, 2001. DVD.

KUBO KUTXA KURSAAL

CARLOS BUNGA

Untitled, 2002. Cardboard, adhesive tape and matte paint, 26x33x28 cm.

Untitled, 2002. Cardboard, adhesive tape, matte paint and plastic.

Projecto Serralves, 2003. Cardboard, adhesive tape, matte tape, light table and slides.

GEERT GOIRIS

Isle Of Skye, 2001. Lambdaprint, 100x129 cm.

(overleaf) **Rhino In Fog**, 2003. Lambdaprint, 100x129 cm.

LAURA HORELLI

Helsinki Shipyard/ Port San Juan, 2002-2003. Video Installation.

POOL BAR

Installation views at *Diner's Crew Lounge & Telephone Service*, San Juan.

Installation views at *Berlin North*, Hamburger Bahnhof.

ANU PENNANEN

From The Monument Project: A Monument For The Invisible / Windows, 2003. 16mm film transferred to DVD.

25

MICHAEL SAILSTORFER

3 Ster mit Ausblick, 2002.

Model (1:3.5) for **Breadboard Construction Marilyn.**

Drawings for **Breadboard Construction Marilyn.**

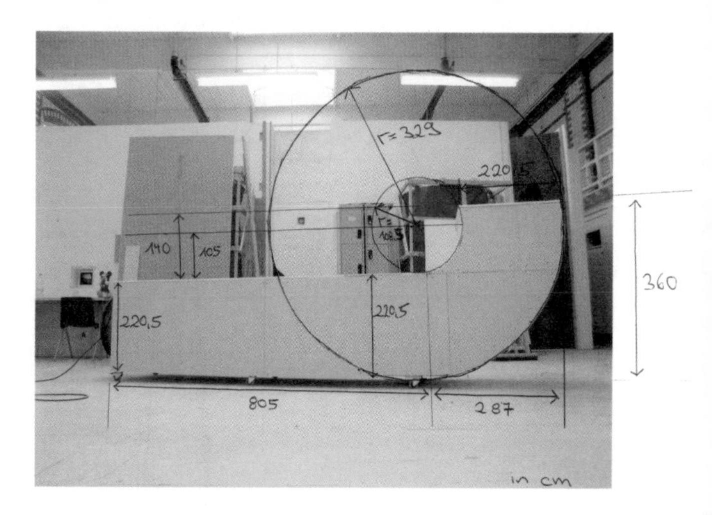

SILKE SCHATZ

Villa Torlonia 1661. Giardini Storici di Roma. Parco Pubblico dal 1978, 2003. Pencil and colour pencil on paper, 101.5 x 137 cm.

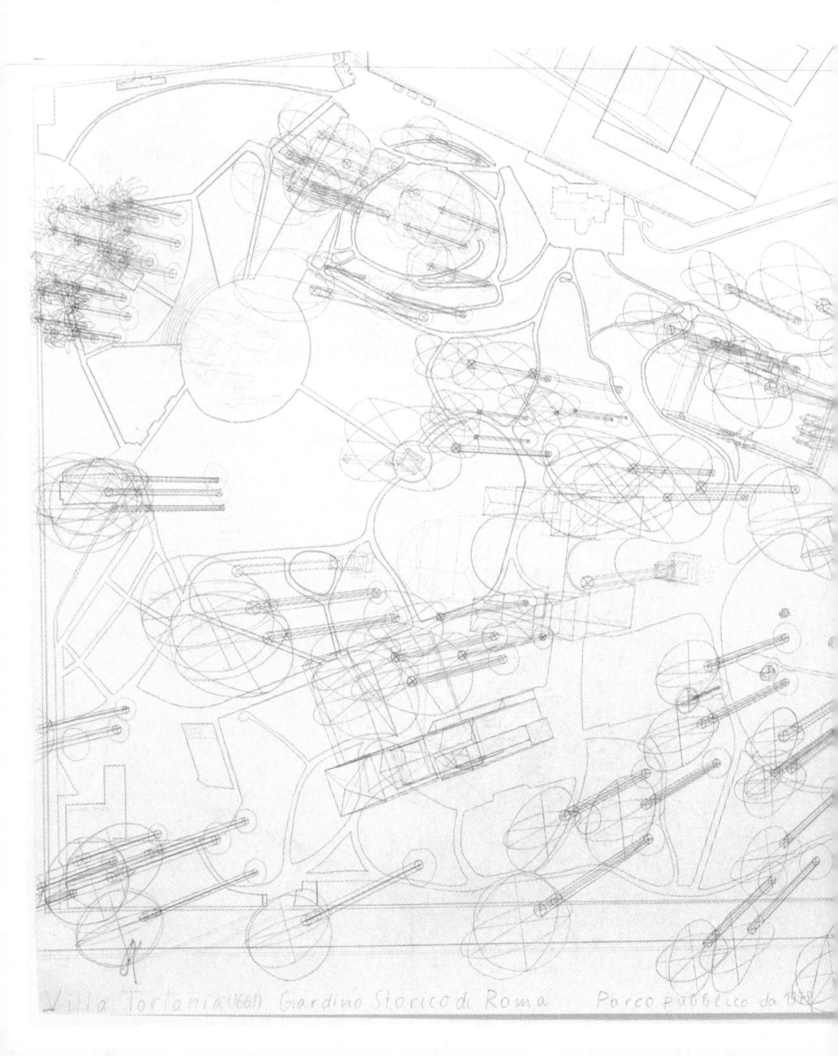

(overleaf) **Hotel Nicol´s San Sebastian**, 2004.
Photographs and newspaper cut-outs on cardboard.

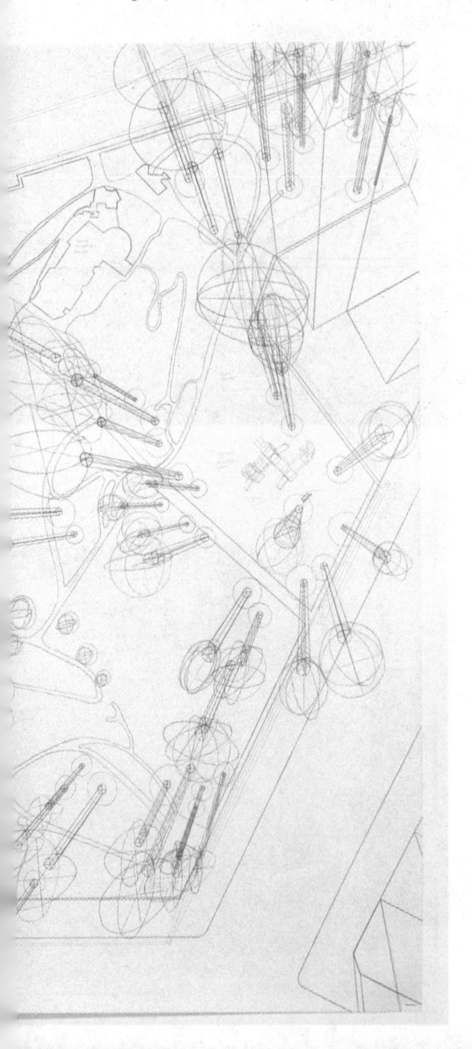

REEDOM FOR THE BASQUE

MARKUS SCHINWALD

Dictio Pii, 2001. 35mm film.

(overleaf) **Diarios (to you)**, 2003 160 slides transferred to DVD.

EYAL SIVAN AND MICHEL KHLEIFI

Route 181, 2003. DVcam.

עצור! גבול לפניך!
STOP! BORDER
IN FRONT OF YOU!
قف! الحدود امامك!
CLIFF HOTEL

VANGELIS VLAHOS

Athens Skyline. View from the top of the Lycabethus hill to the north.

What makes a building a building to remember? Athens Tower (103mt). The tower was the tallest building of the Balkans and Southeastern Europe at the time of its completion (1971). Architect: Ioannis Vikelas.

Georgios Papadopoulos, Greek military officer and political figure, dictator of Greece (1967-1973).

Athens Tower, 2004. Cardboard model.

WEIGHT WATCHERS

ΕΘΕΜΕΛΙΩΣΕ
Γ ΠΑΠΑΔΟΠΟΥΛΟΣ

SOTO

GARRETT PHELAN

Now: Here, 2003. Permanent marker drawing.

Upper Regions
of Consciousness
HEAVENS
GOODS
WORLD OF SPIRITS
FALLACIES
EVILS
HELLS
BATTERY

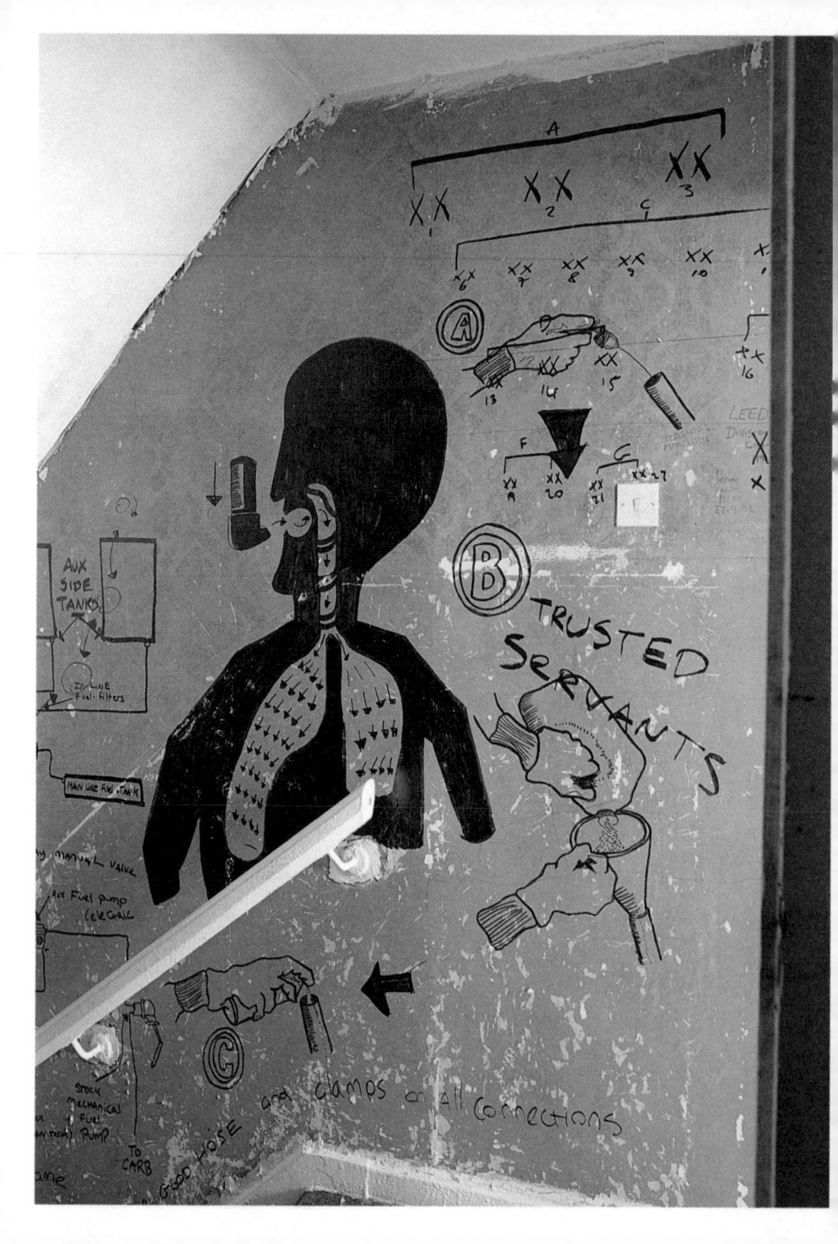
A
B
TRUSTED
SERVANTS
C
AUX
SIDE
TANKS
IN-LINE
Fuel Filters
MAIN LINE FUEL TANK
MANUAL Valve
AUX Fuel pump
Stock
Mechanical
Fuel
PUMP
TO
CARB
GOOD HOSE and clamps on All Connections

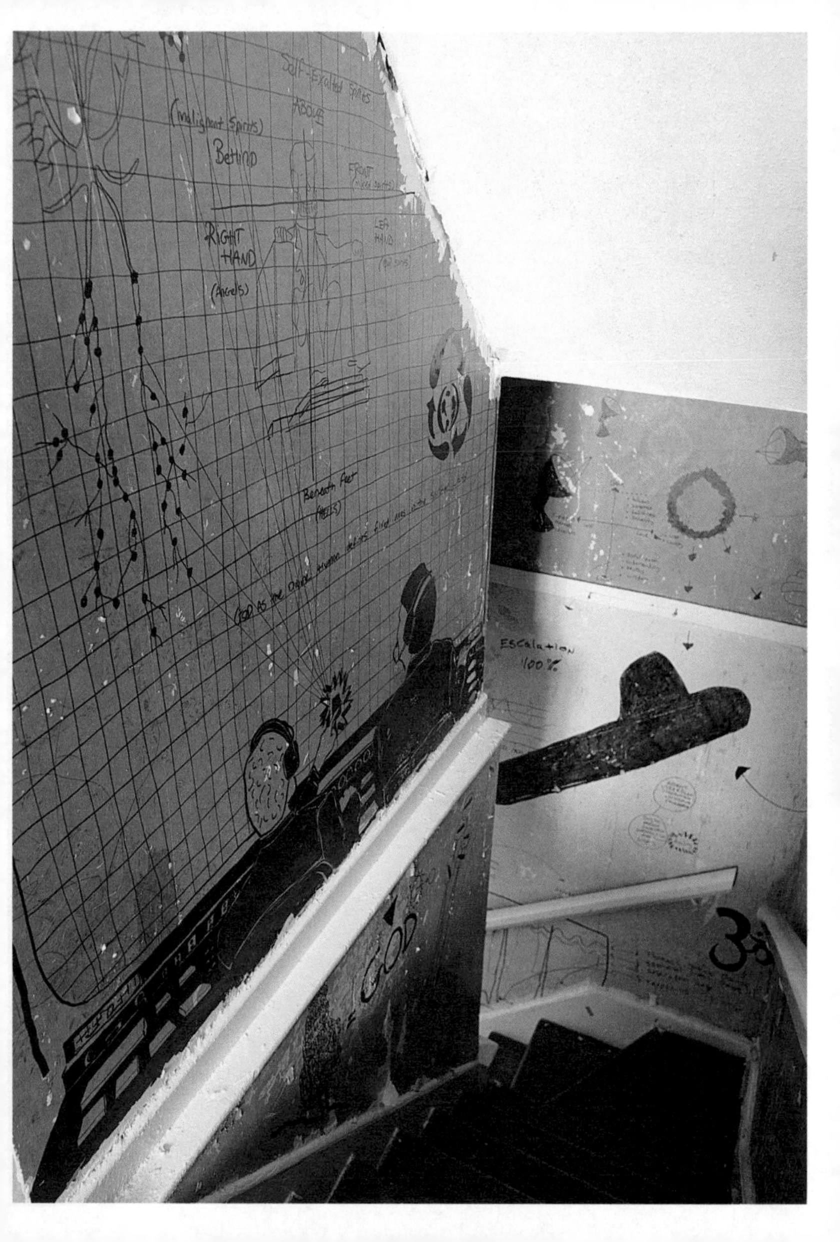
Self-Exalted Spirits
ABOVE
(Malignant Spirits)
BEHIND
FRONT
RIGHT HAND
(Angels)
LEFT HAND
Beneath Feet
(HELLS)
Escalation
100%
GOD

ON THE ROAD

JEREMY DELLER

Tony Blair Mask J-18 Demonstration, London, 2000.
Still from DVD **"Folk Archive"** 2000.

(right) **Memory Bucket**, 2003. Digital prints on paper. 22 photographs, 22x34 cm each.

(overleaf) **Straw Bear Festival**, Cambridgeshire (UK), 2004.
Still from DVD **"Folk Archive"** 2000.

FAMOUS ARTISTS

LEOPOLD KESSLER

Privatised, 2003.
Intervention in Paris.

Do Not Swim - Danger Of Life, 2003.
Intervention in Munich.

MAT'S
HEISSER PFERDELEBERKÄSE

MAT'S

Uncovered, 2002. Intervention in Vienna.
Alarm clock, 2002. Intervention in Amsterdam.
Trashbins, 2004. Intervention in Vienna.

PATRICK TUTTOFUOCO

Velodream, 2001. 10 vehicles, mixed media.

WalkAround, 2002. 10 parts, mixed media.

(overleaf) **BMX-Y project**, 2004.

TRINTXERPE –
TOPO DE LA HERRERA

HÜSEYIN ALPTEKIN

PESCADOS

HOSTAL

CASA CIRIZA

MICOL ASSAËL

Sleeplessness, 2004. Electrical outlets, smoke, windows, ice, compressors. Environment dimensions.

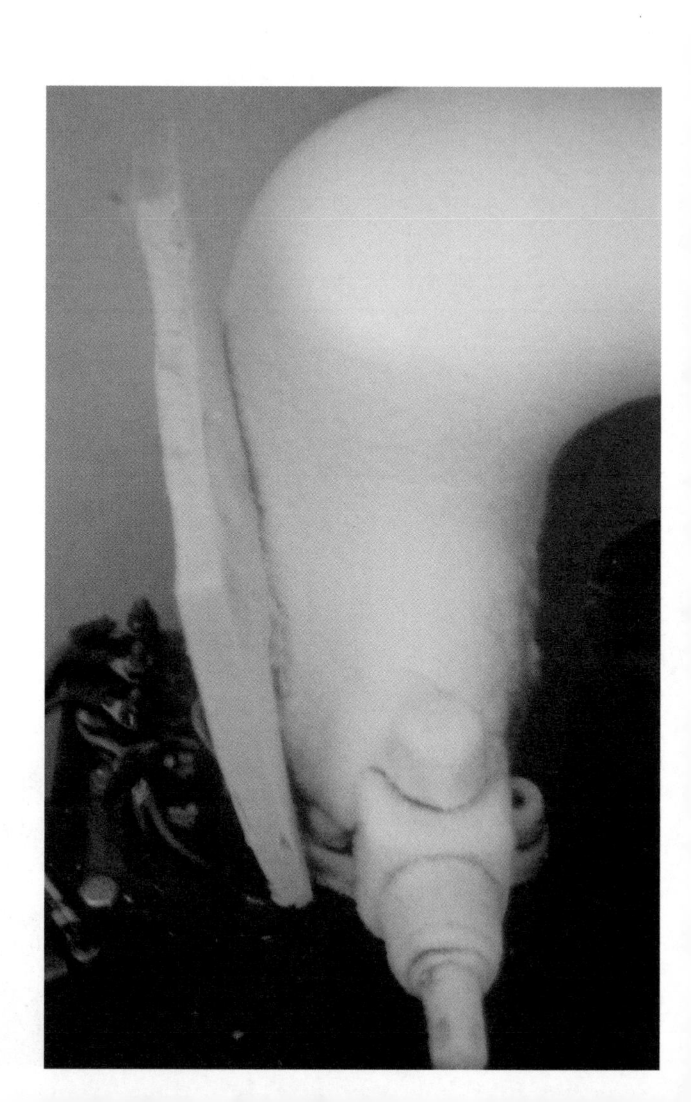

ZBYNĚK BALADRÁN

Carousal, 2003. Archival footage, 8mm black and white film.

Tunnels, 2003. Archival footage, 8mm black and white film.

Now, 2003. Archival footage, 16mm black and white film.

End, 2003. Archival footage, 16mm black and white film.

MARCEL BROODTHAERS

Bateau Tableau (Detail), 1973. 35mm slides.

DUNCAN CAMPBELL

Falls Burns Malone Fiddles, 2003. Slides transferred to DVD.

ISOLATE

ENEMY

ILIYA CHICHKAN AND KYRILL PROTSENKO

Spies Eyes, 2003. Archival footage, 16mm black and white film.

ANGELA DE LA CRUZ

Studio in Progress, 2004.

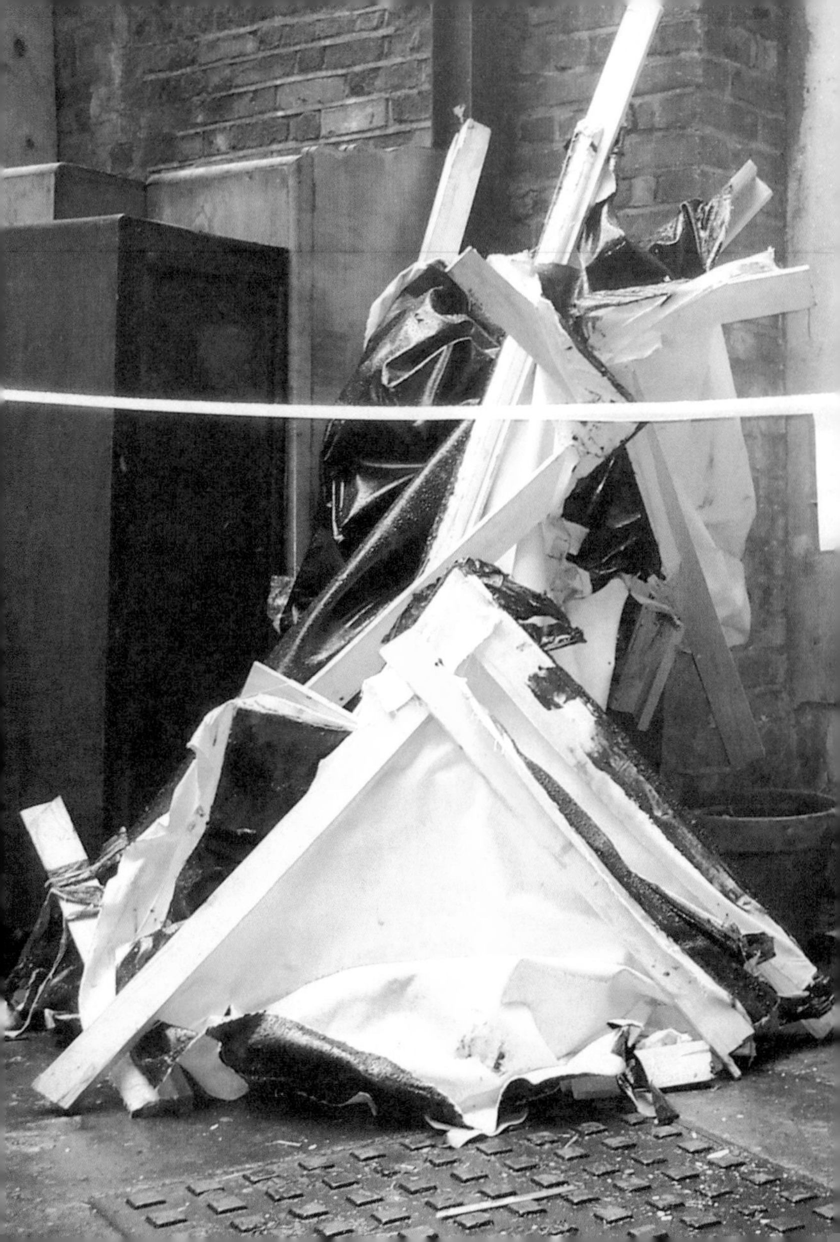

RT WORK
O NOT
REMOVE

D.A.E. DONOSTIAKO ARTE EKINBIDEAK

Operación H, 1963. 35mm film.

Is this the original montage? (...)

The seats are by Oiza, the architecture is by Oiza. (...)

I have been correcting as I go, it's been 41 years, I found the beginning a little disappointing, I would have cut the travelling. Now I know more than I did in the past, I am more self-critical. (...)

I thought the image of the children running closed the film, I remembered this last shot in colour, they were running through a field of poppies —beautiful!— but instead there are some soft-focus shots, which I also like, but I didn't remember the end that way. (...)

The making of a film is a complex action and it needs everyone involved, in equal measure, it is a team venture because each person takes care of one area. It could also be said that there are two possible dimensions in relation to the artistic creation in the form of cinema, the first has to do with what you want to say and the other with the idea you have of the medium: in other words, film as a tool to arrive at what you're trying to say. These are the two dimensions I am referring to, one of them that of the medium itself and the other something that we inaugurate only once in a lifetime. (...)

Excerpts from a conversation with Néstor Basterretxea, 2004.

Film ideal siempre

Una propuesta de D.A.E. Donostiako Arte Ekinbideak.
Por Peio Aguirre y Leire Vergara
en colaboración con Xabier Salaberria y Gorka Eizagirre.

PROYECTA:

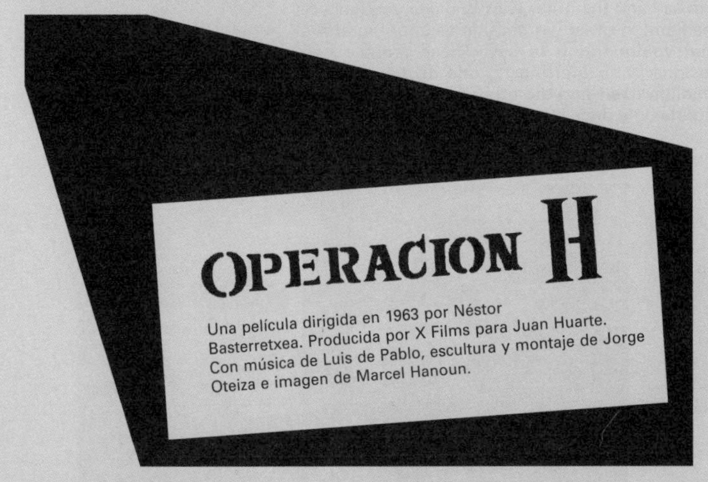

IÑAKI GARMENDIA

KIM HIORTHØY

EVERYTHING
YOU
THOUGHT
WOULD
HAPPEN
WILL
NEVER
HAPPEN

MARK LECKEY

Fiorucci Made Me Hardcore, 1999. DVD.

40:38:01

ASIER MENDIZABAL

Azpeitia
Ordizia

Eibar
Zarautz
Lazkao

P
SS-
PEUGEOT

Azkoitia
Elgoibar
Eibar

Urretxo
Orio
Ordizia

BORIS MIKHAILOV

Dvoyky, 1970s-early 80s. Black and white photographs.

ПРОДУКТ

OKSANA PASAIKO

(overleaf) **Please Don't Leave Me, (A Re-enactment)**, 2004.

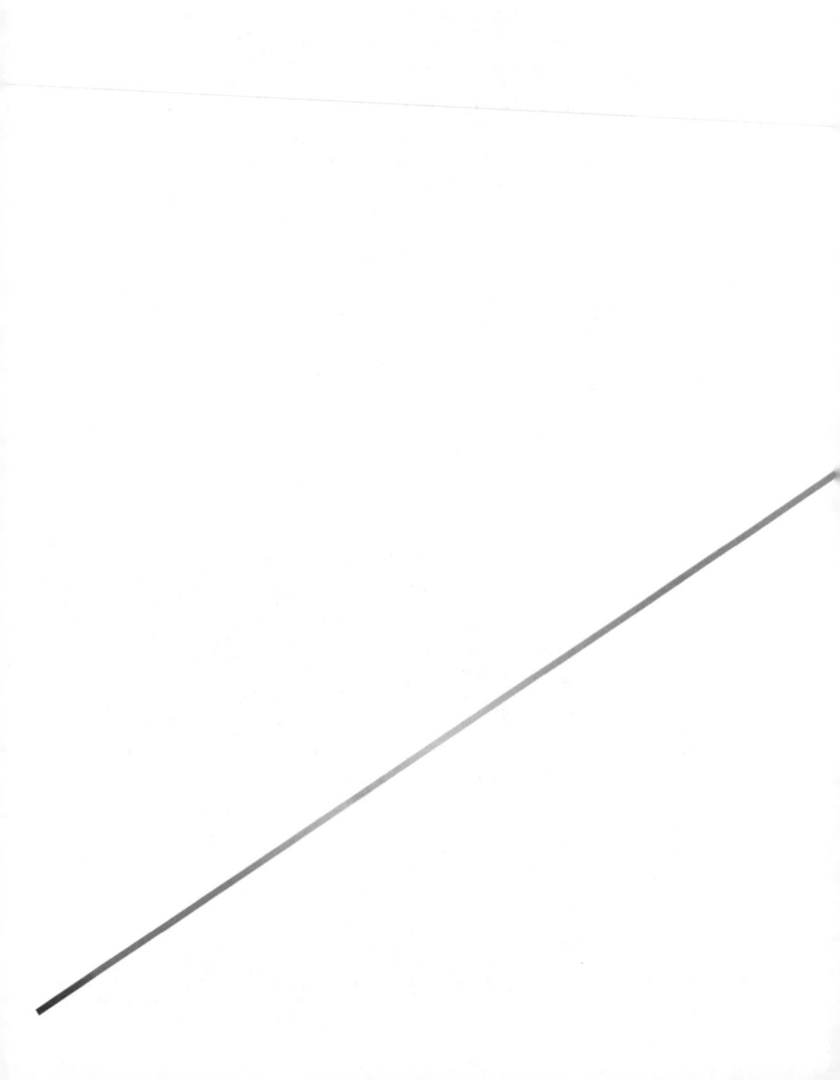

БУДЬ

НЕ

КИДАЙ

ЛАСКА

МЕНЕ

KIRSTEN PIEROTH

Edison's Workbench, 2003.

invent [in'vent] ***v.t.*** **1.** create or design (sth. not existing before): *When was the steam engine ~ed?* (Cf. *discover*, find sth. existing before, but unknown) 2. make up, think of: *~a story (an excuse)*.
inventor ***n***. person who ~s things.
inventive [in'ventiv] ***adj***. able to ~: *an ~ive mind, ~ive powers*.
invention [in'venʃən] ***n***. **1**. [U] inventing: *the ~ of the telephone*; capacity for inventing: *Necessity is the mother of ~*. **2**. [C] sth. invented: *the numerous ~s of Edison; newspaper that are full of ~s (invented, untrue stories)*.

(from *The Advanced Learners Dictionary of Current English*)

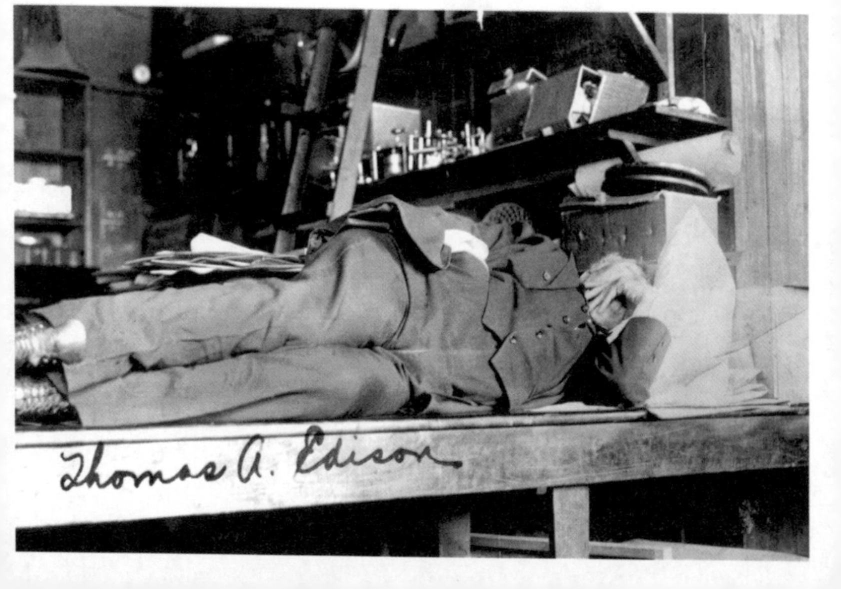
Thomas A. Edison

Thomas G. Edison

PAOLA PIVI

Untitled (Slope), 2003. Grass, wood, scaffolding, 4.7x12.5x7 m

Untitled (Zebras), 2003. Color photograph, 140x178 cm.

E, 2001. Steel, aluminium, motors, photoelectric switches, 267x300 cm.

E, 2001. Detail.

CONRAD SHAWCROSS

Circadium, 2004. Sketches. (overleaf) Mock up.

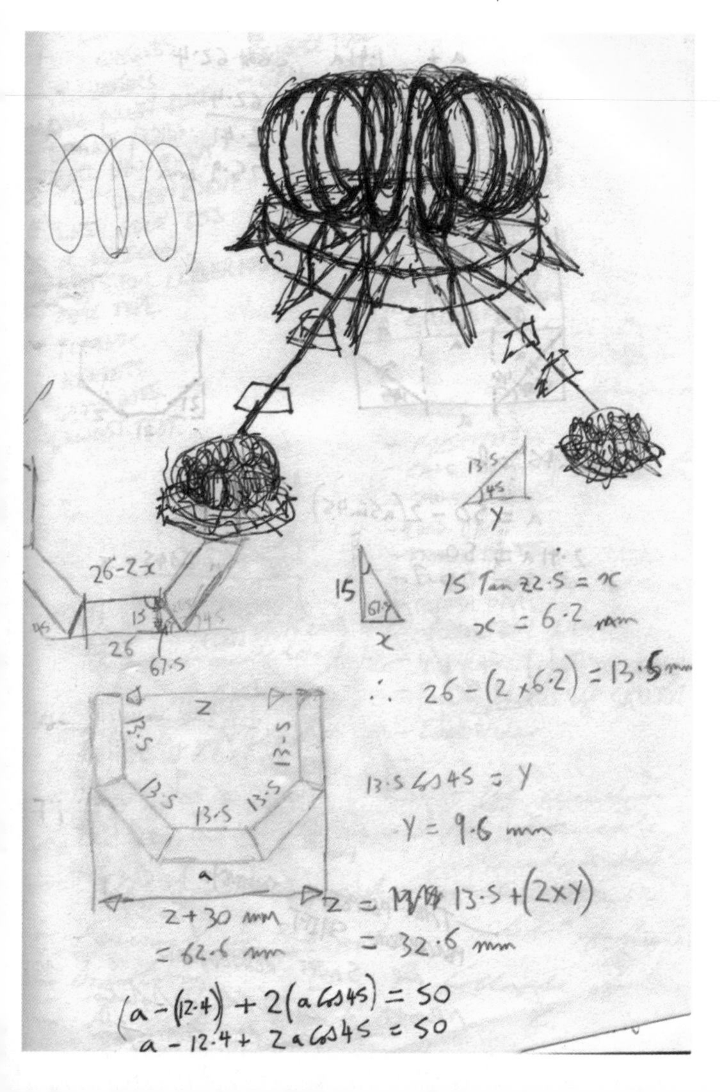

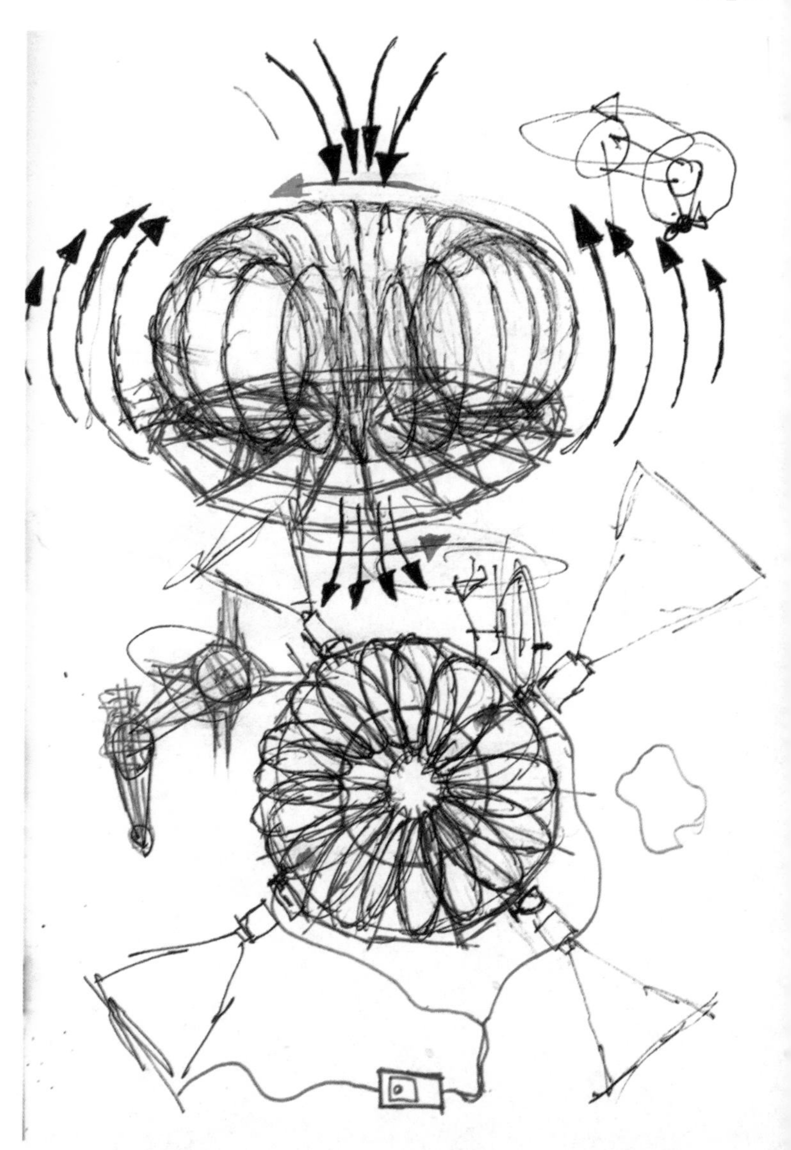

OLIVIER ZABAT

1/3 des yeux - Miguel et les mines. Second part, 2004. Video DV.

(overleaf) **Photo de famille avec missiles**, 2001. 100x150 cm
Color photograph.

DAVID ZINK YI

La Cumbia, 1999. DVD.

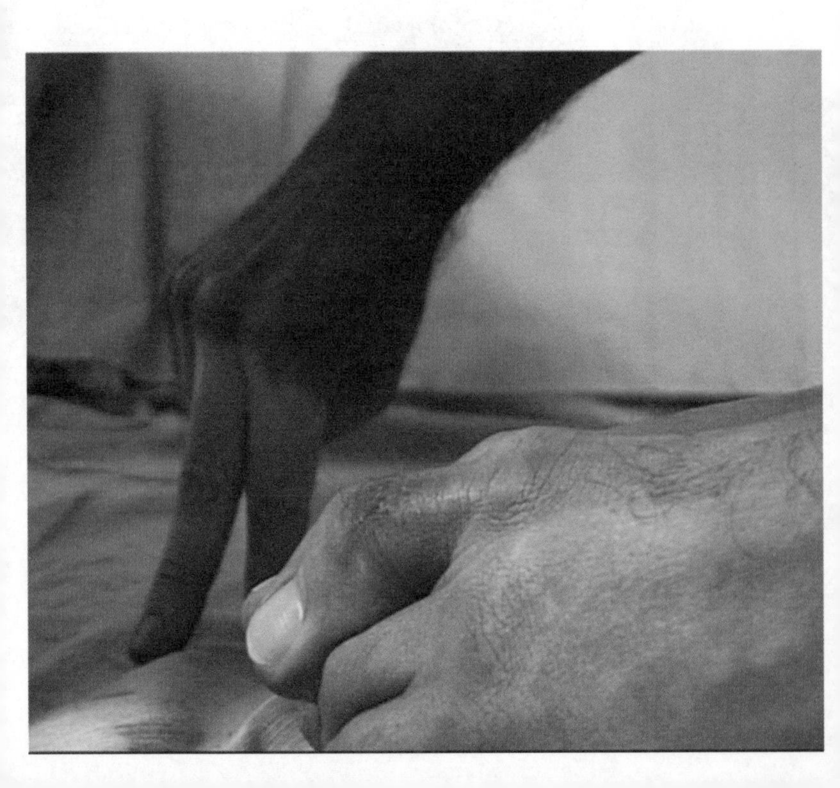

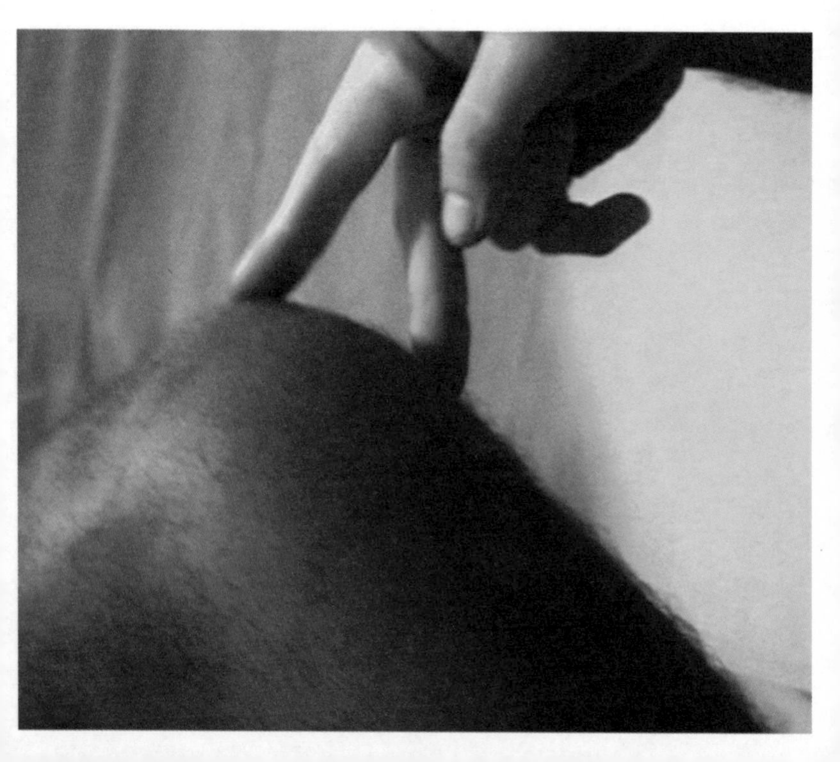

ONDARTXO

JAN DE COCK

Denkmal 2 Astillero Ascorreta 2, Pasajes San Pedro, San Sebastian 2004

10:35:59 pm

MODULE XLVIII

10:36:00 pm

10:36:01 pm

10:36:02 pm

5

the berlage institute - manifesta 5 collaboration

Alejandro Zaera-Polo
Dean, Berlage Institute

The following material was produced as an institutional collaboration between the Berlage Institute in Rotterdam and Manifesta 5, in what I expect to become a model for future practices in architecture and urban design. This collaboration was first initiated by the curators of the Manifesta 5 event in San Sebastian, who were looking for a partnership that would enable this edition of Manifesta to explore the city as a domain of investigation that has now become central to artistic practices. As always, artists would become again the pioneers in discovering the next field of potential: the city. This proposition from Marta Kuzma and Massimiliano Gioni immediately entered into resonance with our own interests at the Berlage Institute.

The city has become today a crucial subject in our civilisation, as both a cultural and an economic device, and remains a subject much in need of a theoretical, speculative revision. No wonder that artists, politicians and philosophers, and not only architects and urban planners, are now deeply engaged in the debate about the city, of which the whole Manifesta series and Manifesta 5 in particular are a clear example.

As an institution, the Berlage Institute occupies a particular position between education and research, between culture and discipline, between theory and practice. It is precisely the singularity of this ambiguous, mediating position that constitutes its biggest potential to develop alternatives to the conventional educational and research models in the discipline of architecture – and in this sense it is an ideal vehicle for Manifesta 5 to engage directly with the practices of architecture and urban planning. But Manifesta 5 was also an ideal vehicle for the Berlage Institute to explore the potentials of direct engagement with real ongoing processes of urban transformation, to become a true laboratory of urban processes instead of just another star-struck academic institution. Our involvement in Manifesta 5 is a step forward in constructing a role that we believe will become increasingly necessary as the processes of urban transformation become more substantial and more critical, as key devices of the synthesis of contemporary cultures and economies: the Urban Mediator.

The Urban Mediator is a figure that does not exist within the usual processes of urban development, which are commonly ruled by a rather limited system of political-economic decision making and in the developed world have become increasingly normative and sclerotic in terms of their ability to produce a more supple and generative integration between the different agents involved in the subject of urban development. As the social and economic effects of these developments become more important, and the mechanisms become more complex, a space of practice is emerging that does not quite fit with the conventional roles of the master planner, the project manager, the architect or the public consultation expert, but lies somewhere in between; a space whose role it is difficult to define in the usual contractual figures.

This is the space that we have tried to occupy with The Office of Alternative Urban Planning (TOOAUP) through this collaboration with Manifesta 5. TOOAUP has been operating in Pasaia in a space where no conventional commissioning process is yet possible, since the structure of decision-making, financing, etc. is too complex to become operative. Pasaia is a location of ravishing beauty and enormous potential, given its proximity to Donosti. However, its development has been hampered by the differences between the three tiers of municipal administration involved: the city of Donosti, the Regional Government, and the National Government as stakeholders of the Port Authority.

TOOAUP has aimed at developing a platform for discussion and engagement between the different forces at play that may serve to unlock the potential oppositions and dialectics between these forces through the development of alternative formats of urban intervention, to be tested for the Manifesta 5 event in a specific installation in Casa Ciriza.

The initial working hypothesis of TOOAUP is based on the notion that a master plan is not adequate in the current situation, going on to replace this with research into prototypical conditions aimed at setting up multiple and simultaneous scales of interventions to become devices of negotiation between the apparently opposing concerns and desires of the stakeholders. This process could be locally implemented, multilaterally or unilaterally, but will always sustain a collective intelligence that allows the prototypes to proliferate beyond the administrative control of any particular agent.

It remains to be seen whether the outcome will be implemented and to what extent: Manifesta 5 is only the first step, the facilitator, for TOOAUP to emerge. After September 2004, when Manifesta 5 is concluded, we cannot say whether TOOAUP will have a future life beyond this experiment. But what is perfectly clear to me is that this collaboration between the Berlage Institute and Manifesta has inaugurated a model for our Institute to become engaged in similar situations around the world, and perhaps for similar institutions to follow.

I would like to thank all of the local institutions in general and their departments — Basque Government, Diputación Foral de Gipuzkoa (Ordenacion del Territorio and Departamento de Cultura), Ayuntamiento de Donostia-San Sebastián (Oficina del Plan General and Plan Estratégico), Ayuntamiento de Pasaia (Departamento de Urbanismo), Oarsoaldea and Autoridad Portuaria de Pasaia — for the receptivity and the support with which they have embraced this exciting project.

SAN SEBASTIAN
TOURISTIC
HIGH INCOME
MARKETED
MANIFESTA 5
PASAJES BAY
INDUSTRIAL
LOW INCOME
OVERSIGHTED
PASAJES SAN JUAN
ONDARTXO
PASAJES SAN PEDRO
PORT AUTHORITY
SAN TELMO
CASA CIRIZA
KURSAAL
3KM
KOLDO MITXELENA
LEZO
PASAJES ANTXO
ARTELEKU
ERRENTERIA

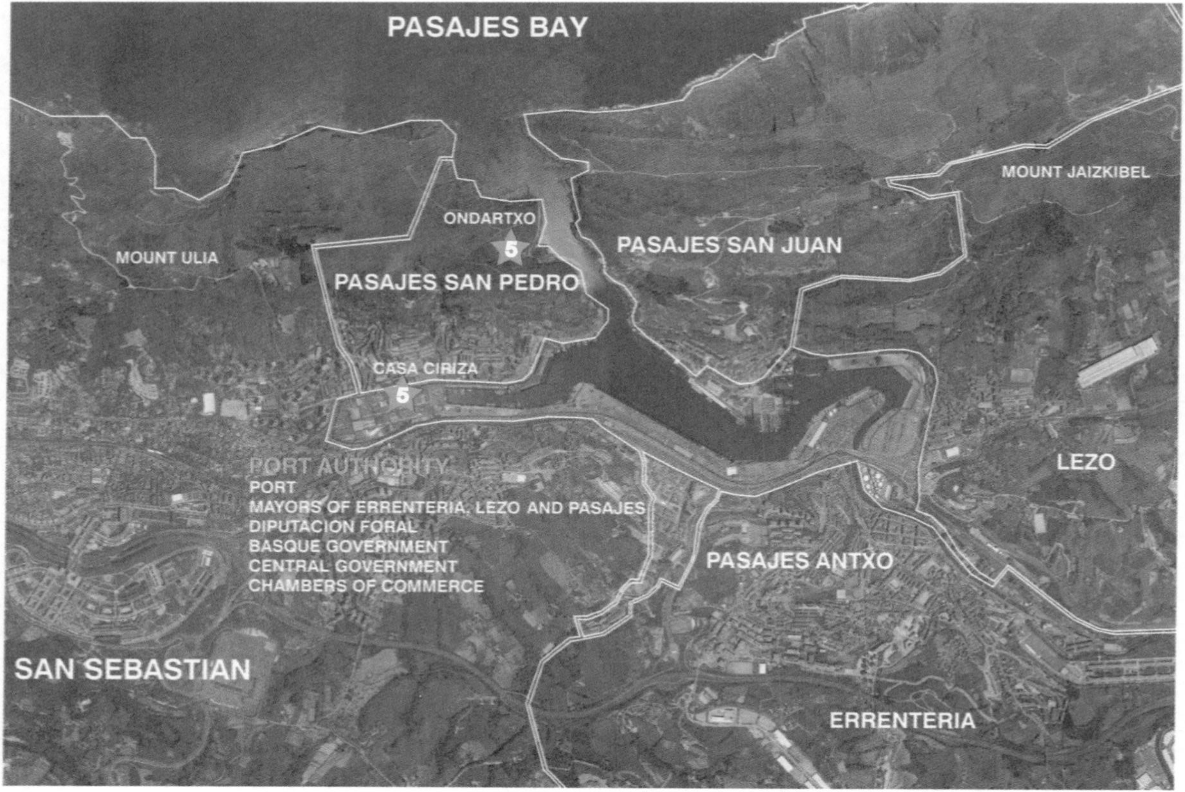

PASAJES BAY

MOUNT JAIZKIBEL

ONDARTXO

5

PASAJES SAN JUAN

MOUNT ULIA

PASAJES SAN PEDRO

CASA CIRIZA

5

PORT AUTHORITY

PORT

MAYORS OF ERRENTERIA, LEZO AND PASAJES

DIPUTACION FORAL

BASQUE GOVERNMENT

CENTRAL GOVERNMENT

CHAMBERS OF COMMERCE

LEZO

PASAJES ANTXO

SAN SEBASTIAN

ERRENTERIA

THE BERLAGE INSTITUTE
IN COLLABORATION WITH MANIFESTA 5

2003 - 2004 Rotterdam / San Sebastián

THE OFFICE OF ALTERNATIVE URBAN PLANNING

Director-Studio Professor: Sebastián Khourian
Consulting Professors: Bernard Cache, Anna Pla Català
Assistants: José Arnaud, Juan Pablo Porta
Berlage Participants: Verónica Arcos, Sannah Belzer, Constanze Hirt, Claudia Strahl, Mónica Villate
Berlage Staff: Alejandro Zaera-Polo + Vedran Mimica
M5 Curators: Marta Kuzma + Massimiliano Gioni

CREATIVE MEDIATION

Performed and written by Sebastián Khourian

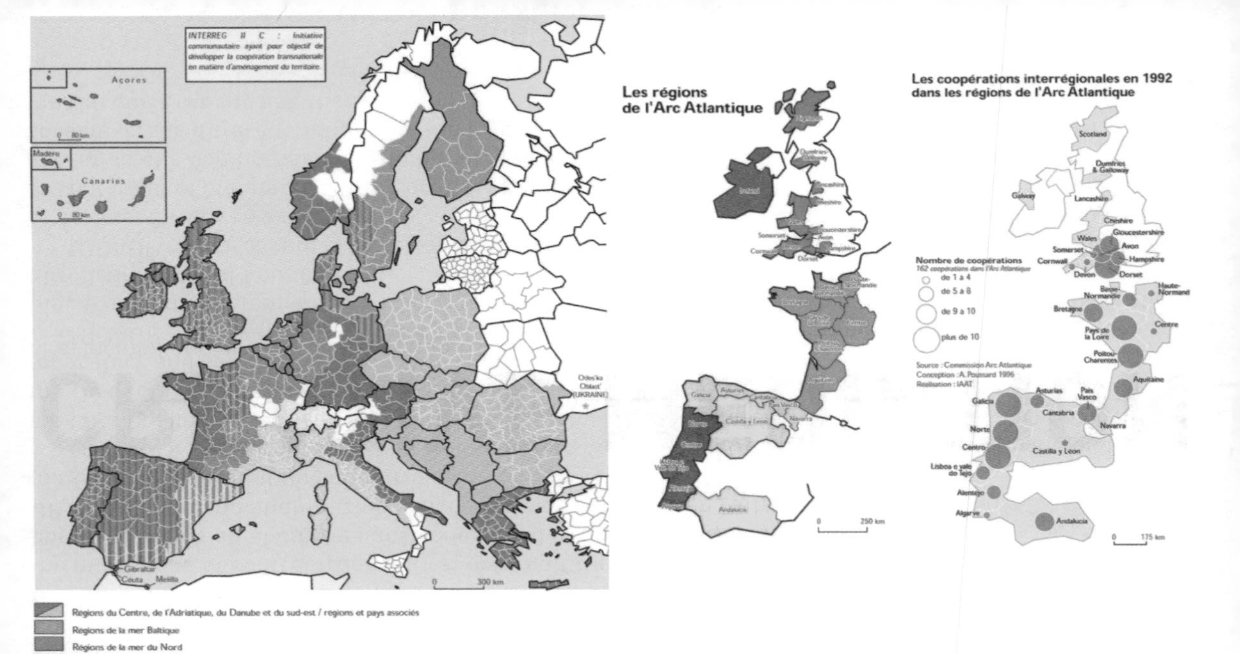
INTERREG II C : Initiative communautaire ayant pour objectif de développer la coopération transnationale en matière d'aménagement du territoire.
Açores
Madère
Canaries
0 80 km
Odes'ka Oblast' (UKRAINE)
Gibraltar
Ceuta
Melilla
0 300 km
Régions du Centre, de l'Adriatique, du Danube et du sud-est / régions et pays associés
Régions de la mer Baltique
Régions de la mer du Nord
Régions métropolitaines de l'Europe du nord
Régions atlantiques / région associée
Régions du sud-ouest européen et de la diagonale continentale
Régions des Alpes latines et de la Méditerranée occidentale / régions et pays associés
Les régions de l'Arc Atlantique
Ireland
Somerset
Cornwall
Dorset
Galicia
Asturias
Cantabria
País Vasco
Navarra
Castilla y León
Norte
Centro
Andalucía
0 250 km
Les coopérations interrégionales en 1992 dans les régions de l'Arc Atlantique
Scotland
Dumfries & Galloway
Galway
Lancashire
Cheshire
Wales
Gloucestershire
Somerset
Avon
Cornwall
Hampshire
Devon
Dorset
Basse-Normandie
Haute-Normand
Bretagne
Pays de la Loire
Centre
Poitou-Charentes
Aquitaine
Asturias
País Vasco
Galicia
Cantabria
Navarra
Norte
Centro
Castilla y León
Lisboa e vale do Tejo
Alentejo
Algarve
Andalucia
Nombre de coopérations
162 coopérations dans l'Arc Atlantique
de 1 à 4
de 5 à 8
de 9 à 10
plus de 10
Source : Commission Arc Atlantique
Conception : A. Poussard 1996
Réalisation : IAAT
0 175 km

TOOAUP

Sometimes naming becomes interesting when it is a given and an uncomfortable enough fact witch demarcates everything you would like to challenge-constitute with practice.

TO a crew of foreign nationals, the practice of exile.

OA rather than operating as an other, under the paradigm of openness, this practice is interested in the migrations of control from central or a multitude of opposing agents towards a distributed field of operations. It is all about responsiveness and not necessarily about progress.

UP discredited and stigmatizing space-based practice, often rather opposed to the time-based multiplicity of oscillating collective systems.

The Office of Alternative Urban Planning was launched on October 30th, 2003 to activate and mediate the process of Manifesta 5. At the initiative of the Manifesta 5 curators in cooperation with the Dean of the Berlage Institute, Alejandro Zaera-Polo, TOOAUP is part of Berlage's postgraduate laboratory and reflects the broader curatorial initiative of the biennial.

TOOAUP has the financial and logistic support of the Basque Government, Diputación Foral de Gipuzkoa and Ayuntamiento de Donostia-San Sebastian, and has also been awarded a grant from the European Cultural Foundation.

TOOAUP research and practice aims at exploring the dynamic between urban organizations and trans-European events. In this current collaboration field of production and relevance, it is in the potential of Manifesta 5, the European Biennial of Contemporary Art, to operate as a territorial operation of a compressed duration that is to be held simultaneously in several locations that are spread across different administrative jurisdictions in the particular context of: the Atlantic arc, the Basque Eurocity and the San Sebastian–Pasajes corridor.

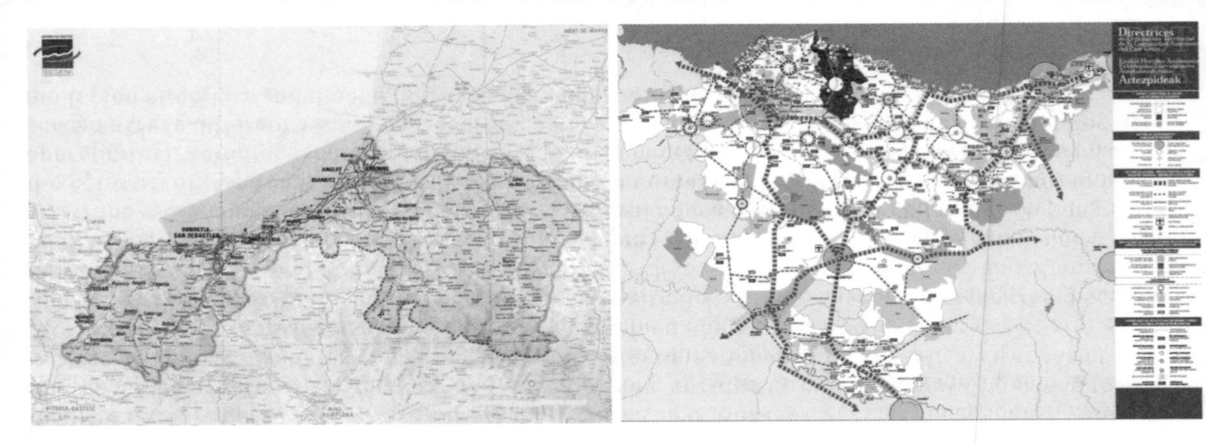

TOOAUP inserts its research and practice in collaboration with Manifesta 5 as a territorial operation into the current urban inertias and dynamics, and by doing so aims at establishing urban mediation as a mode of operation between the stakeholders' opposing concerns, which tend to paralyze the necessary urban regeneration process and initiatives. TOOAUP also aims at triggering debate and implementing projects that are anticipatory in the frame of groundbreaking collective micro-agreements between local agents.

Rather than submitting to the logics in the process of determination of solutions presented as An Exemplary Idea, this practice is more concerned with the development of protocols, techniques, procedures and tools for negotiation as the instrumentality for the engineering of problems and material organizations.

The ambiguity of the relationship between problem and solution — in other words, the degree and kind of continuity between function and form, the mediation between the causes and the effects in a process of determination, or the complex correspondence between the performance and a material organization — constructs a gap that allows for the emergence of a multitude of affiliations and for the management of several levels of production. This ambiguity can become the source of a potential when integrated into a multiplicity of urban and social processes: it allows for a flexible and agile attitude because it is itself the process... rather than being its critique.

However, it is also the channel to the rapid exhaustion of the capabilities and virtualities of an organization and in a project: it could close the possibility of its progressive enrichment.
If its ambiguity is too relaxed, the project can be reduced to a blind set of 'unnecessary' techniques; if it is too tight, the project is reduced to crystallized, dead 'ideas': A diagrammatic hypertrophy in the first case, a representational hypertrophy in the second. Because a project keeps itself alive not only by increasing its technical and material complexity, but also through its agility in turning this increasing complexity in its favour, as a source of potentials. Knowledge, the self-awareness of a project, has to grow as the project grows, without turning itself into a load.
For TOOAUP, architecture is not the byproduct of a multiplicity of processes, but rather the discipline that mediates all those processes. In this sense, TOOAUP's practice has challenged and alienated academia out of its self-indulgent simulacra, and tried to steer it towards the construction of exchange value internal to a new breed of architectural operativity. Also the collaboration has made it clear that this kind of practice tends to constitute an excess of firepower, which was ready to be appropriated, deviated, subsumed and potentiated from the specificity of the other practices involved. Not entirely to our surprise the managerial camp and the political strata were the ones that had been entangled directly or immanently or were in some way surfing the opportunity.

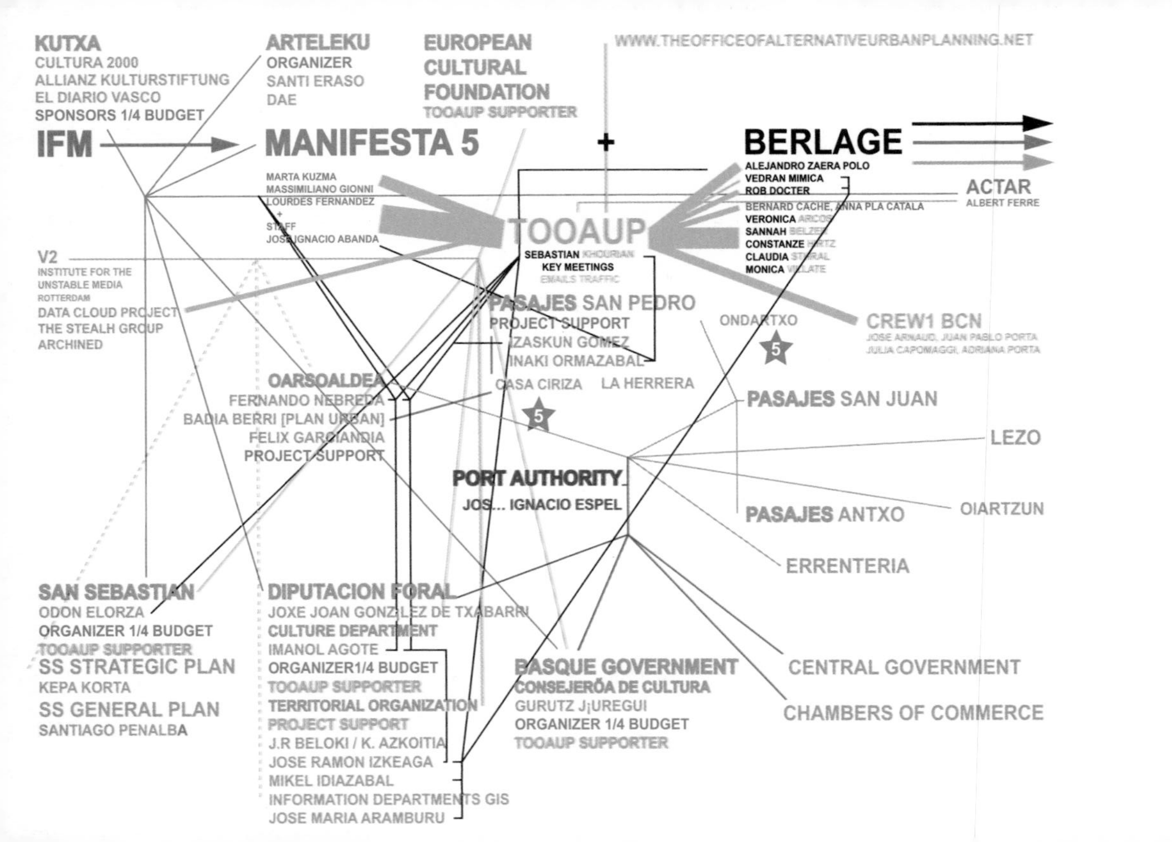

KUTXA
CULTURA 2000
ALLIANZ KULTURSTIFTUNG
EL DIARIO VASCO
SPONSORS 1/4 BUDGET
IFM
ARTELEKU
ORGANIZER
SANTI ERASO
DAE
MANIFESTA 5
MARTA KUZMA
MASSIMILIANO GIONNI
LOURDES FERNANDEZ
+
STAFF
JOSE IGNACIO ABANDA
EUROPEAN
CULTURAL
FOUNDATION
TOOAUP SUPPORTER
+
WWW.THEOFFICEOFALTERNATIVEURBANPLANNING.NET
BERLAGE
ALEJANDRO ZAERA POLO
VEDRAN MIMICA
ROB DOCTER
BERNARD CACHE, ANNA PLA CATALA
VERONICA ARCOS
SANNAH BELZER
CONSTANZE HERTZ
CLAUDIA STHRAL
MONICA VILLATE
ACTAR
ALBERT FERRE
TOOAUP
SEBASTIAN KHOURIAN
KEY MEETINGS
EMAILS TRAFFIC
V2
INSTITUTE FOR THE
UNSTABLE MEDIA
ROTTERDAM
DATA CLOUD PROJECT
THE STEALH GROUP
ARCHINED
PASAJES SAN PEDRO
PROJECT SUPPORT
IZASKUN GOMEZ
INAKI ORMAZABAL
ONDARTXO
CREW1 BCN
JOSE ARNAUD, JUAN PABLO PORTA
JULIA CAPOMAGGI, ADRIANA PORTA
5
OARSOALDEA
FERNANDO NEBREDA
BADIA BERRI [PLAN URBAN]
FELIX GARCIANDIA
PROJECT SUPPORT
CASA CIRIZA
LA HERRERA
5
PASAJES SAN JUAN
LEZO
PORT AUTHORITY
JOS... IGNACIO ESPEL
PASAJES ANTXO
OIARTZUN
ERRENTERIA
SAN SEBASTIAN
ODON ELORZA
ORGANIZER 1/4 BUDGET
TOOAUP SUPPORTER
SS STRATEGIC PLAN
KEPA KORTA
SS GENERAL PLAN
SANTIAGO PENALBA
DIPUTACION FORAL
JOXE JOAN GONZALEZ DE TXABARRI
CULTURE DEPARTMENT
IMANOL AGOTE
ORGANIZER1/4 BUDGET
TOOAUP SUPPORTER
TERRITORIAL ORGANIZATION
PROJECT SUPPORT
J.R BELOKI / K. AZKOITIA
JOSE RAMON IZKEAGA
MIKEL IDIAZABAL
INFORMATION DEPARTMENTS GIS
JOSE MARIA ARAMBURU
BASQUE GOVERNMENT
CONSEJERÕA DE CULTURA
GURUTZ J¡UREGUI
ORGANIZER 1/4 BUDGET
TOOAUP SUPPORTER
CENTRAL GOVERNMENT
CHAMBERS OF COMMERCE

MILIEU

TOOAUP as an instrument attempts to transcend the administrative bottlenecks in place at present between San Sebastian and neighboring Pasaia taking into consideration that Pasaia, as a port overseen by the authority of Madrid, is a town in its own right interested in urban regeneration through economic diversification. The polarity between Donostia-San Sebastian, with the highest per capita income in Gipuzkoa, and neighboring Pasaia, with the lowest, finds correlations in their geographical and political substrata. Pasaia is, within the metropolitan area of Donostia-San Sebastian, a continuous urban area with a strong industrial concentration, important industrial infrastructure and an urban zone in decline. Its social/economic situation is very difficult: obsolete infrastructures, a specific need for restructuring, a high level of long-term unemployment, low economic activity, poverty and exclusion, unattended immigration fluxes, low educational level and a juxtaposed fragmented administration.

The area is on the verge of a substantial process of re-conversion. It is one of the three nodes of the Basque country's poly-nuclear system of capitals and has an advantageous hinge position on the intersection of the Atlantic and the Ebro corridors. In all of the administrative strata, which are well aware of the potentials of the area, efforts have been made to produce studies and projects for positive transformations under their jurisdictions. Although steps have been taken to establish a trans-institutional agency, the fact is that until now all the political manoeuvering has not managed to establish a legitimate agency with the multilaterally capacity to operate successfully in this field.

The main agencies and programs concerning the study, projection, management and evaluation of the urban dynamics are: The Basque Eurocity Bayonne-San Sebastian, the General Plan for Donostia-San Sebastian, the Strategic Plan for Donostia-San Sebastian and the Urban Program of the European Union.

The diagram 'Pasaia Bay Milieu' describes on the one hand the nature of relations between local agents and Manifesta 5, the Berlage Institute and TOOAUP and on the other the individuals with whom communications have been established. Conversations were held with various agents in order to profile our research outputs and to help to open up lines of intervention in the urban milieu that could be adopted by the local agents with or without the agency of The Office of Alternative Urban Planning. The process and content of the research is responsive to the working hypothesis but the outputs are adjustable. The research process aims at developing a consistent knowledge and documentation thought of as virtuality or potential and its outputs as customized actualizations of the prototypical conditions framed for the study.

Our working hypothesis is based on the notion that a master plan is neither recommendable nor feasible in the current situation of the region, but that to carry out research into prototypical conditions could set up multiple-coexistent scales of interventions that would be operative as devices of negotiation between the apparently opposing concerns and desires of the local stakeholders. This process could be locally implemented, multilaterally or unilaterally, but always sustaining a collective intelligence that allows the prototypes to proliferate beyond the administrative control of any particular agent.

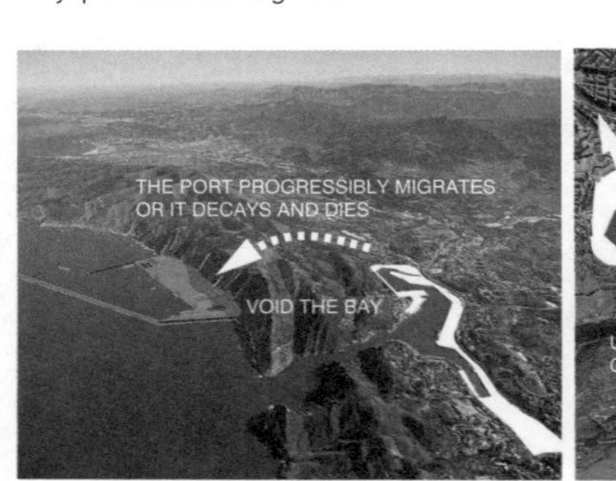

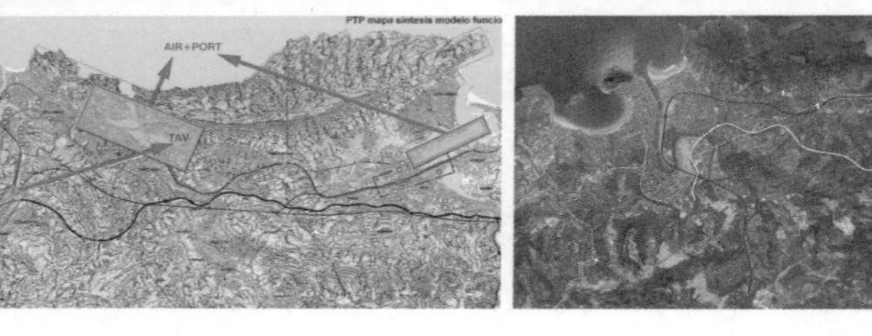

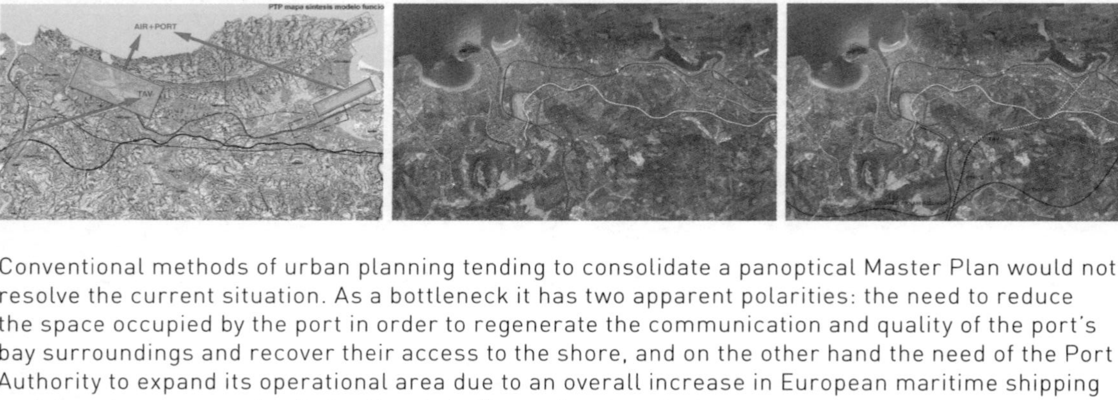

Conventional methods of urban planning tending to consolidate a panoptical Master Plan would not resolve the current situation. As a bottleneck it has two apparent polarities: the need to reduce the space occupied by the port in order to regenerate the communication and quality of the port's bay surroundings and recover their access to the shore, and on the other hand the need of the Port Authority to expand its operational area due to an overall increase in European maritime shipping envisioned as an opportunity for Pasaia in the regional context,

This situation will not be resolved by opting for a pastoral landscaping regeneration of the bay or by establishing a real estate operation that would finance an exterior port: neither approach has any true value on its own.

The regeneration program will have to deal with changes in land ownership, the existence of the port as a land zone that is a barrier, the property of the central government and administered by the Port Authority, is an asset rather than a drawback, because it grants overall control of property investment and value management — value in terms of sustainable profit that goes beyond mere speculation. The municipalities on their own would not be effective in undertaking a process of property investment and value management given their troubled financial status. For them and the other stakeholders, being fairly integrated in a development agency would be the best policy.

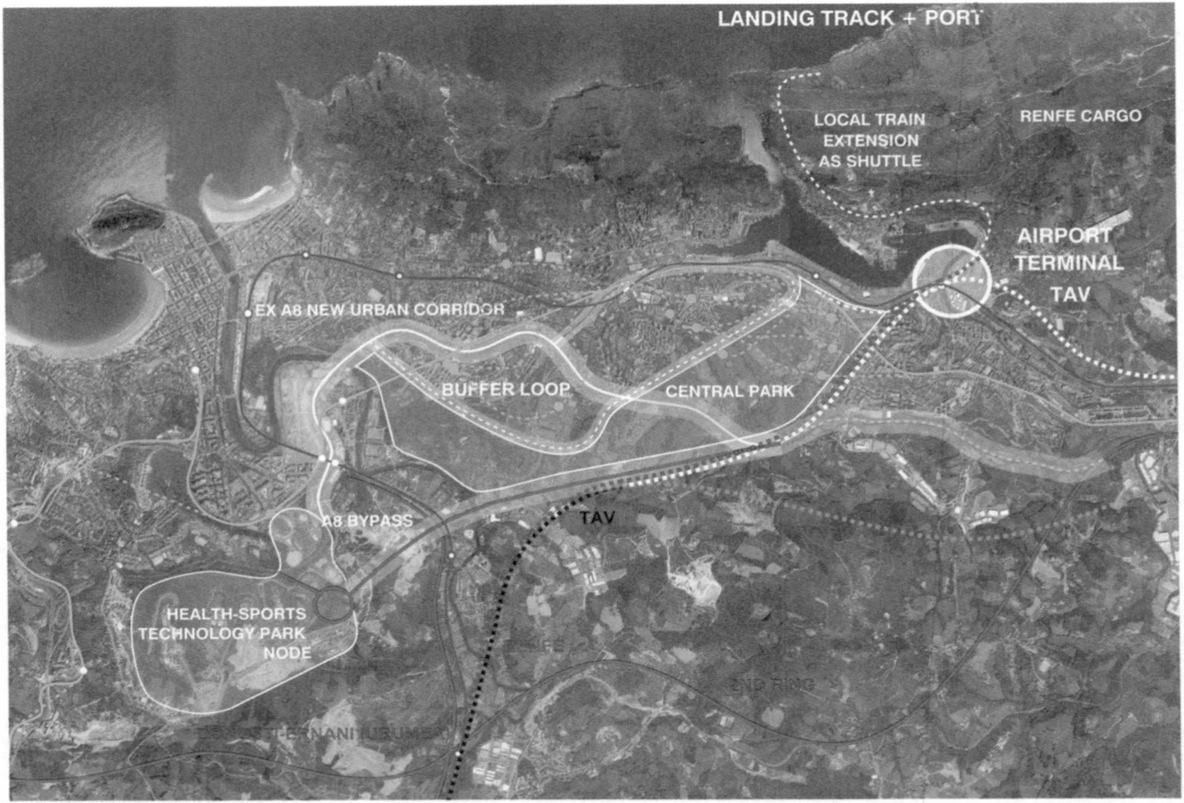

LANDING TRACK + PORT
LOCAL TRAIN
EXTENSION
AS SHUTTLE
RENFE CARGO
AIRPORT
TERMINAL
TAV
EX A8 NEW URBAN CORRIDOR
BUFFER LOOP
CENTRAL PARK
A8 BYPASS
TAV
HEALTH-SPORTS
TECHNOLOGY PARK
NODE
2ND RING

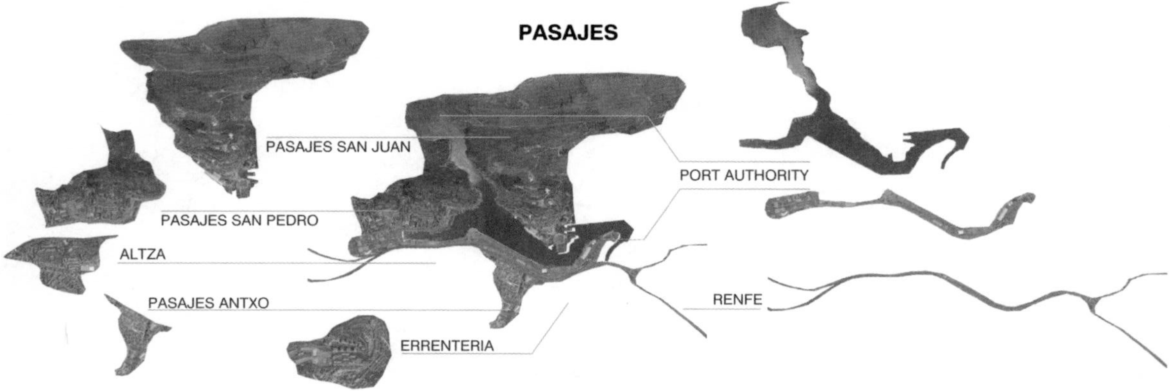

PASAJES

PASAJES SAN JUAN

PASAJES SAN PEDRO

ALTZA

PASAJES ANTXO

ERRENTERIA

PORT AUTHORITY

RENFE

The various agents who link overall regeneration with the realization of an exterior port would campaign for this on the basis that it would bring an economic stimulus to Pasaialdea and allow for the much wanted regeneration of the bay, in spite of the environmental impacts, which would need an extensive process of mitigation.

The debate is highly focused on the construction of the exterior port, which would potentially allow the regeneration of the Bay of Pasaia, rather than on constituting synergetic sets of infrastructural projects at multiple scales. The exterior port is critical. Exterior in the sense of its progressive migration behind the Mount Jaizkibel or exterior because it would decay and die. The Port Authority, in spite of all the geographic and infrastructural constraints, has transformed it into one of the most

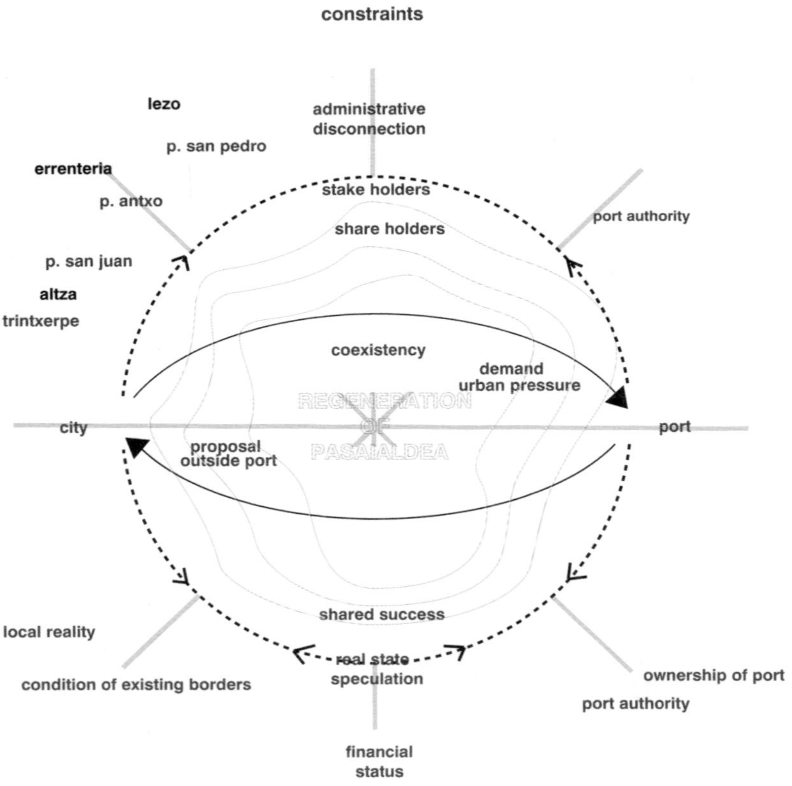

constraints

lezo

p. san pedro

errenteria

p. antxo

p. san juan

altza

trintxerpe

administrative
disconnection

stake holders

share holders

port authority

coexistency

demand
urban pressure

REGENERATION
OF
PASAIALDEA

city

port

proposal
outside port

shared success

real state
speculation

financial
status

local reality

condition of existing borders

ownership of port

port authority

the proposal of urban regeneration
should be consistent with an administrati
milieu represented by a new developing
agency for pasaialdea

impact

local intervention between port and city

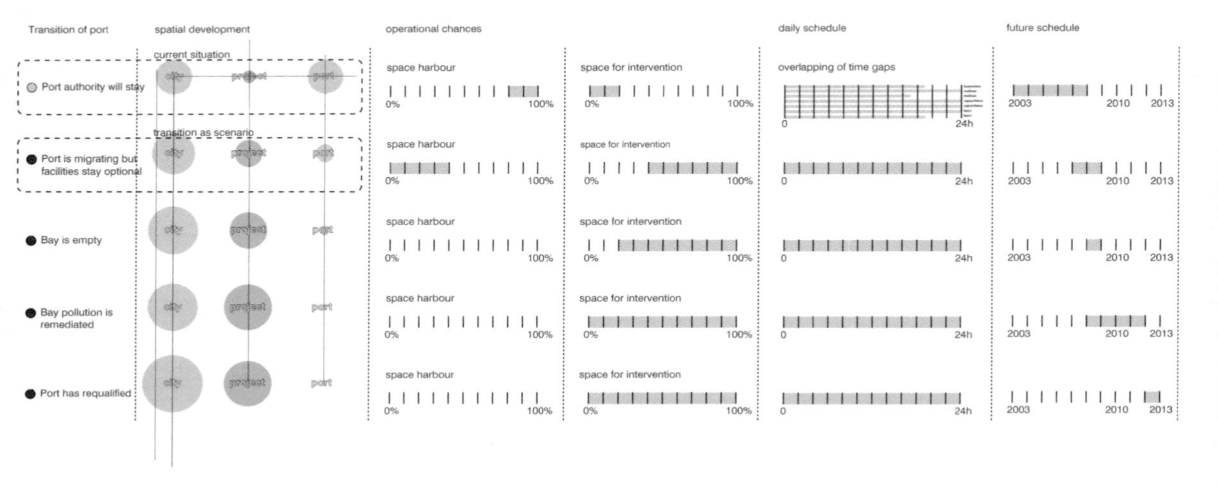

efficient ports of Spain, and the tonnage it handles has steadily increased in recent years, but this is not sustainable given regional conditions and traffic trends. It is critical in the sense of an accumulation of unresolved infrastructural issues with enough inertia to be utilized as the engine for an overall and sustainable qualitative change.

No matter how the port becomes exterior, the complexity and the strata of administration and negotiation involved in a regeneration program such as this determine that it can only be successful if it proves possible to establish the instruments with which the port, associated infrastructures and the city-administered areas can increase their tendency to coexist and co-evolve in a modality of change with distributed benefits and shared success.

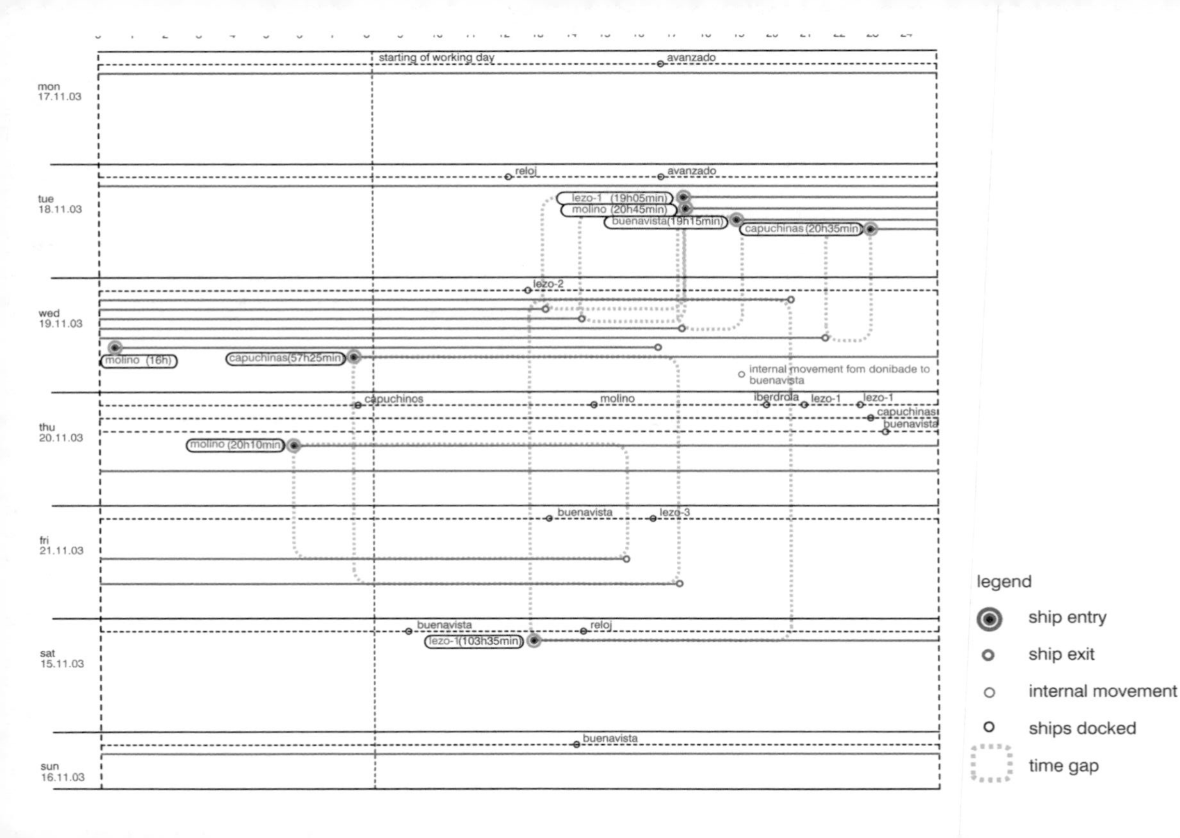
starting of working day
avanzado
mon
17.11.03
reloj
avanzado
tue
18.11.03
lezo-1 (19h05min)
molino (20h45min)
buenavista(19h15min)
capuchinas (20h35min)
lezo-2
wed
19.11.03
molino (16h)
capuchinas(57h25min)
internal movement fom donibade to buenavista
capuchinos
molino
iberdrola
lezo-1
lezo-1
capuchinas
buenavista
thu
20.11.03
molino (20h10min)
buenavista
lezo-3
fri
21.11.03
buenavista
reloj
lezo-1(103h35min)
sat
15.11.03
buenavista
sun
16.11.03
legend
ship entry
ship exit
internal movement
ships docked
time gap

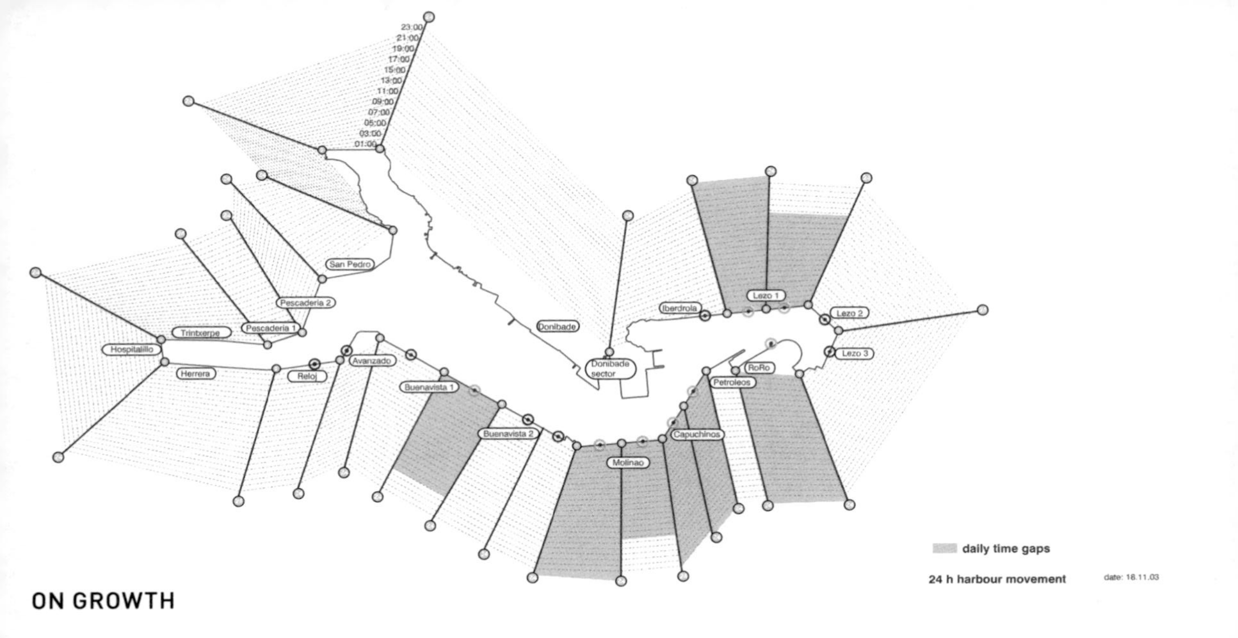

ON GROWTH

Architecture, even when it is conceived as a practice concerned with the engineering of material organizations, can hardly deal with growth. The processes of urban growth do not operate linearly, in spite of all the efforts to naturalize them as representations of variable forms of a concentric spill of surplus. But what is growth? Where do we find it? And why is it relevant?

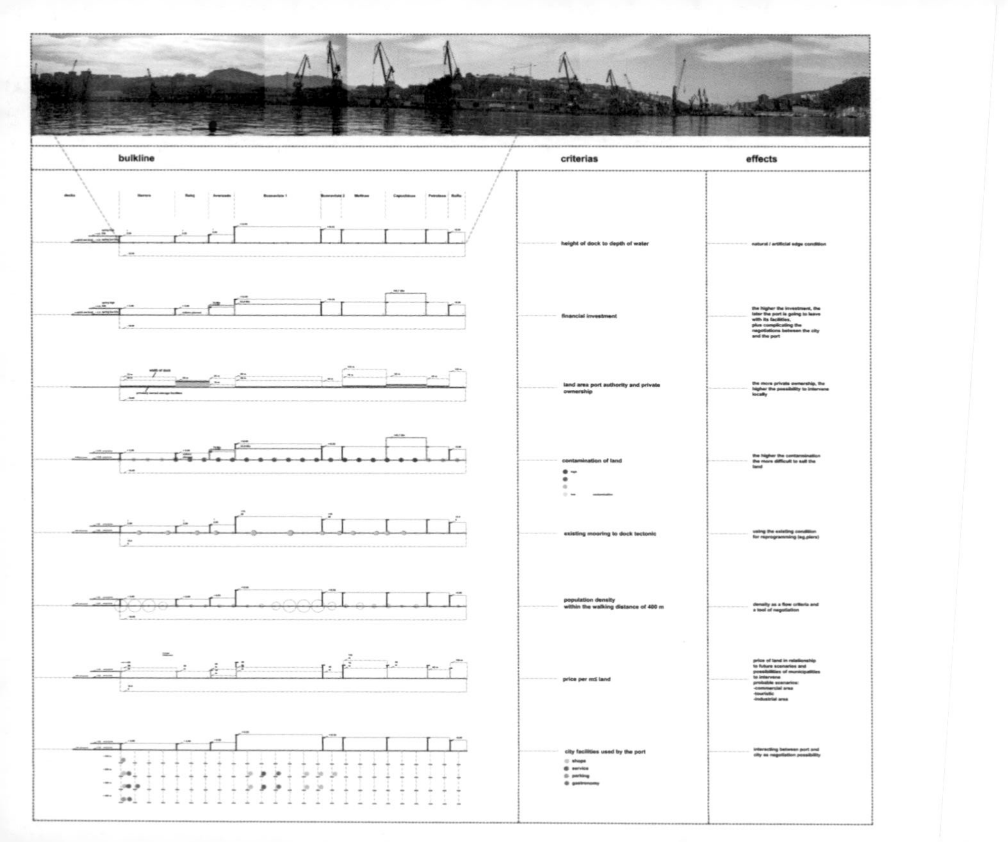
bulkline
criterias
effects
height of dock to depth of water
natural / artificial edge condition
financial investment
the higher the investment, the later the port is going to leave with its facilities, plus complicating the negotiations between the city and the port
land area port authority and private ownership
the more private ownership, the higher the possibility to intervene locally
contamination of land
the higher the contamination the more difficult to sell the land
existing mooring to dock tectonic
using the existing condition for reprogramming (eg.piers)
population density within the walking distance of 400 m
density as a flow criteria and a tool of negotiation
price per m2 land
price of land in relationship to future scenaries and possibilities of municipalities to intervene
probable scenarios:
-commercial area
-touristic
-industrial area
city facilities used by the port
shops
service
parking
gastronomy
intersecting between port and city as negotiation possibility

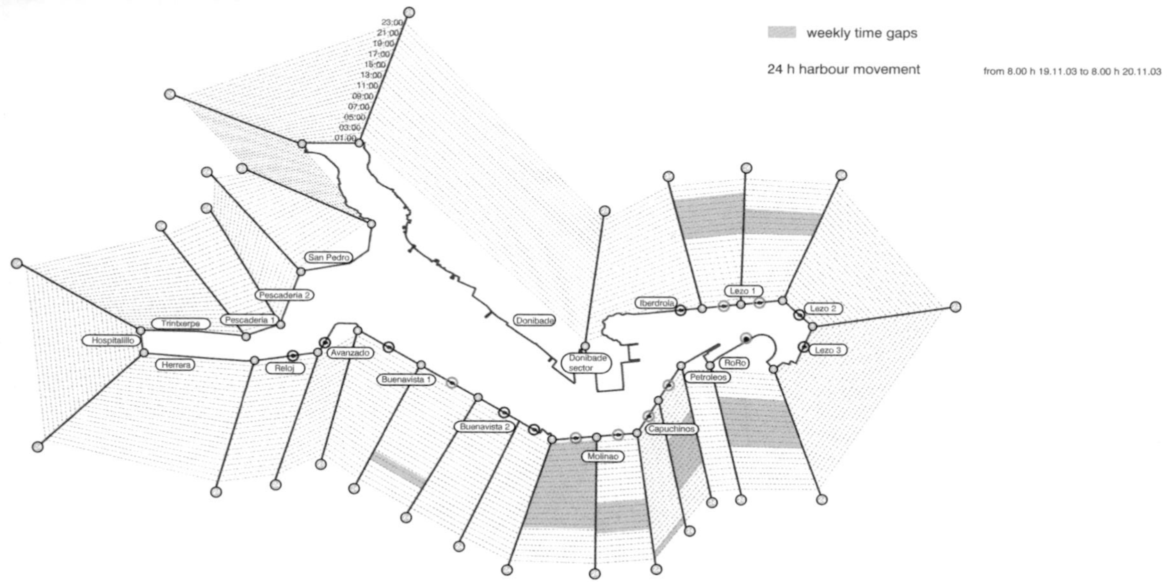

weekly time gaps

24 h harbour movement

from 8.00 h 19.11.03 to 8.00 h 20.11.03

23:00
21:00
19:00
17:00
15:00
13:00
11:00
09:00
07:00
05:00
03:00
01:00

San Pedro
Pescaderia 2
Pescaderia 1
Trintxerpe
Hospitalillo
Herrera
Reloj
Avanzado
Buenavista 1
Buenavista 2
Molinao
Capuchinos
Petroleos
RoRo
Donibade
Donibade sector
Iberdrola
Lezo 1
Lezo 2
Lezo 3

Growth, if reduced to urban renewal strategies, tends to be determined to become a non-reversible process of erosion of memory: an erosion of memory not so much in terms of a quantitative loss of past, but more as a process of loss of a qualitative utilization of the past in terms of the present. (1) A very compressed, crystallized state of matter.

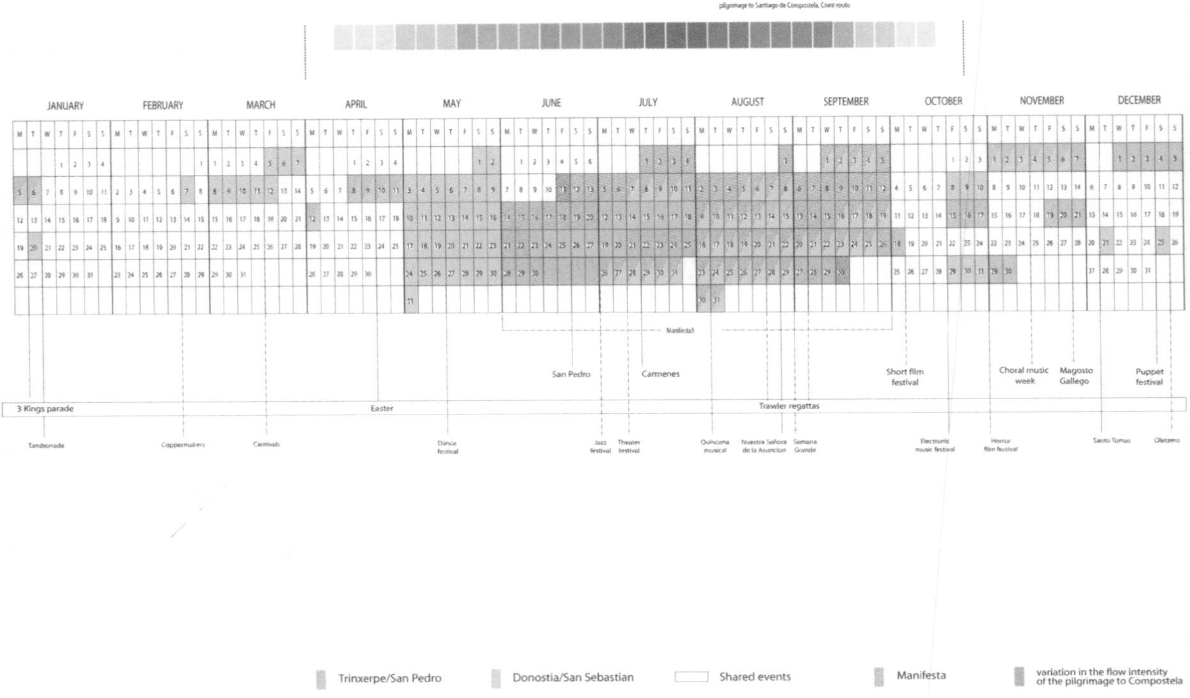

pilgrimage to Santiago de Compostela, Coast route

JANUARY

M	T	W	T	F	S	S
			1	2	3	4
5	6	7	8	9	10	11
12	13	14	15	16	17	18
19	20	21	22	23	24	25
26	27	28	29	30	31	

FEBRUARY

M	T	W	T	F	S	S
						1
2	3	4	5	6	7	8
9	10	11	12	13	14	15
16	17	18	19	20	21	22
23	24	25	26	27	28	29

MARCH

M	T	W	T	F	S	S
1	2	3	4	5	6	7
8	9	10	11	12	13	14
15	16	17	18	19	20	21
22	23	24	25	26	27	28
29	30	31				

APRIL

M	T	W	T	F	S	S
			1	2	3	4
5	6	7	8	9	10	11
12	13	14	15	16	17	18
19	20	21	22	23	24	25
26	27	28	29	30		

MAY

M	T	W	T	F	S	S
					1	2
3	4	5	6	7	8	9
10	11	12	13	14	15	16
17	18	19	20	21	22	23
24	25	26	27	28	29	30
31						

JUNE

M	T	W	T	F	S	S
	1	2	3	4	5	6
7	8	9	10	11	12	13
14	15	16	17	18	19	20
21	22	23	24	25	26	27
28	29	30				

JULY

M	T	W	T	F	S	S
			1	2	3	4
5	6	7	8	9	10	11
12	13	14	15	16	17	18
19	20	21	22	23	24	25
26	27	28	29	30	31	

AUGUST

M	T	W	T	F	S	S
						1
2	3	4	5	6	7	8
9	10	11	12	13	14	15
16	17	18	19	20	21	22
23	24	25	26	27	28	29
30	31					

SEPTEMBER

M	T	W	T	F	S	S
		1	2	3	4	5
6	7	8	9	10	11	12
13	14	15	16	17	18	19
20	21	22	23	24	25	26
27	28	29	30			

OCTOBER

M	T	W	T	F	S	S
				1	2	3
4	5	6	7	8	9	10
11	12	13	14	15	16	17
18	19	20	21	22	23	24
25	26	27	28	29	30	31

NOVEMBER

M	T	W	T	F	S	S
1	2	3	4	5	6	7
8	9	10	11	12	13	14
15	16	17	18	19	20	21
22	23	24	25	26	27	28
29	30					

DECEMBER

M	T	W	T	F	S	S
		1	2	3	4	5
6	7	8	9	10	11	12
13	14	15	16	17	18	19
20	21	22	23	24	25	26
27	28	29	30	31		

Manifesta5

San Pedro

Carmenes

Short film festival

Choral music week

Magosto Gallego

Puppet festival

3 Kings parade

Easter

Trawler regattas

Tamborrada

Coppermakers

Carnivals

Dance festival

Jazz festival

Theater festival

Quincena musical

Nuestra Señora de la Asuncion

Semana Grande

Electronic music festival

Horror film festival

Santo Tomas

Olentzero

Trinxerpe/San Pedro

Donostia/San Sebastian

Shared events

Manifesta

variation in the flow intensity of the pilgrimage to Compostela

When for analytical purpose cities are equated with organisms, their growth is usually framed and placed in a false image: the spatialization of their organs-landmarks and their physical links, an approach that understands the urban field as scattered objects essentialized as discrete functional places, running a clock of predicted outputs and defects.

But instead of senselessly seeking to apprehend the totality or monumentality of cities, a model of growth as temporally emergent switches on a field of material proliferation would be more relevant as a way to engage with their memory, their duration and the vital intensity of their oscillation.

TOOAUP implicitly assumes that the determining factors intrinsic to the study, design, negotiation, management, implementation, construction and decay of an urban organization are an evolutionary process of proliferation.

The complex relationships between structure, function and change in any evolutionary process were initially explored as the core of a rough yet rigorous investigation to determine Performance Specifications, which were then tightened up and instrumentalized into Associative Material Constraints, and were subsequently unfolded, summarized and indexed into a Dynamic Organizational Substrate.

(1) Gilles Deleuze. Bergsonism, 'Memory as virtual coexistence'. 1966.

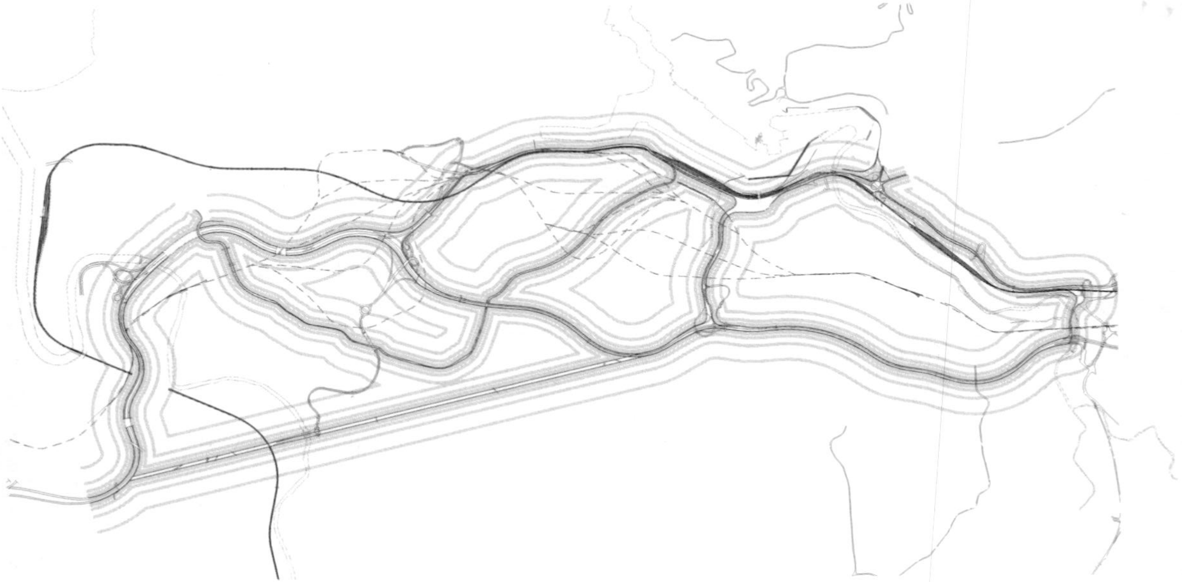

Buffer influence

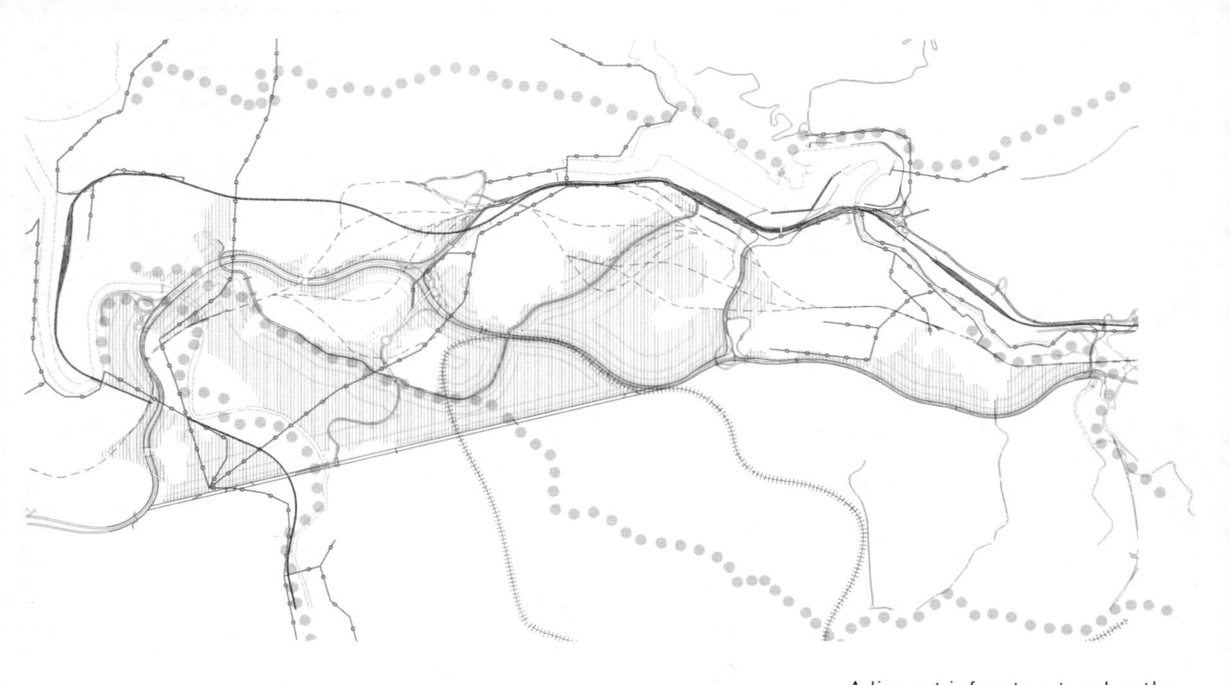

Adjacent infrastructural paths

ON CHANGE

Creative Mediation as a practice is all about steering potential.

To be incorporated in a material organization as an agent, a critical position has to be transposed from a paralyzing autonomy into a drive. In mediation as a practice, 'profiling' has a psychological root, but in architectural terms it engineers life.

Mediation does not construct an 'other' between two subjects or substances; instead it constitutes its own immanence and so is creative. In itself it is a Life, a process of singularization that is carried and actualized in subjects and objects that make it happen. Mediation is also creative in the sense of constituting legitimate problems as a process of anticipating solutions. A speculative problem is solved as soon as it is properly stated. Stating the problem is not simply uncovering it, it is inventing. In order to go beyond partialities, passing from a limited sympathy to an extended generosity, Creative Mediation, as a catalyzer for change, has to operate as a meta-infrastructure.

By virtue of this character, and in strict architectural terms, it is almost a compliment when this practice is pointed to as technocratic by the champions of criticality and poetry ... the last remaining romantics who, unable to cope with the potentials of contemporary practice, project their bitterness while misreading the emergence of a practice based on the utilization of procedures, protocols and techniques as the instrumentalization of a collective drive.

The perplexity is symptomatic of a culture that cannot conceive that interventions of a propositive character could be immanent to an organization without contradictions, oppositions or polarities, that engages in transformations without resorting to equilibrium and homogeneity or far from equilibrium heterogeneity but have instead to give rise to one another as the one and only dynamic.

TOOAUP's practice deals with criticality, political engagement, local identities and so on as the immanence of architectural material rather than as causes or effects in a kind of symbolic exploration of architecture. It is far more productive and sincere to know that architecture on the making is producing these than to position your practice as a magnifying glass, a truth detector that is going to translate its findings into matter: matter has it own will, and by matter we also understand criticality, political engagement, local identities and so on. The fact is that not believing in the architect as the sole producer of symbolic objects, bounds to the notion of duration on material organizations and from that inevitably follows the certainty of not needing at all to set up a critical-political agenda on the projects because they would arise as an intrinsic character of architecture as a collective material practice, the practice should be responsive to them rather than open or supportive.

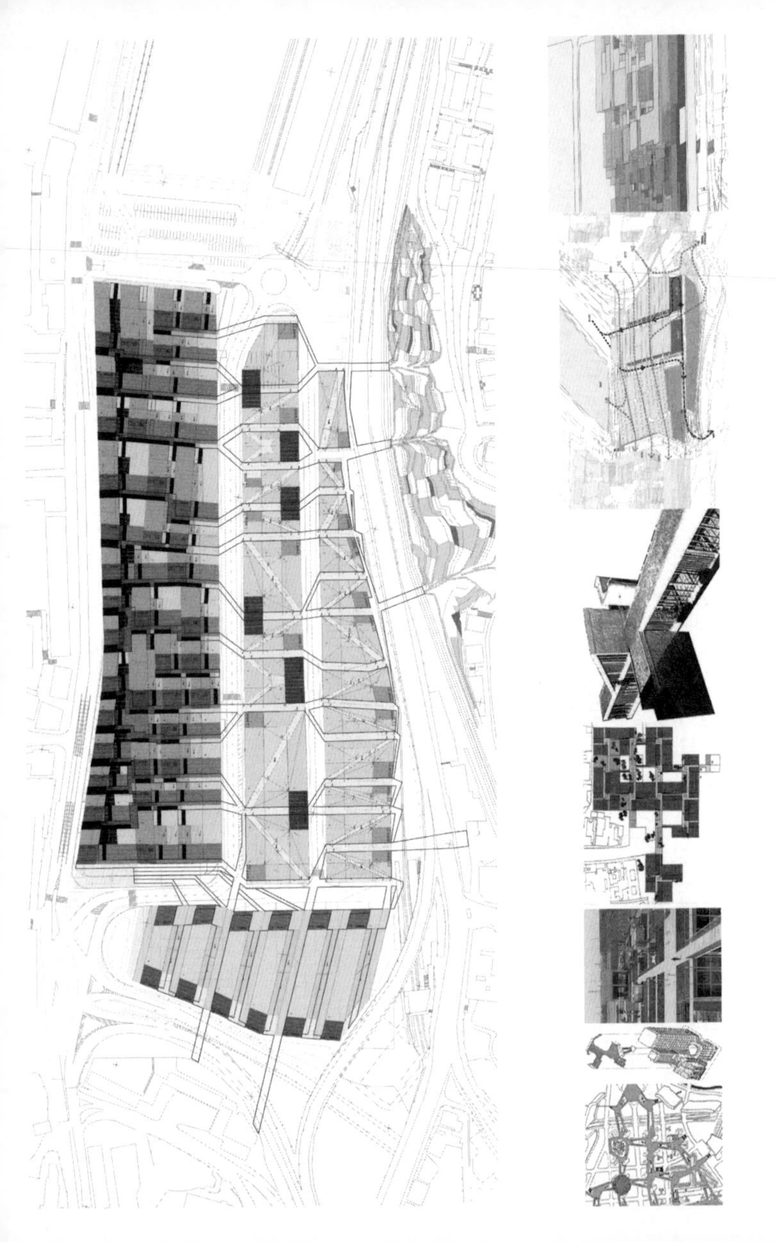

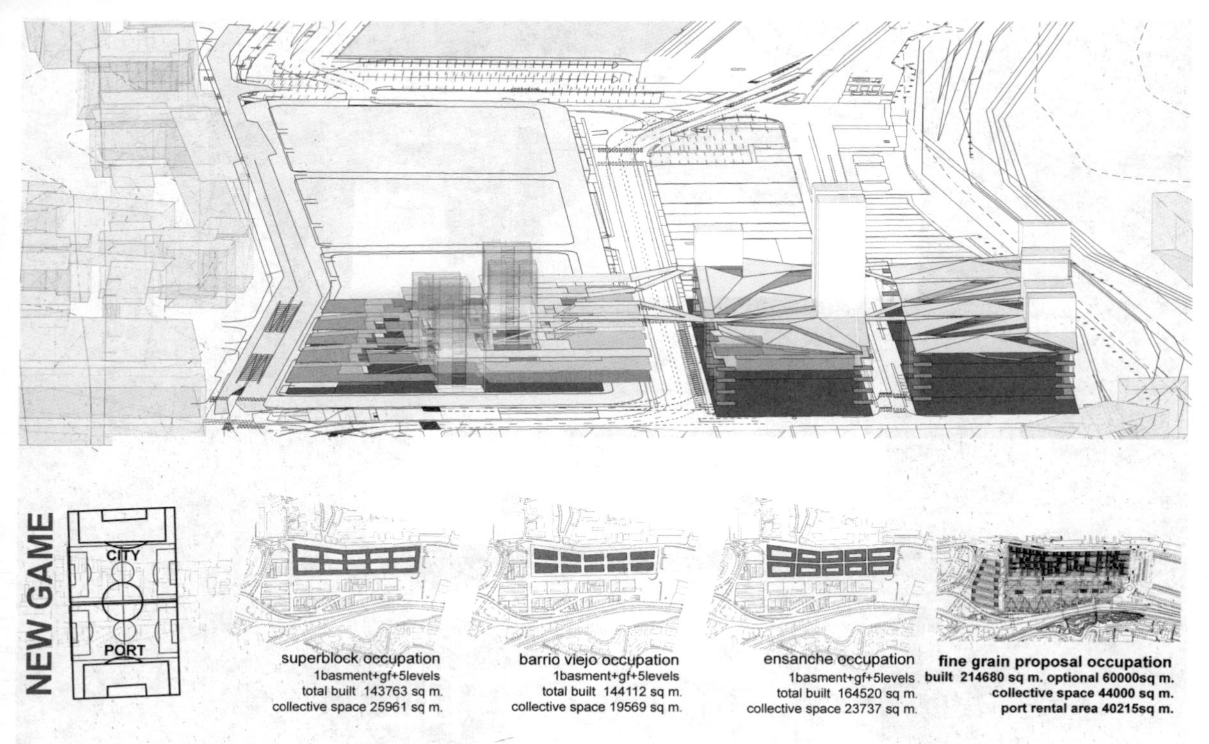
NEW GAME
CITY
PORT
superblock occupation
1basment+gf+5levels
total built 143763 sq m.
collective space 25961 sq m.
barrio viejo occupation
1basment+gf+5levels
total built 144112 sq m.
collective space 19569 sq m.
ensanche occupation
1basment+gf+5levels
total built 164520 sq m.
collective space 23737 sq m.
fine grain proposal occupation
built 214680 sq m. optional 60000sq m.
collective space 44000 sq m.
port rental area 40215sq m.

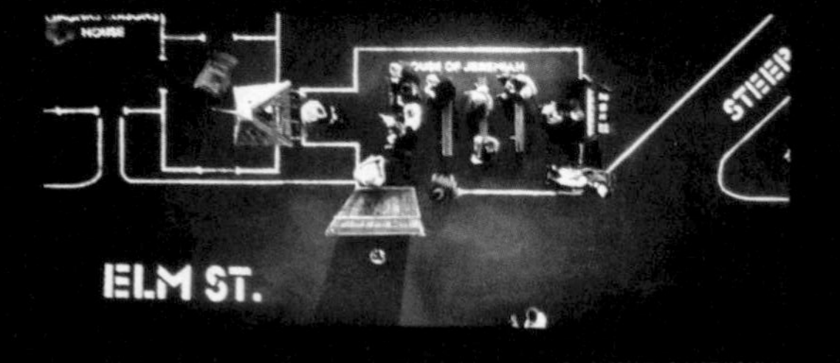
ELM ST.

Después de resumir brevemente
los acontecimientos

ante la lluvia de críticas.

Ground occupation

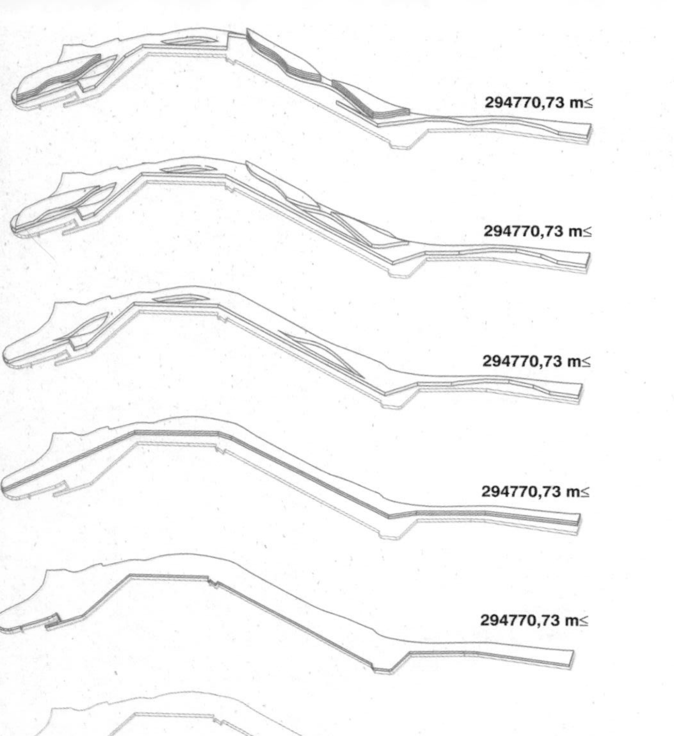

aim of maximum liberation of groud zone
makes areas up to 5 levels necessary
congestion areas are linear to the
existing infrasrtucture (see INDEX/INDICATORS)

stamping the voids
makes zones up to three levels necessary

stamping the voids
extending the urbanline closer to the waterzone

50% covered space
50% free space
two nevels necessery

platform fully covered

amount of money needed for
financing the outside harbour : 800000 Mio Eur
294770,73 m≤ * 3000 Eur/m≤ = 884 Mio Eur

NETWORK

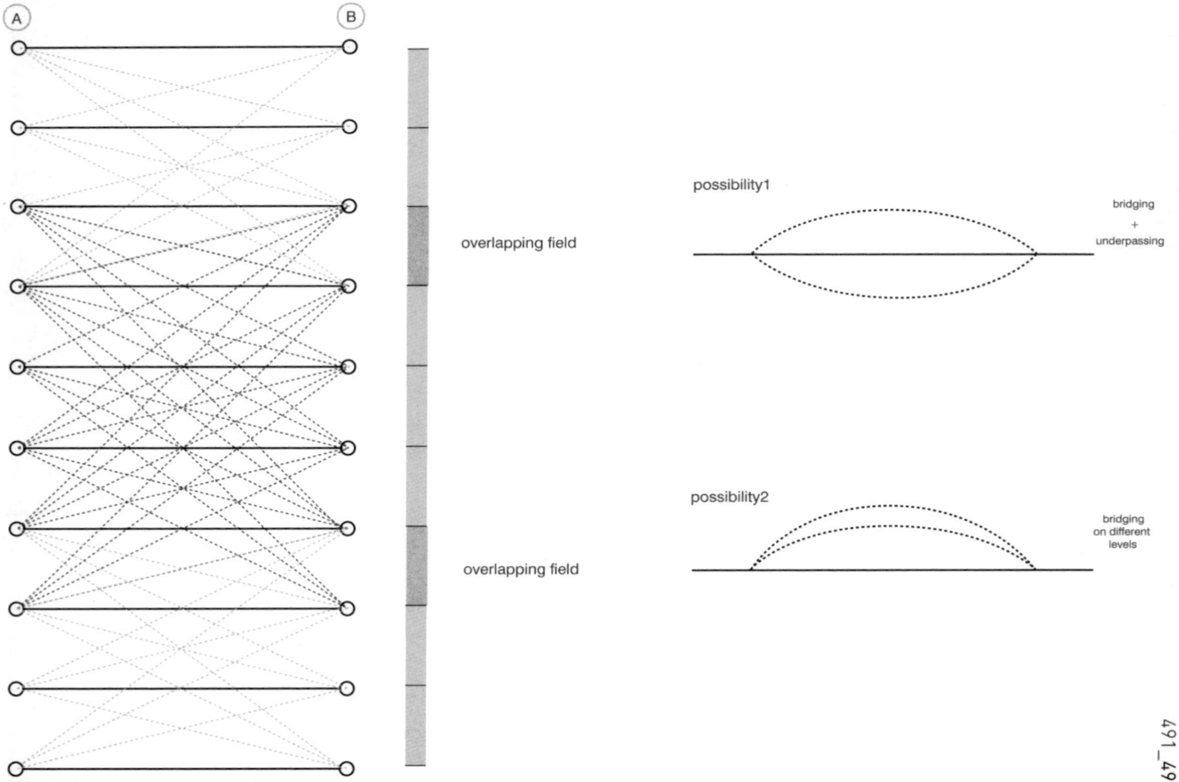

A

B

overlapping field

overlapping field

possibility1

bridging
+
underpassing

possibility2

bridging
on different
levels

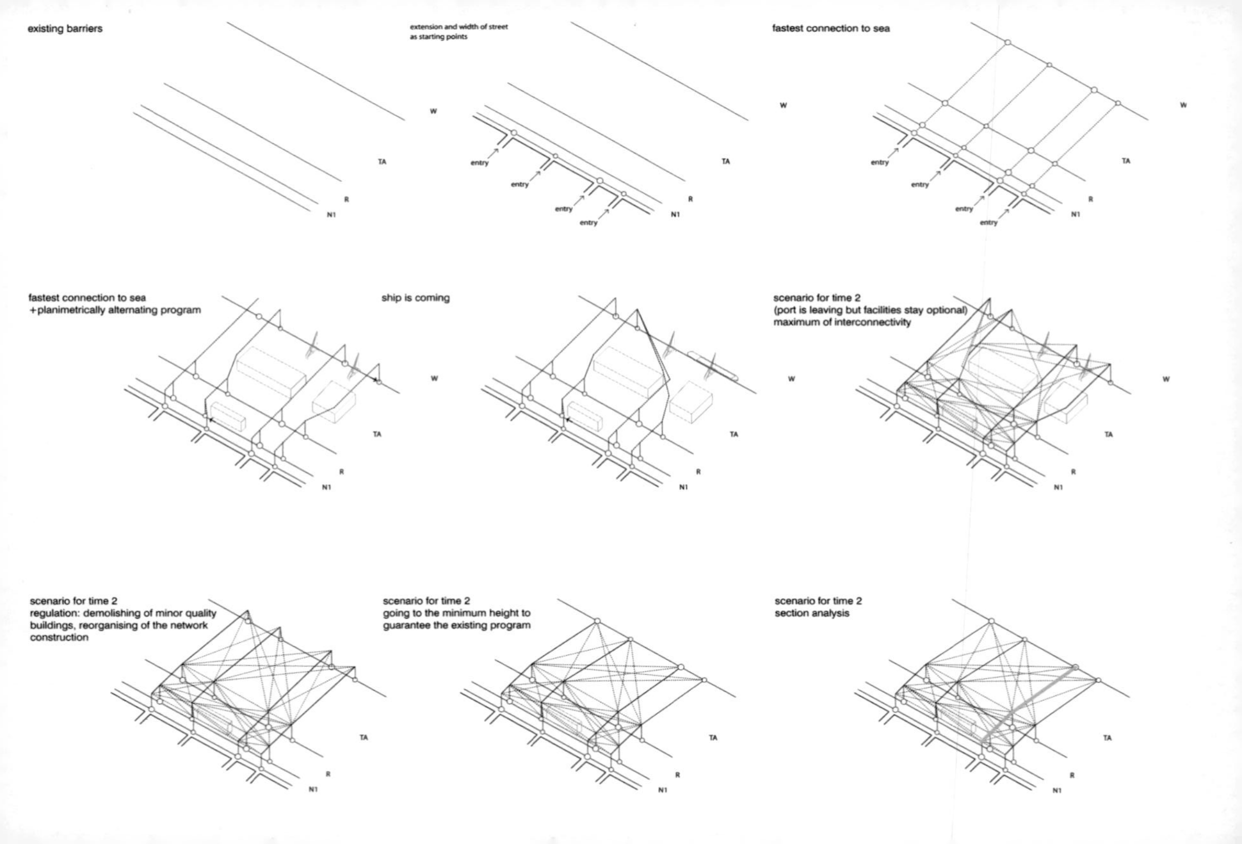
existing barriers
W
TA
R
N1
extension and width of street
as starting points
entry
entry
entry
entry
W
TA
R
N1
fastest connection to sea
entry
entry
entry
entry
W
TA
R
N1
fastest connection to sea
+planimetrically alternating program
W
TA
R
N1
ship is coming
W
TA
R
N1
scenario for time 2
(port is leaving but facilities stay optional)
maximum of interconnectivity
W
TA
R
N1
scenario for time 2
regulation: demolishing of minor quality
buildings, reorganising of the network
construction
TA
R
N1
scenario for time 2
going to the minimum height to
guarantee the existing program
TA
R
N1
scenario for time 2
section analysis
TA
R
N1

scenario for time 2
fields per node

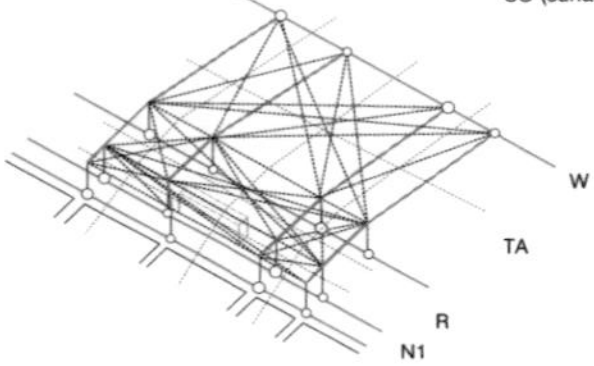

scenario for time 2
SO (surface occupation) per node

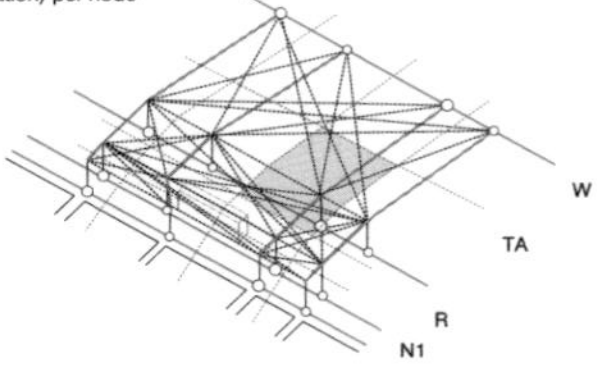

scenario for time 2
VO (volume occupation per node)

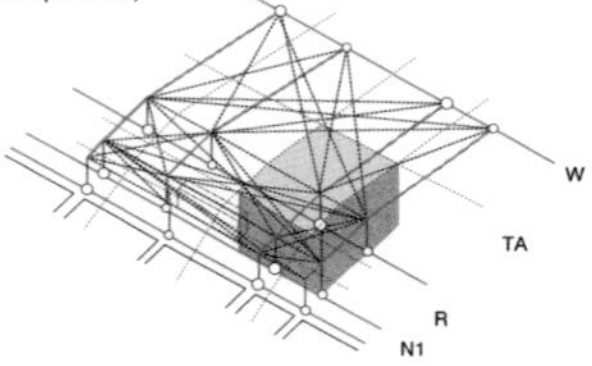

scenario for time 2
IC (infrastructural complexity per node)
defined by span width and height of construction

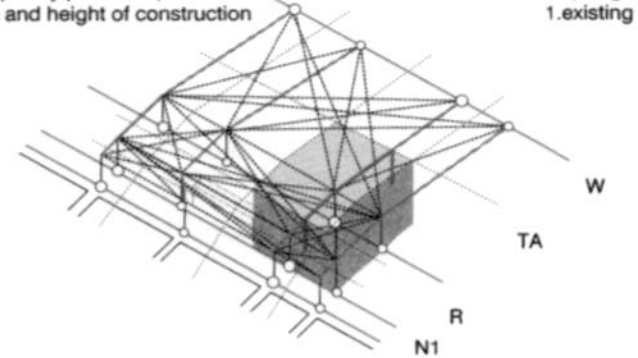

scenario for time 2
IP (integration pedestrian per node)
1.existing network +integration into city fabric

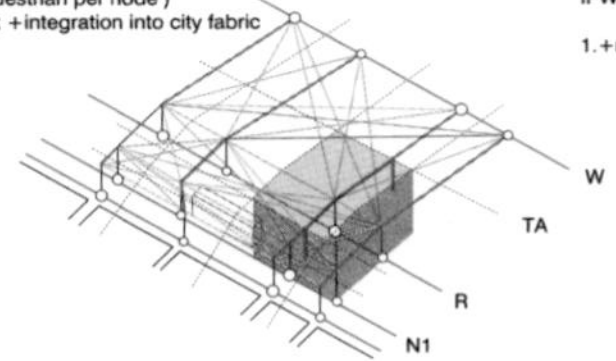

scenario for time 2
IPW(integration pedestrian+way of rights per node)
1.+making use of way of rights

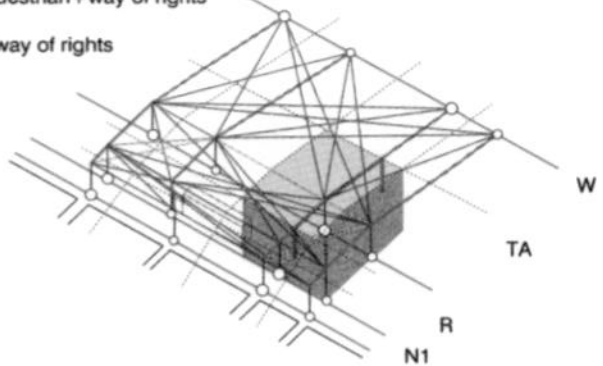

land value per node
indicator (SO/VO/IC/IP/IPW)

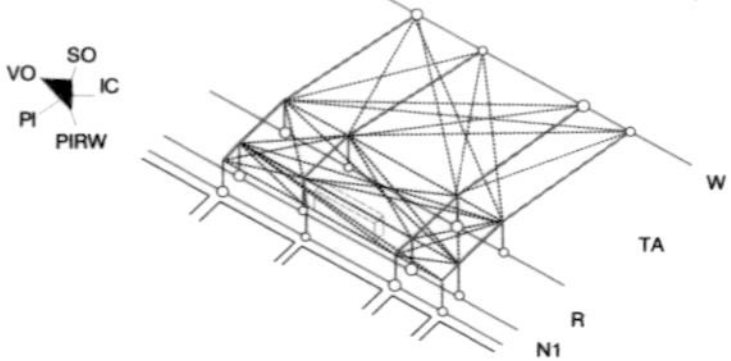

land value per node
indicator (SO/VO/IC/IP/IPW)
transposition of value

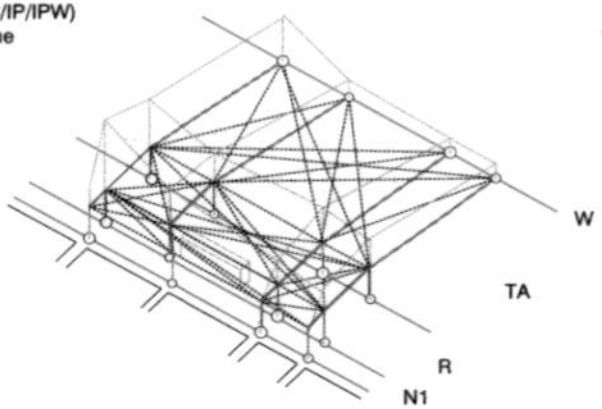

land value per node
index(SO/VO)
transposition of value

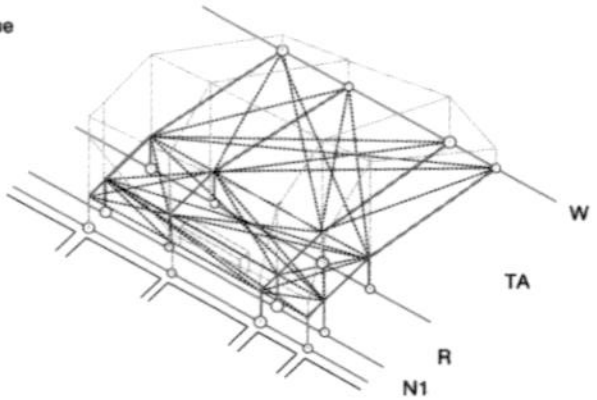

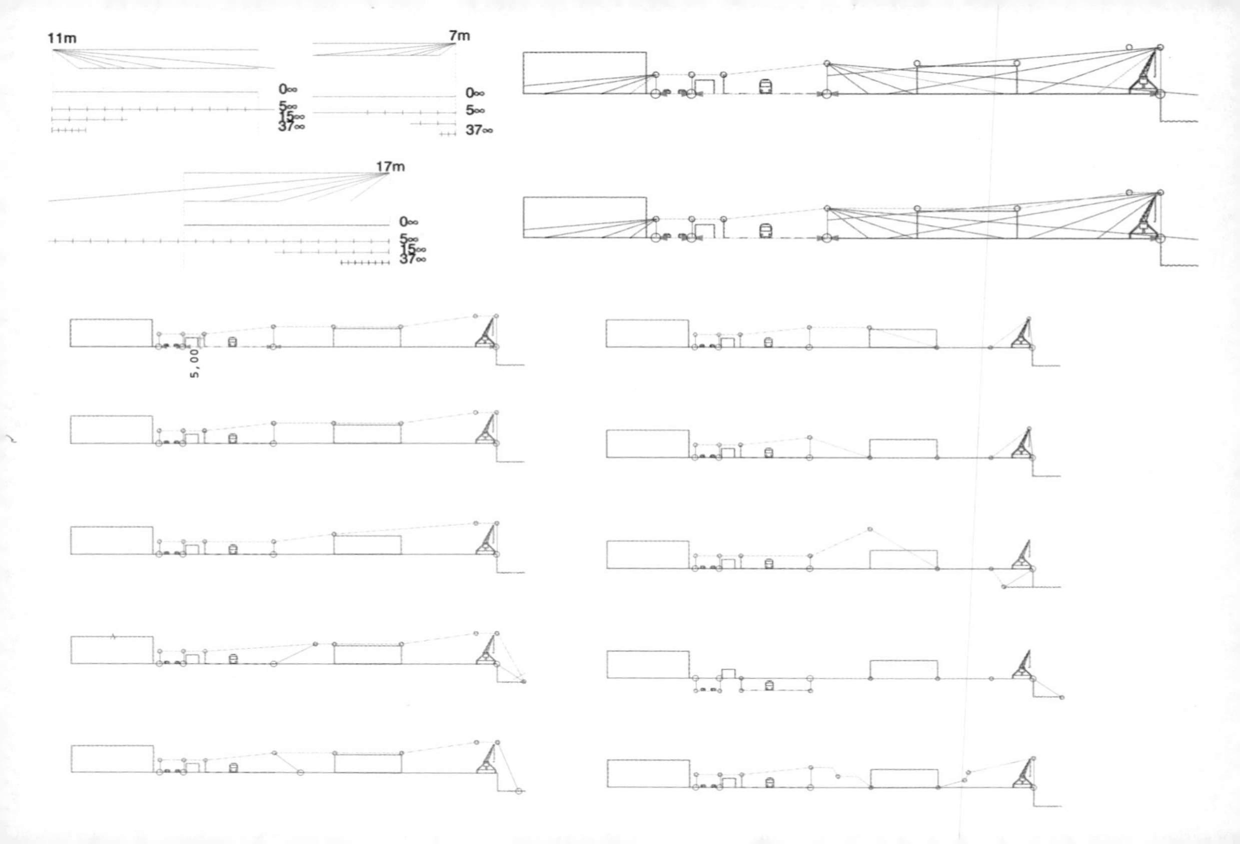
11m
0‰
5‰
15‰
37‰
7m
0‰
5‰
37‰
17m
0‰
5‰
15‰
37‰
5,00

under 1 min
1 min
2 min
3 min
4 min
5 min
6 min
7 min
8 min

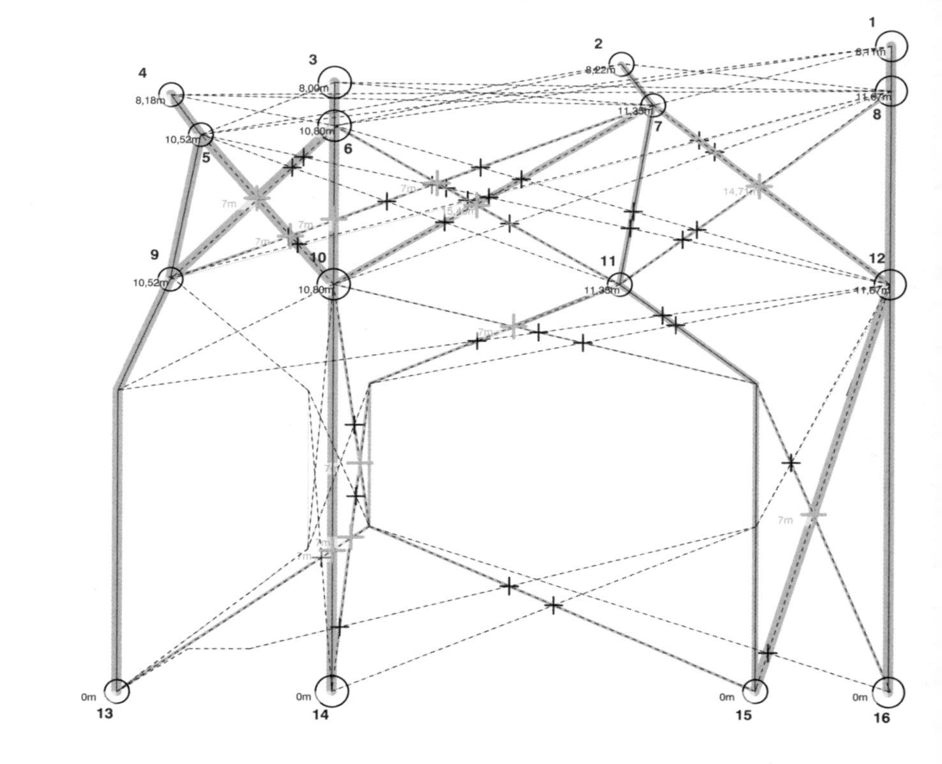
1
8,11m
2
8,22m
3
8,00m
4
8,18m
5
10,52m
6
10,80m
7
11,35m
8
11,67m
9
10,52m
10
10,80m
11
11,35m
12
11,67m
13
0m
14
0m
15
0m
16
0m
7m
14,71m
15,85m

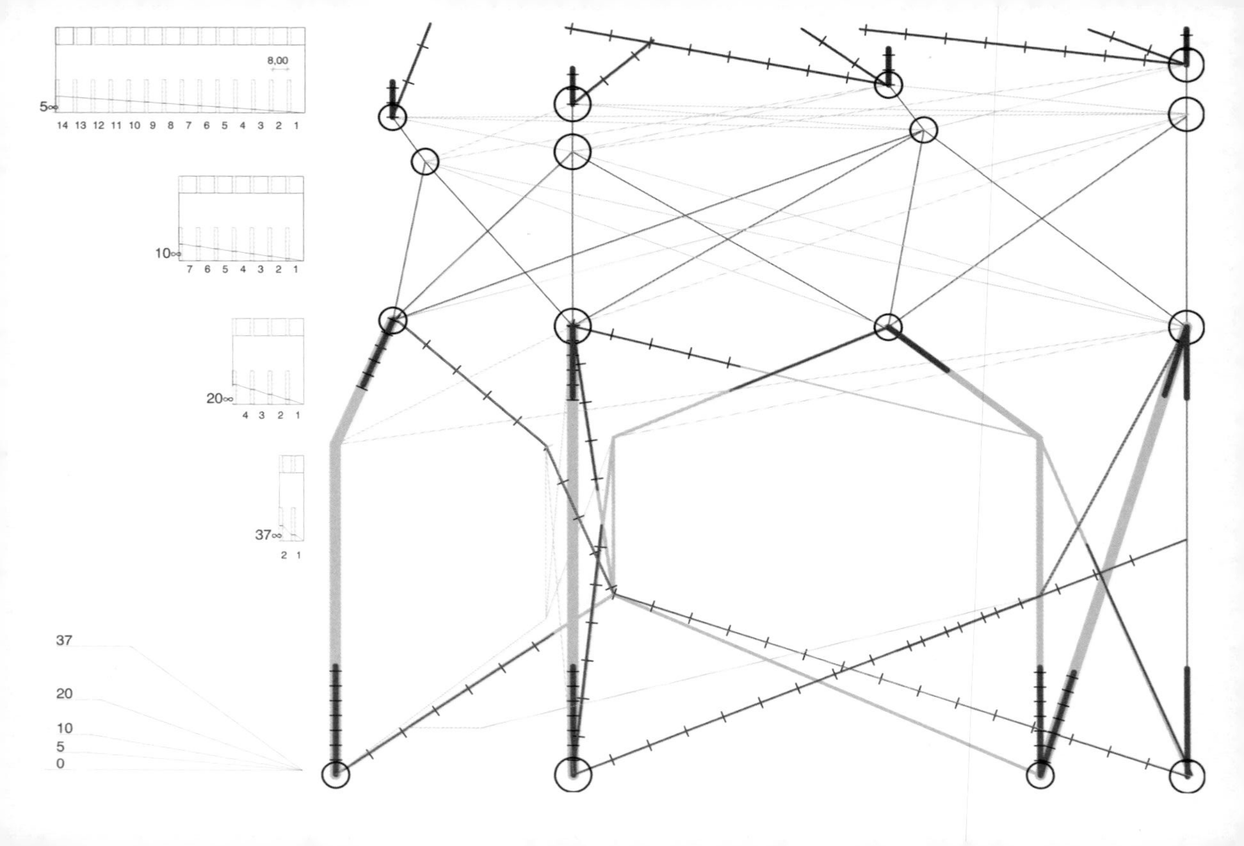
8,00
5‰
14 13 12 11 10 9 8 7 6 5 4 3 2 1
10‰
7 6 5 4 3 2 1
20‰
4 3 2 1
37‰
2 1
37
20
10
5
0

Indicators

SO Surface Occupation

VO Volume Occupation

IC Infrastructural Complexity

PI Pedestrian Integration

PIRW Pedestrian Integration with Rights of Way

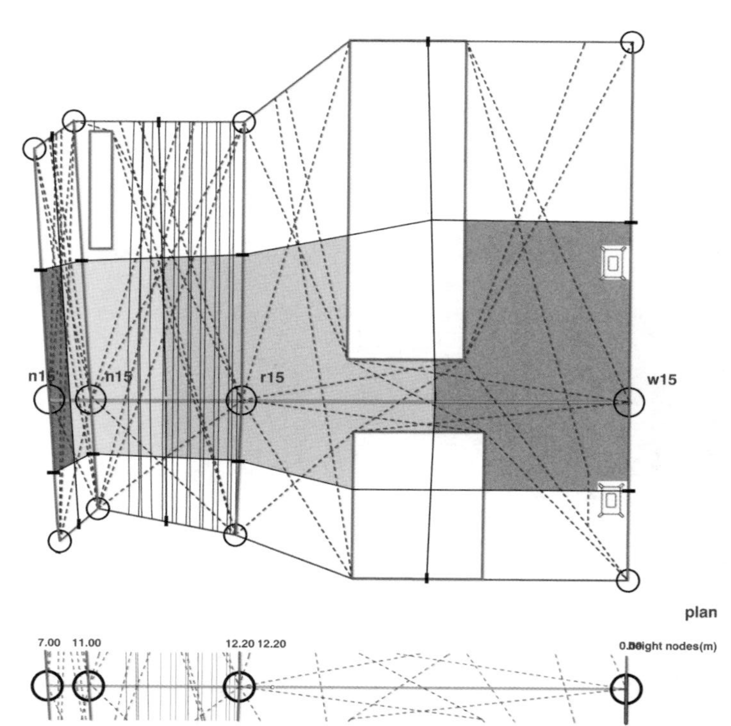

Indicators Index

0	20	40	60	80	100	SO (%)
0	20	40	60	80	100	VO (%)
25	50	75	100			IC (%)
(-)						PI (+)
(-)						PIRW (+)

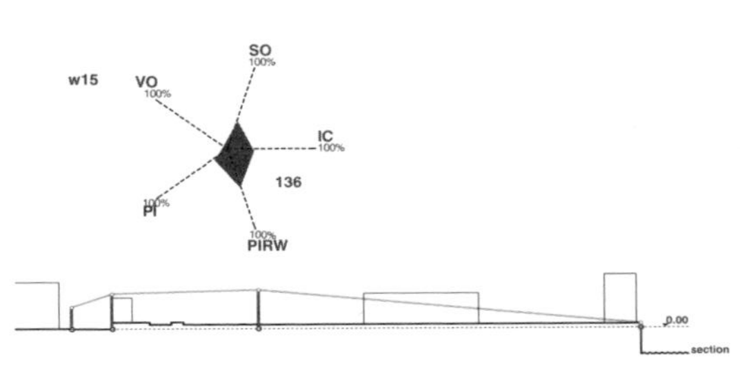

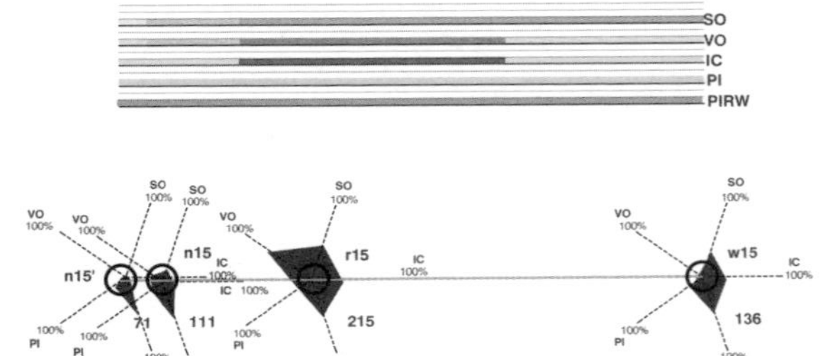

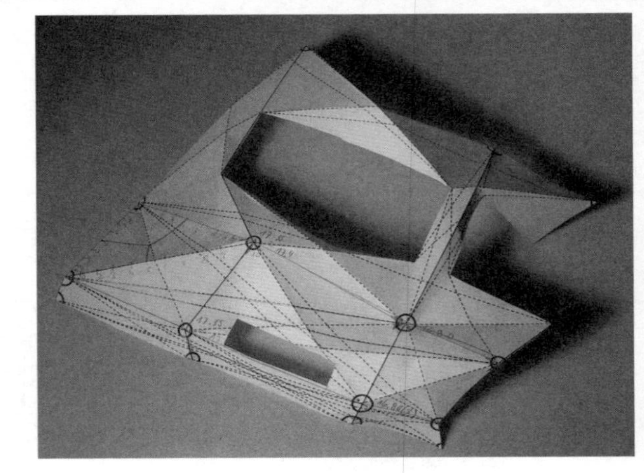

threads

linear threads directing flows of people, energy,water along the site. they are organised along the topographic lines, pathways and connections.they can also include planting and linear architecural elements

nesting voids

clustering voids provide flow regulation and become public species .they describe the unstability of processes and can be used as furnished verge spaces

mats

surface mats provide coverage and can include leisure , touristic and service program

spatial constraints

program

sound

vision

soil contarmination

accessability

tectonic

topography

strategy

bridging

underpassing

covering

mesh network

regulations

financial investment

ownership

human pressure

wind

sun

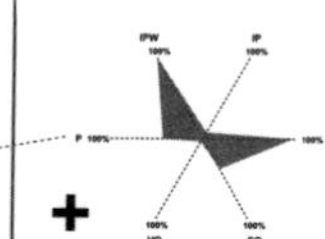

+

indicators

actualisation processes

breaking the rules

irritations

local adjustments

negotiations

design competition

decay

conflicts

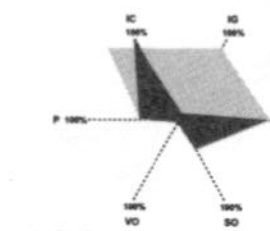

actualisation

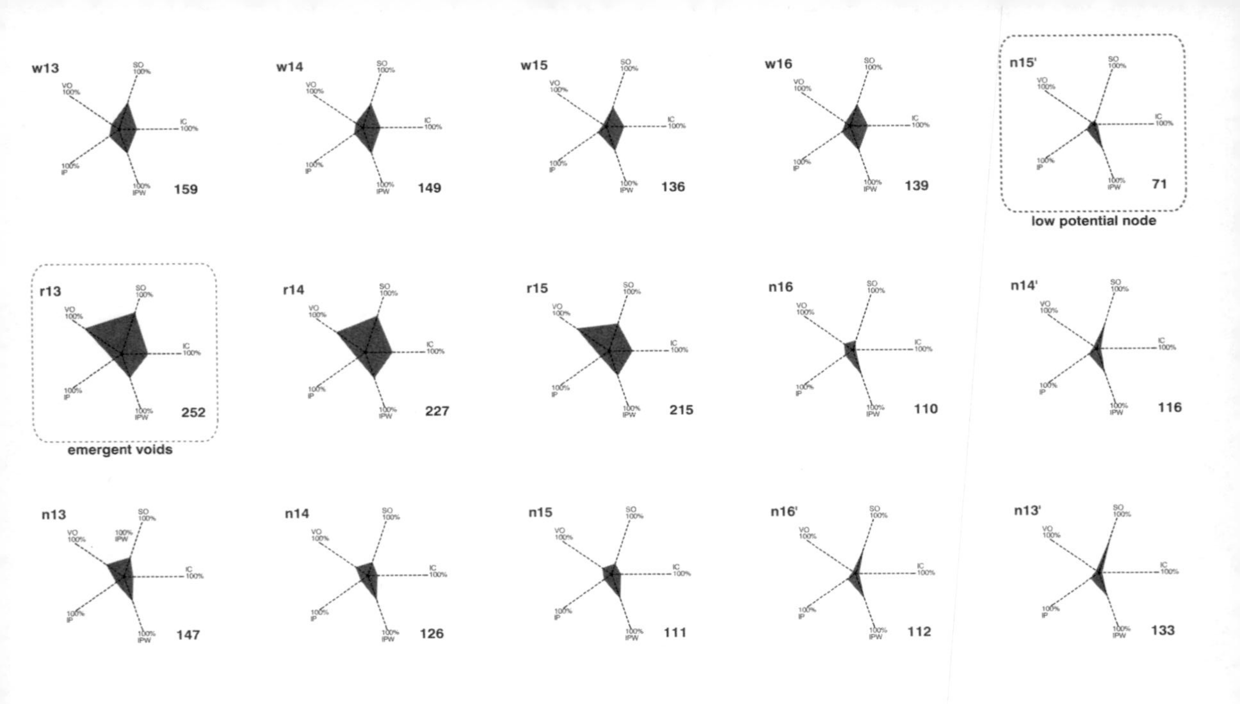
w13
SO 100%
VO 100%
IC 100%
100% IP
100% IPW
159
w14
149
w15
136
w16
139
n15'
71
low potential node
r13
252
emergent voids
r14
227
r15
215
n16
110
n14'
116
n13
147
n14
126
n15
111
n16'
112
n13'
133

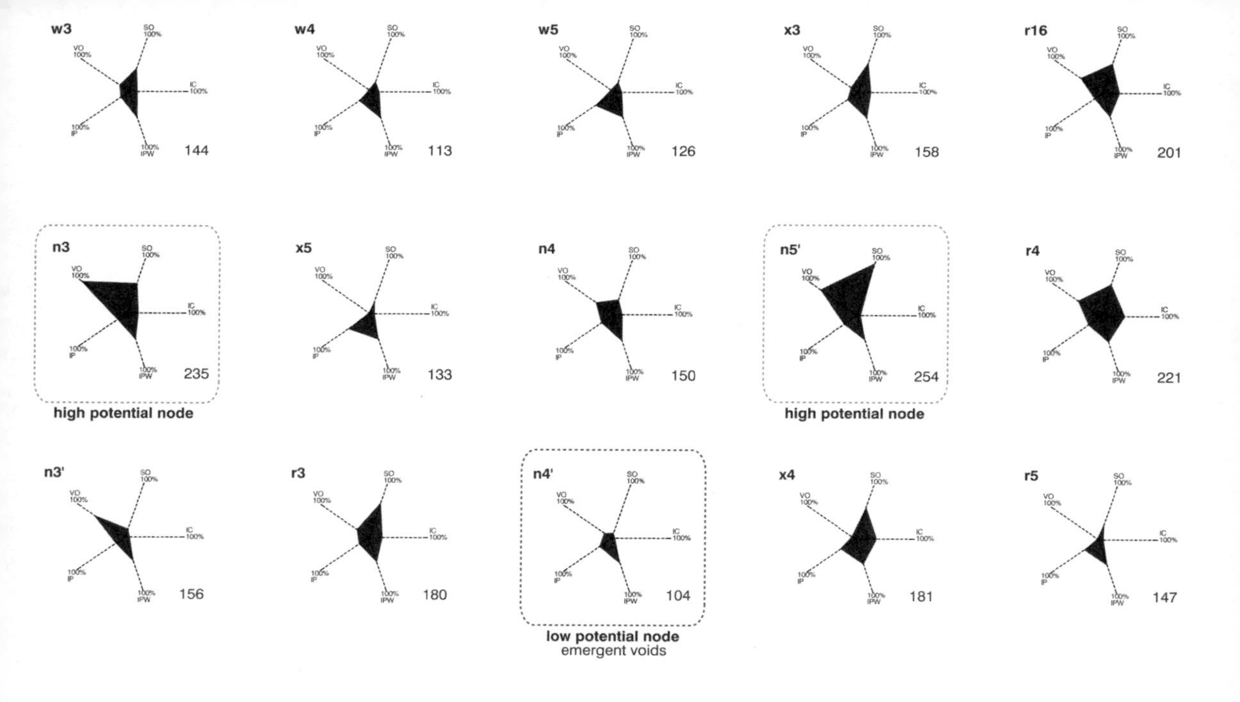
SO 100%
VO 100%
IC 100%
100% IP
100% IPW
w3
144
w4
113
w5
126
x3
158
r16
201
n3
235
high potential node
x5
133
n4
150
n5'
254
high potential node
r4
221
n3'
156
r3
180
n4'
104
low potential node
emergent voids
x4
181
r5
147

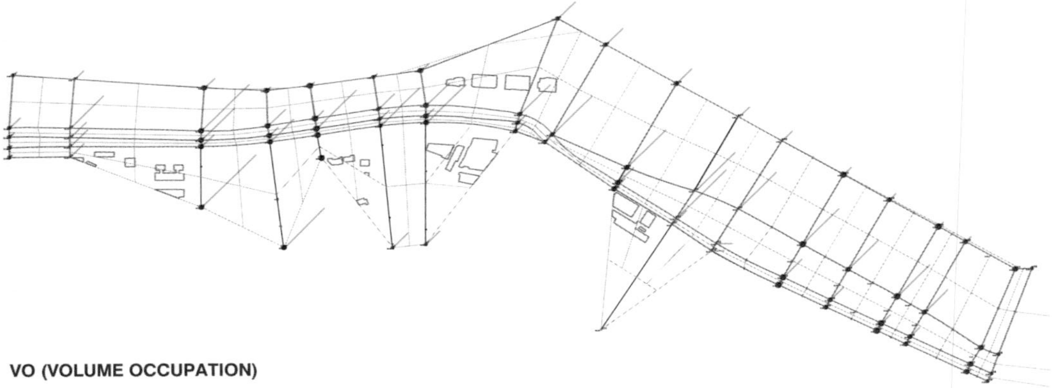

VO (VOLUME OCCUPATION)

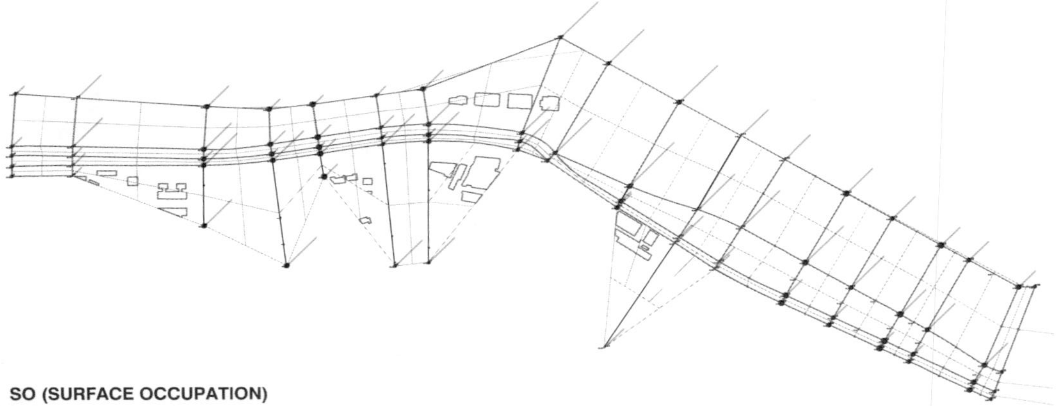

SO (SURFACE OCCUPATION)

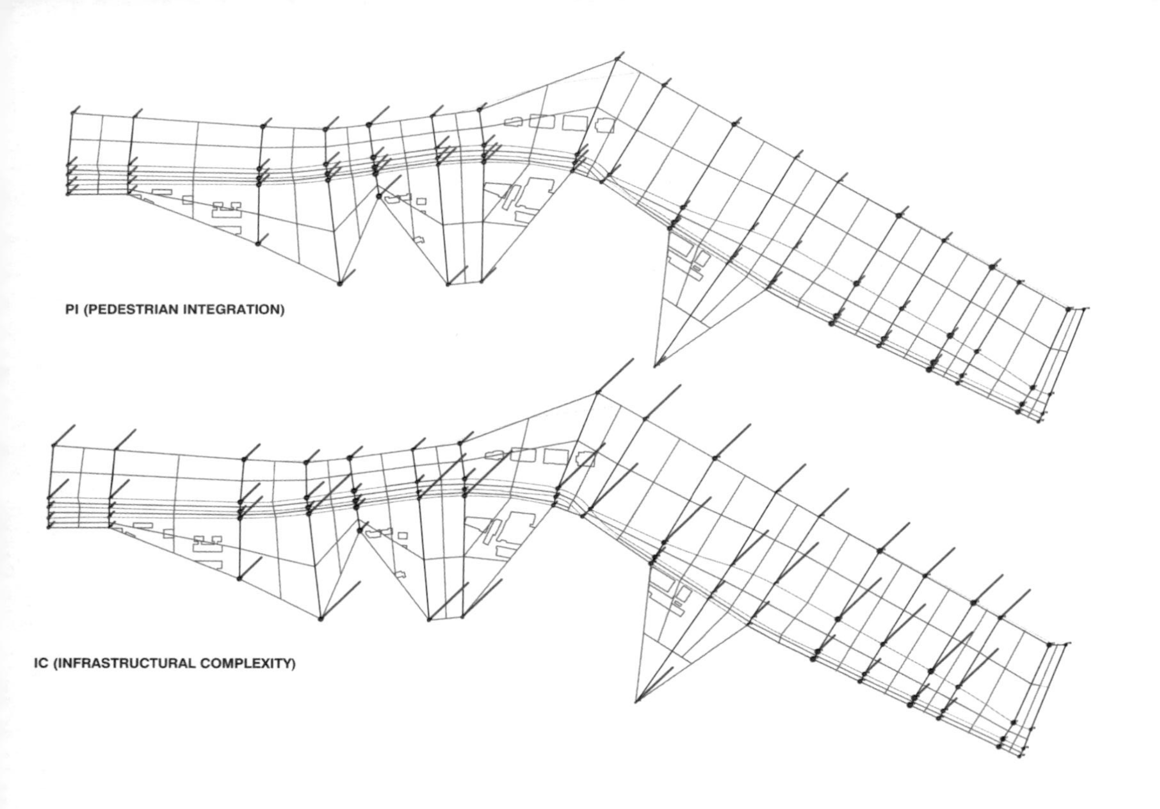
PI (PEDESTRIAN INTEGRATION)
IC (INFRASTRUCTURAL COMPLEXITY)

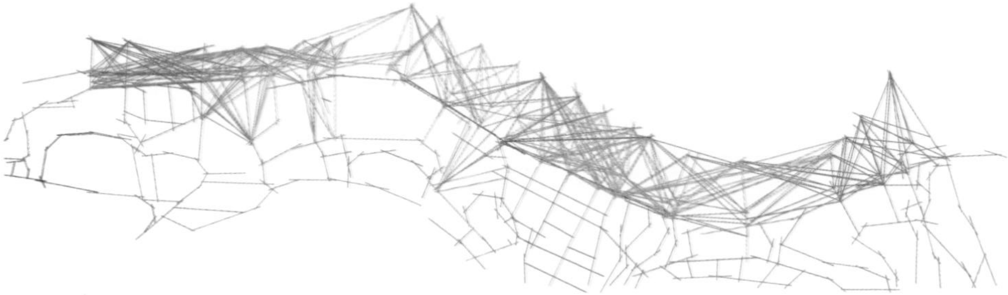

pedestrian streets
+ network

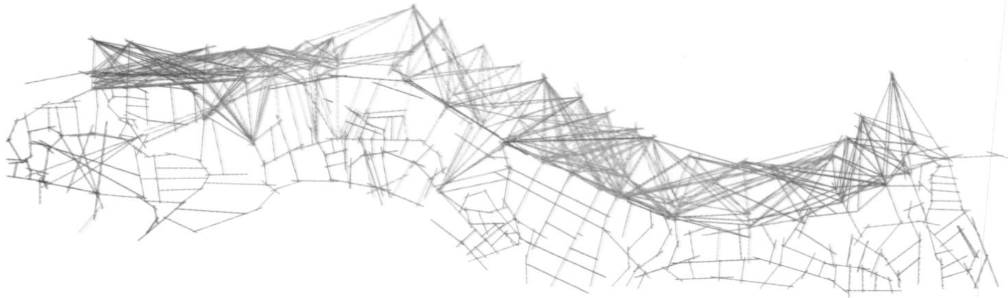

pedestrian streets
+ network
+ rights of way
+ existing voids

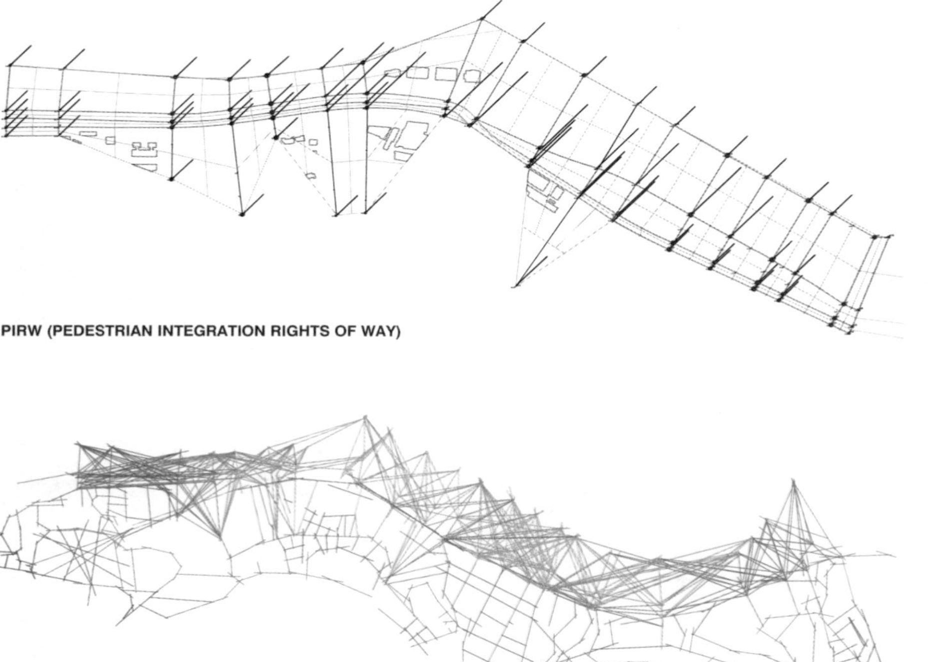

PIRW (PEDESTRIAN INTEGRATION RIGHTS OF WAY)

INTEGRATION PEDESTRIAN (IP) + (IPW)

pedestrian streets
+ network
+ way of rights
+ reorganising according
to ownership

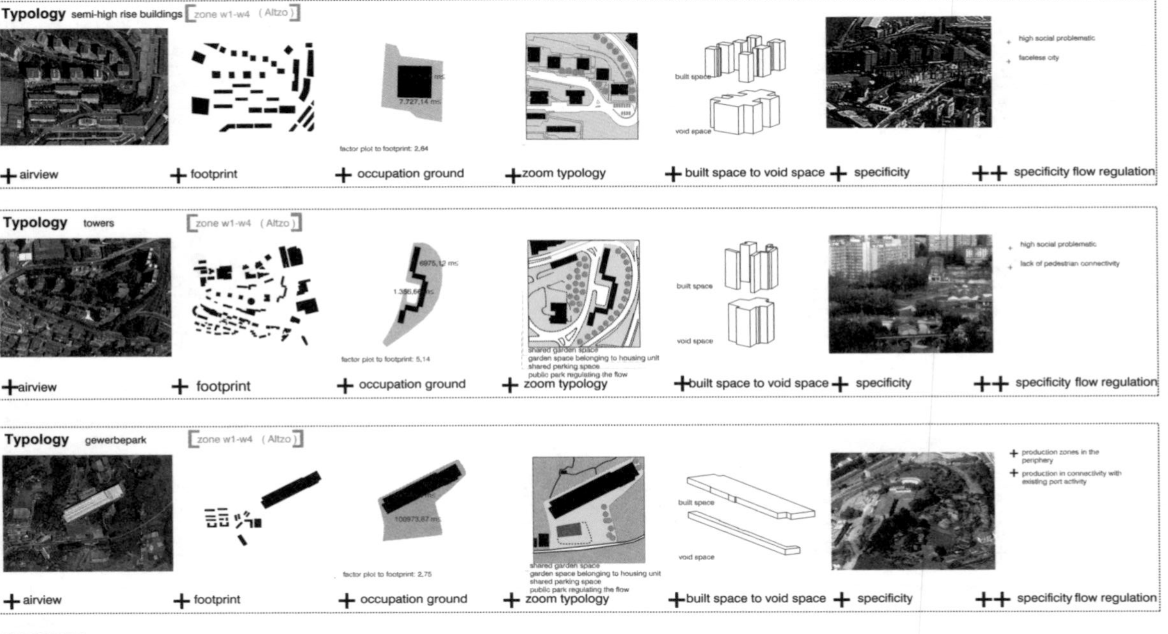
Typology semi-high rise buildings
zone w1-w4 (Altzo)
7.727,14 ms
factor plot to footprint: 2,84
built space
void space
high social problematic
faceless city
+ airview
+ footprint
+ occupation ground
+ zoom typology
+ built space to void space
+ specificity
++ specificity flow regulation
Typology towers
zone w1-w4 (Altzo)
6975,12 ms
factor plot to footprint: 5,14
shared garden space
garden space belonging to housing unit
shared parking space
public park regulating the flow
built space
void space
high social problematic
lack of pedestrian connectivity
+ airview
+ footprint
+ occupation ground
+ zoom typology
+ built space to void space
+ specificity
++ specificity flow regulation
Typology gewerbepark
zone w1-w4 (Altzo)
100973,87 ms
factor plot to footprint: 2,75
shared garden space
garden space belonging to housing unit
shared parking space
public park regulating the flow
built space
void space
+ production zones in the periphery
+ production in connectivity with existing port activity
+ airview
+ footprint
+ occupation ground
+ zoom typology
+ built space to void space
+ specificity
++ specificity flow regulation

TYPOLOGY

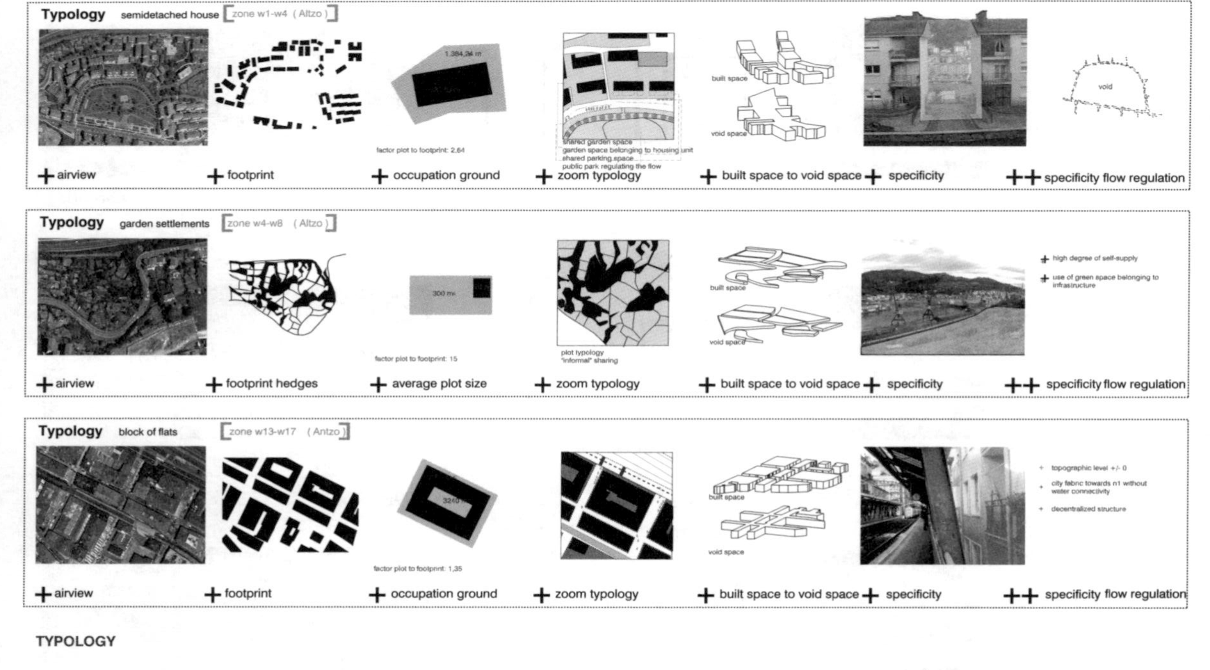
Typology semidetached house
zone w1-w4 (Altzo)
1.384,24 m
factor plot to footprint: 2,64
shared garden space
garden space belonging to housing unit
shared parking space
public park regulating the flow
built space
void space
void
+ airview
+ footprint
+ occupation ground
+ zoom typology
+ built space to void space
+ specificity
++ specificity flow regulation
Typology garden settlements
zone w4-w8 (Altzo)
300 m
factor plot to footprint: 15
plot typology
"informal" sharing
built space
void space
+ high degree of self-supply
+ use of green space belonging to infrastructure
+ airview
+ footprint hedges
+ average plot size
+ zoom typology
+ built space to void space
+ specificity
++ specificity flow regulation
Typology block of flats
zone w13-w17 (Antzo)
3240
factor plot to footprint: 1,35
built space
void space
+ topographic level +/- 0
+ city fabric towards n1 without water connectivity
+ decentralized structure
+ airview
+ footprint
+ occupation ground
+ zoom typology
+ built space to void space
+ specificity
++ specificity flow regulation

TYPOLOGY

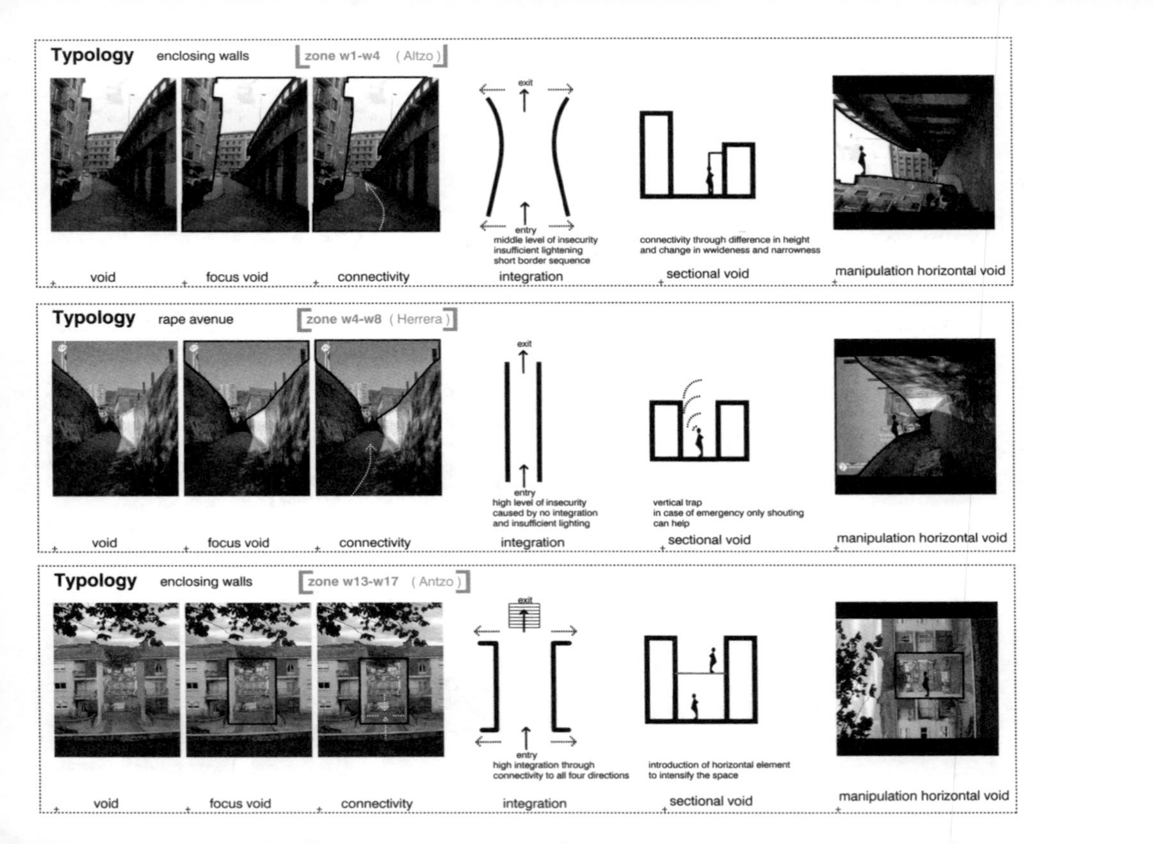
Typology enclosing walls
zone w1-w4 (Altzo)
exit
entry
middle level of insecurity
insufficient lightening
short border sequence
connectivity through difference in height
and change in wwideness and narrowness
void
focus void
connectivity
integration
sectional void
manipulation horizontal void
Typology rape avenue
zone w4-w8 (Herrera)
exit
entry
high level of insecurity
caused by no integration
and insufficient lighting
vertical trap
in case of emergency only shouting
can help
void
focus void
connectivity
integration
sectional void
manipulation horizontal void
Typology enclosing walls
zone w13-w17 (Antzo)
exit
entry
high integration through
connectivity to all four directions
introduction of horizontal element
to intensify the space
void
focus void
connectivity
integration
sectional void
manipulation horizontal void

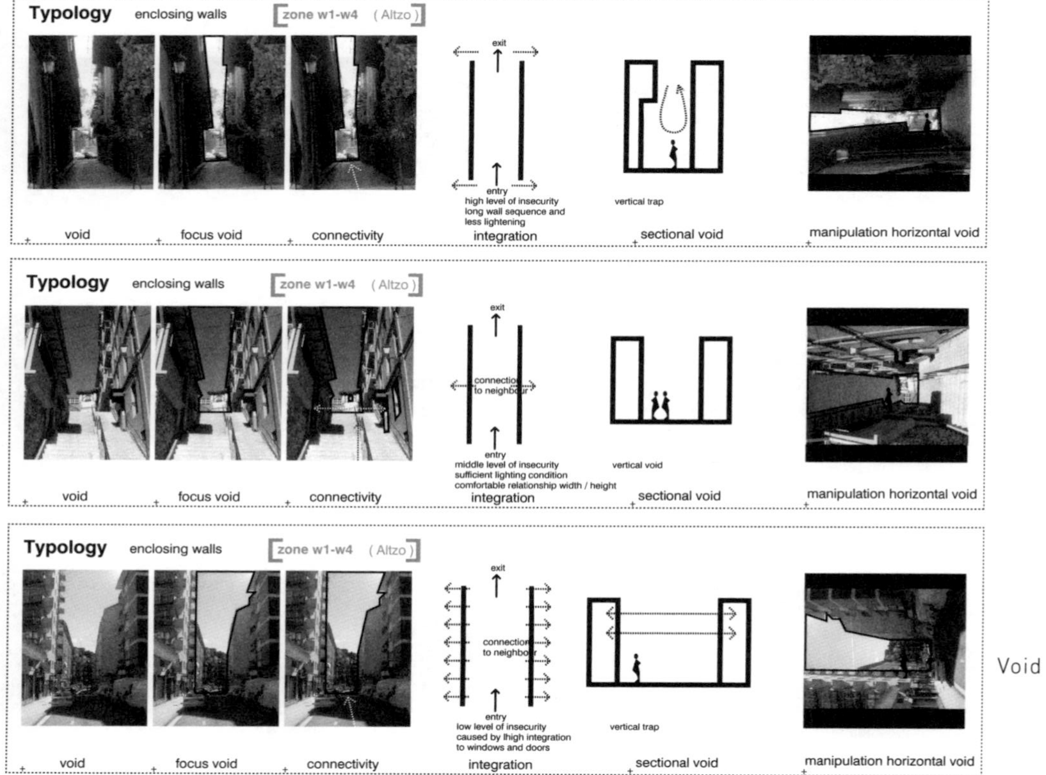

Void catalogue

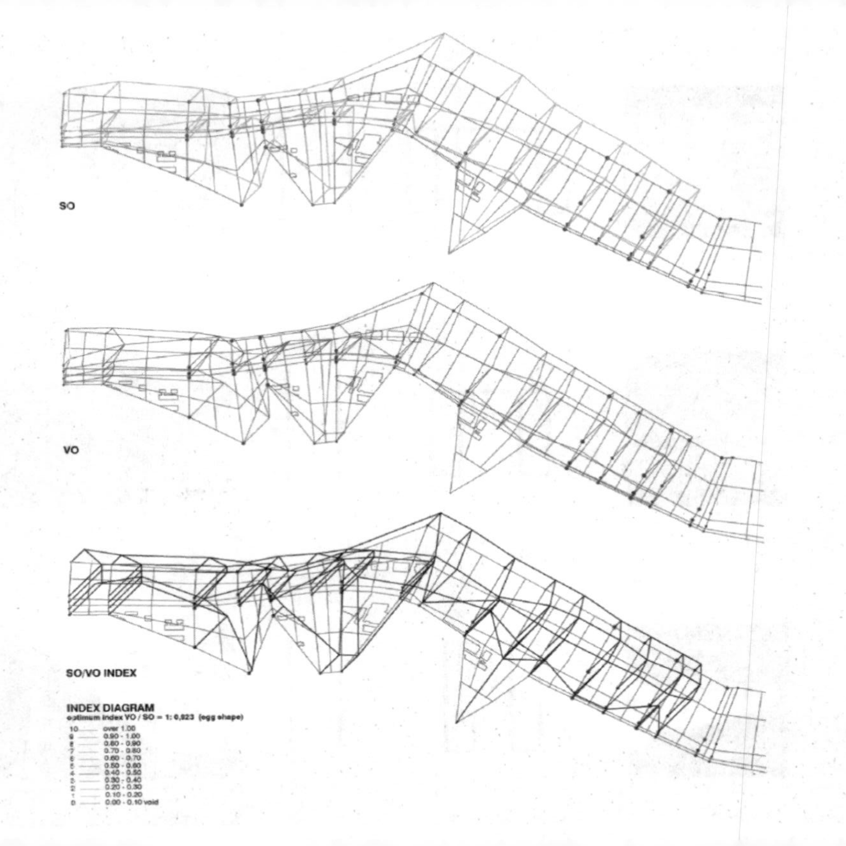
SO
VO
SO/VO INDEX
INDEX DIAGRAM
optimum index VO / SO = 1: 0,823 (egg shape)
10 over 1.00
9 0.90 - 1.00
8 0.80 - 0.90
7 0.70 - 0.80
6 0.60 - 0.70
5 0.50 - 0.60
4 0.40 - 0.50
3 0.30 - 0.40
2 0.20 - 0.30
1 0.10 - 0.20
0 0.00 - 0.10 void

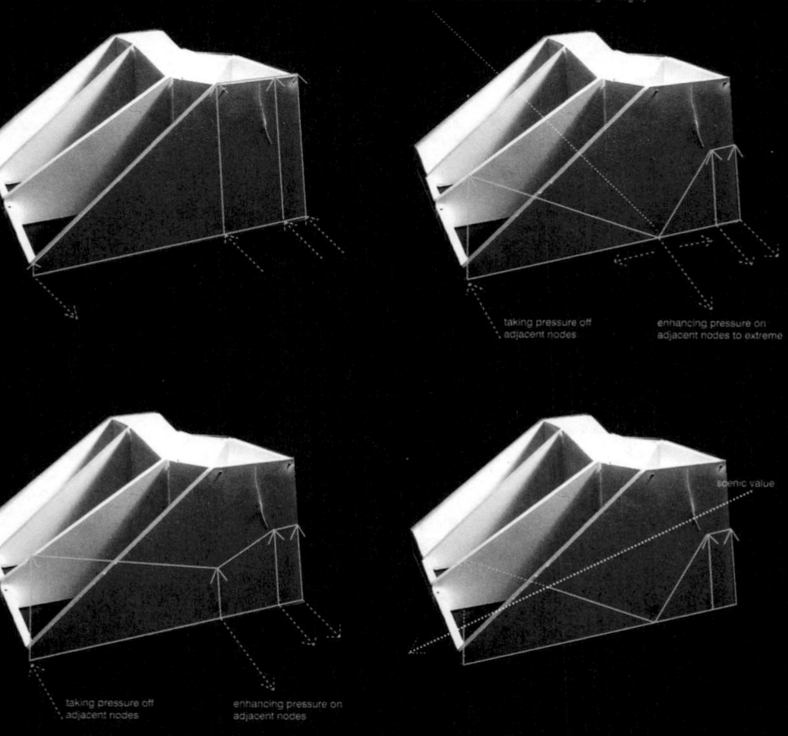
void node with low so/vo index and high integrity
taking pressure off
adjacent nodes
enhancing pressure on
adjacent nodes to extreme
taking pressure off
adjacent nodes
enhancing pressure on
adjacent nodes
scenic value

fastest trajectory to the bulkheadline
maximum voids, just providing of basic infrastructure

integration of highly frequented trajectory according to the integration value
maximum voids, just providing of basic infrastructure

integration of highly frequented trajectory according to the integration value
maximum voids, just providing of basic infrastructure

integration value of nodes

void first order
most connected points according to number of crossings 6times integrated

void second order
second connected points according to distance to other points (max distance 12m)

erasure of potential voids with high SO/VO INDEX

void first order
most connected points according to number of crossings 6times integrated

void second order
second connected points according to distance to other points (max distance 12m)

voids according the most efficient trajectories to the bulkheadline
+ most integrated trajectory

footprint of void foirst order
breaking the existing connections

imprinting foot of void
second order

footprints of void second order becoming congestion regulators

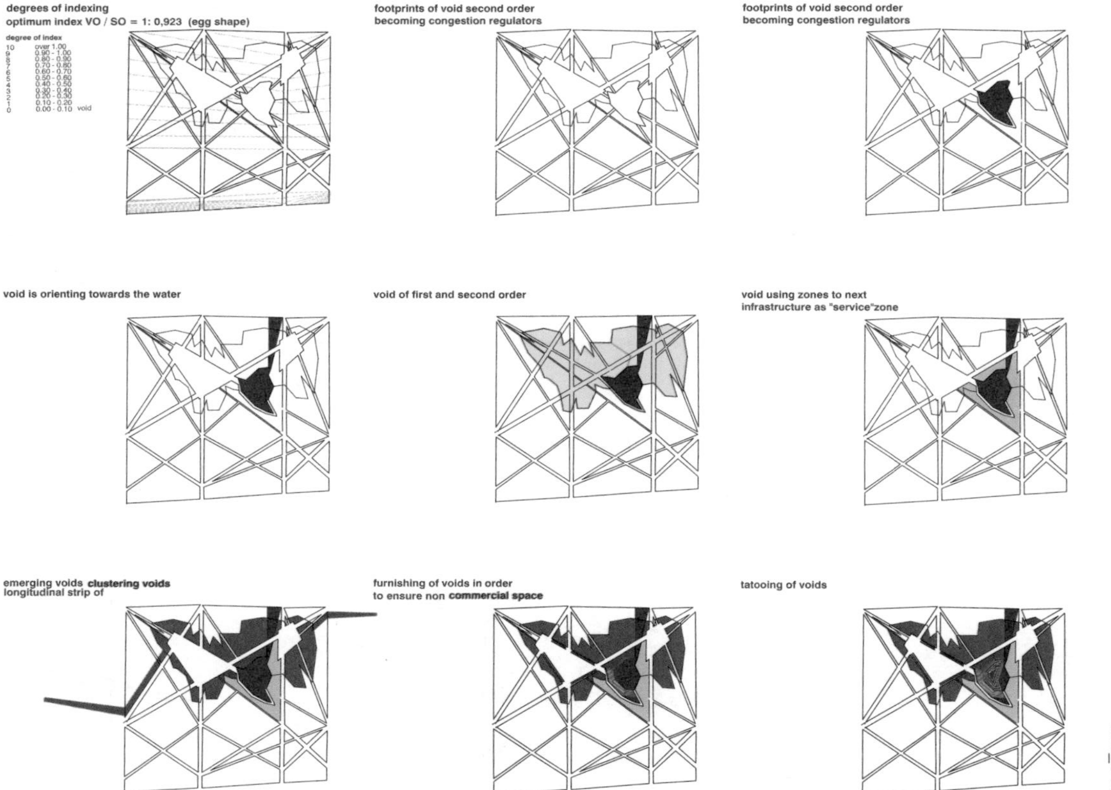
degrees of indexing
optimum index VO / SO = 1: 0,923 (egg shape)
degree of index
10 over 1.00
9 0.90 - 1.00
8 0.80 - 0.90
7 0.70 - 0.80
6 0.60 - 0.70
5 0.50 - 0.60
4 0.40 - 0.50
3 0.30 - 0.40
2 0.20 - 0.30
1 0.10 - 0.20
0 0.00 - 0.10 void
footprints of void second order
becoming congestion regulators
footprints of void second order
becoming congestion regulators
void is orienting towards the water
void of first and second order
void using zones to next
infrastructure as "service"zone
emerging voids clustering voids
longitudinal strip of
furnishing of voids in order
to ensure non commercial space
tatooing of voids

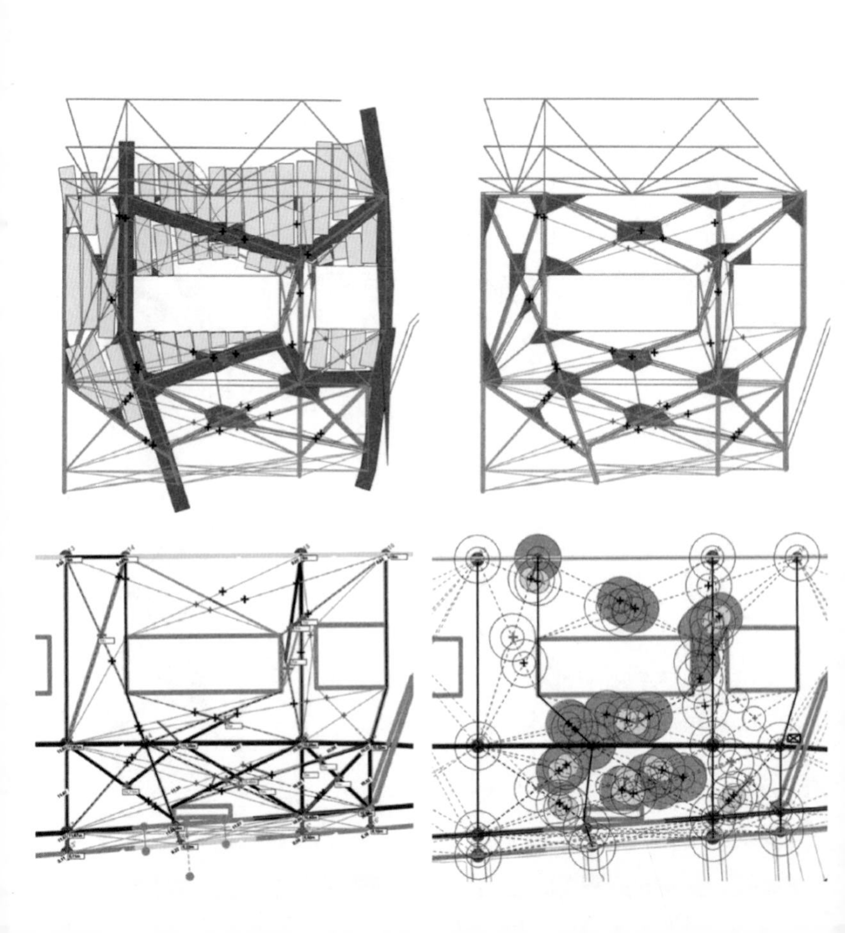

ON FORM (QUOTES)

No one will become a better designer by [...] following any method blindly. If you try to understand the idea that you can create abstract patterns by studying the implication of limited systems of forces, and can create new forms by free combination of these patterns and realize that this will only work if the patterns which you define deal with systems of forces whose internal interaction is very dense, and whose interaction with the other forces in the world is very weak, then in the process of trying to create such diagrams or patterns for yourself you will reach the central idea of what this book is all about. (1)

The pattern is, in short, at the same time a thing that happens in the world and the rule which tells us how to create that thing, and when we must create it. It is both a process and a thing; both a description of a thing which is alive, and a description of the process which will generate that thing. (2) Each pattern is a three-part rule, which expresses a relation between a certain context, a problem, and a solution.

I like to make the distinction between a plan and a recipe. A plan can be reverse engineered from a building but a recipe can't (easily) be reverse engineered from a cake. Our genome is a recipe, not a plan. Recipes seem to serve better as a schema of complex adaptive systems. (3)

The Mediator pattern talks about the relationship between two objects, which often cuts across the intuitive object system partitioning:
Intent: Define an object that encapsulates how a set of objects interact. Mediator promotes loose coupling by preventing objects from referring to each other explicitly, and it lets you vary their interaction independently.

Motivation: Object-oriented design encourages the distribution of behaviour among objects. Such distribution can result in an object structure with many connections between objects; in the worst case, every object ends up knowing about every other.

Though partitioning a system into many objects generally enhances reusability, proliferating interconnections tend to reduce it again. Lots of interconnections make it less likely that an object can work without the support of others: the system acts as though it were monolithic. Moreover, it can be difficult to change the system's behaviour in any significant way, since behaviour is distributed among many objects. As a result, you may be forced to define subclasses to customize the system's behaviour. You can avoid these problems by encapsulating collective behaviour in a separate mediator object. A mediator is responsible for controlling and coordinating the interactions of a group of objects. The mediator serves as an intermediary that keeps objects in the group from referring to each other explicitly. The objects only know the mediator, thereby reducing the number of interconnections.(4)

(2) Christopher Alexander. Notes on the Synthesis of Form. 1964.
(3) Christopher Alexander. Personal communication with Ward Cunningham, 20 February 1996.
(4) Erich Gamma, Design Patterns. Elements of Reusable Object-Oriented Software. 1995.

MEDIATION social disintegration | insecurity | one power occupation | infrastructural disconnectivity | restrictred areas

CAUSE infrastructure - border conditions | absence of collective space | ownership - concessions real state policy

EFFECT infrstructure - continuity | integrated technology parc | ownership - coexistency

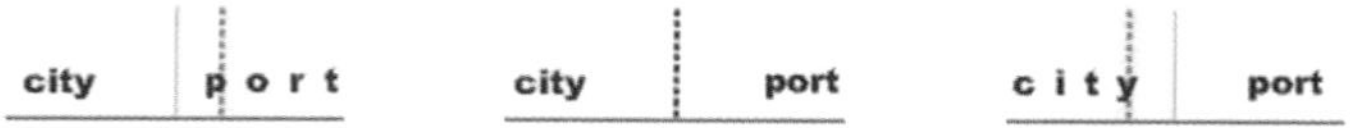

city | p o r t

city | port

c i t y | port

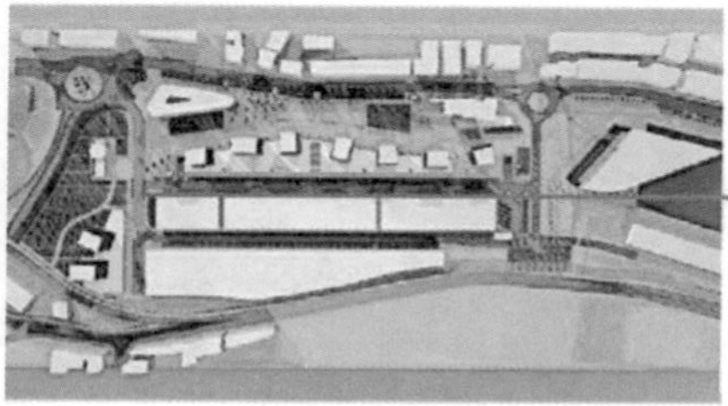

urban planinng

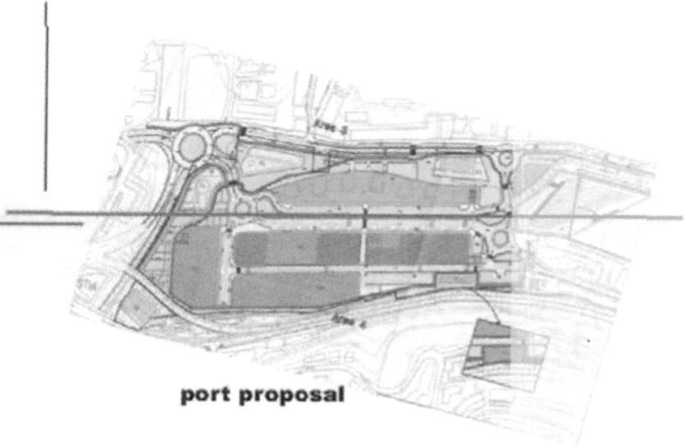

port proposal

11 meters

The quarrel found its peak about an 11 meter line. The port insited on an autonomus road next to the City. Both proposals don't achieve a flexible an d responsive structure to connect both desires.
The process of negociation starts to stagnate. Both suggestions patronize an imaginary wall

11 METER CONFLICT

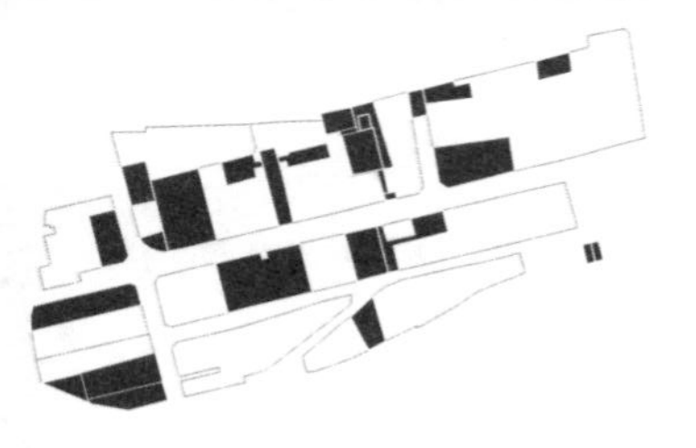
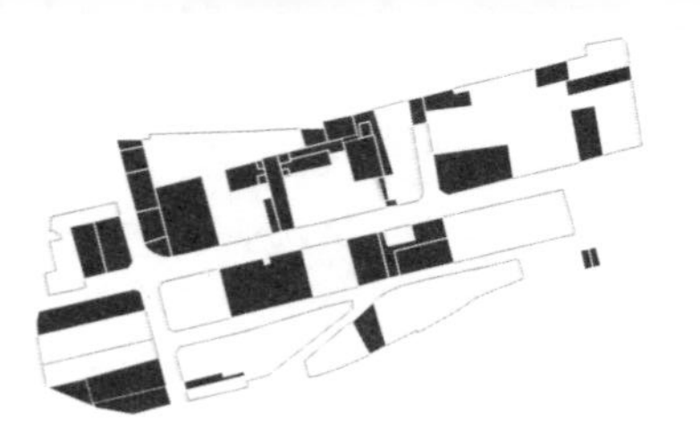
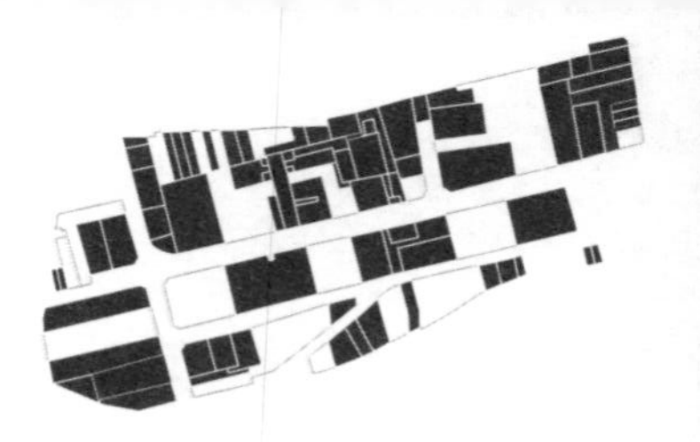
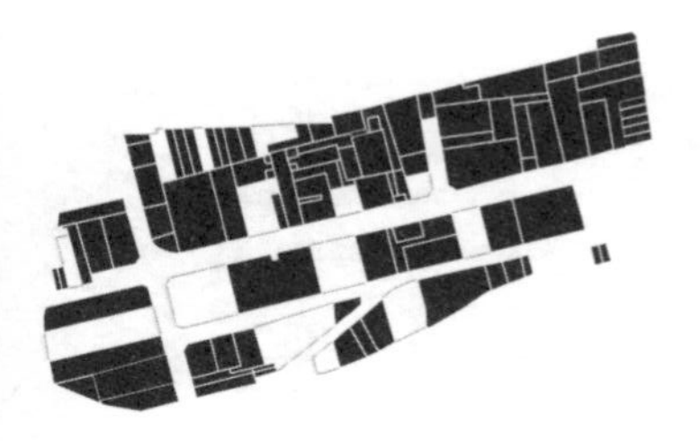
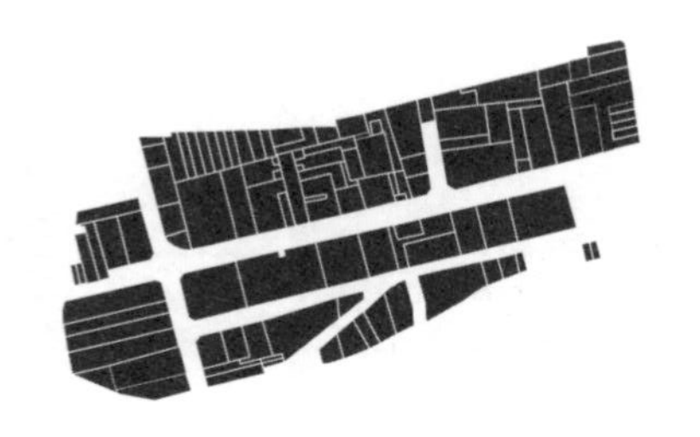

AVAILABLE REAL ESTATES IN TIME

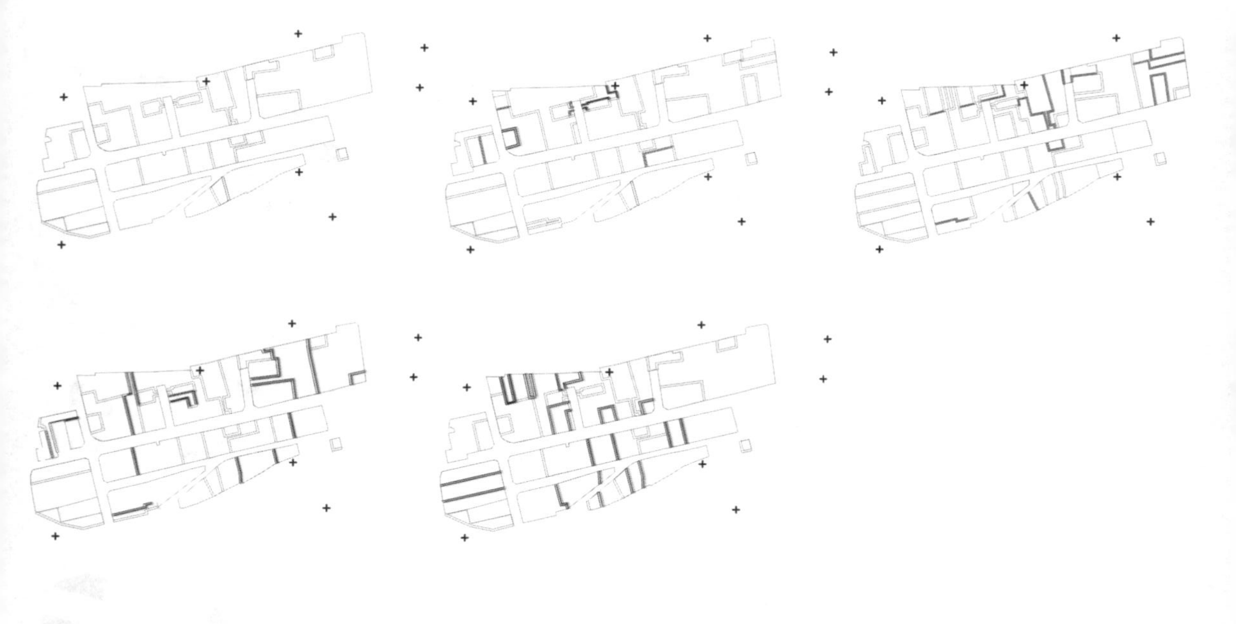

BOUNDARIES WITH NEGOCIATION LIMITATIONS

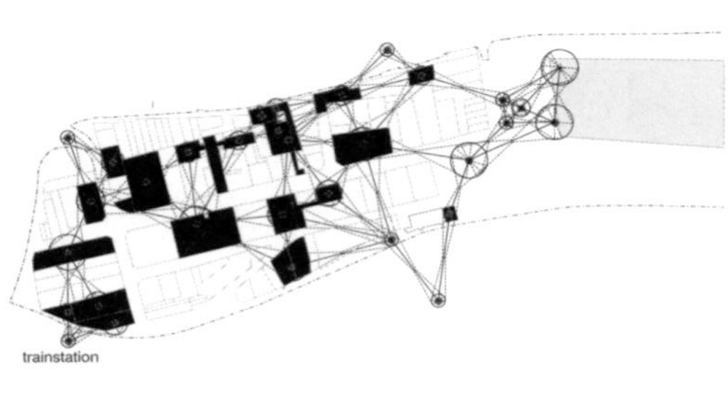

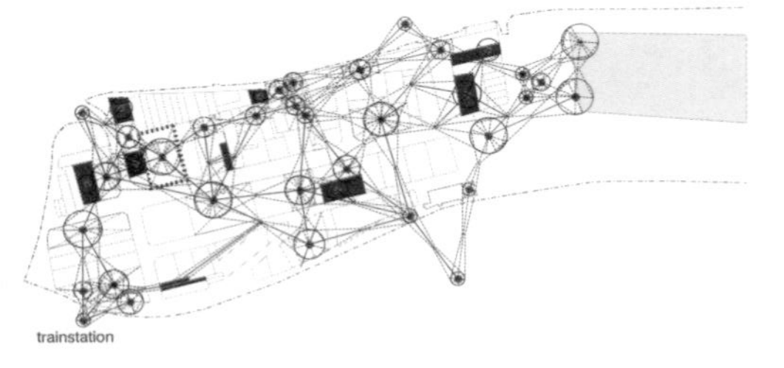

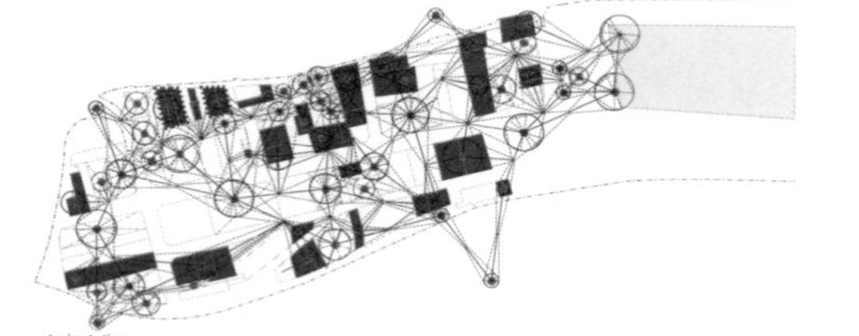

NETWORK GROWTH

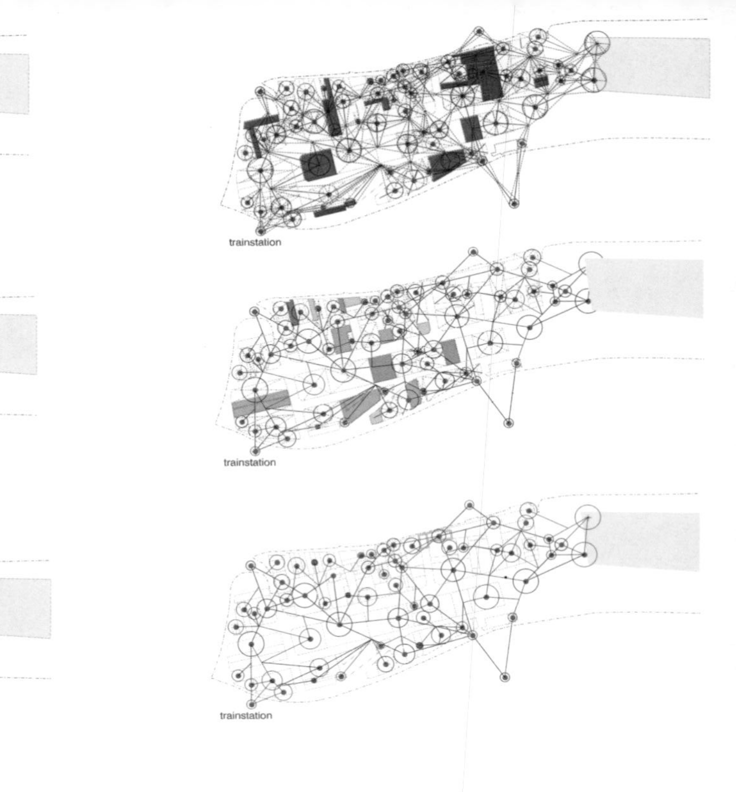

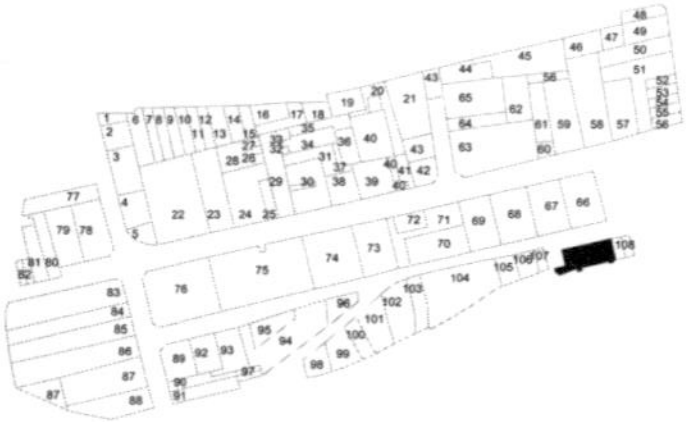

BUILDING 87B

hight:	0
plot:	1434
volumn:	25812
vertical (40%):	15487
horizontal (60%):	10325

PROTOTYPE 87B

radius:	(12/20) 16
hight:	24
wings amount:	0_4
volumn wing:	2581
I1/2	69/26
I3/4	42/34
I4/5	

BUILDING 63

hight:	0
plot:	2046
volumn:	32310
horizontal (60%):	19386
vertical (40%):	12924

PROTOTYPE 63

radius:	(26/15) 20.5
hight:	18
wings amount:	3
volumn wing:	6462
I1/2	
I3/4	
I5/6	

BUILDING 71

hight:	0
plot:	896
volumn:	16128
horizontal (60%):	9677
vertical (40%):	6451

PROTOTYPE 71

radius:	(26/15) 20.5
hight:	18
wings amount:	3
volumn wing:	2419
I1/2	74/74
I3/4	85/55
I5/6	

BUILDING 73

hight:	0
plot:	1060
volumn:	19080
horizontal (60%):	11448
vertical (40%):	7632

PROTOTYPE 73

radius:	(20/12) 16
hight:	18
wings amount:	2_5
volumn wing:	2290
I1/2	84/55
I3/4	61/93
I5/6	121

BUILDING 75

hight:	0
plot:	896
volumn:	16128
horizontal (60%):	9677
vertical (40%):	6451

PROTOTYPE 75

radius:	(26/15) 20.5
hight:	18
wings amount:	3_6
volumn wing:	2419
I1/2	81/104
I3/4	93/113
I5/6	117/73

BUILDING 78

hight:	18
plot:	1003
volumn:	18054
horizontal (60%):	10832
vertical (40%):	7222

PROTOTYPE 78

radius:	(20/11) 15.5
hight:	18
wings amount:	4_5
volumn wing:	2166
I1/2	75/50
I3/4	63/117
I4/5	64

BUILDING 83

hight:	0
plot:	1793
volumn:	32310
horizontal (60%):	19386
vertical (40%):	12924

PROTOTYPE 83

radius:	(26/15) 20.5
hight:	18
wings amount:	2_3
volumn wing:	6462
I1/2	64/69
I3/4	68
I5/6	

BUILDING 87A

hight:	0
plot:	419
volumn:	7542
horizontal (60%):	4525
vertical (40%):	3017

PROTOTYPE 87A

radius:	(13/7) 10
hight:	18
wings amount:	2_3
volumn wing:	1508
I1/2	33/34
I3/4	68
I5/6	

BUILDING 88

hight:	0
plot:	865
volumn:	15570
horizontal (60%):	9342
vertical (40%):	6228

PROTOTYPE 88

radius:	(18/10) 14
hight:	18
wings amount:	0_2
volumn wing:	6462
I1/2	26/54
I3/4	
I5/6	

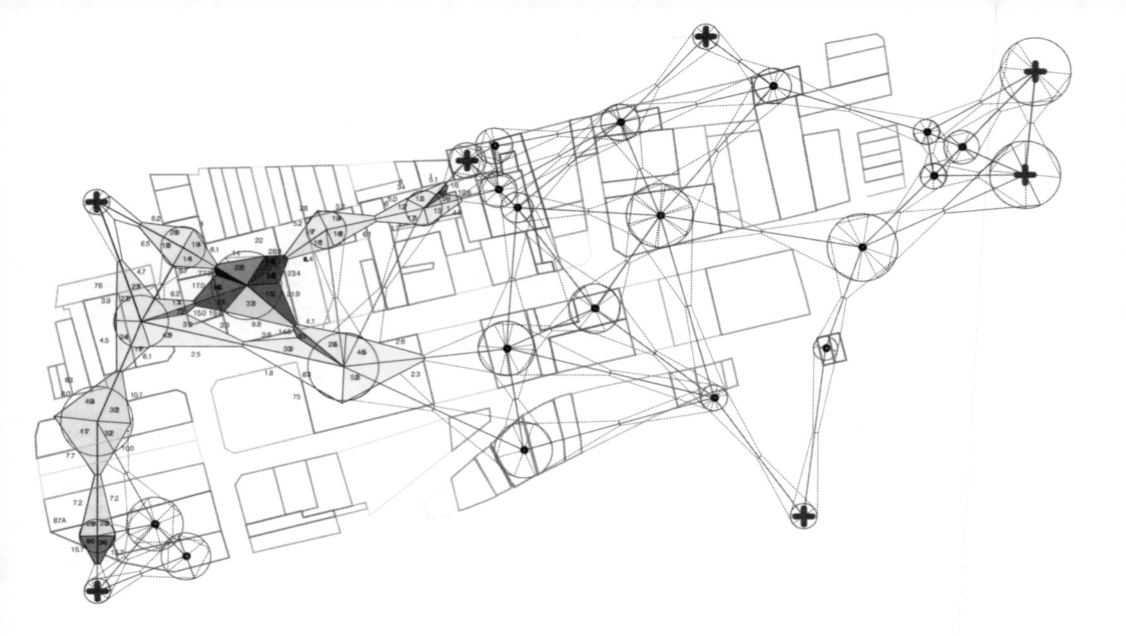

INTENSITIES

The problem is how to deal with the concessions on the port area. On one hand they are used to exert pressure on the City, on the other hand a progressive stage plan exists which should control the giving back areas.
A new system should assure maximal advantage for the port authority in order to finance through its real state an exterior port. For this reason a compensation program is establilshed.
Partly shared plots ensure mutual dependency and prevent a selling off to investors.

	L	M	S
	10%	60%	10%
	90%	40%	90%

city / city

city / port

port / port

occupation L M S

60%

40%

PROTOTYPE 3

radius:	(16/9) 12.5
hight:	18
wings amount:	3
volumn wing:	830
l1/2	56/42
l3/4	50
l4/5	

BUILDING 3

hight:	0
plot:	692
volumn:	4152
vertical (40%):	1661
horizontal (60%):	2491

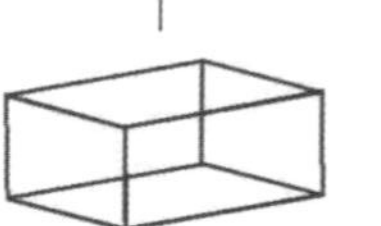

l L_3 V_h l L_1 l V_h R_1 V_h H V_v

PROTOTYPE COMPENSATION

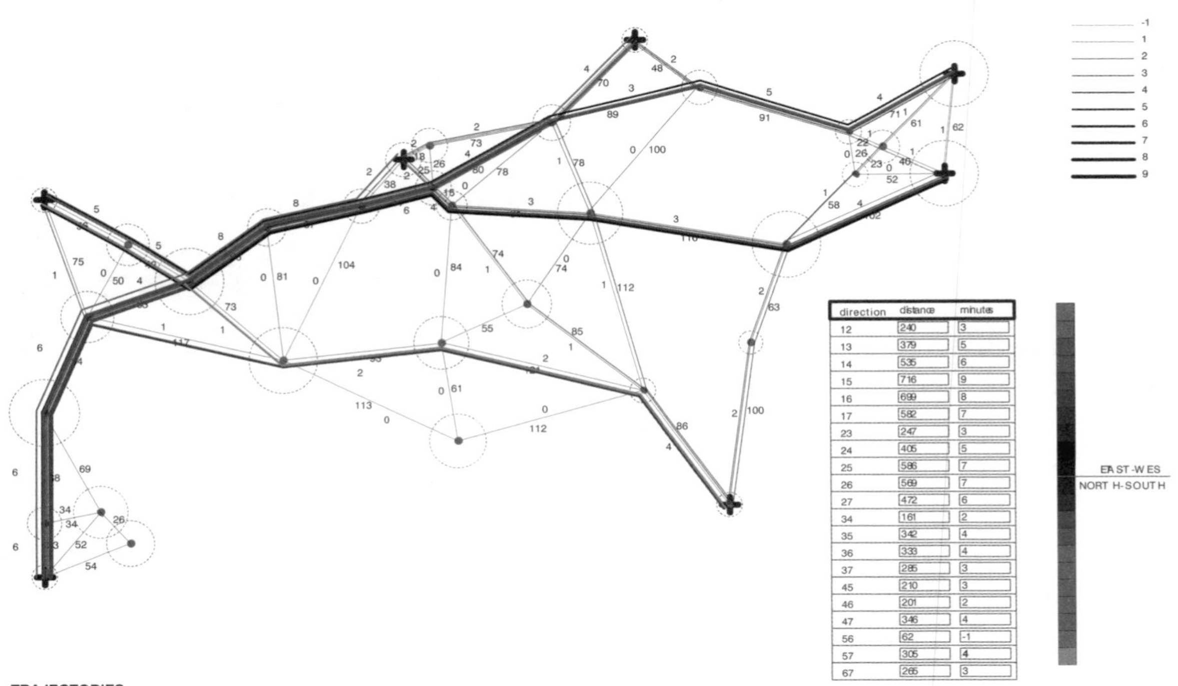

direction	distance	minutes
12	240	3
13	379	5
14	535	6
15	716	9
16	699	8
17	582	7
23	247	3
24	405	5
25	586	7
26	569	7
27	472	6
34	161	2
35	342	4
36	333	4
37	285	3
45	210	3
46	201	2
47	346	4
56	62	-1
57	305	4
67	265	3

TRAJECTORIES

	1	2	3
border	border	gaps	delay
bridging	stable	flexible	instable
time	continuous	interrupted	transitory
value	necessary	efficient	convinient

BORDER BRIDGES

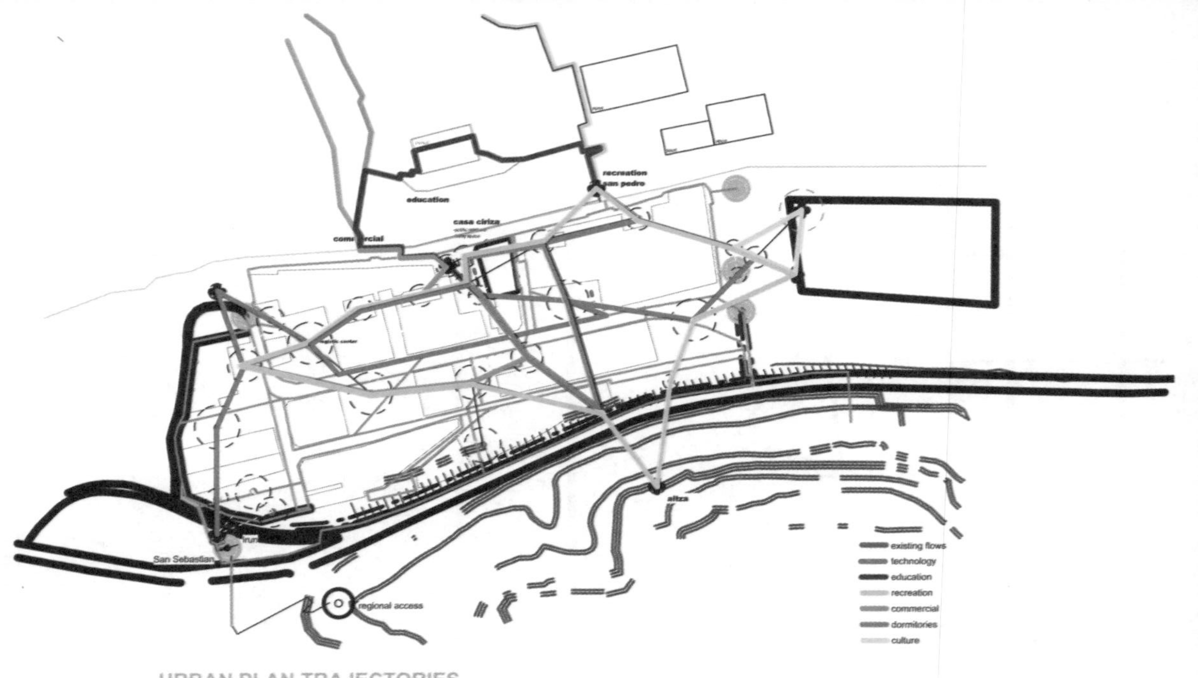

URBAN PLAN TRAJECTORIES

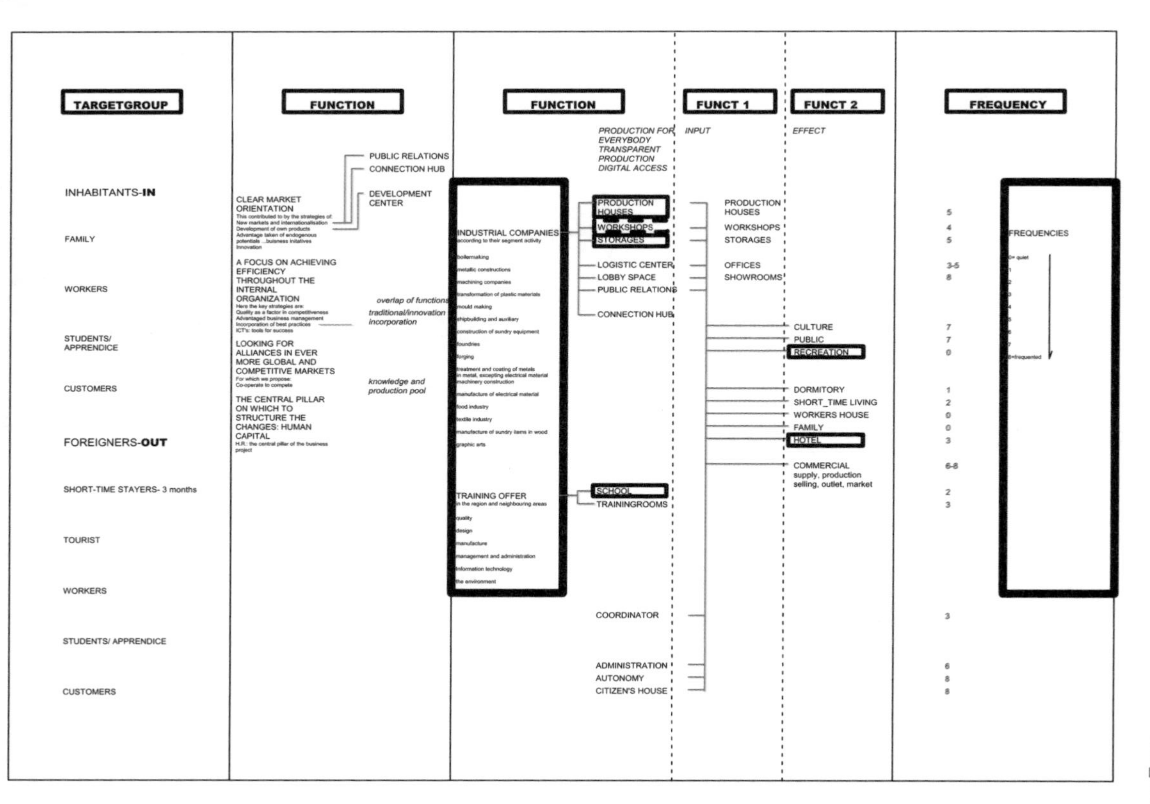

TARGETGROUP
FUNCTION
FUNCTION
FUNCT 1
FUNCT 2
FREQUENCY
INHABITANTS-IN
FAMILY
WORKERS
STUDENTS/ APPRENDICE
CUSTOMERS
FOREIGNERS-OUT
SHORT-TIME STAYERS- 3 months
TOURIST
WORKERS
STUDENTS/ APPRENDICE
CUSTOMERS
CLEAR MARKET ORIENTATION
A FOCUS ON ACHIEVING EFFICIENCY THROUGHOUT THE INTERNAL ORGANIZATION
LOOKING FOR ALLIANCES IN EVER MORE GLOBAL AND COMPETITIVE MARKETS
THE CENTRAL PILLAR ON WHICH TO STRUCTURE THE CHANGES: HUMAN CAPITAL
PUBLIC RELATIONS
CONNECTION HUB
DEVELOPMENT CENTER
overlap of functions
traditional/innovation incorporation
knowledge and production pool
PRODUCTION FOR EVERYBODY
TRANSPARENT PRODUCTION
DIGITAL ACCESS
INDUSTRIAL COMPANIES
according to their segment activity
TRAINING OFFER
in the region and neighbouring areas
PRODUCTION HOUSES
WORKSHOPS
STORAGES
LOGISTIC CENTER
LOBBY SPACE
PUBLIC RELATIONS
CONNECTION HUB
SCHOOL
TRAININGROOMS
COORDINATOR
ADMINISTRATION
AUTONOMY
CITIZEN'S HOUSE
INPUT
PRODUCTION HOUSES
WORKSHOPS
STORAGES
OFFICES
SHOWROOMS
EFFECT
CULTURE
PUBLIC
RECREATION
DORMITORY
SHORT_TIME LIVING
WORKERS HOUSE
FAMILY
HOTEL
COMMERCIAL
supply, production
selling, outlet, market
5
4
5
3-5
8
7
7
0
1
2
0
0
3
6-8
2
3
3
6
8
8
FREQUENCIES

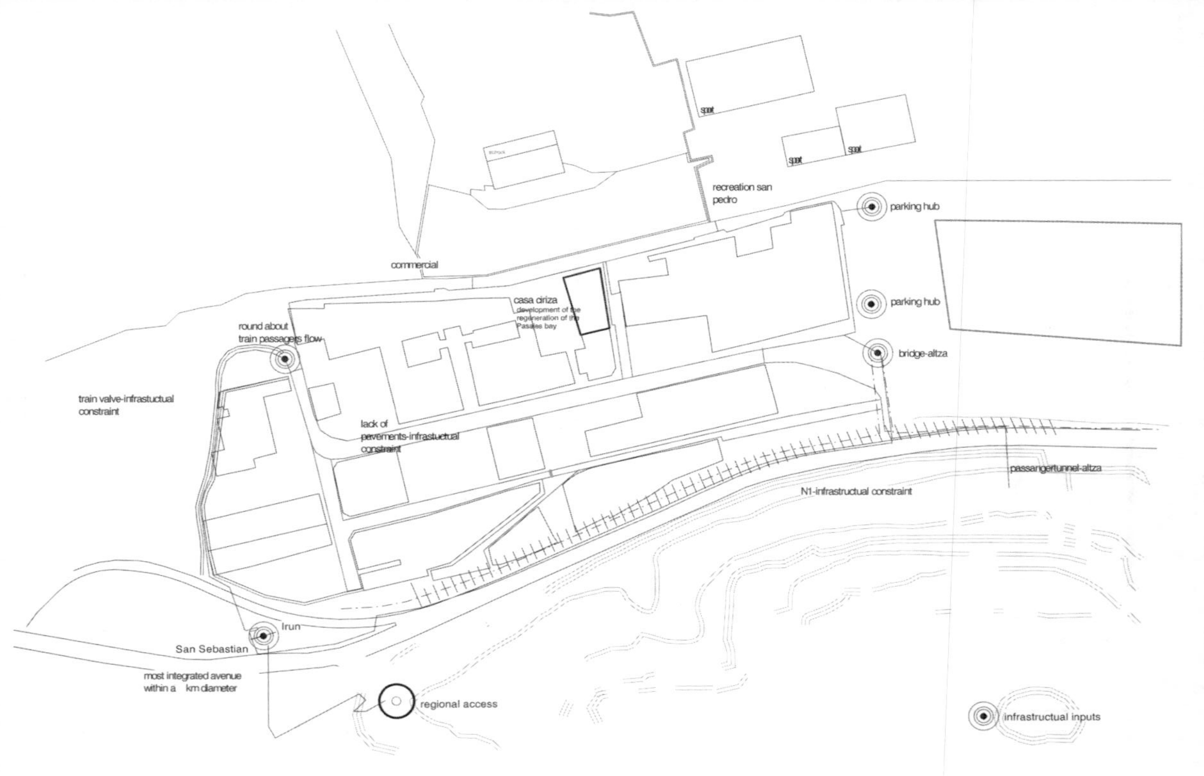

LA HERRERA EXISTING

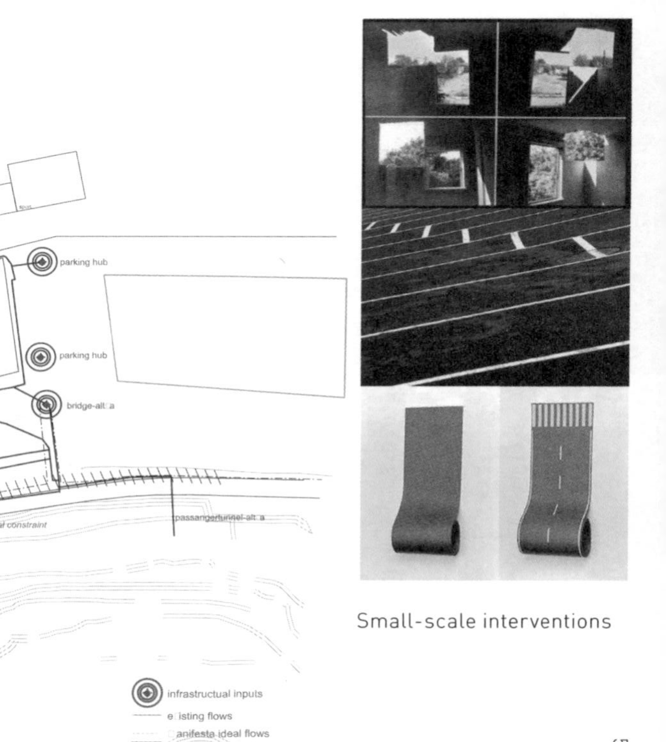

Small-scale interventions

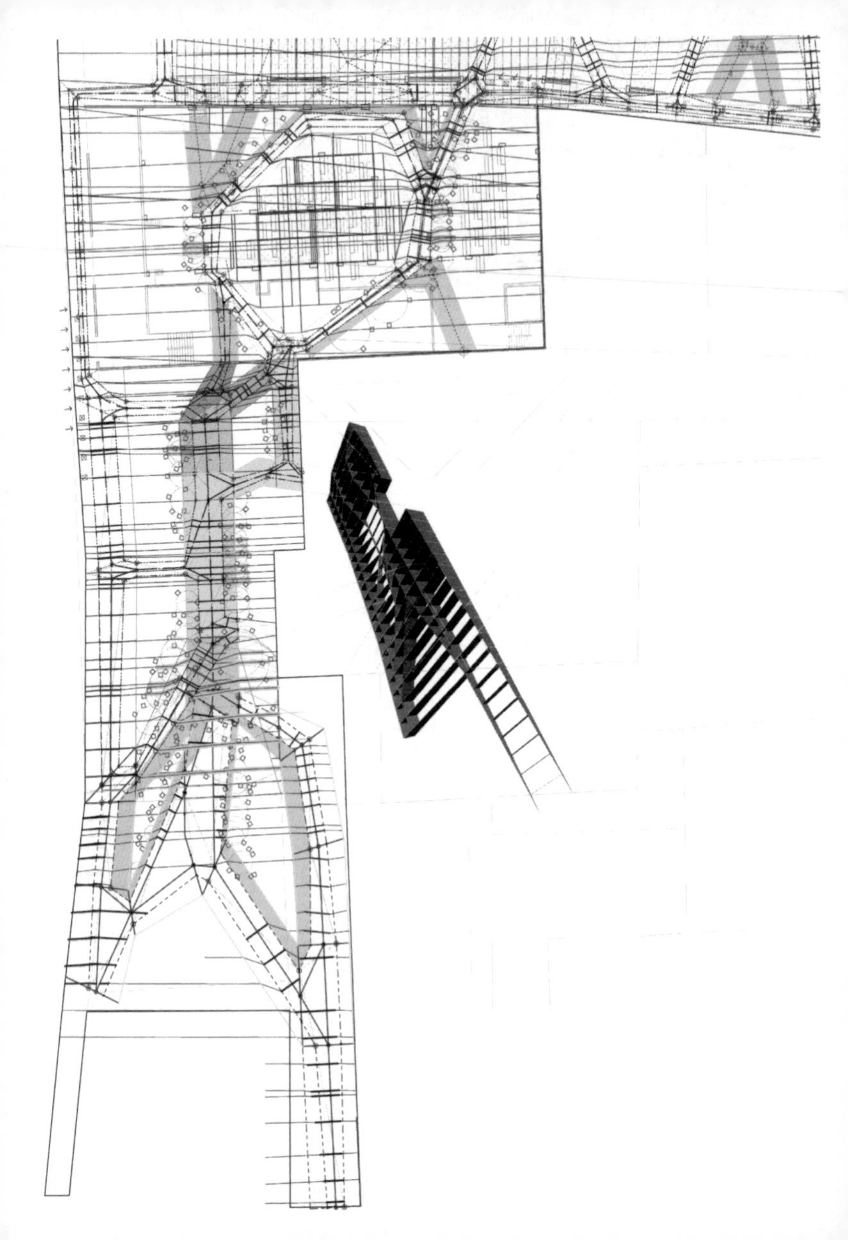

ON CONTINGENCY

It is well known the opposition that practices of everyday life operate on any geometrical panoptical urbanism, but what is not well-known or practiced is an architecture that without resigning its specific modes of control operates in one and only one multiplicity, embedding responsiveness in its constitution as a way of steering contingency and rooting drives.

In this sense a practice of mediation is one that takes frictions, impossibilities, violence, mistrust and struggles and actuates on these energies an Aikido mode exploring the potentials of a practice that do not operate by strategies like any panoptic practice based on the determination of its own place, that proper to it, its place of power and assertion either by tactics, as a practice of opportunity, trickery and wit, surfing time for the next blow, but rather a practice that operates a multiplicity where vital oscillations are responsive to the nature of relationships actuated locally and without contradiction across modalities. The migration of control from a central agent towards a distributed field of operations is all about responsiveness rather than openness. It is concerned with the nature of the elements that are interconnected: ... homogeneously stratifying commands and heterogeneously articulating self-consistent aggregates in an insoluble process of one giving rise to the other.

Any practice that does not see the forces it represses by its own constitution is bound to operate panoptically and lose the capacity of co-evolution with forces or practices that would survive it and by successive iterations mutate into more resistant strains that would undermine its constitution As part of the institutionalized academic and professional globalized apparatus, to seek survival behind the demarcation of knowledge is self-indulgent and conservative, to play at being the contesting grassroots crew is to withdraw into naivety and false charm. We believe in a superlative practice that goes beyond this well-known opposition.

ALDO VAN EYCK'S PLAYGROUNDS

'Van Eyck's humanist rebel playgrounds have a historical significance, not only as successful individual design cases but as an entirely different approach to urbanism, incremental, interstitial, ludic, particiaptory, ground up and polycentered rather than top down and monocentered."

'...how powerful the long term influence of the vision implicit in the physical structure can be in reshaping the relation between people with their surroundings and with each other.'

'...he would be the first to consciously conceive and enact a major new development in post-war planning, what by the 1960s would come to be called an 'incremental' or 'infill' strategy, accomodating immediate user needs, and exploiting opportunities offered by the immediately available sites.'

'Van Eyck's idea of approaching design within a concrete given setting... embedded into real 'circumstances', 'lived-in conditions', 'experienced cases' 'immediate contexts', or 'situations'.

'...Lefebvre argued that the ordinary, forgotten, everyday areas on theperiphery of the metropolitan city were privileged places of poetic experience and social life.'

The infrastructural knots in the city fabric are a reason for its segregation.
The configuration of these infrastructure in the form of a knot actsas a multiple border for the pedestrian flows.
This can be translated into dangerous situations likepedestrians trying to cross a highway, or the presence of crime in these kind of structures, due to the lack of visibility, light or enough people moving.
Around the bay of Pasaia there are two important knots which block the city, knot 01 and knot 02. Which are the frame for the research as prototipical situations.

KNOTS 01 - 02 AS INTENSE ZONES OF INTERVENTION

current situation knot 01

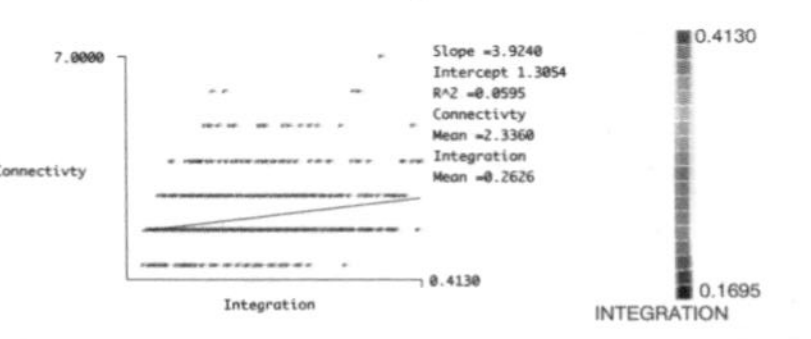

The diagram shows that the most integrated path is located at the south of Herrera station. Which means that is the line that receives more pedestrian movement in the grid. This is due to its strategical location, as the one of the only lines bridging the flows from the south zone of the grid to its north zone. The majority of the lines are segregated, as its shown on the scattergram , the cloud has most of its points on the left side of the integration axis.

proposal knot 01

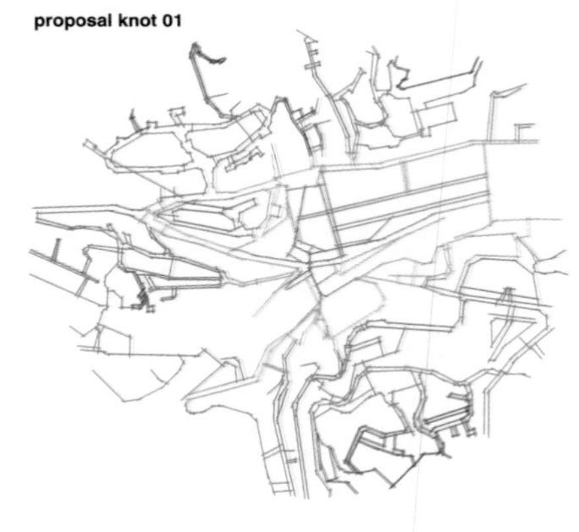

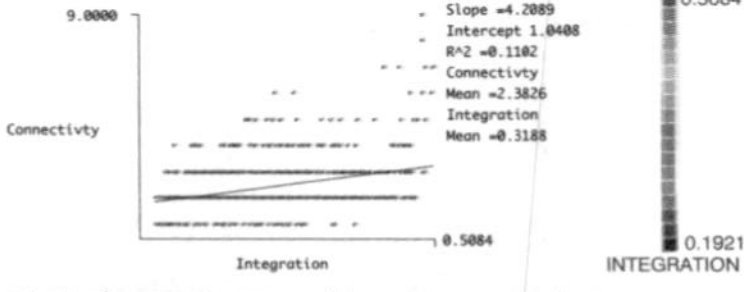

The red colour increased its scope, reaching previous segregated zones.
In the scattergram, the cloud shifted a number of points to the right, showing that the whole system is more integrated.
After a series of interventions -new lines of connection- aiming to bridge segregated zones around knot 01,the diagram shows a notorious improvement in the integration of the whole system. Meaning that the grid will receive more pedestrian movement, which triggers a new imput for the urban development, as a distributed benefit.

integration = ...the 'integration value' of each line reflects its mean linear 'depth' from all other lines in the system. We can then map these integration values from red through purple... Integration values in line maps are of great importance in understanding how urban systems function because it turns out that how much movement passes down each line is very strongly influenced by its 'integration value' calculated in this way, that is by how the line is positioned with respect to the system as a whole.

Bill Hillier, Space is the machine.

INTEGRATION KNOT 01 - PEDESTRIANS

current situation knot 01

proposal knot 01

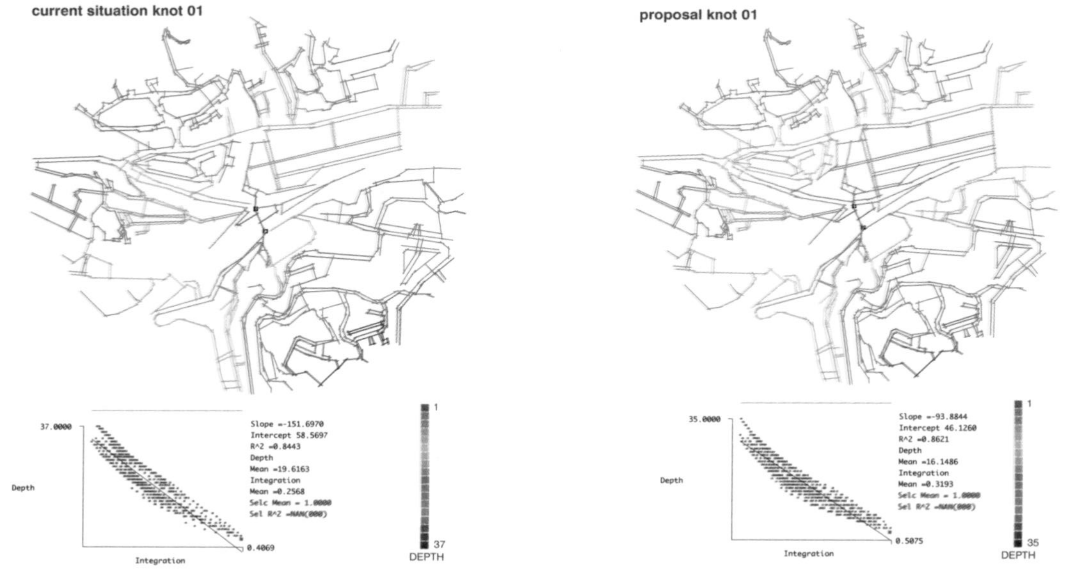

The depth is measured starting from the line at the south of Herrera station, the most integrated line. The diagram shows how the flows are going to move departing from the station. The redder or less depth lines are going to be more visited and the bluer ones less visited.

After a series of interventions bridging knot 01 with its surrounding areas, the diagram shows that its scope has increased, and the maximum depth of the system dicreased from 37 to 35. This means that the movement of the pedestrians coming from the station will move in a larger are, making the whole zone more accesible from the train station.

depth = ...to go from any line to any other one must pass through a certain number of intervening lines. Each line thus has a certain minimum line 'depth' from another, which is not necesarilly a function of distance. It follows that each line has a minimum average line 'depth' from all other lines in the system.
There are substantial differences that govern the influence of the grid on movement in the system: roughly, the less depth to all other lines, the more movement; the more depth the less.

Bill Hillier, Space is the machine.

DEPTH KNOT 01 - PEDESTRIANS

current situation knot 02

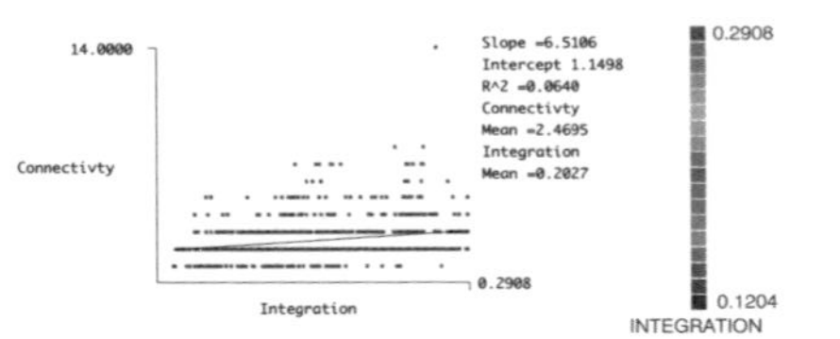

The diagram shows that the most integrated zone is located at the south of knot 02. The lines at the north of the knot, as well as the ones at the west south are segregated.

proposal knot 02

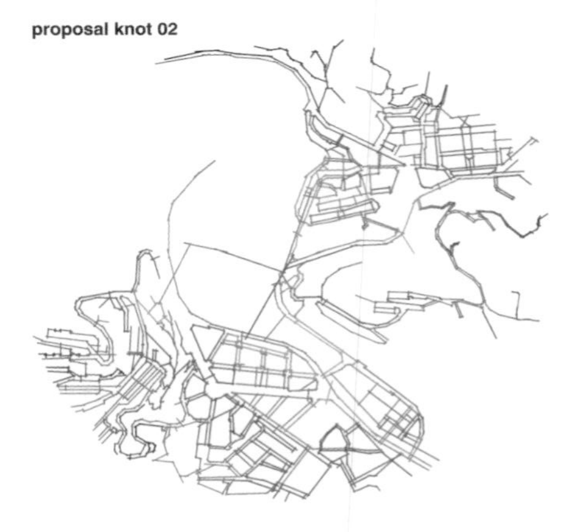

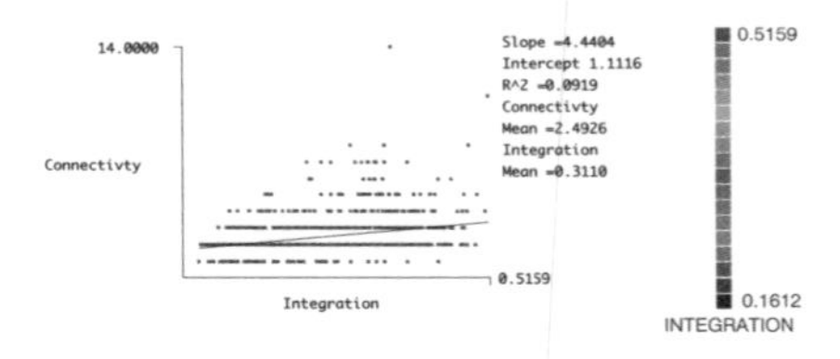

The most integrated zone shifted to knot 02, in this way the "red scope" is able to integrate the north with the south.

INTEGRATION KNOT 02 - PEDESTRIANS

current situation knot 02

The depth is measured starting from the line at the south of knot 02, the most integrated line. The redder or less depth lines are located at the south, and the zone at the north of the zone are segregated from the system.

proposal knot 02

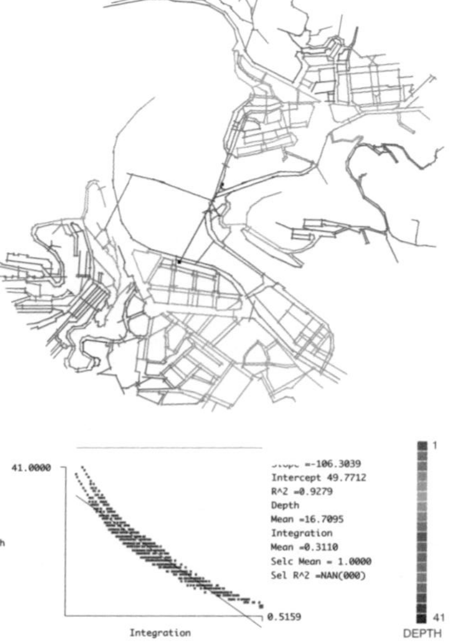

After a series of interventions bridging knot 02 with its surrounding areas, the diagram shows that the most integrated line shifted to the center of the knot. Transforming the system in a more democratic one, integrating to it the north zone. The maximum depth of the system dicreased from 60 to 41.

DEPTH KNOT 02 - PEDESTRIANS

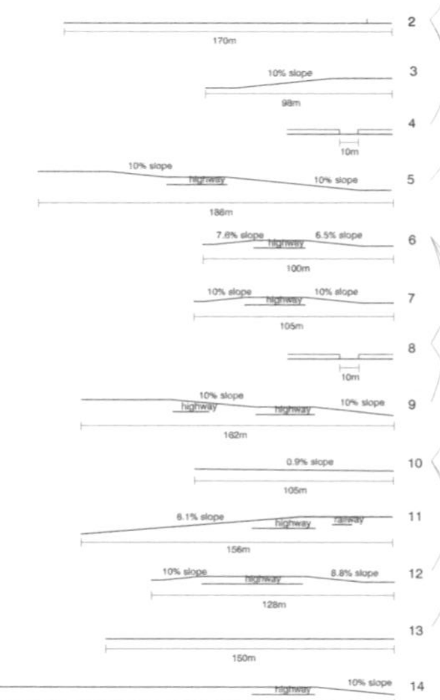

urban prototype = Urban prototypes are engines of change, instruments of new urban form. They are organisational structures, at the same time adaptable to specific environments and stable in their organisational form.

Raoul Bunschoten, Urban flotsam

The prototype is thought as an instrument for urban integration. It bridges physical borders and gaps which are blocking the pedestrian mobility within the city. Its physical form is represented in three categories:
1. surface
2. bridge
3. void

ARCHIPIELAGO KNOT 01 ESTACION HERRERA

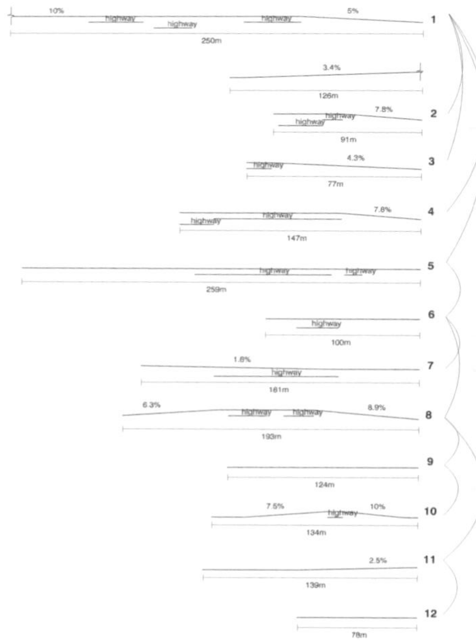

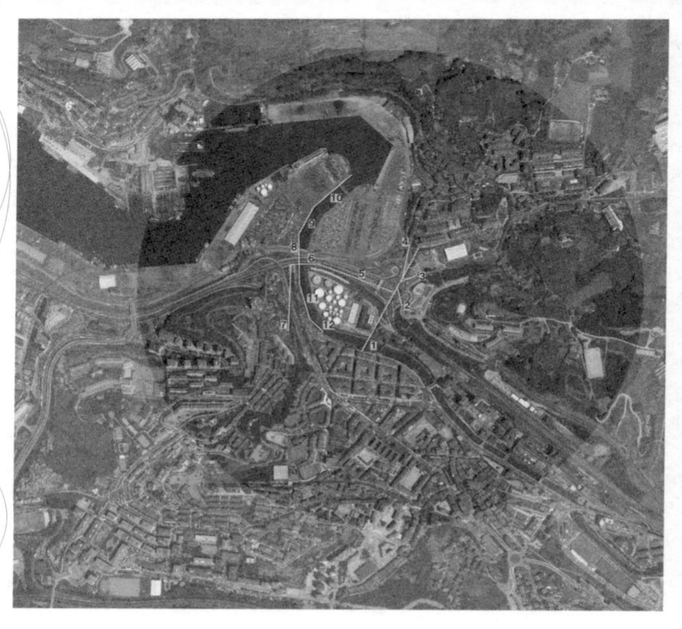

ARCHIPIELAGO KNOT 02 LEZO - RENTERIA

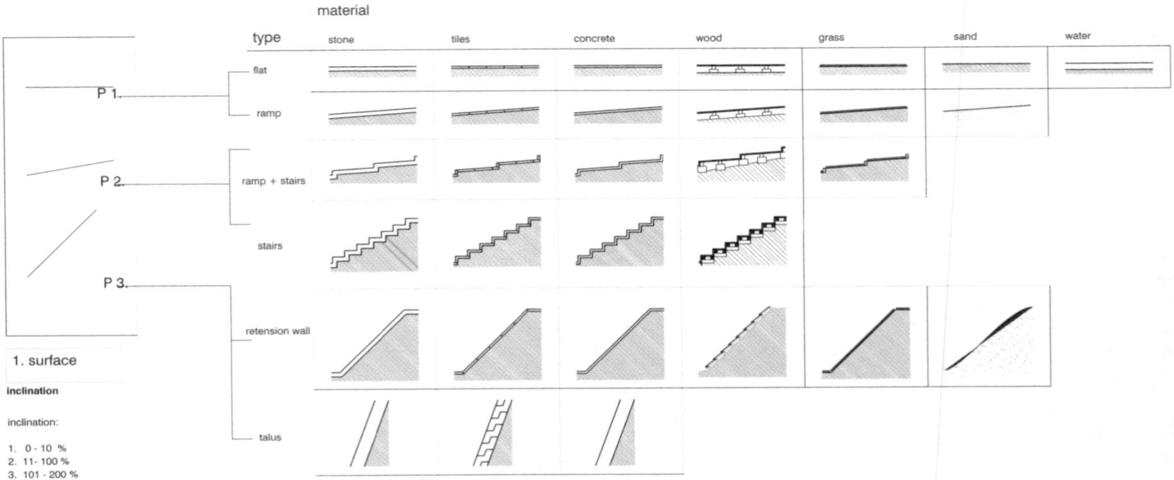

material

type: stone | tiles | concrete | wood | grass | sand | water

P 1. — flat, ramp

P 2. — ramp + stairs, stairs

P 3. — retension wall, talus

1. surface

inclination

inclination:

1. 0 - 10 %
2. 11- 100 %
3. 101 - 200 %

SURFACES CATALOGUE

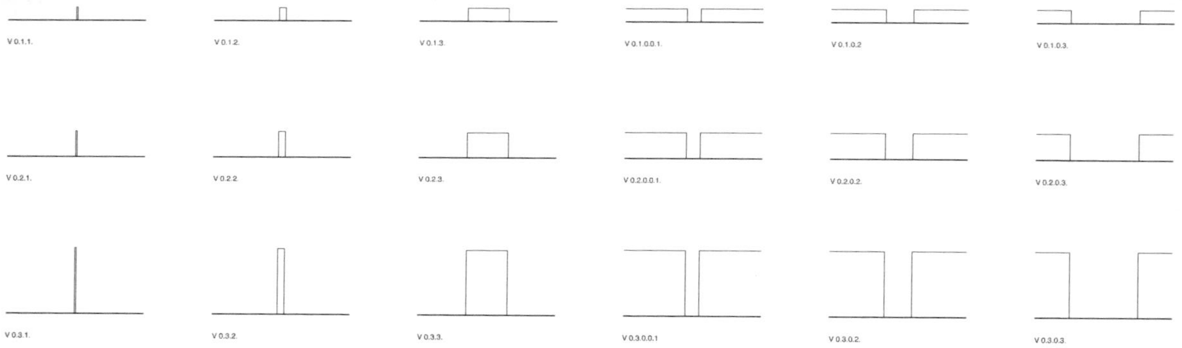

3. void

height + length + width

height:	length:	width:
0.1. 2 - 3 m	0.0.1. 0.2 m	0.0.0.1. 2 m
0.2. 4 - 9 m	0.0.2. 0.3 -1 m	0.0.0.2. 3 - 4 m
0.3. 10 - 20 m	0.0.3. 2 - 6 m	0.0.0.3. 5 - 10 m

VOIDS CATALOGUE

2. bridge

span

span:

0.0.1. 0 - 10 m
0.0.2. 11- 20 m
0.0.3. 21- 50 m

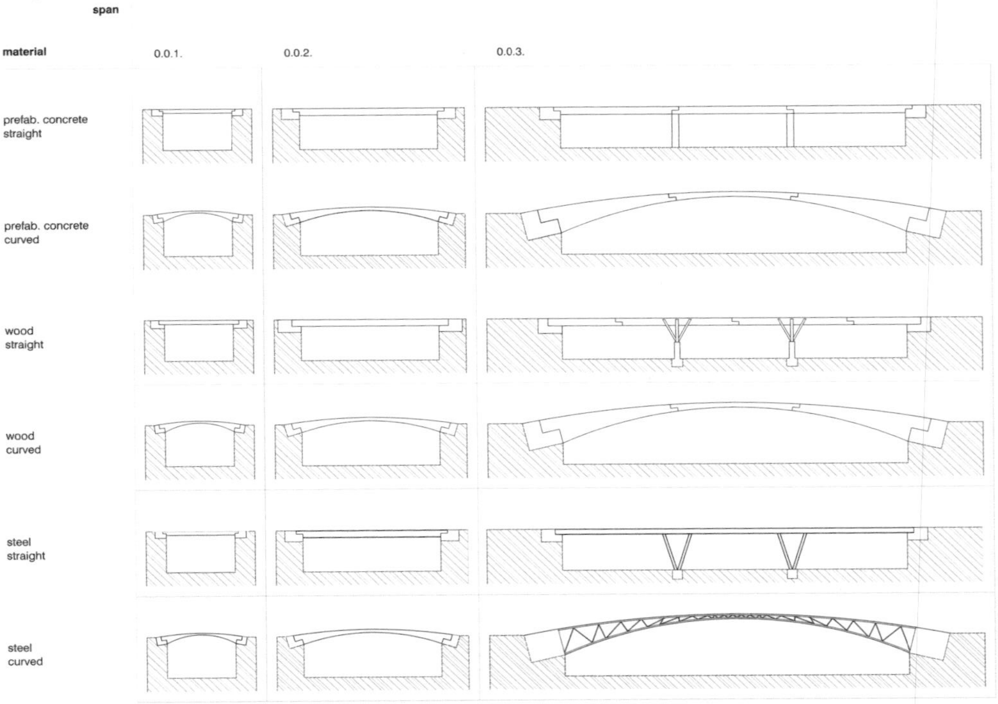

material	0.0.1.	0.0.2.	0.0.3.
prefab. concrete straight			
prefab. concrete curved			
wood straight			
wood curved			
steel straight			
steel curved			

BRIDGES CATALOGUE

0 - 3 m 4 - 9 m 10 - 19 m 20 - 28 m 29 - 40 m 41 - 50 m GRADIENT OF WIDTH AVAILABLE SURFACE

THE WIDTH OF ADJACENT SPACES TO THE PATH GIVES A MAP OF AVAILABLE SURFACE FOR FUTURE PROGRAM

ADJACENT SPACE AND BORDERS

BORDER PERMANENCE

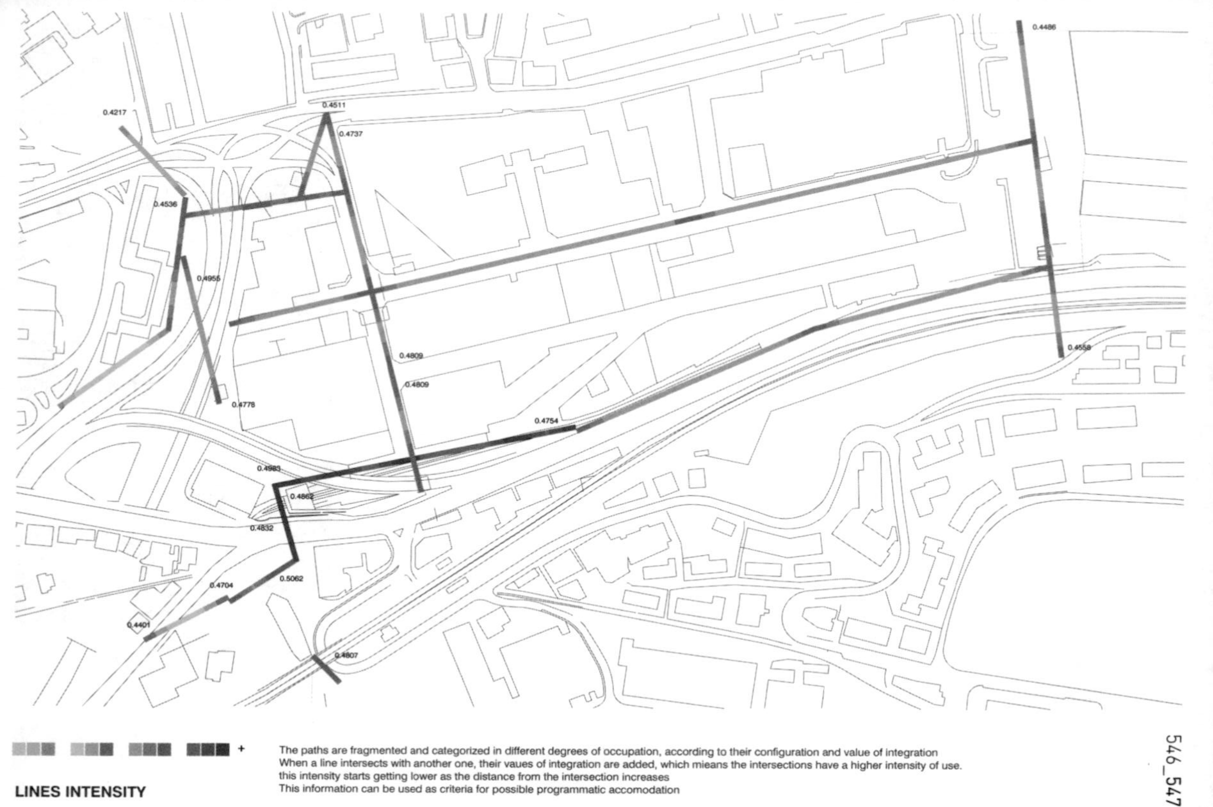

LINES INTENSITY

The paths are fragmented and categorized in different degrees of occupation, according to their configuration and value of integration
When a line intersects with another one, their vaues of integration are added, which mieans the intersections have a higher intensity of use.
this intensity starts getting lower as the distance from the intersection increases
This information can be used as criteria for possible programmatic accomodation

MAXWAN BRIDGES

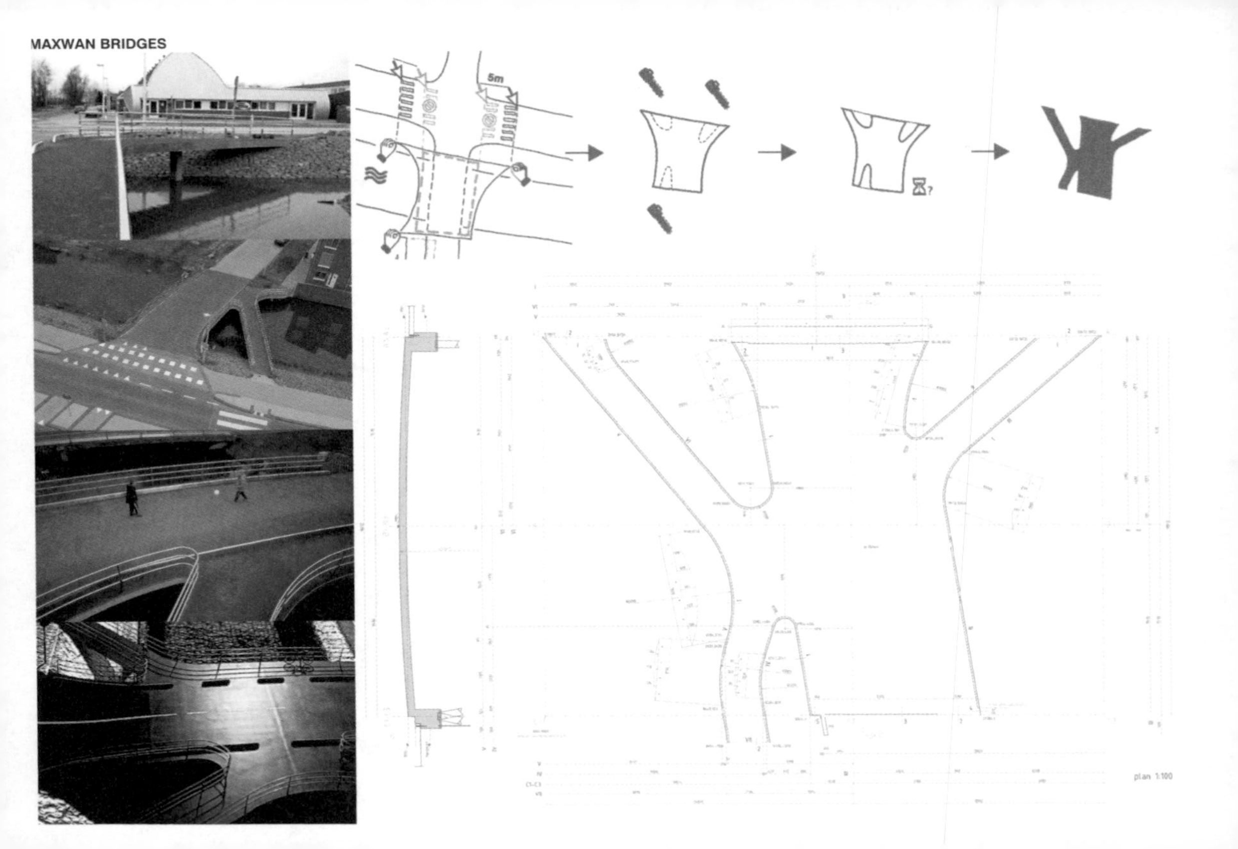

ON PROTOTYPES AND MEDIATIONS

[R]ealism and idealism both go too far, it is a mistake to reduce matter to the perception we have of it, a mistake also to make of it a thing able to produce perceptions in us, but in itself of a different nature than they are. Matter, in our view, is an aggregate of images. And by 'image' we mean a certain existence which is more than that which the idealist calls a representation, but less than that which the realist calls a thing; an existence placed half way between the 'thing' and the 'representation'. (5)

TOOAUP has been developing techniques of control understood as Performance Specifications oscillating in their ecosystem of application at several scales of the Donostia-Pasaia substrate. Initially they were configured as layers of information, and then spatialized as a field of performance. The investigations that were configured as diagrams, scripts, charts, statistics, field maps and spatial analysis were integrated into applications in order to be operative from within the processes of urban growth at various simultaneous scales or in a non-scalar mode.
Performance is an ongoing reverse recipe-making, it deals with thresholds, consistencies and the fluctuation of feedback and decision-making.

The Performance Specifications in each of the domains were developed with a certain degree of associativity that allowed them to be utilized as applications, but the next move was to actualize them as Associative Material Constrains as the determination of a manageable and productive set of cause-effect material relationships, with a built-in consistency, a Rationale that to some degree is anticipatory and has the capacity to assimilate contingency as a vital force, as well as being a prescriptive activator.

Taking advantage of the developed Performance Specifications and Associative Material Constraints as prescriptions to be actualized, deviated and made sustainable as instruments by entering into a process of creative negotiation with their production milieu, a Material Organization will evolve as a result of the progressive meshing of the Performance Specifications with a

Rationale for responsiveness that through the establishment of Associative Material Constraints has determined the modalities and degrees of structure, function and change.

In order to steer the Material Organization, various structural stages of scenario planning could be utilized: this could be understood not merely as an exercise but as its character. Proliferation is fundamental to evaluating the degrees of adaptability of the substrates in order to utilize their configurational character as prototypical conditions.

Prototypes do not need context or site specificity, and although they have limits of applicability, those limits could be expanded via their embedded mediation. As a set of performance specifications they are interesting in being able to activate actualizations and push the envelope of their discipline through a process of creative negotiation.

The movement from the generic applicability of prototypes towards its mediations produces at least two divergent lines, one towards the actual and another towards the virtual, because in the process of gaining actuality the prototype needs to go through an increasing level of sameness in order to be mediated. This sameness is a double bind; it differentiates the prototype by expanding it into its multiple potentials and differentiates its virtuality by forcing actualizations via creative negotiations.

Actualizations operate as the point of inflection in a material flow, they incarnate or anticipate the engagement with multiple agents, so that the organization would tend to become spatialized and sites defined as samples of operation. Sites are not understood merely as locations or as discrete objects but as gradients in a field of dynamic conditions, pinpointed thresholds of a particular interest, provisionally framed and temporally adjusted as in/out switches.

By evolving their differentials, the prototypes are treated as a technology of integration of demands. By programming their machinic response, the prototypes progressively constitute a generic-specific brief where systems and their regime of performance and material qualities are engineered for proliferation.

First, as micro-proposals they are anticipatory, switches on a network of potential that would activate an autogenic process of regeneration utilizing as a continuum the immanent nature of their relationship.

Second, they are demonstrative, needing invariance to operate as control devices that can route contingency by inflecting it into their regime.

An agile utilization of two concepts that although coined by evolutionary biologists have a crucial architectural origin could help to instrumentalize the intrinsic transitions in the growth process, These are exaptations and spandrels.

Exaptation or change of function is a term coined to describe a commonplace occurrence in the evolution of life: for example, a limb or organ evolves originally for a particular function, but later on is recruited to fulfill a new function.

'Spandrels arise non-adaptively as architectural byproducts, but may regulate, and even dominate, the later history of a lineage as a result of their capacity for co-option to a subsequent, and evolutionarily crucial, utility.

In architecture, the prototypical spandrel is the triangular space "left over" on top when a rectangular wall is pierced by a passageway capped with a rounded arch. By extension, a spandrel is any geometric configuration of space inevitably left over as a consequence of some other architectural decision' (6)

Our interest here is not with the pervasive analogical capacity of concepts, it is more with the instrumentalization of two intrinsic architectural categories: the invariant and the differentiation in architectural form and growth.

(5) Henry Bergson. Matter and Memory, Introduction.
(6) S. Jay Gould

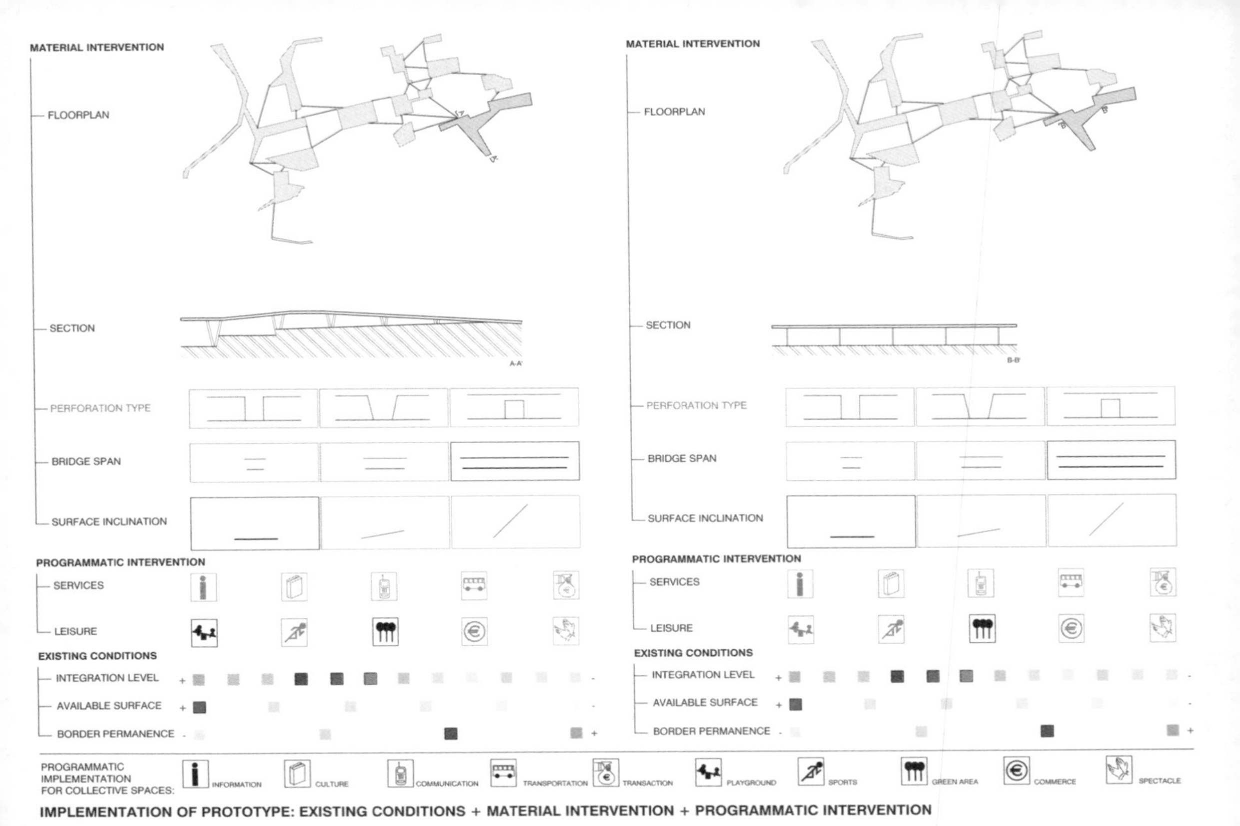

IMPLEMENTATION OF PROTOTYPE: EXISTING CONDITIONS + MATERIAL INTERVENTION + PROGRAMMATIC INTERVENTION

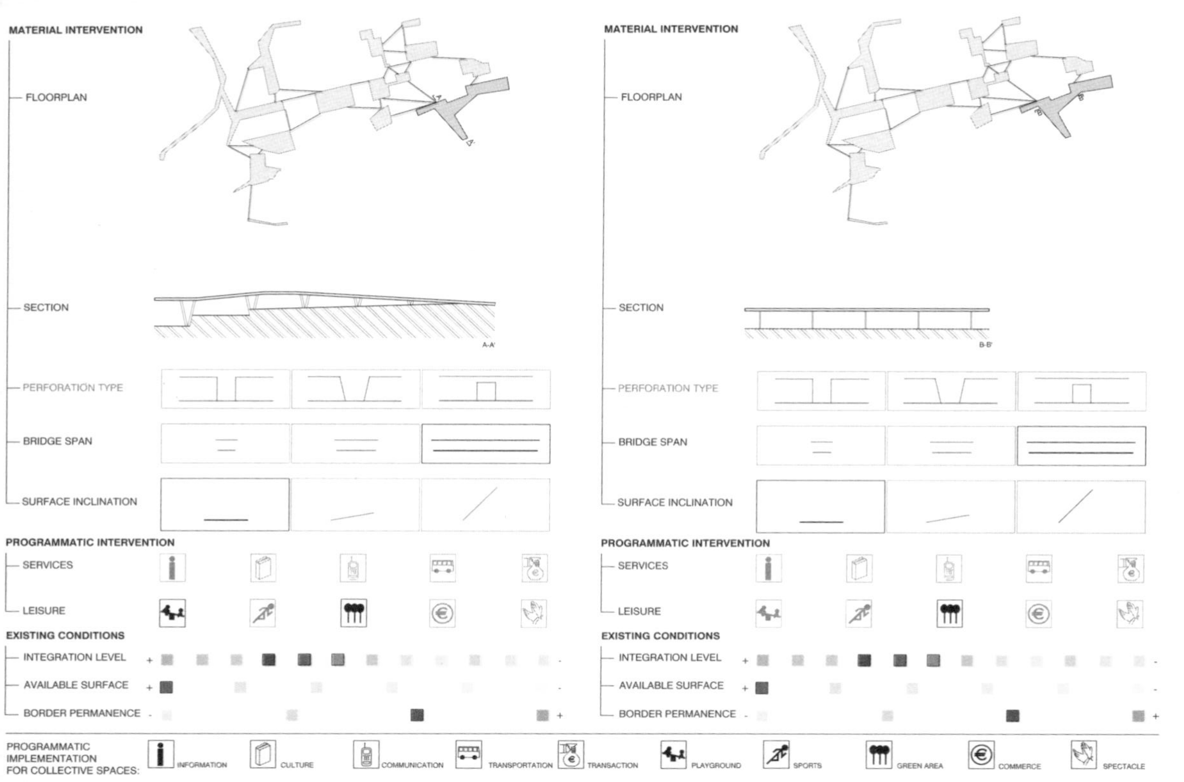

IMPLEMENTATION OF PROTOTYPE: EXISTING CONDITIONS + MATERIAL INTERVENTION + PROGRAMMATIC INTERVENTION

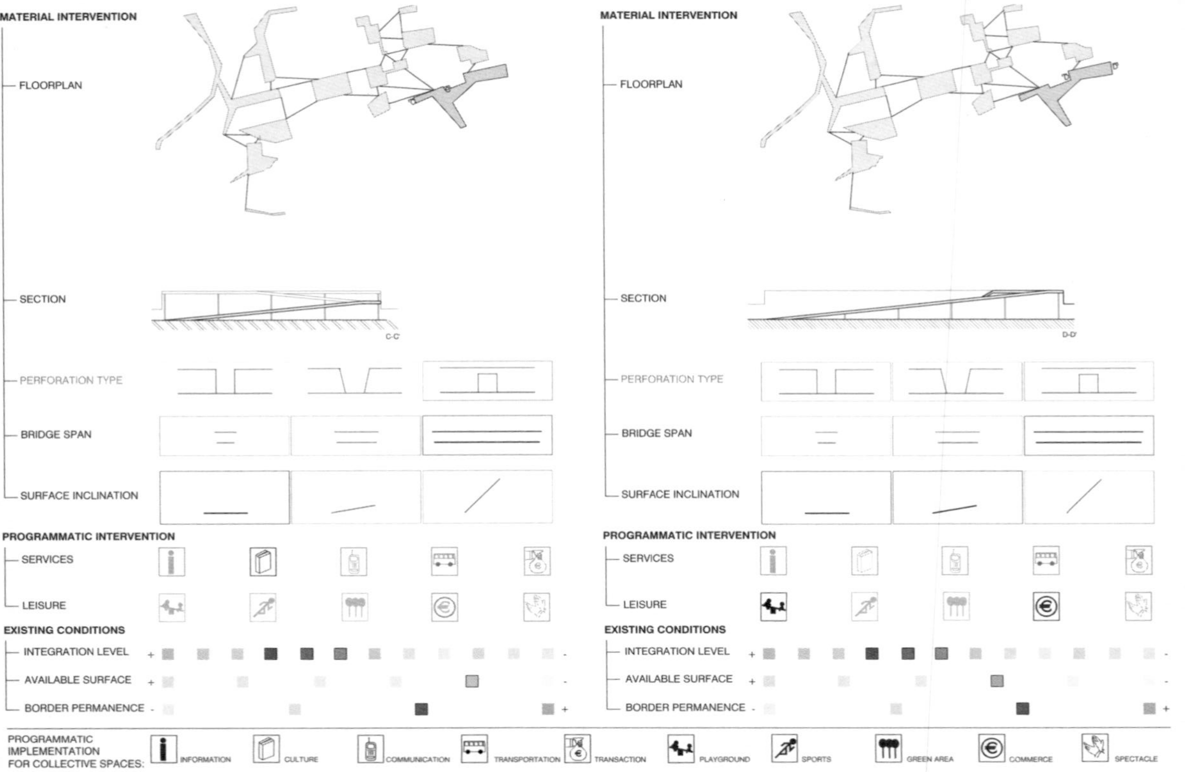

IMPLEMENTATION OF PROTOTYPE: EXISTING CONDITIONS + MATERIAL INTERVENTION + PROGRAMMATIC INTERVENTION

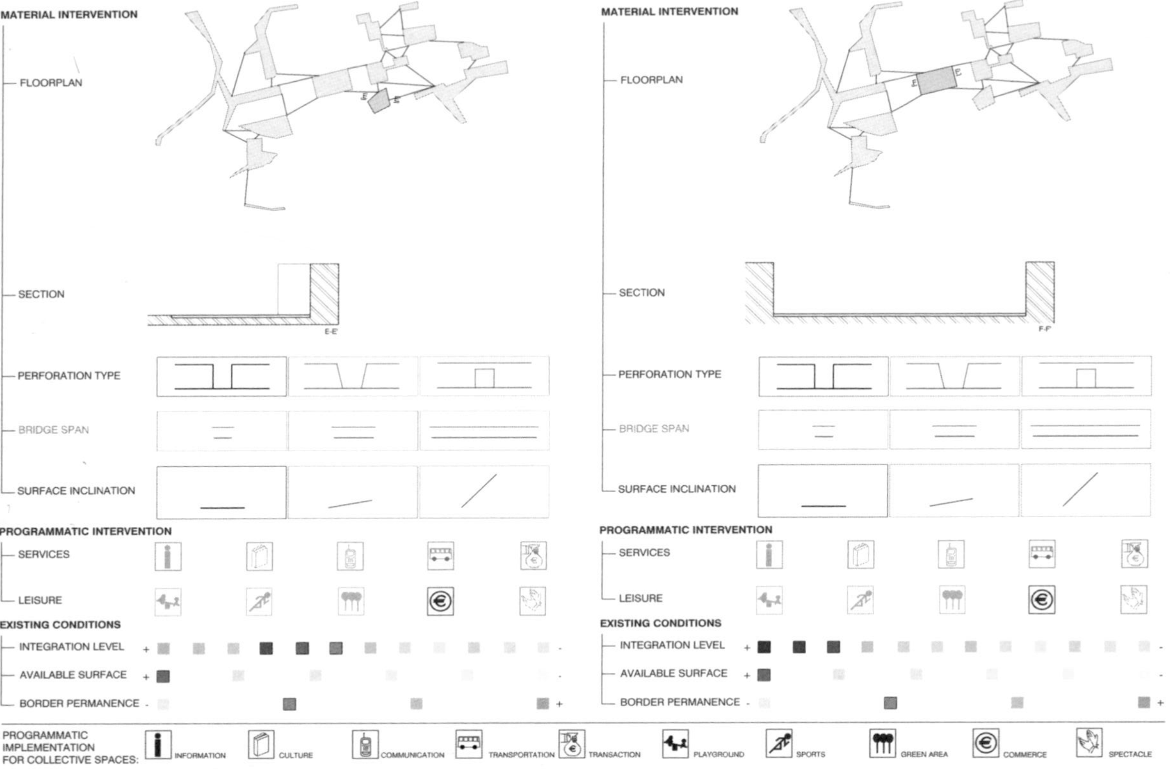

IMPLEMENTATION OF PROTOTYPE: EXISTING CONDITIONS + MATERIAL INTERVENTION + PROGRAMMATIC INTERVENTION

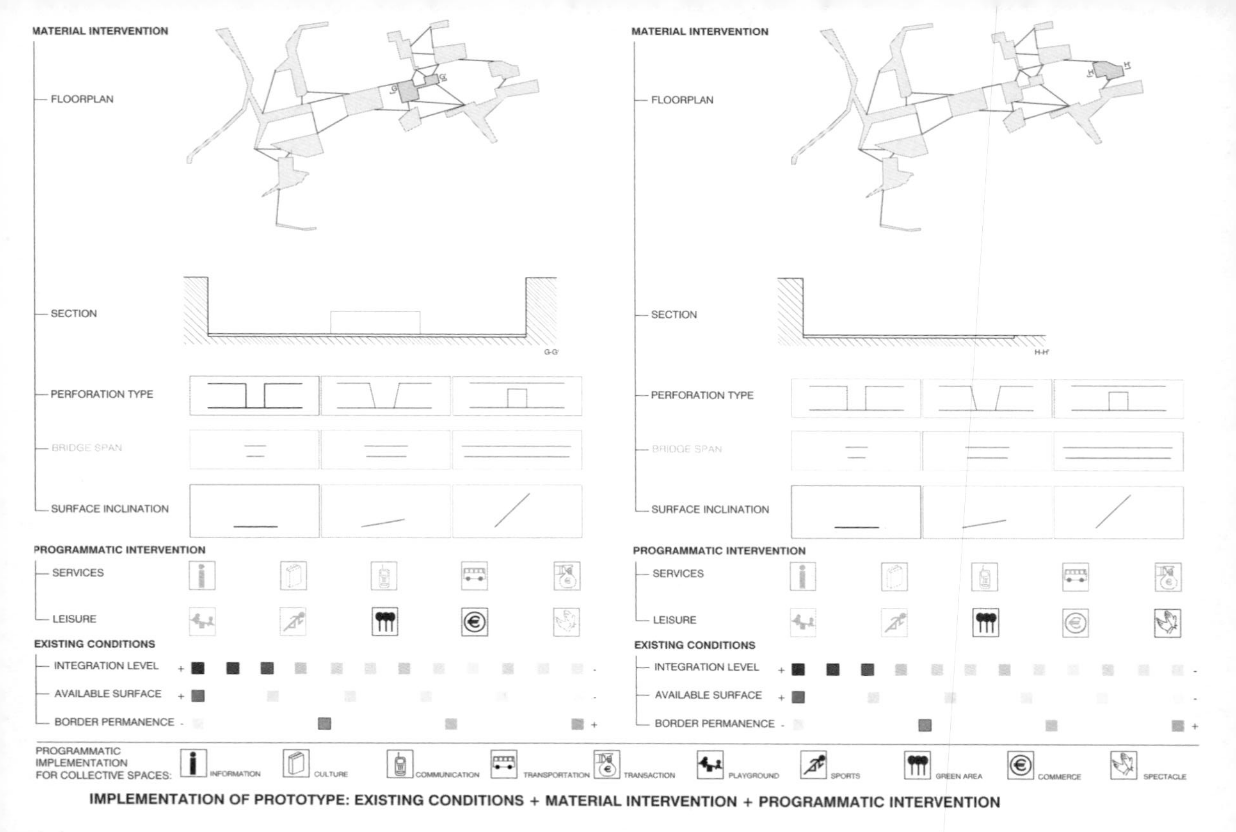

IMPLEMENTATION OF PROTOTYPE: EXISTING CONDITIONS + MATERIAL INTERVENTION + PROGRAMMATIC INTERVENTION

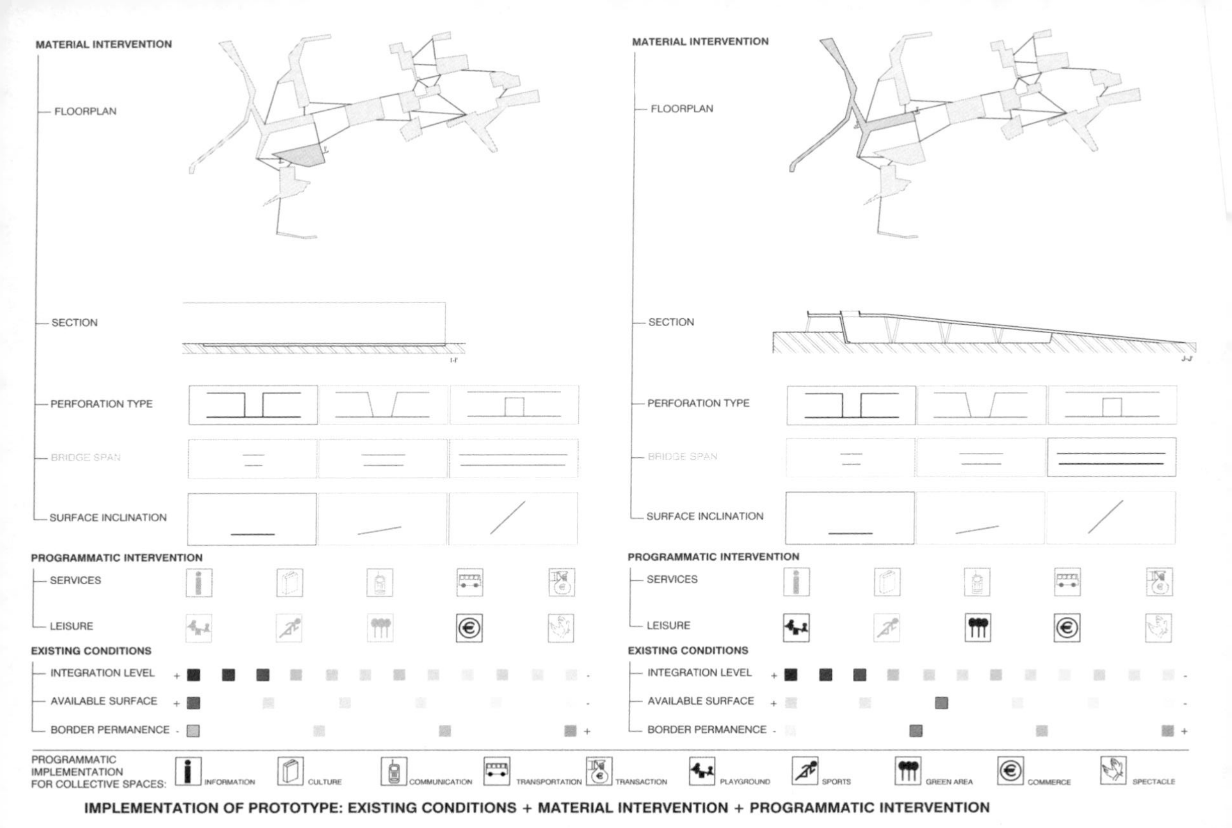

IMPLEMENTATION OF PROTOTYPE: EXISTING CONDITIONS + MATERIAL INTERVENTION + PROGRAMMATIC INTERVENTION

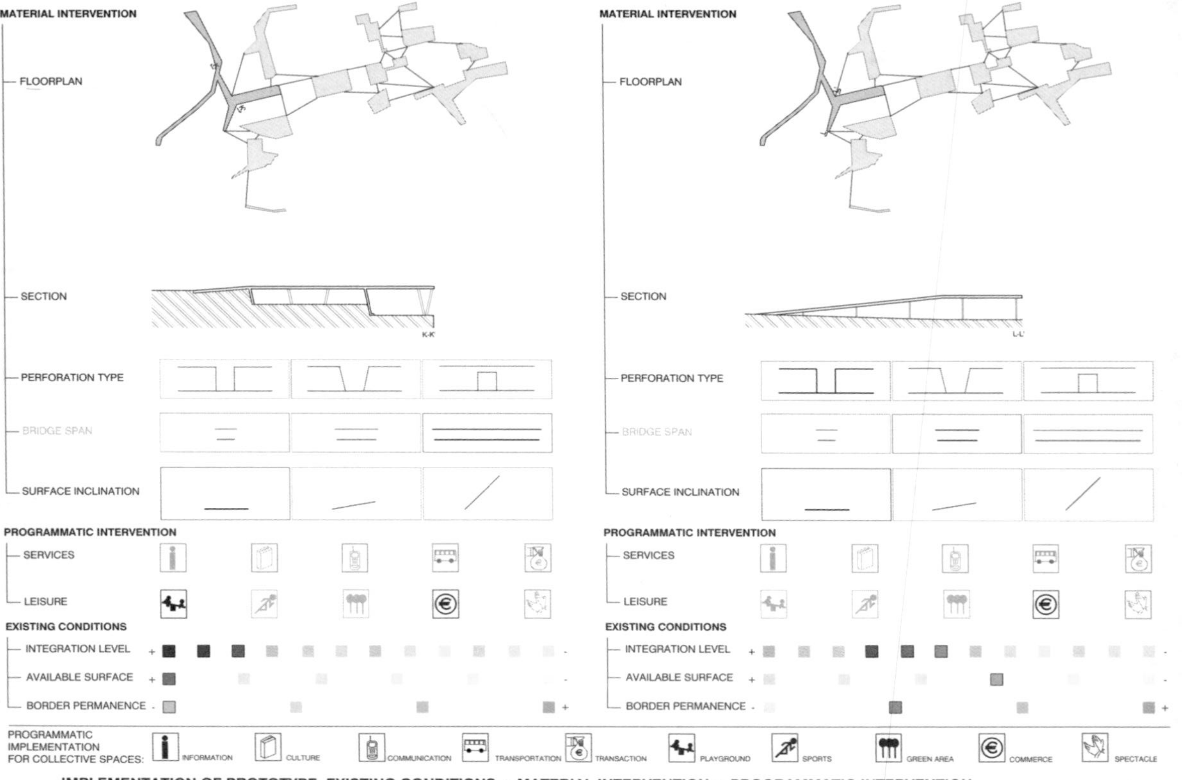

IMPLEMENTATION OF PROTOTYPE: EXISTING CONDITIONS + MATERIAL INTERVENTION + PROGRAMMATIC INTERVENTION

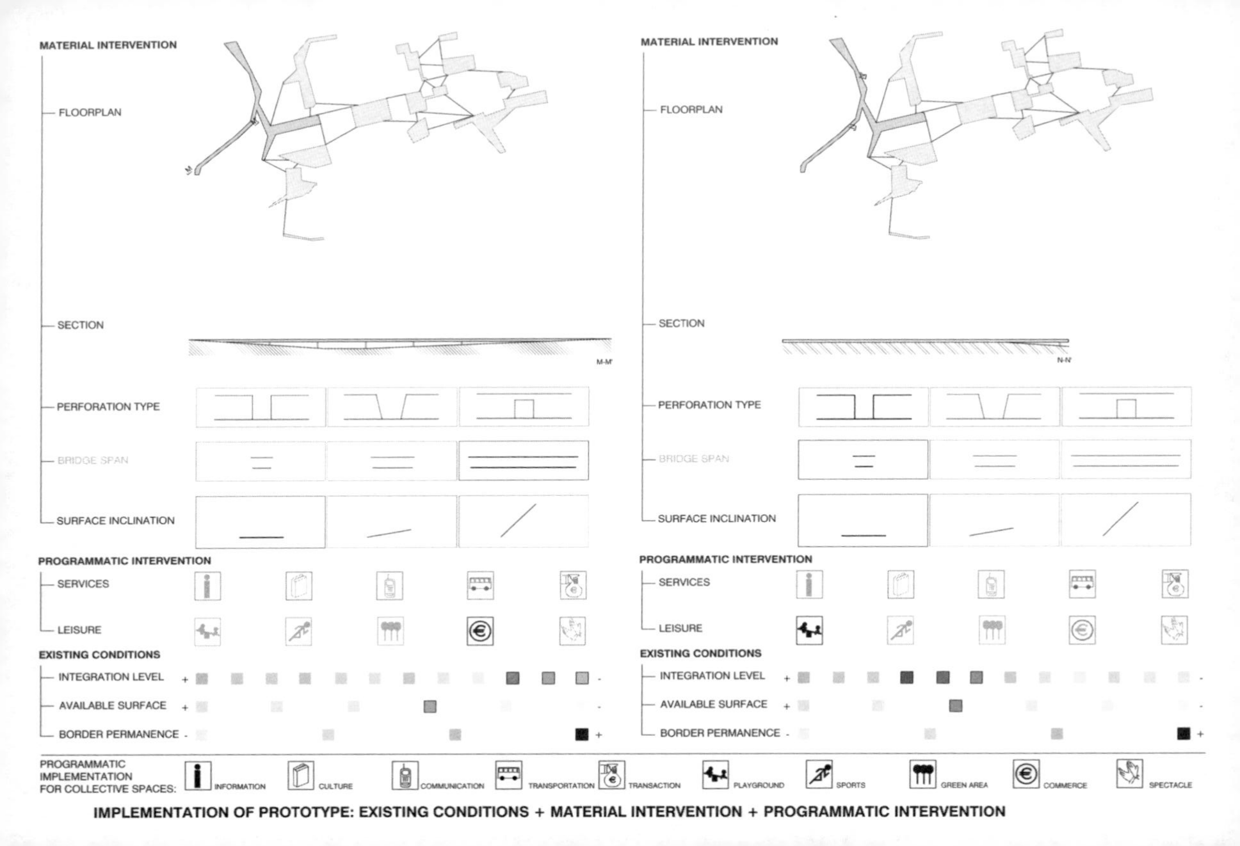

IMPLEMENTATION OF PROTOTYPE: EXISTING CONDITIONS + MATERIAL INTERVENTION + PROGRAMMATIC INTERVENTION

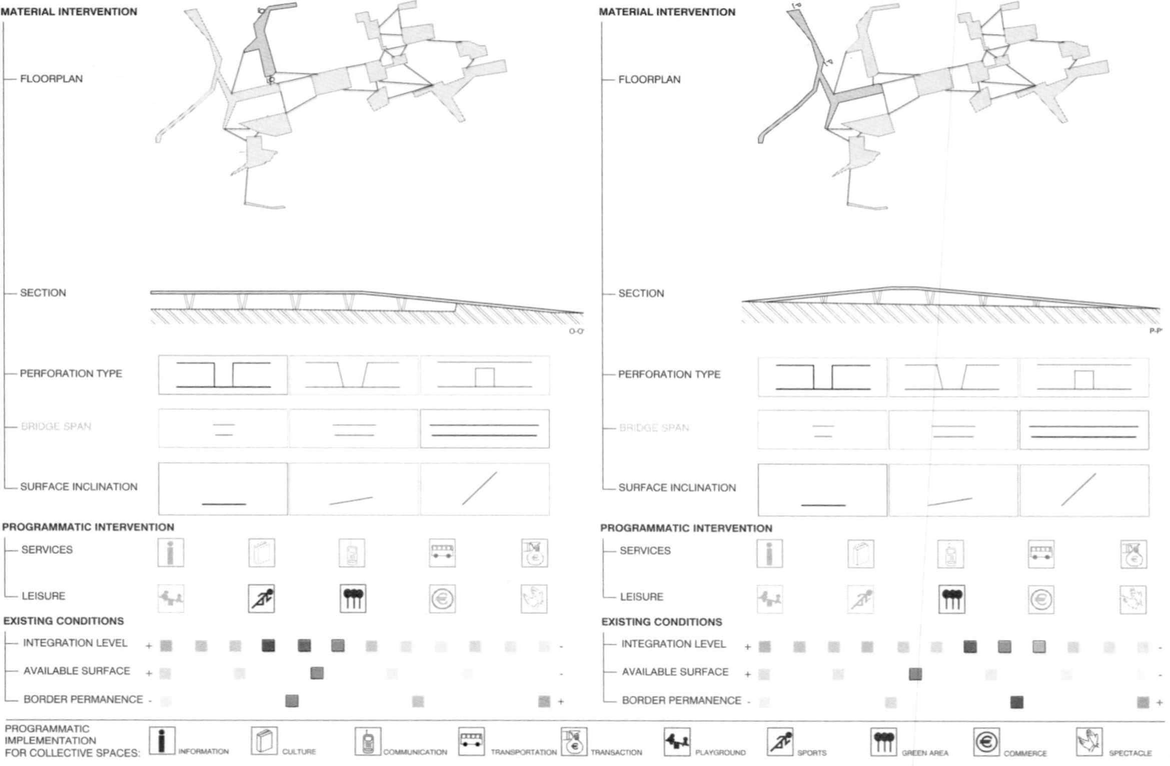

IMPLEMENTATION OF PROTOTYPE: EXISTING CONDITIONS + MATERIAL INTERVENTION + PROGRAMMATIC INTERVENTION

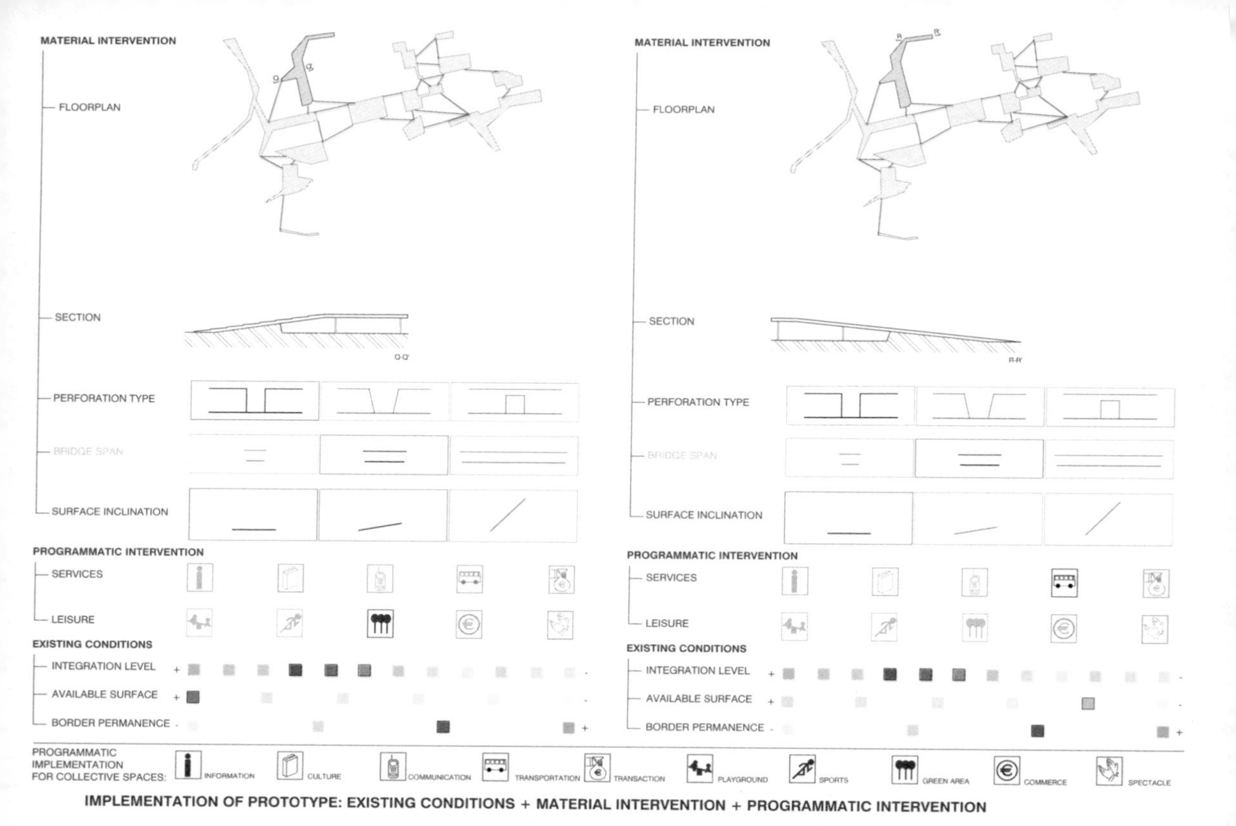

IMPLEMENTATION OF PROTOTYPE: EXISTING CONDITIONS + MATERIAL INTERVENTION + PROGRAMMATIC INTERVENTION

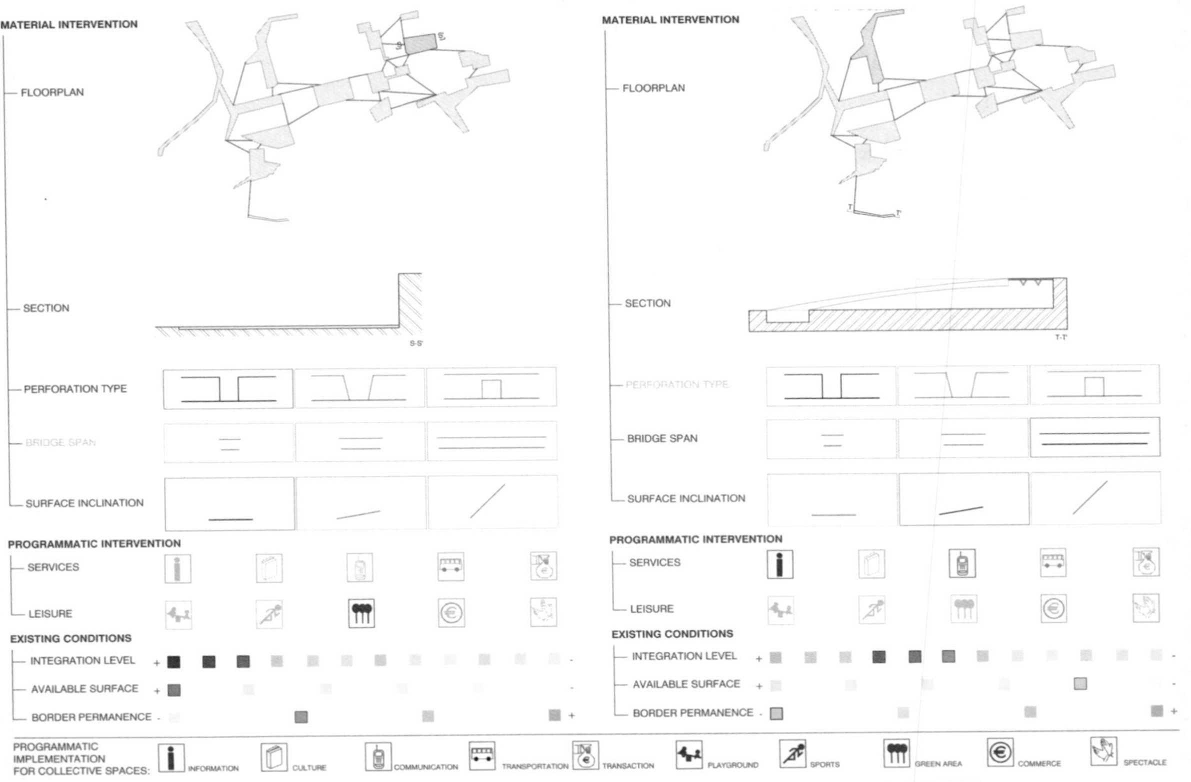

IMPLEMENTATION OF PROTOTYPE: EXISTING CONDITIONS + MATERIAL INTERVENTION + PROGRAMMATIC INTERVENTION

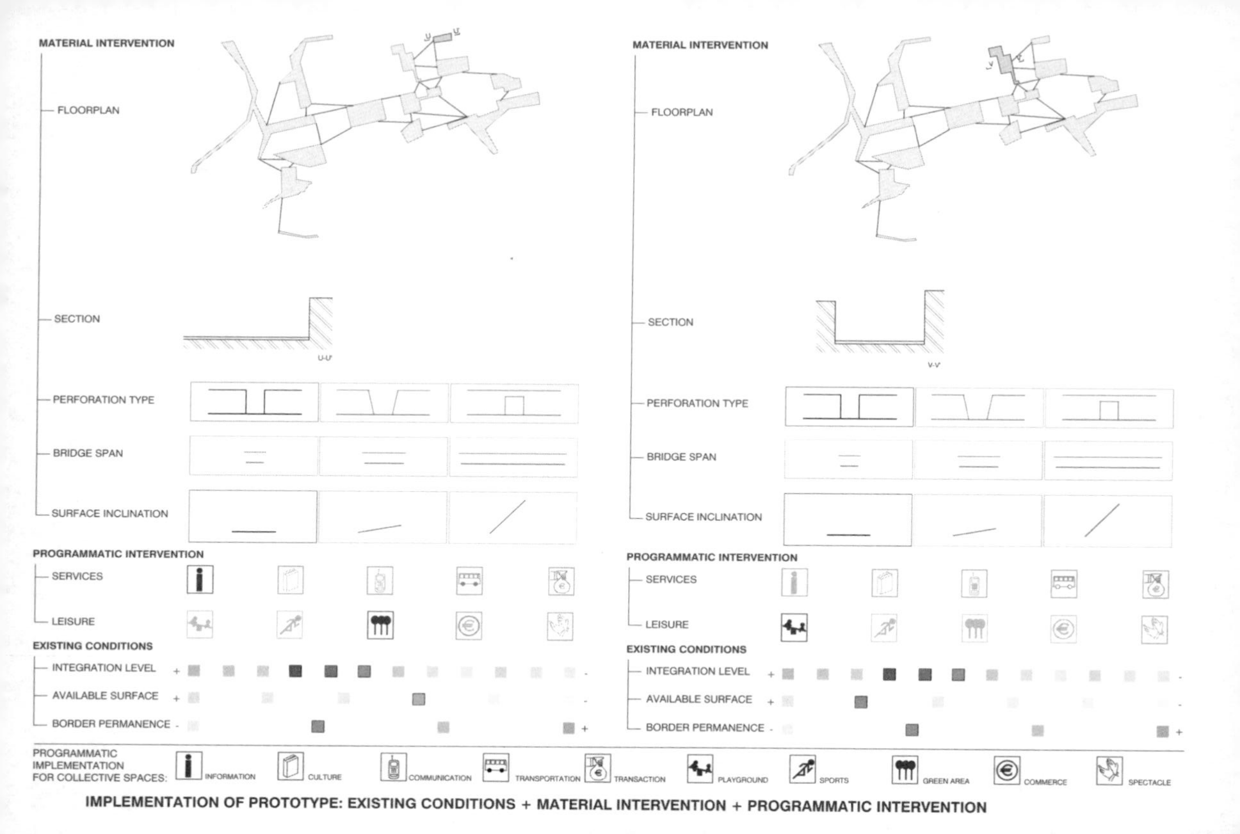

IMPLEMENTATION OF PROTOTYPE: EXISTING CONDITIONS + MATERIAL INTERVENTION + PROGRAMMATIC INTERVENTION

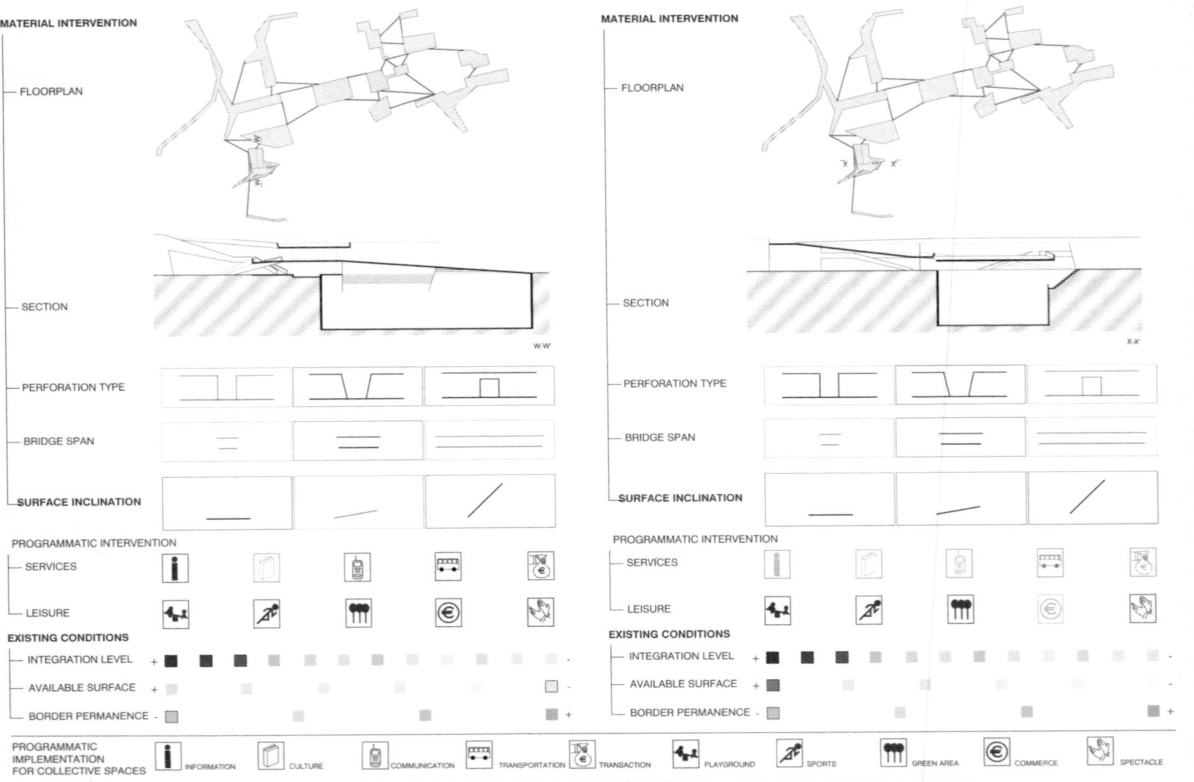

IMPLEMENTATION OF PROTOTYPE: EXISTING CONDITIONS + MATERIAL INTERVENTION + PROGRAMMATIC INTERVENTION

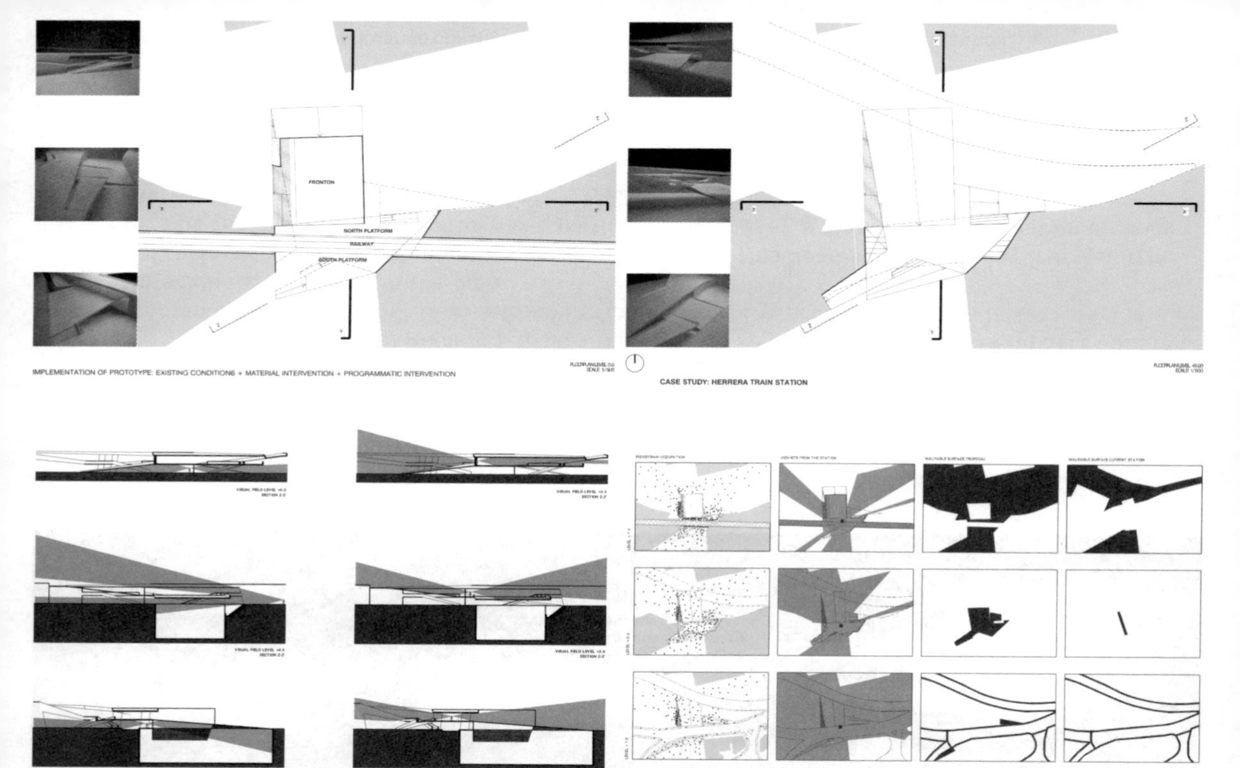
FRONTON
NORTH PLATFORM
RAILWAY
SOUTH PLATFORM
IMPLEMENTATION OF PROTOTYPE: EXISTING CONDITIONS + MATERIAL INTERVENTION + PROGRAMMATIC INTERVENTION
CASE STUDY: HERRERA TRAIN STATION
PEDESTRIAN OCCUPATION
VIEWS FROM THE STATION
WALKABLE SURFACE PROPOSAL
WALKABLE SURFACE CURRENT STATION
CASE STUDY: HERRERA TRAIN STATION
CASE STUDY: HERRERA TRAIN STATION

ON COMMUNICABILITY

There is a frequent failure to make the basic distinction between the couple medium-message and interlocutor vs the production of meaning, and by failing to do so a lack of understanding gets equated with a defect in the former rather than with an intrinsic fact of the production of the latter....as it is said: the black hole at the end of the pipe.
In terms of the production of meaning, when we say 'I believe' this does not refer to any true value in a substance or subject but rather to the participation in a proposal, a modality of affirmation and not its content.

Creative Mediation as a practice engages in a process of determination of consensus operating based on modalities and instrumentalities rather than on devising contents; by operating across as a meta-infrastructure it constitutes a potential, a virtuality that is singularized via actualization processes. In other words, it aims at integrating itself at some level into the memory, the virtual, the potential, and at the same time into the present as a force. Since it is embedded with responsiveness, the degree of deviation operated into the primitive meta-conditions established for mediation is a function of the appropriation, dismissal, utilization and frictions actuated by practices of everyday life.

TOOAUP does not engage in a relation with the city via the apprehension of its monumentality, which inevitably leads to a metaphorical relation and the production of new symbols whose hoped-for effect on the city is emanative, producing through what they give, but being beyond what they give, TOOAUP aims instead at engaging in a relation with the city via the apprehension of its infrastructurality, tending towards establishing an analogical relation and the production of material organizations whose effects on the city are 'immanate' in the cause, rather than emanating from it; their effects are in themselves.

The communicability of the research material is not produced by damping down its complexity but rather by changing register. In this process a modulation has to be operated to constitute an analogical diagram into which 'what is added from one filter to the next are intensive subtractions and it is an addition of subtractions that constitutes modulation and sensible movement as a fall. In short, it is perhaps the notion of modulation in general (and not similitude) that will enable us to understand the nature of analogical language or the diagram.' (7)

(7) Gilles Deleuze. Francis Bacon: The Logic of Sensation.

DATACLOUD: TOOAUP/MANIFESTA_5

DataCloud is an experimental Internet application developed by V2_Institute for the Unstable Media, Rotterdam, in collaboration with STEALTHgroup and ArchiNed with a view to establishing new ways of reading and perceiving multi-layered sets of data, concepts and time-based imagery. It functions as a form of semantic 'knowledge map' that combines the possibilities of various types of media and metadata within the framework of a computer-generated three-dimensional environment. Intended to give its users an insight into and a better understanding of complex collections of information, the Office of Alternative Urban Planning (TOOAUP) version of the DataCloud has been designed to present and moderate TOOAUP, a collaboration between the Berlage Institute and Manifesta 5. DataCloud aims to engage a diverse audience ranging from specialists such as architects, urban designers and municipal planning officials to the more general audience of local residents and international visitors to Manifesta 5, as well as the artistic, cultural and urban research community as a whole.

DataCloud acts as an interactive information tool, allowing users to create relationships based on data objects pulled from the system's databank of TOOAUP project proposals. Users perceive the entire information space as a 'cloud' through which they can 'fly', and which they can reorganise as they choose. The proximity of objects to one another has an 'associative meaning'. Objects that belong together are located closer together (forming small constellations); objects that don't belong together are further away from one another. This idea of an associative, as opposed to a hierarchical, structuring of and navigation through data-objects allows the users to create ideas about urban relationships in new or alternative ways. From a non-linear or immersive cinematographic point of view, DataCloud presents these different data objects, including images, texts, diagrams, videos, and panoramas showing a rich variety of views, analysis and aspects specific to the Pasaia project site.

By searching through the information space and organizing the items, the 3-D constellation will fold and transform, revealing the different topologies of urban data hidden in the cloud. DataCloud can be used to browse this archive, explore the different layers of information and reorganize them to suit the user's particular preferences and interest in the site or the project itself. The system also gives the user the chance not only to view passively and navigate the data elements, but also the opportunity to reflect upon and leave comments on their impression of the TOOAUP project. As such, DataCloud is intended to be used as a tool to develop the broad-based social, urbanistic and political dialogue that such an urban investigation seeks to initiate. Based on the 'clouds' of information selected by the user, and the relationships these form with one another, the user is invited to explore new ways of experiencing, visualising and thinking about future scenarios for this complex area of urban flux and civic potential.

DATACLOUD TOOAUP/MANIFESTA_5 has been produced by:
V2_Institute for the Unstable Media, Rotterdam ←www.v2.nl→
in collaboration with
STEALTHgroup, Rotterdam ←www.stealth-g.net→
ArchiNed www.archined.nl

V2_Institute for the Unstable Media
V2_ is an interdisciplinary center for art and media technology in Rotterdam (NL). The institute is actively engaged in creating and supporting the complex relationships and interactions between different forms of electronic-based media in artistic, cultural and scientific disciplines. V2_'s activities include (public) presentations and conferences (both locally and internationally); media arts research through its media lab; publishing, and developing a comprehensive online media arts and culture archive, as well as the production of the bi-annual Dutch Electronic Art Festival (DEAF).

←http://www.v2.nl→
←http://www.lab.v2.nl→

DataCloud Project History

DataCloud 1.0

The DataCloud Project was initiated in 1998 as DataWolk Hoeksche Waard (DWHW), a project of ArchiNed, AIR Foundation and V2_Lab in collaboration with the Province of Zuid-Holland within the framework of the AIR Southbound event. It contained an experimental Internet site devoted to landscape design for the Hoeksche Waard (an island near Rotterdam) in relation to the Randstad and the Rhine-Scheldt estuary. The site was aimed at designers, policy makers, administrators, inhabitants of the Rotterdam region and other interested parties. The DataWolk Hoeksche Waard won the Dutch National Millennium Competition in the 'Science' category for Architecture and Industrial Design.

← http://www.dwhw.nl→

DataCloud 2.0

In 2001 DataCloud 2.0 was expanded into a 2D information space containing a vast collection of media-objects. Each media-object is of a specific type – image, video, text, 3D model, sound file – and contains its own characteristics in the form of metadata. These characteristics are used for organizing and querying the information space. Users perceive the entire information space as a 'cloud' through which they can 'fly' and which they can reorganize as desired. After an examination of their meta-data, objects in the cloud can be viewed and added to personal collections and storylines. The technical framework on which DataCloud 2.0 is based has been published as open-source software to be used and adapted by other organizations and for a multitude of artistic, cultural and scientific data-manipulation purposes.

← http://datacloud2.v2.nl/→

DataCloud 2.5

In November 2003 DataCloud 2.5 was created as a 3D information space for investigating the changing urban domain of the city of Rotterdam from a cinematographic point of view. Operating as a form of virtual storyboard, DataCloud 2.5 established narratives with which to 'read' the city from numerous vantage points by revealing complex topologies of urban data hidden in the cloud. The project included aspects of interactivity by allowing users to add comments and thus influence the cumulative storyline.

←http://follicle.v2.nl:8080/Datacloud/index.html→

V2_DataCloud Participants:
Anne Nigten (Manager, V2_lab)
Stephen Kovats (TOOAUP/MANIFESTA_5 project coordinator)
Brigit Lichtenegger (Software engineer)
Enric Gili Fort (Interaction design)
Erik Kemperman (Software engineer)
Lenno Verhoog (Designer)
Lobke Hulzink (V2_Lab Project manager)

DataCloud TOOAUP/MANIFESTA_5 external advisors:
Steath_group: Marc Neelen, Ana Djokic ←www.stealth-g.net→

5

FACTOGRAPHY

Police allow nationalists to march in Basque city

By Emma Daly

The New York Times

SAN SEBASTIAN, Spain: Riot police allowed about 3,000 radical Basque nationalists to march Sunday through the sunlit center of San Sebastian shouting pro-independence slogans, despite an official ban on the demonstration.

The decision, fiercely criticized by Madrid, illustrates the difficulty of enforcing the Spanish government's policy of outlawing the separatist movement it says forms an integral part of the terrorist group ETA. Opposition to the measures, which include a ban on Batasuna, a radical separatist political party linked to ETA, is growing among Basque nationalists, even those strongly opposed to ETA's murderous tactics.

"For Freedom," read the banner at a silent protest in Guernica called Saturday by Batasuna's political rival, Eusko Alkartasuna, a member of the coalition running the Basque government. The party shares Batasuna's aim of an independent Basque country, but not its tactics.

Nationalists of all colors feel threatened by Madrid's latest moves: A Spanish judge has suspended all Batasuna activities for three years, while the ruling Popular Party, backed by most of the Spanish Congress, has asked the Supreme Court to outlaw the party it says is part of ETA, which has killed more than 800 people in its war for independence.

"Emotions are running very high, the tension is very noticeable," said Jose Maria Larranaga of the radical nationalist union ELA. "We see this as a kind of coup d'etat against the Basques. I don't agree with ETA, but I also don't agree with banning Batasuna; that is going to create a lot of problems."

In San Sebastian, masked riot police in black jumpsuits stood waiting near the city's gorgeous seafront, packed with revelers and tourists attending an annual rowing regatta. As the demonstration, called in support of Basque prisoners, set off behind a banner declaring, "The Basque Country Needs Freedom," the police moved to block the street.

"It's a disgrace, a shame what those police are doing," said a well-dressed, middle-aged woman walking past. But after taking the names of those leading the march, the police allowed the protest to move on amid traffic on a main, tree-lined avenue.

"They only let us go because there are too many people, and on a day like this, banning the march could cause major trouble," said Leire, who would not give her full name. She was herself imprisoned for 10 years because, she said, "I was a militant separatist — I still am."

As the rally ended, the protesters raised their left fists and sang the Basque nationalist anthem; a few even shouted, "Long live military ETA!"

Leopoldo Barreda, spokesman in the Basque country for the Popular Party, accused the Basque government of "negligence" in allowing the march to proceed.

"There must be some kind of political responsibility, someone must have given the relevant instructions and someone will have to explain why those responsible for maintaining order in the Basque country proved incapable of stopping the terrorists' friends from marching through the streets of San Sebastian," Barreda said.

One of those marching, Joseba Alvarez, is a member of the Basque Parliament for Batasuna, but under the judicial order suspending the party's activities, he is barred from speaking in Batasuna's name, from holding meetings or rallies, and from taking part in politics as a member of Batasuna.

Despite all this, Alvarez says separatists will continue to organize.

"The Basque people engaged in political activities during Franco's time, when there was no legal infrastructure," he said. "If Madrid takes away our basic rights, we will find other ways to continue the struggle for independence." And, he warned, "If you close down all democratic, political routes, it will feed the violence."

Despite concern that the protest Sunday, and another, illegal gathering Saturday evening in Bilbao, would provoke clashes between militant youths and the police, the narrow streets of the historic center were peaceful.

But next weekend another demonstration has been called in Bilbao.

The Spanish government, supported by the opposition Socialist Party, is determined to crush ETA and its supporters. But Batasuna, whose members deny it is a cover for ETA, won 150,000 votes in regional elections in May 2001, and it is the second-largest Basque political group.

Luis Tejido/The Associated Press

Police vans moving in front of demonstrators in San Sebastian, northern Spain, on Sunday, during a protest against the suspension of the nationalist party Batasuna.

CULTURA

Arco

Reconocida internacionalmente, Arco lleva años siendo la exposición española de arte contemporáneo más amplia y vital, la más importante, probablemente, de las que cada año llegan puntuales a su cita. Pero en el mundo del arte no todo es exhibición y belleza. Junto a ello, se han instalado las prácticas dedicadas al robo y a la falsificación que es, sin duda, un problema de primera magnitud en todo el mundo. La Interpol ha señalado que la tercera fuente de criminalidad organizada es el arte, después del tráfico de drogas y del tráfico de armas. Y la Unesco estima que este mercado mueve unos doce mil millones de euros al año.

El número de obras de arte robadas asciende cada año y es un negocio cada vez más floreciente hasta el punto de que se han constituido clanes especializados y redes herméticas que practican el método del encubrimiento sucesivo, basado en la sencilla pero muy eficaz idea de que cuantas más transacciones se realicen, cuantas más personas intervengan en la cadena de operaciones mercantiles, más difícil será probar, finalmente, la mala fe del último comprador.

Desde las falsas declaraciones de robo a las compañías aseguradoras hasta el mercado ilícito de obras robadas, pasando por las tentativas de convencer al ingenuo de que un artista está más cotizado de lo que realmente está, el arte es objeto cotidiano de una de las delincuencias más voraces y sobre la que está implicándose cada vez más el crimen organizado, el bandidismo superlativo, los clanes mafiosos. Drogas, armas y arte componen una tema de comercio ilegal que está situando a la pintura o a la escultura al mismo nivel que la heroína, la cocaína o los misiles nucleares. No cabe duda de que se trata de un extraño y, desde luego, muy peligroso parentesco.

Mientras no haya una legislación internacional unitaria que impida que el arte robado o sencillamente maquillado o falsificado salte fronteras en un mercado ilícito mundial, seguirá habiendo aspectos delictivos dentro del comercio del arte que es, precisamente, un territorio que nunca debería abrirse a tales prácticas.

Juan Carlos ARCE

La Bienal de San Sebastián incluye en su programa la «violencia como resistencia»

El certamen cuenta con el apoyo de Cultura, el Ayuntamiento, la Diputación y el Gobierno vasco

Lo que estaba siendo un unánime acto de condena a Eta y una atractiva presentación en Arco de una prometedora bienal de arte contemporáneo, «Manifiesta 5», que tendrá como escenario San Sebastián en 2004, se tiñó de sombras al final cuando los dos comisarios –un italiano y una ucraniana– designados por la holandesa Fundación Internacional Manifiesta para sentar las bases artísticas de la convocatoria y seleccionar a los 40 artistas invitados tomaron la palabra para anunciar que, entre los temas que éstos tratarán estarán la autodeterminación, la soberanía o la «violencia como resistencia».

Juan Carlos Rodríguez
Madrid

Las paradojas del País Vasco. Mientras que el acto de presentación de «Manifiesta 5» –la quinta edición de la bienal europea de Arte Contemporáneo itinerante y alternativa a Venecia o Kassel que tendrá lugar en 2004 en San Sebastián– se abría con un tajante y unánime «No a Eta» y «No a la Guerra» a los que puso voz el Diputado General de Guipúzcoa, Román Sadupe (PNV), y con un escalofriante testimonio del primer teniente de alcalde del Ayuntamiento de San Sebastián, Ramón Etxezarreta (PSOE) –«esperemos que en 2004 estemos vivos»–, sus dos comisarios, el italiano Massimiliano Gioni y la ucraniana Marta Kuzma, dejaban boquiabierto a más de uno afirmando que parte de sus contenidos y de las obras de los 40 artistas seleccionados tratarán, literalmente, de la autonomía, la autodeterminación y la soberanía. Incluso, Kuzman llegó ayer a hablar de que también versará de la «coherencia e incoherencia de la relación entre el País Vasco y el Estado español»y, sobre todo, del concepto de «violencia como ruptura y resistencia».

Vocablos sorprendentes

Frente a ellos estaba el secretario de Estado de Cultura, Luis Alberto de Cuenca, ya que el Ministerio contribuye económicamente con «Manifiesta 5» e, incluso, ayer anunció que firmará un convenio para apoyar institucionalmente a la bienal –convocada por la Fundación Internacional Manifiesta, con sede en Amsterdam, y responsable artística del evento– y participar en la programación con actividades desarrolladas por las propias unidades del Ministerio, como la Compañía Nacional de Danza o el Centro Dramático Nacional. «Ciertamente me han sorprendido algunos vocablos que he oído –respondió ayer De Cuenca a LA RAZÓN después del acto–, pero no hay todavía ningún programa cerrado y acabado. Seguramente los comisarios no tienen toda la información que habrían de tener sobre el País Vasco, sobre todo porque son extranjeros».

Luis Sevillano

El Secretario de Estado de Cultura, Luis Alberto de Cuenca

Massimiliano Gioni, que también es director artístico de la Fundación Nicola Trussardi en Milán, justificó las alusiones a la autodeterminación y la violencia –aunque la palabra terrorismo no la pronunciaron ninguno de los dos comisarios– como parte del «trabajo preliminar de comprender la realidad del País Vasco» que, según explicó, deben hacer cada uno de los 40 artistas invitados por los dos comisarios a la bienal. «No es más que un postura de observación –matizó el comisario italiano–, somos extranjeros y lo primero que debemos hacer es comprender la realidad del País Vasco». De ejemplo puso que también se hablará de inmigración, de la arquitectura de Donostia, del binomio ciudad-extrarradio o de la «zona fronteriza» de Pasajes. Los comisarios fueron los últimos en intervenir –ya solos en la mesa– y tras ellos no hubo posibilidad de réplica. Todos los discursos políticos, de condena de Eta y de esperanza en la cultura, se oyeron antes de sus ponencias.

Etxezarreta dijo, por ejemplo, que se encontraba en representación de los ciudadanos vivos y de aquellos que están en la memoria y afirmó que «para perdurar y vivir con libertad hay que dotar a la vida de contenidos, como este acontecimiento de creatividad». Su «esperemos estar vivos en 2004» aún retumba. El concejal donostiarra mostró su esperanza de que «Manifesta 5» contribuya a «situar nuestra ciudad y nuestro país» en la vanguardia europea.

«No queremos ser puros»

El diputado general de Guipúzcoa, Román Sudupe, afirmó que las expresiones culturales y artísticas son sinónimo de creación, sinónimo de la mayor de las creaciones: la vida misma. En relación a «Manifesta 5», señaló que supone el reconocimiento internacional del esfuerzo realizado «en aras a la modernización de nuestra sociedad». Sadupe aseguró que «no queremos ser puros, queremos que nos contamine aquello que nos rodea. Y lo queremos hacer de manera amistosa, sin fracturas, desde el respeto y desde el pacto».

La Consejera de Cultura del Gobierno Vasco, Miren Azkarate, afirmó, por su parte, que «Manifesta 5» será un acontecimiento válido y fiable para tomar el pulso y la temperatura al momento actual de la expresión plástica y visual en Europa, «un punto de contacto, de intercambio entre artistas, agentes culturales, escritores y pensadores de museos, centros de arte e instituciones culturales de toda Europa».

Del nuevo CICC a Arteleku

El equipo de comisarios de «Manifiesta 5» ha sido seleccionado por el Patronato de la Fundación Internacional Manifiesta por «sus perspectivas y experiencias anteriores». Gioni está comisariando «The Zone», un proyecto sobre arte italiano en la Bienal de Venecia. Kuzma es comisaria independiente y fue directora del Centro Soros para el Arte Contemporáneo en Kiev. El desarrollo y ejecución del programa y la exposición de «Manifiesta 5» estarán a cargo del equipo directivo formado por Lourdes Fernández y José Miguel Ayerza. El Centro Internacional de Cultura Contemporánea (CICC) –compuesto por el Gobierno Vasco, Diputación Foral de Guipúzcoa y Ayuntamiento de San Sebastián– se responsabilizará de la organización y financiación. El CICC es un proyecto multidisciplinar de creación artística y creativa, que se ubicará en la antigua fábrica de tabaco. Arteleku, centro dedicado a explorar el arte y la cultura contemporánea, será la sede y centro de producción de la bienal.

20 November 2002, El Correo.

MIÉRCOLES 20 DE NOVIEMBRE DE 2002 / Nº 28.993 / PRECIO: 0.80 EUROS

EL CORREO

DE VIZCAYA

A POLÍTICA / 20

La **última encuesta del CIS** dibuja un mapa político vasco muy similar al del 13-M

A ECONOMÍA / 38

Rato anuncia **medidas para elevar la competencia** en el sector servicios

D ENTREVISTA / 44

Urzaiz: «Este equipo sólo es fiable cuando una serie de jugadores estamos en forma»

PARTIDO Y A PIQUE. Momento en el que el 'Prestige' se parte en dos. Poco después se hundió la popa y horas más tarde lo hizo la proa. / MINISTERIO DE DEFENSA

El 'Prestige' se hunde y se convierte en una 'bomba' ecológica

El 'Prestige' reposa en el fondo del Atlántico, a 3.600 metros de profundidad, convertido en una 'bomba' ecológica de efectos imprevisibles. Ayer, el petrolero se partió en dos y se hundió, con 70.000 toneladas de fuel, a 250 kilómetros de las costas gallegas. Los expertos piensan que el crudo se solidificará por las bajas temperaturas, pero no se atreven a asegurar que los tanques no reventarán como consecuencia de la enorme presión submarina. PÁG. 12

«Esto es una porquería»

Los vecinos de los pueblos de la Costa da Morte coruñesa afectados por la marea negra provocada por el petrolero 'Prestige' empiezan a estar hartos de la inoperancia de las labores de limpieza.

El barco se partió y se fue a pique, a 3.600 metros de profundidad, **con 70.000 toneladas de fuel**

Trabajaba en el mercado de fortuna, comprando crudo barato para venderlo al mejor postor

Azkuna descarta el derribo de la Misericordia mientras sea alcalde

Rechaza la alternativa que plantea la UPV para prolongar la Gran Vía hasta Olabeaga

«Destruir el pasado sería un error», dice la entidad social PÁG. 2

104 PÁGINAS

Siete creadores vascos convertirán en obras de arte los tranvías de Bilbao

Eguillor, Euba, Lazkano, Moreno, Sourrouille, Zumeta y Ocáriz participan en el proyecto

Bellas Artes organizará una exposición PÁG. 77

EL DIARIO VASCO

SAN SEBASTIÁN, JUEVES, 6 DE FEBRERO DE 2003 AÑO LXIX. NÚMERO 21.852 / 0,85 EUROS

46 DEPORTES De Pedro cree injusto que le sancionen

DVKIROLAK Campeonato de karate senior

Powell presenta en el Consejo de Seguridad documentos para probar que Irak oculta armas

Según manifestó el secretario de Estado, Bagdad «no hace ningún esfuerzo para desarmarse»

Francia, Rusia y China prefieren dar más tiempo a que los inspectores de la ONU acaben su trabajo

El secretario de Estado norteamericano, Colin Powell, presentó ante la ONU numerosas supuestas pruebas de que Irak no se ha desarmado. Para Bagdad, el informe de Powell fue una comedia y no prueba la existencia de armas prohibidas. PÁGS. 40 A 42

Aznar defiende en el Congreso la guerra preventiva

Zapatero respondió a Aznar que el desarme de Irak es posible sin acciones armadas

Un grupo de artistas fue desalojado por llevar camisetas con el lema «No a la guerra»

PÁGS. 43 Y 44 • EDITORIAL EN PÁG. 23

De las 'galletas' de fuel que llegaban inicialmente se ha pasado a las 'sábanas', tal y como se podía apreciar ayer en la playa de La Concha. [POSTIGO]

Llegada masiva de manchas de fuel al litoral de Euskadi

Arrantzales y trabajadores de la limpieza impiden que el fuel del 'Prestige' se introduzca en la bahía de Txingudi

La costa vasca vivió ayer la peor jornada desde que los vertidos del *Prestige* empezaron a introducirse hace dos meses en el Cantábrico. Enormes fragmentos de la gran mancha de fuel llegaron a casi todas las playas y calas del litoral. Los restos depositados en los arenales eran de un tamaño muy superior al que se ha conocido hasta ahora. La intervención de los barcos pesqueros, que salieron a la mar a recoger el fuel pese al mal tiempo, evitó males aún mayores. Las previsiones meteorológicas para las próximas horas indican que la situación podría empeorar. PÁGS. 2 A 7

104 PÁGINAS

AL DÍA 8

El riesgo de desbordamientos baja en Gipuzkoa pero aumenta en Navarra

POLÍTICA 26

IU-EB reclama a sus socios del Gobierno Vasco la retirada de la reforma electoral

POLÍTICA 27

Cinco detenidos, acusados de dirigir la reorganización de Askatasuna

ECONOMÍA 34

El paro aumentó en 54.229 personas en el mejor enero desde el 2000

16 **February 2003**, El Diario Vasco.

EL DIARIO VASCO

SAN SEBASTIÁN, DOMINGO, **16 DE FEBRERO DE 2003** AÑO LXIX. NÚMERO 21.862 / 1,30 EUROS

EXPECTATIVAS Inversiones en tiempos de guerra

EL SEMANAL Qué se dirime realmente en Irak

Un mundo contra la guerra

La manifestación celebrada en Londres fue una de las más multitudinarias. [PETER MACDIARMID / REUTERS]

- Millones de personas en más de 300 ciudades se opusieron a la intervención armada contra Irak
- Las movilizaciones sobrepasaron las marchas celebradas en todo el mundo contra la Guerra de Vietnam

Un clamor contra la guerra recorrió ayer todo el mundo, sobrepasando las protestas contra la Guerra de Vietnam. Millones de personas se manifestaron en las principales ciudades del planeta para rechazar la opción bélica y reclamar una salida diplomática a la crisis de Irak. En Europa destacaron las multitudinarias marchas que recorrieron Londres, Roma y Madrid, capitales de los países cuyos gobiernos se han mantenido firmes en su apoyo a la intervención militar que abandera EE UU. Bilbao, Vitoria y San Sebastián fueron igualmente escenario de movilizaciones contra la guerra.

Aspecto de la manifestación en San Sebastián. [SARA SANTOS]

Blair dice que los inspectores dispondrán de todo el tiempo para desarmar a Irak

PÁGS. 42 A 47 • EDITORIAL EN PÁG. 23

MAITE PAGAZAURTUNDUA
HERMANA DEL ÚLTIMO ASESINADO POR ETA

«La lucha contra ETA pasa por desalojar a Batasuna de la Alcaldía de Andoain»

Maite Pagazaurtundua, hermana del jefe de la Policía local de Andoain asesinado por ETA, afirma que «la lucha contra ETA pasa por desalojar a Batasuna de la Alcaldía de Andoain. PÁGS. 28 Y 29

Una Real con bajas defiende su liderato ante el Betis

La Real, con bajas, defiende hoy su liderato en el difícil campo del Betis. Alonso, De Pedro y Aranburu no pueden jugar y sí lo harán Boris, Tayfun y Barkero. PÁGS. 52 A 54

La atleta Irantzu Egiguren y su entrenador J. M. Caballero mueren en accidente PÁG. 58

AL DÍA 3
Nuevas oleadas de chapapote llegaron a las playas vascas

ECONOMÍA 36
La venta de coches en Gipuzkoa cayó un 10% en 2002

MUNDO 48
Una bomba contra un tanque mata a 4 soldados israelíes

MUNDO 49
Uribe reafirma su lucha contra el terror en Colombia

CULTURA 76
Artistas vascos eligen sus obras preferidas en Arco

CULTURA 78
Los refugiados de Afganistán se llevan el Oso de Oro

112 PÁGINAS

INTERNATIONAL
Herald Tribune
THE WORLD'S DAILY NEWSPAPER PUBLISHED BY THE NEW YORK TIMES EDITED IN PARIS AND PRINTED IN FRANKFURT
THURSDAY, APRIL 3, 2003

EU clears News Corp. deal for Italian satellite TV

FINANCE | 11

James Cameron's foray as underwater explorer

CULTURE & MORE | 20

A woman takes on the men in the tough world of hockey

SPORTS | 18

UN body warns travelers on SARS

Southern China and Hong Kong on list to avoid

By Thomas Crampton
International Herald Tribune

HONG KONG: The World Health Organization on Wednesday issued a warning against travel to Hong Kong and the southern Chinese province of Guangdong because of the fast-growing outbreak of severe acute respiratory syndrome.

In the first travel alert in its 55-year history addressing an imminent health threat, the United Nations body warned that the illness, known as SARS, may be more infectious than previously feared.

Previously, it had issued travel warnings in case of war or other conflicts.

"We are telling travelers who are planning to go to Hong Kong and Guangdong that they consider postponing their travel," said David Heymann, executive director of communicable diseases at the World Health Organization in Geneva. "We have requested that airports screen passengers who are returning to their countries from these sites."

The disease, which arose out of Guangdong Province, was spread by travelers from Hong Kong to 17 countries on four continents. Perhaps related to the common cold, the disease often develops into life-threatening pneumonia. It has infected more than 2,200 people worldwide and killed more than 75.

"We do not understand the disease completely," Heymann said. "There's no vaccine and there's no drug."

China, which on Wednesday bowed to international pressure to release more information about the outbreak, reported a near 50 percent increase to 1,190 infected patients through March. The number of deaths in China from the disease rose to 46 from 34, according to the World Health Organization.

Cases were reported in Guangxi, Hunan and Sichuan provinces as well as Shanghai for the first time.

"The epidemic is still going on in Guangdong," Heymann said, a statement contrasting with repeated assertions by the Chinese government that the disease outbreak was "under control."

After a delay of more than a week, Beijing also granted permission Wednesday for a team from the World Health Organization to visit Guangdong Province.

Speaking in public for the first time about an outbreak thought to have started last November, China's health minister, Zhang Wenkang, said Wednesday that the situation was improving.

"The number of cases is falling," Zhang said on the state-run CCTV television network. "In Guangdong at the height of the epidemic there were 60 to 70 new cases every day. Now it is fewer than 10."

Canada, grappling with the largest outbreak of the disease outside of Asia, reported two more deaths Tuesday and said that a total of 129 probable cases had

See ALERT, Page 7

U.S. pushes into outskirts of Baghdad

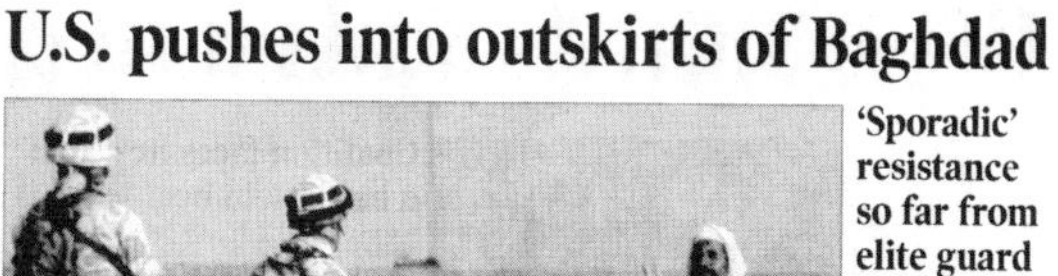

As British coalition forces clashed with Iraqi loyalists in an effort to capture the city of Basra on Wednesday, an Iraqi approached a checkpoint on the Basra outskirts.

Anja Niedringhaus/The Associated Press

'Sporadic' resistance so far from elite guard

By Thomas Fuller
International Herald Tribune

KUWAIT: U.S. Army and Marine divisions approached the outskirts of Baghdad on Wednesday after surging past the remnants of Republican Guard units in a two-pronged attack that met only "sporadic" resistance.

Columns of tanks and armored vehicles several kilometers long rumbled toward the capital in broad daylight, passing burned out Iraqi vehicles and taking dozens of prisoners.

"We've moved to within 30 miles of Baghdad, but there remains tough fighting ahead," said Major General Stanley McChrystal, vice director for operations at the Pentagon.

Other reports said troops had advanced to within 35 kilometers (22 miles) or less, setting the stage for the battle of Baghdad.

On Iraqi television, an announcer read a statement from Saddam Hussein.

"Victory is at hand," the statement said. "Fight them so that Iraq, the bastion of religion and principles, will be secured and our nation will come out of this crisis glorious," the text said.

The announcer said Iraq had "only utilized a third or less" of its army.

Later, images of Saddam meeting top advisers in a windowless room were shown.

But McChrystal said U.S. troops were "clearly threatening" the capital and "threatening the core of the regime."

The real test for the forces will come when they reach Baghdad itself. The Iraqi regime said a few days ago that it expected U.S. troops to encircle the capital this week, and that they would be destroyed once they entered the narrow streets of the city.

American commanders say they will not rush into the Iraqi capital. Reinforcements are arriving in Kuwait and are expected to gradually move north to participate eventually in the battle of Baghdad.

The breakthrough Wednesday came after a pause of over a week for regroupment and resupply. The massive U.S. troop movement began before dawn Wednesday on a moonless and cloudless night.

Southwest of the capital, U.S. Army tanks and armored vehicles dashed through the Karbala Gap, a passage between a large lake and the Euphrates River. They seized a bridge and crossed the Euphrates in the afternoon, clearing the division's last geographic obstacle to its final target.

See WAR, Page 4

WAR IN IRAQ

Blair says Saddam plans to ruin shrines

- Prime Minister Tony Blair said Wednesday that Saddam Hussein planned to damage Muslim shrines and pin the blame on allied troops. *Page 2*
- Political and business calculations are driving a corporate scramble in Western capitals, in hopes of getting slices of postwar Iraqi reconstruction. *Page 3*
- Military officers in Qatar watched the dramatic rescue of a U.S. private unfold through a live video feed. *Page 4*
- With U.S. armored columns closing in on Baghdad, Pentagon leaders say the most dangerous days of the war lie ahead. *Page 5*
- For full recent coverage: *www.iht.com/iraq*

Turkey agrees to expanded role

By Steven R. Weisman with Frank Bruni
The New York Times

ANKARA: The United States reached agreement Wednesday with Turkey to upgrade Turkish support of American military actions in the war with Iraq by permitting use of Turkish territory to supply food, fuel and other necessities to American military forces operating in the northern Iraqi theater.

Turkey also agreed formally for the first time to let American military planes in distress and American service personnel wounded in battle land in Turkish territory, although such help is reported to have occurred informally before now.

The accord was announced Wednesday afternoon by Secretary of State Colin Powell and Turkey's foreign minister, Abdullah Gul, after a full day of meetings intended to repair the damage to Turkish-American relations inflicted when the Turkish Parliament rebuffed an American request last month for use of Turkey as a base from which troops would enter Iraq.

Gul said the new agreement would not require approval by Parliament.

Political analysts and politicians in Turkey said that Turkish leaders were grateful for Powell's visit, which was initiated by the United States.

"It's welcome," said a senior government official in an interview Wednesday. "It's warmly welcome."

A Turkish political analyst, Mensur Akgun, noted that Powell had not visited Turkey during the months of negotiations between Turkey and the United States in advance of the failed March 1 parliamentary resolution. He suggested this visit was overdue.

"It was necessary," Akgun said. "If we'd had Powell's visit before the first of March, we might have had a different outcome from the Parliament."

Powell on Wednesday was telling Turkey some things it wanted to hear: that northern Iraq would remain under coalition control and that Turkey would have a place at the table in the reconstruction of northern Iraq. Details relating to the exact nature of supplies for American forces in northern Iraq were withheld. It was unclear whether the supplies would include weapons, for instance.

But American officials were clearly pleased that Turkey would be playing a more important supporting role in the Iraq war, and that this step in turn would make it easier to secure Congressional backing for the $1 billion in economic assistance for Turkey requested by President George W. Bush.

In a separate part of the agreement Wednesday, Powell said the United States and Turkey would set up a monitoring group to watch the border situation with Iraq to make sure there are no conditions that would compel Turkey to send its troops across the border.

The Bush administration has adamantly said there is no reason for Turkey to intervene. It fears such a move would inflame the Kurdish-dominated region in Iraq.

Turkey says it has no intention of sending its forces in, provided that there is no Kurdish uprising that might threaten Turkish territory or flood Turkey with refugees or lead to attacks on Turkish-speaking peoples of Iraq.

Powell was due to leave Turkey on Wednesday afternoon for Serbia and Montenegro, where he planned to confer with the new prime minister.

U.S. troops near Baghdad

Division seizes bridge, closing in on its target

By Steven Lee Myers
The New York Times

WITH THE 3d INFANTRY DIVISION, in central Iraq

"Six lanes to Baghdad," Lieutenant Colonel Thomas Smith shouted Wednesday as a column of American tanks and armored vehicles lurched slowly toward the bridge over a sharp bend in the Euphrates River. "We'll be home soon."

His exuberance, as it was, was premature. Rounds of Iraqi artillery began landing with a shuddering crack and thump on the west side of the river, each one moving closer to the bridge and sending plumes of whitish smoke skyward.

The bridge — nearly 275 meters (900 feet) across — still stood, but as units of the army's 3d Infantry Division thrust ever closer to Baghdad, Iraqi soldiers detonated explosives packed inside the 10th of 11 twin spans.

Romeo Gacad/Agence France-Presse

U.S. soldiers secured an area close to Karbala on Wednesday.

The blast shattered a concrete beam, shearing its steel girders and convulsing the southern span. As Apache helicopter gunships coursed over groves of palms and Bradley armored fighting vehicles sprayed the opposite bank, soldiers and engineers crossed the Euphrates in rubber boats, attacking a squad of Iraqis beneath the bridge and cutting wires that threatened to blow the northern span.

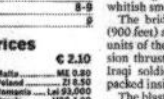

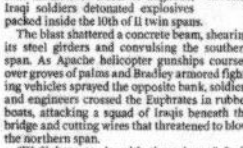

"We'll have to do with three lanes," said Smith, commander of the 1st Brigade's 11th Engineer Battalion, surveying the damage as a cacophony of bullets, mortars and shells reverberated around the river's eastern side.

The seizure of the bridge — after an intense three-hour battle against more than a company of dug-in Iraqi soldiers — cleared the 3d Infantry Division's last geographic obstacle to its final target.

Two weeks after crossing the Iraqi border from Kuwait and 10 hours after rolling through the Karbala gap to the south, routing disorganized and overwhelmed Iraqi forces, the division's forward units seized a growing bridgehead on the Euphrates' eastern shore.

See INFANTRY, Page 4

In this issue *No. 37,346*

Newsstand prices

Germany	€ 2.10		
Albania	US$ 2.00	Malta	ML 0.80
Austria	€ 2.30	Poland	Zl 8.50
Bulgaria	€ 2.55	Romania	Lei 93,000
Czech Rep	CZK 100	Russia	US$ 4.00
France	€ 1.85	Slovakia	SKK 100
Hungary	HUF 450	Turkey	TL 2,700,000
Latvia	Ls 1.85	Ukraine	US$ 5.00
Lithuania	LTL 15	U.S. Mil. (Eur.)	$1.40
Luxembourg	€ 2.00	Yugoslavia	Din 160

To subscribe at home or office, see contact information on **Page 2**

4 198582 002102 40314

OTHER NEWS

- The Turkish Cypriot leader offered concessions to Greek Cypriots in a bid to break a deadlock on UN talks. *Page 7*
- The European Commission initiated disciplinary procedures against France for having violated the EU's public-finance rules in 2002. *Page 11*
- Stock prices around the world staged a sharp, broad advance on Wednesday. *Page 11*

THE DOLLAR | New York

	Wednesday 3 P.M.	Previous
€1 =	$1.0762	$1.0909
£1 =	$1.5656	$1.5778
$1 =	¥118.91	¥118.065
$1 =	SF1.3804	SF1.3543

Full currency rates | *Page 11*

THE MARKETS

	Wednesday 3 P.M.	
The Dow	8,308.39 + 2.96%	+ 238.93
S&P 500	883.24 + 2.88%	+ 24.76
Nasdaq	1,398.65 + 3.73%	+ 50.35

On the Web: *www.iht.com*

EL PAIS

JUEVES 10 DE ABRIL DE 2003
Año XXVIII. Número 9.447

DIARIO INDEPENDIENTE DE LA MAÑANA
www.elpais.es

EDICIÓN **MADRID**
Precio: 1 euro

LAS TROPAS DE EE UU TOMAN BAGDAD EN MEDIO DEL CAOS

El régimen de Sadam se desploma

El Pentágono ignora si el dictador está "oculto, muerto o incapacitado"

Los 'marines' son recibidos con júbilo en barrios populares de la capital iraquí

El mando estadounidense advierte de que aún quedan "combates peligrosos"

Jack Straw: "No queremos ocupar Irak más tiempo del que sea necesario"

Á. ESPINOSA / F. PEREGIL, **Bagdad**
ENVIADOS ESPECIALES

Llegaron los soldados de Estados Unidos a la plaza del Paraíso, frente al hotel Palestina; amarraron una soga a un tanque, se la echaron al cuello de la estatua de Sadam Husein, le pusieron una bandera de EE UU, se la quitaron; y al cabo de media hora derribaron uno de los símbolos más grandes de un régimen obsesionado con los símbolos. Varias decenas de iraquíes empezaron a saltar encima de ella. Después, unos la golpearon con mazas, otros se emplearon a alpargatazos y alguno de los ancianos que rondaban por allí la escupió. La mano derecha de Sadam, la famosa mano que empuñaba fusiles apuntados hacia el cielo, la mano tantas veces levantada indicando el norte a seguir, tantas veces reproducida en miles de estatuas de miles de plazas por todo el país, la mano con la que saludaba a las multitudes desde los balcones... ahora yacía en el suelo, vejada por un muchacho con una camiseta roja del club de fútbol Liverpool. Aún no habían pasado 21 días desde que comenzó la guerra. Y nadie en Bagdad sabía dónde estaba Sadam.

En otra esquina de la ciudad, Alí Husein Abdulhadi cumplió su promesa de vestirse de rojo y salir a bailar para celebrar la caída de Sadam. Su euforia era secundada por miles de personas. Muchos contenían, sin embargo, su alegría, preocupados por los disparos que se oían y por el caos. A primeras horas de la mañana, bandas organizadas y particulares se dedicaban al pillaje de comercios y edificios oficiales. En algunas calles, falsos controles asaltaban a quienes se aventuraban en su camino. En la ciudad no existía ninguna autoridad. Pasa a la **página 2**
Más información en **páginas 3 a 14**
Editorial en la **página 18**

Un soldado tapa con una bandera de Estados Unidos la cara de la estatua de Sadam que presidía una plaza en el centro de Bagdad y que minutos después sería derribada. / ASSOCIATED PRESS

España acepta la versión de EE UU y no exigirá una investigación por la muerte de Couso

El ministro de Defensa, Federico Trillo, calificó ayer de "gravísimo error" la muerte bajo el fuego de un carro de combate de EE UU del cámara de Tele 5 José Couso en el hotel Palestina de Bagdad. El Gobierno dio así por buena la versión del Pentágono de que no hubo ataque deliberado y renuncia a reclamar una investigación.
Páginas 21 a 23 / Editorial en la **página 18**

UN GRUPO extremista israelí pone una bomba en una escuela palestina
INTERNACIONAL. **Página 15**

LA JUEZ DE GESCARTERA decreta la libertad de Camacho bajo fianza de tres millones
ESPAÑA. **Página 26**

EL BARÇA empata en el campo del Juventus (1-1) y el Valencia pierde en el del Inter (1-0)
DEPORTES. **Páginas 53 y 54**

EL FMI rebaja medio punto la previsión de crecimiento de la economía mundial este año
ECONOMÍA. **Página 59**

Muere Jorge Oteiza, el gran escultor y agitador

Jorge Oteiza (Orio, 1908), uno de los máximos representantes de la escultura contemporánea, falleció ayer en la Policlínica de San Sebastián, donde permanecía ingresado desde el pasado 30 de enero. Quien desde hacía muchos años había proclamado su propia muerte artística, falleció en estado de ensoñación, según informaron los médicos que le cuidaban. Autor de una obra mundialmente reconocida, agitador incansable y poseedor de un carácter indomable, dejó escrito su epitafio: "Amo a mi país profundamente; me da rabia (mi país) profundamente. Le doy mi vida. Profundamente le doy mi muerte". Será enterrado hoy en Alzuza (Navarra). **Páginas 39 a 44**

CiberP@ís
Claves criptográficas

España sello a sello

Hoy, cinco sellos de deportes

ETA asegura que no está «en un escenario de tregua» y que abrirá «nuevos frentes»

► Pide el voto nulo porque «traerá avances en la lucha de liberación»

► Arremete contra el PNV y EA y rechaza el plan Ibarretxe

DV. SAN SEBASTIÁN

ETA «no está en un escenario de tregua», considera que el plan Ibarretxe no es válido para sus aspiraciones y sostiene que el voto nulo es la mejor opción que se puede tomar en las elecciones del día 25. Estas tres ideas resumen el mensaje que tres miembros de la organización lanzaron ayer en una comparecencia ante varios periodistas a la que tuvo acceso EiTB para dar a conocer los resultados del proceso asambleario recientemente celebrado en la organización.

En respuesta a una pregunta sobre si se encontraban en tregua, uno de los portavoces de ETA da al traste con los rumores sobre la posibilidad de que la organización estuviera a punto de declarar un alto el fuego. La contestación del activista es, en este punto, contundente. «No. Hay que decir que por parte de ETA no existe ningún alto el fuego táctico», dice. Y no sólo eso, sino que sostiene que «los frentes abiertos hasta ahora siguen abiertos».

Las declaraciones que mostró ayer EiTB son un extracto de las que realizaron los etarras. El diario *Gara*, en su edición digital, mostró poco después algunos detalles más de las palabras de los activistas. Así, cuando se refieren a los frentes que permanecen abiertos, añaden que «algunos frentes se adecuarán y se abrirán otros nuevos».

En la entrevista, los tres etarras comparecen con sus rostros ocultos con capuchas blancas, vestidos con monos oscuros y tocados con txapelas. A sus espaldas figuran la ikurriña, la bandera de Navarra y una enseña con el arrano beltza. La comparecencia se realiza en una habitación en la que se entrevé una pared decorada con un marcado estilo rural.

Los tres miembros de ETA, en un momento de su comparecencia. [DV]

Autodeterminación

Los miembros de la organización muestran sobre una mesa varios ejemplares de su boletín interno, *Zutabe*. En su número de abril, la publicación recoge los resultados del proceso de debate celebrado a lo largo del pasado año. La organización señala que los principios sobre los que debe asentarse una solución para el problema vasco son el derecho de autodeterminación y la territorialidad.

Los tres encapuchados explican que el debate se ha centrado en dos aspectos principales: «de una parte, en el análisis crítico sobre la situación política en la última década, y de otra, en todo lo relativo a la acción armada».

Respecto a la primera de las cuestiones, la situación política, los portavoces de ETA indican que «España ha impuesto un estado de excepción, una dictadura sobre el pueblo vasco». En esta línea, acusan al PP, el PSOE, a la derecha y los socialistas franceses de «la continuidad de la situación de opresión», aunque también critican a quienes «autoproclamándose abertzales renuevan su apuesta por el regionalismo», mencionando expresamente a PNV, EA, Aralar y Abertzaleen Batasuna. «El PNV, con Ibarretxe a la cabeza y con la cobertura de EA, apadrina un nuevo pacto de integración en España», indican.

La organización terrorista no sólo desmintió ayer a quienes aseguraban que mantenía una tregua tras negociar supuestamente con el PNV su apoyo a la consulta popular contenida en el plan Ibarretxe. También desmintió las interpretaciones surgidas con la difusión de su último comunicado, en el que se calificaba de «motivo de alegría» la consulta popular recogida en el plan Ibarretxe. Esta expresión fue tomada como un respaldo a la propuesta del lehendakari y, por parte del Gobierno central, como una prueba de la existencia de un pacto para editar un «Lizarra II».

«Consultar al pueblo es motivo de alegría», afirma uno de los etarras». «De alegría y además algo muy serio. Euskadi Ta Askatasuna –añade– siempre se muestra a favor de eso, y esa es una de las razones de nuestra lucha». En este «motivo de alegría» no figura sin embargo el plan de Ibarretxe. Para ETA, la propuesta del lehendakari «no busca ni una solución ni hacer una consulta para conocer cuál es la opinión de Euskal Herria. El plan de Ibarretxe es excluyente, cerrado y no favorece el arreglo. La propia actitud de Ibarretxe muestra eso». «Nosotros –recalca el portavoz de ETA– pensamos que la solución del conflicto no es cosa exclusiva de una persona, una organización o una única institución, sino el fruto de todas las voluntades y del trabajo en común».

Iniciativas políticas

Los encapuchados reconocen que «la izquierda abertzale tiene dificultades para situarse en un nuevo terreno de juego político que ella misma ha contribuido a crear con su lucha». Tras indicar que «ha llegado el momento de renovar la Alternativa Democrática», los representantes de ETA expresan su intención de «sumar a la actividad armada otras iniciativas políticas», aunque aclaran inmediatamente que «iniciativa no es sinónimo de tregua». Sobre esta última cuestión señalan que «una tregua es un recurso político y militar que ETA podrá activar como elemento de impulso o como consecuencia de un proceso». Además, aseguran que «si se garantizara el respeto a la voluntad de la ciudadanía vasca ETA no tendría que defender por las armas a Euskal Herria».

Los miembros de la organización terrorista hacen un llamamiento por el voto nulo indicando que «nosotros pensamos que esos votos que España ha ilegalizado serán para la defensa y la construcción de Euskal Herria. Votos que traerán avances en la lucha de liberación. Serán votos muy importantes, votos que harán daño al enemigo. Serán votos de dignidad y de lucha». «Muy al contrario, pensamos que los votos que pueda recibir el PNV servirán para garantizar la imposición de hoy día», afirman.

Arzalluz afirma que la organización «apoya a Garzón porque revela un interés común con AuB»

► Rajoy asegura que el mensaje confirma que ETA apuesta «por continuar la lucha armada»

DV. SAN SEBASTIÁN

El presidente del PNV, Xabier Arzalluz, afirmó que, con las declaraciones realizadas ayer, los miembros de ETA «han apoyado o bien al señor Garzón o bien al señor Jiménez de Parga, porque realmente al oirles, es una presunción de que hay un interés común, puesto que salen a pedir el voto para AuB».

En declaraciones a *Radio Euskadi*, Arzalluz, tras ver la aparición «un poco fantasmagórica», de los portavoces de ETA, dijo que «no les acepto a estos señores que irrumpan de esta manera en estas elecciones más o menos democráticas, en las que participa todo el mundo, menos aquellos que han sido excluidos y, si creen que con lo que han dicho de apoyar el voto nulo ayudan a AuB, tenemos una apreciación de las cosas totalmente diferente».

El vicepresidente primero del Gobierno, Mariano Rajoy, señaló que el mensaje de ETA no es «novedad», y aseguró que lo «grave» es que se haya lanzado en la televisión pública ETB, a la que el Gobierno piensa «pedir explicaciones». El anuncio de la organización confirma, según Rajoy, «que está en la independencia, en continuar con la lucha armada y anteponer las supuestas patrias a los derechos individuales, como son la vida, manifestar una opinión o fijar el domicilio».

El consejero de Justicia, Joseba Azkarraga, lamentó que ETA haya rechazado la posibilidad de una tregua y señaló que «tendremos que obligar a esa minoría que intenta sojuzgar a la mayoría de este pueblo, decirle que el único camino viable para avanzar es la paz».

Desde el Gobierno Vasco también reaccionó el consejero de Vivienda y coordinador general de IU-EB, Javier Madrazo, quien afirmó que ETA mostró ayer su «degeneración y enfermedad terminal». Madrazo indicó que el PP «ha vuelto a quedar en evidencia, porque cuando ha habido alguna insinuación de tregua se ha puesto muy nervioso».

Por su parte, el portavoz parlamentario del PSE-EE, Rodolfo Ares, afirmó que el apoyo de ETA al voto nulo «supone la forma que tiene de hacer campaña electoral a favor de unas candidaturas y confirma que estas plataformas anuladas pretendían continuar la actividad de un partido como Batasuna, que ampara y justifica la violencia terrorista».

REACCIONES

XABIER ARZALLUZ (PNV)

► «Al oirles parece que hay un interés común puesto que salen a pedir el voto para AuB»

MARIANO RAJOY (PP)

► «Lo grave es que este mensaje se haya lanzado en una televisión pública»

JAVIER MADRAZO (IU)

► «El PP ha vuelto a quedar en evidencia porque ante la insinuación de una tregua se ha puesto nervioso»

RODOLFO ARES (PSE-EE)

► «Se ha confirmado que las plataformas anuladas querían continuar la actividad de Batasuna»

18 September 2003, El Mundo.

La vanidad hace siempre traición a nuestra prudencia y aun a nuestro interés (Jacinto Benavente)

EL MUNDO

JUEVES 18 DE SEPTIEMBRE DE 2003
Año XV. Número: 5.034

PAIS VASCO / GIPUZKOA

DEL SIGLO VEINTIUNO
Precio: 1 euro. Con DVD: 4.99 euros más

ESPACIO / Pedro Duque: «Entrenar con los rusos ha sido mucho más duro que con los norteamericanos» / 38

Garzón procesa a Bin Laden alegando que el 11-S hubo una víctima española

Considera que esta circunstancia y el que parte de la trama se urdiera en España justifican aplicar la doctrina del Supremo sobre la jurisdicción universal

CARMEN REMIREZ DE GANUZA
MADRID.– El juez Baltasar Garzón ordenó ayer la prisión de Osama bin Laden, el líder de Al Qaeda, y su correspondiente busca y captura, junto a la de otros 15 dirigentes de la organización terrorista islámica.

El juez que protagonizó la persecución penal desde España del dictador chileno Augusto Pinochet vuelve a invocar para ello el principio de justicia universal. Además, esgrime, según la reciente doctrina del Tribunal Supremo, la conexión española de los atentados del 11-S y la existencia de «al menos» una víctima española, Silvia San Pio.

La inclusión del máximo responsable de dichos atentados entre un total de 35 procesados –la mayoría relacionados con la presunta célula de Al Qaeda en España– fue la sorpresa que puso ayer la guinda al auto más esperado y abultado del curso judicial en la Audiencia Nacional.

A lo largo de más de 700 folios, de los que la mitad recogen detalladas transcripciones telefónicas y documentales, Garzón da cuenta de la composición de dicha célula, liderada por Imad Eddin Barakat Yarkas, *Abu Dahdah*; de las relaciones de sus miembros con la cúpula de la organización y de los indicios que la vinculan a los pilotos suicidas y a la propia cobertura de los atentados de Washington y Nueva York. Sigue en **página 25**
Editorial en **página 3**

El PSOE ultima dar un giro al centro con su programa económico

Se comprometerá a no subir los impuestos ni el gasto público, a recortar drásticamente el presupuesto de RTVE y a reformar el mercado laboral

CASIMIRO GARCIA-ABADILLO
MADRID.– El líder del PSOE, José Luis Rodríguez Zapatero, está dispuesto a jugar fuerte en el terreno económico para atraer a las clases medias urbanas. Para ello, ha encargado el diseño de su programa a un grupo de expertos capitaneado por el ex jefe del Servicio de Estudios del BBVA, Miguel Sebastián.

Rodríguez Zapatero cree que los socialistas del siglo XXI no deben tener reparos en asumir algunas recetas centristas de corte liberal que, hasta ahora, eran patrimonio de la derecha reformista. Las líneas maestras del programa económico (aún en la cocina del think tank socialista) han sido adelantadas a EL MUNDO y suponen ciertamente un giro sin precedentes en la trayectoria del PSOE. Sigue en **página 22**

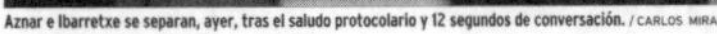
Aznar e Ibarretxe se separan, ayer, tras el saludo protocolario y 12 segundos de conversación. / CARLOS MIRALLES

Carrés: «No renuncies, ¡que es España!» Tejero: «¡Viva España, coño!»

Antena 3 emitirá esta noche el revelador documento sobre el 23-F obtenido por EL MUNDO TV **Págs. 28 y 29**

ZINEMALDIA

La huelga del María Cristina compromete el inicio del Festival

Medem asegura que su filme defiende «la no violencia y el diálogo»

EL CULTURAL

San Sebastián relanza el cine español

Consiga hoy Jules y Jim de la Filmoteca del Cultural por sólo 4,99 €

Ibarretxe acude a un acto convocado por el Rey para conmemorar la Constitución

El Gobierno vasco afirma que se trata de un gesto para demostrar que su plan no rompe con España

FERNANDO GAREA
MADRID.– El lehendakari Juan José Ibarretxe acudió ayer por primera vez a una recepción del Rey y por eso fue el centro de atención en el Palacio Real de Madrid.

Además, su presencia era aún más destacable porque se trataba de la recepción del Monarca a los miembros del Comité de Honor de la Comisión Nacional Organizadora de los actos conmemorativos del XXV Aniversario de la Constitución. Es decir, la misma que pone en cuestión el *plan Ibarretxe*. Sigue en **página 10**
Editorial en **página 3**

IÑIGO IBAÑEZ

Un gol de Kovacevic da el primer triunfo a la Real en la Liga de Campeones

Páginas 50 y 51

XVIII EDICIÓN DE LOS PREMIOS GOYA

La libertad de expresión

DIEGO GALÁN

En cada ceremonia de los Goya se descubre que a lo largo del año ha habido numerosas películas españolas que merecen sobresaliente, y que hay talentos, muchos de ellos anónimos, que las hacen posibles. Tanto si ganan o no esos feos trofeos que llaman estatuillas. Y también se descubre, aunque esa es otra historia, que todos los cineastas están muy enamorados, tienen hijos y una enorme parentela a la que citan como guía telefónica. Parece increíble que quienes son capaces de admirarnos en la pantalla, tengan luego tan escaso sentido del espectáculo. Aunque, por supuesto, no todos ellos. Firme y clara en el escenario estuvo Mercedes Sampietro defendiendo la libertad de expresión, apoyada como una piña por los anteriores presidentes de la Academia: un acto valiente y rotundo, que puede hacer historia.

Las víctimas del terrorismo habían conseguido convertir la película de Julio Medem en el foco de atención. Premiar o no *La pelota vasca* podría equivaler, nada menos, a que la Academia del cine español estuviera o no a favor de ETA, tal es la distorsión con que últimamente se maneja lo que ocurre en este país. Aún habrá alguien más que mantenga este disparate. Y aunque no premiaron finalmente *La pelota vasca*, Medem se llevó la que quizás fue la mayor ovación de la noche cuando Luis Tosar le dedicó su premio. Daba la misma impresión de unión entusiasta que el año pasado se fue haciendo contra la guerra a lo largo de la noche.

Mercedes Sampietro, tercera por la izquierda, junto a los ex presidentes de la Academia de Cine. / BERNARDO PÉREZ

No fue una sorpresa que *Te doy mis ojos*, la magnífica película de Icíar Bollaín con guión de Alicia Luna, acaparara siete premios Goya, todos merecidamente. Había sido, desde su estreno, la clara favorita. La segunda en premios fue *La gran aventura de Mortadelo y Filemón*, a la que correspondieron, lógicamente, cuantos se refieren a una producción de tal envergadura. Pero cualquiera de las otras películas nominadas los podrían haber obtenido igualmente. Y sus actores y sus actrices...

> Ha sido un buen año para el cine español, viendo esta síntesis que los académicos muestran con sus nominaciones

Ha sido un buen año para el cine español, viendo al menos esta síntesis que los académicos muestran con sus nominaciones. Por eso no hay realmente perdedoras, como se insiste en repetir cansinamente uno y otro año. ¿Cómo puede ser perdedora una película si la nominación en sí es ya un triunfo? *Soldados de Salamina*, de sus ocho nominaciones, obtuvo sólo los Goya a los efectos especiales y a la (espléndida) fotografía de Javier Aguirresarobe, pero con igual justicia podría haber conseguido varios premios goyas más. Como otras películas que se quedaron en el tintero, *Las horas del día*, *Carmen*, *La vida mancha*... En esto de las nominaciones y los premios suele haber contradicciones.

Este año, por ejemplo, había dos casos curiosos: *Planta 4ª*, de Antonio Mercero, era candidata a mejor película pero a ningún otro apartado, mientras que Cesc Gay era candidato al mejor director por *En la ciudad*, que no entraba en la categoría de mejor película.

En estrecha pugna con *Suite Habana*, parecía también claro que el Goya a la mejor película de habla hispana recaería en la original y conmovedora *Historias mínimas*, del argentino Carlos Sorín, aunque hubiera pasado desapercibida por nuestras carteleras cuando se estrenó. Carlos Sorín fue uno de los cineastas latinoamericanos que subieron al escenario. Dijeron que éste era el año del cine iberoamericano (acabarán llamándolo hispanoamericano, ya verán).

Un cine, dijo la presidenta de la Academia, Mercedes Sampietro, que quiere reflejar su propia realidad. Como igualmente quiere hacer en ocasiones el cine español, arriesgándose a todos los temas y desde todas las perspectivas. Y en libertad. Ese fue el mensaje de las pegatinas que lucían muchos académicos: un rechazo a los intentos de amordazar el cine y un rechazo indiscutible a la violencia.

El misterio de la pegatina

MARUJA TORRES

La verdad es que nunca me había preocupado e interesado menos narrar en crónica alguna entrega de premios cual la de los de cierto pintor aragonés cuyo nombre no se puede asociar al galardón. Me aburrí como un merengue en una reunión de diabéticos. Y además, con esa sensación de haber sido bien enculada, junto con el ameno público en general.

En fin. Como canta Pablo Milanés, "el tiempo pasa, nos vamos volviendo viejos". Nos vamos volviendo ciegas, también, pues cuando salió Jorge Perugorría creí que era Milanés después de haberse vuelto blanco en donde Jackson recibe a los niños. Al fin supe que era él que llevaba pegatina.

Y nos vamos volviendo sordas y sordos y compañeras y compañeros, puesto que hubo grandes vacíos de sonido ambiental. Hubo momentos, por ejemplo, cuando recién entregado el premio al mejor documental que ¡España! temía recibiera Julio Medem, en aquel mismísimo instante se creó un hueco sonoro digno de Goya, a quien no debo nombrar porque, punto y aparte. Les cuento mi sorda visión.

Julio Medem, a su llegada al Palacio Municipal de Congresos. / CLAUDIO ÁLVAREZ

El premio Los Desastres de la Guerra va, abierto en canal, al primero que me cuente qué puso, argentinamente, Leo Sbaraglia en su pegatina. Le echó retórica al asunto, para dolo del realizador —por cierto, la retransmisión de El Pardo más antigua de la historia de la humanidad—, que no sabía cómo alejarse del candente asunto.

De hecho, habría que premiar, con el galardón Los Premios de Televisión Producen Monstruos, a quienes supieron pasar del plano picado al primerísimo plano sin otear la solapa. Y, al fondo, la orquesta Charatoga y la retransmisión más antigua y franquista que conocemos los veteranos. Menos mal que doña Mercedes, la nueva presidenta de la Academia, le echó un par de ovarios al asunto y exigió lo imposible a nuestros próceres: sentido del humor, que encajen las críticas y que amen el cine. Menos mal que unos cuantos predecesores la apoyaron y, apoyándola, le dijeron al cine español que no está solo.

> Doña Mercedes le echó un par de ovarios y exigió lo imposible a nuestros próceres

Entretanto, la platea bullía de *glamour*. Les juro que lo más interesante que pude otear fue a José Bono, aplaudiendo sin ton ni son.

Por fortuna, el cine no se rinde, y después del año que vivieron peligrosamente sobre todo los iraquíes, y pese a que, en escena, todo fueron alusiones, hay que reconocer el espíritu conciliador de la ceremonia, que, profusa y con política corrección, premió *Te doy mis ojos* —película que ganaría si sacaran las secuencias de terapia de grupo de acémilas y explicaran el vínculo sexual que une a la pareja— y a un montón de hombres y mujeres aquejados de abundancia familiar—.

Mientras que mi favorita, *Torremolinos 75* —o setenta y otro, la ceremonia me ha aplastado—, quedó como quien dice en la cuneta. Gran película.

Volviendo a Los Desastres de la Guerra superpremiun magnum: la música, antigua e inadecuada, un guión inexistente —o existente: no estaba para dejar que hablaran, sino para impedirlo—, salvado por la pericia y el encanto de Diego Luna, desde ya les digo que es preferido de la ciudad, y la siempre eficazmente jezabélica Cayetana, cuyo nombre, oh dioses, cualquiera puede prohibirnos pronunciar en cualquier momento, ligada a Goya. Esa chica lleva muy bien los trajes sin tirantes y es la única que puede permitirse llamar cabecitas a los pesantes premios que reproducen la tremenda testa baturra del pintor.

> Lo más interesante que pude otear fue a José Bono, aplaudiendo sin ton ni son

Digo yo que los españoles deberíamos ir por ahí, a partir de ahora, guarnecidos de prospecto como los medicamentos, para explicar nuestras ideologías y calmar los desmanes. Que es, sin duda, lo que hizo Sbaraglia, pero el cámara no se acercó a su solapa, maldita sea.

7 May 2003, El Correo.

Un carguero encalla en Pasaia y bloquea doce horas la entrada de mercantes

El buque noruego, de 154 metros de eslora y cargado con 10.000 toneladas de pasta de madera, **chocó contra unas rocas de la bocana** y quedó cruzado a la entrada del puerto

JAVIER PEÑALBA SAN SEBASTIÁN

Un carguero de bandera noruega encalló a primera hora de la mañana de ayer en la bocana del puerto de Pasaia y bloqueó durante casi doce horas las salidas y entradas de todos los buques mercantes. Ningún tripulante sufrió daños y los desperfectos en el casco del barco son escasos.

El suceso ocurrió sobre las 7.40. horas cuando el mercante '*Nenominee*', de 154 metros de eslora y que iba cargado con 10.000 toneladas de pasta de madera, comenzó las maniobras para acceder desde el exterior del puerto a aguas de la bahía pasaitarra. El barco había cubierto sin problemas un tercio de los 1.200 metros de los que consta la bocana y, con el práctico a bordo, se disponía a enganchar los cabos de los dos remolcadores que habían salido a su encuentro. En ese instante el mercante se desvió de la ruta y encalló en las rocas de la zona conocida como Cala Burtxa.

Plan de emergencia

Pese al impacto, ninguno de los diecisiete miembros de la tripulación resultó herido. El puerto activó de manera inmediata el plan de emergencia interior, por lo que inspectores de la Capitanía Marítima se desplazaron a la zona y, junto con técnicos especializados y responsables del puerto, subieron a bordo del barco embarrancado.

Asimismo, los dos remolcadores de la empresa Facal que en el momento del siniestro se encontraban junto al buque trataron de retirar el navío de las rocas. Al mismo tiempo, se intentó trasvasar el agua de los tanques de lastre de proa a los de popa, en la creencia de que con ello el carguero se libraría de las rocas. Sin embargo, las operaciones resultaron infructuosas.

El accidente pudo ocurrir por un fallo en el timón o por el fuerte viento

Con el paso de las horas y en fase de bajar mar, las autoridades estimaron que lo más prudente era esperar hasta última hora de la tarde para, de nuevo con la marea alta, reiniciar las labores de retirada del barco. Finalmente, a las siete y media de la tarde, tres remolcadores lograron desencallar el 'Nenominee'. El casco del mercante no sufrió vías de agua.

El siniestro provocó el bloqueo del tránsito portuario de mercantes: Ocho buques tenían previsto acceder en el transcurso del día de ayer a las instalaciones portuarias y otros tantos pretendían partir. Los pesqueros pudieron navegar con absoluta normalidad.

Las autoridades marítimas han abierto una investigación para determinar los motivos por los que el buque encalló. Contemplan la posibilidad de que el barco hubiese sufrido un fallo en el timón. Otras fuentes apuntaron que el accidente se pudo deber a las fuertes rachas de viento que se registraron ayer.

EMBARRANCADO. Varios remolcadores preparan la maniobra para alejar el mercante de la costa. / EFE

El jefe de la Policía dice que Rontealde se confesó responsable del escape

El consejero delegado de la empresa de Barakaldo asegura que **la planta funcionó «perfectamente»** y tacha de «falso» el testimonio del agente

IZASKUN ERRAZTI BARAKALDO

«Era Rontealde: no tuve ninguna duda». Así de contundente se expresó ayer el cabo de la Policía Municipal de Barakaldo que ejercía como jefe de servicio en la mañana de aquel fatídico 21 de otubre de 1994, cuando se produjo el escape de SO_2 tras el que falleció un vecino. «No era la primera vez. Esa fábrica era un viejo problema: lo sé muy bien, he vivido doce años junto a ella». En la segunda sesión del juicio que se celebra en la Audiencia vizcaína contra la empresa química por un delito ecológico con resultado de muerte, el agente recordó aquella «mañana de locos», con los teléfonos «colapsados» por las llamadas de vecinos. Pero también rememoró «claramente» las declaraciones de los directivos de la compañía, que se personaron en la comisaría tras ordenarles «que parasen la producción para prevenir riesgos mayores».

Según el cabo, el director de la planta, José Elizalde, reconoció que minutos antes del escape «habían iniciado el proceso de arranque y que el derivado del azufre no se había disipado bien en la atmósfera».

No obstante, el consejero delegado de Rontealde, Manuel Barrenetxea, que ayer declaró en calidad de testigo, desmintió el testimonio del agente. «Todo funcionó perfectamente», aseguró. «En la fábrica nadie se planteó que se hubiera producido una emisión», añadió el directivo que, sin embargo, dijo no recordar otros aspectos relacionados con lo sucedido aquel día, como su participación en las reuniones a las que fue convocado por la Junta de Calidad del Aire.

Ante estas contradicciones, la abogada del grupo municipal de HB en Barakaldo, Jone Goirizelaia, solicitó la celebración de un careo entre ambos testigos ya que, según explicó, «el reconocimiento de la emisión tóxica es la base del procedimiento». La fiscal y los letrados del Ayuntamiento fabril y Ekologistak Martxan, que también ejercen como acusación particular, apoyaron la demanda. Pero la presidenta del tribunal no lo estimó necesario.

Los gobiernos vasco y catalán presentan a la ONU su red de sostenibilidad

A. ARMADA NUEVA YORK

«No vamos ni contra el Gobierno central ni contra los gobiernos locales. Nos ocupamos de objetivos precisos, como la política de residuos, que no entran en contradicción con los Estados ni con las ciudades». El consejero de Medio Ambiente de la Generalitat catalana, Ramón Espalder, definió así ayer en Nueva York uno de los aspectos de la nueva red de gobiernos regionales, presentada oficialmente en las Naciones Unidas.

Acompañado del consejero de Medio Ambiente del Gobierno vasco, Sabin Intxaurraga, y aprovechando la conferencia sobre el desarrollo sostenible –una cuestión que, a juicio de Intxaurraga, ha estado «desgraciadamente en segunda división de la agenda internacional»–, ambos consejeros hicieron hincapié en la necesidad de impulsar una red de la que hoy forman parte 23 gobiernos regionales de los cinco continentes. Según Intxaurraga, «el desarrollo sostenible es vital para alcanzar la paz, la seguridad, la justicia y el reconocimiento de los derechos humanos».

El consejero catalán señaló que «en cuanto a política de residuos, el Gobierno español no existe», y sin embargo sí figuran en el ámbito europeo los programas puestos en marcha por los gobiernos vasco y catalán. Cataluña y Euskadi forman parte del comité ejecutivo de una red en la que también figuran la Toscana italiana, Renania del Norte-Westfalia (Alemania) y Flandes (Bélgica).

Aprueban el plan que regulará a los funcionarios de la Administración General de Euskadi

AGENCIAS VITORIA

El Ejecutivo vasco ha aprobado el Proyecto de Ley de Ordenación de los Cuerpos y Escalas de la Administración General de la Comunidad Autónoma de Euskadi y de sus Organismos Autónomos, que aporta una nueva estructura del funcionariado, con el objetivo de «apuntalar y garantizar el buen funcionamiento de la Administración Pública de cara al ciudadano», así como «clarificar con mayor detalle el acceso y promoción dentro de la función pública en todas sus escalas».

El nuevo proyecto «profundiza y completa la regulación contenida en la Ley de 1989 de la Función Pública Vasca» y apuntó que afectará a los 4.800 funcionarios al servicio de la Administración General de la Comunidad Autónoma y no a los de las Administraciones forales y locales.

15 URRIA
2003

SANTORAL
Teresa de Jesús y Tecla.
Semana 42. Han pasado 288 días del año.

El Tiempo, hoy

El sol sale a las 08.25 y se pone a las 19.36
La luna sale a las 22.28 y se pone a las 13.22

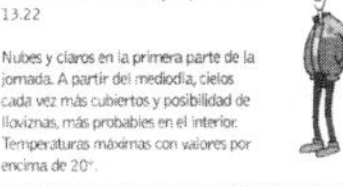

Nubes y claros en la primera parte de la jornada. A partir del mediodía, cielos cada vez más cubiertos y posibilidad de lloviznas, más probables en el interior. Temperaturas máximas con valores por encima de 20°.

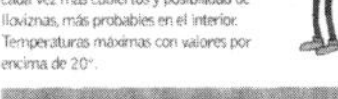

Sorteos y Loterías de ayer

BONOLOTO Martes 14-10-2003
3 · 11 · 12 · 13 · 17 · 31 Complementario **2** Reintegro **1**

CUPÓN ONCE Martes 14-10-2003
25.377 Serie **056** Reintegros **2 · 7**

(Más información en Página 56)

Farmacias de guardia

DONOSTIA

De 9:00 a 22:00: M.T. Pérez Azanza (Urbieta, 24, 427566); J.A. Marco (P. Terranova, 7, 469354); J. Cabezudo (San Francisco, 54, 275448); M.A. Gastelurrutia (P° Larratxo, 98, 352167); 24 horas: O. Unamuno (Garibay, 4, 425938).

GIPUZKOA

Andoain: 24 horas: Arzallus (Aita Larramendi, 16, 300913).
Aretxabaleta-Eskoriatza: J. Fraile (Herriko Plaza, 10, 792199), (Errekabarren, 1, 1° b, 798583). **Arrasate**: J.A. Irizar (Ergin, 11, 791239). **Azpeitia**: 24 horas: Belén Beristain (Urbitarte Auzunea, 3, 811949).
Azkoitia: Pilar Jaén (Ibai-Ondo Kalea, 28, 850660). **Beasain-Ordizia**: Diurno: Jorge de la Cuesta (Avda. de Navarra, 39, Ordizia, 160949); nocturno: Jauregi (Santa María, 2, Ordizia, 160949). **Bergara**: Estella (Matxiategi, 5, 761963).
Deba-Mutriku: Natividad Portillo (Astillero, 2, 669262201). **Eibar**: Mtz. Allue (Ciriaco Agirre, 4, 206984). **Elgoibar**: Zabaleta (Kalebarren, 9, 751384).
Errenteria-Lezo-Pasaia: Iciar Aragón Garbizu (Avda. de Navarra, 77, Errenteria, 344549); nocturno: Enrique Rodríguez (Vicente Elicegi, 7, Errenteria, 516798).
Hernani: Aizpuru (Latxunbe Berri, 11, 336077); nocturno: Arzallus (Aita Larramendi, 16, Andoain, 300913).
Hondarribia: Mayi (Almirante Alonso, s/n, 642191). **Irun**: 24 horas: I. Ollo (Pinar, 13, 611640). **Lasarte-Oria**: Rodríguez (Nagusia, 42, 361774); nocturno: Arzallus (Aita Larramendi, 16, Andoain, 300913).
Legazpi-Urretxu-Zumarraga: 24 horas: Ramón Sarria (Iparragirre, 1, Zumarraga, 721307); Rubén Fenoll (Aizkorri, 12, Legazpi, 734306). **Oiartzun**: A. Agirrezabalaga (Arraskularre, s/n, 491495). **Oñati**: Garate (Kale Barria, 42, 780558). **Tolosa-Villabona**: J.M. Etxebeste (Gernikako Arbolaren, 3, Ibarra, 651040).
Usurbil: Iturralde (Polígono Trece, 9, 363395); nocturno: Arzallus (Aita Larramendi, 16, Andoain, 300913).
Zarautz-Orio-Aia: Mutiozabal (Mayor, 12, Zarautz, 832970). **Zumaia-Getaria-Zestoa**: J. I. Otaño (Gurrutxaga, 4, 861104).

Gipuzkoa

REGENERACIÓN Casi diez años después, la regeneración de Pasaialdea sigue siendo una asignatura pendiente. Todo ello pese a que existe un plan redactado y ayudas previstas.

El Museo Naval, una zona de viviendas y diferentes edificios con oficinas y empresas forman parte del proyecto de regeneración de Pasaia. **DEIA**

El futuro de Pasaia sigue en el aire pese al consenso existente para su regeneración

Carlos Marcos Donostia

ES LA HISTORIA de nunca acabar, aunque todos dicen quererle poner fin. Pasaialdea, una de las zonas más degradadas de Gipuzkoa, requiere una actuación urgente y todo está previsto para ello, incluido el plan de rehabilitación de la dársena de La Herrera; la zona más degradada, con una extensión de 144.000 metros cuadrados.

Sin embargo, los años continúan pasando y las obras siguen sin acometerse. La fecha límite, el 2006. De superarla, no habrá ayudas europeas al proyecto y más de 10 millones de euros caerán en saco roto. La fecha se acerca pero no tanto las posturas entre las diferentes instituciones y organismos involucrados. Léase, Autoridad Portuaria, Ayuntamiento de Pasaia, Diputación de Gipuzkoa...

La Herrera Es la zona más castigada y se contempla la regeneración del 40%

Polémica Se discute la posibilidad de habilitar una vía para el paso de las mercancías

El principal problema responde a que estos terrenos son propiedad del Puerto de Pasaia. La Autoridad Portuaria dice estar dispuesta a cederlos, en parte, al Ayuntamiento pasaitarra; pero advierte de la necesidad de seguir contando con zonas que son consideradas por ambos frentes igual de estratégicas para sus respectivos proyectos.

Es el caso de la dársena de La Herrera. Para el Ayuntamiento pasaitarra es vital actuar en la zona para lograr una regeneración «completa». Para el Puerto, indispensable para mantener su actividad económica mientras no se ejecute el puerto exterior.

En ambos casos se deja bien claro que el Plan Urban para la regeneración de Pasaia y la ejecución del puerto exterior son proyectos diferentes y que poco o nada tienen que ver el uno con el otro, pero los hechos vienen a demostrar que el desarrollo de uno condiciona el proyecto del otro.

El paso de la discordia

El problema no acaba ahí. El paso de un vial destinado al paso de mercancías, que atravesaría el entorno de La Herrera, convertido en un marco idílico con zonas de esparcimiento y museos (Museo Naval o Paco Rabanne) es otro de los puntos que ha tensado aún más la cuerda del conflicto.

La alcaldesa de Pasaia, Izaskun Gómez (PSE-EE), aboga por ac-

EL PAIS

www.elpais.es DIARIO INDEPENDIENTE DE LA MAÑANA FRIDAY, FEBRUARY 20, 2004

ENGLISH EDITION WITH THE INTERNATIONAL HERALD TRIBUNE

Maragall says crisis over ETA truce "resolved"

Carod-Rovira not to return to Catalan government, but to remain ERC head

A. EATWELL, **Madrid**
"The crisis is resolved," Pasqual Maragall, the Socialist premier of Catalonia, declared Thursday a day after his coalition administration was thrown into turmoil by ETA's declaration of a truce limited to the northeastern region.

Maragall spoke after Josep Lluís Carod-Rovira, the leader of the Republican Left (ERC), the second-largest party in the coalition, said he would not return to the administration. Carod-Rovira had previously stepped down as chief minister after admitting to meeting with ETA leaders in France in early January apparently to secure a truce in Catalonia from the Basque terrorist organization.

"I appreciate the efforts of the Republican Left to put an end to this crisis," Maragall said. "The coalition will continue."

ERC will remain in the administration and its powers will remain largely unchanged with Carod-Rovira proposing yesterday that another party member, Josep Bergalló, become chief minister. In addition, and contrary to demands by Spain's governing Popular Party and even Socialist allies, Carod-Rovira will continue to head ERC and will run for Congress in the March 14 general election in representation of Barcelona.

"ERC is an independent political force," Carod-Rovira said, "we make our own decisions about who should lead us and we will not submit to interference from other parties."

The method chosen to "resolve" the crisis nonetheless fell short of the demands for "far-reaching political consequences" made Wednesday by Jose Luis Rodríguez Zapatero, the leader of the Spanish Socialist Workers' Party (PSOE). Yesterday, Zapatero moderated his tone, stressing in a press conference prior to Carod-Rovira's announcement that "neither ETA, nor the PP conditon governments."

Both Prime Minister José María Aznar and his successor and PP candidate Mariano Rajoy stepped up demands yesterday for the Socialists to break the coalition agreement with ERC in Catalonia.

"The agreement with ERC must be broken for reasons of national responsibility and common sense," Aznar said. "It is worth noting that instead of condemning the truce or terrorist acts, [ERC] not only intensifies its defiance but also causes spectacular shame to all Catalans and all Spaniards."

Rajoy argued that by remaining in an alliance with ERC, the Socialists are violating the Antiterrorist Pact that stipulates bipartisan cooperation against terrorism. The PP candidate said that no meeting on the pact would not be convened with the PSOE until it severs its ties with ERC. See EDITORIAL **page 2**

PP acquiesces to election debates but only with all party candidates

Opposition parties see proposal of Rajoy campaign as "unviable"

C. E. C. / A. E., **Madrid**
Spain's governing Popular Party acquiesced Thursday to repeated opposition demands for live televised debates during the election campaign, but it did so with conditions that other parties described as "unviable."

In a letter that was sent to the headquarters of Spanish political parties yesterday morning, Gabriel Elorriaga, the campaign manager of PP candidate Mariano Rajoy, said that the party would accept debates only if "the candidates of all political forces with parliamentary representation participate."

Ostensibly to ensure political plurality, the measure would require candidates from the 12 political parties represented in Congress to take the stand on one television station at any one given time. "It is a way of avoiding the debate citizens really want," Socialist organization secretary José Blanco said, describing that debate as one between Rajoy and Socialist candidate José Luis Rodríguez Zapatero.

For the March 14 election, 600,000 more people are registered to vote than four years ago with eligible voters now numbering 34,570,030.

How private donations have kept PP buoyant

ELECTIONS Pages 4 & 5

Velázquez's Saint Peter is left hanging without a buyer

Despite all the anticipation, the auction of Diego Velázquez's *Tears of Saint Peter* was a disappointment: there was not one single bidder in Madrid's Sala Alcalá on Thursday. Some blame the high asking price of €8 million, though the painting is considered of such importance that the Spanish government in August declared it a "good of cultural interest," which forbids its export to another country.

Israeli tourists travel to Morocco secretly via Spain

I. CEMBRERO, **Madrid**
Yaron Miller, managing director of Flying Carpet, Israel's leading tour operator, doubts whether he will still be able to send Israeli tourists to Morocco. The first group left February 12, but he said there "have been complaints because they have a layover at dawn and have to go through lots of procedures in Palma de Majorca."

In early 2004, Moroccan authorities agreed, according to Israeli sources, to allow tourists from the Hebrew state to enter the country as long as they did not arrive in an Israeli airplane and there were no direct flights from Israel to Morocco. Israeli tourism in Morocco came to a halt in September 2002 after the latest *Intifada* began.

At that time, Flying Carpet spoke to LTE, a Spanish charter company, to organize Thursday flights from Tel Aviv to Palma, where the passengers would connect with another flight, with the same airline, that would take them to Marrakech.

"The travelers go through passport control and customs — their baggage is unloaded — in Palma, where they board another flight with a different code, Miller explains. "It's never a direct flight," he adds, although they get back on the same airplane.

"The first two planes filled up," Miller continues, "but the nine-hour trip turns some clients off" who pay €780 for a 10-day tour.

Morocco's Secretary of State of Foreign Affairs, Taieb Fassi-Fihri, addressed representatives of the main US Jewish organizations in Rabat Tuesday.

"We've answered favorably to Israel's request to expedite the granting of visas and facilitate air transport for Israeli tourists (...)," the *Jerusalem Post* newspaper reported him as saying. His words have outraged legal Muslims, whose organ, *At Tajdid*, fears that this is a first step toward the reopening of the Israeli liaison office in Rabat.

INTERNATIONAL
Herald Tribune
THE WORLD'S DAILY NEWSPAPER PUBLISHED BY THE NEW YORK TIMES EDITED AND PRINTED IN PARIS
THURSDAY, MARCH 11, 2004

A royal gaffe at Covent Garden?
CULTURE & MORE | 9

China's 'Grand Canyon' endangered by dam projects
FOCUS | 2

Disney offers perks to rework Eisner's contract
BUSINESS | 11

Aznar, leaving stage, burnishes his legacy

He points to economy and defends war while working hard on Spain's election

By Elaine Sciolino

MADRID: Years ago, Prime Minister José María Aznar of Spain was called Mr. Nobody because he seemed so pinched and boring. More recently, he has been branded a vassal of the United States for embracing and defending the war against Iraq.

But as he is poised to leave political life after eight years in office, Aznar, a 51-year-old former tax inspector, is running against the clock, both to burnish his legacy and to lead his Popular Party and his handpicked successor to victory over the Socialist Party on Sunday.

To hear Aznar talk about himself, he is a modern-day Winston Churchill who boldly decided to wage war in Iraq in the face of near-total domestic opposition, a miracle maker who transformed Spain into the eighth-largest economy in the world and even a sex symbol with a sense of humor.

In 1996, for example, he said he resisted pressure from aides who urged him to shave off his mustache or risk losing the election.

"I said no," he recalled during a 90-minute interview in Moncloa Palace. "I love it. My wife loves it. A friend of my mother's said, 'A woman who never kissed a man with a mustache has never kissed.' I asked my mother, 'Did this woman's husband have a mustache?' And she said no."

Throughout the campaign, the Popular Party led the Socialists by five to nine percentage points in all the polls, although the lead has narrowed this week. If the lead is retained on Election Day, the only question will be whether the Popular Party keeps its absolute majority of the 350 seats in Parliament or will be forced to rule with one or two smaller parties.

For Aznar, who has honored a pledge not to seek a third term, a Socialist victory would risk the end of eight years of uninterrupted economic growth and higher visibility as a political player in the world.

"What does the word 'Spain' say to you now?" he asked. "Success. That's what it is. That's what's at stake."

The left, he added, "is a disaster" that doesn't "have the leaders or people to govern the country."

"I think there would be a very serious risk of economic and political retreat," he said.

Aznar's low-key approach contrasts with the rough and tumble of Spanish politics. For example, an Aznar ally, Mayor José Manuel Molina of Toledo, spoke Tuesday about a possible Socialist victory, evoking the horror of Hitler's rise to power. Aznar dismissed such talk as unimportant.

"They've compared me to a Doberman," he said of his political enemies, adding, with sarcasm, "You always get this verbal excess in political campaigns."

The Popular Party candidate is Mariano Rajoy, a 48-year-old lawyer who has pledged to adhere to all of Aznar's policies. Even less charismatic than Aznar, Rajoy has nevertheless benefited from the Popular Party's extraordinarily well-disciplined machine and the country's strong economic performance.

"I don't like to be the center of attention or have people think I seek the limelight," Rajoy said in an interview with El País on Sunday.

By contrast, the Socialist candidate, José Luis Rodríguez Zapatero, a 43-year-old lawyer who is a member of Parliament, is more outgoing, but his party is hopelessly disorganized, and he has failed to sway voters.

He has pledged to withdraw Spain's 1,300 troops from Iraq by the summer unless there is a clear United Nations mandate for them to stay, and he has said he would deal with problems like unemployment and a shortage of affordable housing and would fight for greater rights for women and social benefits.

Even though polls indicate that 90 percent of the people opposed Spain's involvement in the Iraq war, Aznar stridently defends his decision to join

See AZNAR, Page 8

Joao Silva for The New York Times

An Iraqi police officer checking the site Wednesday where two American civilians and their interpreter were slain Tuesday.

New tactic heightens terror fear in Iraq

2 American civilians are killed by gunmen dressed as policemen

By John F. Burns

ABU GHARIK, Iraq: Two American civilians working for the Coalition Provisional Authority and an Iraqi interpreter were killed by what Iraqi police officials said Wednesday they believed were four men dressed as Iraqi police officers.

The civilians and the interpreter were driving down from the holy city of Karbala in an unmarked, unprotected vehicle at 6:20 p.m. Tuesday when four men who had been following them opened fire at point-blank range, the police said.

The car, which was traveling on a divided highway, crossed over the median strip, crashed down an embankment and then ran across open ground until it hit an earth banking, where it came to rest.

Iraqi officers at a station more than a kilometer from the scene said they had been alerted to the killings by a passing motorist who had seen the vehicle carrying the killers follow the Americans' vehicle off the road. The motorist saw the attackers resume shooting at the Americans' vehicle after it had come to a halt, the officers said.

The victims appeared to be headed for the regional headquarters of the coalition authority in Hilla, about 100 kilometers, or 60 miles, south of Baghdad, when the attack took place at this village about 13 kilometers southwest of their destination.

The Iraqis say the attackers were dressed in the blue shirts and black trousers of the newly reconstituted Iraqi police service, which has been trained by the Americans.

Dan Senor, a spokesman for the occupation authority, said that identification of the victims would be withheld until the next of kin could be notified.

Senor also said that the occupation authorities were in the process of compiling a report on the killings and that he could not confirm the Iraqi police account identifying the killers as wearing police uniforms.

At the time of the attack, the civilians were about 24 kilometers northeast of Karbala in open country that runs through a landscape of palm groves, wheatfields and natural water pools.

There is a fairly heavy stream of traffic on that road at that time of day and evening. Karbala was the scene last week of the killing of more than 100 people by suicide bombings and other attacks on one of the holiest Shiite celebrations.

Blame for those attacks has been placed by U.S. officials on associates of Abu Mussab al-Zarqawi, a Jordanian-

See IRAQ, Page 8

Bush opts for a fast attack on Kerry

By Adam Nagourney

News Analysis

MIAMI: With a fierce campaign of attacks led by President George W. Bush, an orchestrated barrage of criticism by Republican elected officials and an imminent sweep of hard-hitting television advertisements, the White House is moving with unusual speed and force to try to discredit John Kerry, the president's likely Democratic Party challenger.

Bush's advisers said that in embracing this strategy, they were seeking to take advantage of a window of opportunity when the public was paying attention and making critical first judgments on the likely opponent. Kerry won scores more delegates in four Democratic contests on Tuesday, including here in Florida, and has enjoyed a wave of publicity in the last two weeks.

"There are windows of opportunity in every election cycle, and this is a big window," said Matthew Dowd, one of Bush's senior election strategists. "Will this window of opportunity last for eight months? No. But this is the biggest window of opportunity we'll get until the Democratic convention."

Still, Bush's decision to personally engage his opponent this far before Election Day is highly unusual for an incumbent president, and carries significant risks, Democrats and Republicans said.

It could at least momentarily strip him of the advantage of the platform provided by the White House and his role as commander in chief, dropping him on the same political ground as Kerry, the strategists and officials said.

It risks putting off independent voters, who historically have been alienated by negative campaigning. It could also, some strategists said, numb voters to challenges to Kerry's credibility and credentials by the time the general election campaign comes around.

Douglas Sosnik, who was Bill Clinton's White House political director in 1996, said of Bush, "I think he has very

See CAMPAIGN, Page 8

UPDATE

Jeff Christensen/Reuters

Les Seagraves of Earthlink and Nancy Anderson of Microsoft were among executives of Internet service providers who announced antispam lawsuits on Wednesday. *Page 13*

Outsiders at Shell?

Royal Dutch/Shell investors said that the company may need to bring in outside executives to restore confidence, after a panel reviewing the company's reserves shortfall said it backed the current management. *Page 11*

On the Web: *www.iht.com*

Scientific surprise: ovaries may be replenished

By Natalie Angier

Challenging an 80-year-old biological truth that a female's eggs are made one time only, in limited numbers, researchers have found startling evidence that the ovaries may instead be replenished with new eggs throughout a female's reproductive career.

Dr. Jonathan Tilly and his colleagues at Harvard Medical School and the Massachusetts General Hospital report in Wednesday's issue of the journal Nature that they have discovered multiple signposts of germ-line stem cells in the ovaries of young and adult female mice: powerful and many-talented cells capable of generating a fresh batch of immature egg "seeds," as well as the nourishing ovarian infrastructure needed to bring these oocytes to fruition.

Moreover, the stem cells appear to be quite active, indicating that they are not a pool of insignificant holdovers from fetal development, but rather are busy creating new little egglets and their follicle housing on the surface of the adult ovary. Follicles are fluid-filled capsules in which oocytes (pronounced OH-oh-sites) ripen into fully formed eggs, capable of being fertilized.

If confirmed by other researchers, the results would upend a doctrine adhered to by reproductive biologists for the last 80 years: that a female mammal is born with all the oocytes and follicles she will ever have, and that her stock of eggs is steadily depleted until the procreation pantry is bare.

Males, by contrast, have long been known to possess germ-line stem cells in their testes that make large batches of new sperm throughout adulthood.

And should the process of egg renewal prove to be at work in humans, the ramifications, reproductive biologists agree, are profound.

"The mind boggles at the implications," said Dr. Roger Gosden, scientific director of the Jones Institute for Reproductive Medicine at Eastern Virginia Medical School in Norfolk. "The ability to make more eggs would be a revolution in women's health. In theory, it would allow you to have better control over the timing of menopause, to grow more eggs for one's own fertility treatment, to prevent premature menopause, to recover fertility after chemotherapy, and on and on."

Some results from the new study hint at the existence of egg stem cells in adult women, yet Gosden and others also caution that it is far too early to retire the familiar "no new eggs" doctrine.

"There is still a long march to go, and much strong evidence needs to be provided," said Dr. Ri-Cheng Chian, an expert in egg biology in the department of obstetrics and gynecology at McGill University in Montreal.

The New York Times

Mercenary plot thickens

Equatorial Guinea says it was targeted

By Sharon LaFraniere

JOHANNESBURG: The Zimbabwean authorities threatened Wednesday to execute 64 foreigners from five African countries whose plane was seized Sunday at Harare's airport. The officials said the men were mercenaries on their way to Equatorial Guinea on the West African coast to sow conflict.

The president of Equatorial Guinea, a tiny county whose recent oil discoveries have made it one of the continent's biggest oil producers, said the group was part of a quest by "enemy powers" to overthrow his government.

President Teodoro Obiang Nguema Mbasogo said countries and multinational companies hostile to his 23-year rule had conspired to install a politician now living in exile in Spain in his place.

The operator of the aging Boeing 727 aircraft continued to insist that the plane's only mission was to ferry security guards hired by mining companies to the Democratic Republic of the Congo.

"It is all a dreadful misunderstanding," Charles Burrows, a senior executive of Logo Logistics, told the South African press. But he seemed increasingly a lone voice.

South Africa's minister of foreign affairs said her department was in no hurry to help either the South Africans detained in Zimbabwe or seven other South Africans arrested by the authorities in Equatorial Guinea and accused of plotting a coup.

Nkosozana Dlamini-Zuma told the South African press that "indeed there was a link between the plane and Equatorial Guinea" and that one man arrested in Equatorial Guinea had "spilled the beans."

"They are not exactly innocent travelers finding themselves in a difficult situation," the minister said, adding: "We don't like the idea that South Africa has become a cesspool of mercenaries."

The plane belonged to a small aviation company in Kansas until last week, when an executive of that firm said it was sold. South African aviation officials said the aircraft landed at a small domestic airport near the nation's capital, Pretoria, on Sunday morning, where it took on 64 passengers and a three-member crew.

Besides the 20 South Africans, the passengers included 23 Angolans, 18 Namibians, 2 Congolese and 1 Zimbawean with a South African passport, according to Zimbabwe's state-owned Herald daily.

All were expected to appear in court

See MERCENARIES, Page 8

CHAMPIONS LEAGUE

First knockout round, second leg.

- **Arsenal 2, Celta de Vigo 0.** Arsenal advances, 5-2.
- **AC Milan 4, Sparta Prague 1.** AC Milan advances, 4-1.
- **Monaco 1, Lokomotiv Moscow 0.** Monaco advances on away goals.
- **R. Madrid 1, Bayern Munich 0.** Real Madrid advances, 2-1.

CURRENCIES | New York

	Wednesday 4 P.M.	Previous
€1 =	$1.224	$1.2313
£1 =	$1.8053	$1.8254
$1 =	¥110.78	¥111.4
$1 =	SF1.2872	SF1.2824

Full currency rates | *Page 12*

THE MARKETS

	Wednesday 4 P.M.	
The Dow	10,296.89 - 1.53%	- 160.07
S&P 500	1,123.91 - 1.46%	- 16.67
Nasdaq	1,964.15 - 1.55%	- 31.01

Newsstand prices

France €1.85

Algeria	Din 40	Ivory Coast	CFA 1.500
Andorra	€1.85	Reunion/Antilles	€2.10
Cameroon	CFA 1.500	Senegal	CFA 1.500
Gabon	CFA 1.500	Tunisia	Din 2.500

For information on delivery, or to subscribe in France, call toll-free:
00 800 44 48 78 27

11 March 2004, El País.

EL PAIS

JUEVES 11 DE MARZO DE 2004 · DIARIO INDEPENDIENTE DE LA MAÑANA · EDICIÓN MADRID

Año XXIX. Número 9.779 · www.elpais.es · Precio: 1 euro

EDICIÓN ESPECIAL DE LAS 13 HORAS

Matanza de ETA en Madrid

Más de 170 muertos en cuatro atentados en trenes de cercanías

Las bombas estallaron en plena hora punta en una línea que usan al día 216.000 pasajeros

Avalancha de donantes de sangre en unidades móviles y hospitales de Madrid y Barcelona para los 600 heridos

El Gobierno convoca a los ciudadanos, los partidos suspenden la campaña y la Cámara vasca aplaza el debate del 'plan Ibarretxe'

Aspecto del tren de cercanías que fue centro de una de las explosiones cuando entraba en la estación de Atocha. / GORKA LEJARCEGI

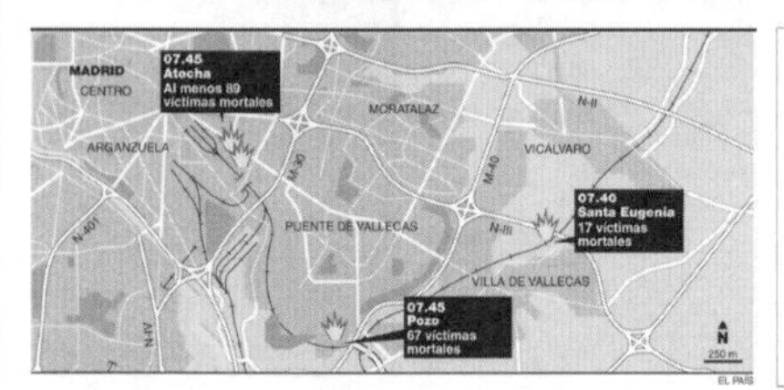

EDITORIAL

11-M

LA FECHA de hoy quedará marcada en negro en la conciencia de los ciudadanos españoles; también en la historia de la infamia: el centenar largo de muertos provocado en tres estaciones de cercanías de Madrid supone la mayor matanza en la siniestra historia del terrorismo que actúa en España, y la catástrofe de mayores dimensiones registrada en la capital desde los bombardeos de la guerra civil. La hipótesis más probable apunta una vez más a ETA, que habría llegado así a la cima de su proceso de degeneración mafiosa. Cuando una organización que invoca móviles políticos llega al punto de no retroceder ante matanzas como la de hoy, significa que ha franqueado cualquier límite de inhibición moral. Pasa a la **página 10**

EL PAIS

VIERNES 12 DE MARZO DE 2004
Año XXIX. Número 9.781

DIARIO INDEPENDIENTE DE LA MAÑANA
www.elpais.es

EDICIÓN MADRID
Precio: 1 euro

Infierno terrorista en Madrid: 192 muertos y 1.400 heridos

Interior investiga la pista de Al Qaeda sin descartar a ETA

Decenas de heridos permanecen junto a las vías instantes después de abandonar el tren que sufrió el atentado en las proximidades de la estación de Atocha. / PABLO TORRES GUERRERO

Diez explosiones en cuatro trenes de cercanías siembran el terror ● La policía encuentra detonadores y una cinta con versos del Corán en Alcalá ● El Rey expresa su "repulsa e indignación" ● Rajoy y Zapatero piden la unidad de los demócratas ● Los partidos suspenden la campaña electoral y se suman a las manifestaciones convocadas hoy en toda España

Cuatro atentados terroristas sincronizados, en los que estallaron 10 de los 13 artefactos explosivos colocados, causaron ayer una matanza en los trenes de cercanías de Madrid. Al menos 190 personas fallecieron y más de 1.400 resultaron heridas en el mayor ataque terrorista en la historia de España y uno de los más sangrientos de Europa. Las bombas estallaron pasadas las 7.30 en la estación de Atocha y en sus cercanías, en la de Santa Eugenia y en el apeadero del Pozo del Tío Raimundo cuando decenas de miles de ciudadanos se dirigían a su trabajo. El Ministerio del Interior informó de que su principal línea de investigación es ETA, pero no descartó la pista de Al Qaeda tras el hallazgo en Alcalá de una cinta con versos del Corán y detonadores en una furgoneta robada.

EDITORIAL

11-M

LA FECHA de ayer quedará marcada en negro en la memoria de españoles y europeos: los casi dos centenares de muertos y más de un millar de heridos provocados por los atentados de Madrid suponen la mayor matanza terrorista en España, y la catástrofe de mayor alcance registrada en la capital desde la Guerra Civil. Este país acaba de experimentar un terrorismo de unas dimensiones y de una crueldad hasta ahora desconocidas. La eventualidad de que sea obra de Al Qaeda y de que tenga relación con el papel jugado por el Gobierno de Aznar en la guerra de Irak introduce una novedad que no puede dejar de sembrar una profunda inquietud. Pasa a la **página 10**

13 March 2004, International Herald Tribune.

INTERNATIONAL
Herald Tribune
THE WORLD'S DAILY NEWSPAPER PUBLISHED BY THE NEW YORK TIMES EDITED AND PRINTED IN PARIS
SATURDAY-SUNDAY, MARCH 13-14, 2004

Write something you regret? Now you can take it back

ITECH | 11

Insurance: what you need and what you really don't

MONEY REPORT | 17

Souren Melikian: Scent of change at Maastricht

ART | 9

Millions of mourners march in Spain

More than a million people gathered in the streets of Madrid on Friday to protest the terrorist bombings. Huge crowds also marched in Barcelona, Seville and other cities.

Europe steps up security

Intelligence officials had expressed fear over rail networks

By Patrick E. Tyler and Don Van Natta

LONDON: Senior European intelligence and security officials in recent months had expressed increasing concern that terrorists would target the still relatively open rail networks of a region that depends heavily on passenger rail transport.

In the aftermath of the terrorist bombings Thursday in Madrid, European leaders and security officials were tightening security at train and subway stations across the region, stepping up police patrols, bomb detection measures and electronic surveillance.

Passenger rail traffic in Europe is more than 12 times the level in the United States, according to European Union figures, and is only surpassed in passenger miles by China and Japan.

France on Friday deployed nearly 500 soldiers to key transportation hubs to beef up local security, especially on the high-speed rail lines from Paris to Lyon and Marseilles. French officials also placed restrictions on private aviation clubs and stepped up chlorination of national water supplies, all part of an elevated alert status ordered by President Jacques Chirac, a spokesman for the National Police said.

A senior French counterterrorism official, who a month ago was trying to cope with a series of security-related cancellations of British Airways and Air France flights to the United States, said in an interview that he was even more concerned about the threat of a terrorist strike on the Paris Métro or the French railway system.

"The trains worry me more than the planes," said the official, who spoke on condition of anonymity.

The French official's concerns have been echoed by Eliza Manningham-Buller, the head of Britain's counterintelligence service known as MI5, who has warned that Al Qaeda has been seeking to stage a large-scale attack in Britain, where officials say air and rail transport is considered the most obvious target.

"We've been focused on the transport sector for some time," a Foreign Office official said. "We've been aware that transport is threatened and that different groups have looked at it."

European transport officials are strongly resisting imposing airport-style security checks — metal detectors and baggage searches — on rail passengers because it would represent a radical transformation of an open transport sector and significantly increase costs.

The Eurostar train that connects

See SECURITY, Page 3

ETA remains top suspect in bombings, Madrid says

By Elaine Sciolino

MADRID: Grief and fury blanketed Spain on Friday evening as the country mourned the victims of the deadliest terrorist attack on a European target since World War II and struggled to learn who was responsible.

From Barcelona to the Canary Islands, millions of people streamed into streets and city squares in a nationwide cry against the violence that left nearly 200 people dead and 1,400 wounded in synchronized explosions on four commuter trains on Thursday in Madrid.

"No to terrorism!" they chanted in the main square in Madrid, which was enveloped in rain and cold. "Assassins! Assassins!"

The center-right government clung to the assumption that the armed Basque separatist group ETA and not Al Qaeda was responsible for the attack, although the evidence is confusing and no scenario has been ruled out.

"So far, none of the intelligence services or security forces we have contacted have provided reliable information to the effect that it could have been an Islamic terrorist organization," Interior Minister Angel Acebes said in a news conference Friday.

He revealed that Spanish investigators had discovered a backpack with an unexploded bomb that contained explosives similar to those used by ETA, a detonator and a cellphone apparently intended as a timing device. And he said that his British counterparts doubted the authenticity of a letter claiming the explosions were the work of Al Qaeda.

ETA has formally denied responsibility for the deadly bomb attacks in Madrid, a Basque newspaper and a TV station said Friday after receiving anonymous telephone calls from the group.

"An ETA message has arrived saying that it bore no responsibility for the attack," a newscaster for ETB Basque public television said.

The political stakes in uncovering the identity of the terrorists are sky-high. Spain is going to the polls on Sunday to choose a new government and Mariano Rajoy, the hand-picked successor of Prime Minister José María Aznar and the Popular Party candidate, is in the lead.

But Aznar's decision to join the American war effort in Iraq and send 1,300 troops there was overwhelmingly opposed by his people. If Al Qaeda is

See SPAIN, Page 4

Grief and anger at a giant morgue

By Doreen Carvajal

MADRID: Spain's Zona Zero is a sprawling convention center of gray halls and endless pavilions, which are usually home to stolid events like the Exhibition of Herbs and Dietetic Products or the International Dental Equipment and Services Show.

But on the Thursday morning that the dental show started, bombs exploded in Madrid, killing about 200 people aboard four crowded commuter trains. Ifema, as the trade fairgrounds are known, was suddenly transformed into a giant temporary morgue.

It is now a place where wives huddle in thick, patchwork blankets, their vacant eyes red without tears. It is the last place where families come when hospitals provide no solace and the only remaining hope is simply bleak news of any kind.

"Leave me in peace!" screamed a slight teenager outside a makeshift Red Cross tent when another body was identified. "Leave me in peace!"

The bodies of the dead have all been brought to one wing, where 60 forensic investigators have been trying to identify the remains. Some 30 bodies may never be identified because they were left unrecognizable in the blasts, the authorities say. Others are the bodies of immigrants, too far from home for families to claim them or know their fates.

Among the fallen are people from 11 countries, mostly from Spain, but also immigrants who came from Central and South American countries who lived in the neighborhoods around the train stations where the bombs struck.

José Flores, an Ecuadorean who moved to Spain nine months ago for a job in construction, stalked the halls of the fairgrounds with a heavy backpack in an unsuccessful search for information about his brother's 26-year-old sister-in-law.

He was so numb that he had trouble recalling what she looked like. She had a beauty spot above her lips, he recalled. She was full of joy. He didn't know whom to blame: "There's nothing that I can say about that."

Every time a body is identified the ritual is the same. Investigators ask for DNA and vivid descriptions of last memories: clothes, complexion, scars, jewelry. Then families are divided alphabetically into different rooms or left to pace the halls. A volunteer psychologist or psychiatrist notifies a waiting family about the results. And then after a consultation and preparation, one relative is escorted to a special

See VICTIMS, Page 4

Attack in Madrid could foster European unity

- The Madrid attacks are an important moment for the European Union, analysts say, because they mark a chance for Europe to coalesce and further establish a common identity, in this case in a show of outrage and grief. *Page 4*
- The question of whether Al Qaeda or the Basque group ETA played a role in an attack is almost certain to have an impact on the national election Sunday. *Page 4*
- Many in Spain say they believe ETA was behind the blast, regardless of the fact that the attack carried few of the group's hallmarks. *Page 4*

Shell pumped numbers

Accounting, not discoveries, added oil

By Stephen Labaton and Jeff Gerth

Arriving on stage in a spaceship and an astronaut suit, Philip Watts, then the senior executive in charge of exploration and production for the Royal Dutch/Shell Group, glowed as he delivered a message of optimism to a conference of 600 company executives in the Dutch city of Maastricht in June 1998.

"I have seen the future, and it was great," he declared.

He was talking about the success of a special management program that had recently addressed a fundamental problem at the company — that it was pumping oil and gas out of the ground faster than it was finding new supplies.

Internal documents show, however, that the program allowed Shell to increase its oil and gas reserves not by major discoveries but by changing its accounting to add reserves that it was not sure could ever be tapped.

Shell's future does not look as great now as it did in 1998. The company, a storied oil giant that traces its roots back to a Dutch oil company and an English seashell importer in the 1890s, ousted Watts as chairman on March 3. He had risen to the top of the company three years ago, in part because of his ability to increase reported reserves, and had been knighted by Queen Elizabeth II in 2003 for his service to Britain.

His departure followed almost two months of investor unrest over the company's decision to cut estimates of its proven reserves by 20 percent, or 3.9 billion barrels.

The U.S. Securities and Exchange Commission, seeking to protect American investors who bought Shell stock and bonds, is now investigating whether he or the company broke the law

See SHELL, Page 15

For white farmers, hope in Zambia

By Sharon LaFraniere

CHISAMBA, Zambia: Douglas Watt is part of a most curious diaspora in southern Africa — prosperous white farmers, vilified as greedy racists and driven out of Zimbabwe, looking for a home.

Watt left the county of his birth almost a year ago after what has become a common encounter there: the husband of a worker in President Robert Mugabe's office politely told him that he was taking over his farm and that Watt had 90 days to get out.

He is one of as many as 140 white Zimbabwean farmers who have relocated to neighboring Zambia, hoping, many say, for a mix of racial harmony and political stability that will enable them to prosper and contribute to black Africa.

Both for the farmers and for the Zambian government, the migration amounts to a new experiment on an issue central to the whole region: How do whites fit in?

While Zimbabwe has been uprooting its white farmers in an aggressive attempt to redistribute colonial-era landholdings, Zambian officials, if a trifle warily, have rolled out the welcome mat.

They are hoping that farmers like Watt will breathe new life into the nation's moribund farming sector, which has been stuck at the rake-and-hoe level since the mid-1970s.

For their part, some of the transplanted farmers say Zimbabwe has taught them that they need to integrate, not just prosper.

Douglas Watt, a farmer from Zimbabwe, walking through a tobacco crop on his new farm in Chisamba, Zambia. Officials there have rolled out the welcome mat.

Watt drove around Zambia for three weeks before he found 650 hectares, or 1,600 acres, to lease near this one-street village, with a post office, police station and food market north of Zambia's capital, Lusaka.

Pasture and brush just 11 months ago, the gently rolling land is now about a meter and a half, or about five feet, high in green tobacco plants tended by 240 workers. Huge yellow sheaves of tobacco are hung to cure in 15 shiny sheds by a new blocklong warehouse.

Watt has sunk $900,000 into his new farm, most of it borrowed from a bank and from Universal Leaf Tobacco, based in Richmond, Virginia.

"I have put every cent I have into this," Watt, 38, said, sitting in the dining room of his new ranch style house. "I've got more invested here than I ever did in Zimbabwe. We will be an asset to the country."

Watt's move continues a long pattern of whites, increasingly uncertain of their welcome, who have

See ZAMBIA, Page 3

CURRENCIES | New York

	Friday 4 P.M.	Previous
€1 =	$1.2223	$1.2338
£1 =	$1.8022	$1.8109
$1 =	¥110.98	¥110.94
$1 =	SF1.2833	SF1.2699

Full currency rates | *Page 14*

THE MARKETS

Friday 4 P.M.		
The Dow	10,240.08 +1.10%	+111.70
S&P 500	1,120.60 +1.25%	+13.82
Nasdaq	1,984.71 +2.10%	+40.82

In this issue *No. 37,639*

Newsstand prices

France € 1.85

Algeria	Din 40	Ivory Coast	CFA 1.500
Andorra	€ 1.85	Reunion/Antilles	€ 2.10
Cameroon	CFA 1.500	Senegal	CFA 1.500
Gabon	CFA 1.500	Tunisia	Din 2.500

For information on delivery, or to subscribe in France, call toll-free:
00 800 44 48 78 27

UPDATE

Air crash inquiry

The former chief of Swiss International Airlines is under criminal investigation in connection with a 2001 Crossair crash, Swiss prosecutors said. *Page 13*

Rival bid for Aventis?

Novartis said it was deciding whether to bid for Aventis, the French-German drug maker that a rival, Sanofi-Synthélabo, is trying to take over. *Page 13*

On the Web: *www.iht.com*

INTERNATIONAL
Herald Tribune
THE WORLD'S DAILY NEWSPAPER PUBLISHED BY THE NEW YORK TIMES EDITED AND PRINTED IN PARIS
TUESDAY, MARCH 16, 2004

The singer Claude Nougaro: An appreciation
CULTURE & MORE | 10

A British designer aims to surpass Martha Stewart
STYLE | 12

Trainers go to new heights in search of an edge
SPORTS | 20

Denis Doyle/The Associated Press
José Luis Rodríguez Zapatero, Spain's prime minister-elect, at a news conference Monday. He said the Iraq war "has been a disaster."

Socialist victor in Spain criticizes Bush and Blair

By Elaine Sciolino

MADRID: Spain's newly elected Socialist prime minister pledged Monday to break with the policies of his predecessor, signaling that his country would no longer march in lockstep with Washington and would withdraw its troops from Iraq in the absence of a United Nations mandate.

In his first remarks to reporters since his party's defeat of the center-right Popular Party candidate on Sunday, the prime minister-elect, José Luis Rodríguez Zapatero, had only scathing criticism for the U.S.-led war in Iraq, which his party opposed, as did 90 percent of the Spanish people, polls show.

"The war has been a disaster, the occupation continues to be a great disaster," Zapatero said on the Spanish radio station Cadena SER. "It hasn't generated anything but more violence and hate. What simply cannot be is that — after it became so clear how badly it was handled — there be no consequences. Mr. Bush and Mr. Blair will have to reflect and engage in some self-criticism, so things like that don't happen again."

He alluded to assertions by Prime Minister José María Aznar of Spain, Prime Minister Tony Blair of Britain and President George W. Bush that the conflict had been justified by the conviction — still unproved — that Iraq possessed weapons of mass destruction that posed an imminent threat.

"You can't organize a war on the basis of lies," Zapatero said. "You can't bomb a people just in case."

In his first news conference later in the day, Zapatero also pledged to repair relations with France and Germany, which were badly damaged when it split with them over the war.

"Spain is going to see eye to eye with Europe again," he said. "Spain is going to be more pro-Europe than ever. I am deeply convinced of that."

Miguel Moratinos, who is likely to be named foreign minister and until recently was a senior career diplomat, explained in a telephone interview that Spain's foreign policy "will be addressed with a whole different spirit."

"We need to engage with the American administration and President Bush in a positive manner but on an equal footing," he said.

In the news conference, Zapatero repeated promises to withdraw Spain's troops from Iraq unless they were put under United Nations control by the end of June, when the United States has promised to hand power over to a provisional Iraqi government.

If Spain withdraws its troops, the sixth-largest foreign force in Iraq, it will pose problems not only for the Bush administration but also for Poland. The Spanish contingent had been set to take control July 1 of the 9,000-strong multinational force now patrolling central and southern Iraq under Polish command.

In Washington, the White House said that Bush had congratulated Zapatero and that the men had pledged to work together to fight terrorism.

"The two leaders said they both looked forward to working together, particularly on our shared commitment to fighting terrorism," the chief White House spokesman, Scott McClellan, said. He did not answer reporters' questions about the administration's view on how the Madrid bombings last week might have influenced the Spanish elections.

At his news conference, Zapatero said his government "is going to be a government that maintains cordial relations with all the governments of the world, and naturally, with the government of the United States."

Asked at the news conference whether Bush had called to congratulate him, Zapatero was cool.

"I have to confess that the list of congratulations is extremely long and at this moment I haven't been able to look over them all," he said. "And I would run the risk of making a mistake, and I don't want to do that."

Zapatero's remarks coincided with

See SPAIN, Page 8

For a school, trains now bring fear

By Doreen Carvajal

SANTA EUGENIA, Spain: When mornings were still reliably ordinary, children rolled heavy backpacks toward a mustard brick schoolhouse overlooking the train tracks and submitted to goodbye kisses.

On Monday, the students still came, but mothers and fathers held them closer before freeing them to enter the primary school — Colegio Ciudad de Valencia de Santa Eugenia — which was draped with a black banner of white handprints and a sign declaring, "No to terrorism."

Goodbyes have more meaning in Santa Eugenia, where many people had friends and relatives who died in the safest place they knew. Eight of the students saw their parents for the last time when they rushed out the gates Thursday to catch a doomed C-2 train line to Madrid that was bombed in a terrorist attack.

"We pass by the station every day," said Rosa Ruiz, 46, as she stood outside the school to drop off two children. "I never dreamed we could die in those trains because of terrorism."

Santa Eugenia is a middle-class suburb of 35,000 people and high rise apartments built in the 1960s about 12 kilometers from Madrid. The trains' rumbling arrival was part of the daily rhythm of the neighborhood, where parents could drop children off early at the public school for a breakfast before joining the commuter rush.

It was almost 8 a.m. last Thursday when the red and white commuter line reached the squat station, which is about 200 meters from the school. Then a backpack stuffed with explosives erupted in the third car in the middle of the train.

Now, people can't walk past their train station without thinking of the shattering blasts, the bodies and the shrill ring of portable telephones that went unanswered within the pockets of the dead.

Six of the victims were mothers of students from the school, and the seventh was a father. A grandfather is still

See CHILDREN, Page 8

The political U-turn: Some see Qaeda victory

By John Vinocur

PARIS: Spain's great electoral upheaval, however fair and open its ground rules and procedure, is being called by some in Europe a victory for terrorism, a precedent that offers Al Qaeda or groups like it the notion that they can alter the democratic process with bombs and murder.

The argument of those who see what they call appeasement gaining the upper hand point to the Socialists' victory as being based on their campaign warning that Islamic terrorists would take revenge on Spain for the support given by the government of Prime Minister José María Aznar to the United States in Iraq.

News Analysis

In this view, after the attack Thursday that killed more than 200 people in Madrid, the Socialist Party's appeal was in its argument that Spain could have insulated itself with a foreign policy in opposition to the Americans and its conditional pledge to pull the Spanish troop contingent of 1,300 men out of Iraq, a compliant gesture that could guarantee the country's future safety.

"Al Qaeda won the election," said a former conservative member of the Spanish Parliament, Pedro Schwartz, now a professor of economics at Universidad San Pablo CEU in Madrid. "It's easy to say, 'We're neutral now, and let the rest of people ready for the bombs.'"

"It's appeasement. The terrorists have gotten away with it. There's no better victory for them than in cowing the enemy."

The Socialists contend that their defeat of Aznar was based on widespread opposition to the Iraq war among Spaniards and what they described as Aznar's lies in trying to focus attention away from Islamic fundamentalists and onto Basque terrorists as the likely culprits. Until pre-election polling stopped in Spain on Thursday, however, surveys showed that Iraq was not a top issue of concern. And as yet, no certainty is at hand on the identity of the group behind the bombings.

Still, Aznar's forces seemed to acknowledge they had made a major strategic error that could have swayed the vote against them. It was only on Sunday, as Spaniards went to the polls, that the ruling Popular Party departed from its line that ETA was the prime suspect. Foreign Minister Ana Palacio said then for the first time that it was impossible to buy off terrorism, whatever its origin, and that Al Qaeda, after all, operating in its own closed circuit of hatred, had attacked Morocco, Indonesia and Turkey, all Muslim countries that opposed the war in Iraq.

This was too late to save the Spanish conservatives, but it was a recurring argument among those who saw the election outcome as giving off dramatic signs of concessions to terrorism.

Friedbert Pflüger, the foreign policy

See TERRORISM, Page 8

The ripples

- A Spanish pullout from Iraq would be bad news for other nations that have contributed troops there. *Page 2*
- The White House sought to shake off the jolt of Spain's political upheaval. *Page 3*
- Analysts say Spain's economic outlook remains solid. *Page 13*

UPDATE

3 Americans dead

BAGHDAD: Three U.S. civilians died Monday in a drive-by shooting in the Iraq city of Mosul, the U.S. military said. Lieutenant Colonel Tom Gilroy of the air force said the three worked for a nongovernmental organization. *(AP)*

CURRENCIES | New York	Monday 4 P.M.	Previous
€1 =	$1.2271	$1.2223
£1 =	$1.8055	$1.8022
$1 =	¥110.32	¥110.98
$1 =	SFr1.2756	SFr1.2833

Full currency rates | Page 12

THE MARKETS	Monday 4 P.M.	
The Dow	10,102.89 -1.34%	-137.19
S&P 500	1,104.35 -1.45%	-16.22
Nasdaq	1,939.20 -2.29%	-45.53

On the Web: *www.iht.com*

In this issue *No. 37,641*

Newsstand prices
France €1.85
Algeria ... Din 40 Ivory Coast ... CFA 1.500
Andorra ... €1.85 Reunion/Antilles ... €2.30
Cameroon ... CFA 1.500 Senegal ... CFA 1.500
Gabon ... CFA 1.500 Tunisia ... Din 2.500

For information on delivery, or to subscribe in France, call toll-free:
00 800 44 48 78 27

Solar system's icy fringe is extended

By John Noble Wilford

Far beyond Pluto, out where the Sun is only a pinpoint of pale light, a frozen world has been found on the dark fringes of the solar system. Astronomers say it is by far the most distant object known to orbit the Sun and the largest one to be detected since the discovery of Pluto in 1930.

With one discovery, it seemed, the solar system got much bigger, glimpses of its outer reaches bringing a sense of reality to what had been remote spheres of hypothesis.

The scientists who detected the object reported Monday that the discovery is likely the first detection of the long-hypothesized Oort Cloud, a sphere of icy bodies thought to reach far beyond the nine planets and perhaps halfway to the nearest star. This is thought to be where many comets come from.

The discoverers described the object as a planetoid and proposed to name it Sedna, after the Inuit goddess who created the sea creatures of the Arctic. The planetoid is about three-quarters the size of Pluto, extremely frigid, peculiarly red and probably a primordial mix of rock and ice.

Of particular significance to scientists is Sedna's remoteness; it is more than three times farther from the Sun than the current distance of Pluto, the outermost of the Sun's family of nine planets. But calculations show that the object, now a relatively close 8 billion miles, or 13 billion kilometers, from Earth, wanders out to as many as 84 billion miles from the Sun and through a frontier never before glimpsed, only imagined.

Michael Brown, an astronomer at the California Institute of Technology in Pasadena who led the discovery team, said that Sedna "is so far away from everything that it must be the first ob-

See PLANET, Page 8

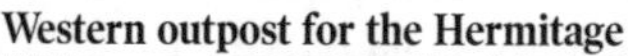

Western outpost for the Hermitage

By Marlise Simons

AMSTERDAM: For much of the 20th century, the Hermitage Museum was a hidden treasure to Western art lovers. Even after the collapse of Communism, it remained for some time off the art circuit's trodden path. So if foreign visitors did not come to St. Petersburg, the museum concluded, the art should seek out the foreigners.

And so it has. In its latest and most ambitious foreign venture, Russia's finest art collection has just inaugurated a large and permanent outpost in Amsterdam.

The first section of Hermitage Amsterdam opened its doors Feb. 28 with a display of ancient Greek jewelry on loan from the mother house. But once the large complex in the heart of Amsterdam is fully remodeled, this will be a permanent satellite museum for the Hermitage, with more than 4,000 square meters of floor space available for rotating exhibitions, or nearly 5,000 square yards.

The Dutch capital is hardly a city that needs a new museum, but the local sponsors of Hermitage Amsterdam believe it is a perfect addition to the Stedelijk, Rijks and Van Gogh Museums.

"The Hermitage is a fabulous source of art from the world over and we'll show work that is not available in this country," said Ernst Veen, director of the new institution. "It will be complementary to our museums. We have enough Dutch masters here, so we will not show theirs."

Hermitage Amsterdam will be the Russian museum's most important foreign satellite, but not its first. Mikhail Piotrovsky, the Hermitage's director, has already opened small outposts in London and Las Vegas and created a successful model for getting Western money to promote Russia's collections abroad. The Hermitage has been given exhibition space at the Venetian Hotel in Las Vegas and the use of five rooms in London's Somerset House, a government-owned palace that is home to the Courtauld Institute Gallery.

The deals made in London, Las Vegas and now Amsterdam include more than just rent-free spaces. All three generate robust contributions for repair and conservation work at the cash-starved Winter Palace, the Hermitage's sprawling and fraying home.

Piotrovsky, who was reached by telephone, seemed suitably pleased with his latest foreign satellite. "London and Las Vegas are our consulates," he said, "and Amsterdam will be our embassy."

By most accounts, the new Amsterdam Hermitage is the result of the friendship between two experienced culture managers, Piotrovsky and Veen. The Dutch museum director, Veen, for more than two decades the director of the Nieuwe Kerk Museum in Amsterdam, a grand 15th-century church with magnificent spaces but no collection of its own, regularly borrowed work from Piotrovsky. They got to know each other well.

"We learned to work together," Veen recalled, saying the two men had co-

See MUSEUM, Page 8

Hollandse Hoogte for The New York Times
Hermitage Amsterdam is settling into Amstelhof and another building.

EL PAIS
www.elpais.es DIARIO INDEPENDIENTE DE LA MAÑANA WEDNESDAY, APRIL 14, 2004
ENGLISH EDITION WITH THE INTERNATIONAL HERALD TRIBUNE

PSOE government is inviting attacks, terrorist video says

Comments attributed to Al Qa'ida lambast Socialist plans in Afghanistan

G. HEDGECOE, **Madrid**
A video cassette found in the Madrid apartment where seven suspected terrorists blew themselves up earlier this month contained a warning that Spain would face new attacks, because the incoming Socialist government had decided to continue "fighting against Muslims."

The cassette was found amidst the rubble of the apartment destroyed by an explosion 10 days ago in an apartment in the Madrid suburb of Leganes. A group of men believed to have masterminded the March 11 terrorist attacks in Madrid as a cell connected to Al Qa'ida, detonated the bomb, which also killed a member of the special police force. Authorities were finally able to comment on the content of the cassette Tuesday, after police finished reassembling it.

The video showed three people in Arab dress and heavily armed reading a communiqué, the Interior Ministry reported.

"Having confirmed that the situation has not changed and after your new leader announced the opening of his term with further fighting against Muslims and the sending of more crusade troops to Afghanistan," the announcement said, "the Companies of Death and Ansar Al Qa'ida have taken the resolution to continue the blessed path of the *jihad* and resistance."

Since winning the general election March 14, incoming Prime Minister José Luis Rodríguez Zapatero has reiterated his pre-election promise to withdraw Spanish forces from Iraq, but he has also proposed to bolster Spain's military presence in Afghanistan, which forms part of a United Nations mission there.

Referring to Spain as Al-Andalus — the name of the nation under the Moorish conquerors — the individuals in the video added that their "brigade" will not leave the country until "your troops leave Muslim bases immediately and without conditions." The message was recorded March 27 — a week before the Leganes explosion occurred — and it gave a deadline of a week, April 4, for Spanish authorities to comply.

"May you know that you will not enjoy safety and know that Bush and his administration will only bring you destruction. We will kill you anywhere and at any time," it said. Continued on **page 3**

Outgoing Prime Minister José María Aznar greets his successor, José Luis Rodríguez Zapatero. / LUIS MAGÁN

Aznar and Zapatero put finishing touches to transfer of powers

Two days ahead of investiture, encounter said to be less tense than before

A.E., **Madrid**
Two days before Socialist leader José Luis Rodríguez Zapatero begins his investiture debate in Congress, Spain's prime minister-elect met Tuesday with his Popular Party predecessor, José María Aznar, at Moncloa Palace, putting the final touches to the transfer of political power in Spain.

The meeting took place in an environment of "cordiality," a government spokesperson said. The encounter brings an end to a series of cross party meetings that have taken place since Aznar and Zapatero's first post-election encounter on March 25, which at the time led to a crossfire of accusations over Spain's role in Iraq and the PP's much-criticized decision to deploy troops there.

Since then, however, the PP has promised to provide the Socialist Party with full information on the current status of all government ministries and the political and administrative processes currently underway.

It is not known whether Aznar and Zapatero discussed the current situation in Iraq yesterday and the rotation of Spain's troops that is due to conclude on April 21. On March 29 the start of the troop rotation was delayed until the government received authorization to proceed from the prime minister-elect, sparking harsh criticism between both parties.

Zapatero has said that he will withdraw Spain's soldiers from Iraq by mid-year unless the United Nations takes far greater control of the country.

Spain advises its citizens not to travel in Iraq

STAFF REPORTER, **Madrid**
The Spanish consulate in Iraq, along with several other European diplomats, issued a warning to its citizens advising them not to travel within the country, only when absolutely necessary. Spaniards were also advised not to travel to the Gulf country.

The announcement followed a week of kidnappings by Iraqi rebels. Tuesday, a coalition spokesperson in Baghdad announced that Iraqi rebels have kidnapped 40 people of 12 nationalities.

Easter road death toll lowest since 1998, 102 killed

M.E., **Madrid**
Fatal traffic accidents during the Easter week holidays reached a 16-year low in 2004, according to Spain's General Traffic Board. Over the 11-day period that ended Monday at midnight, 102 people died in 83 traffic accidents, a 20 percent decrease from last year's holiday.

The worst day was Good Friday, when 22 people died on the roads. See EDITORIAL **p2**

Famed flamenco and lyrical singer Juan Valderrama dies at the age of 87

MIGUEL MORA, **Madrid**
Juanito Valderrama, the last star of flamenco's golden age, died on Monday at his Seville home at 87 years of age. He had suffered from a serious heart condition and was recuperating from a small heart attack he had in February.

Author of dozens of songs, some as popular as *El emigrante*, Juanito Valderrama was best known for his interpretations of lyrical Spanish music.

The tribute record *Don Juan*, which was released in 2001, recovered his work in the field of flamenco and brought him back into the limelight alongside musicians of the stature of Paco de Lucía, Carmen Linares, El Cigala, Juan Habichuela and Miguel Poveda.

The late Juanito Valderrama.

Valderrama had been an indefatigable artist and flamenco lover since a young age. "I don't smoke; I don't drink and I have an extraordinary skill," he said in an interview three years ago. "Nobody has sung this well at my age. What I have is pure art: At six they already told me I was fabulous. And even if I'm not 1.80 meters tall or have green eyes, I've filled theatres for four decades," said Valderrama at the time.

Adored and scorned in almost equal measure, the late *cantaor* was in nothing short of a great artist with a wide-ranging repertoire and an astounding command of most of Spain's traditional music styles.

Life for 500,000 Moroccans this side of the Strait of Gibraltar

For the more than half a million Moroccans resident in Spain, life has changed in their adopted home since March 11

Russian mafia get rich as they lure hundreds here on false pretenses

Once they pay over large sums of money, they realize the promises of bright futures are emptySOCIETY Ps 4 & 5

EL PAIS
www.elpais.es DIARIO INDEPENDIENTE DE LA MAÑANA SATURDAY, APRIL 17, 2004
ENGLISH EDITION WITH THE INTERNATIONAL HERALD TRIBUNE

Parliament votes Socialist Zapatero as Spain's new prime minister

After an eight-year hiatus, the Socialists return to lead the Spanish government

MIKE ELKIN, **Madrid**
After nearly two days of debates, the Spanish Parliament voted in José Luis Rodriguez Zapatero as the new prime minister. Zapatero won the vote 183 to 148, with 19 abstentions.

Zapatero's Spanish Socialist Workers' Party (PSOE) upset José María Aznar's Popular Party (PP) in the general elections that followed the March 11 Madrid bombings. Disenchanted with the PP's handling of the crisis, Spanish citizens voted en mass for the Socialists, who have not held power since 1996.

Spanish King Juan Carlos I will swear in Zapatero Saturday at the royal palace.

One of Zapatero's campaign promises was to withdraw Spanish soldiers from Iraq if the United Nations does not assume control of the situation by June 30, and he has reiterated the promise since the election. About 90 percent of Spaniards opposed the coalition force's invasion of Iraq, despite Aznar's support.

"My stance on the presence of Spanish troops in Iraq is well-known, as are the arguments and reasons," Zapatero said during the debates Thursday. "There's no way to misinterpret them."

In addition to the PSOE's 164 votes in favor, the Valladolid-born lawyer received support from ERC, the Catalan left; BNG, the Galician nationalist party; IU, the United Left; CHA, the Aragonese Junta and CC, the Canary Coalition. The PP voted against with 148 votes. The Catalan and three Basque nationalist parties (CiU, PNV, EA and Na-Bai) abstained.

Upon hearing the final vote, Zapatero grinned as applause filled the hall. Aznar crossed the hall toward his successor and Zapatero met his opponent almost directly in the center of the chamber to shake hands. After doing the same with other PP members, Zapatero turned to greet his supporters, who gravitated around him to offer their congratulations.

Zapatero, a former professor of Constitutional Law at the University of Leon, joined the PSOE in 1979 and was elected to Parliament in 1986 when he was only 26 years old. The party elected him as general secretary in July 2000.

The PSOE first gained power in 1982 under Felipe González, who would lead Spain for the next 14 years. In 1996, Aznar won a tight election race after the PSOE government was marred by corruption scandals and its sponsorship of death squads to liquidate ETA members. In 2000, Aznar won an absolute majority for the PP.

"My promise is to govern for all," Zapatero said during his acceptance speech Friday. "I have confidence in the Spanish society...the best is yet to come. Thank you very much, and let's get to work."

New Prime Minister José Luis Rodríguez Zapatero revels with his wife, Sonsoles, outside the Parliament chambers. / EFE

France's Tavernier defends European cinema against Hollywood machine

E. FERNÁNDEZ SANTOS, **Madrid**
French film director Bertrand Tavernier does not mix words when discussing the uphill battle European filmmakers face against the Hollywood juggernaut.

"We must fight against the dictatorship of immediacy, the dictatorship of image," he said at the Assembly of Spanish Cinematographic Directors during his visit to Madrid Friday.

The problems directors face in Spain are similar to those suffered in France, he said, criticizing the way nations set quotas for domestic and foreign cinema.

Tavernier, who has written several books on American cinema in addition to directing films such as *Round Midnight* and *Daddy Nostalgie*, told his audience that Europe must strive to create an alternative to Hollywood.

In France, he said, the government included a tax to movie tickets. The money was then redirected to aid French cinema.

"If the Americans want to own the French market then they help its survival," Tavernier said. "With this tax it has not only helped many films but also festivals like Cannes. It's a fantastic system. One time Jack Valenti asked me about state funding — he had no idea! 'Jack,' I told him, 'you are the ones that are funding us.'"

Madrid arrests three more suspects of March attacks

M.E., **Madrid**
Spanish police arrested three new suspects in relation to the March 11 bombings in Madrid, a court official said Friday.

The arrests took place Thursday in Madrid. Although authorities did not disclose their identities, officials said they were from Morocco, Egypt and Saudi Arabia. Of the 35 people police have arrested, the majority have been from Morocco. Eighteen suspects are in prison.

Earlier on Friday, Judge Juan del Olmo released six suspects for lack of evidence. Police detained three of the men, Ibrahim Afalah, Hassan Belhadj and Aharouch Said, in Madrid over the past weekend. They testified that they knew the man who rented the apartment in Leganes that seven suspected terrorists blew up on April 3, but that they had no connections to him.

Said reportedly told Del Olmo that he arrived in Spain, like many illegal immigrants, by makeshift boat and had been working in construction. He cried when recounting the difficulties he faced to enter Spain and to then be accused of the bombings.

The other three freed men were detained early this week in Malaga because of their links to Said Berraj, a suspected partner of Serhane ben Abdelmajid Fakhet, the alleged mastermind behind the Madrid bombings that killed 190 people and injured about 1,700. Fakhet died in the Leganes blast.

Two of the men attended the Spanish Institute of Tangier with Berraj in 1992-1993 and the third is the brother-in-law of Berraj's wife. All three denied having any further relation to Berraj.

Investigators believe that Berraj attended a meeting in Turkey in October 2003 with Abdelmajid and Amer Azizi, the supposed Al Qa'ida leader in Europe. At this meeting, authorities say, Azizi helped them plan the Madrid attacks.

On March 9, Berraj left his home and job in Spain and disappeared. Investigators believe he is fleeing or is perhaps one of the three people who died in the Leganes explosion that forensics have still not yet identified.

According to Spain's anti-terror laws, police can hold a suspect for a maximum of five days before he or she must go before a High Court judge. The judge then decides if there is sufficient evidence to open an investigation. If so, the judge can hold the suspect for up to four years before the case goes to trial.

Catalonia travel fair offers stunning destinations for the hot summer months

TRAVEL Ps 4 & 5

7 May 2004, El Diario Vasco.

EL DIARIO VASCO

SAN SEBASTIÁN. **VIERNES, 7 DE MAYO DE 2004** AÑO LXX NÚMERO 22.304 / 0,90 EUROS

DVÓRAME Macaco, ritmos globales desde Barna

EL SEMANAL TV Nuevos en la academia 'UPA'

| JUNTA GENERAL DE SOCIOS DE ELKARGI |

La industria vasca teme el efecto negativo de la ampliación europea y la escasez de materias primas

- Los empresarios destacan la actual situación de incertidumbre derivada de la inestabilidad geopolítica mundial
- Creen que puede ser buen momento para rebajar tensiones, reconducir temas y normalizar relaciones políticas

PÁGS. 54 Y 55

El retraso en el túnel de Arlaban se multará con 6 millones al mes

La Diputación quiere impedir demoras en las obras del tramo Eskoriatza-Arlaban de la A-1

La Diputación adjudicará en breve la obra de la autopista A-1, entre Eskoriatza y Arlaban, que incluye el túnel más largo de la red guipuzcoana, con 3,3 kilómetros. La constructora que gane el concurso se enfrentará a una multa de 6 millones de euros por cada mes de retraso. PÁGS. 2 Y 3

Ibarretxe asegura que cada vez hay más gente de Batasuna que pide una tregua definitiva a ETA

Dice a ETA que «si no respeta la vida es difícil avanzar en un proyecto político»

El lehendakari Juan José Ibarretxe aprovechó ayer la apertura en San Sebastián del I Congreso Internacional por el Derecho Humano a la Paz para volver a reclamar a ETA un alto el fuego, y aseguró que «cada vez son más las personas que dentro de la propia Batasuna exigen a ETA una tregua definitiva y que dé paso a la posibilidad de hacer política». PÁG. 24

La Ararteko denuncia el aislamiento de presos de ETA tras los atentados del 11-M

La Ararteko en funciones, Mertxe Agúndez, denunció ayer en el Parlamento Vasco el aislamiento «en algunas cárceles» de los presos de ETA a raíz de los atentados del 11-M. PÁG. 26

El barril de petróleo rebasa los 37 dólares y amenaza la recuperación de la economía

El precio del petróleo Brent registró ayer otro nuevo máximo en 14 años al superar en Londres los 37 dólares por barril en las primeras horas, aunque por la noche bajó a 35,85 dólares. PÁG. 36

MÁS DENUNCIAS POR TORTURAS A PRESOS IRAQUÍES. El diario *The Washington Post* publicó en su edición de ayer otra serie de fotografías que muestran la humillación y el trato vejatorio de soldados de EE UU a presos iraquíes en una prisión militar cercana a Bagdad. En la imagen, una de las instantáneas publicadas. [THE WASHINGTON POST]

Gran ofensiva de EE UU en Irak

Tropas estadounidenses matan a decenas de chiís en Nayaf y estrechan el cerco sobre Al Sadr

PÁGS. 40 Y 41

Barcelona se transformará en la ciudad de los espectáculos

Fórum acogerá más de 350 eventos culturales a lo largo de 141 días

PÁG. 66

La gran bola sobre el agua, en el ensayo. [EFE]

AL DÍA 4

Tres jubilados holandeses mueren de frío después de perderse en Sierra Nevada en plena ventisca

DEPORTES 46

La posible entrada de Xabi Prieto por Gabilondo reabre el debate sobre la banda izquierda

POLÍTICA 28

El PSOE impone al PP que la comisión sobre el 11-M incluya también los días previos al atentado

DEPORTES 49

El Valencia vence de penalti al Villareal y jugará la final de la UEFA contra el Marsella

EL PAIS

DOMINGO 2 DE MAYO DE 2004
Año XXIX. Número 9.831

DIARIO INDEPENDIENTE DE LA MAÑANA
www.elpais.es

EDICIÓN MADRID
Precio: 1,80 euros

Señora vicepresidenta
La mujer más poderosa de la política en España

Barcelona, capital mundial de la cultura
20 razones para asistir al Fórum 2004 y disfrutar de la nueva reforma de la ciudad

Astronautas del hielo
La aventura de los investigadores españoles en la Antártida

Europa celebra el nacimiento de una gran potencia unificada

Los jefes de Gobierno de la UE ampliada expresan en Dublín sus esperanzas sobre el futuro de la Europa de 455 millones

En las calles de las capitales de los 10 nuevos países miembros se festeja su largamente esperada integración

Tras su reunión con Zapatero, el presidente de la UE anuncia que viajará a Madrid el día 14 con un proyecto de Constitución

CARLOS YÁRNOZ, **Dublín**
ENVIADO ESPECIAL

Fue el día de la Europa unificada. Desde Estonia hasta Chipre, desde Madrid a Varsovia, Europa fue ayer una fiesta, la fiesta de la gran ampliación, la de las alegres bienvenidas a los 10 nuevos socios de la Unión Europea que desde ayer se han sumado a un proyecto que ha derribado los muros que separaban el Este y el Oeste. Reunidos para la ocasión en Dublín, la capital de turno de la UE, los líderes europeos avalaron y celebraron ese Día D de la Europa unida, la que cuenta ya con 25 Estados (un 48% más que hasta ahora), 455 millones de habitantes (un 20% más) y un producto interior bruto de 9,2 billones de euros (sólo un 5% más). Ayer vio la luz la Europa de los 25.

"La ampliación es la prueba del éxito de la Unión Europea", proclamó Bertie Ahern, primer ministro irlandés y actual presidente de la Unión. Es ésta la ampliación que "pone fin a la división artificial que el telón de acero nos impuso durante más de medio siglo", destacó el presidente de la Comisión, Romano Prodi. "No debemos olvidar nunca que de la guerra hemos creado la paz; del odio, el respeto; de la división, la unión; de la dictadura, democracias; de la pobreza, prosperidad". Pasa a la **página 2**

Más información en **páginas 3 a 5**

EFE

LA PRIMERA 'FOTO DE FAMILIA'. Los líderes europeos posaban ayer en Dublín. De izquierda a derecha, en la última fila: el primer ministro búlgaro, **Simeón de Bulgaria;** el polaco, **Leszek Miller;** el belga, **Guy Verhofstadt;** el esloveno, **Anton Rop;** el español, **José Luis Rodríguez Zapatero;** el eslovaco, **Mikulas Dzurinda;** el danés, **Anders Fogh Rasmussen;** el griego, **Kostas Karamanlis;** el italiano, **Silvio Berlusconi,** y el turco, **Recep Tayyip Erdogan.** En segunda fila: el sueco, **Goran Persson;** el maltés, **Lawrence Gonzi;** el húngaro, **Peter Medgyessy;** el portugués, **José Manuel Durão Barroso;** el lituano, **Algirdas Brazauskas;** el alemán, **Gerhard Schröder;** el finlandés, **Matti Vanhanen;** el austriaco, **Wolfgang Schüssel;** el estonio, **Juhan Parts;** el británico, **Tony Blair,** y el checo, **Vladimir Spidla.** En primera fila: el presidente de la Comisión, **Romano Prodi;** el primer ministro de Luxemburgo, **Jean-Claude Juncker;** el presidente rumano, **Ion Iliescu;** la presidenta letona, **Vaira Vike-Frieberga;** el francés, **Jacques Chirac;** el primer ministro irlandés, **Bertie Ahern;** el presidente chipriota, **Tassos Papadopoulos;** el polaco, **Aleksander Kwasniewski;** el primer ministro holandés, **Jan Peter Balkenende;** el presidente del Parlamento Europeo, **Pat Cox,** y el representante de Política Exterior, **Javier Solana.**

Domingo

Un difícil 'puzzle' de 25 países

Una edición especial en la que se analiza la histórica ampliación de la UE, la nueva Europa, del Atlántico a los Urales

ENTREVISTA CON JOSÉ ANTONIO ALONSO

"Es necesaria una ley para poder controlar a los imames de las pequeñas mezquitas"

El ministro del Interior, José Antonio Alonso, es partidario de reformas legales que permitan controlar la predicación de los imames e impedir la propagación del radicalismo islamista. Alonso reflexiona también sobre la conveniencia de crear un registro de actividades religiosas. Sobre el 11-M, el ministro insiste en que en España no se ha pensando ni trabajado sobre el terrorismo islamista. **Páginas 18 y 19**

BIOGRAPHIES

CONTRIBUTORS

ANDREW BENJAMIN

Professor of Critical Theory at Monash University and Visiting Professor of Architectural Theory at the University of Sydney. His recent publications include *Architectural Philosophy* (Continuum 2001) and *Disclosing Spaces. On Painting* (Clinamen 2004).

DAN GRAHAM

1942, Urbana, Illinois.
Dan Graham worked as a gallerist and art critic before embarking on his artistic career in 1965. As both an artist and a theoretician and critic of art and architecture, Graham continues to be a crucial reference in contemporary art's dialogue. His work in the media of video, installation, and sculpture rigorously explore the artistic ramifications of human imposition on the natural and built environment, often situating itself at the intersection of art and architecture. Graham's provocative art and theories also address the historical, social and ideological functions of contemporary cultural systems, including rock music and television. In performances, installations, and architectural/sculptural designs, widely exhibited internationally, Graham manipulates perception with time delay, projections, closed-circuit video, and mirrors, revealing the complex and promiscuous relationships that tie the private to the public, the objective to the subjective.

His solo shows include: Contemporary Art Gallery, Vancouver (Canada), 2003; Museu Serralves, Porto (Portugal); ARC/Musée d'Art Moderne de la Ville de Paris; Kunsthalle, Düsseldorf (Germany); KIASMA, Helsinki, 2001-2002; Kunstwerke, Berlin, 1999; Fundació Antoni Tàpies, Barcelona (Spain), 1998; The Architectural Association School of Architecture, London, 1997; Museum für Gegenwartskunst, Basel (Switzerland), 1996; EA-Generali Foundation, Vienna, 1995; Whitney Museum of American Art, New York (USA), 1994; Boijmans Museum, Rotterdam (The Netherlands), 1993; Wiener Secession, Vienna, 1992; Contemporary Arts Forum, Santa Barbara (USA), 1990.

PETER OSBORNE

Peter Osborne is Professor of Modern European Philosophy at Middlesex University, London and an editor of the journal *Radical Philosophy*. His books include *The Politics of Time: Modernity and Avant-Garde* (1995), *Philosophy in Cultural Theory* (2000) and *Conceptual Art* (Phaidon, 2002). He has contributed widely on questions about the philosophical status and character of contemporary art. Essay topic: Concept and Construction in Contemporary Art.

JORGE OTEIZA

1908-2003

Sculptor, writer, architect and film maker born in Orio, Gipuzkoa, Jorge Oteiza was an artist who over several decades established a critical continuity with the theoretical rationalism and the modern project of the historical avant-gardes.

Winner of the International Sculpture Prize at the São Paulo Biennial in 1957, in 1959 he abandoned the practice of sculpture, considering that he had concluded his experimental enterprise. He wrote innumerable texts and books on aesthetics, anthropology and poetry, among which *Quosque Tandem*, *Ejercicios espirituales en un túnel* and *La ley de los cambios.*

His artistic legacy is now in the Fundación Oteiza in Alzuza, Navarra.

LAWRENCE WEINER

1942, Bronx, New York (USA).

Lawrence Weiner, a central figure of Conceptual art, started exhibiting at the Seth Siegelaub Gallery in 1964. Weiner's early work included experiments with systematic approaches to shaped canvases. A turning point in Weiner's approach came in 1968, when he turned to language as the primary vehicle for his work. All through his numerous installations, films, interventions and sculptures, Weiner has investigated forms of display and distribution that challenge traditional assumptions about the nature of art and objects, which are substituted by verbal description or transfigured into imaginary and poetic statements.

By spreading in different contexts and scenarios, Weiner's work continues to be extremely challenging, and has proved influential for many younger artists.

For this edition of Manifesta, Lawrence Weiner has chosen one of his sculptural fragments to become the title of the exhibition, in an exercise of both expansion and questioning of the traditional formats of exhibition making.

Widely recognized internationally, Weiner's work was featured in many exhibitions worldwide. Solo shows have been mounted by the Tamayo Museum, Mexico City, 2004; the Wexner Center, Columbus (USA), 2002; Kunstmuseum, Wolfsburg (Germany), 2001; Deutsche Guggenheim, Berlin, 2000; CCA, Kitakyushu (Japan), 1999; Boijmans Museum, Rotterdam (The Netherlands), 1996; Ludwig Museum, Cologne (Germany), 1995; Walker Art Center, Minneapolis (USA), 1994; San Francisco Museum of Modern Art (USA), 1992; Dia Center, New York (USA), 1991; Hirshhorn Museum, Washington D.C., 1990.

BAS JAN ADER

1942, Winschoten (The Netherlands)
Missing since 1975

Selected individual exhibitions

Museo Tamayo de Arte Contemporáneo, Bosque de Chapultepec, Mexico DF, 2004.
Modern Art Inc, London, 2004.
Films and Photographs. Galerie Thomas Schulte, Berlin, 2003.
Bas Jan Ader. Galerie Chantal Crousel, Paris, 2003.
Equivocals. Body Figures in Action. Fine Arts School Galleries, Rouen (France), 2002.
Bas Jan Ader. Patrick Painter Inc, Santa Monica (USA), 2002.
Azerty. Centre Georges Pompidou, Paris, 2001.
Bas Jan Ader. Kunstverein Munich (Germany), 2000.
Bas Jan Ader. Kunstverein Bonn (Germany), 2000.
Bas Jan Ader. Kunstverein Braunschweig (Germany), 2000.
Bas Jan Ader. The Art Gallery, University of California, Irvine (USA), 1999.
In Search of the Miraculous: A Homage to Bas Jan Ader. Villandry, London, 1995.
Patrick Painter Editions, Vancouver (Canada), 1995.
Le Magasin, Centre National d'Art Contemporain, Grenoble (France), 1995.
Migrateurs. ARC, Musée d'Art Moderne de la Ville de Paris, 1994.
Nicole Klagsbrun Gallery, New York (USA), 1994.
Bas Jan Ader, Fotowerken en Films. Galerie Pual Andriesse, Amsterdam, 1993.
Bas Jan Ader. Stedelijk Museum, Amsterdam, 1988.
Bas Jan Ader (1942-1975), Keuze uit Nagelaten Werk. Art & Project, Amsterdam, 1985.
Bas Jan Ader. Saman Gallery, Genova (Italy), 1975.
In Search of the Miraculous. Claire S. Copley Gallery, Los Angeles (USA), 1975.
In Search of the Miraculous. Kabinett für Aktuelle Kunst, Bremerhaven (Germany), 1974.
Bas Jan Ader, Broken Fall (Organic). Kabinett für Aktuelle Kunst, Bremerhaven (Germany), 1972.
Bas Jan Ader, a Work on Exhibition Twice Daily. Art & Project, Amsterdam, 1972.
Chouinard Art School, Los Angeles, (USA), 1970.
Implosion, Bas Jan Ader. Claremont Graduate School and University Center, Claremont, (USA), 1967.
Robin Metze Gallery, Pasadena (USA), 1963.

Selected group exhibitions

The Big Nothing. Institute of Contemporary Art, University of Pennsylvania (USA), 2004.
Creeping Revolution 2. Rooseum Center for Contemporary Art Foundation, Stockholm, 2003.
Index Swedish Contemporary Art Foundation, Stockholm, 2003.
Trauer. Atelier Augarten, Österreichische Galerie Belvedere, Vienna, 2003.
Portikus, Stadelschule Art Academy Leinwandhaus, Frankfurt (Germany), 2003.
Geometry of the Face. The National

Museum of Photography, Copenhagen, 2003.
Wish You Were Here. The Art of Adventure. Cleveland Museum of Art, (USA), 2003.
Gestures of Disapparences. Gallery of the Academy of Visual Arts, Leipzig (Germany), 2002.
Hinterlands. Kerstin Engholm Galerie, Vienna, 2002.
En Route. Serpentine Gallery, London, 2002.
Extreme Connoisseurship. Fogg Museum Harvard, Boston (USA), 2001.
Close-Ups-Contemporary Art and Carl Th. Dreyer. Contemporary Art Center, Copenhagen, 1999.
Drawings. Nicole Klagsbrun, New York (USA), 1999.
Sampler. Lousiana Museum of Modern Art, Humlebaek (Denmark), 1997.
More Than Real. Palazzo Reale di Caserta, Naples (Italy), 1996.
Dites-le avec des Fleurs. Galerie Chantal Crousel, Paris, 1996.
Autoreverse 2. Centre National d'Art Contemporain, Grenoble (France), 1996.
Filmabend. Die Filme von Bas Jan Ader. Galerie Daniel Bucholz, Cologne (Germany), 1995.
Album-The Photographic Collection for the Museum Boijmans Van Beuningen. Museum Boijmans Van Beuningen, Rotterdam (The Netherlands), 1995.
Hopeless. Centre for Contemporary Arts, Glasgow (Scotland, UK), 1995.
1965-1975: Reconsidering the Object of Art. Museum of Contemporary Art (Temporary Contemporary), Los Angeles (USA), 1995.
Endurance: The Information. Touring exhibition: ICA, Amsterdam; National Museum of Art, Finland; GAK, Bremen; Dade, Miami (USA); 1995.
Het Gedicht der Zee. Van Gogh Museum, Amsterdam, 1992.
No Rocks Allowed. Centre for Contemporary Art, Rotterdam (The Netherlands), 1992.
Uit de tijd geplukt, Bloemen in Beeldende Kunst en Poëzie. Stedelijk Museum de Lakenhal, Leiden (The Netherlands), 1992.
Künstler aus 25 Jahren Kabinett für aktuelle Kunst. Neues Museum Weserburg, Bremen (Germany), 1992.
Van Vlees en Bloedt (from Meat and Blood), Stedelijk Museum, Schiedam (The Netherlands), 1991.
6080, Attitudes/Concepts/Images. Stedelijk Museum, Amsterdam, 1982.
Een stille ocean. Rijksdienst Beeldende Kunst, The Hague, touring to Delft, Arnheim, Almelo, Amersfoort, and Zwolle (The Netherlands), 1987.
Personal Words. Reality as Metaphor. Travelling exhibition, 1978.
7 Holländische Künstler. Kunstmuseum, Lucerne (Switzerland), 1976.
Mail Art. Kunsthinstorisch Institute, Amsterdam, 1973.
Bas Jan Ader, Bill Leavitt. Nova Scotia College of Art and Design, Halifax (Canada), 1973.
Bas Jan Ader, William Leavitt, Ger Van Elk. Montgomery Art Center, Claremont (USA), 1972.
Bas Jan Ader, Bill Leavitt. California Istitute of Arts, Valencia (USA), 1972.
Sonsbeek buiten e perken. Sonsbeek 71, Anrhem (The Netherlands), 1971.
Prospect 71. Projection. Kunsthalle, Düsseldorf (Germany), 1971.
Vestzaktheater, Groningen (The Netherlands), 1971.
Faculty Show. Mt. San Antonio College, Walnut, (USA), 1969.

Invitational Group Sculpture Exhibition. Cal Poly Gallery, Pomona (USA), 1968.

VICTOR ALIMPIEV
1973, Moscow (Russia)
Lives in Moscow

Education
Moscow Pedagogical University
V. I. Lenin, Art-graphic faculty, Moscow.
New Strategies in Contemporary Art, Open Society Institute (Soros Foundation-Russia), Moscow.
Memory of 1905 Art School, Moscow.

Selected individual exhibitions
For Oleg. Guelman Gallery, Moscow, 2003.
Oleg. Winter Theatre Gallery, with Sergey Vishnevsky, Moscow, 1998.
Oleg, videoversion. Spider & Mouse Gallery, with S. Vishnevsky, Moscow.

Selected group exhibitions
Russian Videoart. Art in General New York (USA), 2004.
Body Display. Wiener Secession, Vienna, 2004.
International Short Film Festival. Oberhausen (Germany), 2003.
Art Moscow Workshops. Moscow, 2003.
Horizon of Realities. MuKHA Museum of Contemporary Art, Antwerp (Belgium), 2003.
Dreams and Conflicts. Bienniale di Venezia, Individual systems, Venice (Italy), 2003.
Art Klyasma. Boarding House Klyazma Reservoir, Moscow, 2003.
Art Frankfurt. TV Gallery Program, Frankfurt (Germany), 2002.
The Urgent reporting. Touring exhibition in Russian cities, 2002.
Art Moscow 2002. TV Gallery Program, Central Artists House, Moscow, 2002.
Son un artista italiano. It is very pleasant! The Russian artist. Piacere! NCCA, Moscow/The Centre of contemporary art Spazio Umano, Milan (Italy), 2002.
Solar Pavilion. Festival of Contemporary Art in the Bay of Pleasure, Boarding House Klyazma Reservoir, Moscow, 2002.
Supervision. Yugnosakhalinsk, Moscow, 2001.
Up-and-Coming. Film Festival, Hannover (Germany), 2001.
International Short Film Festival. Oberhausen (Germany), 2001.
Week of Russian Cinema. Forum Stadtpark, Graz (Austria), 2001.
New York Festival of Russian Films. The Ziegfeld Theater and Clearview Cinemas, New York (USA), 2001.

HÜSEYIN BAHRI ALPTEKIN
1957, Ankara (Turkey)
Lives in Instanbul (Turkey)

Selected individual exhibitions
Georgia on My Mind: B- fact. Leena Kuumola Gallery, with B- fact Group, Helsinki, 2003.
Total Global. Museum für Gegenwartskunst, Basel, 2000.
Sur les Traces de Jules Verne: A Propos de Kiraban. Institut Français, Istanbul (Turkey), 2000
Over the Threshold. Museum Ksiazki, Artystycznej, fabs, Lodz (Poland), 1999.
Kriz: Viva Vaia. Gallery Dulcinea, Istanbul (Turkey), 1999.
Winter Depression. Gallery Nev, Istanbul (Turkey), 1998.
Desert in the Bath. Tvrvk Flrdu, Budapest, 1995.

Selected group exhibitions
Permanent Revolution. The Project Studio, IASPIS, Stockholm, 2004.
*Balkan Bunker Hotel.*The Balkans, A *Crossroad to the Future*. Arte Fiera, Bologna (Italy), 2004.
Community and Art: Artists and Independent Initiatives. Yogyakarta, 2003.
Bunker Research Group. 8th Havana Biennial, Havana, 2003.
B- Fact. Gallery, 1, 1, 1, Istanbul (Turkey), 2003.
B- Fact/ Bunker Research Group. Tirana Biennial, Tirana, 2003.
In den Schlucten des Balkan. Kunsthalle Fredicianum, Kassel (Germany), 2003.
Turkish Art Today. Saitama Contemporary Art Center, Saitama/Tokyo, 2003.
How Latitudes Become Forms. Fondazione Sandretto Re Rebaudengo per l'Arte, Turin (Italy), 2003.
Prophetic Corners. Periferic 6, Contemporary Art Biennial, Lasi (Finland), 2003.
Bal/Kan: Blutt und Honig. Kunst der Gegenwart, Sammlung Essl, Klosterneuburg, Wien, 2003.
Ghosts and Shadows. Platform Contemporary Art Center, Istanbul (Turkey), 2003.
Burada/Here. Platform Contemporary Art Center, Istanbul (Turkey), 2003.
How Latitudes Become Forms: Art in a Global Age. Walker Art Center, Minneapolis (USA), 2003.
Small Brother. National Gallery of Modern Art, Tirana, 2002.
Between the Waterfronts. Galerie Ron Mandos, Rotterdam (The Netherlands), 2002 .
Fundamentalisms of the New Order. Charlottenborg (Denmark), 2002.
In Search of Balkania. Neue Galerie am Landesmuseum Joanneum, Graz (Austria), 2002.
Intersection. Khar- Khorum/Ulaan Baatar, 2002.
4th Cetinje Biennale. Cetinje, Montenegro, 2002.
Under the Sign of the City. Kunst Museum, Bonn (Germany), 2001.
200, 1- 2002 Mutations/Rumour City. TN Probe, Tokyo, 2001.
Conversation. Museum of Contemporary Art, Belgrade, 2001.
Becoming a Place. Project 4L, Istanbul New Museum of Contemporary Art, Istanbul (Turkey), 2001.
Zero_Absolute_the Real. Gallery Marino Cettina, Umag (Croatia), 2001.
Ante- Sound. Center of Contemporary *Art/Inner Spaces*. Poznan (Poland), 2000.
Springtime - New Art from Istanbul. Nikolaj Museum, Copenhagen Contemporary Art Center, Copenhagen, 2000.
Ah Odessa: Tracing Jules Verne. Museum in Progress, Der Standard, 1999.
skorpit: Recent Art from Istanbul. Badischer Kunstverein e.V., Karlsruhe (Germany), 1999.
Haus der Kulturen der Welt, Berlin, 1999.
24th Sao Paulo Biennale, Sao Paulo (Brazil), 1998.
4th Istanbul Biennial, Istanbul (Turkey), 1995.
Little Things. Art in General, New York (USA), 1994.
A Foreigner=A Traveller. Stedelijk Museum, Schiedam (The Netherlands), 1993.

MICOL ASSAËL
1979, Rome (Italy)
Lives in Rome

Education
University La Sapienza, Faculty of Philosophy, Rome.
Classical studies, Rome, 1997.

Selected individual exhibitions
Galleria Bonomo, Bari (Italy), 2004.
Fondazione Sandretto Re Rebaudengo, Turin (Italy), 2004.
Galleria Zero, Milan (Italy), 2004.
La Folie de la Villa Médicis. Villa Medici, Accademia di Francia, Rome, 2002.
Galleria Studio 34, Salerno (Italy), 2001.

Selected group exhibitions
Great Expectations! Fuori Uso, Pescara (Italy), 2003.
Micol Assaël, Nico Dockx, Rikrit Tiravanija, Museum in Progress. San Gimignano (Italy), 2003.
Dreams and Conflicts. Biennale di Venezia, La Zona, Venice (Italy), 2003.
SUB REAL-Reality Survival Strategies. SMART, Project, Amsterdam, 2003.
FullContact. Galleria Civica d'Arte Contemporanea, Siracusa (Italy), 2002.
Prototipi 0.1. Fondazione A. Olivetti, Rome, 2002.
Fatamorgana. Galleria Zero, Piacenza (Italy), 2002.
Exit. Fondazione Sandretto Re Rebaudengo, Turin (Italy), 2002.
Affinités Electives 2. Galerie du Jour: Agnès b. Paris, 2000.
Offered Spaces/Spazi Offerti. S. Casciano dei Bagni (Italy), 2000.
Palazzo Rialto, Roma, 1999.

SVEN AUGUSTIJNEN
1970, Brussels (Belgium)
Lives in Brussels

Selected group exhibitions
World Wide Videofestival 2003. Amsterdam, 2003.
Etablissement d'en face. Brussels, 2002.
A+. Brussels, 2002.
Revolution/Restoration 01, Paranoid Critical Transformation Method. Palais des Beaux Arts, Brussels, 2002.
Argosfestival. Brussels, 2002.
L'Effet Larsen. OK Zentrum für Gegenwartskunst, Linz (Austria), 2001.
Casino Luxembourg. Forum d'Art Contemporain Luxembourg, 2001.
Huis aan de Werf. Utrecht (The Netherlands), 2001.
Argos Festival. Brussels, 2001.
International Filmfestival. Rotterdam (The Netherlands), 2001.
Courtisane. Gent (Belgium), 2001.
14e Festival International du Documentaire. Marseille (France), 2001.
Short Filmfestival. Grimstadt (The Netherlands), 2001.
Docencourt. Lyon (France), 2001.
Palais des Beaux Arts Brussels, 2001.
Festival Gays et Lesbiennes de Bruxelles. Botanique, Brussels, 2001.
Galerie Diana Stigter, Amsterdam, 2001.
Cinema Star. Strassbourg (France), 2001
Bi-Fi. Richard Lohr Loft, New York (USA), 2001.
STUK. Leuven (Belgium), 2001.
Limelight. Kortrijk (Belgium), 2001.
Escale. Düsseldorf (Germany), 2001.
Argos Festival. Brussels, 2001.
Kunstfilmbienale. Cologne (Germany), 2001.
Total Blackout. NICC, Antwerp (Belgium), 2000.
Architectuur Filmfestival. Rotterdam (The Netherlands), 2000.
Metro-Polis. Brussels, 2000.
Galerie Jan Mot, Brussels, 2000.
Escale. Düsseldorf (Germany), 2000.
Splitski Filmski Festival. Split (Croatia), 2000.

3th Panorama of Independent Film-makers. Thessaloniki (Greece), 2000.
Being-together. Marres, Maastricht (The Netherlands), 2000.
Transmediale. Berlin, 2000.
De Appel, Amsterdam, 2000.
17éme Festival Européen du film court de Brest. Le centre d'Art La Passerelle, Brest (France), 2000.
2000 Palestine International Video Festival. Centre Régional d'Art Contemporain Languedoc-Roussillon, Sète (France), 2000.
Kunstfilmbienale. Cologne (Germany), 2000.
24/7. Wilno-New York (USA), 2000.
CAC, Vilnius, 2000.
Once upon a time... MuHKA, Antwerp (Belgium), 2000.
Vacant City. Brussels, 2000.
Urban Dramas, de Singel. Antwerp (Belgium), 2000.
Cinématheque de Toulouse (France), 2000.
Rencontres Urbaines 2000. La Villette, Paris, 2000.
Mladi Levi. Ljubljana, 2000.
Beursschouwburg. Brussels, 2000.
Site. Düsseldorf (Germany), 2000.
Open Days. Jan Van Eyck Academie, Maastricht (The Netherlands), 1999.
W139. Amsterdam, 1999.
HEDAH, Maastricht (The Netherlands), 1998.
T.B.ZES. Antwerp (Belgium), 1998.
Representaties van extreem-rechts. ccBe, Berchem (Belgium), 1998.
KunstenfestivaldesArts. Brussels, 1998.
Kunsthalle, Basel (Switzerland), 1998.
World Wide Videofestival. Amsterdam, 1998.
8e Biennale pour l'Image en Mouvement. Geneva (Switzerland), 1998.
W139. Amsterdam, 1998.
Big Brother, Stroom, Haags centrum voor beeldende kunsten, The Hague, 1998.
De Onzichtbare Stad. Marres, Maastricht, 1998.
The Music in Me, Chapter 2: Regarding Dance. GAK, Bremen (Germany), 1998.
Another World Museum. Gallery Side 2, Tokyo, 1998.
Without Title. MuHKA, in collaboration with Peter Rogiers, Antwerp (Belgium), 1997.
Festival International du Film de l'Art, in collaboration with Les Ballets C. de la B., Paris, 1996.
Springdance Festival 1996, (Prix Essai), Utrecht (The Netherlands), 1996.
Dancing for the Camera: International Festival of Film and Video Dance. Durham (USA), 1996.
Cinémathèque Centre Suzanne Delal, Tel Aviv (Israel), 1996.
Centre Choréographique National de Rennes et de Bretagne, Rennes (France), 1996.
Dance Lumiere. Dancehouse, St. North Carlton, Melbourne (Australia), 1996.
9e Grand Prix International Vidéo Danse. Grasse, Stockholm, 1996.
Vidéoformes. Clermont-Ferrand (France), 1996.
Lost and Found. Maatschappij voor Oude en Nieuwe Media, Amsterdam, 1996.
Centre National de la Dance, Paris, 1996.

Video

Une femme entreprenante, 2003.
François, 2003.
Mission Mont des Arts, 2002.
Johan, 2001.
Le guide du parc, 2001.

Barbarella, collaboration with Willem Oorebeek, 2000.
De Kunstberg... stad op de helling, realised in collaboration with Barbara Visser, 2000.
Ernesto. C'est difficile de voir l'avenir. Je Suis pas encore à demain. Je le verrai petit à petit, collaboration with Koen Augustijnen, 2000.
L'Histoire, video installation, 1998.
Lets op Bach, collaboration with Les Ballets C. de la B., 1998.
La Tristeza Cómplice, realised in collaboration with Les Ballets C. de la B., 1996.
L'école des pickpockets, 1996.

ZBYNĚK BALADRÁN

1973, Prague (Czech Republic)
Lives in Prague

Education

Academy of Fine Arts, Prague, 2003.
Co-founder Display, Space for Contemporary Art, Prague, 2001.
History of Art, Charles University, Prague, 1997.

Selected individual exhibitions

Teorie, Praxe, Expozice. DPzK, Brno (Czech Republic), 2004.
Warianta C. Open gallery, with Erik Binder, Bratislava, 2002.
Target Group. Palais de Tokyo, with Tomas Svoboda, Paris, 2002.
Diorama. BJ Case, Komunardu Street, Prague, 2000.
019. Galerie Jeleni, Prague, 2001.
10. Galerie Eingang, Ostrava (Czech Republic), 2001.
8. Galerie Eskort, Brno (Czech Republic), 2001.

Selected group exhibitions

Interkosmos 2004. Raster, Warsaw, 2004.
Ceskoslovensko. Bratislava, 2003.
Survey 03. Futura, Prague, 2003.
Paradies. Bunker, Alexanderplatz, Berlin, 2003.
Kompression. Wedding, Berlin, 2003.
Forum of Independent Galleries. U Prstenu, GHMP, Prague, 2002.
Wechselstube. der-Ausstellunsgraum, Stuttgart (Germany), 2002.
Uhlopricka. Galerie Eskort, Brno (Czech Republic), 2002.
Premiere vue. Passage de Retz, Paris, 2002.
Artchitektura. GJF, Prague, 2002.
Criss-Cross. Broumov (Czech Republic), 2001.
Prvni a posledni. Galerie V. Spaly, Prague, 2001.
Fotok. MEO, Budapest, 2001.
Kazda kapka... Galerie AVU, Prague, 2000.
Vystava AVU. Manes, Prague, 2000.
Vidiny, Roxy. Galerie NOD, Prague, 1999.
Rickyho gang. Klub Depo, Olomouc (Czech Republic), 1999.
Zelena- Galerie AVU, Prague, 1998.

JOHN BOCK

1965, Gribbohm (Germany)
Lives in Berlin (Germany)

In accordance with the wishes of the artist, no details of his life shall be published.

MICHAËL BORREMANS

1963, Geraardsbergen (Belgium)
Lives in Ghent (Belgium)

Selected individual exhibitions
Museum for Gegenwartskunst, Basel (Switzerland), 2004.
Kunsthalle, Bremerhaven (Germany), 2004.
Zeno X Storage. Borgerhout, Antwerp (Belgium), 2004.
Trickland. David Zwirner Gallery, New York (USA), 2003.
Young and Innocent. Zeno X Gallery, Antwerp (Belgium), 2002.
Vereniging Van Het. SMAK, Ghent (Belgium), 2000.
The Fetish Paintings. Croxhapoxruimte, Ghent (Belgium), 1999.
The Mind and Its Limits. In den Bouw, Kalken (Belgium), 1998.
Huize St.-Jacobus. Ghent (Belgium), 1997.
Cerebral Office, Voorkamer, Lier (Belgium), 1997.
Croxhapoxruimte. Ghent (Belgium), 1996.

Selected group exhibitions
Voorkamer, Lier (Belgium), 2004.
Apparitions. Musée des Beaux-Arts de Tourcoing (France), 2003.
Gelijk het leven is. 50 Jaar Belgische en Internationale Kunst Uit de Collectie. SMAK, Ghent (Belgium), 2003.
Neue Werke im Kupferstichkabinett. Öffentliche Kunstsammlung, Basel (Switzerland), 2003.
The House of Fiction. Sammlung Hauser & Wirth, St. Gallen (Switzerland), 2002.
Pertaining to Painting. Contemporary Arts Museum, Houston (USA), 2002.
Pertaining to Painting. Austin Museum of Art, Austin (USA), 2002.
Works on Paper. Zeno X Gallery, Antwerp (Belgium), 2001.
Was Rubens Een Dribbelaar? Culturel Centrum Berchem (Belgium), 2000.
(With) Drawings into 2000. Van Laere Contemporary Art, Antwerp (Belgium), 1999.
Kunstsalon van Gent, Sint-Pietersabdij, Ghent (Belgium), 1998.
Schilderkunst-Hedendaags-Belgisch. Croxhapox, Ghent (Belgium), 1997.
Alom & Hiernevens. Zwartzusterskiooster (Project Van Voorkamer VZW). Zwartz-usterskiooster, Lier (Belgium), 1997.

SERHIY BRATKOV
1960, Kharkiv (Ukraine)
Lives in Moscow (Russia)

Education
Polytechnical Academy, Kharkiv, Department of industrial electronics, 1983.
Repin Art College, Kharkiv, 1978.

Selected individual exhibitions
Steelworkers. Transit Gallery, Mechelen (Belgium), 2003.
Kids. Espacio Mí nimo, Madrid, 2003.
Souvenirs. Scena Gallery, Moscow, 2003.
Faust and Margherita. Center for Contemporary Art, Kyiv, 2003.
My Moscow. Regina Gallery, Moscow, 2002.
www.girls.ru. LipanjePuntin Gallery, Trieste (Italy), 2002.
Djeti-Kinder-Kids. Kunstverein, Rosen-heim (Germany), 2002.
Fayur-Soyuz. Regina Gallery, Moscow, 2001.
Sailors. Regina Gallery, Moscow, 2000.
Kids. Regina Gallery, Moscow, 2000.
The Daily Journal of Chicatilo. Galerie in der BrotFabrik, Berlin, 1997.
The Medical Cabinet of Prof. Dmitriy Pirogov, Kharkiv Medical Association,

Kharkiv (Ukraine), 1996.
There is no Paradise. Up/Down Gallery, Kharkiv (Ukraine), 1996.
Frozen Landscape: Photo-Action. Soros Center for Contemporary Art, Kyiv, 1995.
In the Haystacks. Galerie in der BrotFabrik, Berlin, 1995.
Forum Stadtpark, Graz (Austria), 1992.
Museum of Contemporary Art, Tel Aviv (Israel), 1990.

Selected group exhibitions
Berlin-Moscow/Moscow-Berlin 1950-2000. Martin-Gropius-Bau, Berlin, 2003.
Dreams and Conflicts. Biennale di Venezia, Tondo/Russian Pavilion , Venice (Italy), 2003.
Neue Ansatze/Zeitgenossische Kunst aus Moskau. Kunsthalle, Düsseldorf (Germany), 2003.
Werkelijkheidshorizonten, Museum van Hedendaagse Kunst, Antwerp (Belgium), 2003.
Sans Consentement. CAN, Neuchâtel (Switzerland), 2002.
Shock&Show. Group 78, Trieste (Italy), 2002.
Photobiennale2002. Manezh, Moscow, 2002.
Biennial of São Paulo (Brasil), 2002.
Brand. Center for Contemporary Art, Kyiv, 2002.
Winter Exhibitions: Tiong Ang, Serhiy Bratkov, David Claerbout, Jose Antonio Hernandez-Diez. Institute of Visual Arts, University of Wisconsin, Milwaukee (USA), 2001.
Inverse Perspectives. Edvik Cultural Centre, Sollentuna (Sweden), 2001.
Contemporary Photographers of the Ukraine. Contemporary Art Centre, Thessaloniki (Greece), 2000.
Two Sides. Center for Contemporary Art, Kyiv, 2000.
Olaf Breuning & Serhiy Bratkov. Cosoi Caponir Museum-Fortress. Kyiv, 2000.
Contemporary Photographers of the Ukraine. Festival Est-Ouest, Die (France), 1999.
3rd Triennale of Photography. Graz (Austria), 1999.
Face Value. Ukrainian Stock Exchange, Kyiv, 1999.
Regards sur l'Ukraine. Passage du Retz, Paris, 1999.
Contemporary Photographers of the Ukraine. École d'art de Mulhouse (France), 1999.
Carte-Blanche à Boris Mikhailov. Cité Internationale des Arts, Paris, 1999.
Photographers from Kharkiv. Gallery Kohlenof, Nuremberg (Germany), 1999.
The Future is Now. Ukrainian Art of 90s. Museum of Contemporary Art, Zagreb, 1999.
Dressed in White. The Art Gallery at Ramapo College, Mahwah, New Jersey (USA), 1998.
Accommodation. Gallery U Iezuitov, Poznan (Poland), 1998.
Public Interest. Gallery of the Artists Union, House of Artists, Kyiv, 1998.
Humanature. Nortalie (Sweden), 1998.
Intermedia. Soros Center for Contemporary Art, Kyiv, 1998.
A Day in the Life, Crimean Project-I. Soros Center for Contemporary Art, Kyiv, 1998.
Symptomatic Anonymity. Soros Center for Contemporary Art, Kyiv, 1997.
Photo Syntheses. Gallery of the Artists Union, House of Artists, Kyiv, 1997.
Intrigue-Provocation. M. Zilinkas Art Gallery, Kaunas (Lithuania), 1997.

Sugar Plum Visions. Soros Center for Contemporary Art, Kyiv, 1997.
Commodity Fetishism. Ukrainian House Cultural Center, Kyiv, 1997.
The Family Album. Mohyla Academy Gallery, Kyiv, 1997.
Bred in the Bone. Soros Center for Contemporary Art, Kyiv, 1995.
Multiple Exposures: Chichkan and Bratkov. Mason Gross Visual Arts School. Rutgers University, New Brunswick, New Jersey (USA), 1995.
The Art of Photography from Ukraine. Mason Gross Visual Arts School, Rutgers University, New Brunswick, New Jersey (USA), 1995.
Black and White. Brama Center for Contemporary Arts, Kyiv, 1995.
Barbaros. Artists Union Gallery, House of Artists, Kyiv, 1995.
Mouth of Medusa. Center for Contemporary Arts Brama, Kyiv, 1995.
Free Zone. Art Museum, Odessa (Ukraine), 1994.
Alchemic Surrender. Battleship *Slavutych*, Sevastopol, Crimea (Ukraine), 1994.
Project for Europe. Turbine Hall, Copenhagen, 1994.
Behind the Fence. Ukrainian Museum of Fine Art, Kharkiv (Ukraine), 1994.
Neoexpressionist Photography: Bratkov, Mikhailov, Solonskiy. Ukrainian Museum of Fine Art, Kharkiv (Ukraine), 1994.
Photography from Kharkiv. Museum of Industrial Culture, Nuremberg (Germany), 1993.
Trans-Kontakt. Kharkiv. New York. New York (USA), 1993, with Boris Mikhailov.
The Art of Contemporary Photography from Russia, Belorussia. Central House of Artists, Moscow, 1993.
Expanse of the Cultural Revolution. Ukrainian House Cultural Center, Kyiv, 1994.
Ukrainian Photography Contemporary. Center for Contemporary Art, Cincinnati (USA), 1992.
Fifth Exhibition of Litera A. House of Artists, Kharkiv (Ukraine), 1992.
Group Show. Gallery Zabo, Nuremberg (Germany), 1992.
Artists from Ukraine. DRK-Forum, Kiel, 1992
150 Years of Photography. Manege, Moscow, 1989.
Will We All Eat One Another and Package It? Gallery Up/Down, Kharkiv (Ukraine), 1991.
Republican Exhibition of Young Artists. House of Artists, Kyiv, 1988.
All-Union Exhibition of Young Artists. Manege, Moscow, 1988.
Art Contacts.Riga, 1988.
New Soviet Photography. Helsinki, 1988.

MARCEL BROODTHAERS

1924, Brussels (Belgium)
Deceased in 1976, Cologne (Germany)

Selected Individual exhibitions

Marcel Broodthaers, Un Jardin d'Hiver... Musée des Beaux-Arts de Nantes (France), 2004.
Marcel Broodthaers: Texte et Photos. SK Stiftung Kultur, Cologne (Germany), 2003.
Palais des Beaux-Arts, Brussels, 2001.
Het Groeningemuseum, Bruges (Belgium), 1998.
Marian Goodman Gallery, New York (USA), 1997.
Marcel Broodthaers: Cinema. Fundació Antoni Tàpies, Barcelona (Spain).
Kunsthalle Düsseldorf (Germany), 1997.
Literarische Ausstellung um Mallarmé

von Marcel Broodthaers. Museum Abeiberg, Mönchengladbach (Germany), 1997.
Marcel Broodthaers, La Lorelei. Musée d'Art Moderne et Contemporain, Geneva (Switzerland), 1996.
Entr'acte. Van Abbemuseum, Eindhoven (The Netherlands), 1995.
Galerie du Jeu de Paume, Paris, 1992.
Museo Nacional Centro de Arte Reina Sofí a, Madrid, 1991.
Walker Art Center, Minneapolis (USA); Museum of Contemporary Art, Los Angeles (USA); Carnegie Museum of Art, Pittsburgh (USA); Palais des Beaux-Arts, Brussels, 1990.
Musée d'Ixelles, Brussels, 1987.
BonneFantenmuseum, Maastricht (The Netherlands), 1987.
Kunsthalle, Bern, 1982.
Moderna Museet, Stockholm, 1982.
Museum Boijmans van Beuningen, Rotterdam (The Netherlands), 1981.
Tate Gallery, London, 1980.

Selected group exhibitions
Dévoler, Vivent les Frac (suite). Institut d'art contemporain, Villeurbanne (France), 2001.
Orbis terrarum. Ways of Worldmaking. Antwerpen Open, Antwerp (Belgium), 1999.
Exploding Cinema. Rotterdam International Film Festival (Marcel Broodthaers, Section Cinéma), Rotterdam (The Netherlands), 1999.
Seeing Time: Selections from the Pamela and Richard Kramlich Collection of Media Art. San Francisco Museum of Modern Art, San Francisco (USA), 1999.
Masterworks from the Collection of Ho-Am Art Museum. Seoul (Korea), 1997.
Documenta X. Kassel (Germany), 1997.
1965-1975: Reconsidering the Object of Art. Museum of Contemporary Art, Los Angeles (USA), 1995.
Departures: Photography 1924-1989. Galerie Julie Kewenig, Cologne (Germany), 1989.
A Historical Surrounding. Museum Boijmans van Beuningen. Rotterdam (The Netherlands); Malmö Konsthall, Malmö (Sweden) 1988.
Sonsbeek 86: International Sculpture Exhibition. Arnhem (The Netherlands), 1986.
Documenta 7. Kassel (Germany), 1982.

CARLOS BUNGA
1976, Porto (Portugal)
Lives in Lisboa (Portugal)

Education
BA in Fine Arts, Escola Superior de Tecnologia, Gestão (Arte e Design), Caldas da Rainha (Portugal), 2003.
Workshop in performance with Rebecca Schneider, Fundação Gulbenkian, 2003.

Selected exhibitions
EDP, Young Artists Award. Serralves Museum, Porto (Portugal), 2003.
Jovens Criadores. Porto (Portugal), 2002.
ESTGAD, Caldas da Rainha (Portugal), 2001.
Caldas Late Night. Caldas da Rainha (Portugal), 2001.
Jovens Criadores. Coimbra (Portugal), 2001.
Interventions in city buildings. Caldas da Rainha (Portugal), 2001.
Caldas Late Night. Caldas da Rainha (Portugal), 2000.

DUNCAN CAMPBELL
1972, Dublin (Ireland)
Lives in Glasgow (Scotland, UK)

Education
MFA in Glasgow School of Art, Glasgow, 1998.
BA in University of Ulster, Belfast, 1996.
National College of Art and Design, Dublin, 1992.
Inchicore Vocational School, Dublin, 1991.

Selected individual exhibitions
Falls Burns Malone Fiddles. Transmission Gallery, Glasgow (Scotland, UK), 2003.
Habitat. Habitat Buchanan Galleries, Glasgow (Scotland, UK), 1999.

Selected group exhibitions
Revolution is Not What it Used to Be. S1 Artspace, Sheffield (UK), 2004.
Old Habits Die Hard. Norwhich Gallery and Kunsternes Hus, Oslo, 2004.
Tongs Ya Bass. Ship Gallery, London, 2004.
Old Habits Die Hard. Sparwasser HQ, Berlin, 2003.
Advertence. Belfast and Dublin, 2003.
Fresh and Upcoming. Frankfurter Kunstverein, Frankfurt (Germany), 2003.
Shadazz. Royal College of Art, London, 2002.
Flicer. De Overslag, Eindhoven (The Netherlands), 2002.
KIASMA, Helsinki, 2002.
Images Passages. Annecy (France), 2001.
Flourish Nights. Flourish Studios, Glasgow (Scotland, UK), 2001.
Retur. Copenhagen, 2001.
What Goes On! The Glasgow Project Room, Glasgow (Scotland, UK), 2001.
D-net Festival. Lux space, London, 2000.
Me We. Project Space, Athens, 2000.
Evolution Isn't over yet. Lugar Comum, Lisbon, 2000.
Video Positive. Liverpool (UK), 2000.
A Day Like Any Other. Kulturhus, Stavanger (Norway), 2000.
Misty in Roots. Fly Gallery, Glasgow (Scotland, UK), 1999.
Fields, Rays and Green Numbers. Transmission exchange with Pineapple Gallery, Malmö (Sweden) 1999.
Evolution Isn't Over Yet. Fruitmarket Gallery, Edinburgh,1999.

CENGIZ ÇEKIL
1945, Bor (Turkey)
Lives in Izmir (Turkey)

Selected individual exhibitions
Melted Paraffin Waxes. Izmir (Turkey), 1999.
The Temporary One. Ankara, 1997.
Seized Letters - Istanbul. Istanbul (Turkey), 1978.

Selected group exhibitions
In the Gorges of the Balkans. Museum Fridericianum, Kassel (Germany), 2003.
Exhibition of New tendencies, 1st Istanbul Biennial. Istanbul (Turkey), 1977.
10 Artists 10 Works. Istanbul (Turkey), 1989.

ILIYA CHICHKAN
1967, Kyiv (Ukraine)
2004 DAAD Residency in Berlin

Selected individual exhibitions
Rabbits on Acid. Remont Gallery,

Belgrade, 2004.
Dog Love. Guelman Gallery, Kyiv, 2003.
P.V.O. Laznya Center for Contemporary Art, Gdansk (Poland), 2002.
Iliya Chichkan. Querini Stampalia, Venice (Italy), 2001.
P.V.O. Gallery RA, Kyiv, 2001.
Acrobats and Rabbits. Regina Gallery, Moscow, 2001.
Sleeping Princes. Gallery One Degree, Skopje, 2000.
Sleeping Princes. School of Fine Arts, Mulhouse (France), 2000.
Mind the Bullocks. Artists Union at the House of Artists, Kyiv, 2000.
Chichkan Party. Ra Gallery, Kyiv, 1996.
Alter Idem. Center for Contemporary Arts Brama, Kyiv, 1994.
Genetical Mutations. Gallery of the Artists Union, Kyiv, 1993.

Selected group exhibition
Entry. Ukrainian Museum of Contemporary Art, Kyiv, 2004.
Photographic Biennial. Turin (Italy), 2003.
Defenders. Art Moscow, 2003.
Donumenta. Rosenheim (Germany), 2003.
Prague Biennial. Prague, 2003.
Atomic Love. Transmediale, Berlin, 2003.
Extra Schengen. Nicelli Airport, Venice (Italy), 2003.
Atomic Love. Center for Contemporary Art, Tel Aviv, 2003.
Photography Biennial. Kyiv, 2003.
Dream Catcher Media Festival. Kyiv, 2002.
KIMAF Media Festival. Kyiv, 2002.
Photography Biennial. Moscow, 2002.
Brand. Soros Center for Contemporary Art, Kyiv, 2001.
Animal Farm. Center for Contemporary Art, Riga (Latvia), 2001.
KIMAF International Media Festival, Kyiv, 2001.
Found Stuff. Odessa (Ukraine), 2001.
Photography Biennial, Moscow, 2000.
Alter Natura: International Media Art Festival, Center for Contemporary Art Gallery, Kyiv, 2000.
New Tendencies. Artists Union at the House of Artists, Kyiv, 2000.
Face Value. Ukrainian Stock Exchange, Kyiv, 1999.
Ab Die Post. Postfuhramt, Berlin, 1999.
Novi Sad Biennial, Novi Sad (Yugoslavia), 1999.
Contemporary Ukrainian Photography. Die (France), 1999.
Carte Blanche à Boris Mykhailov. Cité Internationale des Arts, Paris, 1999.
Regards sur l'Ukraine. Passage du Retz, Paris, 1999.
The Future is Now. Ukrainian Art of the 90s, Museum of Contemporary Art, Zagreb; Museum of Contemporary Art, Maribor (Slovenia), 1999.
Month of Photography. Bratislava, 1998.
Crimean Project II. Livadia Palace, Crimea (Ukraine) and Soros Center for Contemporary Art, Kyiv, 1998.
A Day in the Life. Soros Center for Contemporary Art, Kyiv, 1998.
Public Interest. Gallery of the Artists Union, House of Artists, Kyiv, 1998.
Accommodation. gallery U Iezuitov, Poznan (Poland), 1998.
Intermedia. Soros Center for Contemporary Art, Kyiv, 1998.
Purple and Green. Pretoria Art Museum (South Africa), 1997.
Symptomatic Anonymity. Soros Center for Contemporary Art Gallery, Kyiv, 1997.
Photo Syntheses. Gallery of the Artists Union, House of Artists, Kyiv, 1997.
Green House Affect. Soros Center for Contemporary Art, Kyiv, 1997.

International São Paolo Biennial. São Paolo (Brazil), 1996.
Sugar Plum Vision. Soros Center for Contemporary Art, Kyiv, 1996.
Commodity Fetishism. Ukrainian House Cultural Center, Kyiv, 1996.
The Family Album. Kyiv Mohyla Academy Gallery, Kyiv, 1996-
Hermetic Forest. Soros Center for Contemporary Art, Kyiv, 1996.
After Five Years: Photography Exhibition. Bratislava, 1995.
Multiple Exposures: Illya Chichkan and Serhiy Bratkov. Mason Gross Visual Arts School, Rutgers University, New Brunswick, New Jersey (USA), 1995.
Bred in the Bone. Soros Center for Contemporary Art, Kyiv, 1995.
The Art of Photography from Ukraine. Mason Gross Visual Arts School, Rutgers University, New Brunswick, New Jersey (USA), 1995.
Informatum. Center for Contemporary Art, Ujazdowski Castle, Warsaw, 1995.
Barbaros. Gallery of the Artists Union, House of Artists, Kyiv, 1995.
Mouth of Medusa. Center for Contemporary Arts Brama, Kyiv, 1995.
Project for Europe. Turbine Hall, Copenhagen, 1994.
Osmolovsky Project. Regina Gallery, Moscow, 1994.
Alchemic Surrender. Battleship *Slavutych*, Sevastopol, Crimea (Ukraine), 1994.
Free Zone. Art Museum, Odessa (Ukraine), 1994.
Expanse of the Cultural Revolution. Ukrainian House Cultural Center, Kyiv, 1994.
Angels Over Ukraine, Gallery 369, Edinburgh, 1993.
Artists of the Paris Commune. Artists Union Gallery, Kyiv, 1992.
Stjil. Artists Union Gallery, Kyiv, 1992.
International Festival of Contemporary Art. Avignon (France), 1990.
Republican Exhibition of Young Artists. House of Artists, Kyiv, 1987.

JAN DE COCK
1976, Brussels (Belgium)
Lives in Brussels

Selected individual exhibitions
Denkmal 1a. Luis Campaña, Cologne (Germany), 2004.
Denkmal 9. Henry Van de Velde University Library, Ghent (Belgium), 2004.
Denkmal 10. De Appel, Amsterdam, 2003.
Denkmal 3. Kerstin Engholm Gallery, Vienna, 2003.
Art Brussels, One Man Show. Fons Welters Gallery, Amsterdam, 2002.
Randschade/Collateral Damage Fig.7. SMAK and Museum of Fine Arts, Ghent (Belgium), 2002.
Randschade/Collateral Damage Fig.9. Fons Welters Gallery, Amsterdam, 2002.
Randschade/Collateral Damage Fig.4. Fons Welters Gallery, Amsterdam, 2001.
Argos, Brussels, 2001.

Selected group exhibition
Jeune Peinture Belge. Palais des Beaux-Arts , Brussels, 2003.
Fons Welters Gallery, Amsterdam, 2002.
Randschade/Collateral Damage Fig.5. Watou (Belgium), 2001.
Interaktionen: Natur & Architektur. SMAK and Stadt Borken, Ghent (Belgium), 2001.
Ici et Maintenant/Hier en Nu. Espace 251 Nord, Brussels, 2001.

Coming people. SMAK, Ghent (Belgium), 1999.
Diasporal Thoughts. Tacktoren, Kortrijk (Belgium), 1999.
Beeld in Park. Felix Hap Park, Brussels, 1999.

ANGELA DE LA CRUZ
1965, La Coruña (Spain)
Lives in London (England, UK)

Education
MA in Sculpture and Critical Theory, Slade School of Art, London, 1996.
BA (Hons) in Fine Art, Goldsmiths College, London, 1994.
Foundation, Chelsea College of Art, London, 1990.
Faculty of Philosophy, BA Philosophy, Santiago de Compostela (Spain), 1989.

Selected individual exhibitions
MARCO, Vigo (Spain), 2004.
Lisson Gallery, London, 2004.
Nicolas Krupp Gallery, Basel (Switzerland), 2004.
Gallery Bouhlou, Bergen (Norway), 2003.
Clutter. Galerie Krinzinger, Vienna, 2003.
Anna Schwartz Gallery, Melbourne (Australia), 2002.
Prop. Sturegallerian, Stockholm, 2002.
Perth International Arts Festival, The Church Gallery, Perth (Australia), 2002.
Wetterling Gallery, Stockholm, 2002.
Anthony Wilkinson Gallery, London, 2001.
John Weber Gallery, New York (USA), 2000.
Everyday Painting. Galerie Krinzinger, Vienna, 1999.
One Painting. Lift Gallery, London, 1999.
Larger Than Life. The Ballroom, Royal Festival Hall, London, 1998.
Everyday Painting. Anthony Wilkinson Gallery, London, 1998.
4xSolo. De Markten, Brussels, 1998.
Everyday Painting. John Weber Gallery, New York (USA), 1998.
Galerie In Situ, Aalst (Belgium), 1997.
Untitled. Premises, Hackney, London, 1993.

Selected group exhibitions
Escape Velocities. Spital Space, London, 2004.
A Thing About Painting. Platform Gallery, London, 2004.
Tanya Rumpff Gallery, Haarlem (The Netherlands), 2004.
Fòrum, Barcelona (Spain), 2004.
Chockofuckingblock. Jeffrey Charles Gallery, London, 2003.
Whitechapel Project Space, London, 2003.
Wetterling 1978-2003. Wetterling Gallery, Stockholm, 2003.
Eva Schlegel & Friends. Gallerie 422, Gmunden (Austria), 2002.
Four Women and A Pregnant Man. MGM Gallery, Oslo, 2002.
Art. Bermuda National Gallery, Bermuda, 2002.
Life is Beautiful. Laing Art Gallery, Newcastle (UK), 2002.
Sitting Tenants. Lotta Hammer, London, 2002.
Ingenting (Nothing: Exploring Invisibilities). Rooseum, Malmö (Sweden), 2001.
Record Collection. VTO Gallery, London, 2001.
Nothing: Exploring Invisibilities. Mead Gallery, University of Warwick

Gallery, Warwick (UK), 2001.
Makeshift. University of Brighton Gallery, Brighton (UK), 2001.
Landscape. Barbara Gillman Gallery, Miami (USA), 2000.
3 Rooms. Anthony Wilkinson Gallery, London, 2000.
The Wreck of Hope. The Nunnery, London, 2000.
My Old Man Said Follow the Van. Branch, London, 1999.
Aktuelle Kunst. The Water Tower, Vlissingen (The Netherlands), 1999.
White Out. Gallery Fine, London, 1999.
John Moores 21. Walker Museum & Art Gallery, Liverpool (UK), 1999.
Transgressions and Transformations. Yale University, New Haven (USA), 1999.
Europe on a Shoestring. John Weber Gallery, New York (USA), 1999.
Links-Schilderkunst in Extremis? Provincienhuis, Maastricht (The Netherlands), 1999.
I'm a Virgin. The Waiting Room, Wolverhampton, 1999; Fundación Lázaro Guadiano, Madrid, 1999.
Peinture sur PEINTURE. Salle de Bal, Vienna, 1999.
54x54. MOCA, London, 1999.
England Maximum Diversity. Atelierhaus der Akademie der bildenden Künste, Vienna, 1998.
Contemporary Women Painters. The Hillwood Art Museum, Brookville, New York (USA), 1998.
Speed. The New Langton Arts Centre, San Francisco (USA), 1998.
Destroyer/Creator. John Weber Gallery, New York (USA), 1998.
Take Off. CV/Lebenslauf, Hamburg (Germany), 1997.
Dissolution. Laurent Delaye Gallery, London, 1997.
Fasten Seatbelt. Galerie Krinzinger, Vienna, 1997.
Shuttle. Anthony Wilkinson Fine Art, London, 1997.
Lineart. Galerie In Situ, Aalst (Belgium), 1997.
Stepping Out. 33 Great Sutton Street, London, 1996.
Wasted. Hyena Co., Website, England, 1996.
Art and Design. Academy Editions, London, 1996.
Memory. Riverside Studios, London, 1995.
Making Mischief. St Jamess Street, London, 1994.
Surface Tension. Curwen Gallery, London, 1994.
Rubber Works Installation. Spitalfields Market Project, London, 1993.

D.A.E.
(DONOSTIAKO ARTE EKINBIDEAK)
(since 1999)

Peio Aguirre
1972, Elorrio (Spain)
Lives in Donostia-San Sebastián (Spain)

Leire Vergara
1973, Bilbao (Spain)
Lives in Donostia-San Sebastián (Spain)

Education

Peio Aguirre
Founder of COOP, 1998.
Postgraduate studies, Nantes, 1998.
Responsible for A.K.A., Elorrio, 1997.
Fine Arts, Euskal Herriko Unibertsitatea.

Leire Vergara
Psychology, Universidad de Deusto. Master in Art History and Cultural Studies, Goldsmiths College, London, 1999.

Selected exhibitions, screenings and projects
Lise Harlev, individual project (Denmark), workshop in Arteleku, 2004.
El Cine del Afuera: El Espíritu del Retrato/ Kanpoaldearen Zinema: Erretratuaren Espiritua El Ciclo Audiovisual. Individual project with Jakob Kolding (Denmark), 2003.
Front Line Compilation, catalogue publication, and screening of *Shell-shock Rock* (documentary by John T. Davis), 2003.
Front Line Compilation. Northern Ireland and the Basque Country, 2002.
Superkongresua, Basque Artists Meeting. Organized by Peio Aguirre, Ibon Aranberri, Asier Pérez González and thirty participants, Tilo Schulz (Germany), KLAT (Switzerland), 2001.
Asier Mendizabal (Basque Country), organized by Gorka Eizagirre, 2000.
Itziar Okariz (Basque Country), Iñaki Garmendia (Basque Country), COOP & Nina Sidow (Germany), José Alvaro Perdices (USA), 1999.

JEREMY DELLER
1966, London (England, UK)
Lives in London

Education
MA in Art History, Sussex University Sussex (UK), 1992.
BA in Art History, Courtauld Istitute London, 1988.

Selected individual exhibitions
This is Us. Bard Centre for Curatorial Studies, New York (USA), 2003.
Memory Bucket. ArtPace San Antonio (USA), 2003.
After The Goldrush. Capp St. Residency Project. Wattis Institute, San Francisco (USA), 2002.
Art: Concept Gallery, Paris, 2003.
The Battle of Orgreave. An Artangel Commission. Orgreave, South Yorkshire (UK), 2001.
Folk Archive. Tate Britain, with Alan Kane, London, 2000.
Unconvention. Centre for Visual Arts, Cardiff (Wales, UK), 1999.
Acid Brass. Bluecoat Gallery Commission, Liverpool (UK), 1997.
Low Gallery, Los Angeles (USA), 2001.
The Search for Bez. Cubitt studios Kings Cross, London, 1996.

Selected group exhibitions
The Carnegie International. Pittsburgh (USA), 2004.
Museum of Modern Art, Oxford (UK), 2004.
This Much is Certain. The Royal College of Art, 2004.
Britannia Works. Museum of Contemporary Art, Athens, 2004.
Ill Communication. Contemporary Art Gallery, Dundee (Scotland, UK), 2003.
Electric Earth. Touring exhibition, 2003.
The 4th Sex. Pitti Imagine, Florence (Italy), 2003.
Micro Macro. The Museum of Contemporary Art, Budapest, 2002.
Rock My World. CCAC Wattis Institute, San Francisco (USA), 2002.

ANDREA FACIU
1977, Bucharest (Romania)
Lives in Munich (Germany)

Education
Academy of Arts, Munich (Germany), 2004.
School of Arts *Nicolae Tonitza*, Bucharest, 1991.

Selected group exhibitions
In the Gorges of the Balkans. Kunsthalle Fridericianum, Kassel (Germany), 2003.
Sights. Haus der Kunst, Munich (Germany), 2003.
Vacant Room. Hotel Mariandl, Munich (Germany), 2003.
In the Very Silence. Franziskaner-museum Villingen, Schwenningen (Germany), 2003.
Art on the Ground. Kulturzentrum und Theaterlabor, Schwabhausen (Germany), 2003.
Annual Exhibition. Academy of Arts, Munich (Germany), 2003.
Annual Exhibition. Academy of Arts, Munich (Germany), 2002.
Class Project. Kunstbüro, Hasenbergl (Germany), 2000.
Annual Exhibition. Academy of Arts, Munich (Germany), 1999.

IÑAKI GARMENDIA BARTOLOMÉ
1972, Ordizia (Spain)
Lives in Bilbao (Spain)

Education
Künstlerhaus Bethanien, Berlin, 2004.
Grant from The Culture Dept. of Basque Government, 2001.
Fine Arts, Euskal Herriko Unibertsi-tatea. Bilbao (Spain), 1997.

Selected individual exhibitions
Me Voy a Ir, Me Voy, Estoy Ido. Egiako Kulturetxea D.A.E., Donostia-San Sebastian (Spain), 1998.

Selected group exhibitions
Great Theatre of The World. Taipei Biennial, Fine Arts Museum, Taipei, 2002-2003.
Goierri Konpeti Documentary Premierte/ Front Line Conpilation. D.A.E. Donostia-San Sebastian (Spain), 2002.
Goierri Konpeti Documentary Premierte/ Front Line Conpilation. Touring exhibi-tion: D.A.E.; MNCARS; CCCB; Galerie Le Triangle; Print Temps de Septembre; 2002.
Organisationforms. Skuc Galerija, Ljubjana, 2002.
Super Kongresua. Basque Artists Meeting. Egiako Kulturetxea. D.A.E., Donostia-San Sebastian (Spain), 2001.
Rock Radical Vasco/R.R.V. Installation. Noveles Show. K.M., Donostia-San Sebastian (Spain), 2001.
Exhibition of the workshop directed by A. Bados and T. Badiola. Arteleku, Donostia-San Sebastian (Spain), 1999.
INJUVE 1999. Cí rculo de Bellas Artes, Madrid, 1999.
Kulturetxea. D.A.E., Donostia-San Sebastian (Spain), 1998.

GEERT GOIRIS
1971, Bornem (Belgium)
Lives in Antwerp (Belgium)

Education
Master's Degree in photography, Academy of Fine Arts, Antwerp (Belgium), 2003.
Guest professor, autonomous and

experimental photography, Sint Lukas Higher Institute for Visual Arts, Brussels, 2003.
Member of the Obscuur collective, 2001.
Workshops in the Museum for Photography. Antwerp (Belgium), 2001.
Postgraduate, Higher Institute for Fine Arts. Antwerp (Belgium), 2000.
Member of the board of editors of *Obscuur Tijdschrift*, 2000.
Department of still photography, FAMU Academy of Perfoming Arts, Prague, 1995.
Photography department, Sint Lukas Higher Institute for Visual Arts, Brussels, 1993.

Selected individual exhibitions

The World as We Know It. Prospekto Gallery, with Ville Lenkkeri, Vilnius, 2004.
Lost in Space. Roger Vandaele Editie, Antwerp (Belgium), 2003.
Possibilities. Netwerk Galerij, Aalst (Belgium), 2002.
Frequentie. Lokaal 01, with Kenny Mc. Leod, Antwerp (Belgium), 2002.
Van Wijngaarden Galerie, Amsterdam, 2001.
Surrounded. Galerie Václavy Spály, Prague, 2001.
Kontor in Der Schneiderei, Cologne (Germany), 2001.
Reconstruction. Museum for Photography, Antwerp (Belgium), 2000.

Selected group exhibitions

At Least Begin to Make an End. W 139, Amsterdam, 2003.
Prix Jeune Peinture Belge. Paleis voor schone Kunsten, Brussels, 2003.
Land. Balabanov house, Plovdiv (Bulgaria), 2003.
Provinciale prijs Beeldende Kunst. Koningin Fabiolazaal, Antwerp (Belgium), 2003.
Contemporary Photography from Flanders. Karavanserai Museum, Tbilisi (Georgia), 2003.
Overgangslocaties. Sint-Lukasgalerij, Brussels, 2002.
Blend-Contemporary Photography in Belgium. Caermersklooster, Ghent (Belgium), 2002.
Paramount Basics, Richard Venlet. Museum for Contemporary Art, Antwerp (Belgium), 2002.
Staal / Made in Belgium. Galerie Duchamp, Yvetot Hooghuis, Arnhem (The Netherlands), 2002.
We're Always on the Edge of Wilderness. W 139, Amsterdam, 2001.
goEurope, the Kaleidoscopic Eye. Museum für Photographie, Braunschweig (Germany), 2001.
VLAM Netwerk 2. Hortus Panoramicus, Aalst (Belgium), 2001.
Ici et Maintenant. Tours et taxis, Brussels, 2001.
Introduction a une Philosophie du Presque. De ladder van Pontormo, Ghent (Belgium), 2000.
Short-circuits, Contemporary photography from Flanders. Tallinn (Estonia), 2000.
Geert Goiris/Steve Van Den Bosch. Ruimte IN/OUT, Antwerp (Belgium), 1999.
sPring 98 Young Talent in Antwerp. Antwerp (Belgium), 1998.
Sequentie. Museum Van Humbeek-Piron, Leuven (Belgium), 1998.
Kunst Aanmoedigingsprijs. Amstelveen (The Netherlands), 1998.
Galerie Foto-Medium-Art, Wroclaw

(Poland), 1996.
International Photo Exhibition. Ljubljana, 1995.
Jonge fotografie. Delbekehouse, Antwerp (Belgium), 1993.

KIM HIORTHØY
1973, Trondheim (Norway)
Lives in Oslo (Norway)

Selected individual exhibitions
Life Is Merciless. Andrew Hale, London, 2004.
Jeg er Nesten Alltid Redd. Fotogalleriet, Oslo, 2003.
Trøndelag Kunstnersenter. Trondheim (Norway), 2002.
Tegninger for en Hundrings. Tegnerforbundet Galleri, Oslo, 2001.

Selected group exhibitions
Momentum 04. Moss (Norway), 2004.
Ballpoint. Pentagram Gallery, London, 2004.
Public Address System. Henry Peacock Gallery, London, 2004.
Electric Currents. The Hermitage, St. Petersburg (Russia) 2003.
13. Tomato Gallery, London, 2001.
Inspirert Design. Kunstindustrimuseet, Oslo, 2001.
Design.Scan. Scandinavian Design Center, New York (USA) 2000.
eMotion Picture. Galleri f15, Jeløya (Norway), 2000.
Biennale Syd. Kristiansand Kunstforening (Norway), 1998.
Fellessentralen. Kunstnernes Hus, Oslo, 1998.
Screens. Trondheim (Norway), 1997.
Tegnerforbundet Galleri. Oslo, 1997.
Den Andre Kunsten. UKS, Oslo, 1997.

LAURA HORELLI
1976, Helsinki (Finland)
Lives in Berlin (Germany)

Education
Staatliche Hochschule für Bildende Künste, Städelschule, Klasse Bayrle, Frankfurt a.M. (Germany), 2002.
Department of Time and Space, Academy of Fine Arts, Helsinki, 2001.

Selected individual exhibitions
Galerie im Taxispalais, Innsbruck (Austria), 2004.
Galerie Barbara Weiss, Berlin, 2003.
Kluuvin Gallery, Helsinki, 2001.
Akiyoshidai International Art Village (AIAV), Yamaguchi (Japan), 2000.

Selected group exhibitions
Berlin North. Hamburger Bahnhof, Berlin, 2004.
Kunstbank, Berlin, 2004.
Schrumpfende Städte. Kunstwerke, Berlin, 2004.
In 2052 Malmö will no longer be Swedish. Rooseum, Malmö (Sweden), 2003-2004.
Ill Communication. Contemporary Arts, Dundee (USA), 2003.
GNS. Palais de Tokyo, Paris, 2003.
PR02 [En Ruta]. M&M Proyectos, San Juan, Puerto Rico (USA), 2002.
Rent-a-Bench, Los Angeles (USA), 2002.
Germinations 13. Galeria Arsenal, Bialystok (Poland), 2002.
Plateau of humankind. 49ª Biennale di Venezia, Venice (Italy), 2001.
Ars012. KIASMA, Helsinki, 2001.
Neue Welt. Kunstverein, Frankfurt a.M. (Germany), 2001.

KÜLLI K. KAATS
1975, Tallinn (Estonia)
Lives in Tallinn

Education
Estonian Academy of Arts, Interdisciplinary Arts, M.A. 2000-2003.
Accademia di Belle Arti di Brera, Milan, Italy, 2002-2003.
Estonian Academy of Arts, Faculty of Fine Arts, Department of Graphic Fine Arts (B.A. 2000) 1995-2000.
Estonian Academy of Music, Conducting Department, 1993-1996; 2000-2002 (B.A. 2002).

Selected individual exhibitions
The Catalogue of Birds. Galerii Tuviputka, Estonian Academy of Arts, Tallinn, 2003.
Avifauna, Tallinn City Gallery, 2002.

Selected group exhibitions
My Fatherland is My Love. Artists House, Tartu (Estonia), 2004.
Breath (Estonian video art). Ludwig Museum, Budapest, 2002.
Experiments and Classic, Fideo & Vilm Festival. Pärnu (Estonia), 2002.
12th Tallinn Print Triennial [conditionally existing][conditionally non-existing]. Tallinn, 2001.
Online Auction. The Graduates. ArtLink@Sothebys.com, International Young Art 2001.
Gooseflesh. Video- and performance art festival, Rakvere (Estonia), 2001.
Exhibition of Estonian Art, Artists House, Tartu (Estonia), 2000.
Kiriküüt. Video and film festival, Viljandi (Estonia), 2000.
Your Hidden Life: Estonian Printmaking. Tallinn Art Hall, 1999.
Church 2000. GAADS / Church 24 h. Muhu island (Estonia), 1999.
Raatuse Gallery, Tallinn, 1999.
Media Non Grata. Enter Internet café, Tallinn, 1999.
In Touch. Gallery of the Estonian Academy of Arts, Tallinn, 1998.
Collected Relations. Gallery of the National Library, Tallinn, 1998.

Video art
Blueblackwhite, 2004.
Pigeon, Crow, Seagull, 2003.
The Eye, 2002.
What the Women Want I, II (with Elisabeth Salmin), 2001.
Among the Bird Population III: Choir, 2001.
Among the Bird Population II: The Ward, 2000.
Among the Bird Population I, 2000.
Zefiir Roosa (Pink Zephyr), 2000.
Behave in Cave, 1999.
..., 1999
Emergency Stop, 1999.

Performances
Spring, performance/installation, Tallinn, Tartu (Estonia), 2004.
Tuttpütt Présente (with M. A. students of Interdisciplinary Arts from the Estonian Academy of Arts). Rummu prison (Estonia), 2003.
The Catalogue of Birds. Artistic research in Estonia and Italy, 2002-2003.
Double / Multiple Works. Artistic research (with DIADA laboratorio and Nuova Icona, Italia), Tallinn Children Hospital, 2002.
Man is the Architect of the Universe of Morals (with M.A. students of Interdisciplinary Arts). Estonian Academy of Arts, Tallinn, 2001.
Birth / Don't Teach Me How To Live, Help

Me Financially (with M. A. students of Interdisciplinary Arts). Estonian Academy of Music, Tallinn, 1999.
A-B-R-A-C-A-D-A-B-R-A (with Kristin Kalamees & Katri Sipiläinen). Lone Twin Art Academy, Turku (Finland), 1999.
In the Birds Choir (with students of Estonian Academy of Arts). Muhu island (Estonia), 1999.
Behave in Cave (with Kristin Kalamees, Ly Lestberg & Allan Tõnissoo). Muhu island (Estonia), 1999.

Composition (in music)
Prelude in F, 2001.
External Identification Guide of Estonian Birds. Choir cycle, first performed on May 16, 2001, Teachers Seminar, Tartu (Estonia), 2001.
Little Princess. Cycle of piano pieces, first performed on October 20, 2000, the House of Brotherhood of Blackheads, Tallinn, 2000.

Music in print
External Identification Guide of Estonian Birds. Choir cycle, Edition 49, 2004.
Little Princess, Cycle of piano pieces, *Piano Pieces 2000*, Estonian Music Foundation, 2000.

JOHANNES KAHRS
1965, Bremen (Germany)
Lives in Berlin (Germany)

Selected individual exhibitions
Down'n Out. Zeno X Storage, Antwerp (Belgium), 2003.
Down'n Out. Künstlerhaus Bethanien, Berlin, 2002.
The Drunken Boat. Galerie Almine Rech, Paris, 2002.
A-h. Touring exhibition: SMAK, Ghent (Belgium), 2001; FRAC des Pays de la Loire, Carquefou (France), 2001; Kunstverein, Munich (Germany), 2001.
La Révolution Permanente. Galerie Almine Rech, Paris, 2000.
Night in Sexyland. Zeno X Gallery, Antwerp (Belgium), 2000.
Shot and Painted. Galerie Franck+Schulte, Berlin, 2000.
Last Virgin on the Left. Galerie Signal, Malmö (Sweden), 2000.
Why Don't You Paint My Portrait. Gesellschaft für Aktuelle Kunst, Bremen (Germany), 1998.
Double Stage. 6 Seconds Popular Violence. Galerie Franck+Schulte, Berlin, 1998.
Schwarzes Loch/Weisse Wand. Galerie Franck+Schulte, Berlin, 1998, 1997.
9309- Vorzimmer/4 Klacks. Vereniging Museum voor Hedendaagse Kunst, Ghent (Belgium), 1998.
Hole. Galerie Arndt & Partner, Berlin, 1998.
Thomson Homestead, Slater, Misouri. Galerie Transit, Leuven (Belgium), 1998.
Bild und Malerei. Galerie Wohnmaschine, Berlin, 1995.
Schlag Doch. DAAD Galerie, Berlin, 1994.
Keine Falsche Bewegung. Galerie Mutzek, Berlin, 1993.

Selected group exhibitions
Berlin-Moskau/Moskau-Berlin 1950-2000. Staatliche Tretjakov Galerie, Moscow, 2004.
Voorkamer, Lier (Belgium), 2004.
Was Malerei heute ist. Stiftung Opelvillen, Rüsselheim (Germany), 2004.
Fuori Uso 03. Pescara (Italy), 2003.
Plastik, Plüsh und Politik/Reflexe der

70er Jahre in der Gegenwartskunst. Städtische Galerie Nordhorn, Nordhorn (Germany), 2003.
Berlin-Moskau/Moskau-Berlin 1950-2000. Martin-Gropius-Bau, Berlin, 2003.
Kiss and Ride. Z33/Begijnhof, Hasselt (Belgium), 2003.
Warum! Bilder Diesseits und Jenseits des Menschen. Martin-Gropius-Bau, Berlin, 2003.
A Mains Nues. FRAC Haute-Normandie Sotteville les Rouen (France), 2003.
Deutschemalereizweitausenddrei. Frankfurter Kunstverein, Frankfurt (Germany), 2003.
Great Theater of the World. Taipei Biennial, Taipei, 2002.
Cardinales. MARCO, Vigo (Spain), 2002.
Questions. Studio Massimo de Carlo, Milan (Italy), 2002.
Without Consent. CAN. Centre d'Art, Neuchâtel (Switzerland), 2002.
In/Site/Out. Apex, New York (USA), 2001.
Double-Trouble. Borusan Kültur ve Sanat, Instanbul, 2001.
Moving Pictures. Photography and Film in Contemporary Art. Villa Merkel/ Bahnwärterhaus, Esslingen (Germany), 2001.
Screen. Psychiatrisch Centrum Sleidinge, Sleidinge (Belgium), 2001.
Squatters. Museu Serralves, Porto (Portugal), 2001.
Indoor. SMAK, Ghent (Belgium), 2000.
Children of Berlin. Museum Folkwang, Essen (Germany), 2000.
Dorothea von Stetten Kunstprize. Kunstmuseum, Bonn (Germany); Kunstbank, Berlin, 2000.
Face à l'Autre. FRAC Haute-Normandie, Sotteville les Rouen (France), 1999.
The Children of Berlin. P.S.1, New York (USA), 1999.
Ainsi de Suite 3. Centre d'Art Contemporain, Sète (France), 1999.
Rue Louise Weiss. Centre d'Art Contemporain, Meymac (France), 1999.
Trouble Spot Painting. MuHKA, Antwerp (Belgium), 1999.
Indoor. Musée d'Art Contemporain, Lyon (France), 1999.
Art Club Berlin. AU Base, New York (USA), 1999.
Independance Day. Kunst-Werke, Berlin, 1999.
Drawings. Zeno X Gallery, Antwerp (Belgium), 1999.
EV+A. Limerick City Gallery of Art, Limerick (Ireland), 1999.
Berlin Biennial, Berlin, 1998.
The Cinema Project. Kunstlerhaus Bethanien, Berlin, 1998.
Indoor. Centro Civico per l'Arte Contemporanea, Serre di Rapolano (Italy), 1998.
Le Présent du Futur. FRAC Languedoc-Rousillon, Montpellier (France), 1998.
Kamikaze. Marstall, Berlin, 1998.
Heaven. Private View. P.S.1, New York (USA), 1997.
Selection Fall 1997. Drawing Center, New York (USA), 1997.
Fenêtre sur Cour. Galerie Almine Reich, Paris, 1997.
The Aggression of Beauty. Galerie Arndt & Partner, Berlin, 1996.
Nach Weimar. Kunstsammlungen zu Weimar (Germany), 1996.
Laboratorium Berlin. Moscow. Contemporary Art Center, Moscow, 1996.
Club Berlin. 45ª Biennale di Venezia, Venice (Italy), 1995.
Close Up. Städtische Galerie, Bremen (Germany), 1995.
Filmcuts. Galerie Neugerriemschneider, Berlin, 1995.
Drawings. Galerie Peter Kilchmann,

Zurich (Switzerland), 1995.
A Personal Choice. Galerie Franck+Schulte, Berlin, 1994.
Postconceptual Painting. Kunst-Werke, Berlin, 1994.
Geist und Körper. Deutsches Museum für Geschichte, Berlin, 1990.

LEOPOLD KESSLER
1976, Munich (Germany)
Lives in Vienna (Austria)

Education
Academy of Fine Arts, Munich (Germany), 1998.
Academy of Fine Arts, Vienna, since 1998.

Selected individual exhibitions
Privatisiert. Galerie Corentin Hamel, Paris, 2003.

Selected group exhibitions
Klimatisch im Hoch. Galerie Lisi Hämmerle, Bregenz (Austria), 2003.
VV2. Biennale di Venezia, Venice (Italy), 2003.
Galerie by Night. Studio Galerie, Budapest, 2003.
Critique is not Enough. Shedhalle, Zurich (Switzerland), 2003.
Haunted by Detail. Stichting de Appel, Amsterdam, 2002.
Facing 2. Städtische Galerie, Wels (Austria), 2002.
Parlez vous Français. Galerie Hohenlohe&Kalb, Vienna, 2002.
Interim Plattform. Galerie Kerstin Engholm, Vienna, 2002.
BIG Torino. Biennale of the Youth, Turin (Italy), 2002.
West&Werkstatt. Deichtorhallen, Hamburg (Germany), 2001.
Responsible Transformation. Cittadellarte, Biella (Italy), 2001.
Video etc... Passagengalerie, Vienna, 2001.
Academies of Europe. Castello di Rivoli, Rivoli (Italy), 2000.
Arte al Centro. Cittadellarte, Biella (Italy), 2000.
Nicht aus einer Position. Semperdepot, Vienna, 1999.

MICHEL KHLEIFI
1950, Nazareth (Palestine)
Lives in Brussels (Belgium)

Education
INSAS. Brussels, 1971.

Film
As Script-writer, Director and Producer:
Forbidden Marriages in the Holy Land, 66, documentary, 1995.
Tale Of The Three Jewels. 105' full-length feature film, 1994-1995. Cannes, Quinzaine des Réalisateurs; Isfahan, Golden Butterfly, 1995.
Canticle of the Stones. 100' full-length feature film, 1990. Cannes 1990. Official Selection. Un Certain Regard; Yamagata, Japan, Special Critics Prize; Valencia F.F, Silver Prize.
L'Ordre du Jour. 115' full-length feature film, 1992. Cannes 1987. Quinzaine des Réalisateurs, Prix de la Critique Internationale; San Sebastian (Spain), 1987, Golden Shell; Carthage Film Days, 1988, Golden Tanit.
Wedding in Galilee. 110' full-length feature film, 1985.
Maaloul Celebrates its Destruction. 30' Documentary, 1985.

Fertile Memory, 16mm full-length documentary film, 1980. Cannes 1981, Semaine de La Critique and several international awards.

Television

As Writer/Director & Producer with RTBF (Belgian TV), a series of one-hour documentaries for the weekly program *A suivre: The Road of El-Naim*, a portrait of Naim Khader, PLO representative in Brussels, assassinated in 1981 by Mossad, September 1981.
Ashrafieh, (co-directed with A. Dartevelle), First Prize of the Community of French speaking televisions, documentary series, November 1979.
Peace and the Palestinians, April 1979.
Israeli Settlements in the Sinai, September 1978.
The West Bank, The Palestinians hope?, January 1978.

Theatre

As writer and director:
La Fuite au Paradis. Kunstenfestival des Arts, Brussels, 1998.

MARK LECKEY

1964, London (UK)
Lives in London

Selected individual exhibitions

Parade. Cabinet, London, 2003.
Migros Museum, Zurich (Switzerland), 2003.
Big Box Statue Action.Tate Britain (Tate Egg Live Event), London, 2003.
Mark Leckey's Sound System. Gavin Brown's Enterprise, New York (USA), 2002.
Gavin Brown's Enterprise Corp., New York (USA), 2000.
London, My Part in its Downfall. Galerie Daniel Buchholz, Cologne (Germany), 2000.

Selected group exhibitions

Galerie Daniel Buchholz, Cologne (Germany), 2004.
Ipeg. Bildtonmaschine. Künstlerhaus Bethanien, Berlin, 2004.
Werke aus der Sammlung Boros. Museum für Neue Kunst/ZKM, Karlsruhe (Germany), 2004.
Legende. Film Screening, Filmhaus Kino, Cologne (Germany); Kino Arsenal, Berlin, 2003.
Fast Forward Media Art/Sammlung Goetz, Zentrum für Kunst und Medientechnologie, Karlsruhe (Germany), 2003.
Sample Culture Now. Tate Modern, London, 2003.
Soundsystems. Salzburger Kunstverien, Salzburg (Austria), 2003.
Brighton Photo Biennal, Brighton (UK), 2003.
Rhythm is a Dancer. Kulturhuset, Stockholm, 2003.
Electric Earth. British Council, Touring exhibition in Russian cities, 2003.
Hidden in a Daylight. Foksal Gallery Foundation, Cieszyn (Poland), 2003; Galerie Daniel Buchholz, Cologne (Germany), 2003.
Video Works. De Appel, Amsterdam, 2002.
Electric Dreams. Barbican Centre, London, 2002.
Hotel Sub Rosa. Marc Foxx Gallery, Los Angeles (USA), 2002.
Remix: Contemporary Art and Pop. Tate Liverpool, Liverpool (UK), 2002.
Santa Monica Museum of Modern Art, Los Angeles (USA), 2002.

The Visitors. Théatres du Fantastique, Printemps du Septembre, Toulouse (France), 2001.
Andy Warhol & Sound & Vision. ICA, London, 2001.
Brown. The Approach, London, 2001.
My Generation: 24 hours of Video Art. Truman Brewery, London, 2001.
Century City. Tate Modern, London, 2001.
Protest and Survive. Whitechapel Art Gallery, London, 2000.
Pitti Imagine, Florence (Italy), 2000.
Village Disco. Cabinet Gallery, London, 2000.
Crash. ICA, London, 2000.
London Orphan Society. Openspace, Milan (Italy), 2000.
David Zwirner, New York (USA), 1998.
Gavin Brown's Enterprise, New York (USA), 1996.
ICA New Contemporaries. ICA, London, 1990.

MARIA LUSITANO DA FONSECA MOREIRA SANTOS
1971, Lisbon (Portugal)
Lives in Lisbon

Education
Advanced course on visual arts, MAUMAUS. Escola de Artes Visuais, Lisbon, 2003.
Fase 1 and 2 of Design and Advanced Course of plastic arts Ar.co, Lisbon, 2002.
Faculdade de Medicina de Coimbra, 1997.

Selected group exhibitions
Portugal: 30 artistas abaixo dos 40. Museu Stenersen, Oslo, 2004.
LisbonPhoto com. Museu da Cidade- Pavilhão Preto & Edifí cio INTERPRESS, 2003.
DIA DI BAI. Centro de Artes Visuais, Coimbra (Portugal), 2003.
Prémios EDP. Fundação de Serralves, Porto (Portugal), 2003.
Exposição de Trabalhos de Finalistas e Bolseiros de Ar.co. Centro Cultural de Belém (Portugal), 2002.
Goethe Institut, Lisbon, 2002.
Festival Número. Forum Lisbon, Lisbon, 2002.
Exposição de Finalistas e Bolseiros do Ar.co. Corodoaria Nacional, Lisbon, 2002.
Condutas Privadas. Artemosferas, Porto (Portugal), 2002.
1º ano do Curso Avançado de Artes Plásticas. Ar.co, 2001.
El Dorado; Welcome Center; Escola Maumaus, Lisbon; 2001.

MARK MANDERS
1968, Volkel (The Netherlands)
Lives in Arnhem (The Netherlands)

Selected individual exhibitions
Isolated Rooms. The Art Institute of Chicago (USA), 2003.
Isolated Rooms. The Renaissance Society, Chicago (USA), 2003.
Silent Factory. Pinakothek der Moderne, Munich (Germany), 2003.
Greene Naftali Gallery, New York (USA), 2002.
The Galleries at Moore, Philadelphia (USA), 2002.
Art Gallery of York University, Toronto (Canada), 2002.
Kaleidoscope Night. Kröller/Müller Museum, Otterlo (The Netherlands), 2002.

Yellow Bathtub. Cobra Museum, Amstelveen (The Netherlands), 2002.
Night Drawings. Kabinet Overholland, Stedelijk Museum, Amsterdam, 2000.
Reduced November Room. Greene Naftali Gallery, New York (USA), 2000.
Room with Several Night Drawings and One Reduced Night Scene. The Drawing Center, New York (USA), 2000.
Coloured Room with Black and White Scene. Galerie Friedrich, Berne, 1999.
14 Fragments from Self-portrait as a Building. Staatliche Kunsthalle, Baden (Germany), 1998.
Self-portrait in a Surrounding Area. XXIV São Paulo Biennial, São Paulo (Brazil), 1998.
Zeno X Gallery, Antwerp (Belgium), 1997.
The Douglas Hyde Gallery, Dublin, 1997.
De Appel, Amsterdam, 1997.
Galerie Erika + Otto Friedrich, Berne, 1995.
Zeno X Gallery, Antwerp (Belgium), 1994.
Van Abbemuseum, Eindhoven (Germany), 1994.
MuHKA, Antwerp (Belgium), 1994.

Selected group exhibitions
Sammlung Goetz, Munich (Germany), 2004.
Storage and Display. Programma Art Center, Mexico D.F., 2003.
Contemporary Drawing: Eight Propositions. Museum of Modern Art, New York (USA), 2002.
Documenta 11, Kassel (Germany), 2002.
Tabula. Watou (Belgium), 2002.
Conversation? Recent Acquisitions of the Van Abbemuseum. Athens School of Fine Arts, Athens, 2002.
Free Sport. Greene Naftali Gallery, New York (USA), 2002.
Squatters. Museu de Serralves, Porto (Portugal), 2001.
Plateau of Humankind. Biennale di Venezia, Venice (Italy), 2001.
Post-Nature. Biennale di Venezia, Palazzo Ca'Zenobio, Venice (Italy), 2001.
Dutch Glory. Kabinet Overholland / Stedelijk Museum, Amsterdam, 2001.
Locus Focus. Sonsbeek 9, Arnhem (The Netherlands), 2001.
Museum voor Moderne Kunst, Oostende (Belgium), 2001.
Face to Face. Kabinet Overholland. Stedelijk Museum, Amsterdam, 2000.
Territory. Tokyo Opera City Art Gallery, Tokyo, 2000.
Drawings 2000. Barbara Gladstone Gallery, New York (USA), 2000.
Zeno X Gallery, Antwerp (Belgium), 2000.
3 Räume. 3 Flüsse. Hann Münden (Germany), 1999.
Transmitter. Bonner Kunstverein, Bonn (Germany), 1999.
Zeeuws Museum, Middelburg (The Netherlands), 1999.
Fondazione Sandretto Re Rebaudengo per l'Arte, Turin (Italy), 1999.
De Opening. SMAK, Gent (Belgium), 1999.
Stedelijk Van Abbemuseum, Eindhoven (Germany), 1998.
S.M.A.K. in Watou. Poëziezomers Watou (Belgium), 1998.
Vertical Time. Barbara Gladstone Gallery, New York (USA), 1998.
Fondazione Sandretto Re Rebaudengo per l'Arte, Turin (Italy), 1997.
Belladonna. ICA, London, 1997.
Vereniging voor het Museum van Hedendaagse Kunst, Gent (Belgium), 1996.
Centraal Museum, Utrecht (The Netherlands), 1996.
Zeno X Gallery, Antwerp (Belgium), 1996.
Making a Place. Snug Harbor Cultural

Center, New York (USA), 1996.
Oriëntatie. Stedelijk Museum De Lakenhal, Leiden (The Netherlands), 1995.
Orientasi. National Museum of Modern Art, Jakarta, 1995.
This is the Show and the Show is Many Things. Museum van Hedendaagse Kunst, Gent (Belgium), 1995.
EntrActe 1. Van Abbemuseum, Eindhoven (Germany), 1995.
Films by Dutch Artists. De Vleeshal, Middelburg (The Netherlands), 1995.
Du Concept à l'Image. Art Pays-Bas XXe Siècle. Musée d'Art Moderne de la Ville, Paris, 1994.
En Suite. Vereniging voor het Museum van Hedendaagse Kunst, Gent (Belgium), 1994.
Scuola. Biennale di Venezia, Venice (Italy), 1993.
Sonsbeek 93, Arnhem (The Netherlands), 1993.
Prix de Rome. Museum Fodor, Amsterdam, 1992.

ASIER MENDIZABAL
1973, Ordizia (Spain)
Lives in Bilbao (Spain)

Education
BasisStipendium, grant from Fonds BKVB, Dutch Culture Ministry, 2003.
Fellowship of the Basque Government, with Iñaki Garmendia, 2001.
Residency grant, de-Ateliers, Amsterdam, 2000.
Grant Support to Creation, Diputación de Gipuzkoa, 1998.
Post Graduate diploma, Byam Shaw School of Art, London, 1997.
Workshop directed by Txomin Badiola and Angel Bados, Arteleku, Donostia-San Sebastian, 1997.
Universidad del Paí s Vasco, Fine Arts, Bilbao, 1996.
Erasmus Scholarship, Byam Shaw School of Art, London, 1995.

Selected individual exhibitions
Galerí a T4, Barcelona (Spain), 2003.
De-Ateliers, Amsterdam, 2000.
No Time for Love. D.A.E., Donostia-San Sebastian (Spain), 2000.

Selected group exhibitions
Cine y Casi Cine. Museo Reina Sofí a, Madrid, 2003.
Les Printemps de Septembre. Toulouse (France), 2003.
Lost Territories. Galerie Schroder, L'Aja (Belgium), 2003.
Després de la Notícia. CCCB, Barcelona (Spain), 2003.
Goierri Konpeti. Galerie du Triangle, with Iñaki Garmendia, Bordeaux (France), 2003.
Organisational Forms. Skuç Galerija, Ljubljana, 2002.
Great Theatre of the World. Museum of Fine Arts, Taipei Biennial (Taiwan), 2002.
Gure Artea 2002. Sala Rekalde, Bilbao (Spain), 2002.
Tour/Early Works. De Ateliers, Amsterdam, 2002.
Front Line Compilation. D.A.E. Donostia-San Sebastian (Spain), 2002.
Desartxibo Publicación Para Memoria. Arteleku, Donostia-San Sebastian (Spain), 2002.
Gure Artea 2000. Koldo Mitxelena, Donostia-San Sebastián (Spain), 2000.
Gaur, Hemen, Orain. Museo de Bellas Artes, Bilbao (Spain), 2001.

Flatland Gallery, Utrecht (The Netherlands), 2001.
Parcours d'Incidents. De-Ateliers, with Koenraad Dedobbeleer, Amsterdam, 2001.
Blackout Totale, NICC, with Willem Oorebeek, Antwerp (The Netherlands), 2000.
Intervenciones TV. Festival de Ví deo, Gasteiz-Vitoria (Spain), 2000.
Certamen de Artistas Noveles de Gipuzkoa. Koldo Mitxelena, Donostia-San Sebastian (Spain), 1999.
Exposición del Taller Angel Bados/Txomin Badiola, Reinauguración de Arteleku. Arteleku, Donostia-San Sebastián (Spain), 1998.
Montehermoso-Oihanederra, Gasteiz-Vitoria (Spain), 1998.
Coop. La Central, Donostia-San Sebastian (Spain), 1998.
Sala Barrena, Ordizia (Spain), 1997.
Certamen de Artistas Noveles de Gipuzkoa, Donostia-San Sebastian (Spain), 1997.
Byam Shaw, London, 1997.

BORIS MIKHAILOV
1938, Kharkiv (Ukraine)
Lives in Kharkiv and Berlin (Germany)

Selected individual exhibitions
Palau de la Virreina, Barcelona (Spain), 2004.
Museu Serralves, Porto (Portugal), 2004.
Boris Mikhailov: Private Freuden, Lastende Langeweile, Öffentlicher Zerfall, Eine Retrospektive. Fotomuseum Winterthur (Switzerland), 2003.
TV Mania. Galerie Barbara Weiss, Berlin, 2002.
The Insulted and the Injured. Pace/MacGill Gallery, New York (USA), 2002.
TV Mania. Galerie der Stadt Schwaz, 2002.
Boris Mikhailov: Case History & Heiner Müller Projekt. Haus der Kulturen der Welt, Berlin, 2001.
BildMuseet, Humea (Sweden), 2001.
Orchard Gallery, Derry (England), 2001.
The Photographic Museum, Helsinki, 2001.
Saatchi Gallery, London, 2001.
Boris Mikhailov. The Photographers' Gallery, London, 2000.
Dvir Galerie, Tel Aviv (Israel), 2000.
Galerie Barbara Gross, Munich (Germany), 2000.
Boris Mikhailov. 2000, Hasselblad Award Winner. Hasselblad Center, Göteburg (Sweden), 2000.
By the Ground. Museum of Modern Art, Ljubliana, 1999.
Boris Mikhailov. Querini Stampalia Museum, Venice (Italy), 1999.
Case History. DAAD Galerie, Berlin, 1999.
Case History and Dance. Scalo Galerie, Zurich (Switzerland), 1999.
Boris Mikhailov. Centre National de la Photographie, Paris, 1999.
Boris Mikhailov. Stedelijk Museum, Amsterdam, 1998.
Boris Mikhailov. Les Misérables (About the World). Sprengel Museum, Hannover (Germany), 1998.
Peri Center of Photography, Turku (Finland), 1998.
Photomania. DAAD Galerie, Berlin, 1997.
Crimean Grafomania. Galerie in der Brotfabrik, Berlin, 1997.
Hippolyte Photographie Galerie, Helsinki, 1997.
Boris Mikhailov. Kunsthalle Zurich (Switzerland), 1996.
Boris Mikhailov. A Retrospective. Soros

Center of Contemporary Art, Kyiv, 1996.
After the Fall. The Institute of Contemporary Art, Philadelphia (USA), 1995.
Boris Mikhailov. Portikus, Frankfurt am Main (Germany), 1995.
Hotel Europa, Foto Festival, Rotterdam (The Netherlands), 1994.
Perspektief Photographic Center, Rotterdam (The Netherlands), 1994.
Boris Mikhailov 1970-1991. Forum Stadtpark, Graz (Austria), 1992.
Museum of Contemporary Art, Tel Aviv (Israel), 1990.
Boris Mikhailov: Arles. Paris 1989. Signalhallen, Armémuseum, Stockholm, 1990.
The Missing Picture, Alternative Contemporary Art from the Soviet Union. Visual Arts Center, Lizt (Austria); Cambridge (UK), 1990.

OKSANA PASAIKO

1982 Ruthenia
Lives in Ruthenia

In accordance with the wishes of the artist, no details of her life shall be published.

ANU PENNANEN

1975, Kirkkonummi (Finland)
Lives in Helsinki (Finland)

Education

MFA in the Academy of Fine Arts in Helsinki Department of Time-Based Art, 2003.
BFA in the Turku Polytechnics Arts and Media Department, 2000.
Nordic School of Art Kokkola Finland, 1995.

Selected individual exhibitions

Lamp Works. The Academy of Fine Arts Gallery, Helsinki, 2003.
I Traded my Safety for the Glass Beads of Fantasy. Gallery Just, Turku (Finland), 2000.

Selected group exhibitions

Audiovisual Darcy Ribeiro, Rio de Janeiro (Brazil), 2004.
Heavy Snowflakes. Ex Teresa Arte Actuel, Mexico D.F., 2004.
Momentum. Moss (Norway), 2004.
5th Year Students MFA Spring Exhibition. The Academy of Fine Arts, Helsinki, 2003.
Nuoret 2003, *The Young Artists Exhibition*. Kunsthalle, Helsinki, 2003.
New Media Festival. CMU Art Museum, Chiang Mai (Thailand), 2003.
Enter.video. New Finnish Art. part 3. Embassy of Finland, London, 2003.
LAB. Video Art at Sörnäinen Metro Station. Helsinki, 2002.
Finns Behaving Badly? Finnish Video Art. Gallery Lontar, Jakarta, 2002.
Realm of The Senses. Art Museum, with Johanna Ekman, Turku (Finland), 2000.
2000.katastro.fi. This Moments Futures? Kiasma Museum of Contemporary Art, Helsinki, 1999.
Temporary Media Lab. Kiasma Museum of Contemporary Art, Helsinki, 1999.
Photographs. Gallery Zone, Helsinki, 1998.

GARRETT PHELAN

1965, Dublin (Ireland)
Lives in Dublin

Selected individual exhibitions

RACER RECAPTURED. SS Michael and

John, Essex Street West, Dublin, 2003.
NOW: HERE. Pallas Heights, Dublin, 2003.

Selected group exhibitions

Permaculture. Project, Dublin, 2003.
Affinity Archive. Metropolitan Complex, Dublin, 2003.
National Gallery, Goethe Institute, Dublin, 2003.
How Things Turn Out. Irish Museum of Modern Art, Dublin, 2002.
FRAC. Alsace (France), 2000.
Le Credac d'Ivry sur Seine, Paris, 1999.
Third Annual Santa Fe International Festival of Electro-Acoustic Music, Santa Fe (USA), 1999.
Outside. The Douglas Hyde Gallery, Dublin 1997.
Kerlin Gallery, Dublin, 1997.
Glen Dimplex Artists Award, Dublin, 1997.
Irish Museum of Modern Art, Dublin, 1997.
L'Imaginaire Irlandais. Le Confort Moderne, Poitiers (France), 1996.
LMC, London, 1998.
Invited EV+A, Limerick (UK), 1996.
Kerlin Gallery, Dublin, 1995.

KIRSTEN PIEROTH

1970, Offenbach (Germany)
Lives in Berlin (Germany)

Education

Staatliche Hochschule für Bildende Künste, Städelschule, Frankfurt am Main (Germany), 1999.

Selected individual exhibitions

Klosterfelde, Berlin, 2003.
Mellemdækket Projektrum. Charlottenborg Udstillingsbygning, Copenhagen, 2002.
There Are Two Temperatures: One Outside, One Iinside, with Henrik Olesen. Galleria Franco Noero, Turin (Italy), 2002.
Helga Maria Klosterfelde, Hamburg (Germany), 2001.
Sparwasser HQ, with Kirstine Roepstorff. Berlin, 2001.
Klosterfelde, Berlin, 2000.
Rraum, Frankfurt am Main (Germany), 2000, 1998.
Projektraum Daimlerstraße, with Anke Weyer. Frankfurt am Main (Germany), 1998.

Selected group exhibitions

Adorno. Kunstverein, Frankfurt (Germany), 2003.
SPECTACULAR: The Art of Action. A Program on Performance and the Art Institution. Museum Kunstpalast, Düsseldorf (Germany), 2003.
Open Studio Project. Townhouse Gallery, Cairo, 2003.
Frankenstein. Tanya Bonakdar Gallery, New York (USA), 2003.
GNS. Palais de Tokyo, Paris, 2003.
Dreams and Conflicts. Biennale di Venezia, Utopia Station, Venice (Italy), 2003.
The Berlin Files. Dechiara Gallery, New York, (USA), 2002.
Haunted by Detail. De Appel, Film Programme at Filmmuseum, Amsterdam, 2002.
Efterarsudstillingen 2001. Charlottenborg Udstillingsbygning, Copenhagen, 2001.
Retur. Copenhagen, 2001.
First Biennial of Tirana, Tirana, 2001.
IASPIS Gallery, Stockholm, 2000.
Ausdruck und Sinnbild. Phantombüro, Frankfurt (Germany), 1999.
OTTO hat Besuch. Ausstellungsraum

OTTO, Copenhagen, 1999.
C/o Rathenaustraße, Offenbach (Germany), 1999.
Stuttgart, 17.7.1956-Salem (Wis.)/USA, 3.3.1977. Portikus, Frankfurt (Germany), 1998.
Internationale Buchmesse, Frankfurt (Germany), 1997.
Downtown. Städelsches Kunstinstitut, Frankfurt (Germany), 1997.
Sommerpause. Kunstverein, Offenbach (Germany), 1996.
Wir Begegnen Uns Nicht Zufällig. Haus am Lützowplatz, Berlin, 1995.

PAOLA PIVI

1971, Milan (Italy)
Lives in Milan

Selected individual exhibitions

MACRO, Rome, 2003.
Wrong Gallery, New York (USA), 2003.
Edizioni di Gioielli Elena Levi. Gallery Roma, 2002.
Alicudi Project. Centre d'Art Contemporain, Bretigny sur Orge (France), 2002.
Galerie Emmanuel Perrotin, Paris, 2001.
Galleria Massimo De Carlo, Milan (Italy), 2001.
Alicudi Project. Galerie Michael Neff, Frankfurt (Germany), 2001.
Paola Pivi. Castello di Rivoli, Rivoli (Italy), 2000.
Gallery Massimo De Carlo, Milan (Italy), 1998.

Selected group exhibitions

Dreams and Conflicts. Biennale di Venezia, Venice (Italy), 2003.
Signatures of the Invisible. P.S.1, Brooklyn (USA), 2003.
World Speak Less Dumb. Uplands Gallery, Melbourne (Australia), 2003.
Contemporary Start. Rome, 2003.
ExIT. Fondazione Sandretto Re Rebaudengo, Turin (Italy), 2002.
Tutto Normale. French Academy in Rome, Villa Medici, Rome, 2002.
Magical Machines. Edith Russ-Haus fur Medienkust, Oldenburg (Germany), 2002.
De Gustibus. Palazzo delle Papesse, Siena (Italy), 2002.
Signatures of the Invisible. Centre d'Art Contemporain, Geneva (Switzerland), 2002.
No Return. Museum Abteiberg, Monchengladbach (Germany), 2002.
Ouverture. Palais de Tokyo, Paris, 2002.
Marking the Territory. Irish Museum of Modern Art, Dublin, 2001.
Chain of Vision: Family, Politics and Religion in the Last Generation of Italian Contemporary Art. Hara Museum of Contemporary Art, Tokyo, 2001.
Sonsbeek 9: Locus Focus. Arnhem (The Netherlands), 2001.
Uniform, Order and Disorder. P.S.1 Contemporary Art Center, New York (USA), 2001.
Boom, Manifattura Tabacchi-Manifattura d'Arte – Florence (Italy), 2001.
Play. Openspace, Milan (Italy), 2001.
Signatures of the Invisible. Atlantis Gallery, London, 2001.
Dinamiche della Vita dell'Arte. Galleria d'Arte Moderna e Contemporanea, Bergamo (Italy), 2001.
Uniform, Order and Disorder. Stazione Leopolda, Florence (Italy), 2000.
Migrazioni e multiculturalità. Contemporary Arts Center, Roma, 2000.
Window onto Venus. Havana Biennial exhibition (Cuba), 2000.

Talentum, Tolerare, Prize Querini-Furla for Art. Querini Stampalia Foundation, Venice (Italy), 2000.
Clockwork 2000, P.S.1 National and International Studio Program 1999-2000. Clocktower, New York (USA), 2000.
Identitades Futuras, Reflejos de una Colección. Sala de Exposiciones del Canal de Isabel II, Madrid, 2000.
Au-Delà. Klosterfelde Gallery, Berlin, 1999.
Soggettività e Narrazione, Cinema e Cinema d'Artista. Castello di Rivoli (Italy), 1999.
YOUNG@ALL.AGES. Deweer Art Gallery, Otegem (Belgium), 1999.
L'Autre Sommeil. ARC, Paris, 1999.
Globale Positionen. Museum in Progress, Der Standard, Vienna, 1999.
P.S.1 Italian Bureau Selection 1998-2000. Cittadellarte, Pistoletto Foundation, Biella (Italy), 1999.
Serendipiteit. Watou (Belgium), 1999.
d'APERTutto. 48ª Biennale di Venezia, Venice (Italy), 1999.
Gallery Shanghart, Shanghai (China), 1999.
Zone. Especès d'Espaces. Sandretto Re Rebaudengo Foundation, Guarene d'Alba (Italy), 1999.
Destination is Wherever it Arrives. Salon3, London, 1999.
Simone Berti / Paola Pivi. Galleria SALES, Roma, 1999.
Guarene Arte 98. Sandretto Re Rebaudengo Foundation, Guarene d'Alba (Italy), 1998.
Cannibali. Un'altra sceneggiatura. La Triennale, Milan (Italy), 1998.
Opera Nuova. Fuori Uso 98, Mercato Ortofrutticolo, Pescara (Italy), 1998.
Imitating Christmas. Wiensowski & Harbord, Berlin, 1998.
Light Slow. Galleria Massimo De Carlo, Milan (Italy), 1998.
Opera Prima. Galleria Cesare Manzo, Pescara (Italy), 1997.
Jingle Bells 806. Galleria Massimo De Carlo, Milan (Italy), 1997.
Mercato Globale-Fuori Uso in Provincia- Ex Colonia Stella Maris, Montesilvano (Italy), 1997.
Amplikon. Via Farini, Milan (Italy), 1997.
Invitation to a Pointless Investigation. Via Farini, Milan (Italy), 1997.
A Month on the Lake. Ratti Foundation, Como (Italy), 1996.
Transatlantic. Via Farini, Milan (Italy), 1995.

KYRILL KAZIMIROVICH PROTSENKO
1967, Kyiv (Ukraine)
Lives in Kyiv

Education
Kyiv Academy of Fine Arts.
Member Union Artists of Ukraine.

Selected individual exhibitions
3D Message. with DJ Derbastler, KIMAF, Kyiv, 2002.
Radio Eurasia. Audioexcursion. With DJ Derbastler, Part of Dynamo Machine. Kyiv, 2001.
...CUBA,...POR FAVOR... RA Gallery, Kyiv, 2001.
1 DJs monument, with Illya Chichkan, Kyiv International Media Art Festival, 2000.
Radio Eurasia. with DJ Derbastler Paris, 1999.
No Comment. Central House of Artists, Kyiv, 1997.
Spazio Umano, Milan (Italy), 1997.

The Artifacts of Horizontal or Shit is the Same Everywhere. Central House of Artists, Kyiv, 1995.
Woodbuming. BRAMA Contemporary Art Center, Kyiv, 1995.
World Wide Art Gallery, New York (USA), 1995.
Falling Star. BLANK Gallery, Kyiv, 1994.

Selected group exhibitions
36,6°. RA Gallery, Kyiv, 2003.
EXTRA SCHENGEN. Venice (Italy), 2003.
REBELL MINDS. Berlin, 2002.
Modern and Traditions. Tbilisi (Georgia), 2001.
...undabdiePost!999! Berlin, 1999.
Intermedia. Kyiv, 1998.
The Crimean project. Kyiv, 1998.
The Crimean project 2 . Livadia palace, Crimea (Ukraine), 1998.
Aipe Adria Cinema Festival, Trieste (Italy) ,1997.
Europe...Humanisme. Selest Art (France), 1997.
Loup y es-tu? Espace Diogene, Pézénas (France), 1996.
Dr. Frankenstein study Neochimerism. Odessa (Ukraine), 1995.
Aipe Adria Cinema Festival, Trieste (Italy), 1995.
MonPlaisir. Kyiv, 1994.
The Space of Cultural Revolution. Kyiv, 1994.
Free Zone. Odessa (Ukraine), 1994.
Ukraine National TV, 1994.
Benefit for the National Museum of Ukrainian Art. Auction, Kyiv, 1993.
Prix Futura, Berlin, 1993.
Still. Kyiv , 1992.
Summer. Kyiv, 1992.
Art of Paris Commune. Kyiv, 1991.
Mozart and Sallied. Kyiv, 1991.

MARC QUER
1965, Villepinte (France)
Lives in Marseille (France)
Education
D.E.F.A., Ecole d'Architecture de Marseille (France).
D.N.S.E.P. (Diplôme National Superieur d'Expression Plastique), Ecole des Beaux Arts de Marseille (France).

Selected exhibitions
A Comme Architecture. Galerie Duchamp, Ivetot (France), 2003.
Unisci i Punti. Galleria Neon, Bologna (Italy), 2003.
Comment travailler à l'échelle? La Compagnie, Marseille (France), 2003.
Marcher, c'est Seduisant mais Casse Gueule. Château de Servières, Marseille (France), 2003.
Quatre Coins, on irait s'asseoir sur la Caisse. Pretexte à Danser/FRAC-PACA, La Compagnie, Marseille (France), 2002
Ma Mère ma dit: et ton Métier, alors? Entrée 9, Avignon (France), 2002.
Amenagements Interieurs. Public, Paris, 2002.
Self/In Material Conscience. Fondazione Sandretto, Guarene (Italy), 2002.
Fond Commun de Lecture. Entrée 9, Avignon (France), 2002.
Trouvé, Retrouvé. LME, Marseille (France), 2001.
TELEPOLART. Sol, Murs, Plafond, Marseille (France), 2001.
La Toison d'Or. Sabine Wachters, Fine Arts, Brussels, 2001.
La Santé des Restes. Musée Ziem, Martigues (France) , 2001.
Arte Marsiglia. Centre Culturel Français de Turin (Italy), 2000.
Un Monde dans une Coquille de Noix 2. FRAC-PACA, Marseille (France), 2000.

Prélèvements d'Espaces. Friche de la Belle de Maï, FRAC-PACA, Marseille (France), 2000.
Un Monde dans une Coquille de Noix 1. FRAC-PACA, Marseille (France), 1999.
Mutations Sigulières. Musée des Tapisseries, Aix-en-Provence (France), 1999.
Troisième Festival de l'Art en Vidéo. Musée dArt Contemporain, Lyon (France), 1999.
Transfert. Interface 4, Marseille (France), 1998.
Les Photographies du Portefeuille. Les Ateliers Nadar, Marseille (France), 1998.
Aux Armes...et Caetera. Kuenstlerwerkstatt, Münich (Germany), 1998.
Les Artistes entrent en Gare. Château de Servières, Marseille (France), 1998.
Eternuements. Galerie le Faou, Marseille (France), 1998.
Algérie, France: Images. La Compagnie, Marseille (France), 1998.
Neuf Lavomatiques près de Chez vous. Ergo, Rennes (France), 1998.
Z.U.P. FRAC Poitou-Charentes, Angoulème (France), 1998.
Je vous prête une Oeuvre. Château de Servières, Marseille (France), 1998.
Collections d'Automne. MAC, Marseille (France), 1997.
Normale, Droite, Tordue. Galerie le Faou, Marseille (France), 1997.
La Dernière Roue du Carrosse. Art Dealers 2, Marseille (France), 1997.
Amitiés et Autres Catastrophes, La Carte du Tendre. Crestet Centre d'Art, Vaison-La-Romaine (France), 1997.
Gadget. Sol, Murs, Plafond, Marseille (France), 1997.
Vds Transporter Volkswagen-Contrôl Technique O.K.-1980-TBE. Galerie Redoulés, Toulouse (France), 1997.
Tutto Bene. Interface MMM, Marseille (France), 1997.
Des Chaussures dans le Frigo. Interface MMM, Marseille (France), 1996.
Projets. Sol, Murs, Plafond, Marseille (France), 1996.
Les Nouvelles de l'Art. Galerie Athanor, Marseille (France), 1996.
Souviens-toi, Sylvie. BAD Foundations, Rotterdam (The Netherlands), 1996.
Arta Contemporana în Sudul Frantei. AFAA Musées Nationaux Roumains, Bucarest/Craï ova/Constansta (Romania), 1996.
Laisse le Gras dans le Plat. Anonymes Autochtones, Marseille (France), 1996.

DANIEL ROTH
1969, Schramberg (Germany)
Lives in Karlsruhe (Germany)

Education
Studium an der Staatlichen Akademie der Bildenden Künste, Karlsruhe, bei Harald Klingelhöller, 1996.

Selected individual exhibition
Cabrini Green Forest. Donald Young, Chicago (USA), 2004.
To HMP Weare. Portland, Fons Welters, Amsterdam, 2004.
Museum der Bildenden Künste, Leipzig (Germany), 2003.
Kunstverein, with Johannes Wohnseifer, Aachen (Germany), 2003.
701XXKA, Grazer Kunstverein, Graz (Austria), 2003.
Galerie Karin Günther, with Jeanne Faust, Hamburg (Germany), 2003.
Inside the White Cube, London, 2003.
Schatzhauserwald. Meyer Riegger Galerie, Karlsruhe (Germany), 2002.

The Thermal Bath of the Naked Truth. Vision1, Michele Macarone Inc., New York (USA), 2002.
Artist Space, New York (USA), 2001.
Galerie Fons Welters, Amsterdam, 2001.
Das Linke Bein des Offiziers. Kunsthaus Glarus, Glarus (Switzerland), 2000.
Wie die Leichen der Mafia vorbeitreiben. Galerie Johnen & Schöttle, Köln (Germany), 1999.
Weller Volker. Meyer Riegger Galerie, Karlsruhe (Germany), 1998.
Galerie Thomas Riegger, Karlsruhe (Germany), 1996.

Selected group exhibition

Fiction Mouse on Mars. reviewed & remixed. Kunsthalle Düsseldorf (Germany), 2004.
Actionbutton. Sammlung zeitgenössischer Kunst der BRD, Hamburger Bahnhof, Berlin, 2003.
Unbuilt Cities. Bonner Kunstverein, Bonn (Germany), 2003.
Ars Viva Landschaft 2002. Kunstverein Zwickau, Kunstverein Hamburg (Germany), 2003.
Transfer. Kunstraum, Munich (Germany), 2003.
A Need for Realism. Centrum Stzuki Ujazdowski, Warschau (Poland), 2002.
Ars Viva Landschaft 2002. Kunstverein Zwickau, Kunstverein, Augsburg (Germany), 2002.
Effet Larson. Casino, Luxemburg, 2002.
Persönliche Pläne. Kunsthalle, Basel (Switzerland), 2002.
Centre pour l´image contemporaine, Ghent (Belgium), 2002.
CTRL Space. Zentrum für Kunst- und Medientechnologie, Karlsruhe (Germany), 2001.
Effet Larson. O.K. Centrum für Gegenwartskunst, Linz (Austria), 2001.
Szenarien, oder der Hang zum Theater. Kunstverein, Bonn (Germany), 2001.
Archisculptures. Kunstverein Hannover (Germany), 2001.
Under the Bridge along the River. Casino, Luxembourg, 2001.
Futureworld. Museum Abteiberg, Mönchengladbach (Germany); Museum van Bommel van Dam, Venlo (The Netherlands), 2001.
Superman in Bed. Sammlung Schürmann, Museum am Ostwall, Dortmund (Germany), 2001.
Berlin Biennial, Kunstwerke, Berlin, 2001.
Le Republiche Dell´Arte. Germania, la Costruzione di un´Immagine. Palazzo delle Papesse-Centro Arte Contemporanea, Siena (Italy), 2001.
K&S, Berlin, 2000.
Art in the World 2000. Musée d'Art Moderne de la Ville, Paris, 2000.
Art Agents Gallery, Hamburg (Germany), 2000.
Montreal Biennial (Canada), 2000.
Songlines. Halle für Kunst, Lünburg (Germany), 2000.
Escape-Space. Ursula Blickle Stiftung, Kraichtal (Germany), 2000.
Modell, Modell. Neuer Aachener Kunstverein, Aachen (Germany), 2000.
Hallöchen, Hallöchen. De Lege Ruimte, Ghent (Belgium), 2000.
Xn00. Chalon (France), 2000.
Officina Europa. Galleria d´Arte Moderna, Bologna (Italy), 1999.
A Radiant Future. Forde, Geneva (Switzerland), 1999.
Songs from a Room. Meyer Riegger Galerie, Karlsruhe (Germany), 1998.
Junger Westen, Kunstpreis-Kunsthalle, Recklinghausen (Germany), 1997.

MICHAEL SAILSTORFER
1979, Vilsbiburg (Germany)
Lives in Vienna (Austria)

Education
MA in Fine Art, Goldsmiths College, University of London, 2004.
Akademie der Bildenden Künste, Munich (Germany), 2003.

Selected individual exhibitions
Attitudes, Ghent (Belgium), 2004.
D-IBRB. Transit, Mechelen (Belgium), 2003.
Welttour. Galerie Markus Richter, Berlin, 2003.
Heimatlied. Basement, Galerie Markus Richter, Berlin, 2002.

Selected group exhibitions
Degree Show 2004, MA Fine Art. Goldsmiths College, London, 2004.
Sydney Biennial, Sydney, 2004.
BHF Live Set + Sailstorfer. Galleria Zero, Milan (Italy), 2004.
Wings of Art. Ludwig Forum für internationale Kunst, Aachen (Germany), 2004.
Fuoriuso 2003. Pescara (Italy), 2003.
Head on. Homeroom, Munich (Germany), 2003.
Wir, hier! Lothringer 13/halle, Munich (Germany), 2003.
At Least Begin to Make an End. W 139, Amsterdam, 2002.
Und sie bewegt sich doch! Museumsplatz, Städtische Galerie im Lenbachhaus, Munich (Germany), 2002.
Mit dem Kopf durch Wand! Akademiegalerie, Munich (Germany), 2002.
3 x 1. Galerie Nusser und Baumgart, Munich (Germany), 2002.
Oltre il Giardino. Rimini (Italy), 2002.
Preis der Darmstädter Sezession. Bewerberschau, Ziegelhütte, Darmstadt (Germany), 2002.
Extra Dunkel. Alte Mälzerei, Regensburg (Germany), 2002.
Junger Westen 2001. Kunsthalle Recklinghausen (Germany), 2001.
Acht x Anders. Centro de Arte Joven, Madrid, 2001.

SILKE SCHATZ
1967, Celle (Germany)
Lives in Köln (Germany)

Education
MA, Hochschule für Bildende Künste, Braunschweig (Germany), 1995.
School of the Art Institute, Chicago (USA), 1992.

Selected individual exhibitions
The Kleinfamilie. Anthony Wilkinson Gallery, London, 2003.
Ehemalige Reichsabtei, with Johannes Wohnseifer, Kornelimünster, Aachen (Germany), 2002.
Ich Merkte, Dass was Passiert War, Denn ich bin ja Nicht Dumm. Borgmann Nathusius, Köln (Germany), 2001.
Verorten. Meyer Riegger Galerie, Karlsruhe (Germany), 2001.
Transmission. Anthony Wilkinson, London, 2000.
Schnitt Ausstellungsraum. with Hardwig Schwarz, Köln (Germany), 1999.
Hellwacher Tagtraum. Kunstverein, Braunschweig (Germany), 1999.
Open Eyed Daydream. Brent Sikkema, New York (USA), 1999.
HE IM AT. Meyer Riegger Galerie, Karlsruhe (Germany), 1998.
The Meinersen Show. Künstlerhaus,

Meinersen (Germany), 1997.

Selected group exhibitions

Docu/fiction, Mouse on Mars Reviewed & Remixed. Kunsthalle, Düsseldorf (Germany), 2004.
Mengenbüro/Stirling. The Changing Room, Stirling (Scotland), 2004.
Shaping the Imagination: Artists Explore the Language of Architecture. De Zonnehof, Amersfoort (The Netherlands), 2003.
A Nova Geometria. Galeria Fortes Vilaca, Sao Paulo (Brazil), 2003.
International Paper. UCLA Hammer Museum, Los Angeles (USA), 2003.
Domestic. Apexart, New York (USA), 2002.
Drawing on Space. Project Arts Center, Dublin, 2002.
Come In. Wanderausstellung des Instituts für Auslandsbeziehungen, Stuttgart (Germany), 2002.
Die Kraft der Negation. Theater der Welt, Schauspielhaus Köln (Germany), 2002.
Drawing Book of Space. Fa Projects, London, 2002.
Persönliche Pläne. Kunsthalle, Basel (Switzerland), 2002.
Museum für zeitgenössische Kunst und Art Galerie L-ART, Kyiv, 2002.
A SPORT & A PASTTIME. Greene Naftali, New York (USA), 2001.
New Settlements. Nikolaj Contemporary Art Center, Copenhagen, 2001.
Playing amongst the Ruins. Royal College of Art, London, 2001.
Turning Into A Loop. Gio Marconi, Milan (Italy), 2000.
Kabinett der Zeichnung. Kunstverein, Düsseldorf (Germany), 2000.
Escape-Space. Ursula Blickle Stiftung, Kraichtal (Germany), 2000.
Deutsche Kunst in Moskau. Central House of Artist, Moskow, 2000.
Hallöchen, Hallöchen. De Lege Ruimte, Gent (Belgium), 2000.
ZeitWenden Ausblick Kunstmuseum Bonn (Germany), 1999.
Private Werte. Künstlerwerkstatt Lothringer Straße, Munich (Germany), 1999.
Bildung. Kunstverein, Graz (Austria), 1999.
Lokalzeit/Localtime. 1st. Biennial of Niedersachsen, Schloß Agathenburg, Stade (Germany), 1999.
Silke Schatz et Olivier Dollinger á SKOPIA Art Contemporain. Ghent (Belgium), 1999.
Songs from a Room. Meyer Riegger Galerie, Karlsruhe (Germany), 1998.
Surfacing, Contemporary Drawing. ICA, London, 1998.
OSYGUS. Produzentengalerie, Hamburg (Germany), 1998.
INGIENOOK II. University Galleries of Illinois State University, Illinois (USA), 1998.
Junger Westen. Kunstpreis. Kunsthalle, Recklinghausen (Germany), 1997.
Eröffnung-Opening-Opnum. Villa Minimo, Hannover (Germany), 1997.

MARKUS SCHINWALD

1973, Salzburg (Austria)
Lives in Vienna (Austria)

Education

University fG, Linz (Austria).
Humboldt University, Berlin (Germany).

Selected individual exhibitions

Dictio Pii. Sprengl Museum, Hannover

(Germany), 2004.
Kunstverein, Frankfurt (Germany), 2004.
Ceaseless Blur. TAV Gallery, Taipei, 2003; Gallery Georg Kargl, Vienna, 2003.
...Seconds. Kunstverein, Goldegg (Austria), 2002.
Dictio Pii. Moderna Museet, Stockholm, 2001.
Warp. Tanzquartier, Vienna, 2001.
Oxygen, Flipping through Kiesler. MAK Center for Art and Architecture, Los Angeles (USA), 2000.
Kunstverein, Freiburg (Germany), 1999.
Gallery Karin Günther, Hamburg (Germany), 1999.
GAP. Museum Fridericianum, Kassel (Germany), 1999.
Stage. Museum in Progress, Vienna, 1999.

Selected group exhibitions
3 Condensed Information. Schirn Kunsthalle, Frankfurt (Germany), 2004.
Ulysess. Atelier Augarten, Vienna, 2004.
One in a Million. Austrian Cultural Forum, New York (USA), 2004.
Lodz Biennial (Poland), 2004.
Haus der Kunst, Munich (Germany), 2003.
Adorno. Kunstverein, Frankfurt (Germany), 2003.
Horror der Kunst. Kunstverein, Graz (Austria), 2003.
Re-Produktion 2. Georg Kargl Gallery, Vienna, 2003.
Videodrome. Cosmic Gallery, Paris, 2003.
Dreams and Conflicts. Biennale di Venezia, Utopia Station, Venice (Italy), 2003.
Bewitched, Bothered and Bewildered. Migros Museum, Zurich (Switzerland), 2003.
LAZNIA Centre for Contemporary Art, Gdansk (Poland), 2003.
How Big is the World. Museum of Fine Arts, Kaohsiung (Taiwan), 2003.
In Passing. Pavel House, Potrana (Italy), 2003.
The Air is Blue. Barragan Museum, Mexico D.F., 2003.
Animation: Videos. Centre d'Èdition Contemporaine, Geneva (Switzerland), 2002.
Waiting for the Ice Age. Georg Kargl, Vienna, 2002.
Dialogs. O.K. Center for Contemporary Art, Linz (Austria), 2002.
Untragbar. Museum für Angewandte Kunst, Cologne (Germany), 2001.
Tirana Biennial. Tirana, 2001.
At your Service. Galerie Gasser & Grunert, New York (USA), 2000.
Exit. Chissenhalle Gallery, London, 2000.
Die Neue Künstlergeneration. Kunsthalle, Krems (Austria), 2000.
That's Art. Museum Nordico, Linz (Austria), 2000.
Drive in. Litfastrasse, Vienna, 1999.
Destination is Wherever it Arrives. Salon 3, London, 1999.
Projektwerkstatt. O.K. Center for Contemporary Art, Linz (Austria), 1999.
Expanded Design. Kunstverein Salzburg (Austria), 1999.
Contemporary. Self. Portrait. Sean Kelly Gallery, New York (USA), 1998.
Leisz, Schinwald, Heger/Dejanov. Kunstverein, Graz (Austria), 1998.
Berlin Biennial. Berlin, 1998.
Fast Forward. Kunstverein, Hamburg (Germany), 1998.
Junge Szene. Secession, Vienna, 1998.
Liquid Beauty. Halle für Kunst, Lüneburg (Austria), 1998.

Imitating.... Galerie Wiensowski&Harbord, Berlin, 1998.
Time Out. Kunsthalle, Nürnberg (Germany), 1997.
Sonic Tonic. Läufer, Linz (Austria), 1997.
Inner Space. Galerie 5020, Salzburg (Austria), 1997.
Warming Up. Ballgasse, Vienna, 1997
Falling and suspension. Galerie A4, Wels (Austria), 1997.

CONRAD SHAWCROSS

1977, London (UK)
Lives in London

Education

MFA, Slade School of Art, University College, London, 2001.
BA, Fine Art, Honours, Ruskin School of Art, Oxford (UK), 1998.
Foundation, Chelsea School of Art, London, 1996.

Selected individual exhibitions

The Nervous Systems. Entwistle, London, 2003.

Selected group exhibitions

New Blood. The Saatchi Gallery, London, 2004.
After Life, Death: Remembrance. Redundancy. Reanimation. Bowes Museum, County Durham (UK), 2004.
Dead Game. Museum 52, London, 2003.
It was Bigger than All of Us. Prenelle Gallery, Canary Wharf, London, 2002.
Fame and Promise. 14 Wharf Road, London, 2002.
New Contemporaries 2001. Camden Arts Centre, London; Northern Centre for Contemporary Art, Sunderland (UK), 2001.
Engine II (Communicating at an Unknown Rate). The Old Armory, Harrow Road, London, 2001.
Engine I. Dollard Street Studios, Vauxhall, London, 2000.

EYAL SIVAN

1964, Haifa (Israel)
Lives in Paris (France)

Film

Au sommet de la descente, Fiction, 32 minutes, 2001.
The Specialist, Long-format documentary, 123 minutes, 1999.
Official Selection, Berlin Film Festival, 1999.
Adolf Grimme Prize (Germany), 2001.
Prix de la 7ème Quinzaine du Jeune Cinéma Fançais, Genova (Italy), 2000.
Prix du Festival France Cinéma, Florence (Italy), 1999.
Population in danger, Series of 4 x 13 minutes documentaries, 1996: *Burundi, under Terror; Itsemba, Rwanda One Genocide Later.* Merit Winner, International Film Festival, San Fransisco (USA), 1997.
Special Mention at the Bilbao Documentary Festival Bilbao (Spain), 1997.
Aqabat-jaber, peace with non return. 60' documentary, 1995.
Jerusalem, borderline syndrome. 64' documentary, 1994.
Itgaber, he will overcome. 2 x 85 ' documentary, 1993.
About Science and Values and *About State and Law Israland.* 58' documentary, 1991.
Official Selection, Etats Généraux du Documentaire, Lussas (France), 1991.
Izkor, Slaves of Memory. 97' documen-

tary, 1991. Prix Procirep & Mention Spéciale du Jury FIPA, 1991; Prix d'Investigation, Biennale Européenne du Documentaire, Marseille (France), 1991;
Golden Lens, Tel Aviv (Israel), 1991.
Aqabat jabber, passing through, 81' documentary, 1987. Grand Prix du Jury, Festival *Cinéma du Réel*, Paris, 1987; Golden Crown at the Festikon, Amsterdam, 1988; Prix Air France & Radio France at the Rencontres Ciné-matographiques, Belfort (France), 1988; Jury Prize (Socio-political section), International Film Festival, Oakland (EUA), 1988; Special Jury Mention, Internationale Filmwoche, Mannheim (USA), 1988.

Television Programs
11 TV spots for the *Progressive List for Peace* (Israel), 1988.
Conceptualisation of a thematic evening for Arte entitled *Jerusalem*, Jerusalem, 1994.
Artistic director of *Scalpel*, a series of 13 x 45 minutes documentaries for Arte, 2001.

HITO STEYERL
1966, Munich (Germany)
Lives in Berlin (Germany)

Education
PhD in philosophy.

Selected exhibitions
Berlin Biennial. Berlin, 2004.
Wiener Festwochen. Vienna, 2004.
City of Women. Ljubljana, 2003.
Plattform 1, Documenta 11. Berlin, 2001.
Heimat Kunst. Berlin, 2000.
Continental Shifts. Ludwig Forum für Internationale Kunst, Aachen (Germany), 2000.
Duisburger Filmwoche. Duisburg (Germany), 2000.
Dokumentarfilmfestivals. Munich (Germany), 2001.
Diagonale. Graz (Austria), 2001.
Internationale Kurzfilmtage. Oberhausen (Germany), 2001.
Viennale 2000, Vienna, 2000.
Feminale. Köln (Germany), 2000;
Black International Film Festival 2000, International Festivals, Pesara (Italy).
Translocation. Vienna, 1999.

MISHA STROJ
1974, Ljubljana (Slovenia)
Lives in Vienna (Austria)

Selected individual exhibitions
The Bourgeoise Show. Dunkers Kulturhus, Helsingborg (Sweden), 2003.
Am Fluss (treibt eine Wespe die schläft aber bloß). Kerstin Engholm Galerie, Vienna, 2003.
Research, Berlin, Berlin, 2002.
Sans Press Release. The Mathew Buck-ingham Choice, Apex Art, New York (USA), 2002.
Cinematexas, with E. Einhorn, Texas (USA), 2002.
Schmarotzer. Academy of Fine Arts, Vienna, 2002.
Was glänzt hat kein eigenes Licht. Kerstin Engholm Galerie, Vienna, 2002.
Die Kunst der Stunde... Laznia Center of Contemporary Art, Gdansk (Poland), 2001.
Public Art Project. Glasgow (Scotland, UK), 2000.

Junge Kunst 2000. Dorotheum, Vienna, 2000.
40x50x180, Transart-Symposium. Vienna, 1999.

Selected group exhibitions
Kontext, Form, Troja. Secession, Vienna, 2003.
Transart-Symposium 3, 2000.

TOOAUP - THE OFFICE OF ALTERNATIVE URBAN PLANNING

Verónica Arcos
1974, Punta de Arenas (Chile).
Lives in Rotterdam (The Netherlands).
Graduated Cum Laude at the Universidad Central, Santiago (Chile) in 2001. Arcos's work was exhibited at Air project—an urban installation over the ventilation of the Santiago underground railway—and at the First Architecture Biennale Rotterdam, 2003. During 2003 she worked in Stefano Boeri Arch, Milan (Italy), and in Sadar-Vuga Arhitekti, Ljubljana. She has also been included in collective exhibitions in Kunstwerke, Berlin; Biennale di Venezia, Venice (Italy), and Koper (Slovenia). Her main research focus is the potential of architecture as an urban articulator—when the architectural installation acts not only as an object, but as a key piece within the city's integration, aiming at the activation of dead places, social interaction and appropriation.

José Arnaud Bello
1976, Oaxaca (Mexico).
Lives in Barcelona (Spain).
Graduated at Universidad Iberoamericana, Mexico D.F., MA in Landscape Urbanism at the Architectural Association School of Architecture, London. He has collaborated with Desarrollo Sistematizado de Proyectos, Mexico D.F., Laboratorio Ciudad de México, and Ace Gallery Mexico, Mexico D.F., all between 2001 and 2002. During 2003-2004 he has been teaching at the Berlage Institute, Rotterdam (Netherlands) and at the Architectural Association School of Architecture, London. His work has been featured in several exhibitions and publications.

Sannah Belzer
1979, Rotterdam (Netherlands).
Lives in Rotterdam.
Graduated Cum laude at Design Academy. Belzer joined the Berlage Institute in 2002, also collaborating in the independent projects *Urban Gallery* (with Raoul van Bunschoten), *Border Devices* (with Stefano Boeri) and *34 km of Adriatic Coast* (with Bostjan Vuga). Belzer's work has been exhibited in Turin and Milan (Italy), and in Amsterdam and Rotterdam (Netherlands). Her work has received awards in several competitions and is featured in magazines such as *Elle*, *Frame*, *Detail* and *Architectur*.

Sebastián Khourian
1969, La Plata (Argentina).
Lives in Barcelona (Spain).
Khourian received his architectural degree from Facultad de Arquitectura y Urbanismo, Universidad Nacional de La Plata in 1994, scholar of National Department of Education and the Austrian Academic Exchange Service during 1995 to study at TU Vienna, guest student of architects Enric

Miralles and Peter Cook at Hochschüle für Bildende Künste Städelschule, Frankfurt (Germany) in 1995-1997, Second Candidate at the Organization of American States Scholarship Program, and Scholar of the Fulbright Commission and National Fund for The Arts to study at the Master in Advance Architectural Design, Graduate School of Architecture, Planning and Preservation, Columbia University New York, where graduated in 1998 with the honor Price for Excellence in Design. In 1998, back in Argentina, Khourian starts his academic activity at the Center of Studies of Contemporary Architecture (CEAC), Universidad Torcuato Di Tella, co-directing LabDisDig (Digital Design Lab) responsible for activities related to the use of new digital techniques and tools applied to design. In 1999 under the sponsorship of the CEAC, he developed El Retiro, a proposal for Plaza San Martí n in Buenos Aires with architect Clorindo Testa, and also with the CEAC undertakes a research project on infrastructural systems in the Valentí n Alsina area of Buenos Aires, that later becomes the catalyzer for the theoretical/operative ideas of Meshworks, a field of design practice that he co-directed until 2000. Between 1999 and 2000 he was involved in the Project Development Team of the Metropolitan Design Center, initiated by the Department of Industry, Commerce and Work of Buenos Aires.
Since 2001 Khourian teaches at the Landscape Urbanism MA Program of the Architectural Association School of Architecture, London. In 2002 he was awarded Second Prize by Building Design/Corus for the Young Architect of the Year Award, London. He has currently established his practice in Barcelona and engages in an academic affiliation with the Berlage Institute in Rotterdam.

Juan Pablo Porta
1974, Buenos Aires (Argentina).
Lives in Barcelona (Spain).
Architect graduated at the Universidad de Buenos Aires in 1998, MA in Landscape Urbanism at the Architectural Association, London in 2002. He has collaborated as a teacher in various institutions such as the Universidad de Buenos Aires (Cátedra de Arquitectos Varas), Elisava school of design, Barcelona (Spain), and Universitat Pompeu Fabra, Barcelona (Spain). In 2003 he established the research office Difference Matters, which works on issues of operative capacities and methodology in the design field. Porta is currently dedicated to the construction project of a new general hospital in Cartagena (Spain).

Claudia Strahl
1975, Kempten (Germany).
Lives in Rotterdam (The Netherlands).
BA in architecture from University Wuppertal (Germany) in 2001. While studying, Strahl performed a practice semester at the office Brandlhuber + Kniess b&k+, worked as assistant to Prof. Claus Bury, and as a freelancer at the atelier of Tony Cragg and at various offices in Cologne, Düsseldorf and Wuppertal (Germany).
In 2002 Claudia Strahl received the DAAD scholarship and joined the Berlage Institute Rotterdam (The Netherlands). She also participated in the

First Architecture Biennale Rotterdam, 2003.

Mónica Villate
1976, Bogotá (Colombia).
Lives in Rotterdam (The Netherlands).
BA in Architecture from Universidad Jorge Tadeo Lozano, 2001. Villate joined the Berlage Institute in 2002, where she has been developing her research on architecture as an element not to be made but to be discovered through the study of the different stimuli produced by the city and its individuals.
Villate's work has been featured in publications such as *FiveMinuteCity*, 2002, and *A+U*, 2003, and exhibited at the First Architecture Biennale Rotterdam, and *Territories*, Kunstwerke, Berlin, both in 2003.

Costanze Zehi
1973, Munich (Germany).
Lives in Rotterdam (The Netherlands).
Graduated in architecture at the Fachhochschule München and finished practical training in Berlin. In 2002 Zehi joined the Berlage Institute with the support of a DAAD scholarship, where she has been developing a study on architectural interventions operating as information mediators, which reflect and interact with all the communication processes among the citizens. These interactions should induce mirroring processes that activate participation and communication in public spaces within a City. Her work has been exhibited at the First Architecture Biennale Rotterdam and *Territories*, Kunstwerke, Berlin, both in 2003.

PATRICK TUTTOFUOCO
1974, Milan (Italy)
Lives in Milan

Selected individual exhibitions
My Private #2. Via Pasteur, Milan (Italy), 2004.
Studio Guenzani, Milan (Italy), 2002.
Studio Guenzani, Milan (Italy), 2000.

Selected group exhibitions
On Air:Video in Onda dall'Italia. Galleria Comunale d'Arte Contemporanea, Monfalcone (Italy), 2004.
Dreams and Conflicts. Biennale di Venezia, La Zona, Venice (Italy), 2003.
Art Digital Vidéo. (France), 2002.
Spectacular. Museum Kunstpalast, Düsseldorf (Germany), 2003.
Interferenze Urbane/ Urban Interferences. Europalia, Brussels, 2003.
Framing my View. Galleria Maze, Turin (Italy), 2002.
Centro per le Arti Contemporanee, Rome, 2002.
Exit. Centro d'Arte Contemporanea, Fondazione Sandretto Re Rebaudengo, Turin (Italy), 2002.
Nuovo Spazio Italiano. MART Trento e Rovereto, Palazzo delle Albere, Trento (Italy), 2002.
LArte del Gioco. Museo Archeologico, Aosta (Italy), 2002.
Tensio. Galleria Comunale d'Arte Contemporanea, Monfalcone (Italy), 2002.
Hops! Festival of Visual and Performing Arts. Link, Bologna (Italy), 2001.
Magic and Loss Contemporary Italian Video. Touring exhibition: Lux Centre, London; Artistinvetrina Fendissime, Roma; Man Museo d'Arte Provincia, Nuoro (Italy), 2001.

Turn On. Ikon Gallery, Birmingham (UK), 2001.
Il Dono. Palazzo delle Papesse, Centro Arte Contemporanea, Siena (Italy); Centro Culturale Candiani, Mestre (Italy), 2001.
Boom. Florence (Italy), 2001.
Le Rire d'Echo. Centre d'Art Contemporain, Geneva (Switzerland), 2001.
Turn-up, Clip-on, Plug-in. Teatro Studio, Scandicci (Italy), 2001.
Casino 2001: Quadriennial of Contemporary Art. Stedelijk Museum Voor Actuele Kunst (SMAK); Gent (Belgium), 2001.
Fatica sprecata. Viafarini, Milan (Italy), 2000.
Fuori Uso 2000, The Bridges (Arte in Autostrada). Pescara (Italy), 2000.
L'Art dans le monde 2000. Pont Alexandre III, Paris, 2000.
Video Take. Openbare Bibliotheek, Leuven (Belgium), 2000.
Something Old, Something New, Something Borrowed, Something Blue. Casa Masaccio, San Giovanni Valdarno (Italy), 1999.

SERGEY VISHNEVSKY

1969, Moscow (Russia)
Lives in Moscow

Education

Moscow Pedagogical University.
V. I. Lenin, Art-graphic faculty, Moscow.
New Strategies in Contemporary Art, Open Society Institute (Soros Foundation-Russia), Moscow.
Memory of 1905 Art School, Moscow.

Selected individual exhibitions

Oleg. Winter-Theatre Gallery, with Victor Alimpiev, Moscow, 1998.
Oleg Videoversion. Spider & Mouse Gallery, with Victor Alimpiev, Moscow, 1999.

Selected group exhibitions

Russian Videoart. Art in General, New York (USA), 2004.
International Short Film Festival. Oberhausen (Germany), 2003.
Art Moscow Workshops. Moscow, 2003.
Horizon of Realities. MuKHA Museum of Contemporary Art, Antwerp (Belgium), 2003.
Art Klyasma. Boarding House Klyazma Reservoir, Moscow, 2003.
Son un artista italiano. It is very pleasant! The Russian artist. Piacere! NCCA, Moscow; The Centre of contemporary art Spazio Umano, Milan (Italy), 2002.
Solar Pavilion. Festival of Contemporary Art in the Bay of Pleasure, Boarding House Klyazma Reservoir, Moscow, 2002.
The Urgent Reporting. Touring exhibition Russian cities, 2002.
SuperVision. Yugnosakhalinsk, Moscow, 2001.
Up-and-Coming. Film-Festival, Hannover (Germany), 2001.
Week of Russian Cinema. Graz (Austria), 2001.

VANGELIS VLAHOS

1971, Athens (Greece)
Lives in Athens

Education

MFA in the Manchester Metropolitan University, Manchester (UK), 1997.
BFA in the School of Fine Arts, Athens 1995.

Selected individual exhibitions
Els Hanappe Underground, with Alan Michael, Athens, 2002.
Els Hanappe Underground, Athens, 2001.
Venetia Kapernekas Fine Arts, Inc., New York (USA), 1999.

Selected group exhibitions
3rd biennial for contemporary art, Berlin, 2004.
Breakthrough! Greece 2004: Contemporary Perspectives in the Visual Arts. Alcala 31, Madrid, 2004.
Strange Messengers. The Breeder Projects, Athens, 2003.
Sandroni Rey Gallery, Los Angeles (USA), 2001.
Interplay. Museum of Contemporary Art, Tucson (USA), 1999-2000.
Immediate. Site Gallery, Sheffield (UK), 1999-2000.
Slipstream. Centre for Contemporary Arts, Glasgow (Scotland, UK), 1998.

GILLIAN WEARING
1963, Birmingham (England, UK)
Lives in London

Education
B.A. (Hons.) in Fine Art, Goldsmiths College, University of London, 1990.
B.TECH in Art & Design, Chelsea School of Art, 1987.

Selected individual exhibitions
Kiasma Museum of Contemporary Art, Helsinki, 2004.
Album. Gorney Bravin+Lee, New York (USA), 2003.
Album. Maureen Paley Interim Art, London, 2003.
Mass Observation. Touring exhibition: Museum of Contemporary Art, Chicago; ICA Philapelphia (USA); Musée dArt Contemporain, Montreal, 2003.
Trilogy. Art Gallery, Vancouver (Canada), 2002.
Centro Galego de Arte Contemporánea, Santiago (Spain), 2001.
Unspoken. Kunstverein, Munich (Germany), 2001.
Sous Influence. Musée d'Art Moderne de la Ville, Paris, 2001.
La Caixa, Madrid, 2001.
Bluecoat Gallery, Liverpool (UK), 2001.
Regen Projects, Los Angeles (USA), 2000.
Serpentine Gallery. London, 2000.
Gorney Bravin+Lee. New York (USA), 2000.
Galerie Anne de Villepoix. Paris, 1999.
Gallery Koyanagi, Tokyo, 1998.
Centre d'Art Contemporain, Geneva (Switzerland), 1998.
Jay Gorney Modern Art, New York (USA), 1997.
Wiener Secession, Vienna, 1997.
Kunsthaus Zurich (Switzerland), 1997.
Emi Fontana, Milan (Italy), 1997.
Le Consortium, Dijon (France), 1996.
Western Security. Hayward Gallery, London, 1995.
Maureen Paley Interim Art, London, 1994.

Selected group exhibitions
Social Creatures: How Body Becomes Art. Sprengel Museum, Hannover (Germany), 2004.
Revolving Doors. Fundación Telefónica, Madrid, 2004.
Strange Days. Museum of Contemporary Art, Chicago (USA), 2003.
Synopsis III. Fiction and Reality. National

Museum of Contemporary Art, Athens, 2003.
Happiness: a Survival Guide for Art & Life. Mori Art Museum, Tokyo, 2003.
Outlook, International Art Exhibition 2003. Athens, 2003.
Inaugural Exhibition. Regen Projects, Los Angeles (USA), 2003.
Face Off. Kettles Yard, Cambridge (UK), 2002.
Die Wohltat der Kunst: Post\Feministische Positionen der 90er Jahre aus der Sammlung Goetz. Staatliche Kunsthalle, Baden (Germany), 2002.
Coming of Age. The New Art Gallery, Walsall (Germany), 2002.
To Whom it May Concern. California College of Arts and Crafts, San Francisco (USA), 2002.
I Promise its Political. Museum Ludwig, Cologne (Germany), 2002.
Remix: Contemporary Art and Pop. Tate, Liverpool (UK), 2002.
Bienal de São Paulo. Sao Paulo (Brazil), 2002.
The Video Show. Central Museum, Utrecht (The Netherlands), 2002.
Acquisitions 2001. Part 1: Photographs, Video Installations, Video. National Museum of Contemporary Art, Athens, 2002.
Inner State of Health: The Person in the Mirror of Contemporary Art. Kunstmuseum, Liechtenstein (Germany), 2001; Biennial of Contemporary Art Lyon (France), 2001.
Milano Europa 2001. La Triennale, Milan (Italy), 2001.
Confidence pour Confidence. Casino Luxembourg, 2001.
Video Evidence. Southampton City Art Gallery, Southampton (UK), 2001.
Film Festival Rotterdam. Museum Boijmans Van Beuningen, Rotterdam (The Netherlands), 2001.
Telling Tales: Narrative Impulses in Recent Art. Tate, Liverpool (UK), 2001.
ABBILD Recent Portraiture and Depiction. Landemuseum Joanneum, Graz (Austria), 2001.
No World Without You, Reflections of Identity in New British Art. Herzliya Museum of Art, Tel Aviv (Israel), 2001.
W. Centre d'Art Mobile, Besançon (France), 2001.
Birningham Ikon Gallery, Birmingham (UK), 2001.
Century City. Tate Modern, London, 2001.
Intelligence: New British Art 2000. Tate Britain, London, 2000.
Puerile 69. The Living Art Museum, Reykjaví k, 2000.
Tate Modern Collection. Tate Modern, London; Autowerke, Deichtorhallen, Hamburg (Germany); Contemporary Art Center, Cincinnati (USA), 2000.
Biennial of Sydney. Museum of Contemporary Art, Sydney, 2000.
Docudrama. Bury St. Edmunds Art Gallery, Bury St. Edmunds (UK), 2000.
Tate Britain Collection. Tate Gallery, London, 2000.
Let's Entertain. Walker Art Center, Minneapolis (USA), 2000.
Quotidiana. Castello di Rivoli, Turin (Italy), 2000.
Makeshift. ArtPace, San Antonio (USA), 2000.
Rewind to the Future. Bonner Kunstverein, Bonn (Germany); Neue Berliner Kunstverein, Berlin, 1999.
People. Le Spot, Contemporary Art Centre, Le Havre (UK), 1999.
Hundstage. Gesellschaft für Aktuelle Kunst, Bremen (Germany), 1999.

Ex-Change. La Criee-Centre dArt Contemporain, Rennes (France), 1999.
The Viewing Room. Kansas City Art Institute, Kansas City (USA), 1999.
This Other World of Ours. TV Gallery, Moscow, 1999.
Common People. Fondazione Sandretto Re Rebaudengo per l'Arte, Turin (Italy), 1999.
Sweetie: Female Identity in British Video. The British School at Rome (Italy), 1999.
Searchlight: Consciousness at the Millennium. The California College of Arts and Crafts, Oakland (USA), 1999.
Private Room/Public Space. Almeers Centrum Hedendaagse Kunst, Al Almere (The Netherlands), 1999.
Rattling the Frame: The Photographic Space 1974-1999. SF Camerawork, San Francisco (USA), 1999.
6th International Istanbul Biennial, 1999.
Garden of Eros. Centre Cultural Tecla Sala, Barcelona (Spain), 1999.
La Sphere de L'Intime. Le Printemps de Cahors, Saint-Cloud (France), 1998.
Real/Life: New British Art. Touring exhibition in Japan: Prefectural Museum of Fine Arts, Tochigi; City Art Museum, Fukuoka; Museum of Contemporary Art, Hiroshima; Museum of Contemporary Art, Tokyo, 1998.
Musée du Rochechouart, Rochechouart (France), 1998.
Videorama. Depot, Kunst und Diskussion, Vienna, 1998.
White Noise. Kunsthalle, Berne, 1998
ENGLISH ROSE in Japan, The Ginza Artspace, Tokyo, 1998.
The Turner Prize 1997. Tate Gallery, London, 1997.
Sensation, Saatchi Collection. Royal Academy of Art, London, 1997.
In Visible Light: Photography and Classification in Art, Science and the Everyday. Museum of Modern Art, Oxford (UK), 1997.
Pandaemonium; London Festival of Moving Images, ICA, London, 1996.
I.D. Van Abbe Museum, Eindhoven (The Netherlands), 1996.
Life/Live. ARC/ Musée d'Art Moderne de la Ville, Paris, 1996.
Full House.Young British Art. Kunstmuseum Wolfsburg (Germany), 1996.
Playpen & Corpus Delirium. Kunsthalle Zurich, (Switzerland), 1996.
A/Drift: Scenes from the Penetrable Culture. Center for Curatorial Studies, Bard College, New York (USA), 1996.
The Fifth New York Video Festival. The Film Society of Lincoln Center, New York (USA), 1996.
NOW:HERE. Louisiana Museum of Modern Art, Humlebaek (Denmark), 1996.
Traffic. CAPC Musée Contemporain, Bordeaux (France), 1996.
X/Y. Centre Georges Pompidou, Paris, 1995.
Campo. Biennale di Venezia, Venice (Italy), 1995.
Brilliant! New Art from London. Walker Art Center, Minneapolis (USA), 1995.
Aperto 95. Nouveau Musée, Institut dArt Contemporain, Villeurbanne (France) 1995.
Hotel Mama (Aperto 95), Kunstraum, Vienna, 1995.
Make Believe. Royal College of Art, London, 1995.
Le Shuttle. Künstlerhaus Bethanien, Berlin, 1994.
Uncertain Identity. Galerie Analix B & L Polla, Geneva (Switzerland), 1994.
Okay Behaviour. 303 Gallery, New York (USA), 1993.

Clove 1. The Clove Building, London, 1991.
Empty Gestures. Diorama Art Centre, London, 1991.

CATHY WILKES
1966, Belfast (Northern Ireland, UK)
Lives in Glasgow (Scotland, UK)

Selected individual exhibitions
Raucci/ Santamaria Gallery, Naples (Italy), 2004.
Douglas Hyde Gallery, Dublin, 2004.
Gallerie Giti Nourbaksch, Berlin, 2004.
The Modern Institute, Glasgow (Scotland, UK), 2004.
She Good. Kabinet für Aktuelle Kunst, Bremerhaven (Germany), 2003.
Inverleith House, Edinburgh, 2002.
Migros Museum, Zurich (Switzerland), 2002.
Cubitt Gallery, London, 2001.
Our Misfortune. Transmission, Glasgow (Scotland, UK), 2001.
Mr So and So. Galerie Giti Nourbaksch, Berlin, 2001.

Selected group exhibitions
SMAK, Ghent (Belgium), 2004.
Independence. South London Gallery, London, 2003.
Plunder: Culture as Material. DCA, Dundee (Scotland, UK), 2003.
Happy Outsiders. Zacheta Gallery, Warsaw; City Gallery of Contemporary Art, Katowice (Poland), 2002.
Kwangju Biennial. *Kwangju* (South Korea), 2002.
Circles °4 One for One. ZKM, Karlsruhe (Germany), 2001.
Psycho-Bobble. Galleria Raucci/Santa Maria, Naples (Italy), 2001.
Here and Now. Dundee Contemporary Arts (Scotland, UK), 2001.
Seven Scottish Artists. Grant Selwyn Fine Art, Beverly Hills (USA), 2000.
Film Club 2, with Elizabeth Go. London, 2000.
Beck's Futures. ICA, London; CCA, Glasgow (Scotland, UK); Cornerhouse, Manchester (UK), 2001.
Die Gefahr im Jazz, Berlin, 2000.

AMELIE VON WULFFEN
1966, Breitenbrunn/ Oberpfalz (Germany)
Lives in Berlin (Germany)

Education
Kunstakademie, Munich (Germany), 1994.

Selected individual exhibitions
Galerie Gabi Senn. Vienna, 2003.
Wo die Dämmerung Grün ist. Galerie Ascan Crone, Berlin, 2002.
Museum der römischen Kultur. Kunstverein, Braunschweig (Germany), 2001.
Telos, Munich (Germany), 1999.
Das Schloß, (zus. mit Josef Strau im Rahmen von Snowflake Office). Galerie Walbröl, Düsseldorf (Germany), 1999.

Selected group exhibitions
Dreams and Conflicts. Biennale di Venezia, Venice (Italy), 2003.
Malerei Ausstellung Null Drei Deutschland. Galerie Christian Nagel, Köln (Germany), 2003.
Animation. Kunst Werke, Berlin, 2003.
Ars Viva 02/03-Landschaft. Städtisches Museum, Zwickau (Germany), 2003.
Ars Viva 02/03-Landschaft. Touring exhibition: Kunstverein, Hamburg

(Germany), 2003.
Deutsche Malerei Zweitausendunddrei. Frankfurter Kunstverein, Frankfurt (Germany), 2003.
Banished Poets. Greene Naftali Gallery, New York (USA), 2003.
Ars Viva 02/03. Landschaft. Neue Galerie im Höhmannhaus, Kunstsammlungen Augsburg (Germany), 2002.
Hossa. Centro Cultural Andratx, Mallorca (Spain), 2002.
Unheim, Capricci und Anarchitekturen. Stadthaus, Ulm (Germany), 2002.
Metropolitan. Galerie Jürgen Becker, Hamburg (Germany), 2002.
Tomorrows Fish & Chips. Berlin, 2002.
HIER IST DORT 2. Wiener Secession, Vienna, 2002.
Favoritin, Berlin, 2001.
Galerie Ascan Crone, Hamburg (Germany), 2001.
Greene Naftali Gallery, New York (USA), 2001.
Zero Gravity. Kunstverein, Düsseldorf (Germany), 2001.
Paper. Galerie Borgmann und Nathusius, Köln (Germany), 2001.
Die Gefahr im Jazz. Straßburgerstraße 4, Berlin, 2000.
Hey International Competition Style. TENT, CBK, Rotterdam (The Netherlands), 2000.
Produktivität und Existenz. Kunstamt Kreuzberg/ Bethanien, Berlin, 2000.
Deutsche Kunst in Moskaw. Central House of Artist, Moscow, 2000.
Out of Space. Kölnischer Kunstverein, Köln (Germany), 2000.
Include me Out. Provost Street, London, 2000.
...Laufend Bilder. Kunstverein, Ludwigsburg (Germany), 2000.
Landscape. Galerie Giti Nourbakhsch, Berlin, 2000.
Clara. Galerie Ascan Crone, Hamburg (Germany), 2000.
Freizeit und Überleben. Galerie im Taxispalais, Innsbruck (Austria), 1999.
How is Your Work Going? Galerie Nagel, Berlin, 1999.
Snowflake Office. Greene Naftali Gallery, New York (USA), 1999.
Off the Wall. New Work on Paper from Berlin. DNA Gallery, Provincetown (USA), 1995.
Die Utopie des Designs. Kunstverein München, als Teil einer Projektgruppe, Munich (Germany), 1994.

YEVGENIY YUFIT
1961, St. Petersburg (Russia)
Lives in St. Petersburg

Selected exhibitions and Films screenings
Filmmuseum, Munich (Germany), 2004.
ICA, London, 2003.
32nd International Film Festival, Rotterdam (The Netherlands), 2003.
MOMA, New York (USA), 2003.
Yale University, New Haven (USA), 2002.
Anthology Film Archives, New York (USA), 2001.
University of Pittsburgh (USA), 2001.
After the Wall. Touring exhibition: Moderna Museet, Stockholm; Ludwig Museum, Budapest; Hamburger Bahnhof, Berlin; 2000.
MOMA, New York (USA), 1999.
Archipelago, Stockholm, 1998.
Stedelijk Museum, Amsterdam, 1997.
Exhibition of Contemporary St. Petersburg Artists. St. Petersburg (Russia), 1997.
MOMA, New York (USA), 1997.
The State Russian Museum,

St. Petersburg (Russia), 1997.
Harvard Film Archive, Boston (USA), 1996.
Film Society of The Lincoln Center, New York (USA), 1995.
Berlin Film Academy, Berlin, 1995.

OLIVIER ZABAT
1965, Grenoble (France)
Lives in Paris (France)

Education
AFAA, Section nouvelles images, Villa Medicis Hors Les Murs, 2002.
FIACRE, Section vidéo et nouvelles technologies, Ministère de la Culture, 1998.
AFAA, Section arts plastiques, Villa Medicis Hors les Murs, 1996.
Mastère des Beaux-Arts, Paris, 1991.
Diplôme Supérieur des Beaux-Arts, Grenoble (France), 1990.

Selected individual exhibitions
Pequeno Desfile Urbano. Centro Cultural Banco do Brasil, Rio de Janeiro (Brazil).

Selected group exhibitions
Le Prototype Cinématographique, Festival du Film de Vendôme, Vendôme (France), 2004.
Festival Internacional de Cine Independiente (BAFICI), Buenos Aires, 2004.
Alternative Histories of Modern Conflict in the Projected Image, 1914-2003. Imperial War Museum, London, 2003.
L'Envers du Monde. Espace Paul Ricard, Paris, 2003.
MK2 Bibliothèque, Paris, 2003.
Es is Schwer, das Reale zu Berühren. Kunstverein München, Munich (Germany), 2003.
Based upon True Stories/After the War. Festival International du Film de Rotterdam, Rotterdam (The Netherlands), 2003.
Entre Vues. Festival de Cinéma de Belfort, Belfort (France), 2002.
Mémoires Vives. Galerie Nationale du Jeu de Paume, Paris, 2002.
What? A Tale in Free Images. Memlingmuseum, Bruges (Belgium), 2002.
Festival International du Documentaire de Marseille. Le Variétés, Marseille (France), 2002.
7èmes Vidéogrammes. Vidéochroniques, Marseille (France), 2002.
Festival International du Cinéma Nouvelle Génération. Cité Internationale, Lyon (France), 2002.
Catastrophe. Internationale Kurzfilmtage, Oberhausen (Germany), 2002.
Les Vertus sont des Titres, les Souffrances sont des Droits. FRAC, Poitou-Charente (France), 2002.
Productions Vidéos et Films Récents ou Inédits. Projection au Centre Georges Pompidou, Paris, 2002.
Boxer. Kunsthalle Tirol, Innsbruck (Austria), 2002.
Traversées. Musée d'Art Moderne de la Ville de Paris, 2002.
New Video Brazil. Pacific Film Archive/ Berkeley Museum, Berkeley (USA), 2002.
Absences-Fraever. Touring exhibition in Norway, 2002.
Du Bist die Welt. Festival Fest Wochen-Künstlerhaus, Vienna, 2002.
A Look Apart. Walker Art Center, Minneapolis (USA), 2002.
My generation. Atlantis Gallery, London, 2002.

DAVID ZINK YI
1973, Lima (Peru)
Lives in Berlin (Germany)

Education
Universität der Künste, Berlin, 2003.
Akademie der bildenden Künste, Munich (Germany), 1999.
Woodcarving Diploma, Berufsfach-schule, Munich (Germany), 1998.

Selected individual exhibitions
Hauser und Wirth, Zurich (Switzerland), 2004.
Johann König, Berlin, 2004.
De Adentro y Afuera. Johann König, Berlin, 2003.

Selected group exhibitions
Falckenberg Collection, Hamburg (Germany), 2003.
Nation. Kunstverein Frankfurt/Main (Germany), 2003.
Kino der Kälte. Medienkunstarchiv, Vienna, 2002.
Eyes Look into the Wall: Current Trends in Video Art. Brandenburgischer Kustv-erein, Potsdam (Germany), 2001.
Dedicated to Yi Yen Wu. Kunsthaus Raskolnikow, Dresden (Germany), 2001.
K2 Gallery, Leipzig (Germany), 2000.
Z-2000. Akademie der Künste, Berlin, 2000.

DARIUS ŽIURA
1968, Vilnius (Lithuania)
Lives in Vilnius

Education
Department of Painting, Vilnius Academy of Arts, 1997.

Selected individual exhibitions
Another Space. Contemporary Art Centre, Vilnius, 1999.
0253. Laiptai Gallery, Vilnius, 1994.
ZH2O. Akademija Gallery, Vilnius, 1993.

Selected group exhibitions
Violence of Tone. Gallery W139, Amsterdam, 2004.
Parallel Progressions 3. Contemporary Art Centre, Vilnius, 2003.
Centre of Attraction. 8th Baltic Triennial of International Art, 2002.
ARS 01. Kiasma, Helsinki, 2001.
Exotica. Contemporary Art Centre, Vilnius, 2001.
Self-Esteem. Lithuanian Art 01. Contem-porary Art Centre, Vilnius, 2001.
World Wide Video Festival. Amsterdam, 2001.
Sound+image. Contemporary Art Centre, Vilnius, 1999.
Lithuanian Art 1989. 1999: The Ten Years. Contemporary Art Centre, Vilnius, 1999.
Art in Lithuania 95. Contemporary Art Centre, Vilnius, 1995.
For Beauty. Soros Contemporary Art Center (Lithuania), 1995.
Change of Rules. Nortälje Art Hall, 1996.
After Painting. Contemporary Art Centre, Vilnius, 1998.
From Outside to The Side. Willa Werner, Octhrup (Germany), 1998.
Time Space Movement Art Festival. Paide (Estonia), 1998.
Hinspiel. Rückspiel. HDK Gallery, Berlin, 1997.
Personal Time. Touring exhibition: The Zacheta Gallery of Contemporary Art, Warsaw, 1996.

CREDITS

COURTESY, PHOTOGRAPHY AND CREDITS

Bas Jan Ader
pp. 258-261 Courtesy: Bas Jan Ader Estate / Patrick Painter Editions, Hong Kong-Vancouver.

Micol Assaël
pp. 372-375 Courtesy: Galleria Bonomo, Bari.

Sven Augustijnen
pp. 224-231 Courtesy: Galerie Jan Mot, Brussels

John Bock
p. 262 Camera, editing: Marc Aschenbrenner. Courtesy: Klosterfelde, Berlin; Anton Kern, NY.
p. 263 Photo: Knut Klaßen. Courtesy: Klosterfelde, Berlin; Anton Kern, NY.
pp. 264-265 Photo: Knut Klaßen. Courtesy: Klosterfelde, Berlin; Anton Kern, NY.

Michaël Borremans
p. 228 Photo: Peter Cox. Private collection. Courtesy: Zeno X Gallery, Antwerp.
p. 229 Photo: Felix Tirry. Private collection. Courtesy: Zeno X Gallery, Antwerp.
p. 230 Photo: Felix Tirry. Courtesy: Zeno X Gallery, Antwerp.
p. 231 Courtesy: Zeno X Gallery, Antwerp.

Marcel Broodthaers
pp. 380-383 Courtesy: Walker Art Center, Minneapolis; T. B. Walker Acquisition Fund, 1997.

Duncan Campbell
pp. 384-387 Courtesy: Belfast Exposed and Community Visual Images, Belfast.

D.A.E.
pp. 396-399 Courtesy: Archivo Filmoteca Vasca.

Angela de la Cruz
pp. 392-395 Photo: Colin Guillemet and Anthony Wilkinson. Courtesy: Krinzinger, Vienna; Lisson Gallery, London; Amma Schwartz, Melbourne.

Jeremy Deller
pp. 354, 356, 357 Courtesy of Art: Concept, Paris.
p. 355 Courtesy: Art: Concept, Paris. Originally commissioned by ArtPace, A Foundation for Contemporary Art, San Antonio.

Laura Horelli
pp. 316-319 Courtesy: Galerie Barbara Weiss, Berlin. Produced with the support of Puerto Rico 2002 (En Ruta), M&M Proyectos, Paula Toppila, FRAME and the City of Helsinki Cultural and Library Committee.

Johannes Kahrs
pp. 240-241 Courtesy: Galerie Almine Rech, Paris.
pp. 242-243 Collection Centre Georges Pompidou, Paris. Courtesy: Galerie Almine Rech, Paris.

Mark Leckey
pp. 408-411 Courtesy: Galerie Daniel Buchholz, Cologne; Cabinet, London; GBE, New York.

Boris Mikhailov
pp. 416-419 Courtesy: Barbara Weiss, Berlin.

Anu Pennanen
pp. 320-323 Courtesy: the artist and Vitra Productions.

Paola Pivi
p. 428 Photo: Hugo Glendinning.
p. 429 Photo: Hugo Glendinning. Courtesy: Galerie Emmanuel Perrotin, Paris.
pp. 430-431 Photo: Attilio Maranzano. Courtesy: Galerie Emmanuel Perrotin, Paris.

Marc Quer
pp. 282-285 Courtesy: Collection Ville de Marseille – Fond Communal d'Art Contemporain.

Daniel Roth
pp. 244-247 Courtesy: the artist and Galerie Meyer Riegger, Karlsruhe.

Michael Sailstorfer
pp. 324-325 Courtesy: the artist and Zero, Milan; Gallery Zink und Gegner, Munich.

Silke Schatz
pp. 328-329 Courtesy: Galerie Meyer Riegger, Karlsruhe.

Markus Schinwald
pp. 334-335 Courtesy: Gallery Georg Karl, Vienna.

Eyal Sivan / Michel Khleifi
pp. 336-339 Courtesy: Momento Distribution, Paris.

Patrick Tuttofuoco
p. 360 Photo: Dirk Pawels. Courtesy: Studio Guenzani, Milan.
p. 361 Photo: Roberto Marossi. Private Collection. Courtesy: Studio Guenzani, Milan.

Gillian Wearing
pp. 290-293 Courtesy: Maureen Paley – Interim Art, London.

Cathy Wilkes
p. 252 Courtesy: Private collection, Italy.
p. 253 Courtesy: The Modern Institute, Glasgow.
pp. 254-255 Courtesy: The Modern Institute, Glasgow.

Amelie von Wulffen
p. 294 Private collection. Courtesy: Greene Naftali Gallery, New York.
p. 295 Courtesy: Greene Naftali Gallery, New York; Galerie Ascan Crone, Andreas Osarek, Berlin.
pp. 296-297 Private collection. Courtesy: Galerie Ascan Crone, Andreas Osarek, Berlin.

David Zink Yi
pp. 440-443 Courtesy: Johann König, Berlin.

All other images appear courtesy of the artists.

MANIFESTA 5 has been organized by the Centro Internacional de Cultura Contemporánea, S.A. and International Foundation Manifesta

---

CENTRO INTERNACIONAL DE CULTURA CONTEMPORÁNEA, S.A.

President
Joxe Juan Gonzalez de Txabarri
General Deputy
Territorial Council of Gipuzkoa

Board

Territorial Council of Gipuzkoa
Imanol Agote
Head of the Department of Culture

Pilar Goya
Head of Comunication and Assessment

Fernando Tapia
Head of Social and
Institutional relationships

Xabier Huitzi
Head of Basque Language Planning

Donostia-San Sebastian City Council
Odón Elorza
Mayor

Ramón Etxezarreta
Culture Delegate

Juan Carlos Etxezarreta
Tecnical Secretary

María San Gil
PP Councillor

Mikel Ubillos
EA Councillor

JoséRamón de Miguel
IU Vocal

Basque Government
Miren Karmele Azcarate
Minister of Culture

Gurutz Larrañaga
Vice- Minister of Culture

Aranzazu Arzamendi
Director of Cultural Heritage
of the Department of Culture

Miren Lorea Bilbao Artetx
Director of Services of the Department
of Culture

JoséAntonio Arbelaiz
Director of Cultural Creation
and Diffusion of the
Department of Culture

MANIFESTA 5

Management Team
Lourdes Fernández and
JoséMiguel Ayerza
Curators
Marta Kuzma and Massimiliano Gioni
Production
JoséIgnacio Abanda
Communication and External Relations
Carmen Ruiz
Curators' assistants
Tevi de la Torre and Saioa Riba Inda
Production assitants
Elixabete Azpiroz and
César Hernández
Press/Communication assistant
Eider Córdoba
Direction Secretary
Begoña Galparsoro
Administration
Jon Iturrioz, Urtzi Basterrika
and Ane Orcolaga

Voluntary's Programme
Production
Olaia Ibarzabal, Isabel Fernández,
Arantxa Vázquez, Eneko Calvo,
Leticia Aristi, Hugh Mc Carthy, Aitor
Bea, Ane Abalde and Gorka Merchan
Communication
Elisabet Eguibar and Zuriñe Yriarte
Press
Ainara Odriozola, Nere Lujanbio,
Ane Rodriguez and Lierni Ibargutxi
Curators' assistants
Cecilia P. Alemani,
Paul W. Brewer and Victor Palacios
Artists' assistants
Julio Martín, Vanessa Alfate,
Susana Segurola, Lourdes Sánchez,
Ainara Arbizu

Catalogue
Gianluca Alviti
Zuriñe Uriarte
Graphic image
Zuriñe Uriarte
Web
Eli Korta
Inauguration Programme
Ana Espinosa, Jose Ramón
Garmendia, Inazio Zurutuza,
Nerea Garmendia, Javier Cantero,
Izaskun Gómez, Irene Yurrebaso,
Usua Ramírez, Leire Peñagaricano,
Edurne Aristi, Endike Olacieregi
and Iñaki Saez

Berlage Institute
Olaia Garona, Ibai Rigby
and Ohiana Kerexeta

And all those people who have
subsequently joined the work team

Team Arteleku
Natalia Barbería, Amalur Gaztañaga,
Miren Eraso, Lourdes Urrutia,
Gemma Gil and Gabi Corbella

Work teams at the exhibition venues
Koldo Mitxelena, Kubo Kutxa Kursaal,
Museo San Telmo, Casa Ciriza,
Ondartxo and Aquarium

Work teams at the
Donostia-San Sebastian City Council,
Pasaia City Council,
Territorial Council of Gipuzkoa,
Basque Government
and Port Authority of Pasaia

INTERNATIONAL FOUNDATION MANIFESTA

President
Henry Meyric Hughes

Director
Hedwig Fijen

Board
Daniel Birnbaum, Director of Portikus, Frankfurt

Francesco Bonami, Chief Curator of the Contemporary Art Museum, Chicago; Director Biennale di Venezia 2003 and Curator Manifesta 3

Iara Boubnova, Institute of Contemporary Art, Sophia; Curator Manifesta 4

Lourdes Fernández, General Coordinator Manifesta 5

Martin Fritz, Honor Treasurer, Vienna

Maaretta Jaukkuri, Chief Curator Museum of Contemporary Art (KIASMA), Helsinki

Gilane Tawadros, INIVA - Institute of International Visual Arts, London

Vicente Todolí, Director Tate Modern, London

Igor Zabel, Senior curator, Moderna Galerija, Ljubljana

Honorary Members
Gijs van Tuyl, Former Director Netherlands Office of Fine Arts, Director Kunstmuseum Wolfsburg, Wolfsburg

Joop van Caldenborgh, Chairman National Committee. Manifesta 1 1993-1997; Collector; Director Caldic Chemie, Rotterdam

Geert Dales, Treasurer National Committee. Manifesta 1 1993-1997, currently Mayor of the City of Leeuwarden

Marlene Dumas, Member of the National Committee. Manifesta 1; 1993-1997; artist, Amsterdam

Jolie van Leeuwen, Project Manager Manifesta 1; advisor, Amsterdam

Rosa Martínez, Curator Manifesta 1; former curator 5th Istanbul Biennial; former curator Santa Fe Biennial; independent curator and art critic based in Barcelona

Viktor Misiano, Curator Manifesta 1; founder Moscow Art Magazine; independent curator and Deputy Director of ROSIZO, the State Centre for Museums and Exhibitions

Andrew Renton, Curator Manifesta 1; independent curator; art critic based in London

Hans-Ulrich Obrist, Curator Manifesta 1, former Board Member IFM 1994-2002; art critic; independant curator and Curator Musée d'Art Moderne de la Ville de Paris

Katalyn Neray, Chief Curator Manifesta 1994-1996; Director Ludwig Museum, Budapest

Lilijana Stepani, Advisory Board and Board Member IFM 1993-2000; Director MGLC, Medarodni Graficni Likovni Center, Ljubljana

Anda Rottenberg, Advisory Board 1993-1997; former Director Zacheta Gallery, Warsaw

RenéBlock, Advisory Board 1993-1997, Director Museum Fridericianum, Kassel

Svenrobert Lundquist
Advisory Board 1993-1997; former Director Konsthallen Göteborg; currently working as an artist

Maria Lind
Curator Manifesta 2, co-Director Kunstverein München

Barbara VanderLinden
Curator Manifesta 2; former Board Member IFM 1997-2002; Director Roomade, Brussels

Robert Fleck
Curator Manifesta 2; Director Deichtorhallen Hamburg

Enrico Lunghi
Director Manifesta 2; Board Member IFM 1996-2000; Director Casino Luxembourg, Luxembourg

Jo Kox
Project Manager Manifesta 2 1996-1998; Financial Manager Casino Luxembourg

Erna Hennicot Schoepgess
Minister of Culture; Higher Education and Research, Luxembourg

Ole Bouman
Curator Manifesta 3; independent curator and Chief Editor ARCHIS Magazine, Amsterdam

Maria Hlavajova
Curator Manifesta 3; Director BAK, Utrecht

Kathrin Rhomberg
Curator Manifesta 3; Director Kölnischer Kunstverein, Cologne

Andreja Rihter
Minister of Culture Slovenia during Manifesta 3, Ljubljana

Majda Sirca
Current Minister of Culture Slovenia, Ljubljana

Mitja Rotovnik
Project Manager Manifesta 3 1998-2000; Director Cankarjev Dom, Ljubljana

Chris Dercon
Former Board Member IFM 1994-2002; Director Haus der Kunst, Munich

Vasif Kortun
Former Board Member IFM; Director Platform Garanti Contemporary Art Center, Istanbul

Kasper König
Former Board Member IFM 1994-2002; Director Ludwig Museum, Cologne

Stephanie Moisdon
Co-Curator Manifesta 4; independent curator and Founding Director Bureau de Video (BDV) in Paris

Nuria Enguita Mayo
Curator Manifesta 4; senior curator FundacióTàpies, Barcelona

Dieter Buroch
Manager Manifesta 4; Director Artists House Mousonturm, Frankfurt am Main

Coordinator
Marieke van Hal

Archive
Julia Schleyerbach

ADVISORY COMMITTEE

President
Xanti Eraso
Director Arteleku

Antón Aizpitarte
Director Patronato de Cultura del Ayuntamiento de Donostia-San Sebastián

Ibon Aranbarri
Artist invited in Manifesta 4

Leire Bergara
D.A.E

Norka Chiapuso
Director Feria de Teatro de Donostia-San Sebastián

Luis Chillida
Chillida Leku

JoséAntonio Echenique
Director XV Musical

Ricardo Echepare
Director of the summer courses at the Universidad del País Vasco/EHU

Guadalupe Echeverría
Director École des beaux arts de Bourdeaux

Julían Flórez
Director General Vicomtech

Kepa Korta
Director Plan Estratégico de Donostia-San Sebastián

Frank Larkade
Director Consonni

Francisco Javier Lopez Landatxe
Director Koldo Mitxelena

Bartomeu Marí
Director of exhibitions at the MACBA

Miguel Martín
Director Festival de Jazz de Donostia-San Sebastián

Alberto Martínez-Aranbarri
Director Obra Social de Kutxa

Mikel Olaciregui
Director Festival Internacional de Cine de Donostia-San Sebastián

Petra Pérez
Representative of the Galeristas del Pais Vasco

JoséLuis Rebordinos
Responsible of the film unit at Donostia Kultura

Socorro Romano
Director Museo Naval

Ana Salaberría
Responsible of the exhibition room at the Centro Koldo Mitxelena

Vicente Zaragüeta
President Aquarium

MANIFESTA 5 HAS BEEN POSSIBLE WITH THE SUPPORT AND COLLABORATION OF

Gobierno Vasco
Diputación Foral de Gipuzkoa
Ayuntamineto de Donostia-San Sebastián

European Commission's Culture 2000, Belgium
Allianz Kulturstiftung, Germany
Kutxa, Spain
El Diario Vasco, Spain

European Cultural Foundation, The Netherlands
Mondriaan Foundation, The Netherlands
Vidi Square, Belgium
Ministerio de Cultura, Spain
Fomento de Contrucciones y Contratas, Spain

Aquarium, Spain
Association Française d'Action Artistìque, France
Association Tranzit, Czech Republic
Astigarraga Auto, Spain
Ayuntamiento de Pasaia, Spain
Azkar, Spain
Bataplan, Spain
Berlage Institute, The Netherlands
British Council, United Kingdom
Center for Contemporary Art at the Kyiv Mohyla Academy, Ukraine
Center for Contemporary Art, Estonia
Centro de Atracción y Turismo , Spain
Centro Informatico Municipal, Ayuntamiento de Donostia-San Sebastián , Spain
Comet, Spain
Convention Bureau, Spain
Critical Voices, Ireland
Donostia Cultura, Spain
Erictel. Communication Systems, Spain
Federal Office of Culture, Switzerland
Finnish Fund for Art Exchange, Finland
Fundação Calouste Gulbenkian Serviço de Belas-Artes , Portugal
Gipuzkoako Foru Aldundiko Lurralde antolaketa eta sustapenerako departamentua/ Departamento para la ordenación y promoción territorial de la Diputación Foral de Gipuzkoa, Spain
Institut für Auslandsbeziehungen e.V., Germany
Instituto das Artes. Ministério da Cultura, Portugal
International Renaissance Foundation, Ukraine
Luso-American Foundation, Portugal
Ministry of Culture and Tourism, Turkey
Ministerie van de Vlaamse Gemeenschap, Belgium
Office for Contemporary Art, Norway
Prosegur, Spain
Plan Urban, Spain
Puerto de Pasajes, Autoridad Portuaria de Pasajes, Spain
Scottish Arts Council, United Kingdom
Teledonosti, Spain
Untitled Art Consulting, Spain

MANIFESTA 5 HAS BEEN POSSIBLE WITH THE SUPPORT AND COLLABORATION OF

Organizers

KULTURA SAILA
DEPARTAMENTO DE CULTURA

Gipuzkoako Foru Aldundia
Diputación Foral de Gipuzkoa

Sponsors

Cultura 2000

Collaborating Entities

Other collaborators

Udal Informatika Zentrua
Centro Informático Municipal

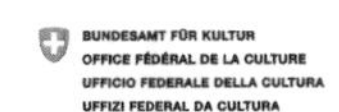

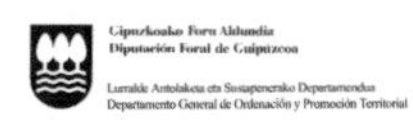

OFFICE FOR CONTEMPORARY ART NORWAY

UNTITLED Art Consulting Consultoría de Arte

manifesta°
International Foundation

Manifesta, Arte Garaikidearen Bienal Europarra,
Amsterdamen (Holanda) egoitza duen Manifesta Nazioarteko
Fundazioak sortua eta sustatua da.
Manifesta, la Bienal Europea de Arte Contemporáneo,
fue creada y estáapoyada por la Fundación Internacional Manifesta,
con base en Ámsterdam, Holanda.
Manifesta, the European Biennial of Contemporary Art,
is initiated and supported by the International Foundation Manifesta
an organisation based in Amsterdam, The Netherlands.

Manifesta 5 wishes to thank the artists for their precious contribution and their enthusiasm. Our warmest acknowledgements also to the staff and everyone who made this exhibition possible.

MANIFESTA 5 WISHES TO THANK THE FOLLOWING FOR THEIR COLLABORATION, COOPERATION AND SUPPORT:

Albania
Petrit Hoxha
Edi Muka

Australia
Anna Schwartz Gallery

Austria
Galerie Krinzinger
Georg Kargl Gallery
Kerstin Engholm

Belgium
Marie Puck Broodthaers
Chris Dehondt
Robert Michel
Jan Mot
Koraalberg Art Gallery
Mr and Mrs. Schutyser
Zeno X

Canada
Patrick Painter Inc.

Croatia
Natasa Illic
Branka Stipancic

Czech Republic
Vít Havránek
Ludvik H. Lavacek

Denmark
Galerie Asbaek
Jacob Fabricius
Catherine Lefèvre

Estonia
Anders Härm
Sirje Helme
Centre for Contemporary Art, Tallinn

Finland
Henna Harri
FRAME
ISEA Biennale of Electronic Art
Tapio Makela
Marketta Seppala
Paula Toppila

France
Alison Gingeras
Thomas Boutoux
Tony Brown
Collection Ville de Marseille – Fonds Comunal d'Art Contemporain, Marseille
Art: Concept
CAPC-Musée d'Art Contemporain, Bordeaux
Centre Georges Pompidou
DGAC Atelier des Artistes
Corinne Diserens
Ecole des Beaux Arts, Paris
Flach Pyramide International
Fonds Communal Ville de Marseille
Galerie Almine Rech
Galerie Corentin Hamel
Galerie Emmanuel Perrotin
Stephanie Moisdon Tremblay
Momento Distribution
Musée d'Art Moderne de la Ville de Paris
Annette Neve
Hans Ulrich Obrist
The International Herald Tribune
Thierry Ollat

Germany
Daniel Birnbaum
Rene Block
DAAD (Deutscher Akademische Austauschdienst)
Anselm Franke
Galerie Barbara Thumm
Galerie Barbara Weiss
Galerie Daniel Buchholz
Galerie Ascan Crone
Jens Hoffmann
Lena Kiessler
Johann König
Kapinos Gallery
Klosterfelde
Kunstlerhaus Bethanien
Dr. Friedrich Meschede
Dr. Ute Meta Bauer
Meyer Riegger Galerie
Giti Nourbakhsch
Christopher Tannert

Greece
The Breeder
Marina Fokidis
Katerina Gregos
Els Hanappe Underground
Dakis Joannou
Xenia Kalpaktsoglou

Ireland
Tara Byrne
Phil Collins
Valerie Connor
Brian Hand
Darragh Hogan
Critical Voices
Iseult Dunne
Peter Murray

Israel
Raffi Gamzou

Italy
50th Venice Biennial
Claudia Ardizzoni
Ilaria Bonacossa
Luca Cerizza
Caroline Corbetta
Josef Dalle Nogare
Massimo De Carlo
Flavio Del Monte
Galleria Bonomo

Studio Guenzani
Heinz Peter Hager
Flavia Fossi Margutti
Colonello Marco Marinaro
Barbara Roncari
Beatrice Trussardi
Massimo Vianello
Paolo Zani

Kazakhstan
Valeria Ibraera

Latvia
Ieva Kalnina
Solvita Kreese

Lithuania
Contemporary Art Center Vilnius
Lolita Jablonskiene
Raimundes Malasauskas
Birute Pankunaite
Soros Center for Contemporary Art

Macedonia
Zlatko Teodosievski

Montenegro
Petar Cukovic

The Netherlands
Alex Adriaansens
Anke Bangma
Ole Bauman
Berlage Institute
Lexter Brak
De Appel
Catherine David
Ann Deemester
Annet Dekker
Tom van Gestel
Jos Houweling
Jean Bernard Koeman
Marije Langelaar
Winy Maas
Annette Mullick
Martijn van Nieuwenhuyzen
Thomas Peutz
Vanessa Reed
Rijksakademie
Smart Space
Stedelijk Buro
V2
Esther Vossen
W139
Barbara Wesseling

Norway
Christiane Erharter
Eivind Furnesvik
Fotogalleriet, Oslo
Office of Contemporary Art Norway

Portugal
Juergen Bock
Manuel da Costa Cabral
Nuno Faria
Joao Fernandes
Fondation Gulbenkian
Luís Serpa
Filomena Soares
Maumaus
Museo Serralves
Pedro Oliveira

Poland
Foksal Gallery

Romania
Iara Boubnova

Russia
Joseph Beckstein
Daria Beskina
Ekaterina Lazareva
Victor Misiano
Vladimir Ovrachenko
Regina Gallery
Soros Center for Contemporary Art, St. Petersburg
Olesya Turkina

Slovenia
Natasa Petresin
Moderna Galerija Ljubljana

Spain
Andoni Luis Aduriz
Agata, amigos del tango
Xavier Agote
Fernando Aizpiri
Peio Aldazabal
Angel Alvarez
Carlota Alvarez Basso
Alberto Anaut
Joxe Anta
Maria Jesús Aranburu
Jaione Askasibar
Asociación Brasil cultural ABCDE
Asociación guipuzcoana de jubilados
Asociación Vecinos de Pasajes de San Pedro
Autoridad Portuaria de Pasajes
Txomin Badiola
Rocio Bardín
Sofia Barroso
Nestor Basterretxea
Patxi Bastarrika
Santiago Beltrán
Felix Belza
Pep Benlloch
Fernando Berridi
Esther Boulandier
Damián Casado
C.A.T. Donostia-San Sebastián
Cementos Rezola
Centro Kursaal
JoséMaría Civit
Pepe Cobo
Susana Corcuera
Lorena Corral
Juan Cruz
Tomás Cuesta
Deia, Diario de Gipuzkoa
Josune Diez Etxezarreta
Norberto Doctor
Josetxo Domínguez
Fernando Dueñas
Guadalupe Echevarria
Hasier Etxeberria
E.I.B.E. Amigos de las ballenas y los delfines
Ehgam
El Correo Español del Pueblo Vasco
Elkartu, Federación de discapacitados físicos
El País
El Mundo
Nuria Enguita Mayo
Jose Ignacio Espel
Gorka Espiau
Esgrimistas
Iñgo Espinosa
Filmoteca Vasca
Fomento de Donostia-San Sebastián
Fermín Fraile
Juan Pablo Fusi
Galería Colón XVI
Galería Fucares
Galería Pepe Cobo
Galería Senda
Galeria Vanguardia
Felix Garciandía
Mª Carmen Garmendia
Gehitu
Izaskun Gómez
Rosina Gómez de Baeza
Javier González Durana
Juan Huarte
Juan Carlos Huércanos
Mikel Idiazabal
Mª Jose Inchausti
Olatz Iriondo
Denis Itxaso
Jose Ramon Izkeaga
Miren Jaio
Alberto de Juan
Kepa Korta

La Paquera de Jerez
Xavier Laka
Mariasun Landa Lizaralde
La Razón
Franck Larkade
Jose Antonio Larrañaga
Evelyne Lehalle
Pedro Manterola
Tomás March
Bartomeu Marí
Miguel Martín
Celina Martín
Chus Martínez
Massa d'Or Produccions
Eneko Matilla
Libe Mendizábal
MID_E
Motos clásicas
Mugatxoan
Joxean Muñoz
Jose Ignacio Murua
Manu Narváez
Museo Naval
Fernando Nebreda
Okupgraf
Margarita Otaegui
Augustín Perez Rubio
Christoph Pingel
Plan Estratégico de Donostia-San Sebastián
Josep Ramoneda
Ana Rivilla
Sancho Rodríguez
Telmo Rodríguez
Socorro Romano
Alberto Rosales
Antonio Rosales
Javier Sada
Eva Salaberria
Ignacio Salazar-Simpson
Mario Sangalli
María San Gil
Jesús Silva
JoséAntonio Sistiaga
Roman Sudupe
Tattoo
Begoña del Teso
Universidad de Deusto. Campus de Donostia-San Sebastián
Eugenio Urdanbide
Carlos Urroz
Pablo del Val
Manolo Borja-Villel
Vicente Zaragüeta
Octavio Zaya

Sweden
Lena Essling
Anders Kreuger

Switzerland
Adrienne and Peter Biberstein
Yvana Enzler
Andreas Münch
Serge Ziegler Galerie
Staub Galerie

Turkey
Halil Altindere
Yesmin Dikmen
Vasif Kortun
Ministry of Culture and Tourism
Platform
Sh Rodney Sharkey

Ukraine
Anna Bernandska
Center for Contemporary Art, Kyiv
DJ Derbastler
Natalia Filomenko
Institute of Unstable Thoughts
International Renaissance Foundation
Liudmilla Motsiuk
Olesya Ostrovska
Oleh Sokolov
Oleksandr Soloviov
Olya Zhuk

United Kingdom
CCA
Margaret Dalzell
Kate Davis
Dan Gunn
Entwistle Gallery
Martin Herbert
Louise Higham
IBID Projects (London – Vilnius)
Claire Jackson
Tracy Kelly
Lisson Gallery
Adam Lowe
Maureen Paley - Interim Art
The Modern Institute
Gerrie Van Noord
Peter Osborne
Sue Pirnie
Timothy Taylor Gallery
Toby Webster
Tramway
Transmission
White Cube
Wilkinson Gallery
Zenomap

United States
Mary Sue Ader
Bard Centre for Curatorial Studies,
Annandale on Hudson, NY
Francesco Bonami
Maurizio Cattelan
Sylvia Chivaratanond
Corinna Durland
Kathleen Eagan
Gavin Brown Enterprise
Douglas Fogle
Marian Goodman
Dan Graham
Carol Greene
Eugene Hutz
Hanna Schouwink
Ali Subotnick
Philippe Vergne
Walker Art Center
Lawrence Weiner
David Zwirner

Yugoslavia
Stevan Vukovic

And to all establishments
and individuals from the city
of Donostia-San Sebastian
for their close collaboration in
the organization of this Biennial.